The Glannon Guide to Contracts

The Glannon Guide to Contracts

Learning Contracts Through Multiple-Choice Questions and Analysis

Third Edition

Professor Theodore Silver
Touro College, Jacob D. Fuchsberg Law Center

ASPEN
PUBLISHING

Cover images: iStock.com/pixhook; iStock.com/GlobaliStock (inset)

To contact Customer Service, e-mail customer.service@aspenpublishing.com, call 1-800-950-5259, or mail correspondence to:

       Aspen Publishing
       Attn: Order Department
       PO Box 990
       Frederick, MD 21705

Printed in the United States of America.

5 6 7 8 9 0

ISBN 978-1-4548-9234-2

Library of Congress Cataloging-in-Publication Data

Names: Silver, Theodore, author.
Title: The Glannon guide to contracts: learning contracts through
  multiple-choice questions and analysis / Professor Theodore Silver, Touro
  College, Jacob D. Fuchsberg Law Center.
Description: Third edition. | Frederick, MD: Aspen Publishing, [2019] | Includes
  bibliographical references and index.
Identifiers: LCCN 2018060363 | ISBN 9781454892342
Subjects: LCSH: Contracts—United States—Problems, exercises, etc. | LCGFT:
  Study guides.
Classification: LCC KF801.Z9 S49 2019 | DDC 346.7302/2—dc23
LC record available at https://lccn.loc.gov/2018060363

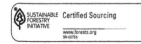

About Aspen Publishing

Aspen Publishing is a leading provider of educational content and digital learning solutions to law schools in the U.S. and around the world. Aspen provides best-in-class solutions for legal education through authoritative textbooks, written by renowned authors, and breakthrough products such as Connected eBooks, Connected Quizzing, and PracticePerfect.

The Aspen Casebook Series (famously known among law faculty and students as the "red and black" casebooks) encompasses hundreds of highly regarded textbooks in more than eighty disciplines, from large enrollment courses, such as Torts and Contracts to emerging electives such as Sustainability and the Law of Policing. Study aids such as the *Examples & Explanations* and the *Emanuel Law Outlines* series, both highly popular collections, help law students master complex subject matter.

Major products, programs, and initiatives include:

- **Connected eBooks** are enhanced digital textbooks and study aids that come with a suite of online content and learning tools designed to maximize student success. Designed in collaboration with hundreds of faculty and students, the Connected eBook is a significant leap forward in the legal education learning tools available to students.

- **Connected Quizzing** is an easy-to-use formative assessment tool that tests law students' understanding and provides timely feedback to improve learning outcomes. Delivered through CasebookConnect.com, the learning platform already used by students to access their Aspen casebooks, Connected Quizzing is simple to implement and integrates seamlessly with law school course curricula.

- **PracticePerfect** is a visually engaging, interactive study aid to explain commonly encountered legal doctrines through easy-to-understand animated videos, illustrative examples, and numerous practice questions. Developed by a team of experts, PracticePerfect is the ideal study companion for today's law students.

- The **Aspen Learning Library** enables law schools to provide their students with access to the most popular study aids on the market across all of their courses. Available through an annual subscription, the online library consists of study aids in e-book, audio, and video formats with full text search, note-taking, and highlighting capabilities.

- Aspen's **Digital Bookshelf** is an institutional-level online education bookshelf, consolidating everything students and professors need to ensure success. This program ensures that every student has access to affordable course materials from day one.

- **Leading Edge** is a community centered on thinking differently about legal education and putting those thoughts into actionable strategies. At the core of the program is the Leading Edge Conference, an annual gathering of legal education thought leaders looking to pool ideas and identify promising directions of exploration.

To all first-year law students everywhere

Contents

Acknowledgments

The author would like to thank everyone at Aspen Publishing, especially Rick Mixter, Christine Hannan, Dana Wilson, Lisa Wehrle, and Susan McClung.

The author also gratefully acknowledges the contribution of his research assistant, David J. Wood, Esq.

The Glannon Guide to Contracts

1

You *Must* Read This Very Short Introduction

For too many students, first-year contracts is a heartache, plaguing them perpetually with this demoralizing thought: "I do my work, I go to class, I listen, I participate, and still — I don't know what it's all about or what my teacher wants me to know."

We're here to spare you that sorrowful plight — to grab hold of contract law, tear away its veil of mystery, and flood it with such bright light as lets you see it for what it is: a course, like any other — easily understandable with ordinary work and thought.

And How Do You Do *That*?

We bathe this book in simple illustration after simple illustration after simple illustration. We surround our user-friendly teaching with *stories*, each one simple, easy to read, and at the same time tied to a complex legal concept — as intricate as any contracts case can be.

We "hold off" on stating any legal rule until first we show you why the law created it. Others will burden you with abstract precepts of law in a truncated incomprehensible form, followed by lackluster illustrations of their application. But that's not our way. We *first*, with a simple story, show you a problem in need of a legal solution; *then* describe the legal rule designed to solve it. With further illustration, we show you, too, how contract law (like so much law) makes new problems, even as it solves others. Moreover, we speak forthrightly to the misconceptions that surround so many rules of contract law and thus afford you depth of understanding. That's what your professor wants and that's what we'll provide: *depth of understanding* — mastery that leads straight to a high and happy grade.

This book stands on its own; it's a comprehensive contracts course in itself. Yet most students will (and should) use it as a companion to their first-year contracts class as taught by their professors. And while we're on that subject, know this:

Contracts Professors Aren't Cut from a Single Cloth

Contracts teachers vary in the way they organize their syllabi. Some begin with the topic of contract formation (Chapters 2-11), some with consideration (Chapters 12-14), and others with remedies (Chapters 25-30). Hence, this book has *three beginnings*.

1. If your professor starts with contract formation (offer, acceptance, "mutual assent," "mechanics of a bargain"), begin this book at Chapter 2 and read through Chapter 11.
2. If your professor begins with consideration ("exchange," "mutuality of obligation," "the necessity of a bargain"), you should nonetheless begin with Chapter 2, but you need only read sections A, B, and D. (And you may, if you like, skip the multiple-choice questions. You'll address those when your class covers the topic of contract formation. That's when you'll read Chapters 2-11 in full.) After reading Chapter 2, sections A, B, and D, turn to Chapter 12 and read through Chapter 14. Those chapters address consideration per se, but you'll better understand that whole topic if first you read Chapter 2, sections A, B, and D. We can't overemphasize that truth.
3. If your professor begins with remedies, start at Chapter 25 and read through Chapter 30.

Furthermore, for any topic in contracts, teachers differ in their thoroughness of coverage. Professor X thoroughly covers "this" topic and gives short shrift to "that" one. Professor Y shortcuts "this" topic and belabors the other. That's a problem; when a teacher sweeps through a topic at high speed, she leaves her students confused.

When That Happens Come to Us

Suppose your class leaves you totally "unglued" as to the relationships among "reliance," "restitution," "unjust enrichment," "quasi-contract," "benefit conferred," and "quantum meruit." When that happens (and certainly it will), head straight for our Chapter 28; we'll glue you back together. Read our stories and—*very important*—tackle our multiple-choice questions.

About the Multiple-Choice Questions

This is a *Glannon* Guide, so it's studded through and through with multiple-choice questions, each followed by elaborate analysis and explanation. The questions show you, rule by rule, that you do or don't know your "stuff" — completely, absolutely. Answer incorrectly, and the analysis reveals your error. Answer correctly, and it tells you whether your *reasoning* was right (or whether you just "got lucky").

About Our Appendix

In a perfect world, every law student would first understand our legal system and the *history* of law that makes up, specifically, her first-year courses. Then she would take the courses themselves. Hence, some might say we should offer you all of that in the very next chapter, before turning to contract law itself. But we won't do that, and here's why.

We Don't Want to Begin by Boring You

With the next chapter's first page, you'll dive into contract law, head first (as we, your lifeguards, keep you safe from drowning). Quickly, you'll see that contracts — learned *our* way — is fun. Were we to start with stuff that's in the Appendix, we'd turn you off — fast — and *that* we refuse to do.

When *Do* I Read the Appendix?

We don't ask, ever, that you read it as a whole, all in one "swallow." Instead, we send you now and again to certain of its sections. When you're in the midst of this or that chapter, we'll ask that you stop, turn to the Appendix, and read one of its parts. Know, too, that the Appendix stands on its own as a great introduction to law, the history of law and, especially, the history of *contract* law. And, since this is a *Glannon* Guide, the Appendix, too, is replete with multiple-choice questions, analyses, and explanations.

At some point, you might decide to read the appendix from beginning to end, and thus deepen your mastery of law — *all* law. But that's up to you. Read the sections to which we point you — *when* we point you, and all will be well. You'll learn ever so much more, and you'll keep a smile on our faces.

Finally: Have *Fun*

With this book as your constant companion, you'll love contracts, and that's what we want. For you, we want contracts to be engaging, enlightening fun. So turn the page and let the fun begin!

2

How to Form a Contract: The Basics

A. Contracts Arise by Offer, Acceptance (and Consideration)

Nonlawyers often think "contract" means a *writing*, formally drafted and ceremoniously signed. They're wrong. Many contracts do inhere in signed writings, and we call them "written contracts." Many arise from speech alone. They're "oral contracts." Some arise without words at all. They're born of communicative *behavior*, with nary a word of type or talk. Those are "contracts implied in fact." All such creatures are, to be sure, *contracts*, and all arise by the same legal mechanism: *Two (or more) parties form a contract when they **mutually assent to a bargain** that exacts from each some consideration.* Ordinarily, they do so by process of offer and acceptance and so we say: *Two parties form a contract when one makes an **offer** that the other **accepts**, each providing consideration to the other.* Equally fundamental to the law of contracts, therefore, are these two topics: (1) offer and acceptance, and (2) consideration.

5

For that reason, some professors begin their courses with consideration. If yours does that, then begin this book with this Chapter 2, sections A, B, and D. Then read Chapters 12-14. Come back here to Chapter 2 when your professor takes up offer and acceptance. If your professor begins with offer and acceptance, keep reading this chapter and continue with Chapters 3-11. Chapters 2-11 tackle offer and acceptance — the "ins," the "outs," and the bottom lines.

1. Offer and Acceptance: The Easy Part and the Hard Part

It's easy to *say* "offer" and "accept." It's easy, too, to memorize their legal definitions, which we'll soon present. But it's not so easy (at first) to apply those words to two "real" parties conducting "real" communications. The challenge is to watch what they do, hear what they say, read what they write, and reach a reasoned legal opinion as to (a) whether one of them made an offer and, if he did, (b) whether the other accepted. With respect to offer and acceptance, *that's* the "hard part."

2. Sometimes the Hard Part Is Easy: Dan, George, Donna, and Gale

Dan and George are strangers standing in a movie line. Dan says to George, "I hereby make you an offer." George responds, "I accept." These chaps used the *words* "offer" and "accept," but Dan did not *make* an offer, which means George had nothing *to* accept. Between Dan and George, there is no offer, no acceptance, and no contract.

Donna and Gale are strangers, seated next to each other in the movie theater. Donna wants to make a phone call but hasn't brought her mobile phone. Meanwhile, Gale, without her glasses, is struggling to see the screen. Donna says to Gale, "I'll lend you a pair of theater binoculars for the duration of the movie, if you'll lend me your cell phone for fifteen minutes, right now." Gale responds, "Sure." These two didn't *say* "offer," "accept," or "contract," but Donna made an offer, Gale accepted it, and the ladies formed a contract.

B.   The Meaning of Offer

When Dan said, "I hereby make an offer," George couldn't know what "deal" Dan meant to propose. On the other hand, when Donna proposed to swap binoculars for phone, Gale should plainly have seen that Donna proposed exactly that — to swap binoculars for phone. And therein lies the critical difference between the stories. Donna proposed a genuine exchange, a bargain, a swap, a trade, a quid pro quo — an "I'll do this if you'll do that." Dan did no such thing. Donna made an offer; Dan did not. And with that, we're ready to define "offer."

Restatement (Second) of Contracts[1] §24 defines it thus:

> An offer is the manifestation of willingness to enter into a bargain, so made as to justify another person in understanding that his assent to that bargain is invited and will conclude it.

Look at the fifth word, "manifestation." As known to the law it denotes an outward showing, not an inward state of mind. Under some (exceptional) circumstances, we *manifest* thoughts or feelings we don't really possess. One who cries leads others to believe she's unhappy. She *manifests* sadness. Yet, hearing that her first grandchild was born, she might cry for joy. With tears streaming down her cheeks, she *manifests* sadness, but isn't sad. One who is deep in intense, silent contemplation, on the threshold of revelation, might lead reasonable persons to think her apathetic. She *manifests* apathy, but she is in fact thoughtfully engaged.

Resting, as it does, on the word "manifestation," the law's definition of "offer" refers to a person who does, says, or writes that which *would lead a reasonable person to believe* that she stands ready and willing to make a bargain. Whether she manifests such willingness turns not on what she truly wants or intends, but on what, to a reasonable person, she *appears* to want and intend. Occasionally, then, one may unwittingly manifest willingness to enter into a bargain when not truly possessed of any such purpose.

Suppose Carlos stands by his lawnmower and says, in a serious tone, "I want to sell my lawnmower for $100." Carlos thus manifests a wish to sell *that* lawnmower, even if in his own mind he's thinking of another of his lawnmowers stored in a garage three miles away.

Mindful, now, of what "manifest" means, let's break the Restatement's definition of offer into three pieces.

Piece 1: *An offer is a manifestation . . .* To make an offer, Party A must make an outward showing or communication to Party B. He may do so with *speech, writing, or behavior.*

Piece 2: *. . . of a willingness to enter a bargain . . .* A's communication must be such as would lead a reasonable person in B's position to understand (1) that A wishes to form a *bargain*, meaning an arrangement that calls on each party to do something for the other; and (2) *what*, specifically, he expects that each will do.

---

1. For a large number of legal topics, an entity called the American Law Institute has written a so-called Restatement of the Law. For some topics, including Contracts, it has written a Restatement and then revised it. Hence there now exist, as they're commonly known, (1) a "Restatement (First) Contracts," issued in 1932, and (2) a "Restatement (Second) Contracts," issued in 1979. It's not law, but it is what's called "good authority." Learn more about the Restatements — what they are and what they are not — in the Appendix, section C.

Piece 3: *. . . so made as to justify another person in believing . . . his assent . . . is invited . . . and will conclude it.* The communication must be such as would, under the prevailing circumstances, cause a reasonable person in B's position to think, "A asks me to say 'yes,' and, if I do, each of us is firmly committed to the other; we have a deal."

Suppose Alice sits on the hood of a small car and in a serious tone says to Bob, a stranger: "I need my car washed urgently — right now. I'll pay you $200 to do it. Is it a deal?" By law, Alice has offered to pay Bob $200 to wash the small automobile on which she's sitting. That's true even if Alice later proves, indisputably — with incontrovertible evidence — that she was "only joking." It is likewise true if Alice proves that she does not own the little vehicle on which she's sitting and that *her* car, a mammoth limousine, is located 900 miles away.

One makes an offer by doing or stating that which, *under the operative circumstances,* would cause a reasonable person to believe that (1) a definite exchange has been proposed to him, and (2) his assent will "seal the deal." The circumstances under which Alice makes her statement include the physical location from which she makes it. Seeing that she's perched atop the little car, a reasonable listener in Bob's position would understand "my car" to mean "*this* car." Since Bob would reasonably think Alice to mean "this car," then, in the law's eyes, that *is* what she means, whether she knows it or not. Stated otherwise, the law holds Alice not to the meaning she truly harbors in her head, but to the meaning she *manifests*.

QUESTION 1. On April 1, Fay sends to Mort this signed fax message: "Mort — April is upon us. I need your services — this Wednesday, please, at 11 A.M. I'll be ready with cash. Okay?" What additional circumstance, if proven, would most clearly mean that Fay's message constitutes an offer?

A. Mort is a skilled landscaper, mechanic, and carpenter, and at various times in the past Fay has hired him to perform services related to those skills.
B. Every April for the previous twelve years Mort has trimmed the trees in Fay's front yard, for which Fay has each time paid him $125.
C. Fay does not know Mort, but has heard that he is a skilled landscaper.
D. By signed writing, Mort responds to Fay: "Yes, I'll be there."
E. By signed writing, Mort responds to Fay: "I'll be glad to help you, but my fee is now $35 per hour."

ANALYSIS. Go back to Restatement (Second) §24 and read it. (That's easy.) Think of its *meaning* and apply it. (That's *not* so easy.) To determine that a given communication is an offer, examine (a) the communication itself, and (b) the circumstances under which it's made. Then ask yourself: "In my opinion, would a reasonable person receiving this communication understand that a definite bargain is proposed to him and that his assent will 'seal' the deal?"

Fay wrote only this: "April is upon us. I need your services. I'll be ready with cash." Viewed objectively, Fay's message communicates almost nothing. It's like Dan's statement to George made in the movie line. Fay's words, by themselves, could not cause a man in Mort's position sensibly to draw any conclusion as to what she wants him to do or how much "cash" she'll pay him.

Yet under some *circumstances*, Mort might reasonably take Fay's little fax as a definite proposition of specified terms. This question asks that we identify such a circumstance. Among the answer choices we're to find some fact that, if added to the story, would logically cause Mort to understand, specifically, what Fay wants of him, what she'll pay him in exchange, and that he need only express his assent to "close the deal."

D and **E** concern Mort's *response* to Fay's message. They don't concern Fay's statement or the circumstances under which she makes it. In no way do they address *the meaning of* "offer." **D** and **E** are wrong.

Consider **A**. If Mort were operating under the circumstance it describes, how would he naturally interpret Fay's message? He might think Fay has for him some work tied to landscaping, mechanics, or carpentry, and that she stands ready to pay some amount of money for his service. But he couldn't know with any specificity what Fay actually wants him to do or how much she's ready to pay.

C tells us that Fay has heard that Mort is a capable landscaper — and, so what? **C** tells us something about Fay's state of mind, but it tells *Mort* nothing of what Fay proposes. **C** is wrong.

And what of **B**? It tells us that every April, for twelve years, Mort has trimmed Fay's trees for $125. Mindful of that history — that *circumstance* — a reasonable person in Mort's position would justifiably conclude that Fay once again wants her trees trimmed, and that she's ready to pay, as before, $125 in cash. **B** is right.

QUESTION 2. Over the fourteen years, 2005 to 2018, Andrea has visited Frank's diner for breakfast about four times weekly between 6:30 A.M. and 11:45 A.M., each time ordering two soft-boiled eggs with toast, and each time paying the menu price for those items. Also over these fourteen years, Andrea has come to Frank's diner about three times weekly for lunch between 12:15 P.M. and 3:30 P.M., each time ordering two *hard*-boiled eggs with toast and paying the menu price. At noon sharp on January 3, 2019 Andrea steps into Frank's diner and sits at a table. Which of the following additional facts would best justify the legal conclusion that on that day, Andrea has made an offer to Frank in which she proposes to buy soft-boiled eggs for the menu price?

A. Unbeknownst to Frank, Andrea had breakfast today at 7:30 A.M. in another diner, which she also has frequented regularly for fourteen years.

> **B.** Unbeknownst to Frank or Andrea, Andrea's wristwatch is running one hour slow, and Andrea believes the time to be 11:00 A.M.
> **C.** Frank does not serve breakfast after 11:50 A.M. and begins serving lunch at noon.
> **D.** A moment after taking her seat, Andrea says, "Eggs and toast, please."
> **E.** A moment after taking her seat, Andrea says, "Another morning — the usual please."

ANALYSIS. A fourteen-year history gives Frank every reason to know that Andrea has soft-boiled eggs for breakfast and hard-boiled eggs for lunch. He should know, too, that when Andrea wants breakfast she normally arrives before 11:45 A.M.; for lunch she comes no sooner than 12:15 P.M.

Today, Andrea arrives *at* 12:00 P.M. and takes a seat. By doing so she communicates *something*. Frank might justifiably believe that Andrea is proposing to purchase, for the menu price, toast and two eggs. But, because it's exactly noon, he can't justifiably determine whether she wants her eggs hard or soft boiled. Absent additional circumstances, Andrea has *not* made an offer.

Go back to Restatement (Second) §24 and again take hold of its meaning. Then read each answer choice and, in your mind, add to the story its stated fact. Determine which one, in your opinion, means that Andrea has offered to buy soft-boiled eggs at the menu price.

Neither **A** nor **B** relates to the substance of Andrea's communication or any circumstance of which Frank should know. If Andrea had breakfast earlier in the day or if her watch is fast, Frank has no reason to know anything about it. Neither fact can affect his reasonable understanding of what Andrea means by "eggs and toast." **A** and **B** are wrong.

According to **D**, Andrea asks for eggs and toast. At noon sharp, Frank has no way reasonably to conclude that she wants the eggs hard or soft boiled. **D** is wrong.

According to **C**, Frank doesn't serve breakfast after 11:50 A.M. If Frank has reason to think that Andrea knows that policy, he might be justified in believing that Andrea wants lunch. On the one hand, we're not told that Andrea knows the policy or that Frank has any reason to think she does. Nonetheless, some students might assume that Frank has told Andrea of his policy and that he should conclude that she wants hard-boiled eggs. **C** isn't bad, but maybe **E** is better.

In **E**, Andrea refers to her "morning . . . usual." On hearing the word "morning," Frank *should* understand that Andrea proposes to buy toast and soft-boiled eggs for the menu price. **E** is right.

Remember, even with the facts added by **E**, Frank need not give Andrea what she wants. Andrea has made an offer, but since Frank has yet to accept it, the parties do not (yet) have a contract.

For the meaning of offer, we've looked thus far to Restatement (Second) §24. But *the Restatement isn't law.* (See the Appendix, section C.) We're not confined to its definition of offer (or of anything else it puts forth). We might properly define the term "offer" in a variety of ways. Consider these:

> *An offer is any communication that leads its recipient reasonably to conclude that he is asked to join in an exchange, explicit in terms, and that his assent will create a binding agreement.*
>
> *An offer is any act or expression that, under prevailing circumstances, naturally causes its witness or recipient to conclude that a bargain of specified terms is available to her and that her assent will finalize it.*
>
> *One makes an offer by communicating that which would justifiably lead another to think she is asked to partake of an exchange, specific in its terms, and that her accession will conclude it.*

All of these formulations correctly characterize an offer. They're not "official," but neither is the Restatement. Offer is a common law concept, susceptible to many formulations. Be familiar with the Restatement definition because courts, authorities, and some teachers lean on it all too heavily. But don't think that its words are law. Don't think, either, that memorizing the Restatement's definition of "offer" or *anyone's* definition of "offer" (or any definition of *anything*) means you've learned the law. Knowing words is important only if you comprehend their meaning. Law is about *meaning,* not words. The lawyer must work well with words as the tools by which she gives and takes meaning. It's all about *meaning.* Words are the conducting wire, meaning is the power.

QUESTION 3. Vortech Inc. supplied industrial chemicals to a large number of customers, including Hartco Inc. After years of doing business with Hartco, Vortech sent Hartco this document:

DEFINITIVE OFFER TO SELL

We have available a variety of alcohol- and ammonia-based cleaning products, many of which you've purchased in the past. We wish to sell some or all of the products in good quantities at favorable prices. Let us know, please, if you wish to purchase any now. Please describe specifically the product(s) you want to purchase and the exact quantities you wish to acquire. This is a definite offer, and we look forward to your acceptance.

Did Vortech make Hartco an offer?

A. Yes, because Vortech described its message as a "definite offer"
B. Yes, because Vortech did not restrict Hartco to purchasing any particular product and left it free to choose among many

C. No, because a seller cannot bind a prospective buyer without that buyer's assent
D. No, because Vortech did not refer to cleaning chemicals by name
E. No, because Vortech was nebulous as to the transaction it suggested

ANALYSIS.   Think about the *meaning* of offer. Ask yourself: "Under these circumstances could Hartco reasonably see in Vortech's message a proposal for a definite bargain — an explicit exchange?"

Vortech expresses its wish to sell a "variety" of products, in "good quantities" at "favorable" prices. Vortech doesn't specify *what* it will sell or what price Hartco must pay for whatever it is. Hartco cannot justifiably believe that Vortech has contemplated a true exchange of specified terms. The writing is not an offer — it's too vague.

Since your answer is "no," confine yourself to **C**, **D**, and **E**. Ignore **A** and **B** (for now).

C states that a buyer can't bind a seller unless the seller assents. That's wholly true and wholly irrelevant. You're asked not whether Hartco and Vortech formed a *contract*, but whether Vortech made Hartco an *offer*. No prospective buyer or seller acting on her own can create a contract, but either can make an *offer*. **C** is bad; keep looking.

According to **D**, Vortech's message fails as an offer because it does not refer to products "by name." That's tempting. The problem with Vortech's message is indefiniteness — failure to propose a clear, specific exchange. Named products are more specific than unnamed ones. Still, **D** isn't good. Were we to supplement Vortech's message with product names but nothing else, the message would still fail to specify quantity or price. It would still fail to propose a bargain of *specified terms*. **D** is wrong. **E** features the words "nebulous," "transaction," and "suggested" — words that don't usually arise in connection with this subject. For that reason, the question writer hopes you'll dismiss it.

Surprise her. Read not for buzzwords but for *meaning*. **E** means Vortech's message fails as an offer because it's too indefinite ("nebulous") as to any exchange ("transaction") it proposed ("suggested"). *That* correctly tells us why Vortech's proposal is not an offer; it doesn't adequately specify its terms. But before settling "for keeps" on **E**, look quickly at **A** and **B**.

According to **A**, Vortech's document *is* an offer because Vortech *calls* it one. You know better. Whether a communication qualifies as an offer doesn't depend on the name it carries. One may use the *word* "offer" without making one (as Dan did when talking to George in the movie line). Reciprocally, one may make an offer without using the word (as Donna did when speaking to Gale in the movie theater). **A** is wrong.

B targets your prejudice. From childhood we learn that freedom is good (which it is) and that it's generally better than restriction (which it is). On that basis, some students imagine that **B** just "must be" right. But it's wrong. The freedom to which **B** refers is the very reason Vortech's message fails as an offer. The freedom inheres in the nonspecificity of the Vortech message, which leaves Hartco "free" to consider what chemical he might want to buy, in what quantity, and at what price — which is why it fails outright to propose a definite bargain. **B** is wrong, and **E** is right.

QUESTION 4. Eunice, age 97, is fond of her younger neighbor Alison, age 26. On Wednesday, May 12, Eunice plans to move from her home in Washington State to New Mexico. On the evening before the move, she leaves Alison this voicemail message: "You've told me that you need a car. My car is nearly new, but I've decided to give up driving. In gratitude for our long friendship, I offer you my car. I'll sign the title certificate over to you and mark the box that reads 'transferred as gift.' I'll leave the certificate in your mailbox. I'm leaving for New Mexico tomorrow. Our next contact will probably be by mail." By leaving the voicemail message, Eunice

A. did make an offer because she described her definite good faith intention to convey property to Alison.
B. did make an offer because she expressed an explicit, unconditional plan, asking no response from Alison.
C. did not make an offer because she did not require that Alison pay money for the car.
D. did not make an offer because she did not call for a return performance from Alison.
E. did not make an offer because she proposed not a commercial transaction but an informal arrangement between friends.

ANALYSIS.   Here's another "yes, because," "no, because" question (with "did" and "did not" replacing "yes" and "no"). Steer clear of the answer choices until you first conceive *your own* answer and reasoning.

One makes an offer by proposing a bargain — an exchange — a swap — an "I'll do this if you'll do that." Eunice didn't do that. As a reasonable person, Alice cannot conclude that Eunice asks anything in return for the car; Eunice proposes no *bargain*. Rather, she promises a gift. She's free to do that, but she hasn't made an offer. Hence, the parties can't form a contract. (As you'll learn from Chapter 12, Eunice need not honor her promise; she's free to break it.)

Now we've conceived of an answer and reason: Eunice made no offer because her message proposed no *bargain*. Reading for meaning and not for words, look first at the answer choices beginning with "did not," ignoring for now those that begin with "did."

E implies that one can make an offer only if she communicates in a commercial setting. You know better. One may make an offer to anyone in any setting — commercial, noncommercial, friendly, or unfriendly. **E** is wrong.

C looks better. It notes that Eunice asked for no money. If Eunice had asked for money she'd be asking, plainly, for a quid pro quo, and her message would be an offer. C seems correct, but before writing it in stone (or ink), let's look at D. D uses the phrase "return performance," which means "something done or given in exchange." According to D, Eunice made no offer because she did not ask that Alison do anything in return for the car. That sounds right for the same reason that C sounds right. So which is better — C or D? Look at the difference between them.

According to C, the message fails as an offer because it asks Alison for no money. One can make an offer without asking the other for money. One may make an offer in which money plays no role at all. X may propose to wash Y's windows in exchange for Y's sweeping X's floor. In the movie theater, Donna made an offer by proposing to exchange binoculars for a cell phone. D recognizes that an offer requires not a request for money, but the solicitation of *some* performance that might or might not involve monetary payment. That makes D better than C.

Before settling on D, look at A and B. A ignores the absence of a proposed bargain and implies that one always makes an offer if she proclaims a plan to transfer property. That's wrong (and the happy words "definite good faith intention" can't make it right. Read for *meaning*, not words).

B accurately describes Eunice's message, but tells us that she *did* make an offer. That Eunice's plan is unconditional means it asks nothing back from Alison. For that reason alone, it can't be an offer. Because it calls for no response, it does not ask for Alison's assent. That too means it can't be an offer. With A and B out of our way, we know that D is right.

C. The General Significance (and Insignificance) of Writings and Signatures

We know that one can make an offer by speech, writing, or behavior. As you'll soon see, the same goes for acceptance. Hence, as stated at the beginning of this chapter: Two parties may form a contract with or without a writing. That raises a simple question: If two parties can form a contract without a writing, why do they so often create one?

Here's the answer: To do something is one thing. To *prove* you did it is another. Suppose you pay April's telephone bill in cash, at the phone company office. You take a receipt but lose it. One month later, the company bills you for May and asserts that you still owe for April.

You know you've paid April's bill, and you so inform the company. If the company finds a record of your payment and agrees that you've paid, there's no problem. But suppose it finds no such record and sues you for April's bill.

As a plaintiff, the phone company bears the burden of proof; it *must* introduce some evidence that you did not pay, or the court will dismiss its case.

At trial, a phone company employee testifies that (1) the company normally keeps records of all customer payments, and (2) it has no record of your April payment. Your attorney cross-examines the employee: "To your knowledge, has the phone company ever lost a record?" The employee answers, "No, not to my knowledge."

The phone company has introduced evidence tending to show that you did not pay April's bill. As a defendant, you have the opportunity to present evidence showing that you did pay the bill. A receipt signed by phone company personnel would be compelling evidence; with that, you'd surely win. But you don't have one. What evidence can you offer? You can testify that you remember paying April's bill in cash. The jury might believe you, in which case you'll win. But the jury might find the phone company's evidence more compelling than yours, in which case you'll lose. Even though you really did pay April's bill, you'll have to pay it again.

Similarly, two parties, Anastasia and Bob, might form a contract by speech alone. If Bob later denies having done so and there exists no writing that documents their agreement, Anastasia will have trouble proving that the contract ever was made. That is not to say she *can't* prove it; she might have other evidence sufficient to convince a court that the parties formed a contract, notwithstanding Bob's denial. Indeed, plaintiffs often succeed in proving they've formed contracts without a writing. Nonetheless, when two parties form a contract, a writing is compelling evidence that they did so, and it is evidence, also, of the terms on which they agreed.

Hence, when two parties put their contract in writing, they do so in contemplation of a future dispute, for reasons of evidence and proof — proof that they formed a contract and proof of its terms. (Some contracts, however, are enforceable *only* if they are recorded in writing, a matter addressed in Chapter 15.)

D. The Meaning of Acceptance, Power to Accept, and Identity of the Offeree

1. Acceptance

One accepts an offer if he writes, says, or does that which would lead a reasonable person in the offeror's position to believe that he has assented, unconditionally, to all terms of the offeror's proposed bargain. Restatement (Second) of Contracts §50(1) states it this way:

> Acceptance of an offer is the manifestation of assent to the terms thereof made by the offeree[.]

As in the Restatement's definition of "offer," we read the word "manifesta-tion." The legal meanings of offer and acceptance are alike in this way: They turn not on one's genuine intentions but on his *manifest* intentions. If, in response to an offer, an offeree says or does that which the offeror would reasonably interpret as "Yes, I assent," then the offeree accepts. So, whether one *makes* or *accepts* an offer depends not on what he truly intends but on the intentions a reasonable person would ascribe to his words or behavior.

2. *Power to Accept*

The "power to accept" an offer rests only in an *offeree*. As Restatement (Second) §50(1) provides: "Acceptance of an offer is the manifestation of assent to the terms thereof made *by the offeree*[.]" If A makes an offer to B, and C says, "I accept," there is no contract. C has *attempted* to accept, but he is not, alas, an offeree and has no power to do so.

3. *Identity of the Offeree*

That an offer allows for acceptance only by an offeree raises this question: How do we identify an offeree? As with the creation of an offer, the answer turns on the offeror's *manifest intent* — on what reasonable persons would believe when interpreting the offeror's acts, statements, or writings. Put another way: *With respect to any offer, an offeree is any person who, under the circumstances, reasonably believes that the offeror's proposal is made to him and that his assent is invited.* Restatement (Second) §29(1) states it thus:

> The manifested intention of the offeror determines the person or persons in whom is created a power of acceptance.

James, Nancy, and May

Nancy and May are flutists. James visits them, and there follows this conversation:

> **James:** "Hey, Nancy, if you'll give me five flute lessons, one on each of the five consecutive Thursdays, beginning this coming Thursday, from 8:00 P.M. to 9:00 P.M., I'll pay $50 per lesson. Is that a deal?
> **May:** "Yes, I'll do it."
> **Nancy:** "Yes, I'll do it."

James began with "Hey, Nancy," and so manifested his intent to address *Nancy*. Nancy was the offeree; May was not. Nancy had the "power to accept"; May did not. May's assent is no acceptance. After May speaks, James's offer lives on, Nancy having power to accept it. When Nancy says, "Yes, I'll do it," she and James form a contract.

As in the case above, an offeror's manifest intention might create only one offeree, thus vesting the power to accept in one person only. The offeror might also create two or more offerees, vesting a power to accept in both (or all) of them, providing also, however, that if one offeree accepts, the others lose their power to do so. Consider again, the conversation among James, Nancy, and May, slightly modified:

> **James:** "Hey, you two — I want five flute lessons, one on each of the five consecutive Thursdays, beginning this coming Thursday, from 8:00 P.M. to 9:00 P.M.; I'll pay $50 per lesson. Is that a deal?"
> **May:** "I'll do it."
> **Nancy:** "I'll do it."

Reasonable persons in May's or Nancy's position should understand James to mean, "I'd like to have five flute lessons, and I don't care who provides them. I do not, however, want ten lessons. So, if one of you agrees, it's too late for the other." When May assents, she exercises her power of acceptance; Nancy loses hers.

An offeror might make an offer to two or more persons as a "team," providing that a contract will arise only if *all* of them assent. In that case, all offerees together "share" the power of acceptance; acceptance arises only if all manifest assent. Suppose, for example, Alan says to Beth, Chad, and Trey: "Hey, you three, if you'll perform at my wedding — Beth at the piano, Chad at the drums, and Trey at the bass — I'll pay $500." The three offerees should understand that Alan wants performance from all three together or none at all. If only one or two of the three offerees assent, there is no acceptance. If all assent, they furnish acceptance and a contract arises.

Finally, an offeror might make an offer to two or more persons separately, allowing all to accept. Suppose Libroco makes this written announcement to the public: "We will pay $5 to every person who reads our new book, *Cat Tail* and, by August 18, sends us a written review."[2] Any person who reads the announcement is justified in believing that she is invited to assent. Every one of them has a power of acceptance independent of the others. Suppose 5,000 persons read the book and, by August 18, send their reviews. With its 5,000 offerees, Libroco forms 5,000 contracts.

Restatement (Second) §29(b) speaks to all such possibilities with this one sentence:

> An offer may create a power of acceptance in a specified person or in one or more of a specified group or class of persons, acting separately or together, or

---

2. But see Chapter 5 as to whether and when an advertisement constitutes an offer.

to anyone or everyone who makes a specified promise or renders a specified performance.

Realize that one cannot make an acceptance unless he first receives an offer. Suppose Phillip turns to Mei and says, "I was thinking, maybe, of selling this diamond ring for a very good price." Mei responds, "I accept." By law, Mei did *not* accept, for the simple reason that Phillip made her no offer. *Without an offer, there can be no acceptance.*

QUESTION 5. In the town of Hampshire there live two women named Harriett Folger. One lives at 14 *Chelton* Lane. The townsfolk know her to be an industrial quality control engineer. She is also a talented seamstress but, as she is well aware, no one knows that. The other Harriett Folger, of 14 *Chester* Lane, is a seamstress, renowned for the high quality of her work. Farah Fuilan, also of Hampshire, writes and signs this letter:

> Dear Ms. Folger,
>
> As is well known, you are a gifted seamstress. I have a dress in need of repair. I'd like you to examine it and determine whether you can fix it. I'll pay you $100 to do just that much. I'd like to meet next Saturday — at 1:00 P.M. if that works for you. Are you agreeable?
>
> Sincerely yours,
>
> Farah Fuilan

Confused as to which Harriett lives where, Farah addresses her letter to Harriett the engineer at 14 *Chelton* Lane. Harriett receives the letter, opens it, and writes back to Farah: "Yes, absolutely. I am agreeable. Let's meet this coming Saturday at 1:00 P.M., my home."

Farah then learns of her error. She contacts Harriett the engineer and tells her, "By error, I sent my letter to you. I now know that I should have sent it to Harriett Folger the seamstress, at 14 *Chester* Lane." The engineer responds, "You do not know it, but I too am a capable seamstress. You sent the letter to me, I accepted your offer, and we have a contract." Farah asserts that she and Harriett (the engineer) did not form a contract. Her position is best supported by which fact?

A. Farah honestly wished to contact the other Harriett and, under the circumstances, her error was reasonably understandable.
B. Harriett knew that her abilities as a seamstress were unknown to the community.
C. Harriett's principal professional activity is in the field of engineering.
D. Farah cannot be bound to an agreement she did not intend to make.

ANALYSIS.   Think, first, of the relevant law: Two parties A and B form a contract when A makes an offer *to B* and B accepts it. B can't accept an offer if A has not made her one.

Let's ask: Did Farah make an offer to Harriett? Harriett was "well aware" that the community knew her not at all as a seamstress. Seeing that Farah's letter referred to a "well known . . . gifted seamstress," she should have known that Farah meant to make her offer to the other Harriett Folger; that was Farah's *manifest* intention. Harriett of *Chelton* Lane was not Farah's offeree. Possessed of no offer, *that* Harriett had nothing to accept. Her response, "I am agreeable" was not an acceptance, and the parties formed no contract. Among the answer choices, the right one will reflect *that* reasoning.

A refers to Farah's *honest* intent and the understandability of her error. Neither of these factors states the reason for which these parties failed to form a contract. They failed to form a contract because legally, Farah made no offer to Harriett. **C** reminds us that Harriett is not a professional seamstress. But that doesn't matter. What matters is this: Harriett knows that the community is ignorant of her abilities as a seamstress and so should have believed that Farah did not intend to make a proposal to *her*. **C** is wrong. **D** makes the false statement that one cannot be bound to a contract contrary to her actual intention. *We know that's wrong.* Contracts arise not by actual intention, but by manifest intention. **D** is for the dumper.

B refers to Harriett's knowledge that the community did not know her as a seamstress. Extend your reasoning from there. Understanding that she was not known as a seamstress, Harriett *should* have understood that Farah did not intend to engage her as one. That's the thought for which we're looking, so **B** is right.

QUESTION 6. Martha secured a patent for a biomedical device she called "Gutmate." Believing that Deborah was a qualified manufacturer of biomedical devices, Martha sent Deborah the Gutmate plans and designs, together with a note: "I am prepared to hire you as manufacturer of Gutmate. I have little capital and propose, therefore, to convey to you a share of the patent ownership in exchange for your services. I invite your acceptance." Deborah responded, by writing: "Yes, we have a deal."

Does Deborah's response constitute an acceptance?

A. Yes, because Deborah expressed her assent, clearly and unequivocally
B. Yes, because Martha explicitly invited Deborah to accept
C. No, because Martha's writing omits to describe Deborah as a qualified manufacturer
D. No, because Martha's writing proposes no definite bargain
E. No, because it did not present the word "accept" or "acceptance"

ANALYSIS.   You are asked to decide only this: that Deborah's response is or is not an acceptance. Martha's message makes no offer because it specifies no exchange. Most blatantly, it fails to indicate how large a "share" of the patent ownership Martha will convey. Because Martha made no offer, Deborah can give no acceptance.

Look among the choices for one that reaches the right conclusion ("no") for the right reason: Martha made no offer.

Choice **C** raises the reddest of "red herrings." One certainly may make an offer without reciting the offeree's qualifications to perform. The offeree may, likewise, accept. Nothing in **C** explains why Deborah's response fails as an acceptance. **E** implies that one may accept only by using the *word* "accept," and that, of course, is nonsense.

According to **D**, Deborah did not accept because Martha proposed no definite bargain. That's the test writer's way of noting that Martha made no offer, and that *is* the reason that Deborah could not accept. **D** seems certainly to be right, but for safety's sake let's look at **A** and **B**.

A tells us that Deborah plainly and unambiguously expressed her "assent." But that to which she assented was *not an offer,* meaning her assent was not an acceptance. **B** suggests that one gives an acceptance if someone else asks for her assent, and she responds by giving it. Choice **B**, like choice **A**, fails to account for the fact that an *acceptance must follow from an offer* and that Martha, in this case, did not make one. **A**, **B**, and **C** are wrong. **D** is right.

E.   Acceptance by Silence

If circumstances are such that a reasonable offeror should interpret the offeree's silence as assent, then *silence is acceptance.*

Wallace Washes Willa's Windows

In April, for $75, Wallace washed Willa's windows. Willa then told Wallace that she would likely want him to wash her windows again in six months. Six months later, in October, Wallace called Willa and asked if she'd like him to wash her windows again. She said "yes," he did so, and Willa again paid him $75. The same occurred every April and every October for eleven years.

On April 2 of the twelfth year, Wallace telephoned Willa and left this voicemail message: "I'll be by on Tuesday April 9 to wash the windows. Let me know, please, if that's a problem." Willa listened to the message and made no response.

Hearing nothing from Willa, Wallace appeared at Willa's home, ready to wash the windows. Willa told him that she no longer wished to have her windows washed.

Has Willa Breached a Contract?

Yes, probably. With his voicemail message of April 2, Wallace made an offer. In view of his request that Willa report any "problem" she had with his plan, and in light of the eleven-year history, Wallace was justified in believing

1. that if Willa did not want his services, she would come forth and say so and, therefore,
2. that Willa, with her silence, said, in effect, "yes, come on April 9; I have no problem with that."

This exemplifies the (rather rare) case in which *silence is acceptance.*

So What's the Rule?

You already know the rule because you know the meaning of acceptance. Silence may constitute acceptance because, under some circumstances, an offeree manifests assent by doing and saying — nothing. *An offeree's silence constitutes her acceptance when, under the circumstances, the offeror would naturally expect the offeree to come forth and speak up if she wished not to accept the offer.*

Restatement (Second) §26 (illustration) explains:

> Where an offeree fails to reply to an offer, his silence and inaction operate as an acceptance [if] because of previous dealings or otherwise, it is reasonable that the offeree should notify the offeror if he does not intend to accept.

QUESTION 7. RakeCo is a landscaper and CondoHome a residential condominium community. In each of the years 2009-2018, the two parties formed a written contract under which CondoHome paid RakeCo $90,000 and RakeCo attended to CondoHome's landscaping during the months of April through October. On February 1, 2019, CondoHome contacts RakeCo:

(1) February 1, **CondoHome** (by signed writing): We have received no contract for this year. Please assure us that you'll take care of our landscaping this coming spring through fall.

(2) February 4, **RakeCo** (by signed writing): Yes, of course we will. We have raised our fees by about 3 percent to all customers. In your case, our fee will be $93,000, not $90,000. None of our customers has objected to this modest increase, and we assume you will not object either. We'll be making all of our plans firm on April 1. You'll let us know, of course, if you have any comment.

> On February 7, CondoHome reads RakeCo's February 4 message and issues no response. On April 2, CondoHome advises RakeCo that for 2019 it has contracted with HoeCo, another landscaper, whose fee was $91,000, and that it will not accept RakeCo's services.
>
> RakeCo brings an action against CondoHome, alleging that the parties had formed a contract requiring that CondoHome retain RakeCo as its landscaper for April-October 2019 and pay its $93,000 fee. CondoHome contends that it never accepted RakeCo's February 1 offer, wherefore the parties formed no such contract.
>
> If judgment is for RakeCo, the reason will most likely be that
>
> A. RakeCo could sensibly understand that if CondoHome wanted not to accept RakeCo's offer, it would have said so before April 1.
> B. RakeCo did not impose the 3 percent fee increase on CondoHome alone, but rather imposed it on all of its customers.
> C. CondoHome should reasonably have anticipated that RakeCo might, after ten years, increase its fees.
> D. Before contracting with HoeCo, CondoHome owed RakeCo the opportunity to match HoeCo's price.

ANALYSIS. On February 4, RakeCo made CondoCo an offer. If these parties formed a contract it must be because RakeCo was justified in taking CondoCo's silence as assent.

Let's assess the answer choices. Choice **D** implies this rule: If Party X repeatedly buys from Party Y and then finds Party Z offering the same commodity at a lower price, Y may not contract with Z until it first gives X the chance to meet Z's price. Ridiculous; there's no such rule. **D** is wrong.

C is wrong too. Maybe CondoHome should have expected an increase in RakeCo's fee. But that doesn't mean CondoHome must pay it. Neither does it turn CondoHome's silence into acceptance. **B** implies that because RakeCo raised its price to *all* its customers, CondoHome's silence constitutes acceptance. That, too, is wrong. Whether RakeCo imposed its increase on all of its customers or on CondoHome only, CondoHome's silence is acceptance only if RakeCo should reasonably understand it as such. **B** is wrong.

What about choice **A**? RakeCo advised CondoHome that "We'll be making all of our plans firm on April 1," and asked that CondoHome contact it "with any comment." Quite arguably, CondoHome should reasonably have believed (sensibly understood) that to mean: "If you wish not to have us perform the work this year, please let us know by April 1." And, in view of the parties' history, RakeCo might, *on* April 1, be perfectly justified in reading CondoHome's silence thus: "We have no objection to your proposal; we accept it." A court might (*might*) see the situation in just that way and, for that reason, rule that CondoHome's silence was an acceptance of RakeCo's offer.

That's why **A** is right.

F.   Acceptance by Dominion

Suppose DirtCo, showing no return address, mails to 1,000 private homes a bottle of its laundry detergent, "LaundraLust," together with this message:

> Dear Homeowner:
>
> We offer you this bottle of LaundraLust for $1.89, and we'll send you another 11 bottles, one per month, for which you will pay (in advance) that same price of $1.89 per bottle. To accept this offer you need only keep this bottle we've sent you.

That's Cute. The Homeowner Accepts by Keeping the Bottle?

No, he doesn't. *An offeree accepts when she says, writes, or does that which, under the prevailing circumstances, would cause a reasonable person in the offeror's position to believe that she has assented, unconditionally, to the offeror's proposed bargain.*

That's law. No offeror can alter it. A reasonable person in DirtCo's position would understand that when one receives a product without asking for it, without notice of a return address, he will likely keep it for the simple reason that he doesn't know what else to do. An offeror cannot manufacture an acceptance by decreeing that he will treat the offeree's natural behavior as assent. Hence, DirtCo cannot reasonably believe that a homeowner who retains the LaundraLust assents to its offer.

So the Homeowner Gets to Keep and Use the LaundraLust for Free?

No, he doesn't. If the offeree keeps the property he makes himself a *bailee*.[3] By common law, he must return DirtCo's detergent when DirtCo asks to have it back. If, however, the offeree (homeowner) *exercises dominion* over the property, meaning that he uses it, sells it, gives it away, or otherwise treats it as his own, then he accepts DirtCo's offer and must pay the offered price. If he refuses to do so, he commits contractual breach.

---

3. When you "check" your coat at a restaurant you bail it; you're the bailor, the restaurant is the bailee. The bailee must keep and care for the coat, until you ask to have it back, treating it all the while as *your* property. The same is so when you leave your car in a commercial parking lot. Further, the common law *implies* a bailment when you lose your property and another finds it. You are the bailor and the finder is the bailee. The finder has the obligation to care for the property and, ultimately, to return it to you if and when you claim it. (That's a common law rule, but *statutes* in most jurisdictions allow the finder to bring the found property to the local police and thus be relieved of his responsibility as bailee.) Bailment is an expansive legal topic in its own right. The subject has spawned multi-volume works, some of them more than a hundred years old. The topic's tentacles touch a great many fields of law including contracts, as discussed in this section.

Restatement (Second) of Contracts §69 (2) provides (in part):

An offeree who does any act inconsistent with the offeror's ownership of offered property is bound in accordance with the offered terms unless they are manifestly unreasonable.

That means this: *If Party A delivers property to Party B, offering it for sale to Party B, and Party B in some way treats the property as his own, then Party B accepts Party A's offer to purchase the property — unless the terms of the offer are manifestly unreasonable.*

"Manifestly Unreasonable"? What's That?

Suppose:

1. Seller sends Homeowner a can of shoe polish together with an offer to sell it for *$12 million*, and
2. Homeowner uses it.

On learning that Homeowner has used the product, Seller cannot, as a reasonable person, believe that Homeowner manifested assent to pay the $12 million.

The offeree's exercise of dominion does not, in that case, constitute acceptance. (It probably does, however, constitute the tort of conversion.[4])

Can the Offeree Leave the Property in His Mailbox? And If He Takes It Into His Possession, Can He Ever Discard It?

Yes, and yes. If the offeree leaves the seller's property where he finds it (at his doorstep or in his mailbox, for example) he bears no responsibility for its care or return. If he takes custody of it and thus becomes a bailee he may, after a reasonable time, discard it.[5]

But Know This: Where the Offeror Uses U.S. Mail, a Federal Statute Supersedes this Common Law Rule

A federal statute now provides, generally, that if, on his own initiative, a Party A *mails* property to a Party B together with an offer to sell it, Party B may take and keep the property as his gift.

---

4. One commits the tort of conversion and thus becomes a "converter" when, without consent or other justification, he exercises such dominion and control over another's property as properly belongs to a true owner, wherefore the law allows the true owner, in essence, to recover from the defendant the value of the property and thus, in effect, to require that he buy it. See *Am. Jur. 2d Conversion §2, Restatement 2d Torts §222A*. If a bailee treats a bailor's property as though it is his own, he commits conversion.

5. None of this is quite so simple as we might like it to be. Bailment, once again, is a topic unto itself and it happens to cross paths, here, with contracts. In general, however, when one becomes an "involuntary bailee," as happens in these scenarios, he may, after a reasonable time, conclude that the bailor has abandoned the property—and then—discard it.

39 U.S.C. §3009(b) provides:

> [Any unordered merchandise sent by U.S. mail] may be treated as a gift by the recipient, who shall have the right to retain, use, discard, or dispose of it in any manner he sees fit without any obligation whatsoever to the sender.

The federal statute applies only where the offeror uses the *U.S. mails* to send the unordered merchandise. Where he employs some other mode of delivery, the common law continues to operate.

Can You Restate That Please, Your Way?

(1) If (other than by U.S. mail), without any request, one receives property together with the owner's offer to sell it, then the recipient may (a) leave the property where he finds it and be free of any responsibility, or (b) take custody, hold it as a bailee, and, after a reasonable time, discard it, or (c) exercise dominion by using it, selling it, gifting it, or otherwise treating it as his own. In case (c), he accepts the owner's offer (unless its terms are manifestly unreasonable) and, by contract, must pay the owner's price. On the other hand (2) If such receipt arises by U.S. mail, then the property belongs wholly and absolutely to the recipient.

QUESTION 8. CupCo manufactured disposable cups and sold them to distributors. SupCo was a distributor of disposable cups, and on all the cups it sold, stamped its own name and imprint. On August 1, in its own truck, CupCo sent SupCo two thousand disposable coffee cups, in boxes, together with this message:

> We provide herewith two thousand of our new CoffeeFriend coffee cups. We assume you'll want to sell them to your own customers. If you keep them, we'll assume that you've decided to buy, and we'll bill you $125. If you do not wish to buy, please return to us within fifteen days, COD; we will pay the shipping charges.

Which of the following would most likely mean that SupCo accepts CupCo's offer?

A. SupCo keeps the cups in their unopened boxes for more than fifteen days.
B. SupCo writes to CupCo: "We will keep the cups until you come to get them."
C. SupCo writes to CupCo: "We very much like the cups."
D. SupCo stamps its own name and imprint on the cups.

ANALYSIS. On its own initiative CupCo sent its cups to SupCo. Notwithstanding CupCo's message, mere silence on SupCo's part will not constitute acceptance. Rather, SupCo will accept if either (a) it contacts CupCo and assents to its offer, or (b) exercises dominion over the cups. According to Choice **A** SupCo keeps possession of the cups but does not even open the boxes in which they came. In doing that, it does not accept the offer but, instead, makes itself a bailee. **A** is wrong. **B** is wrong too. By telling CupCo that the cups are available for pickup, SupCo once again makes itself a bailee.

What of **C**? Maybe the message, "we very much like the cups," manifests assent to CupCo's offer. Were it not for **D**, **C** would be best. But **D** is plainly better. By stamping its name on the cups SupCo treated them as its own; it exercised dominion over them and thus accepted CupCo's offer. **D** is right.

G.   The Closer

> **QUESTION 9.** Paula, President of PowerCo, owns ten million gallons of diesel fuel and needs a refinery to process it during the coming autumn so she can sell it during the winter. Olivia owns and operates a diesel fuel refinery and Frank, her competitor, owns and operates one as well. On a Monday in August, Paul, Olivia, and Frank meet, each with a pad of note paper. They discuss Paula's need to have her ten million gallons of diesel fuel refined during the coming autumn. Olivia advises Paula that she has the capacity to do the job. Frank advises her that he, too, has that same capacity.
>
> On two separate sheets of paper from her pad, Paula writes, "PowerCo is prepared to pay $7 million now for a guarantee that our ten million gallons of grade-two diesel fuel oil will be refined on or before October 10 of this year." After she signs both writings Paula says, "Here, this is for the two of you." She then hands one to Frank and the other to Olivia. Frank and Olivia read the writing, and the three parties separate.
>
> On the next day, Tuesday, Frank personally delivers to Paula this written message, "I accept your offer of yesterday." On the same day, Olivia reaches Paula by telephone and says, "I accept the offer you made yesterday." Which of the following additional facts most likely means that Paula is obliged to purchase diesel fuel from Olivia and not from Frank?
>
> A. Frank did not sign the writing that he delivered to Paula.
> B. Olivia reached Paula by telephone before Frank arrived at Paula's office.
> C. When Frank wrote the words "I accept your offer of yesterday," he had lost Paula's writing and no longer had it in his possession.

> **D.** On Wednesday, Olivia sent by certified mail a signed writing in which she stated: "I hereby reaffirm acceptance, made by telephone on Tuesday, of Monday's offer."

ANALYSIS.   With respect to any offer, the offeree is she who reasonably believes the offeror has invited *her* assent. Paula makes her offer by signed writing, orally addressed to "the two of you." Hence, both Olivia and Frank are offerees. Yet Paula made plain her wish to have refined only ten million gallons of fuel. Consequently, her offerees should know that she invites acceptance from either of them, but not both. As with James, Nancy, and May (section D above), Paula's offer starts a "race" between two offerees; both have power to accept, but *each loses the power if the other exercises it first*. Olivia accepts the offer if she is first to manifest her assent.

Choice **A** implies that an unsigned writing is legally ineffective. Nonlawyers might believe that, but it's not true. As discussed in section C above, signatures have significance — primarily for purposes of evidence.[6] Nonetheless, one may offer or accept without a writing, or with a writing that's unsigned.

C and **D** cite facts that are legally irrelevant. According to **C**, Frank lost Paula's writing before writing his words of acceptance. The law nowhere requires that an offeree have in his possession some written record of the offer when he decides to accept it. **D** states that Olivia sent by certified mail a signed writing reaffirming the acceptance she made by telephone. To that, we say, "so what?" With the phone call she accepted Paula's offer. A second acceptance means nothing (but, as discussed in section C, the writing creates good *evidence* of the acceptance).

According to **B**, Olivia was first to contact Paula and express her assent. That means she accepted the offer so that she and Paula formed a contract. Simultaneously, Frank lost his power to accept. When he handed Paula his writing, he did nothing of legal import; the writing is a "legal nullity." **B** is right.

 ## Silver's Picks

1.	**B**
2.	**E**
3.	**E**
4.	**D**
5.	**B**
6.	**D**
7.	**A**
8.	**D**
9.	**B**

---

6. But, again, Chapter 15 discusses exceptions to that rule.

3

Understand the Relationships Among Three Critical Phrases

A. Manifest Intention (Again)

Think again of the lawnmower case described in Chapter 2, section B: Carlos stands by a lawnmower and says, in a serious tone, "I want to sell my lawnmower for $100." Even if Carlos means to describe another lawnmower miles away, a reasonable person, seeing and hearing him, would think he's talking of the mower standing right there. Regardless of Carlos's true intention, *that's* the intention to which the law holds him; it's his "manifest intention." *A party's manifest intention, then, is the intention that, under all prevailing circumstances, a reasonable person would attribute to her on seeing what she does, hearing what she says, or reading what she writes.* Where contract law refers to "intention," it almost always means *manifest* intention.

> A contract has, strictly speaking, nothing to do with the personal, or individual, intent of the parties. A contract is an obligation attached by . . . acts . . . . [and] words[.] . . . [W]hatever was the [parties'] understanding, it is of not the slightest consequence, unless it took form in some acts or words, which,

being reasonably interpreted, would have such meaning to ordinary [persons.] ... [T]he question always remains for the court to interpret the reasonable meaning of the acts of the parties, by word or deed, and no characterization of its effect by either party thereafter, however truthful, is material.

Hotchkiss v. National City Bank of New York, 200 F. 287, 293-294 (S.D.N.Y. 1911).

A party's manifest intention, then, is the intention that, under all prevailing circumstances, a reasonable person would attribute to her on seeing what she does, hearing what she says, or reading what she writes. Where contract law refers to "intention," that's what it means; it means *manifest* intention.

B.   Objective Theory of Contracts

That brings us to the "objective theory of contracts," a pretentious little phrase that refers to the legal doctrine we've been discussing: *A party's intentions are not those that she subjectively carries in her own mind but rather those that an objective reasonable person would, under all surrounding circumstances, attribute to her words and behavior.*

In the lawnmower example, a judge, lawyer, professor, or writer who refers to the objective theory of contracts means only that Carlos, by law, is deemed to be offering for sale the very lawnmower standing next to him because a reasonable *objective* person would so conclude. For all time, by and large, contract law has subscribed to the objective theory. Authoritative statements to that effect arise as early as the 1400s when, during the reign of Edward IV, an English court wrote: "It is a trite learning that the thought of man is not triable, for the devil himself knows not the thought of man." Brian, in YB 17 Edw. IV, 2. A wide range of jurists and scholars have agreed, and all modern courts are in accord:

> [T]he law imputes to a person an intention corresponding to the reasonable meaning of his words and acts.

Howell v. Smith, 128 S.E.2d 144 (N.C. 1962); Roper v. Clanton, 258 S.W.2d 283 (Mo. App. 1953); Marefield Meadows, Inc. v. Lorenz, 427 S.E.2d 363 (Va. 1993).

Yet many commentators write of a historical debate between those who believed in the objective theory of contract and those who endorsed a *subjective* one. According to proponents of the subjective theory, no two persons could form a contract unless they truly, in their heads, intended to be bound by a single set of terms. A difference of genuine intent or interpretation, if proven, meant the parties formed no contract.

But the truth seems to be that no learned authority — of any century — ever fully expounded a system of contract law based on subjective intent. So, even though some literature *refers to* a historical competition between subjective and objective theorists, it's not clear that there ever truly was any such contest.[1] In any case, all modern authorities agree that the objective theory of contracts is law.[2] And yet, opinions feature sometimes, still, the unfortunate phrase "meeting of the minds."

C.   "Meeting of the Minds"

At its heart, the objective theory of contracts means this: When two persons form an agreement, each is entitled to enjoy his *reasonable expectations and beliefs and, in turn, must fulfill those of the other*. On that principle, we define "offer" as a *manifestation* of willingness to enter a bargain that *justifies* another person in believing his assent is invited. Because we so define "offer," one who reasonably believes that a bargain is proposed to him does indeed have power to assent to it and thus finalize a contract, even if the offeror truly intends no such thing. And it matters not that offeror and offeree, *in their own heads*, give different meanings to the offeror's words or behavior. By law, words and behaviors have such meaning as *reasonable* persons would give them under the prevailing circumstances.

Similarly, we define acceptance as a *manifestation* of assent, so that when the offeror reasonably believes the offeree has assented, the parties form a contract, even if the offeree truly intended no such thing. It matters not that offeror and offeree, *in their own heads*, give different meanings to the offeree's words. By law, they have such meaning as *reasonable* persons would give them under the prevailing circumstances.

1. But Aren't All Words Susceptible to Many Reasonable Interpretations?

Under most circumstances, according to the law, no. Under most circumstances, communicative words or behaviors have but one reasonable

---

1.   Referring to the so-called historical debate between proponents of the "objective" and "subjective" contract theories, Professor Perillo writes,

> A more accurate account of the origins of the objective theory is that objective approaches have predominated in the common law of contracts since time immemorial. The account is not seamless; there was a brief but almost inconsequential flirtation with subjective approaches in the mid-nineteenth century. The flirtation produced the rhetoric of a subjective approach but had little effect on the outcome of cases involving the formation or interpretation of contracts[.]

Joseph M. Perillo, *The Origins of the Objective Theory of Contract Formation and Interpretation*, 69 Fordham L. Rev. 427, 428 (2000).

2.   "[T]he law "long ago discarded . . . subjective intent[.]" John E. Murray, *Convention on Contracts for the International Sale of Goods* (1988). "Secret intent [is] immaterial, only overt acts constitute intent." 1 Samuel Williston, *Treatise on the Law of Contracts* §22 (1922). "Maryland follows the objective law of contract interpretation and construction. [W]hat is meant is not what the parties to the contract intended it to mean, but what a reasonable person in the position of the parties would have thought it meant." Young v. Anne Arundel County, 807 A.2d 651 (Md. 2002).

interpretation. *Rarely*, however, quirks of circumstance arise in which one's words and behaviors are susceptible to two very different interpretations, both of them perfectly reasonable. In those uncommon cases, if the misunderstanding is material[3] to the purported agreement, the parties do *not* form a contract. That too squares with the objective theory.

Illustration: *Ilsa v. Ike*

On Ike's used car lot, there stands a 2004 Jaguar XYZ with a "blue book" value of $20,000. Also on the lot is a 2018 Chevrolet Capricious with a "blue book" value of $12,000. At noon on September 10, Ike posts (a) on the Jaguar a sign that reads: "ONCE IN A LIFETIME DEAL! This Beautiful 2004 JAGUAR XYZ For Sale Now at the GIVE-AWAY PRICE of $15,000," and (b) on the Chevrolet a sign that reads: "ONCE IN A LIFETIME DEAL! This Beautiful 2018 Chevrolet Capricious For Sale Now at the GIVE-AWAY PRICE of $9,000."

At 12:05 P.M., some guy named Victor sees the signs and decides to make mischief. He puts the $9,000 sign on the Jaguar and the $15,000 sign on the Chevrolet. At 12:06 P.M., Ilsa arrives at the lot and sees the signs. Believing that $9,000 is, most certainly, a very low price for the Jaguar, she enters Ike's office and asks, "Are you serious about the $9,000 price on the windshield outside? For $9,000 you're really selling *that vehicle*?" "Yes," says Ike. "That vehicle is a great car for a great price." Ilsa responds, "Well, then I'll take it." Ike replies, "And you've got it. It's a deal. Here, let's quickly make up a writing, and we'll sign a more formal one later."

On paper, Ike quickly writes: "There now sits on the lot of the undersigned Ike Irkton ("Seller") a vehicle bearing a price tag of $9,000. Seller and the undersigned Ilsa Ilis ("Buyer") do agree that on or about this day March 15, 2018, Seller will sell and Buyer will buy that vehicle for $9,000." Ilsa then signs the writing, which means that she is the offeror. Ike then signs, meaning he accepts Ilsa's offer. (As is fully discussed in Chapter 5, section C, when two parties sign a written contractual document, by law, usually, the first to sign makes an offer to the other of all that is written in the document. When the other signs, he accepts the offer.)

Ike and Ilsa then walk out to the lot. Distraught when he sees how his signs have been moved, so that the $9,000 price tag sits on the Jaguar, Ike proclaims, "Someone has moved my signs around. Did you actually think this beautiful Jaguar was available for $9,000?" Ilsa responds, "You wrote 'give-away price' and yes, I truly thought the car was available for $9,000; that's a give-away price. So that's our deal." "Oh, no, it's not," counters Ike, "I posted on the Jaguar a price of $15,000. Somebody moved this $9,000 sign from the Chevrolet to the Jaguar and the $15,000 Jaguar sign to the Chevrolet."

---

3. The word "material" pops up throughout the law of contract. It refers to that which is significant. When we say "material misunderstanding," we refer to a misunderstanding that significantly affects the burdens and benefits that the contract visits on one or both its parties.

Nonetheless, Ilsa insists that she is entitled to buy the Jaguar for $9,000. Ike insists otherwise.

With reference to their conversation and signed writing, these two parties gave two different meanings to "that vehicle," *both of which, under these peculiar circumstances, were reasonable ones.*

Now Let's Think What, by Law, That *Really* Means

When Ilsa signed the writing, she *thought* she was offering $9,000 for the Jaguar, but Ike reasonably believed she was offering that price for the Chevrolet. Legally, that means without her knowing it, *Ilsa did offer to pay $9,000 for the Chevrolet*. When Ike then signed the writing, he *thought* he was accepting Ilsa's offer to buy the Chevrolet for $9,000. But Ilsa reasonably believed Ike had agreed to sell her the Jaguar for $9,000. *So, regardless of what Ike thought, he agreed to sell the Jaguar for $9,000.* These two failed to form a contract for this simple reason: Ilsa made an offer to buy the Chevrolet, and Ike accepted an offer to sell the Jaguar. These were their legal intentions (opposite to their true intentions). Between them, there was no offer and acceptance. Simple. That's it.

All courts and (competent) lawyers would agree that Ilsa and Ike formed no contract. Yet faced with situations like this — where two parties give different interpretations to the same words, both of them reasonable — many courts have had trouble articulating the real reason for their conclusions. They have resorted instead to the unhappy, misconceived words, "meeting of the minds."

For example, a court deciding *Ilsa v. Ike* would surely reach the right result but, in doing so, publish a misleading opinion like this:

> Each of these parties behaved honestly. Plaintiff Ilsa Ilis genuinely thought the "give-away" $9,000 advertised price pertained to the Jaguar; she offered to purchase that car for that amount. Defendant accepted the offer, but believed that for $9,000 he was to sell the Chevrolet.
>
> The law does not impose a contract on two persons, each of whom honestly believes the bargain to be one thing while the other believes it to be another. Notwithstanding their offer and acceptance, and because of their good faith misunderstanding, we hold that these parties failed to form a contract for the simple reason that they did not achieve a meeting of the minds, without which no offer and acceptance can make a contract.

For the wrong reason, this court reached the right result. No true "meeting of the minds" is necessary — *ever* — to the formation of a contract. Any and every (competent) court in the nation would hold, and every (learned) lawyer would agree, that the offeror who stands next to a lawnmower offering to sell "my lawnmower" offers to sell the very lawnmower in front of her regardless of her own true intention. No one would care that the offeror's and offeree's minds don't "meet."

Properly understood, the objective theory of contracts explains the result in *Ilsa v. Ike* without reference to any failed "meetings" between "minds." Ike and Ilsa failed to form a contract because they failed to achieve offer and acceptance. When Ilsa offered to purchase "that vehicle" for $9,000, Ike reasonably understood "that vehicle" to mean the Chevrolet. Consequently, *by law*, Ilsa *did offer to buy the Chevrolet.* She did not, of course, in her own mind, want to buy the Chevrolet, but when she said "that vehicle," her words had such *legal* meaning as would be given them by a reasonable person in Ike's position. Ike, under the circumstances, *wrongly but reasonably* believed that Ilsa was referring to the Chevrolet. Consequently, that was Ilsa's legal intention; Ilsa offered to buy the Chevrolet for $9,000 although she herself did not know that.

When Ike told Ilsa she could have "that vehicle" for $9,000, Ilsa *wrongly but reasonably* understood *that he was referring to the Jaguar.* The parties then signed a writing, Ilsa first and Ike second. The writing (which, in any event, normally supersedes the conversation)[4] also bore the phrase "that vehicle." Ilsa as offeror *manifested* an intention to buy the Chevrolet, for $9,000 and, legally, that's what she offered. Ike *manifested* an intention to sell the Jaguar for $9,000 and that, legally, is what he "accepted" — an offer never made to him. By law, Ilsa offered to buy a Chevrolet and Ike agreed to sell a Jaguar (all opposite to the parties' true intentions).

Ilsa did not, of course, in her own mind, want to buy the Chevrolet, but when she said "that vehicle," her words had such *legal* meaning as would be given them by a reasonable person in Ike's position. Ike under the circumstances, *wrongly but reasonably* believed that Ilsa was referring to the Chevrolet. These parties failed to form a contract because they didn't achieve an offer and acceptance; Ilsa made an offer that Ike did not accept. Conceptually, "meeting of the minds" has no proper place in this or any other contractual analysis.

2. The Famous Case of the Peerless

The English case of Raffles v. Wichelhaus, 2 H. & C. 906 (Ct. Exchq. 1864), involved a buyer and seller who attempted to contract for the sale of cotton. The 1864 case report does not indicate which of the parties was offeror or which was offeree, but we can imagine it either way 'round; the issue and result are the same. So let's suppose that Seller was the offeror.

Seller offered to sell cotton to Buyer, the cotton to be delivered to Buyer at Liverpool on a ship called *Peerless*, which was to sail from Bombay to Liverpool. Buyer accepted the offer, and the parties thus thought they had contracted for the purchase and sale of cotton to be delivered to Buyer at Liverpool aboard the ship *Peerless* sailing from Bombay.

Unbeknownst to either party, two separate ships named *Peerless* were scheduled to sail from Bombay to Liverpool during the relevant period, one

---

4. Chapter 19.

arriving in October, the other in December. When Seller made his offer and specified *Peerless*, he knew nothing of the October *Peerless* and had no reason to know of it. He, in his own mind, meant to designate the December ship, the only *Peerless* of which he knew. Yet, when Buyer accepted the offer, he knew nothing of the December ship and had no reason to know of it. He, in his own mind, understood *Peerless* to mean the ship arriving at Liverpool in October. Consequently, the parties thought they had agreed on the ship by which the goods would land in Liverpool (and, therefore, the month in which the goods would arrive). Yet they had not done so. Each had his own understanding of the name *Peerless*, and *both understandings, under the circumstances, were reasonable.*

In October, a ship *Peerless* arrived at Liverpool. Buyer sought to claim his cotton and found it was not on board. In December, the other *Peerless* arrived at Liverpool with the cotton on board. Buyer refused to take it, insisting that Seller should have delivered it on the October ship *Peerless*, the one on which he thought the parties had agreed. Seller brought an action against Buyer, alleging that Buyer was obliged to take and pay for the goods delivered on the December ship, the one on which *he* thought the parties had agreed.

The court ruled that the parties formed no contract at all, adopting the argument (apparently) that they had failed to achieve *consensus ad idem* (meaning agreement of idea; meeting of the minds): "[I]t appears that two ships called the 'Peerless' were about to sail from Bombay [to Liverpool.] . . . That being so, there was no *consensus ad idem*, and therefore no binding contract." Raffles v. Wichelhaus, 2 H. & C. 906, 907-908 (Ct. Exchq. 1864).[5]

In *Peerless*, as in *Ilsa v. Ike* above, the two pertinent parties, each thinking *reasonably*, gave different meanings to the same words. In *Ilsa v. Ike*, this rare happening arose from the underlying unlikelihood that within a few minutes after the seller posted two prices on two cars, a meddler should switch them 'round, and a passer-by should immediately offer to buy one of them for "that price."

In *Peerless*, the rare happening arose because of another unlikelihood — that two cargo ships bearing the same name sailed from Bombay to Liverpool at or about the same time. *Peerless* too is readily susceptible to analysis via the objective theory. When Seller offered to sell goods delivered on the *Peerless*, he meant the December ship. But Buyer, knowing only of the October ship, reasonably (but wrongly) understood that Seller was referring to that one. Consequently, Seller, despite what he thought, offered to sell goods to be delivered on the October ship. Buyer, when he purported to accept, agreeing to buy goods on the *Peerless*, meant the October ship, but Seller reasonably understood him to mean the December ship. Consequently, in his attempt to accept,

---

5. Like many English opinions of old, this one was written by a court reporter; it summarizes counsels' arguments and then reports the court's decision.

Buyer did not accept the offer made to him. For that reason — for failure of offer and acceptance — the parties formed no contract.

When a judge rules that two parties form no contract because they fail to achieve a "meeting of the minds," she means (but may not know she means) the two parties gave materially[6] different meanings to the same word or phrase and that *both interpretations were reasonable*. Restatement (Second) of Contracts §20(1) provides:

> There is no manifestation of mutual assent to an exchange if the parties attach materially different meanings to their manifestations and . . . neither party knows or has reason to know the meaning attached by the other[.]

That jumble of words is the Restatement's *Peerless* provision. (See Restatement (Second) §20 illus. 2.) It means that two parties fail to form a contract if to the same word or phrase each gives a materially different interpretation, both of them reasonable under the prevailing circumstance. In such cases, the parties fail to form a contract because the meaning of the offeror's offer *as the offeree reasonably construes it* differs from the meaning of the offeree's purported acceptance *as the offeror reasonably construes it.*

Hence, even though the parties shake hands or sign their names to the *same set of words*, the offeror proposes one thing and the offeree "accepts" another. The parties achieve no offer and acceptance, and *that's* why they fail to form a contract. A failed "meeting of the minds" has naught to do with it.[7]

3. *"Latent Ambiguity"*

Some speak of "latent ambiguity" instead of (or together with) a failed "meeting of the minds." The phrase "latent ambiguity" belongs to the same situation as does "meeting of the minds": "Latent ambiguity" means a word or phrase that, as expressed and meant by one party, carries a materially different meaning for the other, *both meanings being reasonable* under the operative circumstances. In *Ilsa v. Ike*, the phrase "that vehicle" represents a latent ambiguity; so does the name "Peerless" in *Raffles v. Wichelhaus*. Hence, where some say that two parties fail to form a contract because they fail to achieve a "meeting of the minds," others say (or add) that the contract fails for "latent ambiguity." These identical statements are identically flawed. We hope they'll someday pass away to be superseded by a proper understanding of cases like *Ilsa v. Ike* and *Peerless*,

---

6. In the *Peerless* case, for example, the difference between the October and December ships is *material* — significant. If instead one ship arrived at 12:00 noon on October 5 and the second at 12:10 P.M. on October 5, the difference would be *immaterial* — insignificant. Materiality is ordinarily a question of fact for the jury (or the court in a bench trial).

7. See Murray, *supra* note 2: ("[T]he unfortunate phrase 'meeting of the minds' . . . [arises] only where there is no preponderance of objective evidence favoring [the reasonableness of] one interpretation over another."). To make matters worse, when dealing with two parties each of whom attributed different but reasonable meanings to the same word or phrase, many courts employ the misbegotten phrase "unilateral mistake." (See Chapter 22, section E.)

for which this is truly the rule: *Where (as is rare) (a) two contracting parties give different interpretations to one of their contractual terms, and (b) (as is rare), under the prevailing circumstances, both interpretations are reasonable, then the two parties fail to form a contract, not because they fail to achieve a "meeting of the minds," but because the offer, as reasonably construed by the offeree, does not correspond to the acceptance as reasonably construed by the offeror, meaning that the parties do not achieve offer and acceptance and, for that reason, do not form a contract.*

Let's revisit *Peerless* and alter the facts. Suppose that (a) Buyer takes the word "Peerless" to mean the ship due in October, *having a reason* to know that Seller thinks "Peerless" means the ship due in December, but (b) Seller has no reason to know that Buyer thinks "Peerless" means the ship due in October. In that case, Buyer's interpretation is unreasonable. By presumption of law, no reasonable person will stand by his interpretation of a contractual term if he knows (or should know) that the other contracting party interprets it differently. Consequently, with the *Peerless* case thus (hypothetically) altered, Seller's interpretation is ineffective; "Peerless" means the ship due in December.

Let's state that abstractly:

Contract formation never requires — ever — any true meeting of any mind with any other; rather (1) if, to the contractual terms on which they purport to agree, two parties A and B give materially different interpretations and (2) A knows or has reason to know of B's interpretation, but (3) B has no reason to know of A's interpretation then, in that case, (4) A's interpretation is not reasonable, and the parties form a contract according to B's interpretation.

Let's Illustrate That

Chelsea has two white bookcases in her den, one on the east wall, one on the west wall. Between the two bookcases there sits, on the floor, Chelsea's desk. For some twenty years, Chelsea has stored her large unabridged dictionary in the western bookcase. One day, however, she leaves it on her desk, and her nine-year-old son moves it from the desk to the *eastern* shelf. There it remains.

Six months later, Chelsea invites to her home Otis, a painter. She says to him, "I'd like you to paint a bookcase for me today— now. It's in the den. It's white and I want it painted black." Otis enters the den without Chelsea and, seeing two bookcases, shouts to her: "Both these bookcases are white. Which do you want me to paint?" Chelsea responds, "The one with the big unabridged dictionary on it." Otis then says, "Okay, I'll paint that bookcase for $100." Chelsea says, "yes, that bookcase, agreed." Two hours later, when Chelsea sees which bookcase Otis has painted, she proclaims, "Oh, I meant for you to paint the *other* bookcase. That's where I always store the dictionary. I can't pay you for this work; it's not the work I intended you to do."

At the time these parties formed their contract, they honestly attributed different meanings to the words "that bookcase." Otis took those words to mean the bookcase that actually held the dictionary, which was in fact the eastern bookcase. Chelsea meant to specify the western bookcase, the one on which she honestly thought the dictionary sat. And although both parties were honest in their divergent understandings, Chelsea's understanding, by law, *was not reasonable*. Chelsea *should* have known — she had *reasonable opportunity* to know — that the dictionary was in the eastern bookcase. It was she who absentmindedly left the book on the desk six months earlier, whereupon her nine-year-old son, with access to the desk, placed it on the eastern bookcase. Without herself examining the bookcases, speaking from another room, Chelsea directed Otis to the bookcase with the big unabridged dictionary on it.

With precision, let's examine the parties' statements in terms of their legal significance.

Chelsea: I'd like you to paint a bookcase for me today — now. It's in the den. It's white, and I want it painted black.	Invitation to deal
Otis *[entering the room without Chelsea]:* Both these bookcases are white. Which do you want me to paint?	Invitation to deal
Chelsea: The one with the big unabridged dictionary on it.	Invitation to deal
Otis: Okay, I'll paint the bookcase for $100.	*Offer:* Chelsea *should* understand Otis to say "I'll paint the *eastern* bookcase for $100."
Chelsea: Yes, that bookcase, agreed.	*Acceptance:* Otis reasonably understands Chelsea to say "Yes, paint the *eastern* bookcase for $100."

By offer and acceptance, these parties formed a contract respecting the *eastern* bookcase.

Analogy to Negligence/Fault.   Chelsea's absentminded failure to replace the dictionary on the western shelf six months earlier, and her failure, before answering Otis's question, to verify that the book was, in fact, on the eastern shelf amount to a kind of negligence or fault. Chelsea is like the driver who by absentmindedness passes through a red traffic light and causes a collision. Consequently, when assessing the situation in which two parties give different meanings to some term of their agreement, we may ask whether (a) the parties are equally blameless (or blameworthy), as in *Peerless* and *Ilsa v. Ike*; or (b) one of the parties is somehow at fault for the misunderstanding, as in the case of Chelsea and Otis.

If, via something akin to negligence, one of the parties is at fault for the misunderstanding, then, by law, her understanding of the relevant term is not a reasonable one. Consequently, the parties do form a contract and the disputed term carries the meaning given it by the other party — the party who is not at fault. Restatement (Second) §20(2) articulates this same principle:

> The manifestations of the parties are operative in accordance with the meaning attached to them by one of the parties if . . . (b) that party has no reason

to know of any different meaning attached by the other, and the other has reason to know the meaning attached by the first party.

If we apply the Restatement rule to Chelsea and Otis, we find that:

1. Chelsea and Otis attached different meanings to the words "that bookcase."
2. Otis, understanding the phrase to designate the eastern bookcase, had no reason to know of any other meaning attached by Chelsea.
3. Chelsea, intending the phrase to designate the western bookcase, *did* have reason to know the meaning attached by Otis; it was she who left the dictionary out of place and thus caused the misunderstanding.

Consequently, notwithstanding their divergent interpretations of the term, the parties do form a contract for painting of the *eastern* bookcase.

4. Let's Put It All Together in One Big Rule

If two parties, A and B, do all that is otherwise necessary to form a contract, but they attribute materially different meanings to a word or phrase on which they think they agree, then:

(a) where, under the circumstances, both interpretations are reasonable, the relevant term constitutes what some unfortunately call a "latent ambiguity" (to which others erroneously refer with the phrase "meeting of the minds," which phrase has no legitimate place in the law) and the parties form no contract;

(b) (i) where, under the circumstances, one of the interpretations is unreasonable and the other reasonable, then the parties do form a contract and the disputed term carries the reasonable interpretation, and (ii) where one of the parties, Party A, knows of the interpretation given by the other, Party B, but Party B does not know of the interpretation given by Party A, then Party A's interpretation is, by law, unreasonable, and Party B's is reasonable.

The *Peerless* and *Ilsa v. Ike* cases fall within subsentence (a) above, and cases like those cause some courts, regrettably, to invoke the phrase "meeting of the minds." The Chelsea-Otis case falls within subsentence (b)(ii) above. And once again, the rule just stated and the rule of Restatement §20(2) reflect the *objective* theory of contracts, even when some authorities (and professors) fail to see that truth.

QUESTION 1. Sam keeps two bicycles in his garage, a red one that sits at the back of the garage hidden behind old furniture, and a blue one that sits at the front, in plain view. Although Sam placed both bicycles in his garage, he has forgotten all about the blue one; he remembers only the red one hidden at the back. On Monday, Babs visits Sam and sees the blue bike in the front of the garage. On Tuesday, Babs telephones Sam:

> **Babs:** I saw the bicycle in your garage yesterday. I'd like to buy it — today. Will you take $90?
>
> **Sam:** Ninety dollars — yes, definitely. Come over, we'll take it out of the garage, you'll pay me, and it's yours. And by the way, I think that's a reasonable price.

Babs arrives at Sam's garage. As she moves toward the blue bike in plain view, the parties talk.

> **Sam:** Oh, you meant *that* one? I'd forgotten all about it. I thought you meant the bike at the back of the garage, although I see now that it's hidden.
>
> **Babs:** Well, I want the bike that's right here in front of me. That's the one for which I offered $90.

Sam refuses to sell the blue bike for $90, insisting that it is worth $105. Babs brings an action alleging that Sam breached their contract by failing to sell her the blue bike for $90. Sam contends that because of their misunderstanding, the parties formed no contract. The court rules that the parties did form a contract for the sale of the blue bike. If the court properly understands the law, it might articulate as its reason that

I. **By law,** the parties "intended" to contract for the sale of the blue bike.
II. Sam expressly stated that he thought the $90 price was reasonable.
III. **By law,** Babs offered to buy the blue bike, and Sam accepted her offer.
IV. Sam had reason to know that with the words "the bicycle in your garage," Babs was referring to the blue bike, and Babs had no reason to know that in saying "it's yours" Sam was referring to the red one.

A. I and II
B. I and III
C. I, II, and IV
D. I, III, and IV

ANALYSIS.   Grab hold of the rule given in section C.4 above. In attempting to form a contract for the purchase and sale of "the bicycle in [Sam's] garage," these parties attached different meanings to those critical words. Babs did not know and *had no reason to know* that a red bike sat hidden in the back of the garage. Sam, although he had forgotten about the blue bike, *had reason* to know of it; he had put both bikes in the garage. Consequently, Sam should have known that the garage housed two bikes and that Babs had seen only the blue one. For those reasons, the case is not like *Peerless* or *Ilsa v. Ike*. Rather, it resembles *Otis v. Chelsea*.

Stated otherwise, Babs made an offer, and Sam accepted. When Babs offered to purchase the bicycle in Sam's garage, Sam *should have understood her to mean* the blue bike at the front of the garage. By law, therefore, that's the bicycle Babs offered to buy. When Sam said, "yes, definitely . . . ," Babs *reasonably understood* him to mean he would sell her the blue bicycle. By law, therefore, Sam agreed to sell the blue bike regardless of what he, in his own head, meant to say. He accepted Babs's offer.

Stated yet another way, these parties had corresponding manifest intentions. A reasonable person in Sam's position would understand that Babs intended to buy the blue bike. Consequently, that was her manifest intention. A reasonable person in Babs's position would understand that Sam meant to sell the blue bike. Consequently, that was Sam's manifest intention. The manifest intentions "match," and the parties form a contract.

Option I states that irrespective of their misunderstanding, the parties *legally "intended"* to contract for the sale of the blue bike. That is precisely correct and precisely on point. Hence, the right answer must include option I. Option II reports that Sam expressly acknowledged the reasonableness of Babs's proposed price, a fact that's off point. When Sam said, "yes, definitely . . ." he accepted Babs's offer; the parties formed their contract. That he then said he thought the price reasonable is irrelevant. That eliminates **C** because it includes option II.

We're left with **D**, which includes options I, III, and IV. Option I, we know, is correct. Option III correctly observes that regardless of their misunderstanding, Babs and Sam achieved offer and acceptance, which perhaps *best* explains the result. Option IV correctly observes that Sam had reason to know of Babs's understanding and that Babs had no reason to know of Sam's. That reasoning reflects the rule given in C.4 above, and in Restatement (Second) §20(2) and means, once again, that the parties achieved an offer and acceptance. Options I, III, and IV make correct statements, option II does not, and **D** is right.

D. Who Decides What Is and Is Not Reasonable?

In all fields of law, "reasonable" refers to that which ordinary reasonable persons would do or perceive under all circumstances surrounding their situation. That is so whether we speak of reasonable belief, reasonable perception, reasonable time, "reasonably prudent person" (with respect to negligence), or reasonable—anything.

Ordinarily, "reasonableness" creates a question of fact, and questions of fact go to juries (except in a "bench trial"). After hearing evidence of the circumstances surrounding the relevant parties, the jury ordinarily decides the matter of "reasonableness" whether it relates to time, behavior, belief, or anything else. *Any* question of fact, however, can become a question of law. If in a given litigation the judge believes that no sensible juror can find "this" or "that" thing to be unreasonable, she'll decide "as a matter of law" that it *is* reasonable. If she thinks that no sensible juror can find this or that thing to be reasonable, she'll decide "as a matter of law" that it's *un*reasonable.[8]

---

8. As you'll learn in your Civil Procedure class, such, in part, are the import of a "directed verdict," a "judgment notwithstanding the verdict," and a "nonsuit."

E.   The Closer

QUESTION 2. On January 3, 2019, Yantzi Yard prepared this document, unsigned:

CONTRACT

The undersigned seller, Zalia Zorinsky ("Seller"), and the undersigned buyer, Yantzi Yard ("Buyer"), do hereby agree that:

(1) On January 20, 2019 Seller will convey to Buyer all jewelry that she owns, and

(2) In exchange, Buyer will, upon receiving such jewelry, pay Seller the sum of $5.

SELLER: **BUYER:**

Signature: _____   Signature: _____

Zalia Zorinsky   Yantzi Yard

Later that same day, Yantzi approached Zalia with the paper in hand. The parties were casually acquainted, neither knowing the other well. On meeting, they spoke.

Zalia: Hi. What paper are you holding?

Yantzi: I'm glad you asked. I'm making a study of signatures; I'm interested to know if there really is an identifiable difference between a male and female signature. You can help me. Would you sign your name at the bottom of this paper — right on the line that says "signature"?

Yantzi showed Zalia the bottom of the paper and so leaned himself over as to conceal from Zalia all but this:

Signature: _____
        Zalia Zorinsky

Zalia, happy to help, signed her name as Yantzi had asked.

Signature: _*Zalia Zorinsky*_
        Zalia Zorinsky

Yantzi thanked Zalia, bid her farewell, and then signed his own name to the writing that Zalia had just unwittingly signed.

Have Zalia and Yantzi formed a contract according to the terms of the signed writing?

A. Yes, because the writing would be admissible evidence of the fact that they formed a contract according to the terms of the writing

B. Yes, because Yantzi's signature signified his acceptance of Zalia's offer

C. No, because the parties did not achieve a "meeting of the minds"

D. No, because neither party made an offer, so that neither could issue an acceptance

ANALYSIS.   Evaluate the events according to law. Yantzi hid the paper's contents when he presented it to Zalia, professing to ask for a sample of her signature. As a reasonable person, Zalia had no cause to believe that the paper bore any purported contractual terms at all. Consequently, Zalia's signature was not an offer — of anything. When Yantzi then took hold of the document, complete with Zalia's signature, Yantzi knew that Zalia had not seen its text. As a reasonable person, therefore, Yantzi should have known that Zalia did not intend to propose any bargain to *him*. Hence, Zalia made no offer to Yantzi, and Yantzi's signature accepted nothing. Neither party made an offer to the other, meaning that neither was an offeree and neither had anything *to* accept.

Plainly then, the answer is "no," these parties did not form a contract — not at all. Whatever the correct answer, its meaning must reflect the reasoning we've just put forth. A correct answer might be, for example:

- No, because the parties never achieved offer and acceptance
- No, because neither party accepted an offer from the other
- No, because neither party manifested an intention to propose or assent to a bargain
- No, because neither party empowered the other to accept an offer

A begins with "yes," so it's wrong. It then states that the writing would be admissible evidence *tending to prove* that the parties formed a contract. That's true. As discussed in Chapter 2, section C, a signed writing that describes a mutual exchange of promises or performances is *evidence* that the two relevant parties formed a contract. But the appearance of what seems to be a contractual writing does not mean, absolutely, that the parties formed a contract. Plaintiff might sue defendant for breach and produce a "signed" "contractual writing." Defendant might prove that she never did sign the document, meaning that some forger did so instead. Other circumstances, too, beyond forgery might well prove that what seems to be a contractual writing does not, in truth, represent a contract.

In this case, a court would admit the writing as evidence of a contract, but when presented with the facts (and the story is presented to us as *fact*), it would rule that notwithstanding the writing, these parties failed to form a contract. So **A** is out.

B is wrong, too. By telling us that Yantzi accepted Zalia's offer, it states, implicitly, that Zalia *made* an offer, which she did not. **C**, too, is a loser. It invokes that war-torn phrase "meeting of the minds," which applies, if ever, only when the parties give different meanings to their words, acts, or expressions, *both of them reasonable* (see section C of this chapter). That hasn't happened here. In signing her name, Zalia could have but one reasonable understanding; she was providing Yantzi with a sample of her signature — nothing more. Likewise, that's the only reasonable interpretation Yantzi could have given Zalia's willingness to sign. Because there was but one reasonable way to interpret Zalia's willingness to sign, "meeting of the minds" is out of place.

We come to **D**, which states that the parties did not form a contract because neither made an offer to the other, which means that neither made an acceptance. **D** is "just right."[9] When Yantzi presented the paper to Zalia, he made not even an invitation to deal. That means Zalia's signature was no offer, which means that Yantzi's signature was no acceptance, which means that **D** is right.

 # Silver's Picks

1.   **D**
2.   **D**

---

9. See *The Three Bears*: Goldilocks's statement to herself on tasting Baby Bear's porridge.

4

More About Offers: Invitations to Deal and Indefiniteness

A. Invitation to Deal
B. Contracts Void for Vagueness, Indefiniteness, or Uncertainty
C. When Material Terms Aren't Expressly Specified: "Gap Fillers"
D. The Closers
⬦ Silver's Picks

A. Invitation to Deal

Let's listen again to Martha from Chapter 2, section D:

> I am prepared to hire you as manufacturer of Gutmate. I have little capital,
> so I propose to convey to you a share of the patent ownership in exchange
> for your services. I invite your acceptance.

Martha proposes no bargain and makes no offer. Yet she suggests the *possibility* of a bargain not fully shaped. The law tags such an expression with the labels "preliminary negotiation," "preliminary inquiry," "invitation for an offer," "solicitation of an offer," or, most commonly — "invitation to deal." "Invitation to deal" and these other phrases describe a communication that looks toward *the possibility* of a bargain but lacks the definiteness necessary to an offer, like this one:

> Dear Alex: Your yacht is lovely. I believe it to be worth about $300,000. I'm ready
> to buy it for that amount. Are you agreeable? — Jaden

That's an offer. But suppose Alex had written this:

> Dear Alex:Your yacht is lovely. I suspect it's worth about $300,000. Have you thought of selling it? — Jaden

That second writing alludes to the *possibility* that Jaden and Alex will buy and sell the yacht. It invites Alex to think along those lines and make a response. Because it suggests that one of the parties *might* ultimately make an offer to the other, *it is not an offer, but an invitation to deal.*

We call a communication "invitation to deal" to tell ourselves not what it is, but what it is *not* — an offer. We say, "X made no offer — only an invitation to deal." Some preface the phrase with the word "mere": "X's letter was not an offer, but a mere invitation to deal."

1. *Invitation to Deal as a Circumstance*

An invitation to deal is not an offer, but it's a *circumstance* that might turn some subsequent communication *into* an offer. Suppose Tom says to Jane, "How about Sunday, at my home from 7 to 10, at $15 per hour?" Standing alone, that question means nothing. It proposes no bargain; certainly it's no offer. But consider it as statement (5) of this conversation:

(1) **Tom:** Hi, Jane. I must go out this coming Sunday. Might you baby-sit Jennifer?
(2) **Jane:** Maybe. What hours and what pay?
(3) **Tom:** I'm not sure about the hours. I'm thinking to pay $10 or $12 per hour. What's your usual charge?
(4) **Jane:** I don't have one; I haven't done this in a while.
(5) **Tom:** How about Sunday, at my home from 7 to 10, at $15 per hour?
(6) **Jane:** Okay, great.

Statements 1 through 4 are invitations to deal. They also represent *circumstances* that surround statement 5. In light of those circumstances — statements 1-4 — Jane should hear statement 5 to mean "I hereby propose that you baby-sit Jennifer on Sunday night at my home from 7 to 10, in exchange for which I will pay you $15 per hour." Hence, statement 5 is an offer because the prior invitations to deal should tell Jane what, *with* statement 5, Tom means to propose. For, as Justice Holmes wrote, "the character of every act depends upon the circumstances in which it is done." Schenck v. United States, 249 U.S. 47, 52 (1919).

QUESTION 1. Jackson, a building contractor, contacts Leister, an electrical contractor.

> **Jackson:** I'm undertaking a construction project for Faith Hospital in Tuttontown. I need an electrical contractor. Interested?
> **Leister:** Yes, definitely, I accept.
> **Jackson:** Great. Can you come by my office tomorrow at 8:00 A.M., to iron out the details?
> **Leister:** Yes, I'll be there.

At 7:00 A.M. the next day, Leister contacts Jackson announcing that she will neither keep the appointment nor serve as his electrical contractor. Is Leister in breach of contract?

A. Yes, because Jackson made an offer and Leister accepted it
B. Yes, because the parties manifested a mutual interest in forming a bargain
C. No, because Jackson's first statement proposed no bargain
D. No, because Leister timely notified Jackson of her altered decision

---

ANALYSIS.   Leister can't breach a contract on Tuesday unless she forms one on Monday. On Monday, Jackson, speaking first, described insufficient detail to pose a bargain. His statement looked toward the *possibility* of a bargain, but was far too vague actually to propose one. Jackson made only an invitation to deal. Receiving no offer, Leister had nothing to accept. *Saying,* "I accept," she expressed only her wish to continue discussion. She too made a mere invitation to deal. Hence, the correct answer must say "no," Leister committed no breach because, with their "mere" invitations to deal, these parties never formed a contract.

A and B begin with "yes," so they're wrong. According to A, Jackson made an offer and Leister accepted it. That didn't happen. Jackson made only an invitation to deal. The statement in B is true. Speaking as they did, Jackson and Leister clearly expressed their *interest* in making a deal. But that means only that they began discussion — they started to negotiate.

We're left with C and D, both of which properly say "no," Leister is not in breach. For its reason, D tells us that Leister "timely" told Jackson that she had changed her mind. And — so what? With or without Leister's notice to Jackson, these parties failed to form a contract. D is wrong.

We come to C, which says that Leister breached no contract because Jackson's first statement proposed no bargain. That's true; it didn't. It was a mere preliminary negotiation (another phrase for "invitation to deal"). Yet if Jackson *had* proposed a bargain — if he had made an offer — then with Leister's response, "I accept," these folks would have formed a contract. Precisely because Jackson proposed no bargain they did *not* form one. That's why Leister committed no breach. **C is right.**

2. *Offer or Invitation to Deal? Sometimes It's Arguable*

Between offer and invitation to deal there lies no bright line. As with any precept of law, statutory, regulatory, common law, or constitutional, some cases lie at the extremes and allow for little argument. Others lie nearer the middle and create opposing positions, each of them rational and reasonable.

Read these statements, each one separate from the other:

1. "Nice bike. I might think of buying it, say, for $900. Have you any interest in selling?"
2. "I like that bike. Would you, do you think, sell it for $900?"
3. "I wish, today, to purchase that bike for $900. Are you prepared to sell?"

All (competent) judges would agree that statement 1 is a mere inquiry, a preliminary negotiation, an invitation to deal. All would agree, too, that statement 3 is an offer. Statement 2's status, however, is arguable. One judge might call it an offer. Another might brand it an invitation to deal. It's "in the middle." (If we modified statement 2 by changing "would" to "will" and by deleting the words "do you think" it would read, "Will you sell it for $900?" *That* would be an offer.)

QUESTION 2. Dov owned retail store property at 199 Trumbull Avenue. Without naming a price, Portia expressed a tentative interest in buying it, and wished to know its market value. For that purpose, with Dov's permission, Portia hired and paid two professionals, both of whom reported to her and to Dov that it was worth approximately $450,000. Immediately thereafter the parties exchanged these signed writings:

(1) **Portia:** As you know, I'm interested in your 199 Trumbull Avenue property, evaluated by two appraisers at $450,000. Will you sell it to me for that amount?

(2) **Dov:** I'll take no less than $500,000. Talk to me when you're ready to pay that price.

(3) **Portia:** Very well, $500,000 it is.

Portia then tendered[1] to Dov a $500,000 certified check and demanded that Dov convey the property. Dov refused and Portia sued, alleging breach of contract. Dov maintained that he breached no contract

---

1. One "tenders" a performance when she shows that she is ready, willing, and able to deliver it. If A is to paint B's house, and A arrives at the site, equipment in hand, and says, "I'm ready to begin," she has tendered her performance. Here, we say that Portia tendered a $500,000 certified check. We mean that she came to Dov and said something like, "I have in my hands a $500,000 certified check. Here it is. Take it." Or, she contacted Dov by telephone, email, or fax: "I have a $500,000 certified check in my hands. Where shall I send it?"

because he and Portia never formed one. Which of the following judicial statements plausibly constitutes a proper assessment of the conflict?

I. Writing 1 was a mere invitation to deal. Writing 2, likewise, continued as a preliminary negotiation, manifesting Dov's willingness only to *consider* an offer of $500,000. Writing 3 was Portia's offer to buy for $500,000, which Dov did not accept. The parties formed no contract and Dov is not in breach.

II. Knowing of Portia's interest in the property and allowing her to have it appraised, Dov implicitly offered to sell the property at any price reasonably close to the appraised value. With writing 1, Portia proclaimed her willingness to purchase for $450,000 and thereby accepted Dov's offer. The parties formed a contract and Dov is in breach.

III. Writing 1 was a mere inquiry — an invitation to deal. Writing 2 was Dov's offer to sell for $500,000, and writing 3 was Portia's acceptance. The parties formed a contract and Dov *is* in breach.

A. I
B. I and II
C. I and III
D. II and III
E. I, II, and III

ANALYSIS. All legal doctrines and distinctions sit on a spectrum, each having a middle zone that's home to the arguable cases — the cases in which one judge might see it "this way" and another "that way." Those are, as well, the cases that drive two opposing lawyers to court, each convinced that she should win. Here, we're asked to examine three judicial statements and determine which, in our opinion, *represent plausible judicial resolutions of this controversy.* Let's (a) read the parties' signed writings, (b) determine whether each is (i) clearly one thing or another, or (ii) *arguably* one thing or another and, on the basis (c) determine which of the three judicial statements I, II, and III is/are plausibly correct.

What's writing 1? It speaks to a particular property and price. Plainly, it shows Portia's interest in buying the property. On the other hand, it presents not a statement but a question. We think that it's most likely — but not certainly — a preliminary inquiry/invitation to deal. That's *our* legal opinion. Yet we think, to a possibility of 20 percent perhaps, that some judge, some lawyer (or you) might call it an offer. That would be their (or, maybe, your) legal opinion. Difference in opinion makes horse races and — money for lawyers.

If writing 1 is an invitation to deal, might we say that writing 2 is an offer? Maybe. Dov expresses his unwillingness to take less than $500,000, and tells Portia to "talk to me" when she's ready to pay that amount. Should someone in Portia's position believe that Dov has *definitively expressed his willingness* to sell the property for $500,000? Let's say, with a confidence of about 65/35, that the answer is "no," meaning that we think there's a 35 percent chance the answer is "yes." Hence, 65/35 (*we* say) — writing 2 is not an offer, but an invitation to deal.

What of writing 3? Plainly, Portia manifests her unequivocal willingness to buy the land for $500,000. Writing 3 qualifies as an offer, but Dov doesn't accept it, which means the parties don't form a contract. Yet, if writing 2 is an offer (which we said is *possible*), then writing 3 seems certainly to be an acceptance, in which case the parties do form a contract.

So maybe these parties form a contract and maybe they don't. There are at least two plausible ways in which to evaluate their interactions.

> **Probably:** Writing 1 is Portia's invitation to deal, writing 2 is Dov's invitation to deal, and writing 3 is Portia's offer, to which Dov gives no acceptance, meaning the parties form no contract.
>
> **But just maybe:** Writing 1 is an invitation to deal, writing 2 an offer, and writing 3 an acceptance, meaning that the parties do form a contract.

Option I describes what we've just called probable. It says writings 1 and 2 are invitations to deal, and writing 3 an offer for which there follows no acceptance.

Option II is nonsense. No reasonable person in Portia's position could believe that by allowing for the appraisal, Dov manifests an intention (offered) to sell the property for a price equal to its assessed value. Option II is wrong (and the seductive words "reasonably close" don't make it right).

To option III, we say "35 percent possible." It calls writing 1 an invitation to deal, writing 2 an offer, and writing 3 an acceptance. Options I and III are plausible, II is not. C is right (*we* say; maybe you disagree).

B.   Contracts Void for Vagueness, Indefiniteness, or Uncertainty

Suppose Abram says to Beth, "I have an offer for you." Beth asks, "What's the offer?" Abram responds, "Some tickets to this Friday night's Asteroid game." Beth replies, "I accept."

Abram uses the word "offer" but plainly does not make one. Consequently, Beth accepts nothing and these parties form no contract. In assessing their interaction we need *think* nothing more, but there's more we must *say*.

We know that a contract requires, first, that one party make an offer to another. That simple truth underlies a host of dubious and superfluous common law statements with which we must reckon, like them or not. Most courts would describe Abram's and Beth's situation like this:

> The terms on which the parties agreed are insufficiently specific, and their contact is *void for vagueness*.

In that same vein, others would say:

> If not reasonably certain as to their material terms, contracts are unenforceable and where any kind of property is bought and sold, material terms include quantity and price. These parties specified neither quantity nor price; their contract is *void for vagueness*.

Consider these two writings signed by EnnerCo and MotoCo.

EnnerCo to MotoCo: Offer to Sell — Large quantity of Grade A Kerosel just received by us at bargain price. We wish to pass savings to you. Will sell some to you at discount price. Please let us know if you accept.
MotoCo to EnnerCo: Purchase Order — Re your offer of yesterday. We accept. What quantities are available and at what prices?

EnnerCo issued a mere invitation to deal. Although MotoCo wrote "we accept," it, too, made only an invitation to deal. Hence, these two companies formed no contract; they ended their communications before either made an offer to the other. Restatement (Second) of Contracts §33(1) explains it (very badly) like this:

> Even though a manifestation of intention is intended to be understood as an offer, it cannot be accepted so as to form a contract unless the terms of the contract are reasonably certain.[2]

---

2. Here, again, the Restatement writers stumble through legal terrain blindly, mindlessly, complacently — after the fashion of Mr. Magoo. With respect to a communication from Party X to Party Y, we know that the meanings of "intend," "intention," and "intended" do not pertain to what is, truly, in X's head. Rather, they turn on the intent that Y reasonably ascribes to X by virtue of X's words and acts. Stated otherwise (and pretentiously), X's communication is subject to the "objective theory of contracts." (See Chapter 2, section B and Chapter 3, section B.)

Yet the Restatement writers give us this sentence: "Even though a manifestation of intention is intended ... [.]" They should have written something like: "Unless its terms are reasonably certain, no person can justifiably interpret a proposal so to believe that (i) the issuer manifests a willingness to enter a bargain or (ii) that his assent to that bargain is invited, or (iii) that his assent will conclude it." At the very least they should have written: "Unless its terms are reasonably certain, no proposal constitutes an offer, meaning that no party can accept it, meaning that such a proposal and a purported acceptance do not create a contract."

Further, the Restatement refers to the *acceptance* of a *manifestation*; in language and concept, there is no such thing. One assents to a proposal or accepts an offer, but cannot "accept" a "manifestation." Finally, the writers refer to "the contract," when in fact they mean to say that there is none. In essence, they write, "No person can accept a manifestation unless the terms of the contract are reasonably certain." We ask, "What contract?" The writers have just referred not to a "contract" but to a "manifestation."

For these among other reasons we say, simply, that the Restatement writers know not what they do (but we do not *forgive* them).

Hence, in the MotoCo-EnnerCo case, the Restatement rightly tells us that the parties formed no contract. All (competent) authorities would reach that same conclusion. Unfortunately, however, some (misguided) ones would *explain* their conclusion by writing that the parties' "contract" is "void for vagueness," "indefiniteness," or "uncertainty as to material terms" — failing to state that the parties formed no contract at all.

QUESTION 3. On August 9, BuyCo and SellCo began communicating with these signed writings:

> **August 9, BuyCo:** We understand that you now own the original oil painting *Nightbird*, which is, of course, priceless. Nonetheless, we hereby offer to buy it, and we'd like to hear back from you on any other matters you deem significant, including price. Perhaps an appraiser's report would be helpful. We look forward to your response.

> **August 11, SellCo:** Thanks for your offer regarding our priceless painting, *Nightbird*. We accept, and we'll be in touch within ten days.

Ten days later, on August 21, together with an appraiser's report that values it at $950,000, SellCo tendered delivery of the painting to BuyCo and demanded that BuyCo pay $950,000. BuyCo rejected the delivery and refused to pay anything, maintaining that "we never formed a final intention to buy."

SellCo sues BuyCo for breach. Correctly deciding for Buyco, a court might make which of the following statements, whether or not it is a correct conception of law?

  I. The contract at issue is void for indefiniteness.
 II. The contract at issue is void for vagueness.
III. The parties formed no contract because they agreed that the painting was "priceless."
 IV. The parties formed no contract because neither made an offer to the other.
  V. The parties formed no contract because BuyCo did not fully intend to purchase the painting.

  A. I
  B. I and II
  C. I, II, and III
  D. I, II, and IV
  E. I, II, IV, and V

ANALYSIS.   BuyCo's "offer" is too vague truly to constitute an offer, meaning that SellCo accepted nothing. The "contract" on which Sellco sues is no contract at all.

Regrettably, some courts (and teachers) would characterize the case by writing that (1) "The parties' contract is void for indefiniteness, vagueness, and uncertainty." Better judicial thinkers (in markedly short supply) would explain that (2) "These two parties formed *no contract at all*, because neither made an offer to the other." The second statement is conceptually correct. The first is not. Yet, from too many courts (and others) the *first* is what we read and hear. For that unhappy reason any option, I-IV, that resembles statements (1) or (2) correctly responds to *this question*.

Options I and II speak of a contract void for "indefiniteness" and "vagueness." Both reflect incorrect conceptions of law, but *correct answers to this question* because, regrettably, they represent statements that judges, lawyers, and teachers do still make.

Option III is nonsense. Two parties may describe an item of property as "priceless" or "worthless" and still contract to buy and sell it.

Option IV states that neither party made an offer to the other. *That's* the truth. In a perfect legal world, all judges would decide this case upon that observation; IV is accurate.

Option V implies that two parties can't form a contract unless both truly intend to be bound. From Chapter 2, sections B and D, and Chapter 3, section B we know that's wrong. Contract law decrees that one's "intentions" are his *manifest* intentions — the intentions another would reasonably attribute to him through his words and acts. Options I, II, and IV "belong"; III and V do not. **D** is right.

C.   When Material Terms Aren't Expressly Specified: "Gap Fillers"

Notwithstanding the oft-repeated doctrines of vagueness, indefiniteness, and uncertainty, today's contract law does not require that an offer and acceptance show black and white specificity for every material term. If two parties omit to mention some important matter and thus leave a "gap" in their agreement, the law often concludes quite correctly that as to the unmentioned matter, notwithstanding their seeming silence, the parties justifiably understood that they had agreed on some term that each of them, as reasonable persons, should have ascribed to their agreement. Consider this interaction between RentCo and BuildCo:

BuildCo: Do you have a ten-ton forklift available tomorrow from 9 to 6?
RentCo: Yes, we do. We'll be glad to reserve it for you.
BuildCo: Thank you, please do. I'll take it.

These parties seem certainly to believe they've formed a binding arrangement, but by omitting to discuss price, they've left their agreement with a "gap." Modern law fills it by attributing to these parties a mutual understanding that BuildCo was to pay RentCo a price that would be reasonable under the circumstances. If when the time comes for BuildCo to pay up, the parties can't agree on a price, one might, theoretically, sue the other. By law these two have agreed on a "reasonable price," just as though they had actually spoken those two words. When two parties can't agree on what one of their contractual terms means, it's the court's job to interpret it. In this case, a court will decide what price is a reasonable one. Depending on the evidence, that might be

1. the price that BuildCo has paid RentCo in the past for the same or similar machinery; or
2. the price that RentCo normally charges to other customers, if any, to whom it rents the same or similar machinery; or
3. the price that other businesses in RentCo's field normally charge for the same or similar equipment; or
4. RentCo's direct and indirect costs plus some ordinary margin of profit; or
5. any other amount that, on the evidence, a court identifies as a "reasonable price."

1. Why the Law Fills Gaps

The truth be known, most contracts create more gap than specificity. Most contracting parties leave most of their agreed terms unstated. In fact, no two contracting parties ever *can* specify, in words, even a small portion of the terms to which they agree. They might agree that work is to be finished by "New Year's Day" without stating whether they mean the Euro-American new year, Greek new year, or Chinese new year. They might agree on delivery at 10:00, without specifying "P.M." or "A.M." They might even agree on "10:00 A.M." without specifying eastern standard, eastern daylight, or Greenwich mean time. They might establish a price of "$1,000" without stating that the applicable dollar is American, not Canadian or Australian.

All human expression takes its meaning not from words, but from one person's reasonable interpretation *of* words, made in view of the circumstances under which another uses them. The point goes deep to the matters of communication and language, and it's critical to the law of contract.

Let's Probe It a Little More

At 6:30 P.M., setting the table, moving a platter from stove to dining room, Henry asks Wanda, "Shall we have dinner?" If Wanda processes only the four words actually spoken, her mind will be awash in a whirl of confusion: "Does

Henry mean we should have dinner now or at some unstated time in the future? Where does he propose to have dinner? Here at home? Elsewhere? When he says 'dinner,' does he mean a European-style afternoon meal or an American-style evening meal? And what does he mean by 'have' dinner? 'Hold' it? 'Own' it? 'Consume' it? I can't answer. I don't know what he's asking."

Henry's statement *is* full of gaps, but if Wanda is a (half-way) reasonable person who lives a (half-way) normal (American) life — who sees both the clock and the action around her, she knows that Henry has invited her to sit down with him for dinner here and now at 6:30 P.M. according to the time zone in which they live.

When others speak or write to us, we understand them *in light of surrounding circumstance.* With inference and intuition, day in and day out, we all "fill" communicative "gaps." Absent that, none of us could communicate anything, ever, to anyone — not in any mode, language, or dialect.

In very abstract terms, we might say that *contract law's essential purpose is to fulfill the reasonable expectations that all of us have of those with whom we form agreements.* For that reason, contract law "fills gaps" and in doing so charges all of us with such knowledge, understanding, belief, purpose, inference, and intention as would naturally apply to reasonable persons in like circumstances.

Be ready to read and hear the phrases "void for vagueness," and "void for indefiniteness." Speak, write, and repeat them if a teacher so insists. But in your own heart and brain, know that:

There is no place for the words "void for indefiniteness" if each of two parties does and/or says and/or writes what should lead the other to understand that she believes herself bound by an agreement whose terms are sufficiently specific as to make clear

(a) *what each party is obliged to do and, therefore,*
(b) *what each is entitled to expect from the other.*

2. Gap Filling Under the UCC, Article 2

Here's How Article 2 of the UCC Attempts to State What We've Written Just Above

UCC §2-204(3):

> Even if one or more terms are left open, a contract for sale does not fail for indefiniteness if the parties have intended to make a contract and there is a reasonably certain basis for giving an appropriate remedy.

As usual, the provision is badly structured and difficult to apprehend[3] but, once again, it means to say what we have written just above.

---

3. Further (as too is usual), it misconceives the law itself, for the drafters use the word "intended" when they should use words akin to "manifest an intent."

So What's Up with Those Last Words, "Reasonably Certain Basis for Giving an Appropriate Remedy"?

They're the Code's (ridiculous) way of describing an agreement whose terms are sufficiently specific as to tell a reasonable person/court/jury (a) what each party is obliged to do and, therefore, (b) what each is entitled to expect from the other.

For Example.   Suppose D manufactures batteries — a great many types for a large number of purposes. P is an automobile manufacturer. In 2019, for the first time, P and D deal with each other, forming what they call a "contract." On paper, they sign their names to this: "Whereas P needs batteries for its business, P will sell batteries to D during the calendar years 2019 and 2020."

During that two-year period, D delivers no batteries to P. P sues D. The judge reads the paper and concludes that she can't enforce its terms because they're "void for indefiniteness."

Now Know This.   When a judge decides that a "contract" is void for "indefiniteness" or "vagueness," there runs through her mind something like this:

> I can't tell to what, if anything, these parties agreed. I don't know what, if anything, each is obliged to do for the other. Hence, I don't know what, if anything, each party should expect *from* the other. The writing refers to the delivery of batteries, but it gives me no clue as to (1) *how many* batteries D was to deliver, (2) *when* during the two-year period she was obliged to deliver them, (3) *what kind* of batteries she was obliged to deliver, or (4) *how much* P was obliged to pay her.
>
> Having no idea of what, if anything, D was obliged to do, I can't tell whether she did or did not "breach." Not knowing to what, if anything, P was entitled, I don't know what damages, if any, he suffered. Hence, I don't know how, if at all, to compensate him for what he calls a "breach."

That last sentence is equivalent to this one: "There is no basis on which to give an appropriate remedy."

So It All Comes to This.   To say that a purported contract provides a "basis on which to give an appropriate remedy" is to say that we can fill its gaps by imputing to the parties such intentions as would be reasonable under all prevailing circumstances. Reciprocally, to say that a purported contract does not provide a "basis on which to give an appropriate remedy" is to modernize the phrase "void for vagueness/indefiniteness," which means that the purported "contract" is no contract at all.

More About Article 2's Gap Filling; Price of Goods

Suppose P and D write this: "During the years 2019 and 2020, whenever P so requests, D will deliver to P Type X-IV automotive batteries in any quantity that P requests, except that D shall not be obliged to deliver any units in excess of 40,000 during any 30-day period."

In black and white dollars and cents, these parties do not mention price and so leave their agreement with a "price gap." As is so of all contractual gaps, a judge or jury might have sufficient basis on which to fill this one by deciding what, under the prevailing circumstances, two reasonable parties should reasonably have understood to be the price on which they agreed. Maybe it's D's current catalog price, or the price charged by other wholesalers of the same or similar product in the same or similar location, or something that "makes sense" in light of what the parties said and did under all surrounding conditions.

> And in that regard, UCC §2-305(1) gives us a gap filler directed especially to price:[4]

> The parties if they so intend can conclude a contract for sale even though the price is not settled. In such a case the price is a reasonable price[.]

The statute tells us that if (as to the purchase and sale of goods), Buyer and Seller mutually "intend"[5] to bind themselves by an agreement, they form a contract even if they omit to mention price. If, when the time comes for Seller to deliver and/or for Buyer to "pay up," the two cannot agree on the amount to be paid, one party might sue the other. At trial, each party presents evidence as to what price is reasonable, and the court (with or without a jury) decides the question, naming an amount in dollars and cents.[6]

If the Parties Don't "Intend to Make a Contract," We Don't Fill Gaps

S is a widget wholesaler who sells widgets to retailers. B is a widget retailer. The parties conduct their first interaction.

> **B:** I need size 12 widgets. Do you carry them?
> **S:** We accept. How many cases do you want?
> **B:** First of all, I'm glad you have accepted. We have a deal. Now, how many units come in a case?

---

4. The provision mentions one particular form of gap: price. Hence, it is by and large redundant of UCC §2-204(3), which addresses all gaps in general.

5. Always (*always*) remember that in contract law "intend" does not carry its ordinary meaning. To say that Parties 1 and 2 "intend" to conclude a contract is to mean that each such party leads the other reasonably to *understand* that he intends to conclude a contract. That's why the Restatement's definitions of "offer" and "acceptance" include the word "manifestation" (Chapter 2, sections B and D and such underlies the "objective theory of contracts" Chapter 3, section B).

6. The Code does not expressly provide a "gap filler" as to a missing term for quantity. If two parties purport to form a contract for the sale of goods and make no statement that expressly or implicitly provides for quantity, Article 2 does not allow a court to fill the resulting "gap" with "reasonable quantity."

S: Yes, we have a deal. Each case is packed with 100 units. How many cases do you want?

B: What's the price per case?

S: That depends on how many cases you want.

B: How much for ten cases?

S: I'll get back to you.

These two speak of widgets size 12, but they don't specify price, quantity, delivery time, or anything else. Furthermore, we can't "fill" those "gaps." We fill gaps only after first deciding that the parties "have 'intended' to make a contract" (UCC §2-204(3)). With their questions and answers, to and fro, neither of these guys manifests "willingness to enter into a bargain so made as to justify [the other] in understanding that his assent to that bargain is invited and will conclude it." That means neither made an offer to the other (Restatement (Second) of Contracts §24; Chapter 2, section B). That means neither had any offer *to* accept, and *that* means the parties did not "intend" to conclude a contract. When that's the case, we can't and we don't fill gaps.

QUESTIONS 4-6. SportCo operates a chain of sporting goods stores, and BallCo manufactures a variety of articles tied to sports. BallCo publishes a price catalog, which it updates from time to time, ordinarily sending the current edition to all of its regular customers.

In 2009, BallCo published an updated price catalog in which it posted a price of $288 per gross (144) of baseballs. BallCo published no new catalog until January 2019, when it did publish one, setting the price of baseballs at $319 per gross.

During the years 2009-2018, SportCo had ordered a total of 100,000 gross of BallCo's baseballs and paid, always, the catalog price of $288 per gross. In March 2019, the parties exchanged these signed writings:

(1) **March 1, SportCo writes:** Purchase Order — Please ship immediately to our warehouse at 4400 Raritan Way, Coppertown, PA, 10,000 gross of your baseballs. Will expect invoice with delivery. Thank you.

(2) **March 2, BallCo writes: Sales Confirmation** — Thank you for your order. Will ship promptly, with invoice.

(3) **March 3, SportCo writes:** With apologies we must cancel our recent order for 10,000 gross of baseballs. Please do not ship.

BallCo insists that SportCo is contractually obliged to purchase the baseballs. SportCo maintains that because they never discussed price, the parties did not form a contract.

> **QUESTION 4.** Pursuant to UCC Article 2, is SportCo's position correct?
>
> A. Yes, because when goods are sold, price is a material term
> B. Yes, because no two parties form a contract unless one puts to the other a bargain of reasonably specific terms
> C. No, because the parties implicitly agreed on a "reasonable price"
> D. No, because BallCo changed its published price only once in ten years

---

ANALYSIS. UCC Article 2 provides that two parties can contract for the sale of goods without mentioning price, so long as they mutually manifest an intention to be bound. These parties have done that; SportCo made an offer and BallCo accepted; they contracted to buy and sell 10,000 baseballs — implicitly by law — at a reasonable price.

You're not told, specifically, that BallCo has or has not sent SportCo the 2009 or 2019 catalogs, but that matter affects the *numerical value* of the reasonable price, not formation of a contract. If BallCo has not sent SportCo either catalog, a court surely will find enough evidence to name *a* reasonable price — probably $288 or $319. Hence, under UCC §2-305, these parties did form a contract.

A and **B** are wrong for declaring that these companies formed no contract. That leaves **C** and **D. D** tells us that a contract arose because the seller changed its published price only once between 2009 and 2019. That doesn't explain how or why these parties formed a contract. If BallCo had revised its pricing every year, then, still, this latest transaction would create a contract.

C correctly refers to the rule of UCC §2-305. These parties formed a contract because, notwithstanding their failure explicitly to specify price, each manifested to the other an intention to be bound. By law they agreed on a "reasonable price" to be determined by a court if they, themselves, should be unable to agree on what price is "reasonable." That's why **C** is right.

> **QUESTION 5.** For this question only, assume that BallCo sent SportCo its 2009 catalog but not the one it published in 2019. When BallCo insists that SportCo must buy the baseballs, SportCo agrees and stands ready to pay $288 per gross. BallCo demands $319, the price set forth in its 2019 catalog. All other facts are as originally set forth. Probably, BallCo is entitled to be paid
>
> A. $288, because that is the price it has repeatedly charged SportCo, and SportCo had no notice that the price had been changed.
> B. $288, because it is unreasonable for a seller suddenly to publish a higher price to a long-time buyer who has customarily and in good faith paid a lower one.

C. $319, because under these circumstances a buyer should reasonably expect to pay according to a seller's published price list.

D. nothing, because a buyer need not pay a price to which he has not agreed.

ANALYSIS.   These parties have a contract. You're to determine the amount the court would likely name as a "reasonable price." BallCo did not provide SportCo with its latest catalog. Together with the relevant history, that fact probably puts the reasonable price at $288.

Quickly eliminate **D**. It does not recognize a contract. Discard **B**, too; it's not founded in law. Certainly a seller may raise prices to any or all of its buyers no matter how long their business relationships are, notwithstanding that all have acted in "good faith."

We're left with **A** and **C**. Which one better represents a likely judicial ruling? **C** ignores a relevant fact — that BallCo failed to apprise SportCo of the increased price. If a seller revises its price catalog and fails to so notify one of its regular buyers, is it really *reasonable* that this buyer be obliged, implicitly, to pay the increased price of which it had no reason to know? We think not. Under these circumstances, each party should reasonably have understood that the $288 price continues. **A** is right. (That's what *we* think. How about you?)

QUESTION 6. For this question only, assume that BallCo did send SportCo a copy of its 2019 catalog, but that SportCo never examined it. When BallCo insists that SportCo must buy the baseballs, SportCo agrees and stands ready to pay $288 per gross. BallCo demands $319, the price set forth in its 2019 catalog. All other facts are as originally set forth. Probably, BallCo is entitled to be paid

A. $288, because that is the price it has repeatedly charged SportCo, and SportCo had no actual knowledge of the price change.

B. $288, because it is unreasonable suddenly to publish a higher price to a long-time buyer who has customarily and in good faith paid a lower one.

C. $319, because under these circumstances a buyer should reasonably expect to pay according to a seller's published price list.

D. nothing, because a buyer need not pay a price to which he has not agreed.

ANALYSIS.   These choices are the same as those of Question 5, but the facts differ. Here, BallCo did provide SportCo with a new price catalog, but SportCo didn't read it. That changes everything. Reading SportCo's proposal under these circumstances, BallCo was justified in believing that SportCo expected to pay the current catalog price of $319. And if SportCo's personnel had read the catalog (as would ideally reasonable persons), they would have taken BallCo's acceptance to *mean* "will ship promptly, with invoice showing current catalog price of $319."

B and D are bad just as they were for Question 5. We're left again with A and C. A is wrong for stating that "SportCo had no actual knowledge that the price had been changed." SportCo had *reason to know* of the price increase; it had the new price catalog but failed to read it. C correctly states that $319 is a reasonable price because SportCo had access to the new price list. C is right.

3. The "Agreement to Agree"

Consider this interaction between two strangers, Victor and Michael:

> **Victor:** I need software that will keep track of my various accounting records. Can you create that for me? If so, how long will it take and what will be your fee?
> **Michael:** Well, that depends on the program's complexity. I don't know what you need.
> **Victor:** I understand. For how long will you warranty your work?
> **Michael:** That too depends on what ultimately I do. Why don't we agree now that I'll write a program for you? Later on, and before I begin work, we'll agree on its specifications, the price, and a warranty period.
> **Victor:** It's a deal.

Michael's second response to Victor consigns to some future agreement almost all terms of the contemplated exchange. For that reason, it proposes no definite bargain. The interactions between these two were so utterly nonspecific as to constitute only a series of invitations to deal, meaning that neither made an offer to the other. These parties could not and did not form a contract.

Yet, most courts don't characterize this kind of interaction in quite that way. Instead they invoke what passes for a doctrine regarding the "agreement to agree": *Where two parties purport to reach a final binding arrangement, but leave material terms for later negotiation or agreement, they form only an "agreement to agree," which is not a contract. See Mays v. Trump Indiana, Inc.*, 255 F.3d 351 (7th Cir. 2001); *Rule v. Brine, Inc.*, 85 F.3d 1002 (2d Cir. 1996).

Like rules that speak to "vagueness/indefiniteness," this one, repeated over the centuries, passes for—but isn't—a correct statement of law. Know when to invoke it. Know, too, that the "agreement to agree" is but one species of an agreement that does not flesh out every one of its details. It is subject, therefore, to gap filling. If, from the relevant communications and circumstances, a modern court (a) concludes that two parties mutually manifested their intention to form a binding agreement (meaning that they achieved offer and acceptance), and (b) finds a rational means by which to fill the gap, it might do so. Such is an emerging trend under the common law. For the sale of goods it is statutory doctrine. Look more fully at UCC §2-305(1):

> (1) The parties if they so intend may conclude a contract for sale even if the price is not settled. In such a case the price is a reasonable price at the time for delivery, if:
>> (a) nothing is said as to price; or
>> (b) the price is left to be agreed by the parties and they fail to agree; or
>> (c) the price is to be fixed in terms of some agreed market or other standard as set or recorded by a third person or agency and it is not so set or recorded.

QUESTION 7. BanaCo and StatCo deal in electrical equipment. In its catalog StatCo lists the prices for some of its products, but not for #4 conducting wire. On July 11, BanaCo sends StatCo this signed written message: "We wish immediately to have 4,000 feet of your #4 conducting wire. We do not see the item listed in your catalog, so we propose that price will be agreed on later. Please ship." On July 12, StatCo responds with this signed writing: "Thank you. We will ship." Have BanaCo and StatCo formed a contract?

A. Yes, because where goods are bought and sold, price is not a material term
B. Yes, because notwithstanding the open price term, their interaction reflects finality of agreement
C. No, because two parties do not form a contract if they agree that a material term will be subject to future agreement
D. No, because a seller who declines to publish its price shows an intention not to sell

ANALYSIS. The transaction concerns the sale of goods, meaning that UCC Article 2 governs. The communications are unequivocal, meaning that each party manifested its "intent" to conclude a contract. Even without specificity of price the writings create a contract under UCC §2-305. The parties must buy and sell at a "reasonable price." If, ultimately, they cannot agree on a price that's reasonable and one sues the other, a court will decide the question. Stated otherwise, the court will fill the gap.

C and D reach wrong conclusions. UCC §2-305 tells us that these parties did form a contract. Furthermore, C and D make legal misstatements. Two parties may, at times, form a contract even when they leave a material term for future agreement. UCC §2-305 tells us that as to the sale of goods, that's surely true for price. And, it represents the modern common law trend as well. As for

D: that for some product or other, a seller omits to publish his price does not mean, necessarily, that he lacks the "intent" to sell it.

A is tempting, but it's not quite right. It's true that two parties who buy and sell goods may form a contract without explicitly *specifying* price, but price *is*, nonetheless, a material term.

B is best. It tells us that the parties' interaction reflects "finality of agreement," meaning it shows (manifests) their "intent" to create a contract. When buyer and seller do that, they form one even if they don't mention price. By law, they agree to a "reasonable price." **B** is right.

4. Gap Filling Goes Only So Far

Gap filling has its limits. The law goes only so far in supplying terms that the parties fail to specify. For example, where a real estate lease gives the tenant an option to renew at a rent to be agreed on in the future, most courts decline to imply a "reasonable rent." Martin Delicatessen v. Schumacher, 417 N.E.2d 541 (N.Y. 1981). It remains law, therefore, that when two parties describe their agreement with such indefiniteness as prevents a court from identifying their bargain — **prevents it from giving "an appropriate remedy"** — they form no contract or, as some say, "the contract fails for indefiniteness." That's true under Code and common law.

D.   The Closers

> **QUESTIONS 8-10.** Beginning on October 1, FuelCo and HeatCo exchange signed writings:
>
> (1) **October 1, FuelCo to HeatCo:** Offer to Sell — Shipment of Bortex Coal Kindler just received at reduced price. Prepared within next ten days to sell to you any quantity. Please accept promptly.
> (2) **October 2, HeatCo to FuelCo:** Purchase Order — Re your offer of yesterday. We accept. What quantities are available, and at what prices?
> (3) **October 3, FuelCo to HeatCo:** Offer to Sell — Available: 13 tons. Price depends on amount ordered. What quantity shall we ship? Others are making orders. Supply is shrinking. Please respond soon.
> (4) **October 4, HeatCo to FuelCo:** Offer to Buy — Re Bortex — will want all 13 tons delivered to our warehouse. Need price.
> (5) **October 5, FuelCo to HeatCo:** Offer to Sell — Can deliver. Price: $800 per ton = $10,400. Please advise.

(6) **October 6, HeatCo to Fuelco:** Purchase Order — Thank you. We expect delivery.

(7) **October 7, FuelCo to HeatCo: Purchase Confirmation — Okay.** A.M. **or** P.M. **delivery?**

QUESTION 8. Which of writings 1-7 are best characterized as invitations to deal?

A. 2, 3, and 4
B. 1, 2, 3, and 4
C. 1, 3, 5, and 7
D. 1, 2, 3, 4, and 7
E. All of writings 1-7

QUESTION 9. Which of writings 1-7 most likely constitutes an offer?

A. 5
B. 5 and 6
C. 4, 5, and 6
D. 4, 5, 6, and 7
E. None of writings 1-7

QUESTION 10. Which of the following italicized modifications would most likely convert the indicated writing to an offer?

A. Writing 1 is modified to read: "Shipment of Bortex Coal Kindler just received at reduced price. Prepared within next ten days to sell to you any quantity. Please accept promptly *and advise us of the price you are willing to pay.*"
B. Writing 2 is modified to read: "Re your offer of yesterday. We accept. *We need 18 tons, $300 per ton. Please ship immediately.*"
C. Writing 3 is modified to read: "*We have 13 tons now available and will hold all until we hear from you.* Price depends on amount ordered. Please respond soon."
D. Writing 4 is modified to read: "Re Bortex—will *certainly* want all 13 tons delivered to our warehouse. Need price. *Subject to price we have definite deal.*"

ANALYSIS.   Whether a communication constitutes an offer *does not depend on what the author calls it.* A communication called "acceptance" might be an offer. A communication called "offer" might be an invitation to deal or, for that matter, an acceptance. Labels don't matter (much). Mindful of what makes an offer, look at each of the writings and ask "Is this an offer and, if not, what is it?"

No reasonable person could read writing 1 to propose a definite bargain. It looks to the possible sale of a particular good, but mentions neither price nor quantity. If HeatCo were to respond by writing, "We accept," neither party could know *what* HeatCo had accepted. Writing 1 is an invitation to deal.

Writing 2 purports to "accept." But in writing 1, FuelCo made no offer, so in writing 2, HeatCo can't accept one. Neither does this "purchase order" propose any bargain of its own. It's not an acceptance, and it's not an offer. It's another invitation to deal.

Writings 3 and 4 advance the negotiations, but neither proposes an explicit bargain. Writing 3 tells HeatCo that 13 tons are available, and writing 4 tells FuelCo that HeatCo wants all of it, delivered on October 8, depending on price. Neither party has yet proposed to the other a definite bargain.

Heatco receives writing 5 and should interpret it thus:

> We're ready to sell you all 13 tons, to be delivered on October 8.
> Price: $800 per ton. Say yes and we have a deal.

That's an offer.

With writing 6, HeatCo plainly manifests its assent, and the parties form a contract. So what's writing 7? It contemplates no exchange. It's not even an invitation to deal. There's no special name for it. It's a communication by which FuelCo courteously asks HeatCo to state a preferred delivery time. If HeatCo states its preference, FuelCo might or might not honor it. The parties formed their contract with communications 5 (offer) and 6 (acceptance). Legally, writing 7 is nothing.

Let's answer all three closers:

Question 8 asks that we identify invitations to deal. We've already found them in writings 1-4, and nowhere else. The answer is **B**.

Question 9 asks that we find an offer. We've done that too. It's in writing 5. The answer is **A**.

Question 10 asks that we reconsider the writings with modifications and determine which would most likely amount to an offer. **A**'s modification of writing 1 mentions price but does not specify it. Neither does it specify quantity. It remains an invitation to deal. **C** modifies writing 3 in that FuelCo promises to keep all 13 tons available until HeatCo responds. That's a sweet gesture, but HeatCo can't be held to it. HeatCo has made no offer, and the parties have no contract.

D alters writing 4 so that it presents the constructions "certainly" and "definite deal." Still, this certain and definite deal is "subject to price." The statement remains an invitation to deal.

B revises writing 2 so that HeatCo proclaims readiness to buy 18 tons of product at $300 per ton for immediate shipment. It doesn't name the product, but in light of writing 1, FuelCo should clearly understand that "18 tons" means 18 tons of Bortex Coal Kindler. As modified, writing 2 *is* an offer. That's why **B** is right.

Silver's Picks

1.   C
2.   C
3.   D
4.   C
5.   A
6.   C
7.   B
8.   B
9.   A
10.   B

5

More About Offers: Advertisements, Solicitations, and Signatures

A. Advertisements, Rewards, and Price Tags
B. Bid Solicitations and Auctions
C. Written Proposals and the Significance of Signatures
D. The Closer
✦ Silver's Picks

A. Advertisements, Rewards, and Price Tags

An offer needs an offeree, as Restatement (Second) of Contracts §24 makes clear:

> An offer is the manifestation of willingness to enter into a bargain, so made as to justify another person in understanding that his assent to that bargain is invited and will conclude it.

From Chapter 2, section D, we know that an offeree is one who reasonably believes that the offeror means to communicate with *him*. If Party A proposes a bargain but there is no Party B who reasonably believes the proposal is made to him, then Party A makes no offer.

1. For That Reason the Ordinary Advertisement Is Not an Offer

Suppose in a newspaper with circulation of 500,000, one sees: "*Lasser's Appliances now offers 32-inch Tanyo television sets, $199.*" In the law's eyes, Lasser's message does not lead a reasonable person to believe that *her* assent will definitely finalize a "deal." Sayeth the law: One should not conclude that Lasser has a number of units sufficient to supply all of the ad's readers. Rather, according to the law, one who reads this ad should understand that Lasser's asks *her* for an *offer to buy* the TV for $199.

Right or wrong, that's the general common law rule: *The ordinary advertisement is not an offer, but an invitation to deal.* It's the advertiser's suggestion that the reader make an offer to buy the advertised product, which offer, of course, the offeror/seller may accept or or not. The rule applies to any "ordinary" advertisement — print, broadcast, billboard, mail, or Internet "pop-up."

The Advertisement That's *Not* Ordinary

Yet, if an advertiser indicates that she is addressing a discrete group of persons who conform to some specific criteria, *then her ad is an offer.*

Suppose Store publishes this: "1 Black Lapin Stole, Beautiful, Worth $139.50, This Saturday, $1.00. FIRST COME, FIRST SERVED." Customer, a reasonable person, reads the ad. She understands that the store has only one stole to sell. Justifiably, she thinks this:

> The store is telling me that (1) for $1.00 it will sell one black lapin stole to one person, and (2) in order to accept the offer I must be first to visit the store on Saturday.[1]

At 1:00 A.M. on Saturday, Customer stands herself outside Store's door. When Store opens at 9:00 A.M., she enters and asks to buy the stole. Store and Customer do form a contract because *this* advertisement is not the "ordinary" one; it's not an open-ended publication to all the world that names a good (or service) and a price. Rather, this advertisement quantifies, precisely, the number of goods available and, of course, a price. Further — and this might matter — it makes plain the manner in which one is to accept the offer.[2] In this case, one accepts if he is first to visit the store on Saturday. Notwithstanding the court's imprecise, tortuous prose, that was, by and large, its ruling in Lefkowitz v. Great Minneapolis Surplus Store, 86 N.W.2d 689, 691 (Minn. 1957).[3]

---

1. There seems to be not one authority who understands that such an advertisement embodies two separate messages, each with its own legal consequence. First, it proposes a bargain: one stole for $1 to one person. Second, it identifies the manner in which an offeree is to accept, to wit, by being first to arrive at the store on the day in question. Had the store not, in the ad, included the reference to "first come, first served," then, presumably, any person would be free to accept if she communicated her assent in any (reasonable) manner. You'll know what we're talking about when you read Chapter 9. (Furthermore, as discussed in footnote 3 below, the offer does not truly propose 1 stole for $1.00. Rather it offers an *option* to purchase the stole for that price.)

2. In a similar case, a plaintiff contended that defendant's advertisement was an offer, and the court decided it was not. The court took note of the *Lefkowitz* (lapin stole) case, but ruled that the case at hand was unlike *Lefkowitz* because "[the advertisement] made no mention of the steps a potential offeree would be required to take to accept the alleged offer[.]" Leonard v. Pepsico, 88 F. Supp. 2d 116 (S.D.N.Y 1999).

3. Contrary to what many (way *too* many) teachers say, the plaintiff by entering the store did not form a contract *to buy the stole.* Once he came through the door, he was free according to his own

Referring obliquely to that case, Restatement (Second) §26, (illustration) explains:

> A, a clothing merchant, advertises overcoats of a certain kind for sale at $50. This is not an offer, but an invitation to the public to come and purchase. The addition of the words "Out they go Saturday; First Come, First Served" might make the advertisement an offer.

Suppose an advertiser publishes this: "Blue-colored contact lenses; $50/pair to all brown-eyed adults who live in Orange County. Dial 1-800-909-9090." The ad designates a group of persons who conform to highly specified criteria — brown-eyed persons living in Orange County. Further (and once again, this might matter), it specifies the manner in which the offerees are to accept. Probably, it's an offer.

Read This Ad; Probably It's an Offer.   "Collector wants every extant copy of Leland's *Gypsy Sorcery and Fortune Telling*. Will pay $25 for every copy sent to 455 Wayland Street, Hanlin, Massachusetts on or before January 1, 2020." The advertiser addresses a specified group of persons: all persons who have a copy of the book. In the law's eyes, any person who owns a copy of the book justifiably believes that the offer is made to her and that she concludes a bargain by sending it to the Massachusetts address.

So What's the Rule?   *(1) An ordinary advertisement directed to the general public is not an offer; it's a mere invitation to deal, but (2) if an advertisement leads a reasonable person to understand that acceptance is limited to a discrete, specifically identifiable person or group of persons to which she herself belongs — then it's an offer to her, and (3) it is all the more likely to be an offer if it specifies the manner in which she and the other offerees are to accept.*

2. Offers of Reward

One makes an ordinary reward offer when she promises money to a person who does something — apprehends the suspect, finds the missing dog, returns the lost wallet. A reward offer is an advertisement, but *not* an "ordinary" one. Every person who knows of it should understand (1) that the advertiser has exactly one reward to give out, and (2) that she accepts only if she is first to perform the requested act. Suppose Ariela loses her wallet. Hoping to recover it, she publishes this message: "$200 reward for the return of my wallet: black

---

choice to buy the stole or not. Properly construed, defendant proposed this bargain: "We will convey to one person an option — the right to buy, *if he wants to* — one lapin stole for $1.00. You may accept the offer by coming to us, as our first visitor, this coming Saturday." The store proposed not an exchange of $1.00 for a lapin stole, but the exchange of (a) an *option* to buy the lapin stole for $1.00 for (b) one's arrival at the store as first visitor on the day in question. Hence, the *Lefkowitz* case concerns, really, the formation of an *option contract* — a matter that you'll understand when you read Chapter 6, section B.

leather, lost near 103rd Street train station. Return to Ariela Martinez, 14 Wayne Way, Scottsdale, AZ. 760-444-7301." All who know of Ariela's offer are offerees. In order to accept, of course, one must be *the* person who returns her wallet. Hence, although all persons are offerees, each knows (should know) that only one of them can actually accept.[4]

QUESTION 1. In a national newspaper, Genelco publishes this:

Genelco will pay $45 per share of Westelco common stock to any and every person who agrees to sell us one or more such shares, stating his readiness to do so by signed, notarized written letter mailed no later than May 9, 2019, to Genelco Corporate Headquarters, 110-94 Corporate Plaza, Hartstown, Colorado 41567. After we receive your writing, we will arrange, within 30 days, to make payment and collect your share certificates.

Well before May 9, 2019, Jacqueline sends Genelco this signed, notarized letter: "I have three shares to sell and I accept your offer." With the letter she includes photocopies of her three share certificates. Has Jacqueline formed a contract with Genelco?

A. Yes, because she specifically wrote the words "accept your offer"
B. Yes, because she manifested assent to Genelco's proposed bargain
C. No, because Genelco's message was an advertisement made to the public
D. No, because Genelco asked for an indication of commitment, not photocopied certificates

---

ANALYSIS. Expressly addressing *all persons* who own Westelco shares, Genelco addresses itself to those persons who own stock in Westelco, and manifests its readiness to buy any and every such share. Its ad is not an "ordinary" one. It's an offer. Jacqueline accepted and the parties formed a contract.

Both **C** and **D** state that the parties have no contract, so both are wrong. According to **C**, Genelco's message is an advertisement to the public and for that reason doesn't constitute an offer. The relevant rule provides that *ordinary* advertisements are not offers. This is no ordinary one, and **C** is wrong.

D implies that an offeree fails to accept if she supplies the offeree with something more than he requested. There is no such rule. **D** is wrong.

A states that the parties formed a contract because Jacqueline used the *words* "offer" and "accept." Nonsense. One may write the word "offer" a

---

4. A reward offer is an offer for a unilateral contract as described in Chapter 9, sections A, B, and C.

thousand times and fail to make an offer. And she may *make* an offer using that word not once. One may accept an offer without using the word "accept," and she may use that word without accepting.

What of **B?** With precision, Genelco identifies its offerees. The ad is an offer, Jacqueline accepted it, the parties formed a contract, and **B** is right.

3. *Retail Store Price Tags*

Traditional common law provides that when a product sits on a retailer's shelf, its price tag represents not an offer but an invitation to deal, inviting the buyer to take the item from the shelf, present it to the cashier, and thus manifest his willingness to pay the stated price. By placing the item on the seller's counter, the buyer makes his offer to buy at the tagged price. The seller is free to accept or not.

Lately, however, that old rule is giving way to a new one. Some courts now hold, under UCC Article 2, that a retailer offers his good for sale when he puts it on his shelf and tags it with a price. See Annot. 78 A.L.R.3d 696 (1977). In construing and developing the common law, the nation's courts may well begin to rule that even in the absence of statute, a retailer makes an offer when he places an article on his shelf together with a price tag. The law on that point is in flux.

B. Bid Solicitations and Auctions

Think of an auction. The auctioneer puts on the block an item of jewelry and asks for bids. Under the law, he makes an invitation to deal — a request for offers. When Bidder 1 bids $50, he offers to buy for $50. When Bidder 2 bids $60, she offers to buy for $60. When Bidder 3 bids $70, she offers to buy for $70. If the auctioneer then says, "sold for $70," he accepts the third offer, and the parties form a contract.

The same logic applies when a business puts out a request for bids. Suppose DevelopCo publicizes this message: "Now seeking bids from construction engineering planners for building and development of Shalemart Plaza, specifications detailed on the next 100 pages." DevelopCo has asked for bids, which means it has asked for offers, which means it has made an invitation to deal. Each bid that follows is an offer, which DevelopCo is free to accept or not.

Suppose, on the other hand, that DevelopCo writes its message thus: "For building and development of Shalemart Plaza, we need a construction engineering planner. Lowest bidder will be hired." That's an offer. It's addressed to a specified group of persons — construction engineering planners. And, furthermore, it tells them how to accept — by submitting the lowest bid.

QUESTION 2. Acting as Martha's legal representative, Blairehouse Auctioneers announces by newspaper advertisement that it will sell at auction the Remington painting *Color on Canvas* at 3:00 P.M. on September 19. At the appointed time, with hundreds in attendance, the auctioneer begins: "Do I hear $40?" Jack bids $40, Jane bids $50, Jack bids $60, and Jane bids $80. The auctioneer cries out for $90. No one responds, and he says, "Going once, twice—sold for $80!" One second later, Jane declares, "I take back my bid; I don't want the painting. Sell it to the man who just bid $60." Is Jane contractually obliged to buy the painting for $80?

A. Yes, because the seller's representative acceded unequivocally to Jane's express preparedness to purchase for a stated price
B. Yes, but only if Jane was aware that one who bids at an auction occupies the legal status of an offeror
C. No, because the auctioneer offered to sell for $90, and Jane failed to raise her bid to that amount
D. No, because an auctioneer's request for bids represents only an invitation to deal

ANALYSIS.   *A contract arises by offer and acceptance.* An auctioneer makes invitations to deal, and bidders make offers. This auctioneer heard three bids and accepted none of them. When Jane made a fourth bid, offering to buy for $80, the auctioneer, not *immediately* accepting her offer, asked *for an offer* of $90, but none came forth. He then accepted Jane's $80 offer, and the parties formed a contract. The answer, therefore, should be "yes" — Jane has an obligation to buy. The reason? Jane made an offer and the auctioneer accepted.

C states that the parties did not form a contract. For that reason, it's wrong. Further, it incorrectly implies that the auctioneer offered to sell the painting for $90. Let's be clear: The auctioneer never offered to sell the painting, at any price. He *asked* for offers from prospective buyers (the bidders). With his barkings, he made repeated invitations to deal.

D correctly states that a request for bids is only an invitation to deal. Yet, it reaches the wrong conclusion. Yes — the auctioneer made only invitations to deal, but all were followed by offers, one of which he accepted (Jane's).

B tells us that Jane must buy the painting. That much is right, but the rest is nonsense. One may make an offer without knowing, legally, that she has done so. In contract law, as in (almost) every other legal arena, the legal status of one's behavior does not turn on her knowledge of law. One who intentionally kills another commits murder whether he knows it or not. Offer securities for public sale without first registering with the SEC, and you violate federal law, know it or not. B is wrong.

A presents not one of the relevant "buzz" words — neither "auction," "bid," "offer," nor "acceptance." Read for *meaning*, not for words. "Seller's representative" means the auctioneer. "Unequivocally acceded to" means "definitely assented to." "Jane's express preparedness to purchase for a stated price" means "Jane's offer." In short, **A** *means* "yes, because the auctioneer accepted Jane's offer." **A** is right.

C.   Written Proposals and the Significance of Signatures

Let's think now about written proposals and the significance of signatures. Look at three versions of a letter from Kirk to Beverly, all written on Kirk's personal letterhead. The letters differ one from another as to a small portion of text and as to who does or does not sign them.

Version 1

Dear Beverly,

I'd like to have you tutor my son Manny in his pre-calculus course — 15 weekly one-hour sessions, beginning this coming Thursday, $75 per hour. If you're agreeable, please sign and return the document to me. Thanks.

Agreed: Agreed:

_____   _____
           Kirk Grandel   Beverly Charlotte

Version 2

Dear Beverly,

I'd like to have you tutor my son Manny in his pre-calculus course — 15 weekly one-hour sessions, beginning this coming Thursday, $75 per hour. If you're agreeable, please sign and return the document to me. Thanks.

Agreed: Agreed:

Kirk Grandel
_____   _____
           Kirk Grandel   Beverly Charlotte

Version 3

Dear Beverly,

I'd like to have you tutor my son Manny in his pre-calculus course — 15 weekly one-hour sessions, beginning this coming Thursday at $75 per hour. If you're agreeable, please sign and return the document to me. Do that and we have a deal; we'll expect to see you this coming Thursday at 7:30 P.M.

Thanks.

Agreed: Agreed:

_____   _____
         Kirk Grandel   Beverly Charlotte

1. Offer or Invitation to Deal?

Let's analyze. With version 1 Kirk seems certainly to show that he is ready and willing to enter a bargain. Yet he leaves blank the space provided for his own signature. So let's ask: With Kirk's signature line left blank, should Beverly believe that *her* signature alone will "seal the deal?" Or, with Kirk's signature missing, should she construe the letter as a mere invitation to deal, asking *Beverly* to sign, and thus make an offer to Kirk on Kirk's stated terms? The answer is, probably, that Kirk's message (version 1), unsigned, is a mere invitation to deal. To explain, we resort to that simple, pliable, ubiquitous word "ordinarily." In the law's eyes, a written proposal with blank signature lines should, *ordinarily*, cause the reasonable person to realize that the proposor intends signatures to serve as the final showings of assent.

Here, in version 1, with Kirk's signature missing, Beverly should know that *her* signature will not conclude the bargain. She should realize that Kirk, omitting his own signature, reserves the right to have the final word. He doesn't make an offer but, instead, *asks* for one that he'll then be free to accept or not. In version 2, because Kirk signs his name on the signature line, Beverly should understand that he has proposed to her a definite bargain and, by signing *her* name, she'll accept it.

To summarize: a proposal or "draft contract" that bears a marked space for the proposor's signature is, ordinarily, an offer if the proposor signs. It's an invitation to deal if he doesn't.

2. But "Ordinarily" Doesn't Mean "Always"

To say that a "draft" bearing the proposor's blank signature line is ordinarily an invitation to deal is to say that in *some* cases (the extraordinary ones), it's *not* an invitation to deal but an offer.

Look at version 3 and ask if it's an offer. Ordinarily, the answer would be "no" because it shows a blank space for Kirk's signature. But the proposal isn't "ordinary." Very clearly and specifically, it advises Beverly that her signature will finalize the arrangement:

"If you're agreeable, please sign. . . . Do that and we have a deal; we'll expect to see you this coming Thursday at 7:30 P.M." In light of that language, Kirk's missing signature loses significance. Signed or not, his writing describes a bargain and asks for Beverly's assent. As a reasonable person, Beverly should believe that to "seal the deal," she need only sign and return the document. Hence, version 3 is an offer. If Beverly signs, the parties have a contract, and that's so even if Kirk *never* signs. (Beverly should demand that Kirk sign anyway, so that she has all the more evidence of his assent and hence that he and she formed a contract.)

D.   The Closer

QUESTION 3.   By telephone, Stephen Quadra of ConCo contacts Amanda Johnson of WebCo to say that ConCo wants to purchase all of WebCo's stock in WebCo's subsidiary corporation, FenCo. The parties talk. At the end of their chat Amanda tells Stephen, "I'll send you a draft contract." Stephen responds, "I'll be expecting it." Amanda then sends Stephen this *unsigned* document:

CONTRACT FOR STOCK PURCHASE:

The undersigned parties, ConCo and WebCo, hereby agree that:

(1) For $10,000,000 (ten million dollars) ConCo ("Buyer") will purchase from WebCo ("Seller") all shares in the FenCo Corporation, the transaction to occur on this next coming November 15, 2019.

ConCo Inc.   WebCo Inc.

By: _____   By: _____
Stephen Quadra,   Amanda Johnson,
President   *President*

Where indicated, Stephen signs the document and returns it to Amanda. The written exchange probably creates:

  I. a contract between ConCo and WebCo.
  II. an invitation to deal from ConCo to WebCo.
 III. an invitation to deal from WebCo to ConCo.
 IV. an offer from ConCo to WebCo.
  V. an offer from WebCo to ConCo.

A. I
B. II and III
C. II and IV
D. III and IV

ANALYSIS. Between these parties there pass two written communications: (1) WebCo's unsigned writing to ConCo, and (2) the same writing, returned to WebCo *signed* by ConCo. The first shows WebCo's definite interest in entering a bargain, quite specific in its terms. But let's ask: Should a reasonable party in ConCo's position believe (a) that its own assent will conclude the bargain, or instead (b) that WebCo has reserved for itself the "final say?" Asked another way: As read by a reasonable person in ConCo's position, does WebCo's writing (a) make an offer to ConCo, meaning that ConCo's signature will create a contract, or (b) ask that ConCo make an offer to WebCo meaning that WebCo's writing is an invitation to deal — that ConCo's signature will create an offer *to* WebCo?

WebCo designated space for two signatures, but sent the writing to ConCo unsigned. Ordinarily, then, ConCo should conclude that WebCo, reserving the right to sign last, has the "final say" — that ConCo's own signature will not finalize an agreement. Since there appears no extraordinary language or circumstance, this is the "ordinary" situation. WebCo's unsigned letter to ConCo is an invitation to deal.

By signing the letter and sending it back, ConCo takes the terms of WebCo's invitation and turns them into its own offer; *ConCo* makes an offer to *WebCo*. Hence, options III and IV are correct, but I, II, and V are not. These parties have not yet formed a contract because WebCo has not yet accepted ConCo's offer. In this written exchange, ConCo made no invitation to deal, and WebCo made no offer. Rather WebCo made the invitation to deal and ConCo the offer. (During the preliminary telephone conversation, ConCo did make an invitation to deal. The question, however, asks only about the written exchange.) **D** is right.

 # Silver's Picks

1.   **B**
2.   **A**
3.   **D**

6

How Offers Die

A. Termination by the Offeror's Revocation (and the "Option Contract")

Jeff wants Ellen to frame a painting.

(1) **Jeff:** Ellen, I'll pay $90 plus the cost of supplies if you'll frame this painting. I'd like it done by next Friday. Deal?

(2) **Ellen:** I'm not sure. I'll let you know tomorrow morning.

(3) **Jeff:** Never mind. I'll get someone else.

(4) **Ellen:** No, please don't. I'll do it. I'll do it by Friday; I accept.

Jeff and Ellen have *not* formed a contract. With statement 1, Jeff made an offer. With statement 2, Ellen said she'd consider the matter, but did not accept. In statement 3, Jeff *revoked the offer*; he "took it back." That put the offer to an end; Ellen lost her power to accept. With statement 4, Ellen tried to accept, but she spoke too late. The offer was gone — with the wind. Ellen had nothing *to* accept, and the parties formed no contract.

An Offeror Can Take His Offer Back?

Yes, absolutely. At any time *before an offeree accepts*, an offeror is free to revoke. He can do so even if he promises he won't. Imagine, for instance, that the foregoing dialogue went like this:

(1) **Jeff:** "Ellen, I will pay you $90 plus the cost of supplies if you will frame this painting. I'd like it done by next Friday. My offer stands until tomorrow at noon; I won't take it back. I promise."
(2) **Ellen:** "Well, thank you. I'll let you know tomorrow morning."
(3) **Jeff:** "On second thought — never mind, I'll get someone else."
(4) **Ellen:** "No, please don't. I'll do it. I'll do it by Friday; I accept."

Even with *that* dialogue, these parties form no contract because Jeff revoked before Ellen attempted to accept. That was his right, even though he had *promised* to hold his offer open. With the offer withdrawn, Ellen lost her power to accept. At statement 4, her *attempt* to accept was ineffective, and the parties formed no contract.

Restatement (Second) of Contracts §42 together with its comment (a) states the rule:

> An offeree's power of acceptance is terminated when the offeree receives from the offeror a manifestation of an intention not to enter into the proposed contract[.] ... [An] offer is revocable even though it expressly states the contrary[.]

Underlying that rule is another one, fundamental to the whole of contract law: *One party cannot be bound to an agreement unless the other is bound as well.* As to any proposed agreement between two parties, *one party is bound only if both are bound.* If one remains free to contract or not, then the other must be equally free.

That fundamental tenet stands behind the offeror's right to revoke (and also underlies rules regarding consideration discussed in Chapters 12-14). If the law were to prevent Jeff from withdrawing his offer while Ellen made her decision to accept or not, then it would bind Jeff without binding Ellen. Picture Ellen, freely pondering her decision — free to bind herself or not. Meanwhile, Jeff is at Ellen's mercy. If she snaps her fingers with an "I accept," Jeff is bound. His hands are tied while Ellen's are free. *That*, contract law will not abide. When two parties contemplate a contract, both are bound or neither is bound.

QUESTION 1. WesCo and JenCo exchange these signed writings:

(1) **WesCo:** We need 25,000 units of Bantex 44. Please quote us a price.
(2) **Jenco (by signed writing):** We have no Bantex 44 in stock. We probably can acquire the 25,000 units you request and deliver them within 20 days, but before we research that possibility, you should know that our current price is $8/unit. Interested?
(3) **WesCo:** Your delivery terms are fine, but we are prepared to pay only $6/unit. Please procure product and ship for $6/unit.
(4) **JenCo:** Would you consider paying $7/unit?

> (5) **WesCo:** No, thank you. We've changed our mind about the purchase; we'll do without the Bantex.
> (6) **JenCo:** We are able, after all, to order the 25,000 units, and we accept your offer to pay $6/unit. Will deliver.
>
> Thereafter JenCo contacts WesCo announcing that delivery is imminent. WesCo again advises JenCo that it no longer wants the goods and won't accept them. JenCo sues WesCo for breach. WesCo claims it formed no contract. Which of the following judicial conclusions properly supports a decision for WesCo?
>
> A. Neither party made an offer to the other.
> B. JenCo made an offer, but WesCo did not accept it.
> C. WesCo made an offer, but JenCo did not accept it.
> D. Each party made an offer, but neither made an acceptance.

ANALYSIS. In order to decide in WesCo's favor a judge must conclude that the parties exchanged no offer and acceptance. Examine the parties' communications. In statement 1, WesCo showed its interest in buying goods. It asked about price, but made no definite proposal. WesCo put forth only an invitation to deal. Then, uncertain of access to the product, Jenco named its price, but committed to nothing. It, too, made a mere invitation to deal. In statement 3, WesCo responded with an *offer* to buy at $6/unit. It remained for JenCo to accept while the offer remained operative. At statement 4, JenCo responded but did not accept. And, with statement 5, WesCo revoked: "We've changed our mind . . . we'll do without the Bantex." In Restatement terms, JenCo received "from the offeror a manifestation of an intention not to enter into the proposed contract." At statement 6, Jenco tried to accept — too late, for the offer was gone.

According to **A**, neither party made an offer. Wrong. With statement 3, WesCo did make an offer. According to **B**, JenCo made an offer. That's wrong too. JenCo made two invitations to deal (statements 2 and 4), and at statement 6, a failed attempt to accept WesCo's offer. It never made an offer of its own. Choice **D** states that both parties made offers, which is false because JenCo did not.

According to **C**, WesCo made an offer but JenCo failed to accept it. That's true: WesCo made an offer in statement 3, but revoked it in statement 5. JenCo *tried* to accept in statement 6, but had nothing to accept. Just as **C** states, "WesCo made an offer, but JenCo did not accept it." **C** is right.

But One Can *Purchase* an Irrevocable Offer—The "Option Contract"

Although an offeror may revoke his offer at any time before the offeree accepts, one may nonetheless *purchase* an irrevocable offer by forming with the offeror an "option contract."

Victoria and Pamela

Wanting to sell her building, Victoria contacts Pamela and the parties exchange these signed writings:

(1) **Victoria:** I own a building described in the Frontier County land records at volume 202, page 348. Its address is 4040 Thirteenth Avenue. I will sell it to you for $8 million.
(2) **Pamela:** I'd like to think about it. Will you allow me 120 days to make up my mind?
(3) **Victoria:** Yes. I'll hold the offer open for 120 days.

As we now know, Victoria is free to revoke the offer notwithstanding her promise to hold it open. Pamela has no legal assurance that the building will be available to her for 120 days or even 120 seconds.

Now consider *this* exchange:

(1) **Vanessa:** I own a building described in the Frontier County land records at volume 195, page 420. Its address is 4040 Twelfth Avenue. I will sell it to you for $8 million.
(2) **Peter:** I need time to think it over. I'll pay you $10,000 tomorrow morning if you'll agree to hold the offer open for 120 days.
(3) **Vanessa:** Agreed.

Wanting time to consider Vanessa's offer without risking its revocation, Peter responds, in statement 2, with an offer of his own (which we call a "counter-offer"; see Chapter 7, section A). He proposes to *pay money* in exchange for Vanessa's promise not to revoke her offer. Vanessa accepts and the parties form a contract.

What That Contract Requires

The contract does not require that these parties buy and sell the building. Rather, it requires that Peter pay Vanessa $10,000 and that Vanessa hold open for 120 days her offer to sell Peter the building for $8 million. In essence, for $10,000, Peter has *bought* from Vanessa an irrevocable offer. Reciprocally, for $10,000, Vanessa has sold Peter that same irrevocable offer. For 120 days, *by contract*, Peter has the *option* to accept it or not. If he decides to accept — to "exercise his option" — then he must pay Vanessa $8 million and Vanessa must convey the building. If he decides not to accept, he loses his $10,000, having received exactly what he paid for — a form of "insurance" — an offer, irrevocable for 120 days called, also, a "120-day option on Vanessa's building."

But I Thought an Offeror Can *Always* Revoke Her Offer at Any Time Before the Offeree Accepts

That's right; an offer is revocable at any time before the offeree accepts. But a *contract* in which an offeror agrees not to revoke her offer is, like any other contract, fully enforceable. Between Vanessa and Peter there stands not a simple offer from one to the other, but a *contract* by which both are bound. Like any other contract, it arose by offer and acceptance (statements 2 and 3 above). And to this sort of contract, we give the special name "option contract": *An option contract is a contract in which (a) a Party 1 ("optionee") gives value to a Party 2 ("optionor") and, in exchange, with respect to some other prospective contract, (b) Party 2 (optionor) promises, for some agreed period, to hold irrevocable an offer so that Party 1 (optionee) for that period has the option to accept it or not.*

Let's apply that definition to Vanessa and Peter.

> "*An option contract is a contract . . .*"

An option contract is, first of all, *a contract*. It must arise through its own offer and acceptance. This one arose through Peter's offer at statement 2, accepted by Vanessa at statement 3.

> "*. . . in which . . .*"

An option contract is a particular *kind* of contract about to be described.

> " *. . . a first person ("optionee") gives value to a second ("optionor") . . .*"

Peter, the optionee, gives value to Vanessa, the optionor, by way of his promise to pay $10,000.

> "**with respect to some other prospective contract**"

Vanessa and Peter contemplate the possibility of another contract not yet formed — a contract for the sale to Peter of Vanessa's land for $8 million.

> "**the second (optionor) agrees, for some specified period, to hold irrevocable some offer so that the optionee for that period has the option to accept it or not, as he wishes.**"

Vanessa promises that for 120 days she will hold her offer irrevocable so that Peter may, at any time during that period, accept it, if and as he chooses.[1]

Option contracts come with their own lexicon of words and phrases:

OPTION CONTRACT VOCABULARY LIST

Option: one's contractual right to accept an offer held irrevocable for some specified period.

Optionor: party who sells an option to another.

Optionee: party who buys an option from another.

Option price: price the optionee pays for his option.

Strike price: price the optionee will pay if she exercises her option. (Beware: Some people use "option price" to mean "strike price.")

Option period: time period during which the optionor must hold her offer irrevocable.

---

1. For additional illustrations of option contracts, see Restatement (Second) of Contracts §25 illus. 1, 2.

Exercise: optionee's decision to accept the irrevocable offer. Know too that if from Party S, Party B buys an option to purchase, for example, a parcel of land, some will say that B has "an option on" the land. Hence, the colloquial phrase "option on" means, really, "option to buy."

QUESTION 2. By signed writing, Party G makes this offer: "My 300-acre farm is for sale immediately. The land is described at volume 2084, page 782 of the Harrison County Land Records. Price: $10 million, all cash, payable immediately." Party H reads the offer and responds, whereupon G and H exchange writings. Among the exchanges shown below, which creates an option contract?

A. (1) **Party H:** I'll pay you $1 million one month from today if you give me five years to decide that I do or do not wish to buy the farm for an additional $9 million.
(2) **Party G:** Agreed.

B. (1) **Party H:** I'm interested. I'll pay you $1 million one month from today. In five years, I'll pay you the remaining $9 million and at that time you'll transfer the farm to me. Agreed?
(2) **Party G:** Agreed.

C. (1) **Party H:** I'm interested, but I'd like to buy an option to purchase the farm. Agreed?
(2) **Party G:** Agreed. The option period will be five years, the option price $1 million, and the strike price $9 million.

D. (1) **Party H:** I'm interested, but I need five years to make a decision. Agreed?
(2) **Party G:** Agreed.

ANALYSIS. An option contract is, first, a contract. If an interaction fails to form *a contract*, it cannot form an option contract. Consider **D**. At statement 1, in response to G's initial offer to sell the farm, H asks for five years in which to make a decision. With statement 2, in exchange for nothing, G agrees, meaning she purports to make her offer irrevocable for five years. Legally, we know, she can't do that; notwithstanding her promise, she retains the right to revoke. G has made, still, only her initial offer to sell the farm, and H has not accepted it. The parties have no contract, meaning they have no option contract. **D** is wrong.

Now for **C**. With statement 1, H expresses *interest* in forming an "option contract" but makes no offer to do so. He provides no terms—no option price, no option period, no strike price. Hence, in responding to G's offer, H makes a mere invitation to deal. With statement 2, Party G truly *offers* H an option to buy the farm. She identifies the option period (five years), the option price

($1 million), and the strike price ($9 million). Party H does not respond, and so we're left with G's unaccepted offer to sell H an option on the farm. The parties form no contract, so **C** is wrong.

In **B**, the parties do form a contract. Party H responds to Party G's initial offer not with an acceptance but with a counteroffer, which means an offer in response to an offer. (See Chapter 7, section A.) He proposes definitely to purchase the farm *not* immediately and *not* for "all cash, payable immediately." Rather, he offers to pay $1 million in one month and $9 million five years later, at which time Party G is to convey ownership of the farm. That's an offer, and with statement 2 Party H accepts it. The parties form a contract that leaves neither one with any options at all. These parties *must* buy and sell. Hence, they form a contract, but not an option contract. **B** is wrong.

We're left with **A**. Again Party H receives G's offer and responds with an offer of his own. He proposes to pay $1 million in exchange for the right to buy the farm at any time within the next five years, by paying — if he chooses to buy — another $9 million. Hence H offers to buy, for $1 million, G's five-year irrevocable offer to sell the farm for (an additional) $9 million. Party G accepts the offer, and the parties thus form a contract — and, more specifically, an option contract. Some would say, "G sold H an option on her farm," or "H bought an option on G's farm." Whatever they say, **A** is right.

B. Termination by the Offeree's Rejection

If in response to an offer, the offeree says "no," she rejects the offer and thus terminates it. Consider this interaction, occurring at 11 A.M.:

> **Party A:** I'll pay you $50 if you'll wash all of my windows by noon today.
> **Party B:** No, thank you.
> **Party B (again):** I've changed my mind. I accept your offer.

By saying "no," B rejected A's offer and thus "killed" it. B changed her mind and tried to accept the offer, but she spoke too late. By saying "no" she rejected the offer and put it to an end; she lost her power to accept. The parties have no contract.

Now consider this interaction, also occurring at 11 A.M.:

> **Party C:** I'll pay you $50 if you'll wash all of my windows by noon today.
> **Party D:** I wish I could, but I can't wash all of the windows in one hour.
> **Party D (again):** I've changed my mind. I can do it. I accept.

At 11 A.M. Party C made an offer. Party D expressed her wish to finalize the bargain, but stated also that she could not give the requested performance within the specified time. By law, to say "I wish I could, but I can't" is to say "no" (nicely). Party D rejected C's offer. She "killed" it. Her subsequent attempt to accept was ineffective.

The rule, then, is this: *An offeree rejects an offer and thereby terminates it when she leads the offeror reasonably to believe that she has decided not to accept.* Restatement (Second) §38(2) states it this way: "A manifestation of intention not to accept an offer is a rejection. . . ." Section 39(2) adds: "An offeree's power of acceptance is terminated by his rejection of the offer. . . ."

If an offeree responds to an offer not with "yes" or "no" but with "maybe," she neither accepts nor rejects. The offer continues in effect, and the offeree retains her power to accept. Consider this little chat:

> **Party A:** I'll pay you $50 if you'll wash all of my windows by noon today.
> **Party B:** Well, I'll think about it.
> **Party B (again):** I've thought about it. I can do it. I accept.

In her first statement, B manifests neither acceptance nor rejection. She indicates that she'll *consider* A's proposal. The offer continues in force, just as though B had said nothing. Then, with her second statement, B accepts, and the parties form a contract. Accordingly, Restatement (Second) §38(2) provides:

> A manifestation of intention not to accept an offer is a rejection unless the offeree manifests an intention to take it under further advisement.

QUESTION 3. On March 1, Dennis Storme telephones Mariah Wilson and leaves her this voicemail message:

(1) **March 1, Dennis (voicemail message):** Hello, I'm Dennis Storme. You come highly recommended as a math tutor, and I'd like you to tutor my daughter Susan in trigonometry. Would you get back to me so that we can discuss the possibilities?

(2) **March 2, Mariah (voicemail message):** Hello, Mr. Storme, this is Mariah Wilson. I would be happy to tutor Susan. I have only one opening at present—Saturday mornings from 10:30 A.M. to noon. My fee is $90 for the 90 minutes. I am prepared to commit to the next ten Saturdays. After that, we can consider whether Susan needs any additional tutoring.

(3) **March 3, Dennis (fax):** Thank you for your return call. I cannot work with the hours you mention. Would you be able to tutor on Saturday evenings?

(4) **March 4, Mariah (voicemail message):** No, Mr. Storme, I'm sorry that I cannot tutor Susan on Saturday evenings. Exactly as stated in my last message, I am available for the next ten Saturdays from

> 10:30 A.M. to noon and would be pleased to tutor Susan on those days at those hours.
>
> (5) **March 5, Dennis (fax):** Very well—we're agreed. Saturday mornings from 10:30 A.M. to noon; I'll find some way to see that we can do it.
>
> Legally, is Mariah free *not* to tutor Susan?
>
> A. Yes, because Dennis's March 5 message was too indefinite to create a contract
> B. Yes, because on March 3, Dennis lost his power to accept Mariah's March 2 offer
> C. No, because on March 3, Dennis plainly continued in his willingness to purchase Mariah's services
> D. No, because on March 5, Dennis effectively assented to the terms that Mariah had set forth on March 4

ANALYSIS. The question is whether these parties formed a contract — whether one of them made an offer that the other accepted while the offer still lived. On March 1, Dennis spoke to the possibility of purchasing Mariah's tutoring services. He mentioned neither fee nor hours. He made an invitation to deal. On March 2, Mariah responded with an offer. On March 3, Dennis stated that he "could not work" with the hours she had specified. Put otherwise, he expressed an intention not to accept the offer. He thereby rejected it and thus lost his power ever to accept; the March 3 offer was "dead." But on March 4, Mariah restated her proposal and thus made the offer anew. When Dennis assented, he accepted the offer — the March 4 offer — and the parties formed a contract.

A and B are wrong; they tell us that Mariah *is* free to withhold her services, meaning that the parties formed no contract. It's true, as A states, that Dennis's first message was an invitation to deal. It's also true, as B indicates, that when Dennis rejected Mariah's first offer, he lost his power to accept it. Still, there later arose Mariah's new offer, which Dennis accepted.

C and D correctly imply that these parties did form a contract. Yet choice C erroneously suggests that on March 3, Dennis's plain willingness to secure Mariah's services somehow creates a contract. Nonsense. On March 3, Dennis rejected Mariah's first offer and lost his power to accept it; the offer "died," notwithstanding that Dennis continued in his willingness to secure Mariah's services. **D** has it right: These parties formed a contract because on March 4 Mariah made her offer anew; she made a *new offer* (whose terms were the same as those she offered on March 3). On March 5, Dennis accepted, and the parties were bound in contract. **D is right.**

C.   Passage of Time

Offers are mortal things; they die. We know already that an offeror may kill his own offer by revocation and that the offeree may kill it by rejection. Know now that without revocation or rejection, every unaccepted offer dies of "old age"— by "decay." The offeror may expressly provide for that by tagging his offer with a "shelf life." Suppose Barnette sends to Chadwell this signed writing: "We are prepared to replace all of the windows in your building at 444 Weston Street, with our new double-insulated windows, #820. Our price: $90,000, payable in advance. Offer good for ten days."

Barnette may revoke its offer, of course, any time before Chadwell accepts. *The offer's last sentence does not and cannot alter that truth.* The last sentence means this: If neither party acts for ten days, the offer expires "for passage of a time stated in the offer." The offer dies on its own, and the offeree loses his power to accept.

When the offeror does *not* tie his offer to a timer, the law limits its life to a "reasonable time." Had Barnette not set a ten-day timer on his offer but instead stayed silent on that subject then, by law, after a "reasonable time," his offer would die on its own. (As to who decides what is a "reasonable" time, please revisit Chapter 3, section D.)

QUESTION 4. Vlad telephones Esther and tells her, "I stand ready to clean your carpet for $125 on any Friday morning you choose." Esther repeats, "Any Friday morning?" Vlad answers, "Yes, my Fridays are clear." Esther responds, "I'll get back to you." "Very well," says Vlad, "I look forward to hearing from you." *For two years* neither party communicates with the other. Esther then telephones Vlad: "I accept your offer. Please come this Friday morning." Have these parties formed a contract?

A. Yes, because Vlad made an offer and Esther accepted
B. Yes, because Vlad expressly stated that "any Friday morning" would be appropriate
C. No, because Esther failed to accept while Vlad's offer was operative
D. No, because Esther rejected the offer by saying "I'll get back to you"

ANALYSIS.   Vlad made an offer, tying it to no time limit. By law it expired after a reasonable time. As in all other contexts, reasonableness is ordinarily a question of fact, representing what reasonable persons would do and expect under the prevailing circumstances. No reasonable person in Esther's position could believe that Vlad intended his offer to live for two years. When Esther attempted to accept, the offer's life — *a reasonable period of time* — had expired. We don't know exactly just *when* it expired, but we know for this offer, that a reasonable time passed, probably after a month, and certainly after two months, let alone two years.

A and B state that the parties did form a contract, so they're wrong. As for choice A, Esther did not issue an acceptance. She *attempted* to accept. But in that effort she failed; one cannot accept an offer that no longer lives. Regarding B, Vlad's reference to "any Friday morning" could not justify Esther in believing that the offer was eternally open. She ought to have understood Vlad to mean "the next few Friday mornings." D correctly states that the parties did not form a contract, but its reasoning is wrong. Esther did not reject Vlad's offer. She said she'd be in touch again. "No" rejects, "maybe" does not. C tells us that Esther attempted to accept Vlad's offer when the offer was no longer "operative," meaning that Esther had lost her power to accept. That's exactly right. When Esther tried to accept the offer, it was long gone. Therefore, Esther attempted to accept after the offer had terminated and so failed to form a contract. For that reason, C is right.

D. Death or Incapacity of Offeror or Offeree

If one dies, his "estate" lives on in his place. Hence, when two parties form a contract and one of them then dies, the contract lives on and, in effect, the surviving party has a contract with the decedent's "estate." Through its executor, the estate asserts the decedent's contractual rights, and must fulfill his contractual duties. (You'll learn all about that when you study wills, trusts, and estates.) That does *not* mean that the decedent's heirs or beneficiaries must fulfill his contracts. Rather, the estate must fulfill them, resorting to assets the decedent leaves behind.

Suppose Tom borrows $800,000 from Lender and dies before making any repayment. In addition to the $800,000 borrowed from Lender, Tom has, at his death, $200,000, so that his estate's assets are, in total, $1 million. Tom's will leaves "everything I own to my son and daughter, Jack and Jill." The estate owes Lender $800,000, but Jack and Jill owe him nothing. From its $1 million, the estate first pays its debt. Jack and Jill take the $200,000 that remains. If the estate's value falls below $800,000, Lender takes whatever it has. As for the rest that's owed him, Lender loses out; he gets nothing more. After the estate pays Lender all that it has, it's empty. Jack and Jill get nothing, even though Tom, their father, wanted to leave them everything he had.

On January 1, Bess and Lloyd interact:

> **Bess:** I'd like to borrow $100. I'll repay it in six months at a 6 percent annual interest rate, meaning that in six months I'll pay you $103.
> **Lloyd:** I'll make the loan, but I can't do so until February 1, one month from now. Further, I want the interest paid at the outset. That means

that you'll pay me $3 on February 1, I'll then lend you $100 on that same day, and you will repay me the full $100 six months later — on August 1. Agreed?

Bess: Agreed.

The parties have a contract. If Lloyd dies two weeks later, on January 15, the contract with Bess lives on. From Bess, on February 1, Lloyd's estate is entitled to $3 and, on that same day, it must lend her $100, with Bess to repay it — to the estate — on (or before) August 1.

A Contract Survives Either of Its Parties, But an Offer Does *Not* Survive an Offeror or Offeree

Let's modify the original interaction:

Bess: I'd like to borrow $100. I'll repay it in six months at a 6 percent annual interest rate, meaning that in six months I'll pay you $103.

Lloyd: I'll make the loan, but I can't do so until February 1, one month from now. You'll repay me six months from then — on August 1 together with, as you say, $3 in interest.

Bess: Let me think about that. I'll let you know by January 25. Okay?

Lloyd: Yes, that's fine.

Plainly, these folks have no contract. Bess made an offer and Lloyd responded with an offer of his own (a "counteroffer") leaving Bess with power to accept it or not. If Lloyd dies on January 15, his offer dies too; *it* doesn't pass to his estate. If Bess then contacts Lloyd's executor, announcing her acceptance, no contract arises. The same is so if Bess should die with Lloyd alive, his offer still outstanding. Bess's power to accept does not pass to her estate; her death terminates Lloyd's offer.

Analogous rules apply to mental incompetence. If two parties form a *contract* and one then suffers mental incompetence, the contract continues. An "administrator" or "conservator" acts for the incompetent party. On his behalf, she asserts contractual rights and, using the incompetent party's assets, fulfills his contractual duties (perhaps by commissioning another to perform as his substitute). Yet if one makes an *offer* and he or his offeree suffers that fate, the offer terminates — as it does when either party dies. Restatement (Second) §48 addresses both unhappy events:

An offeree's power of acceptance is terminated when the offeree or offeror dies or is deprived of legal [mental] capacity to enter into the proposed contract.

QUESTIONS 5-7. On July 1, Wharton and Xavier create a contract under which Xavier will pay Wharton $9,000 and Wharton will repair Xavier's large yacht, the *Largesse*. Wharton is to begin work on August 1 and on that day Xavier is to pay him $4,500. Wharton is to finish work on August 31, and Xavier is then to pay the remaining $4,500. Also on July 1, just after they have formed their contract, the parties converse:

Xavier: I have another, smaller yacht. It needs that very same repair. For an additional $5,000 will you repair the smaller yacht just after you finish repairing this one?

Wharton: I'll think it over and let you know within two weeks.

Xavier: That's fine. Contact me by phone, fax, or email.

QUESTION 5. One week later, on July 8, Xavier dies. As a result, Wharton loses

   I. his rights regarding the larger yacht.
  II. his rights regarding the smaller yacht.
  A. I only
  B. II only
  C. Both I and II
  D. Neither I nor II

ANALYSIS.   If two parties form a contract, and one or both then die, the contract continues. Yet if one makes an offer, not yet accepted, it terminates if offeror or offeree dies.

As to the larger yacht, these parties formed a contract. When Xavier died, the contract continued. Wharton retained his rights and duties. Xavier's estate must pay Wharton $4,500 on August 1, and Wharton must repair the yacht. The estate must then pay Wharton $4,500 more when he finishes the work on August 31. As to the smaller yacht, the parties formed no contract. Xavier made an offer, Wharton responded with a "maybe," and Xavier then died. The offer terminated, and Wharton lost his power — his *right* — to accept it.

Option I makes a false statement, which means that **A** and **C** are wrong. Regarding the smaller yacht, Xavier made an offer, but on Xavier's death it expired; the parties formed no contract. Option II makes an accurate statement, so **D** is wrong. Wharton retains his rights under the existing contract, but loses his right to accept the outstanding offer. **B** is right.

QUESTION 6. Assume, now, that neither party dies. Instead, on July 8, Xavier becomes mentally incompetent. As a result, Wharton loses

  I. his rights regarding the larger yacht.
  II. his rights regarding the smaller yacht.
  A. I only
  B. II only
  C. Both I and II
  D. Neither I nor II

ANALYSIS. On mental incompetence and death, the law has like effects. Contracts survive. Offers don't. Again, **B** is right.

QUESTION 7. Assume now that both parties remain alive and well. On July 8, Xavier contacts Wharton and says, "I've changed my mind about both yachts. Repair neither one." As a result, Wharton loses

  I. his rights regarding the larger yacht.
  II. his rights regarding the smaller yacht.
  A. I
  B. II
  C. Both I and II
  D. Neither I nor II

ANALYSIS. Regarding the larger yacht, the parties have a contract. Xavier's statement does not alter that fact. Regarding the smaller yacht, there stood only an offer from Xavier to Wharton, which, with his statement, Xavier revoked. Wharton loses his right to accept the offer. As for the larger yacht, he retains his contractual rights (and duties). Again, **B** is right.

E.   The Closers

QUESTIONS 8 & 9

Eyon owns all of the stock in Eyon Inc. He has heard that Orlin, who owns all of the stock in Orlin Inc., might wish to sell it. In December, the two exchange these signed writings:

December 1, 2019, Eyon: I may wish, within the next year, to purchase all of your stock in Orlin. I'll pay $15 million, but I need one year—until November 30, 2020—to make my decision. I am prepared to pay $100,000 tomorrow, December 2, in order to have from you this commitment: If, during this next year, I wish to make the purchase, you'll sell for that price.

December 1, 2019, Orlin: Agreed. Please send the payment.

Eyon sends Orlin $100,000. On December 2, Orlin receives it. Then, on May 1, 2020, Orlin contacts Eyon:

May 1, 2020, Orlin: Not hearing from you in five months, I have decided not to sell you the stock. I revoke my offer and will return your $100,000.

May 1, 2020, Eyon: No, no, no; that's not acceptable. As we agreed, I may still wish to purchase the stock and I will make my decision on or before November 30.

QUESTION 8. Does Eyon retain the right, through November 30 to purchase the stock?

A. Yes, because on December 1 he acquired a one-year option to do so
B. Yes, because he proposed to pay the $100,000 within one day
C. No, because corporate stock is not a good
D. No, because Orlin stood ready to return Eyon's $100,000

ANALYSIS.   With his first statement, Eyon offered Orlin $100,000 for Orlin's promise to sell Eyon the Orlin stock for $15 million should Eyon choose to buy it during the next year. Stated in plain, simple, ordinary, pretentious legalese, Eyon offered to buy an option on Orlin's stock, to be exercised within one year, with an option price of $100,000, and a strike price of $15 million. Orlin accepted, and the parties formed an option contract.

We're asked whether Eyon retained the right to purchase the stock until November 30. Plainly, the answer is "yes." **C** and **D** say "no," so they're wrong. **C** reasons that corporate stock is not a good, and that's true. But option contracts do not arise from UCC Article 2 and they're not confined to the sale of goods. Option contracts are but one species of contract under the common law. They might concern goods, services, or anything else. **D** says "no" because Orlin offered to return Eyon's $100,000 payment. When two parties form a contract, neither can escape it by returning what the other has given him under its terms. By law, "a deal is a deal." Hence, **D** is wrong.

B says "yes," but its reasoning is askew. When Eyon made his offer, he proposed to pay $100,000 the next day, December 2. When one promises a performance, whether he promises it for today, tomorrow, or after the Second Coming — he gives value. *A promise is value. A promise, itself, is consideration.* Had Eyon proposed to pay Orlin in one week, one month, one year, or five years, then still these parties would form an option contract requiring that (a) Orlin, through November 30, stand ready to sell his stock and (b) Eyon pay Orlin $100,000 — at whenever time he agreed to do so. **B** is wrong.

A tells us that Eyon retains his right to buy the stock because he bought an option to do so. Therein lies the simple truth, and the truth shall set us free (usually). **A** is right.

QUESTION 9. Which of the following most accurately characterizes the transaction?

A. Eyon offered to buy stock from Orlin.
B. Orlin sold Eyon an option to purchase stock.
C. Eyon was optionor and Orlin optionee.
D. Eyon presented Orlin with an invitation to deal.

ANALYSIS.   Orlin sold Eyon a one-year option to buy stock. Stated the other way 'round, Eyon purchased *from* Orlin an option to buy the stock. Whichever statement we make, Orlin was the optionor and Eyon the optionee. **A, C,** and **D** mischaracterize the transaction. As for **A,** Eyon never offered to buy stock. He offered to buy *the right* to do so at his option. What of **C**? Orlin sold the option, so he is the optionor. Eyon *bought* it, so he is the optionee. And **D**? Never did either party make an invitation to deal. From the first, Eyon offered to buy an option. Orlin accepted, and Eyon paid him the option price. Hence, Orlin sold Eyon an option to purchase his stock. That's why **B** is right.

Silver's Picks

1.   C
2.   A
3.   D
4.   C
5.   B
6.   B
7.   B
8.   A
9.   B

7

Counteroffer and the Mirror-Image Rule

A. Counteroffer as Rejection
B. The Mirror-Image Rule
C. A "Mere Inquiry" Doesn't Reject
D. The Closer
◈ Silver's Picks

A. Counteroffer as Rejection

One might receive an offer and respond by proposing a change in its terms, thereby making an offer of his own, commonly called a "counteroffer."

The Photocopier, Case 1

Party A: I can repair your photocopier by Saturday morning for $320. Okay?
Party B: Do it by Friday morning and we have a deal. Agreed?

Party A made an offer and B responded with a "counteroffer." *With respect to any original offer, a counteroffer is an offer made by the original offeree to the original offeror, similar in subject matter but different in terms.* Restatement (Second) of Contracts §39(1) puts it thus:

> A counteroffer is an offer made by an offeree to his offeror relating to the same matter as the original offer and proposing a substituted bargain differing from that proposed by the original offer.

Common law provides, ordinarily, that when Party A makes an offer to Party B, who then responds with a counteroffer, A justifiably believes that B has rejected the offer initially made to him. At the front of (almost) every counteroffer, the law writes, "no, I reject your offer." By law, Party B responded to A with this:

> No, I reject your offer. Do it by Friday morning and we have a deal. Agreed?

With the words "no, I reject" implied by law, B's counteroffer has these two effects: (1) it rejects A's original offer, so that B can no longer accept it; and (2) it turns A into an offeree affording him the power to accept B's counteroffer, which is after all, an *offer*.

Let's continue the dialogue and see what that means.

(1) **Party A:** I can repair the photocopier by Saturday morning for $320. Okay?
(2) **Party B:** [No, I reject your offer.] Do it by Friday morning and we have a deal. Agreed?
(3) **Party A:** I can't do that.
(4) **Party B:** Okay. I accept your initial offer — Saturday it is.
(5) **Party A:** No. I've changed my mind about the price; it will be $380.

Neither party made an offer that the other accepted. With statement 1, A made an offer to which B, in statement 2, made a counteroffer meaning that he (1) put his own offer "on the table" and (2) rejected A's offer, thus shoving it from the table into the dumper. With statement 3, A rejected B's counteroffer, leaving the table empty. With statement 4, B tried to accept A's original offer, but he spoke too late. That offer died when, with his counteroffer at statement 2, B rejected it. With statement 5, A then made a new offer, which B is free to accept or not.

About a counteroffer we now know this: It rejects the offer to which it responds. Beyond that, it's an offer like any other. The party who makes it is an offeror (although he was first an offeree). The party who receives it (originally an offeror) is an offeree, free to accept it or not, for so long as it lives — for so long as it does not expire by revocation, rejection, or any other means.

Sometimes a Counteroffer Does Not Reject

By implication of law, as just discussed, a counteroffer "ordinarily" acts as a rejection, meaning that an *ordinary* counteroffer rejects the offer that it answers. But one might overcome the law's implication by making a counteroffer that is not "ordinary."

The Photocopier, Case 2

(1) **Party A:** I can repair the photocopier by Saturday morning for $320. Okay?
(2) **Party B:** I'll think about that; I might want to accept. Meanwhile, know this: If you'll do the work by Friday morning, we have a deal. Agreed?

(3) **Party A:** I can't do that.
(4) **Party B:** Okay. I accept your initial offer — Saturday it is.
(5) **Party A:** I've changed my mind about the price; it will be $380.

With statement 1, A makes an offer and B, with statement 2, answers with a counteroffer, *making clear his wish to preserve A's original offer.* B's counteroffer is not the "ordinary" one. It overcomes the law's implication that it acts as a rejection. Hence, *this* counteroffer does *not* work a rejection. Party A's offer remains effective, and with statement 4, B accepts it. When, at statement 5, A attempts to revoke his offer and make a new one (at a higher price), he speaks too late. With statement 4, the parties form a contract.

Neither does a counteroffer operate as a rejection if the original offer*or* makes plain that he will not so interpret it.

The Photocopier, Case 3

(1) **Party A:** I can repair the photocopier by Saturday morning for $320. Propose a change in terms, if you like. I won't take that as a "no."
(2) **Party B:** I can't wait until Saturday. If you can do it by Friday morning, we have a deal. Agreed?
(3) **Party A:** I can't do that.
(4) **Party B:** Okay. I accept your initial offer — Saturday it is.

With statement 1, A made an offer and plainly told B that he would not take a counteroffer as a rejection. B made a counteroffer and, with statement 3, A rejected it. Meanwhile, A's original offer remained operative. With statement 4, B accepted it. The parties formed a contract according to A's original offer.

The rule is: *One who makes a counteroffer rejects the offer to which he responds, unless (a) he affirmatively manifests his wish to keep the offer under consideration, or (b) the original offeror manifests his intention not to treat it as a rejection.* Restatement (Second) §39(2) states it (badly) like this:

> An offeree's power of acceptance is terminated by his making of a counteroffer unless the offeror has manifested a contrary intention or unless the counteroffer manifests a contrary intention of the offeree.

In the second photocopier case, the counteroffer manifested "a contrary intention of the [original] offeree" because it included the words "I might want to accept." In the third photocopier case, Party A, the offeror, "manifested a contrary intention" by saying: "Propose a change in terms, if you like. I won't take that as a 'no.'"

B.   The Mirror-Image Rule

The common law features this long-standing rule: *To accept an offer, the offeree must manifest an assent that mirrors the offeror's proposal in any and every respect. She must show agreement to each and every one of the offeror's proposed terms without alteration.* This "mirror-image rule" reflects the simple logical notion that a party can accept only such offer as is actually made to her.

Suppose A and B conduct this conversation:

Party A: I'll wash your car, right now, for $30.
Party B: I accept, but don't wash the car, paint the house instead, and I'll pay you $3,000.

You need no special rule named "mirror image" to conclude that these parties formed no contract. Party B spoke the *words* "I accept," but plainly did not assent to the offer before her. She stated her willingness to enter a bargain *not* offered. She accepted — nothing. To say that acceptance requires a mirror image of the offer is to say only that there can be no acceptance of an offer not made. That's all there is to the mirror-image rule. Don't let anyone tell you otherwise.

This so-called rule applies, of course, whether the difference between offer and acceptance is dramatic or trivial. If Party X offers apples, Party Y can't accept bananas. If Party X offers red apples, Party Y can't accept green ones. If Party X offers a quart of skim milk for $1.00, Party Y cannot accept a quart of whole milk for $0.99. Again, *one cannot accept an offer not made.*

Now consider this little conversation:

Party A: I'll wash your car for $30. I'll begin work on Tuesday morning at 9:00.
Party B: I accept, but please begin on Tuesday morning at 9:01.

Party B assented to an offer not made; 9:00 is not 9:01. Consequently, he failed to accept, and the parties formed no contract.

When faced with a problem in which one party makes an offer and the second party purports to accept, but alters the offeror's terms, *say* this: "Because of the mirror-image rule the parties form no contract." But *understand* this: The mirror-image rule means only that a contract requires an offer and an acceptance — *of that offer.*

Now let's ask: When A makes an offer and B issues a non-mirror-image response, what then sits on the "table"? Return to A's and B's exchange over the Tuesday morning car wash. On the table sits (1) A's offer to B, *dead,* because B rejected it, and (2) B's counteroffer to A, which A is free to accept or not.

The rule is: *If an offeree purports to accept an offer but changes or adds to its terms, then he makes a counteroffer, which, of course, (ordinarily) rejects the initial offer and leaves the original offeror free to accept or not.* As one court reasoned, "The acceptance may not impose additional conditions on the offer, nor may it add limitations. 'An acceptance which is equivocal or upon condition or with a limitation is a counteroffer. . . .'" Ardente v. Horan, 366 A.2d 162,

165 (R.I. 1976) (quoting John Hancock Mut. Life Ins. Co. v. Dietlin, 199 A.2d 311, 313 (R.I. 1964)). Restatement (Second) §59 states it thus:

> A reply to an offer which purports to accept it but is conditional on the offer-or's assent to terms additional to or different from those offered is not an acceptance, but is a counteroffer.

QUESTIONS 1 & 2. Sidney says to Rena: "I'd like to use your recording studio this coming Tuesday from 9 A.M. to noon. Will you rent it to me, and if so, what will you charge?" Rena responds: "Yes, definitely, I accept. The charge is $100 per hour, but on that day the studio is available only from noon to 3 P.M."

QUESTION 1. Which of the following responses from Sidney would most likely create a contract?

A. "Fine, noon to 3 P.M. it is, but I can pay only $250."
B. "Fine, noon to 3 P.M. it is, but I can't afford $300."
C. "Fine, noon to 3 P.M. it is, but let's make it $95 per hour."
D. "Fine."

ANALYSIS.   An offeree's statement of assent constitutes acceptance only if it "mirrors" the offer. Sidney first issued a preliminary inquiry — an invitation to deal — expressing interest in renting Rena's studio on Tuesday morning. Rena responded with an offer to rent the studio on Tuesday afternoon for a specific period at a specific price.

Sidney's responses cited at **A, B,** and **C** show no assent *to Rena's offer*. In each, Sidney is unwilling to pay her proposed price. But at **D,** he assents to all of Rena's terms without alteration. **D** is right.

QUESTION 2. Assume that Sidney responds to Rena: "Well, that's a high price, and I'd feel better with a price of $95. But that's *my* problem — you've got a deal." Have the parties formed a contract?

A. Yes, because Sidney assented fully to the terms Rena proposed
B. Yes, because Sidney's proposed price of $95 differs only slightly from Rena's proposed price of $100
C. No, because Sidney did not manifest complete satisfaction with Rena's proposed price term
D. No, because as to time, Rena's offer did not conform to Sidney's original proposal

---

ANALYSIS. On learning of an offeror's proposed terms, an offeree might moan, gripe, groan, wail, or whine. But if he answers "yes" to *all* of them, he accepts. Here, Sidney expresses dismay over the $300 price but does, ultimately, accede to it and to all else that Rena proposes. The parties form a contract.

C and **D** are wrong because they tell us that the parties fail to form a contract. According to **C**, an offeree accepts only if he shows "complete satisfaction" with the offeror's terms. There is no such rule. Grumpy or glad, sour or sad, the offeree who assents, fully, to the offeror's terms accepts her offer. **D** suggests that the difference between Sidney's invitation to deal and Rena's offer somehow defeats the contract. We know better. Parties may exchange multiple invitations to deal, offers, and counteroffers, each differing from every other. If one party ultimately makes an offer that the other accepts, they hatch a contract.

B implies that an offeree may accept with a response that alters the offeror's terms, so long as the change is minor. There's no such rule. One who purportedly assents to an offer but varies its terms — ever so slightly — fails to accept. Again, one cannot accept an offer not made.

A correctly states the result and reason. Sidney's response, in the end, does express assent to all that Rena proposes. Notwithstanding his disgruntlement as to price, he responds, "But that's *my* problem — you've got a deal." The parties achieve offer and acceptance, and so form a contract. **A** is right.

C. A "Mere Inquiry" Doesn't Reject

We know now that the common law ordinarily sees a counteroffer as a rejection of the offer it answers. Yet, it sees no rejection in the offeree's simple inquiry about a possible change in terms.

The Photocopier, Case 4

    (1) **Party A:** I can repair the photocopier by Saturday morning for $320. Okay?
    (2) **Party B:** Can you do it by Friday?
    (3) **Party A:** No.
    (4) **Party B:** I accept your initial offer — Saturday it is.
    (5) **Party A:** I've changed my mind about the price; it will be $380.

With statement 1, A made an offer. With statement 2, B said neither yes nor no. Neither did he make a counteroffer to which the law would impute a rejection. Rather, *he asked a question about a possible change in terms.* When an offeree does that, the law places the words "maybe, but" at the front of his statement: "[Maybe, but] Can you do it by Friday?"

Can We State a Rule About That?

Of course we can: *A counteroffer ordinarily operates as a rejection of the offer to which it responds, but a counteroffer differs from a "mere inquiry" as to a change in terms, and such an inquiry is neither a counteroffer nor a rejection.*

Restatement (Second) §39 cmt. b puts it this way:

> [A] mere inquiry regarding the possibility of different terms, a request for a better offer, or a comment upon the terms of the offer, is ordinarily not a counteroffer[.] . . . [I]t does not terminate the offeree's power to accept[.]

Remember too (from section A above) that even a true counteroffer does not act as a rejection if the offeror or offeree expressly makes plain that such should not be so.

Combining the three precepts, we arrive at this more comprehensive rule: *(1) A counteroffer operates as a rejection, unless (a) when making his counteroffer the offeree states (or plainly implies) that he wishes further to consider the original offer, or (b) the offeror or offeree makes plain that the counteroffer will not/does not constitute a rejection, and (2) a mere inquiry as to a change in the offeror's proposal is neither a counteroffer nor a rejection.*[1]

QUESTION 3. On October 30, Tien brings a box full of silverware to Alex's store, "Shine, Sheen, and Show-It-Off."

(1) **Tien:** I'd like you to polish all of my silverware by November 1.
(2) **Alex:** I can do the job by November 5, for $75.
(3) **Tien:** What do you think about November 3?
(4) **Alex:** No, I can't do that either. In fact, I've just realized that I can't do it, even by November 5. How about November 7? Deal?

After Alex makes statement 4,

A. the parties have no contract, but Tien is empowered to accept Alex's offer to complete the job by November 5.
B. the parties have no contract, but Tien is empowered to accept Alex's offer to complete the job by November 7.
C. the parties have a contract requiring that Alex complete the job by November 5.
D. the parties have a contract requiring that Alex complete the job by November 7.

---

1. [A] valid "acceptance must be absolute and unqualified." . . . "A qualified acceptance constitutes a rejection terminating the offer; it is a new proposal or counter-offer which must be accepted by the former offeror now turned offeree before a binding contract results. . . ." "A mere inquiry regarding the possibility of different terms, a request for a better offer, or a comment upon the terms of the offer, is ordinarily not a counter-offer." Comdisco Inc. v. Xerox Corp., 930 F.2d 26 (9th Cir. 1991) (citations omitted).

ANALYSIS.   Characterize each communication as an invitation to deal, offer, counteroffer, rejection, revocation, inquiry, acceptance — or whatever. Then, for each statement 1-4, assess the legal consequence.

Tien talks first: "I'd like you to polish all of my silverware by November 1." Arguably, that's an invitation to deal, and arguably it's an offer. Tien says nothing about price, but no communication is wholly complete as to all details. Recall the matter of gap fillers (Chapter 4, section C). The law (a court) might impute to Tien's statement an implied willingness to pay a *reasonable* price, or the "going price." On the other hand, it might not. We don't know. Whether Tien's first statement be an offer or invitation to deal is a question you must answer with your best, most thoughtful, educated guess (known also as your legal opinion).

Yet, the answer doesn't matter. If Tien does make an offer, Alex doesn't accept it. Rather, with statement 2, Alex makes a counteroffer, complete with price. Hence, Alex rejects Tien's offer. With statement 3, Tien poses a mere inquiry; Alex's offer remains effective, leaving Tien with power to accept it for so long as it lives. But with statement 4, it dies; Alex revokes and, simultaneously, makes a new offer proposing to finish the work by November 7.

After all is said, there stands Alex's offer to complete the job by November 7 for $75. Tien has not accepted it, meaning the parties have formed no contract.

C and **D**, therefore, are wrong. **A** states that the parties have not formed a contract, but describes Tien's right to accept Alex's offer to complete the work by November 5. That offer died when Alex revoked it. **A** is wrong.

And **B**? It describes Alex's offer, open for Tien's acceptance, to finish the work by November 7. **B** is right.

D.   The Closer

QUESTION 4. Which altered conversation from Question 3 above would most likely mean that Tien and Alex form a contract?

A. (1) **Tien:** I'd like you to polish all of my silverware by November 1.
   (2) **Alex:** Why sure, let me check my calendar.

B. (1) **Tien:** I'd like you to polish all of my silverware by November 1.
   (2) **Alex:** Why sure, give me the silver.

C. (1) **Tien:** I'd like you to polish all of my silverware by November 1.
   (2) **Alex:** I can do the job by November 5, for $75.
   (3) **Tien:** I accept, but you must finish by November 3.

D. (1) **Tien:** I'd like you to polish all of my silverware by November 1.
   (2) **Alex:** I can do the job by November 5, for $75.

(3) **Tien:** What do you think about November 3?

(4) **Alex:** No, I'm afraid not. In fact, I've just realized that I can't do it, even by November 5. I can do it by November 7. Okay?

(5) **Tien:** No. I accept your initial offer — November 5.

ANALYSIS. A, C, and D report conversations that plainly terminate without offer and acceptance. B is questionable. As earlier discussed, Tien's proposal, missing a price term, might be an offer and might be only an invitation to deal. If it's an offer, then — in that case — Alex clearly accepts it with his response, "why sure, give me the silver." We can't confidently conclude that **B** creates a contract, for there remains an arguable question (an "issue") as to how we should characterize Tien's first statement. *Arguably*, it's an offer, meaning, *arguably*, the parties formed a contract. **B does not *clearly* create a contract, but assessed against A, C, or D, it most *likely* does so. B is right.**

 # Silver's Picks

1.　　**D**
2.　　**A**
3.　　**B**
4.　　**B**

8

When Acceptance, Revocation, and Rejection Take Effect

A. Acceptance Is Effective on Dispatch; Revocation and Rejection on Receipt

On Monday, A telephones B and makes her an offer. On Tuesday, B writes and mails a letter to A, expressing her assent. On Wednesday, not having yet received the letter, A telephones B and says, "I revoke." B protests: "I've already accepted — by letter mailed yesterday." A responds, "I haven't received it. Again, I revoke."

Let's ask: Did A effectively revoke, or did he speak too late? Let's answer: *Acceptance is effective when dispatched by the offeree, whereas revocation and rejection are not effective until received by the offeror or offeree, as the case may be.* Regarding acceptance, Restatement (Second) of Contracts §63(a) provides:

> [A]n acceptance ... [is effective] as soon as put out of the offeree's possession, without regard to whether it ever reaches the offeror.

That rule often goes by the nickname "mailbox rule."

Regarding revocation, Restatement (Second) §42 provides:

> An offeree's power of acceptance is terminated when the offeree receives from the offeror a manifestation of an intention not to enter into the proposed contract.

Regarding rejection, Restatement (Second) §40 tells us:

> Rejection or counteroffer [sent] by mail . . . does not terminate the power of acceptance until received by the offeror[.]

So:

Acceptance	*is effective when*	The offeree *dispatches* it
Rejection	*is effective when*	The offeror *receives* it
Revocation	*is effective when*	The offeree *receives* it

Let's ask: When is a rejection or revocation "received"? Let's answer: *One receives a written revocation or rejection when it reaches a destination at which she, in ordinary course, receives communications.* If, orally, with A's voice directly to B's ear, A issues a rejection or revocation to B, it is received immediately. When ordinary mail arrives in one's mailbox, she receives it. When an email arrives in one's "inbox," she receives it. When a message churns through one's fax machine, she receives it. And, by the same logic, when a message is left on one's voicemail, she receives it. Furthermore, one receives each such communication regardless of when or whether she ever reads or hears it. Restatement (Second) §68 provides:

> A written revocation [or] rejection . . . is received when the writing comes into the possession of the person addressed, or of some person authorized by him to receive it for him, or when it is deposited in some place which he has authorized as the place for this or similar communications to be deposited for him.

Back to Parties A and B

On Wednesday, B dropped her letter in a mailbox and accepted A's offer; the parties formed a contract.

Notwithstanding that on Wednesday A knew nothing of B's letter, he had no power to revoke; B had accepted A's offer. Concomitantly, when B mailed her letter and thus accepted the offer, she lost her power to reject. If, before her letter reached A, she had changed her mind, telephoned A, and announced her rejection, she would accomplish nothing. If one accepts an offer she cannot then reject it.

QUESTIONS 1 & 2. On May 1, Hal tells Gretta, "I'd like you to install my new Betaline video system. When might you do it, and what would you charge?" Gretta responds, "I can do the work on May 9 for $250."

Hal replies, "Let me think it over," to which Gretta says, "Fine." On May 2, Gretta writes, dates, and drops in the mail a letter addressed to Hal: "Sorry, I can't install your Betaline system." On May 3, Hal writes, dates, and drops in the mail a letter addressed to Gretta: "I accept your offer." On May 4, Hal receives Gretta's May 2 letter of revocation. On May 5, Gretta receives Hal's May 3 letter of acceptance.

QUESTION 1. On May 2, just after Gretta deposits in the mail a letter of revocation, her offer to Hal

A. remains effective because the letter has not yet reached Hal.
B. remains effective because Hal has had no reasonable opportunity to read the letter.
C. is no longer effective because the letter constitutes a revocation.
D. is no longer effective because she no longer intends to honor it.

ANALYSIS. On May 1, Hal makes an invitation to deal, and on that same day Gretta makes an offer. Then, on May 2, Gretta attempts to announce a revocation; it operates when *received* by Hal. On May 2, therefore, Gretta's offer remains effective, which eliminates **C** and **D**. According to **C**, Gretta's offer terminates because her letter revokes it. That's wrong; the letter is ineffective until Hal receives it. **D** states that the offer terminates because Gretta no longer *intends* to honor it. That's contrary to law. An offeror's *intent* to terminate her offer means nothing. Revocation requires a *communication*, received by the offeree.

A and **B** correctly conclude that the offer remains effective, but as to reasoning, one is right and the other wrong. According to **B**, the offer lives on because Hal has had no reasonable opportunity to read Gretta's letter. That's not the law. Revocation is effective as soon as the offeree *receives* it, whether or not he has had the opportunity to give it attention, and whether or not he ever does so. **B** is wrong. **A** tells us that the offer survives because, as of May 2, Gretta's letter has not reached Hal, meaning he has not *received* it. That's the law. **A** is right.

QUESTION 2. These parties form a contract

A. on May 3.
B. on May 4.
C. on May 5.
D. not at all.

ANALYSIS. On May 3, Hal dispatches his acceptance wherefore, on that day, the parties form a contract. That's so, even though Hal receives Gretta's revocation before Gretta receives Hal's acceptance. Acceptance is effective on *dispatch* — in this case, on May 3. Revocation is effective on *receipt* — in this case, on May 4. Hal's acceptance precedes Gretta's revocation, and the parties form a contract. Again, that's so even though Hal knew of Gretta's attempted revocation before Gretta knew of Hal's acceptance.

Now, it's simple. Since these parties did create a contract, **D** is wrong. Because they did so not on May 4 or 5, but on May 3, **B** and **C** are wrong. That means **A** is right.

B. Exception: Acceptance That Follows Rejection Is *Not* Effective on Dispatch

Suppose (1) on Monday, A makes an offer to B, (2) on Tuesday, B dispatches to A this first message: "I reject your offer," (3) on Wednesday, B dispatches to A this second message: "I've changed my mind. I accept." When an offeree sends out those two messages in *that* order, the acceptance is *not* effective on dispatch. Rather, the message that first reaches the offeror dictates the outcome. If A receives the acceptance on Thursday and the rejection on Friday, the acceptance governs, the parties form a contract, and the purported rejection is a nullity. If, however, A receives the rejection on Thursday and the acceptance on Friday, the rejection governs. The offer terminates, and the parties form no contract. When, on Friday, the acceptance arrives, it acts as a new offer from B to A.

Think of It This Way

In a race between the offeree's acceptance and the offeror's revocation, the offeree's acceptance is effective when he dispatches it. The offeror's revocation is not effective until the offeree receives it. The law governs the outcome according to which of the two events is first to occur — offeree's dispatch of acceptance or offeree's receipt of offeror's revocation.

But in a race between the offeree's rejection and then, upon a change of mind, his acceptance, dispatch is irrelevant. If the rejection is first to reach the offeror, then the offer is rejected. When the message of acceptance then reaches the offeror, it acts as a new offer from the offeree to the offeror. On the other hand, if the acceptance is first to reach the offeror, then the acceptance is effective. When the rejection then reaches the offeror, it's legally insignificant.

Restatement (Second) §40 (with characteristic clumsiness) states it thus:

> [A written] . . . acceptance started after the sending of an otherwise effective rejection . . . is only a counter-offer unless the acceptance is received by the offeror before he receives the rejection or counteroffer.

These Restatement folk — this coterie of dreadful draftsmen — mean to tell us that *if*, in response to an offer, the offeree first dispatches, as message 1, a rejection and subsequently dispatches as message 2, an acceptance, *then* (1) the parties form a contract if the offeror first receives the acceptance, but (2) the offer dies if he first receives the rejection. The would-be acceptance becomes a new offer from (original) offeree to (original) offeror.

Acceptance	*is effective when*	The offeree *dispatches* it
Rejection	*is effective when*	The offeror *receives* it
Revocation	*is effective when*	The offeree *receives* it

BUT, If
(1) Offeree dispatches rejection;
(2) Offeree changes her mind and dispatches acceptance;
THEN

The first to reach the offeror governs the outcome.

QUESTION 3. Eve builds furniture. Ray wants her to make him a desk, the work to be done in Ray's home, with wood that he supplies. Throughout September, the parties discuss the desk in great detail and Ray tells Eve that he wants to have it by November 1. On September 30, the parties fully, finally, and precisely identify the dimensions, design, and specifications suitable to Ray's needs, but neither has yet made an offer to the other. On October 1, Eve mails to Ray this six-word message: "I will build it for $1,000." On October 5, the message reaches Ray's mailbox and Ray reads it. On October 6, Ray mails a three-word response: "That's too much." On October 7, Ray writes again and mails to Eve this four-word message: "On reconsideration, I accept." Eve receives the October 6 mailing on October 9, and the October 7 mailing on October 10. She telephones Ray and says, "I have changed my mind. I won't build the desk." Have Eve and Ray formed a contract?

A. No; Eve's October 1 mailing does not mention price, and so lacks the specificity necessary to an offer.
B. No; although each made an offer, neither made an effective acceptance.
C. Yes; their September discussions implicitly add all necessary specificity to their October communications.
D. Yes; all of their communications, taken together, manifest mutual assent to a bargain.

ANALYSIS. Acceptance, 'tis said, is effective on dispatch. In truth, that is so when the offeree's attempt to accept "races against" the offeror's attempt to revoke (as in Questions 1 and 2 above). But it's not so when an offeree's rejection races with his own subsequent attempt to accept. In that case, the law honors the message that first reaches the offeror.

After receiving Eve's offer, Ray dispatched a rejection and then, on changing his mind, an acceptance. Eve first received the rejection; the offer died. On Friday, Eve received the (would-be) acceptance, which now served only as a new offer from Ray to Eve. By telephone, Eve rejected it, and the parties formed no contract.

Examine choices **A** and **C**. As **C** implies, it's true that the October communications are, on their face, devoid of specificity. Standing on their own, they are a bunch of invitations to deal. It's true too, as **C** suggests, that the parties should certainly have understood their October communications to incorporate the details they identified on September 30, which identified a price of $1,000. Consequently, Eve's October 1 message proposed a price of $1,000 and did constitute an offer. **A** is wrong. But the offer never spawned a contract because Ray rejected it on October 6. **C** is wrong too.

D states that the October communications, all together, manifest "mutual assent" to a bargain. They don't. They embody an offer from each party and a rejection from the other:

And **B**? It correctly states that the parties form no contract because their communications embody (1) Eve's offer, rejected by Ray and (2) Ray's offer, rejected by Eve. Each party made an offer, but neither accepted. **B** is right.

C.   Revocation by Indirect Message

Effective revocation requires no *direct* communication from offeror to offeree. If an offeree learns not from the offeror but from some other source that the offeror will not honor her offer, then the offer is effectively revoked.

Colin and Dorothy

On November 1, Dorothy learns that she'll need a chauffeur on the evening of November 17. On November 2, she contacts Colin, who offers to provide the service for $300, stating that for five days his offer will stand firm and irrevocable. By law therefore, Colin's offer will expire on November 7 unless, before that day, Colin revokes or Dorothy rejects. (Remember that until an offeree accepts, an offeror may freely revoke his offer even if he promises that he won't; Chapter 6, section A.)

While Dorothy ponders the offer, she meets Arnesto, a trustworthy friend. Arnesto tells her, accurately, that he and Colin have formed a contract under which Colin will serve as Arnesto's chauffeur for all of November 17, day and night. Dorothy then knows (or, more precisely, *should know*) that Colin is no longer available to serve as her chauffeur on that day. Colin's offer is thus revoked, even though Colin himself did not communicate that fact to Dorothy.

Restatement (Second) §43 provides:

> An offeree's power of acceptance is terminated when the offeror takes definite action inconsistent with an intention to enter into the proposed contract and the offeree acquires reliable information to that effect.

After Colin made his offer to Dorothy, he took the "definite action" of forming a contract with Arnesto. That action is inconsistent with a plan to enter a contract with Dorothy. Then, from Arnesto, Dorothy acquired reliable information of what Colin had done.

QUESTIONS 4 & 5. On July 1, by telephone, Dick offers to sell Domina 100,000 paper clips for $200, the clips to be delivered to Domina's address on August 1. Dick says, "My offer expires on July 10."

QUESTION 4. Suppose that on July 2 Domina learns from a reliable source that Dick has sold all his paper clips to another party. On July 2, with regard to Dick's offer, Domina

A. loses her power to accept because Dick no longer has possession of the paper clips.
B. loses her power to accept because she has cause to know that Dick is no longer willing to sell her the paper clips.
C. retains her power to accept because Dick has not himself communicated to her his intention to withdraw his offer.
D. retains her power to accept because Dick's offer does not expire until July 10.

QUESTION 5. For this question assume that the event of July 2 (described in Question 4) does not occur. Instead, on

July 3: There sits in Domina's email inbox a message from Dick advising her that he withdraws his offer.
July 5: In the U.S. mail, Domina deposits a signed letter addressed to Dick: "I accept."
July 6: Domina reads Dick's July 3 email.
July 8: Dick receives Domina's July 5 mailing.

Have Dick and Domina formed a contract?

A. Yes, as of July 5
B. Yes, as of July 8
C. No, because by July 5 Domina had lost her power to accept
D. No, because on July 6 Domina lost her power to accept

ANALYSIS.   On July 1, Dick made an offer that, he proclaimed, would expire on July 10. By law, Dick's statement meant only that his offer would expire on July 10, unless rejected or revoked before that date. Dick remained free to revoke at *any* time before Domina accepted (Chapter 6, section A). His promise to hold it irrevocable meant nothing. An offer is revoked when the offeror so informs the offeree or, when from some other reliable source, the offeree learns (or should understand) that the offeror intends not to honor his offer.

As for Question 4.   On July 2, Domina acquired reliable information that Dick had sold his paper clips to another buyer. She should then have understood that he no longer intended to sell them to her. Dick's offer underwent revocation, and Domina lost her power to accept.

Both choices **C** and **D** state that Dorothy retained her power of acceptance, which she did not. As for a reason, **C** tells us that Dick did not personally advise Domina that he had withdrawn his offer. The reasoning is wrong; we now know that an offer may be revoked without any communication from offeror to offeree, so long as the offeree somewhere acquires reliable information that the offeror will not honor his offer. **C** is wrong. **D** cites as a reason that Dick's offer, by its terms, would not expire until July 10. Wrong reasoning again. *Unless and until it is accepted, an offer is revocable even if the offeror states otherwise.* Dick's offer was revocable for so long as Domina did not accept it.

Both **A** and **B** correctly tell us that Domina lost her power to accept. As its reason, **A** states that "Dick is no longer in possession" of the paper clips. That Dick *parted* with possession of the paper clips did not by itself revoke his offer. Rather, the offer underwent revocation when and because Domina learned that Dick did not intend to stand by it. Choice **B** correctly explains that the offer was revoked because Domina should have known that Dick was no longer willing to sell her the paper clips; he had sold them to another. Hence, **A** is wrong and **B** is right. (If these two had formed a *contract* for the sale of the paper clips and Dick then sold them to another, Dick would be in breach.)

As for Question 5.   Dick made an offer on July 1. On July 3, he dispatched a revocation, not by U.S. mail, but by *email*, meaning that Domina received it almost immediately— when it reached her inbox. Hence, on July 3, Dick's offer died. Domina's (purported) acceptance, mailed on July 5, did not create an acceptance. For on that day Domina had no offer on her "table." (Her attempt to accept acted as a new offer from her to Dick.)

A and **B** tell us that the parties did form a contract. They're wrong. Both **C** and **D** correctly state that the parties failed to form a contract because Domina lost her power to accept. According to **D**, Domina lost it on July 6 — the date on which she read Dick's message. That's wrong too. Dick's revocation took effect on July 3, when Donna received it. According to **C**, Domina "had" lost her power to accept "by" July 5. That's why the parties formed no contract, and that's why **C** is right.

D. The Closers

QUESTIONS 6 & 7. On October 1, Bella spoke with Sally:

> **October 1, Bella:** I have a large document that I want you to photocopy. It's 50,000 pages, and I need 10 copies. Can you do it?
> **Sally:** Oh, I think so, certainly. Let me get back to you with a price and timetable.
> **October 4, Sally (by fax):** Regarding the job: I can complete it by October 10 for $15,000.

Later on that same day at 1:00 P.M., Bella composed this signed writing: "Thanks. I'll bring you the document tomorrow morning, October 5." Bella attempted to transmit that writing by fax, but she saw that her fax machine did not function.

QUESTION 6. Assume that Bella then took the document to a hand courier. At 1:20 P.M. she paid the courier his $15 fee, and he promised to deliver the document by 3:00 P.M.. Bella returned to her own office. At 2:00 P.M. the courier set out for Sally's office. At 2:30 P.M. before he arrived, Sally telephoned Bella:

> **Sally:** I can't do the copy job.
> **Bella:** I've already accepted your offer with a message that you'll receive by hand delivery.
> **Sally:** I don't yet have it and, as I said, I withdraw the offer.

Bella sues Sally alleging breach of contract. Sally responds by asserting that the parties never formed a contract because she effectively revoked her offer. Among the following, which represents a judicial decision most consistent with law?

A. When Sally sent Bella her fax of October 4, she accepted Bella's offer. Consequently, the parties formed a contract.
B. When Bella left her document with the courier, she accepted Sally's offer. Consequently, the parties formed a contract.
C. When Sally announced her revocation, she had no notice of Bella's writing. Consequently, the parties did not form a contract.
D. Bella took no action in reliance on the agreement, and Sally's withdrawal caused her no harm. Consequently, the parties did not form a contract.

ANALYSIS.   Begin here: (1) When an offeree accepts an offer, the parties form a contract and the offeror can no longer revoke; (2) acceptance is effective on dispatch or — as the Restatement tells us — when "put out of the offeree's possession."

On October 1, the parties exchanged invitations to deal. At noon on October 4, Sally made an offer, and at 1:20 P.M., Bella left with a courier her message of acceptance, thus — *putting it out of her possession*. Bella thus accepted the offer; at 1:20 P.M., the parties formed a contract.

A states that Sally accepted Bella's "offer" by faxing her on October 4. That's wrong because Bella never made an offer. On October 1, Bella made only an invitation to deal. It was *Sally* who, on October 4, made an offer to Bella.

C reports that Sally had no notice of Bella's acceptance, an irrelevant fact (in this case). Whether known to Sally or not, Bella's letter worked an acceptance *when dispatched*.

D raises another irrelevancy: that Sally attempted to revoke her offer when Bella had not relied on the "agreement." If two parties undergo offer and acceptance, *they form a contract* whether either relies on it or not.

When Bella deposited her letter with the courier, she put it out of her possession and thus accepted Sally's offer. The parties formed a contract, and Sally lost her power to revoke. **B** is right.

QUESTION 7. Assume now that when Bella discovered she could not fax her message, she took it at 1:20 P.M. to Binko's Fax Service. There she found a long line of customers waiting to use Binko's only working fax machine. Rather than join the line, Bella left her document with Rob, a Binko employee. She paid Rob Binko's $2 fax fee and supplied him with Sally's fax number. Bob promised to dispatch the document as soon as the machine should become available. Bella returned to her office, and at 2:00 P.M. telephoned Binko's. Rob answered and Bella asked, "Have you faxed the document?" "No, not yet," Bob answered. "Do you still want me to do so?" "Yes, definitely," said Bella, to which Rob replied, "We'll send it by 2:30 P.M." At 2:15 P.M., Sally telephoned Bella:

> **Sally:** I can't do your copy job.
> **Bella:** I've already accepted your offer with a signed writing that I left with Binko's. You'll have it by fax within fifteen minutes.
> **Sally:** Well, I don't have it now and, again, I withdraw my offer.

Bella sues Sally alleging breach of contract. Sally responds by asserting that the parties never formed a contract because she effectively revoked her offer. Among the following, which represents a judicial decision that is arguably correct? (Note: Two decisions might, of course, reach opposite results although each is *arguably* correct.)

I. Bella accepted Sally's offer when she paid Binko's fee and left her writing to be faxed. Consequently, by 2:15 P.M. she had accepted Sally's offer. Sally's revocation was ineffective.

II. For so long as Binko's had not yet sent Bella's message by fax, Bella retained the right to countermand her instruction and to have the document returned to her. Consequently, at 2:15 P.M., she had *not put it out of her possession, meaning that she had not* accepted Sally's offer, and that Sally effectively revoked it.

A. I only
B. II only
C. Both I and II
D. Neither I nor II

ANALYSIS. The issue is whether, by 2:15 P.M. on October 4, Bella had accepted Sally's offer. The relevant *rule* is clear, but the result is not. Acceptance is effective when "put out of the offeree's possession." As to the meaning of that phrase, this case raises an issue: When Bella left her letter with Binko's, did she put it "out of her possession"? Bella's lawyer might argue: "My client did certainly part with physical possession of her letter. She moved it from her own hands into Binko's. Moreover, she left Binko's premises and returned to her office. At 2:15 P.M., Binko's had the letter. Bella did not. It was out of her possession, and her acceptance was complete."

Sally's lawyer might argue: "For so long as Binko's had not sent the message to Sally, Bella had the right to abort its dispatch. She had the right to telephone Rob and direct him not to send it. The writing thus remained in Bella's control and hence in her 'possession.' For that reason, Bella had not, by 2:15 P.M., accepted Sally's offer. Sally's revocation was effective."

Both positions are credible; neither is "right" or "wrong" until a judge chooses between them. Knowing not which argument a judge will endorse and knowing that both have merit, we say **C** is right.

 # Silver's Picks

1.	**A**
2.	**A**
3.	**B**
4.	**B**
5.	**C**
6.	**B**
7.	**C**

9

Mode or Manner of Acceptance; Unilateral and Bilateral Contracts

A. Master or Mistress of the Offer

As taught in Chapter 2, section D, acceptance is the offeree's unconditional assent to the offeror's proposed bargain. One might communicate assent in a variety of ways, including mail, fax, smoke signal, drumbeat, talk, wink, or nod. All of that raises this question: Does the law place limits on the mode or manner in which the offeree may effectively express her assent?

The answer is "yes." Traditional common law provides that in making his offer, the offeror may impose on the offeree any requirements he chooses as to mode or manner of acceptance. If the offeror requires that the offeree accept by writing, sent in ordinary postal mail, then no other expression of assent will suffice. If the offeror requires a certified letter, then a certified letter it must be. If the offeror requires acceptance by telephone, email, fax, stamp of foot, nod of head, wink of eye, blast of horn, or bark of dog — the offeree who shows assent in any other way fails to accept.

That common law rule — that the offeror is empowered to decree the mode or manner by which the offeree may accept — often goes by this unfortunate shorthand: "The offeror is master of his offer." (Or, as modernized (by *us*), "The offeror is master or mistress of the offer.") That ill-born (stupid) expression means that the offeror is entitled to require that the offeree accept in "this" or "that" way, and that the offeree's attempt to accept in any other way is ineffective.

Viewed in full, Restatement (Second) of Contracts §50(1) states that rule in its last nine words:

> Acceptance of an offer is a manifestation of assent to the terms thereof made by the offeree *in a manner invited or required by the offer.*

Further, Restatement (Second) §60 provides:

> If an offer prescribes the place, time or manner of acceptance, its terms in this respect must be complied with in order to create a contract.

That provision, too, reflects the common law rule that the "offeror is master or mistress of the offer."

B.   When the Offeror Does Not Designate a Mode of Acceptance

Most offerors do not exercise their power as "master" or "mistress." Most are silent as to how the offeree should accept. Suppose that in a signed writing, sent by ordinary mail, Andrew offers to redesign Zelda's patio deck for $10,000, the work to be finished by September 10. Andrew writes not a word about how Zelda should accept, and that raises this question: If Zelda wants to accept, how does she do so?

Modern common law provides: *When the offeror imposes no requirements as to the mode or manner in which the offeree must accept, then the offeree may do so in any way that is reasonable under the prevailing circumstances.* Restatement (Second) §30(2) states:

> Unless otherwise indicated by the language or the circumstances, an offer invites acceptance in any manner and by any medium reasonable in the circumstances.

Under any given circumstance a whole variety of methods might constitute reasonable modes of acceptance. But the law presumes that it is always reasonable for an offeree to accept in the same mode or manner as that in which the offeror made his offer. Restatement (Second) §60 states it this way:

> Unless circumstances known to the offeree indicate otherwise, a medium of acceptance is reasonable if it is the one used by the offeror[.]

If the offeree attempts to accept in some communicative manner different from the one used by the offeror, there arises the question of whether the same was "reasonable." And, as to who decides what's "reasonable," please revisit Chapter 3, section D.

Andrew made his offer by signed writing and expressed no requirement as to how Zelda might accept. That means Zelda may accept in any manner reasonable under the circumstances. Probably, therefore, she may accept by telephone call, email, fax message, or face-to-face statement. Certainly and absolutely, she may accept by signed letter sent via ordinary mail, for that is the very means by which Andrew made his offer.

QUESTION 1. By signed writing sent and delivered by certified U.S. mail, TonCo offers to purchase from DumpCo 500 refuse collection trucks, each one for $290,000. In its last sentence, TonCo writes, "Please let us know if you wish to accept." DumpCo wants to accept and asks its attorney by what mode or manner it should do so. Wanting to give TonCo the best possible advice, the attorney should suggest that acceptance be made with a

A. hand-delivered message to TonCo's receptionist.
B. signed writing sent by fax.
C. signed writing sent by certified U.S. mail.
D. telephone voicemail message, followed by a signed writing sent via fax.

ANALYSIS. If an offeror expressly prescribes the manner in which the offeree may accept, the offeree may accept only that way. If, as is usual, the offeror makes no such prescription, the offeree may accept in any manner "reasonable" under the circumstances.

Every choice **A** through **D** likely describes a reasonable mode of acceptance. Yet, we're asked to name the one that's best. If an offeror states nothing as to how his offeree should accept, then it's reasonable, *always*, that the offeree do so in the manner by which the offeror made the offer. **C** names the mode of communication that the offeror used in making its offer. Hence, among the options, **C** is best, so **C** is right.

C. Bilateral and Unilateral Contracts: What They Are and How They Differ

Suppose Anthony offers to pay Barbara $500 to install software. Barbara accepts, and the parties form a contract. At the moment they do so, each party has an unfulfilled duty to the other. Anthony has yet to pay the $500. Barbara has yet to install the software. In legalese, an unfulfilled contractual obligation is an "executory duty." Both these parties, therefore, have executory duties. Stated another way, "the contract is executory on both sides."

When Barbara installs the software, the contract ceases to be executory on her side. It's executory on Andrew's side only. When Andrew pays Barbara, the contract is no longer executory at all. Both parties have fulfilled their duties.[1]

Think back now to the moment at which these two formed their contract — the moment at which Barbara accepted Andrew's offer. The contract was, then, executory on both sides. That means it was a "bilateral contract": *A bilateral contract is a contract that, at the moment of formation, is executory on both sides.* When Barbara installs the software, the parties have a "bilateral contract executory on Andrew's side only." We name the contract, still, "bilateral" because at the *moment of formation* it *was* executory on both sides.

Aren't *All* Contracts Executory on Both Sides at the Moment They're Formed?

Surprisingly, no. Suppose Maria says to Charles, "I'll pay you $50 to remove all snow from my driveway. You may accept only by *doing the job* — all of it — by removing all snow from my driveway. Do that and you will accept my offer. Fail to do that and you won't." Charles, of course, is free to begin the work or not. Even if he does begin, he's free to finish or walk away. If he finishes, then and only then — at that very moment — does he accept Maria's offer. Only *then* — at *that* moment — do the parties form a contract.

Suppose Charles begins shoveling at 4:00 and removes the driveway's last little snow crystal two hours later, at 6:00. At that moment, he accepts Maria's offer and the parties form a contract. Curiously, *that contract requires nothing of Charles.*

Why Not? *How* Not?

In allowing Charles to accept her offer only by *doing* all that she asks of him, Maria leaves Charles free to begin or not the shoveling of snow. Even if he

---

1. It is, perhaps, oxymoronic to speak of a "contract no longer executory on anyone's part." For if both contracting parties fulfill all of their duties, the contract, in a sense, ceases to exist. As to that lego-philosophical question, we can offer only this: If and only if a "dead person" is a person, then a "contract executory on nobody's part" is a contract. If a dead person is not a person, then a contract executory on nobody's part is not a contract. Take your pick.

does begin, he's free to finish or walk away because, Maria, the "mistress of her offer" allowed Charles to accept only by removing all snow from her driveway. The way that Maria has set it up, the parties form a contract only if and when Charles completes work, not a moment before. At 6:00, Charles does complete the work and there occur, simultaneously, these two events: (1) the parties form a contract, and (2) Charles completes his part of it. Consequently and curiously, the contract, from the instant it's born, leaves Charles without any duty at all. And *that* means the parties form a "unilateral contract": *Two parties form a unilateral contract when an offeror allows an offeree to accept only by full performance, and the offeree does then provide full performance; from the moment of formation the contract is executory only on the offeror's part.*

QUESTION 2. By fax, MoveCo makes SpaceCo this offer: "We'll handle all of your shipping needs for one full year if you'll allow us to store in your warehouse all of our excess inventory. Agreed?" By fax, SpaceCo responds, "Agreed." The parties have formed a

A. unilateral contract, because the decision to accept the offer was left unilaterally in SpaceCo's hands.

B. unilateral contract, because MoveCo did not limit the means by which SpaceCo might accept.

C. bilateral contract, because when SpaceCo sent its fax, each party acquired a duty to the other.

D. bilateral contract, because when MoveCo received SpaceCo's fax, each party acquired a duty to the other.

ANALYSIS. To determine that two parties create a bilateral or unilateral contract, identify the moment of formation — the moment of acceptance — and ask yourself: "*At* that moment, is the contract (a) executory on both sides, or (b) executory on the offeror's side only?" If the answer is (a), the parties form a bilateral contract. If it's (b), they form a unilateral contract.

Because acceptance is (generally) effective on dispatch, this contract arose when MoveCo *sent* SpaceCo its fax, "Agreed." At that moment, neither party had completed (or even begun) performance. MoveCo owed service to SpaceCo, and SpaceCo owed service to MoveCo. From its formation, the contract was executory on both sides, wherefore the parties formed a bilateral contract.

A and **B** are wrong because they tell us the parties have formed a unilateral contract. **A** gives this reason: The decision to accept the offer was left "unilaterally" to SpaceCo. *Every* offer leaves the offeree with the power to accept or not. For so long as an offer lives, the offeree is free to accept it or not, a fact that's irrelevant to the difference between bilateral and unilateral contracts. The question writer hopes that in some befuddled way you'll fix on the word "unilaterally" and select this very wrong answer. Don't do it. Bear in mind the *meaning* for which you're searching: that the contract is bilateral because, at the instant of formation, it leaves each party with a duty owed to the other.

B correctly indicates that MoveCo placed no limit on how SpaceCo might accept its offer. That fact suggests the creation of a *bi*lateral contract. After all, if an offeree is free to accept by any reasonable mode, he need not accept by full performance, and acceptance by full performance is the *sine qua non* of the unilateral contract.

What about **C** and **D**? **D** correctly states that the parties formed a bilateral contract, but its reason is wrong. Acceptance is effective on dispatch. The contract arose not when MoveCo *received* SpaceCo's fax, but when SpaceCo *sent* it as stated in **C**. That distinction represents the only difference between choices **D** and **C**. Because of that difference, **D** is wrong and **C** is right.

QUESTION 3. Isaac makes an offer to Joan: "If you'll type my manuscript, I'll pay you $6,000." Joan responds: "If I want to accept, how shall I do so?" To that, Isaac says: "You may accept by doing the work — all of it; that's the only way." Thereafter, Joan does type Isaac's manuscript, fully and properly. The parties thus form a

A. unilateral contract, since on making her acceptance Joan is free of further obligation.

B. unilateral contract, since only Joan is called on to deliver an actual service.

C. unilateral contract, since only Isaac is required to make a payment of money.

D. bilateral contract, since the two parties are mutually bound only upon Joan's completion of performance.

ANALYSIS.   Identify the point at which the parties form their contract and ask: "At that moment, (a) does each party owe a duty to the other, or (b) does only the offeror owe a duty to the offeree?" If the answer is (a), the parties create a bilateral contract. If it's (b), they create a unilateral contract.

Isaac allows Joan to accept only by fully performing the work he wants of her. When Joan does that, the parties form their contract. At that moment, offeror Isaac owes Joan her payment, but offeree Joan owes Isaac nothing. From its inception, the contract is executory on the offeror's side only; it's a unilateral contract. The right answer will reach that conclusion for that reason.

D tells us that the parties formed a bilateral contract, so it's wrong. Further, **D** gives as its reason that the parties are mutually bound (which means "form a contract") only when Jane completes her performance. That's the very reason that these parties form a *unilateral* contract. **B** reaches the right conclusion for the wrong reason. The parties form a unilateral contract, it states, because only one party is required to deliver "service."

It's true that only Joan delivers service (and that Isaac must pay money). That, however, is wholly irrelevant to the question. Suppose Party A says to Party B, "I'll cut your hair for $25. You may accept my offer only by paying me the $25 — all of it." If and only if B pays A $25, the parties form a contract and, at that moment, B has fully performed so that the contract is executory only on A's side. Whether the offeror is to pay money, deliver a good, or perform service is irrelevant to the difference between a unilateral and bilateral contract.

C makes the reciprocal error, suggesting that a contract is a unilateral one if only one party is required to pay money. That, too, is false. **A** — happy day — is right. The contract is a unilateral one for this reason: When offeree Jane made her acceptance, and thus formed the contract, she owed to Isaac, the offeror, no duty. Her acceptance *was* her performance. **A** is right.

D. Unilateral and Bilateral Contracts: Vocabulary and — A Warning

Know the meaning of "offer for a unilateral contract." It refers to an offer that, if accepted, creates a unilateral contract. Hence: *An offer for a unilateral contract is an offer in which the offeror allows the offeree to accept only by delivering all (not part) of the performance asked of her.* If the offeree does complete that performance, then in the same instant there occur three events: (1) the offeree fulfills her part in the exchange, (2) the contract arises, and (3) an executory duty is created on the offeror's side, and only on the offeror's side.

If an offeror allows his offeree to accept by doing anything *other* than fully performing her side of the bargain, he makes an "offer for a bilateral contract." If he allows the offeror to accept by word, writing, smoke signal, or email, he makes an offer for a bilateral contract, because the resulting contract subjects each party to a duty owed to the other — an executory duty — a duty yet unfulfilled. If the offeror permits the offeree to accept by completing *half* her performance, he makes an offer for a bilateral contract. Hence, if and when the offeree completes half her performance, the contract arises. It leaves the offeree with an obligation, still, to furnish the second half, and it leaves the offeror with the duty, still, to furnish all of his performance. From the moment it arises, it is executory on both sides.

Watch Out for These Misleading Phrases: "Promise in Exchange for an Act" and "Promise in Exchange for a Promise"

Many authorities (and teachers, who certainly should know better) carelessly describe an offer for a unilateral contract as one in which the offeror proposes to give his "promise in exchange for an act." These same folks describe an offer for a bilateral contract as one in which the offeror proposes to give his "promise in exchange for a promise." Those statements are misleading and misconceived, so we'll correct them.

Suppose Beth says to David, "I'll pay you $200 to install my stereo components and my computer system. You may accept only by fully installing both the stereo and computer systems." In response, David installs both systems. Beth required that David accept by completing *all* that her offer asked — by installing both the computer and stereo systems. When he completes both jobs, David accepts the offer, and the parties form a contract. At the moment of formation, the contract is executory only on Beth's part; she is obliged to pay. David owes Beth nothing because, at the moment he accepts and forms the contract, he completes all that is required of him. The parties form a unilateral contract — a contract that from the moment of formation is executory only on the offeror's/Beth's side.

Suppose, instead, that Beth says to David, "I'll pay you $200 to install my stereo components and my computer system. You may accept by fully installing *just* the stereo components." Beth requires that David accept her offer by performing *an* act, but not by performing, fully, his part of the proposed exchange. Suppose David installs the stereo equipment. By doing so, he accepts the offer and the parties form their contract. At that moment, each party owes a duty to the other. David must, still, install the computer system, and Beth must, still, pay him (after he does, in fact, install the computer system). The parties form a bilateral contract, *even though the offer required the offeree to accept by performing an act.*

QUESTION 4. Frank is a puppeteer. Evelyn telephones him and the parties speak:
(1) **Evelyn:** My little boy is turning two. Will you present a puppet show at the party I'm holding that day?
(2) **Frank:** What day?
(3) **Evelyn:** Saturday, September 28, my home: 459 Urbana Way, Munsey.
(4) **Frank:** Yes, I'm available at any time that day. My show is twenty minutes long and my fee is $350. If you wish to contract with me you must, please, send a check for one-half that amount. The remainder will be due after I conclude the show on September 28.

(5) **Evelyn:** I accept right now; it's a deal.

Frank and Evelyn have formed

A. a unilateral contract, because there remains only on Frank's part the duty to deliver a performance; Evelyn is obliged only to pay money.
B. a bilateral contract, because Frank's proposal calls on each party to provide some performance to the other.
C. no contract, because the offeree has not accepted the offer.
D. no contract, because neither party has made an offer to the other.

ANALYSIS. With statements 1 through 3, the parties conduct a negotiation. All three statements are invitations to deal. None is an offer.

With statement 4, Frank makes an offer. In light of all circumstances (including, notably, statements 1 through 3), Evelyn should understand that Frank, having made a reasonably definite proposal, awaits her assent. He proposes to deliver a puppet show in a specified place, for a specified fee, on a specified day, at any hour Evelyn might name.

Separately (and unlike most offerors), Frank exercised his privilege as master of the offer. He allowed Evelyn to accept only by sending him a check for a specified amount. With statement 5, Evelyn purported to accept, but not in the manner that Frank prescribed. Consequently, she failed to accept, and these parties formed no contract.

A and **B** tell us that the parties formed a contract, and both are wrong for that reason alone. Further, **A** states that the parties formed a unilateral contract because Frank had a duty to deliver a performance and Evelyn had only a duty to pay money. The truth is that neither party had any duty whatever because Evelyn failed to accept Frank's offer. **A** is misconceived for yet another reason. Suppose Frank had not prescribed any mode of acceptance. Evelyn's statement that she accepts "right now" would create a contract. It would leave Frank with the duty to deliver a puppet show and Evelyn with an obligation to pay. The contract, from its inception, would be executory on both sides — a *bi*lateral contract.

B incorrectly implies that an offer calls for a bilateral contract if it proposes that two parties exchange performances. That's an essential feature of *every* offer whether it contemplates a bilateral or unilateral contract. By definition, an offer proposes a *bargain*. Hence, *all* true offers call for an exchange — a *quid pro quo* — an "I'll do this if you'll do that." (Chapter 2, sections A, B, and C.) **B** is wrong.

D correctly concludes that these two have formed no contract, but it falsely states that neither made an offer. Frank did make an offer, so **D** is wrong. With statement 5, Evelyn attempted to accept, but failed to do so because she did not send Frank a check, as Frank had required. Choice **C** tells us that the parties formed no contract and correctly states the reason: The offeree (Evelyn) did not accept Frank's offer. **C** is right.

And do know this: Frank's offer was "an offer for a bilateral contract." It required that Evelyn accept by performing an act, but not by performing *all* that the offer asked of her. She was to accept by sending Frank a check for one-half his fee. If she had done that a contract would arise, and each party would, still, owe a duty to the other: Frank would be obliged to deliver the show and Evelyn would be obliged, thereafter, to pay Frank the rest of his fee.

E.   Offers for Unilateral vs. Bilateral Contracts: Why We Care

The difference between an offer for a unilateral and bilateral contract relates only to this question: What must the offeree do to accept? That, in turn, calls for *construction of the offer*, and that's what the whole topic is (or should be) about.

The typical controversy in which the distinction is significant involves (1) an offer, (2) the offeree's *attempt* to accept, followed by either (3) the offeror's attempt to revoke or the offeree's attempt to reject. There then arises this question: Was the attempted revocation or rejection effective or did it come too late? That, in turn, raises this question: Was the attempted *acceptance* effective? And *that* question requires that we determine what the offer allows as to mode or manner of acceptance.

Suppose Marjorie says to David, "If you'll publish my advertisement, I'll pay $1,500." David replies, "I accept." Marjorie then says, "I've changed my mind, I withdraw my offer." Whether these parties formed a contract depends on the meaning, legally, of Marjorie's statement, "If you'll publish my advertisement[.]" Does it (1) describe the performance Marjorie wants *and* the only manner by which David may accept, or does it (2) identify only the performance sought without addressing mode of acceptance?

Under older common law (before 1920 or so), an offer looked to a unilateral contract unless the language plainly and expressly allowed for an acceptance by some mode other than full performance. Older courts would have construed Marjorie's offer thus: "If you'll publish my advertisement, I'll pay $1,500. *To accept, you must publish the advertisement.*"

Modern common law takes the opposite view: Unless otherwise clearly and plainly stated, an offer permits acceptance by any mode reasonable under the circumstances (as already described above in section B). If the offeror demands acceptance by full performance, his offer must make that plain, clear, and explicit. He'll have to write or say something like: "You may accept only by complete performance," or "Our agreement takes effect only after you finish the performance described in this offer," or "I will not allow for acceptance by promise. Rather, I require full performance." Marjorie made no such statement. Modern courts would construe her offer thus: "If you'll publish my advertisement, I'll pay $1,500. *You may accept this offer in any ordinary way including, of course, the way in which I've made the offer — by simple speech.*"

QUESTION 5. On September 15, Jonathan and Mandy start to exchange signed writings:

(1) **September 15, Jonathan:** I wish to have you repave the parking lot located at my business facility on 100 Grande Street, work to be done, please, this Saturday, September 19. There will be no one on the premises that day, so you'll be able to work without interference. I will pay $25,000 on completion. I am interested in real performance, not empty promises. Please respond.

(2) **September 16, Mandy:** I understand your needs and concerns. You have my solemn promise that I'll complete the work you have requested on September 19; it's a deal.

(3) **September 17, Jonathan:** Thank you for your response, but I've decided not to repave the lots this year. I hope to be in touch with you in the future; my offer is withdrawn.

(4) **September 18, Mandy:** We formed a contract on the 16th; I intend to perform and expect you to pay.

Have Mandy and Jonathan formed a contract?

A. Yes, because Jonathan's offer contemplated a unilateral contract, and on September 16 Mandy agreed to deliver full performance

B. Yes, because on September 15 Jonathan plainly demanded acceptance by promise, and one day later, Mandy made the necessary promise

C. No, because Jonathan's offer was for a unilateral contract, and by September 17 Mandy had not paved the lots to which Jonathan's offer referred

D. No, because Jonathan's September 15 communication was silent as to mode of acceptance and therefore constituted not an offer but an invitation to deal

---

ANALYSIS. The problem probes the difference between offers for unilateral and bilateral contracts. On September 15, Jonathan makes an offer, and on the 16th, Mandy assents to its terms. If the assent qualifies as an acceptance, the parties form a contract, and Jonathan's subsequent attempt to revoke is ineffective. If, on the other hand, Mandy's assent is not an acceptance, the parties form no contract. Jonathan effectively revokes on the 17th, and Mandy loses her power to accept.

Whether Mandy effectively accepted Jonathan's offer depends on whether Jonathan (a) allowed her to accept by promise, as she attempted to do, or (b) required that she accept by full performance as, by September 17, she had not done. In legalese, the question is whether Jonathan made "an offer for a unilateral contract," or "an offer for a bilateral contract." If the offer was for a unilateral contract, Jonathan effectively revoked before Mandy accepted. If it was for a bilateral contract, Mandy accepted before Jonathan tried to revoke.

Examine Jonathan's offer. It features no words like "if you wish to accept" or "you are required to accept in this way" or "you may accept by." Arguably, therefore, Jonathan allowed Mandy to accept in any reasonable way, which she tried to do. Arguably, on the other hand, Jonathan required an acceptance by full performance when he wrote: "I am interested in real performance, not empty promises. Please respond." *Arguably*, Mandy should understand that to mean: "If you want to accept, you must deliver full performance; a promise will not suffice." *Arguably*, then again, Mandy, as a reasonable person, would note that (1) the sentences do not in "black and white" demand acceptance by performance; (2) Jonathan expresses no contempt for promises in general, but only for "empty" ones; and (3) the words "please respond" suggest that he invites a verbal assent.

Whether these parties formed a contract is open to argument. The answer might be "yes" and it might be "no," but none is correct unless *accompanied by an appropriate rationale*. The correct answer will be akin to (a) "Yes, because Jonathan made an offer for a bilateral contract and Mandy effectively accepted before he tried to revoke," or (b) "No, because Jonathan made an offer for a unilateral contract, and he revoked before Mandy fully performed." Knowing what we're looking for, let's examine the answer choices.

A and **B** say "yes." As its reason, **A** states that Jonathan's offer was for a unilateral contract and Mandy promised to perform. The reasoning is backwards. An offer for a unilateral contract does not create a contract when the offeree *promises* performance. Acceptance requires that she *actually* perform — fully. **B** reasons that Jonathan "plainly" demanded acceptance by promise and that Mandy gave the necessary promise. Maybe Jonathan *allowed* Mandy to accept by promise, but he did not "plainly" demand that she do so. **B** is weak — *very* weak.

Let's assess the "no" options. **D** tells us that Jonathan's first writing was silent as to mode of acceptance. Arguably, that's true. True or false, however, such silence would not negate the creation of an offer. To constitute an offer, a communication need *not* explicitly provide for a manner of acceptance. Failure to address mode of acceptance means, simply, that any reasonable mode will suffice. **D** rests on an erroneous premise; it's wrong.

We're left with **C**. "No," it states, the parties formed no contract. Why not? Because Jonathan's offer looked toward a unilateral contract and by September

17, the day on which Jonathan tried to revoke, Mandy had not accepted; she had not "paved the lots to which Jonathan's offer referred." **C** posits an offer for a unilateral contract and supplies the appropriate reasoning. **C** is right.

Realize that a "yes" answer would be correct if it carried the proper reasoning. Suppose, for example, that one of the options read: "Yes, because Jonathan made no express requirement that Mandy accept only by full performance." With that rationale, a "yes" answer would be right.

F.   Notice to the Offeror

Julia lives in New York but owns a rental home in New Mexico where her tenant resides. On December 31, the tenant vacates. Lei is Julia's long-time friend, living in New Mexico about 200 miles from the rental home. Julia wants Lei to inspect the rental property, arrange for any necessary repairs, clean the premises, and thus ready it for a new tenant. To that end, on January 1, Julia contacts Lei by telephone and says, "My tenant has moved out. I'll pay you $1,000 if you'll travel to the rental home, inspect it, arrange for any necessary repairs, clean all of the rooms, and thus ready the house for a new tenant by January 10. You may accept only by doing all that I ask. Naturally, you may stay in the home as you complete all of this work." Lei responds, "Very well." She travels to the home and by January 5 completes the work. She does not, however, contact Julia to notify her of that fact. Rather, Lei leaves New Mexico for a vacation overseas.

On January 10, Julia wants to know if Lei has or has not accepted her offer. For that purpose, she tries to reach Lei by telephone, fax, and email. Receiving no response she finds herself in a bind. If Lei *has* done the work, she and Julia have a contract, requiring that Julia pay Lei $1,000. If Lei has not done the work, Julia is free to hire someone else to do it instead.

To spare an offeror that dilemma, modern common law provides: *Where an offeree, B, accepts by performance and should understand that the offeror, A, has no meaningful way to know that she has done so, B must notify A that she has in fact performed. If, within a reasonable time, B fails to give A such notice, then A, the offeror, is discharged from her contractual obligation.*

Restatement (Second) §62(2) provides:

> If an offeree who accepts by rendering a performance has reason to know that the offeror has no adequate means of learning of the performance with reasonable promptness and certainty, the contractual duty of the offeror is discharged unless
>
> (a) the offeree exercises reasonable diligence to notify the offeror of acceptance, or
>
> (b) the offeror learns of the performance within a reasonable time, or
>
> (c) the offer indicates that notification of acceptance is not required.

Lei gave her performance some 3,000 miles from Julia's location. She then left the country. She ought to have recognized that Julia was without adequate means of learning that she had, in fact, readied the house for a new tenant. After some reasonable time passes and Lei fails, still, to notify Julia that she has done the work asked of her, Julia is discharged from her duty; she need not pay Lei.

QUESTION 6. Harry operates a horse farm in Colorado. Tom, his brother, lives in Connecticut. Dick is Tom's friend, living near Harry in Colorado. Both Tom and Dick know Harry as rather an irresponsible chap. In 2019, Harry urgently needs money and he telephones his brother Tom to ask for a loan. Tom then sends his friend Dick this signed letter: "My brother Harry needs $100,000. If you make him a loan in that amount, I'll guarantee it. If he doesn't repay, I will. Accept my offer by making the loan."

Dick does then immediately lend Harry $100,000, on the understanding that Harry will repay it in five years. Five years later in 2024, Harry fails to pay. Dick contacts Tom and demands that Tom pay him the $100,000 Harry owed. Tom refuses. Dick brings an action against Tom, alleging that Tom has breached a contractual duty to repay Harry's debt. Tom contends that he has no such duty. What additional fact, if proven, would best support Tom's position?

A. Dick made the loan to Harry, expecting that Harry would not be able to repay it.

B. At no time before 2024 did Dick or Harry inform Tom that the loan had been made.

C. In the past, Tom had guaranteed some of Harry's debts, and Harry had always repaid them.

D. When the five years expired, Harry, unable to repay the loan, promised that he would repay it after one additional year.

ANALYSIS. Tom required that Dick accept his offer by actually lending Harry $100,000; he made an offer for a unilateral contract. When Dick did that he accepted the offer and Tom acquired a contractual duty to pay Harry's debt if Harry himself failed to do so. Because Dick knew Harry to be an irresponsible chap, he had reason to believe that Harry would not advise Tom of the loan. Tom was in a bind similar to Julia's. He lacked adequate means by which to learn that Dick had made the loan — he had no good way to know that Dick had accepted his offer. Consequently, Dick himself had an obligation to tell Tom that he had made the loan. If Dick failed to do that and if Tom did not otherwise learn of the loan, the law discharges Tom from his obligation under the contract with Dick. With that, examine the options and find the facts that would most likely free Tom of his contractual duty.

A, **C**, and **D** cite matters of irrelevance. They describe no facts that would affect Tom's duty to pay Harry's debt. **B**, however, gives us this: Neither Dick nor Harry advised Tom that the loan had been made. As just discussed, that fact discharges Tom's obligation. **B** is right.

G.   Reward Offers Look to Unilateral Contracts

From Chapter 2, section D, we know that the "power to accept" an offer rests only in an *offeree* and that one is an offeree only if, under the circumstances, he reasonably believes the offeror's proposal is made to *him*. The simplest of logic tells us that if one does not know, even, that some offer has been made, he cannot possibly think it was made to *him* and that he cannot be an offeree. Please keep that in mind.

From Chapter 5, section A, we know that an offer of reward is, of course, an offer. Further, all legal authorities agree that a reward offer is an offer for a unilateral contract. Even if the offeror does not so specify, one may accept only by doing, in full, what the offeror requests.

Suppose Offeror publishes this notice: "REWARD — $1,000 for safe return of LOST DOG. White poodle, answers to the name 'George,' lost near corner of Main and High Streets." The posting proposes a bargain in which Offeree is to return the lost dog and, in exchange, Offeror will pay $1,000. The law generally regards reward offers as offers for unilateral contracts; one cannot accept the offer by *promising* to find and return the dog. Rather, in order to accept one must *actually find and return the dog*. If and when some person does return the dog then, simultaneously, he (1) accepts the offer, (2) performs his part of the bargain, and (3) leaves the contract just formed executory only on the offeror's part; it remains only for the offeror to pay the reward.

Suppose Ernest loses his laptop computer and publishes a notice offering $1,000 for its return. Not knowing of Ernest's offer, Jorge finds a laptop computer, turns it on, and learns that it belongs to Ernest. He returns it to Ernest as would any honest person. *Subsequently*, he learns of Ernest's reward offer and asks that Ernest pay him the reward.

Ernest need *not* pay him. Not knowing of the reward offer, Jorge was not an offeree. In returning the computer, therefore, he did not accept the offer. That chain of logic creates this rule: *In order to accept an offer of reward, one must (a) know of the offer, and (b) complete the performance for which the offeror asks.* Restatement (Second) §51 cmt. a provides:

> [I]n cases of offers of reward, it is ordinarily essential to the acceptance of the offer that the offeree know of the proposal made. In general, performance completed before the offer comes to the offeree's knowledge does not have reference to the offer, and the terms of the offer are not satisfied by such action.

H. The Closers

Sadie is the author of a short story called "Cookie Jar," and she owns its copyright. By handwritten fax, on May 8, Baldwin sends Sadie this message: "I am prepared immediately to purchase from you the copyright to your story 'Cookie Jar' for the price of $300,000, half ($150,000) in advance, to be paid on June 1 and half ($150,000) to be paid on July 1, on which latter date (July 1) you will actually transfer copyright ownership to me. Please get back to me no later than May 15 with your written response. Handwriting is fine."

Sadie considers Baldwin's offer. On May 14, she has not made a decision and on that day, by fax, sends Baldwin this handwritten message: "I continue to consider your offer. Might you extend the May 15 deadline by one week — to May 22? At 11:00 P.M. on May 15, Sadie has received no response.

QUESTION 7. For this question, assume that at 11:30 P.M. on May 15, with no response from Baldwin, Sadie telephones Baldwin and leaves him this voicemail message: "I accept your offer of May 8." Baldwin retrieves the voicemail message the following morning, May 16. Then, on the afternoon of May 16, Sadie sends Baldwin this handwritten fax: "In accordance with my voicemail message of last night, May 15, I accept your May 8 offer." In all probability these parties

A. have formed a contract because, within a reasonable time of leaving her voicemail message, Sadie sent Baldwin a handwritten fax message confirming her assent.
B. have formed a contract because voicemail represents a reasonable mode of communication in modern-day transactions.
C. have not formed a contract because Sadie failed timely to express her assent in the manner prescribed by Baldwin.
D. have not formed a contract because Sadie could not reasonably expect that Baldwin would hear her voicemail message before May 16.

> **QUESTION 8.** For this question, assume that at 11:00 P.M. on May 15,
> Sadie sends Baldwin this *email* message: "I accept your May 8 offer." The
> message posts to Baldwin's inbox at 11:01 P.M. but Baldwin does not read
> it until the following morning, May 16. In all probability these parties
>
> **A.** have formed a contract because Sadie accepted Baldwin's offer
> according to the time and manner prescribed in the May 8
> communication.
> **B.** have formed a contract because by May 15, Sadie formed a definite
> intent to assent to all terms of Baldwin's proposal.
> **C.** have not formed a contract because Sadie did not express her assent
> in handwriting.
> **D.** have not formed a contract because Sadie rejected the offer on
> May 14.

ANALYSIS. Baldwin is "master of his offer"; Sadie accepts it only if she manifests her assent in such manner as Baldwin prescribes. Further, she must do so before the offer expires by rejection, revocation, or passage of time (Chapter 6). By requiring that Sadie respond "no later than May 15," Baldwin has limited his offer's life to a moment before midnight, May 16. In order to accept, Sadie must manifest her assent *in writing*, no later than that hour on that day.

As for Question 7. Sadie's May 14 fax message is no acceptance; it doesn't show assent to Baldwin's proposal. Neither, however, does it reject. Sadie advised Baldwin that she was not ready to make a decision and asked whether she might have more time. (Recall from Chapter 7, section C, that an offeree does not reject an offer by inquiring about a possible change in terms. That applies to an inquiry about terms of the bargain itself or about terms as to time and manner of acceptance.) Baldwin's offer remains open through May 15.

Late on May 15, Sadie does make an expression of assent. She dispatches it — puts it out of her possession — but does *not* do so in writing as Baldwin prescribes. Consequently, at the stroke of midnight that begins the day of May 16 Sadie fails to accept and the offer expires. It does not save Sadie that on May 16 she follows her voicemail with a writing; the writing comes too late.

A tells us that the parties did form a contract. For that reason alone, it's wrong, and the happy phrase "reasonable time" can't make it right. That Sadie issued a writing one day after leaving her voicemail means not a thing. She failed to comply with the "master's" decree and so failed to accept.

And **B**? Voicemail is a reasonable mode of communication. If Baldwin had prescribed no special mode of acceptance, the voicemail would have done the job. But B overlooks this critical fact: Exercising his rights as "master," Baldwin required a written acceptance. Sadie could accept in no other way. **B** is wrong.

D correctly concludes that the parties failed to form a contract, but its reasoning is askew. Acceptance is effective on *dispatch* — when the offeree puts it out of her possession (Chapter 8, section A). That Baldwin would not likely *hear* the telephone message until May 16 would not negate the timeliness of a voicemail acceptance if, in this case, voicemail had been a proper mode of acceptance. Sadie dispatched her message on time, but not *in the right way*.

That leaves **C**, which tells us that the parties failed to form a contract because Sadie did not, while the offer lived, assent to its terms in the manner prescribed by the offeror. **C** is right.

As for Question 8.   An email message is a writing. Hence, Sadie dispatched a *written* message of acceptance *on* May 15. She sent it timely, in the appropriate mode. No rejection or revocation preceded the message, and for all of these reasons, the parties formed a contract.

C and **D** tell us that the parties formed no contract, so they're wrong, as is their reasoning. **C** implies that Sadie was empowered to accept only by handwriting. Ridiculous. Baldwin called for a *written* response. He stated that handwriting would be "fine," but he didn't require it; he required only *a* writing. On May 15, Sadie sent him an email. That's a writing. **C** is wrong. **D** states that Sadie rejected on May 14. She did no such thing; she made a mere inquiry.

B correctly tells us that the parties formed a contract, but its reasoning is all wrong. Way back in Chapters 2 and 3, we learned that neither offer nor acceptance springs from what is in one's head. They arise through another's reasonable understanding of her words and acts. **B** is not only wrong; it insults our intelligence.

That leaves **A**, which for the right reason, correctly states that these two formed a contract. Acceptance in this case required that Sadie manifest her assent by May 15 in writing. That's what Sadie did, and so was born a beautiful brand-new baby contract. It matters not that Baldwin first read the message on the following day because, as we know, acceptance is effective on dispatch (Chapter 8, section A). **A** is right.

 # Silver's Picks

1.	C
2.	C
3.	A
4.	C
5.	C
6.	B
7.	C
8.	A

10

More About the Offeree Who Accepts by Performing an Act

A. When the Offeror Requires Acceptance by *Act*

Chapter 9, section A, taught you that the offeror is mistress of her offer; it's in her power to prescribe the mode/manner by which the offeree may accept. (If she prescribes no such mode, then the offeree may accept in any reasonable manner.)

X and Y, Case 1

X offers money to Y in exchange for Y's performance of acts 1, 2, and 3, expressly allowing that Y accept only by completing all three acts. That means Y does not accept until he does, in fact, complete all three acts. By *beginning* to perform one of the acts, Y does not accept and the parties do not, at that time, form a contract. Only when Y *completes* all three acts, do they form a (unilateral) contract.

X and Y, Case 2

If X makes to Y the same offer of money in exchange for acts 1, 2, and 3, but allows Y to accept by completing only act 1, then the parties create no contract until Y does, in fact, complete act 1. When Y *begins* to perform act 1, the parties do not yet have a contract. Only when Y *completes* act 1 do they form a (bilateral) contract.

In both cases 1 and 2, Y demands that X accept by *completing* one or more acts, and the fact that Y begins to perform does not create a contract.

1. That Makes for a Problem: Sam, Sally, and a Flagpole

We know generally that an offeror may revoke at any time before the offeree accepts. Strictly applied, that rule leads to an unsettling result when an offeree (a) is allowed to accept only by completing some act and (b) *begins* to perform it. In the classic illustration, Sam says to Sally, "I'll pay you $100 if you climb to the top of this 100-foot flagpole. You may accept only by fully performing — by reaching the top of the flagpole." Sally begins to climb. After twenty minutes, when she is but an inch from the top, Sam shouts up to her, "I revoke my offer." Sally hangs one inch from the top of the flagpole with nothing to show for it — no contract, no action for breach (and, of course, a long climb downward).

2. Is That Fair? Older Authorities Said "Yes"

If before beginning her climb Sally had consulted her attorney, she would have known that the offeror had the right to revoke at any time before she reached the flagpole's tippy-top. She would have known the rules of the "game" and could have chosen to "play" or not. She might have responded with a counteroffer, *promising* to climb the pole in exchange for Sam's promise of $100. Sam would then be free to accept or not. Because Sally does not put to Sam any such counteroffer, but instead begins her climb in response *to* Sam's offer (for a unilateral contract), older authorities deemed it perfectly fair that Sam retain his right to revoke at any time before Sally *completes* the climb. In abstract terms, the older rule was that *an offeror who allowed his offeree to accept only by completing some act retained the power to revoke at any time before the offeree completed the act, even if the offeree had begun performance and nearly completed it.*

3. Modern Law Doesn't Buy That

Modern thought finds injustice in the offeror's right to revoke his offer after an offeree begins to perform the act necessary to his acceptance. The common law now provides, generally, *when an offeror allows an offeree to accept only by performing some act(s) and the offeree begins to perform, the offeror loses his right to revoke.*

It remains so, under modern law, that to accept Sam's offer, Sally must complete the climb; she must reach the top of the pole. Beginning the climb does not constitute acceptance but, when Sally starts up the pole, Sam loses his right to revoke. As she makes her ascent, Sally knows that Sam cannot take back his offer.

Yet, Sam's offer may still expire by events discussed in Chapter 6, sections C, D, and E. The rule, then is this: *If an offeror requires that his offeree accept by performing some act(s) and the offeree begins to perform, then (1) the offer becomes permanently irrevocable, but (2) the offer may expire by any of the other usual means: rejection, passage of a stated time, passage of a reasonable time, and death or incapacity of the offeror or offeree, and (3) the relevant contract does not arise unless and until the offeree completes performance before the offer expires through any such event.*

QUESTIONS 1 & 2. SurveCo surveys and inspects homes for prospective buyers. Peter contemplates buying a home. On June 1, the two parties exchange emails:

(1) **Peter:** I'm contemplating the purchase of a home located at 587 Greenery Way in Heightland. I'd like you to survey it, inspect it, and send me a written report on or before June 18 at 5:00 P.M. Are you able to do that, and what is your fee?

(2) **SurveCo:** Certainly we can accommodate you. We'll begin the survey on June 12 and, if we fail to finish it that same day, we'll certainly finish by June 18 at 5:00 P.M. For the survey and report, our fee is $1,200.

(3) **Peter:** Thank you. I am prepared to proceed on your terms, with a deadline of June 18 at 5:00 P.M. and with this additional understanding: You may accept my offer only by completing all of the work for which I ask.

(4) **SurveCo:** We accept your terms.

QUESTION 1. Assume that at 10:00 A.M. on June 12, SurveCo begins the survey and inspection. By 3:00 P.M., it has completed 75 percent of the work. At 4:00 P.M., Peter contacts SurveCo and declares his offer revoked.

Just after Peter makes his 4:00 announcement, do the parties have a contract that (a) requires SurveCo to complete the inspection and survey, with written report; and (b) requires Peter to pay SurveCo $1,200?

A. Yes, because at statement 4 SurveCo accepted Peter's offer
B. Yes, because on June 12 SurveCo began performance
C. No, because SurveCo has not, at that time, accepted Peter's offer
D. Yes, because Peter's power to revoke would first arise on June 18 at 5:00 P.M.

QUESTION 2. Now assume that SurveCo begins its survey and inspection on June 12 at 10:00 A.M. and completes it that same day. On June 13, SurveCo emails Peter to announce that its on-site work is complete, adding, "We wish to complete the written report by June 18, but we cannot do so. We'll finish it on or before June 25." Peter emails back, "That is not acceptable. I wish not to do further business with you." Later that same day, SurveCo emails Peter again to say that it *can* complete the report by June 18. Peter is firm: "As I wrote earlier, I no longer wish to do business with you." On June 18, SurveCo submits the written report. Does Peter owe SurveCo $1,200?

A. Yes, because on June 12 Peter's offer was permanently irrevocable
B. Yes, because the parties formed a contract on June 12
C. No, because on June 13, Surveco believed it could not complete its performance by June 18.
D. No, because on June 13, SurveCo lost its power to accept

ANALYSIS. Examine the first email exchange and ask: Did one of the parties make an offer to the other and, if so, did the other accept? At statement 1, Peter expressed his interest in purchasing SurveCo's services. Failing to propose a fee, he made a mere invitation to deal. At statement 2, SurveCo named a fee and stated its readiness to do the work by June 18. Probably, SurveCo made an offer. Yet if it did, Peter didn't accept. Peter took hold of SurveCo's terms, added a new one, and presented it back to SurveCo. He made a counteroffer.

Peter's counteroffer provided that SurveCo could accept only by completing all of its work, thus proposing a unilateral contract. These parties could form no contract unless SurveCo completed the survey/inspection and report by June 18, Peter's prescribed deadline. When SurveCo began performance, Peter lost his power to revoke. Nonetheless, the offer remained subject to expiration by rejection, by passage of time stated in the offer, or by Peter's death or incompetence.

As for Question 1. Question 1 states that SurveCo began performance on June 12. At that moment, Peter permanently lost his power to revoke, but the parties did not then form a contract. Peter allowed that SurveCo could accept only with a full performance, complete by June 18.

A and B tell us that the parties have formed the contemplated contract. On that basis alone, both are wrong. Their reasoning is erroneous too. As to A, we know that with statement 4, SurveCo did *not* accept the offer because Peter allowed it to accept only by complete performance. As to B, SurveCo's beginning of performance is not an acceptance. It does render Peter's offer irrevocable, but it doesn't form a contract.

D states that Peter would acquire a power to revoke at 5:00 P.M. *Wrong.* When SurveCo began its performance, Peter *permanently* lost his power to revoke. At 5:00 P.M. on June 15, Peter's offer was to expire — by passage of a time stated in the offer. Peter can't *revoke* his offer under any circumstance.

C speaketh truth. The parties had no contract because on June 12, just after Peter announced his wish to revoke, SurveCo had not completed its performance, meaning it had not accepted Peter's offer. That's why C is right. (SurveCo has the right, still, to continue its work and accept the offer by completing it before 5:00 P.M. on June 18. But as of June 12, just after Peter announces his wish to revoke, these parties have no contract.)

As for Question 2.   According to Question 2, SurveCo finished the inspection and survey on June 12. Yet to accept Peter's offer, SurveCo had still to submit its written report by June 18. On June 13, SurveCo announced to Peter that it *wished* to finish the report by that date but could not do so. From Chapter 6, section C, remember this: "I wish I could but I can't" means "no; I reject your offer." Hence, with its June 13 announcement, SurveCo rejected Peter's offer. Even though SurveCo moved a long way toward completion, it ultimately said "no." Notwithstanding that Peter's offer was irrevocable, SurveCo's *rejection* put it to death. SurveCo's subsequent attempt to accept was ineffective.

A states that Peter must pay the $1,200 because his offer turned irrevocable on June 12. It's true that the offer turned irrevocable on that day, but it died nonetheless on June 13 when SurveCo rejected it. Hence, A is wrong. B states that the parties formed a contract on June 12. Wrong again; a contract requires offer and acceptance, and the "master" of this offer decreed that SurveCo would accept only if it *completely* performed on or before June 18 at 5:00 P.M. On June 12, SurveCo had not written its report and, therefore, had not accepted the offer. C correctly states that Peter owes nothing to SurveCo, but its reasoning is whacked. What SurveCo did or did not believe on June 13 is irrelevant. It's what SurveCo outwardly expressed that matters. Peter's offer expired on June 12 because SurveCo *told* Peter that it could not complete performance in accordance with the offer's terms; it rejected Peter's offer.

D, alas, tells us that Peter owes nothing to SurveCo and correctly states the reason: "On June 13, SurveCo lost its power to accept." On that day, Peter's offer, although irrevocable, expired by rejection, and so SurveCo did lose its power to accept. D is right.

4. How the Restatement Words the Modern Rule

The Restatement expresses this same modern view by rather a gratuitous, pretentious (and silly) use of the phrase "option contract" (Chapter 6, section B). Rather than state simply that an offer becomes irrevocable when it demands acceptance by act and the offeree begins to perform that act, Restatement (Second) of Contracts §45(1) provides:

> Where an offer invites an offeree to accept by rendering a performance and does not invite a promissory acceptance, an option contract is created when the offeree . . . begins the invited performance. . . .

According to the Restatement, the offeree's payment for the "option" inheres in the very fact that he begins to perform the requested act: "[T]he beginning of performance furnishes [payment] for an option contract." Restatement (Second) §45 cmt. d.

In substance and effect, the Restatement rule is exactly the same as the one stated in section A.3 above. The offeree who begins to perform buys an "option" to complete the act, which is tantamount to providing that the offeror's offer becomes irrevocable. In wording and legal "theory," however, the Restatement rule is different. The Restatement reaches its result by creating these fictions:

When This Happens in Fact	The Restatement Draws This Legal Conclusion
Offeror: If you will register my copyright with the U.S. copyright office, I will pay you $1,000. In order to accept you must actually register the copyright. Offeree begins the process of registering the copyright.	Offeror makes two offers: (1) to pay the offeree for registering the copyright, and (2) to give the offeree the option to complete that performance if he begins it. Offeree accepts offer 2 and the parties thus form an "option" contract. That option contract represents this bargain: • offeree has begun the registration process, in exchange for which • offeror must hold offer 1 permanently irrevocable, because the offeree has the "option" to complete his performance.

As noted earlier, the offer remains subject to termination by the offeree's rejection, passage of time, or death or incapacity.

So, what should you know exactly? First, know the rule stated in section A.3 above. Second, know that the Restatement (Second) §45 means to state that very same rule in its own stupid way.

QUESTION 3. Naomi, a former governor, hopes to publish her memoirs. On August 25, she submits a manuscript to Publisher, who telephones her after reading it: "Your manuscript is excellent. If you will rewrite the last chapter so that it describes your plans for the future and submit it within 30 days, we will publish the manuscript and pay you a royalty of 10 percent on gross sales. Our agreement takes effect when you submit the revised chapter." On September 2, Naomi begins to revise the last chapter. Later that day, Publisher calls to say, "I'm sorry, but we've decided against publishing the book." Under modern common law, Publisher's attempt to revoke is ineffective because

> **I.** Publisher did not communicate its revocation by signed writing.
> **II.** Publisher's offer became irrevocable when Naomi began to revise the final chapter.
> **III.** The parties formed an option contract when Naomi began to revise the final chapter.
> **A.** I only
> **B.** I and II only
> **C.** II and III only
> **D.** I, II, and III

ANALYSIS.   Publisher made an offer and allowed Naomi to accept only by full performance. In order to accept she actually had to revise and submit the final chapter. Naomi began the revision, meaning that Publisher's offer became irrevocable. Or, in Restatement terms, the parties formed an "option contract" under which Naomi acquired the "option" to complete the revision and thus to accept Publisher's offer. For these reasons, Publisher's subsequent attempt to revoke was ineffective.

Item I proclaims that the Publisher failed to revoke because it did not communicate its revocation by signed writing. There is no such rule. Publisher's offer became irrevocable when Naomi began to write the revision. If Publisher had attempted to revoke by sworn statement, smoke signal, or signed writing, he would fail because his offer was irrevocable. Option I is false, which eliminates **A**, **B**, and **D**.

Items II and III correctly explain why Publisher's revocation is ineffective. In plain English, item II tells us that Publisher lost his right to revoke when Naomi began to revise her last chapter. Item III makes the same statement in Restatement jargonese: When Naomi began the revision, the parties formed an "option contract," affording Nancy the "option" to *complete* the revision and thus accept the offer. Because options II and III make true statements, **C** is right.

QUESTION 4. Ivis owns a patent on a machine technology called Manutrix. Anton wishes to purchase from her an exclusive license to build and sell Manutrix machinery. For that purpose, he contacts Ivis by signed writing:

(1) **Anton:** I wish to buy an exclusive license to use your Manutrix technology for five years. In exchange, I'll pay you $300,000 in each such year.

(2) **Ivis:** I'm agreeable to the fee and to the five-year term, but I need some assurance that you will be able to make the payments each year.

> Bring to me a letter from your bank showing that your bank balance is, as of now, at least $1 million. Do that and we have a deal.
>
> Anton asks his bank to issue the letter. The bank agrees to do so and tells Anton it will be written and ready in five days. Before the bank issues the letter, Ivis contacts Anton: "I've changed my mind. I'm not willing to sell you the license." Which of the following accurately characterizes the parties' legal rights and duties?
>
> I. Ivis and Anton have a contract requiring that Ivis sell Anton the exclusive license.
> II. Ivis and Anton have an option contract under which Anton has the option to purchase the exclusive license from Ivis.
> III. Ivis and Anton have an option contract under which Ivis has the option to sell the exclusive license to Anton.
> IV. Ivis made an offer, and Anton has the power to accept it or not.
> A. I only
> B. I and II only
> C. II and IV only
> D. III and IV only

ANALYSIS.   In statement 1, Anton made an offer to Ivis, and in statement 2, Ivis responded with a counteroffer, allowing Anton to accept it only by performing an act — by presenting Ivis with a bank letter attesting to his balance. When Anton *began* his effort to obtain the letter, he rendered Ivis's offer irrevocable. In Restatement terms, the parties formed an "option contract" affording Anton the option, if he chose, to acquire the bank letter, deliver it to Ivis, and thus accept Ivis's offer. When Ivis told Anton that she had changed her mind, she made an ineffective attempt to revoke. The parties did not form a contract for the sale of the license. Rather, Anton acquired the irrevocable right to accept Ivis's offer and thereby form a contract that would entitle (and oblige) him to purchase it.

Item I states that the parties do have a contract for the sale of the license; for that reason it's wrong. Item IV properly reports that Anton is Ivis's offeree with power still to accept Ivis's offer. That's correct: Ivis's offer is irrevocable and thus leaves Anton with power to accept it notwithstanding Ivis's attempt to revoke. The right answer must include item IV but exclude item I, meaning that **C** or **D** is right, depending on the correctness of items II and III. Both II and III describe an option contract. Item III reports that *Ivis* has an option to *sell* the license. Item II reports that *Anton* has an option to *purchase* the license.

Anton is possessed of an irrevocable offer to purchase the license. If he wishes to purchase, he need only wait for his bank to issue the letter and then deliver it to Ivis. If he does not wish to purchase, he need only abort his efforts. It is for *Anton to decide*, as he wishes, that he will or will not accept Ivis's offer. In Restatement terms, Anton has an "option" to purchase the license. Ivis, meanwhile, has no option but to await Anton's decision. Item II correctly states that Anton has an option to purchase the license. Item III incorrectly states that Ivis has an option to sell it. Items II and IV make true statements, and that's why **C** is right.

In Chapter 9, section F, you learned this: When an offeree accepts by completing performance, the offeror has some right to learn of it. If the offeree should understand that the offeror has no reasonable means by which to do so then, within a reasonable time of completing performance (and hence accepting the offer), the offeree or some other party must tell the offeror that he has done so, or the offeror's contractual duty is discharged — the law undoes it; it ceases to exist.

Similarly, an offeror has a right to know if his offer has become irrevocable. Suppose A makes an offer to B, requiring that B accept by furnishing some or all of his performance. B begins to perform, which means that A's offer becomes irrevocable. Suppose that A has no meaningful way to *learn* that B has begun performance and B should know that. A must, within a reasonable time, have notice that B has begun performance.

B.   When the Offeror Allows the Offeree to Accept by Promise *or* Performance

We know now that if an offeror *requires* her offeree to accept by completing an act, her offer becomes irrevocable when the offeree begins to perform. Let's deal now with the offeror who permits an offeree to accept by promise *or* performance.

Suppose Bill wants to purchase Leah's computer and makes her this offer: "I'll buy your computer for $300. You may accept my offer by delivering the computer or by promising, right now, that you'll deliver it. The promise or the performance will constitute acceptance." Bill has *allowed* Leah to accept by delivering the computer, but he has not *required* that she do so. He has allowed, also, that she accept by promise. In such a case, the offeree's beginning of performance is, by law, *her promise to complete it*. Hence, by *beginning performance*, the offeree accepts the offer and forms a contract. Restatement (Second) §62 provides:

> (1) Where an offer invites an offeree to choose between acceptance by promise and acceptance by performance, the . . . beginning of the invited performance . . . is an acceptance[.]
> (2) Such an acceptance operates as a promise to render complete performance.

Further, as we already know, if the offeror is silent as to the mode or manner of acceptance, the offeree may accept in any manner that is reasonable (Restatement (Second) §30(2); Chapter 9, section B). If performance of an act is a reasonable mode of acceptance, then the offeror has implicitly permitted the offeree to accept by promise or performance. In that case, too, when the offeree *begins* to perform, he accepts the offer and the parties form a contract. *Once again, the beginning of performance operates as an acceptance when and only when expressly or by implication of law, the offeror has allowed the offeree to accept by promise* **or** *performance of an act(s). If the offeror has allowed the offeree to accept only by performance of an act(s), then the beginning of performance does not operate as an acceptance. Rather, it renders the offer irrevocable.*

QUESTION 5. On April 1, Sylvia mails her accountant Jared statements of income and deductions for the preceding tax year, together with this letter: "I enclose records relevant to my income for this past tax year. If you'll prepare my state and federal tax returns, I will, of course, pay you the usual fee." On April 4, Jared receives and reads the letter. On April 5, he begins work on Sylvia's tax return. The two parties have

  I. a contract in which Jared must prepare Sylvia's tax return and Sylvia must pay Jared's usual fee.
 II. an option contract in which Jared has the option to complete Sylvia's tax return.

A. I only
B. II only
C. I and II
D. Neither I nor II

ANALYSIS. Sylvia made Jared an offer. She was silent as to how Jared should accept. By implication of law, therefore, she permitted him to accept in any reasonable way, meaning that he was free to accept (a) by promise communicated in any reasonable way or (b) by preparing the tax return. That, in turn, means that Sylvia allowed Jared to accept by performance but did not *require* that he do so. She allowed him to accept by promise *or* performance. When Jared began to perform he accepted Sylvia's offer, meaning that the beginning of his performance operated as his promise to complete it.

As item I states, these parties formed a contract requiring that Jared complete the tax return and that Sylvia pay his fee. Item II incorrectly states that the parties formed an option contract. If Sylvia had *required* that Jared accept by performance, his beginning of the performance would have rendered the offer irrevocable, thus affording him the option to complete it. But that's not this case. Item I makes a true statement and item II a false one. **A** is right.

QUESTION 6. On Monday at 10:00 A.M., Luella brings her computer to Norman, a computer repair technician. Told to leave it on the front desk with a note describing its dysfunction, Luella does so, writing: "Computer won't boot. Please repair. I'll pay your normal fee, of course. I'll come in tomorrow, Tuesday, to check on the status." Later that same Monday at 3:00 P.M., Norman begins work on the computer. At 5:00 P.M., Luella telephones Norman and tells him not to repair the computer. Norman responds, "Too late. I've already begun to fix it." "Well, you didn't tell me that you were beginning the work," Luella says, "and I'm directing you now not to repair the computer." Norman contends that he and Luella have formed a contract. In response, Luella cites the fact that Norman did not immediately inform her that he had begun performance. On that basis Luella contends that she and Norman have not formed a contract. Is she right?

A. Yes; the beginning of performance does not operate as an acceptance unless and until the offeror obtains such notice
B. Yes; Norman's failure to give such notice shows bad faith on his part
C. No; by leaving her computer at Norman's facility, Luella waived her right to such notice
D. No; Luella's stated plan to return to the facility on Tuesday gave Norman reason to believe that Luella would acquire such notice

---

ANALYSIS.   When Luella left her computer at the front desk together with her note, she made an offer. She did not expressly require that Norman accept by giving full performance, but plainly she *permitted* him to do so. By implication of law, she allowed him to accept by promise *or* performance. Consequently, when Norman began to repair the computer he accepted Luella's offer, and the parties formed a contract requiring that Norman repair the computer and that Luella pay his usual fee.

If Norman had reason to believe that Luella would not learn within a reasonable time that he had begun performance, he himself would be obliged, also within a reasonable time, to notify her that he had done so. But Luella's note gave Norman every reason to believe that on Tuesday Luella would learn that he had begun his work. Hence, he had no obligation to notify her that he had done so.

We're looking for the answer "no." **A** and **B** say "yes," which makes them wrong. Predictably, they also misstate law and fact. According to **A**, Norman's beginning of performance was not an acceptance. That's wrong; when an offeror permits — but does not require — that an offeree accept by performing an act, the offeree's beginning of performance *is* acceptance. **B** invokes the time-honored phrase "bad faith." There is not a whit of dishonesty ("bad faith") in Norman's failure to notify Luella that he has begun performance.

According to **C**, Luella gave up ("waived") her right to notice by leaving the computer at Norman's facility. There is no such rule. **C** is wrong. But **D** hits the bull's eye. It tells us that these parties formed a contract notwithstanding Norman's failure to notify Luella that he had begun performance. The reason, it reports, is that Luella announced her plan to visit Norman on Tuesday. That gave Norman reason to believe that within a reasonable time Luella would learn that he had begun to perform. **D** is right.

C.   The Closers

In the same week, Judge World issued decisions in two bench trials.[1] In the first, she concluded that the litigating parties had formed a contract. In the second, she concluded that they had not. Please read both her opinions.

Opinion 1: *PoolCo v. Silver Oaks Country Club*
The question is whether Plaintiff and Defendant formed a contract.
Upon the evidence, I find these facts:

(1) On August 1, Defendant Silver Oaks Country Club contacted Plaintiff PoolCo and wrote, in pertinent part: "At summer's end, beginning on September 22, we wish to have you winterize all four of our swimming pools, just as you have done in the past. As in the past, we will pay your full fee of $90,000 only when you complete the work, with no payment to be made in advance. Will you do the work for us?"
(2) On August 2, by signed writing, Plaintiff responded: "Certainly."
(3) On August 3, Defendant again contacted Plaintiff: "We have changed our minds and do not wish to have you winterize our pools this year."

Defendant's August 1 communication was, undoubtedly, an offer. The issue is whether (a) Defendant required that Plaintiff accept by complete performance, thus making an offer for a unilateral contract; or (b) Defendant allowed for acceptance by promise, thus making an offer for a bilateral contract. Plaintiff did not begin performance. Let's suppose that the offer was for a unilateral contract. In that case, since Plaintiff did

---

1. Bench trial means a trial without a jury, which, depending on the circumstances, may be perfectly proper. In a bench trial, the judge has the obligations of finding fact and applying the law (as she construes it).

not begin performance, Defendant effectively revoked on August 3, and the parties formed no contract. If Defendant's offer was for a bilateral contract, Plaintiff's August 2 response accepted it. Defendant's attempt to revoke on August 3 was ineffective.

Defendant cites its language of August 3: "As in the past, we will pay your full fee of $90,000 only when you complete the work, with no payment to be made in advance." That language, says Defendant, creates an offer for a unilateral contract. I disagree. There is a difference between an offer that provides for no payment in advance and one that allows the offeree to *accept* only by completing performance. Unless otherwise indicated by the language or circumstances, an offer invites acceptance in any manner and by any medium reasonable in the circumstances. Restatement (Second) of Contracts §30(2).

In its communication of August 1, Defendant nowhere stated or implied that it would allow Plaintiff to accept only by performance. Indeed, with the last sentence of its August 1 communication, it asked for a promissory acceptance: "Will you do the work?" That question justified Plaintiff in believing that Defendant sought a promissory acceptance.

Defendant made an offer for a bilateral contract, and on August 2 Plaintiff accepted. Defendant's subsequent attempt to revoke was ineffective.

Opinion 2: *PoolCo v. High Oaks Country Club*
The question is whether Plaintiff and Defendant formed a contract.
I find these facts:

(1) On August 1, Defendant High Oaks Country Club contacted Plaintiff PoolCo: "At the end of summer, beginning on or about September 22, we ask that you winterize our three swimming pools. We will take as your acceptance only your completion of the work, at which point we, as usual, will pay your full fee of $90,000, no money to be paid until the work is complete. We ask that you let us know if and when you intend to begin the work."

(2) On August 2, by signed writing, Plaintiff responded: "We'll begin on September 23."

(3) On August 3, Defendant again contacted Plaintiff: "We have had a change of plans. We revoke our offer of August 21. Don't winterize our pools." Defendant's August 1 communication was an offer. The issue is whether (a) Defendant required that Plaintiff accept by complete performance, thus making an offer for a unilateral contract, or (b) Defendant allowed Plaintiff to accept by promise, thus making an offer for a bilateral contract. Plaintiff did not begin performance. Hence, if the offer was for a unilateral contract, Defendant effectively revoked on August 3 and the

> parties formed no contract. If Defendant's offer was for a bilateral contract, Plaintiff's August 2 response accepted it. Defendant's attempt to revoke on August 3 was ineffective.
>
> Citing this Court's very recent decision, *PoolCo v. Silver Oaks*, Plaintiff argues that Defendant's offer allowed for acceptance by promise — that Defendant's reference to "completion of the work" referred only to the time at which it would pay, not to the form of acceptance it demanded.
>
> As in *Silver Oaks*, Defendant offered to pay only when Plaintiff completed the work. But here, Defendant wrote, also: "We do not seek a promissory commitment, but will take as your acceptance only your completion of the work[.]" In *Silver Oaks*, Defendant's offer carried no language of like meaning. This Defendant made an offer for a unilateral contract. Hence, Plaintiff's response of August 2 was no acceptance. And, since Plaintiff did not begin performance, Defendant effectively revoked on August 3, and these parties formed no contract.

QUESTION 7. The judge found that the parties formed a contract in Case 1, but not in Case 2. Which of the following best describes the reason for which she arrived at the different results?

A. In one case, the offeror was willing to make payment before the offeror completed its work; in the other, it was not.

B. In one case, the offeree responded with words of definitive assent; in the other, it did not.

C. In one case, the offeree manifested a willingness to enter a bargain; in the other, it did not.

D. In one case, the offeror specified the allowable mode of acceptance; in the other, it did not.

ANALYSIS. Evidently, before deciding these two cases, the judge read this book (particularly Chapter 9, section D). She knows that if the offeror wishes to allow acceptance only by full performance, he must make that plain, clear, and explicit. In each case, therefore, she tests the offer for the high level of specificity that such a restriction requires. In Case 1, she does not find it. Rather, in Case 1, she decides that by the terms of its offer, Defendant proposed to *make payment* only after performance was complete, but she finds no indication that complete performance was necessary to *acceptance*. In Case 2, she found what she believed to be the necessary specificity: "We will take as your acceptance only your completion of the work[.]" In one case, she found the necessary specificity. In the other, she did not. That's exactly what **D** tells us; **D** is right.

   A makes a false statement. In *both* cases, the offeror proposed to pay only after the offeree completed the work. (In Case 1, however (according to the judge), the offeror did not require that the offeree complete the work in order to *accept* the offer.) **A** is wrong. As for **B**, it's true that in Case 1, PoolCo responds with "Certainly," whereas in Case 2, it responds, "We will begin on September 23." The first response is more definitive than the second, but the judge does not seem to think that matters. In her mind, both are sufficiently definite to constitute an acceptance so long as the relevant offer allows for acceptance by promise. For in *both* cases, she writes, "If . . . Defendant's offer was for a bilateral contract, then Plaintiff's August 2 response accepted it." She does not think that in Case 2, PoolCo's response is too tenuous to be an acceptance. So **B** is wrong.

   C states that one of the defendants made an offer and the other did not. That's plainly false. In both cases, the judge writes, "Defendant's August 1 communication was an offer." For that reason, **C** is wrong. And once again, **D** is right.

QUESTION 8. For both decisions, in the second sentence of the second paragraph, the judge writes, "Since Plaintiff did not begin performance, Defendant effectively revoked on August 3." She wrote that because in either case, if Defendant's offer had looked toward a unilateral contract, then Plaintiff's beginning of performance

   I. would have rendered the offer irrevocable.
   II. would have formed an option contract.
   A. I only
   B. II only
   C. Both I and II
   D. Neither I nor II

ANALYSIS.   Modern common law provides that when an offeror allows for acceptance only by complete performance, the offeree's beginning of performance renders the offer irrevocable. In describing that rule, Restatement (Second) §45(1) invokes the phrase "option contract." Statements I and II have the same meaning, and both are true. **C** is right.

Silver's Picks

1. C
2. D
3. C
4. C
5. A
6. D
7. D
8. C

11

Uniform Commercial Code: Offer and Acceptance

A. The "Firm Offer"

YOU MUST (PLEASE) READ, NOW, APPENDIX SECTIONS A AND D. Then, come see us back here. (We'll wait.)

Having read Appendix sections A and D, you know what the Uniform Commercial Code is and that its Article 2 concerns contracts for the sale of goods. And you know that where Article 2 conflicts with the common law, Article 2 governs. But, once again, that is true only as to contracts for the sale of goods. As for contracts pertaining to anything else, the common law is alive and well (except where it differs from some miscellaneous statute. (Appendix, section D.4.)

Chapter 6, section A, taught you that (a) an offeror may revoke her offer at any time before the offeree accepts, and (b) she may do so even if she proclaims her offer irrevocable. That represents long-standing *common law*. Statutes, however, supersede the common law. When a federal or state legislature enacts a statute that conflicts with the common law, the statute governs. That's a precept of the common law itself. The common law renders itself subordinate to statutes. *Statutes supersede the common law.*

1. UCC §2-205

The Uniform Commercial Code (UCC) is a statute in every state. Its Article 2 governs contracts for the sale of goods, meaning, generally, "movable things." *Some* — not all — but *some* of the provisions within UCC Article 2 apply only to "merchants," so let's define that word as Article 2 uses it: *With respect to the sale of some kind of good, a merchant is one who (a) deals professionally in that kind of good or (b) holds himself out as having special knowledge related to that kind of good.* As to the sale of a piano, a piano dealer is a merchant. So are a piano teacher and piano tuner. As to the sale of a power saw, a hardware retailer is a merchant, as is a power tool manufacturer, a power tool mechanic, and a carpenter. (See, if you wish, UCC §2-104(1); it's wholly incomprehensible.)

UCC §2-205 provides that if a merchant makes an offer in a signed writing and proclaims it irrevocable for some particular period of time, then it *is* irrevocable for that period of time:

> An offer by a merchant to buy or sell goods in a signed writing which by its terms gives assurances that it will be held open is not revocable . . . during the time stated[.]

Let's take that apart.

UCC §2-205 provides that an offer proclaiming itself irrevocable for two days or two weeks or two months is irrevocable for the stated time if and only if it is (a) made by a merchant (b) offering to buy or sell goods,[1] (c) in a signed writing. Suppose Bill, a clothespin manufacturer, uses miniature springs in manufacturing them. By signed writing Bill offers to buy miniature springs from Sam. In his last sentence he writes, "Our offer is irrevocable for ten days." The common law would leave Bill free to revoke any time before Sam accepts. However, because Bill (a) deals professionally in clothespins which, in turn, are made with miniature springs meaning, for this transaction, that he is a merchant, who (b) made an offer to buy goods and (c) made that offer by signed writing — UCC §2-205 applies. Bill proclaimed his offer to be irrevocable for ten days and it *is* irrevocable for ten days.

---

1. As explained in Appendix section D, all provisions of UCC Article 2 apply only to contracts for the sale of goods. They don't apply to contracts for the sale of service, to contracts for the sale of real property, or to contracts for the sale of intangible property such as patents, copyrights, stocks, bonds, and other securities.

QUESTION 1. Sally manufactures valves. Betty manufactures tires. On
June 1, Sally sends Betty this signed writing: "I am prepared to sell you
our standard tire valve #19 at 40 cents per unit, quantity 100 units
delivered to your facility. You have six weeks to consider this offer; during
that period we will not withdraw it." When Sally hears nothing from
Betty, she writes again on June 14: "I now withdraw our offer of June 1."
On June 19, Betty writes back: "I accept your offer of June 1." As of June
20, Betty and Sally

A. are parties to a contract because Sally made an offer and Betty
   accepted it.
B. are parties to a contract because the common law provides that Sally,
   as merchant, is bound by her promise to hold her offer open.
C. are parties to a contract because Betty is a merchant.
D. are parties to a contract because Betty responded to Sally on June 19
   by signed writing.
E. are not parties to a contract because Sally revoked her offer before
   Betty attempted to accept it.

ANALYSIS.   Because tire valves are goods ("movable things"), UCC Article 2
governs the transaction. On June 1, Sally makes an offer, representing that for
six weeks she will not revoke it. She (a) is a merchant (b) who made an offer
to sell goods, and (c) did so in a signed writing. UCC §2-205 holds her to her
word; for six weeks her offer is irrevocable. Two weeks later, her attempt to
revoke is ineffective. On June 19, her offer is, still, alive and well. Betty accepts
and the parties form a contract.

E states that Sally and Betty formed no contract because "Sally revoked
her offer before Betty attempted to accept it." That's exactly what did *not* happen. Sally *attempted* to revoke, but UCC §2-205 denied her that privilege. The
offer survived. When Betty accepted, the parties formed a contract. E is wrong.

We're left with A, B, C, and D, all of which correctly conclude that these
parties formed a contract. But only one of them states the relevant reason.
Many students jump at D, because (1) they see the phrase "signed writing" as a
familiar face and grab hold of it, or (2) they hurriedly misread it to state: "are
parties to a contract because Sally set forth her offer in a signed writing." If
D truly read that way, it would be correct. D refers not to Sally's offer but to
Betty's response. Where UCC §2-205 mentions "signed writing" it refers not to
the offeree's acceptance, but to the *merchant's offer*. If Betty had tried to accept
orally or by unsigned writing, or in any other (reasonable) way, then still the
parties would form a contract. So it's not true that these parties formed a contract *because* Betty responded to Sally by signed writing. D is wrong.

And C? It proclaims that the parties formed a contract "because Betty is
a merchant." Again, that's wrong. UCC §2-205 operates when the offer*or* is a

merchant and puts forth her offer in a signed writing. The offeree need not be a merchant and need not respond by signed writing. If **C** were to tell us that Betty and Sally "are parties to a contract because *Sally* is a merchant," then it would be right. But it tells us no such thing. **C** is wrong.

B is wrong because it speaks not of the UCC but of the common law. It states that Sally and Betty "are parties to a contract because the *common law* provides that Sally, as merchant, is bound by her promise to hold her offer open." The common law provides no such thing. Under the common law, an offeror, merchant or not, is free to revoke her offer even if she promises she won't do that. **B** would be correct if it replaced "common law" with "Uniform Commercial Code," but as truly written, it's wrong.

B, **C**, and **D** teach this lesson: Read the answer choices for what they truly state. Read *every* word. If consciously or unconsciously you overlook or misread a single one, your error will turn 'round and bite you.

A tells the simple truth. Sally made an offer, and on June 19 it remained effective notwithstanding her failed attempt, on June 14, to revoke. Betty accepted and so there was born a contract. **A** is right.

2. *The Three-Month Limitation*

UCC §2-205 allows a merchant to make her offer irrevocable, but puts a ceiling on the period for which she may do so:

> An offer by a merchant to buy or sell goods in a signed writing which by its terms will be held open is not revocable . . . during the time stated . . . *but in no event may such period of irrevocability exceed three months*[.]

Stated otherwise, UCC §2-205 comes to this:

If a merchant's signed, written offer to buy or sell goods proclaims itself irrevocable, then it is irrevocable for the shorter of (a) the period identified in the offer or (b) three months.

If the offeror states that her offer is irrevocable for one week, then it's irrevocable for one week. If she says it's irrevocable for two months, it's irrevocable for two months. If she proclaims that it's irrevocable for three months, it's irrevocable for three months. But, if she tells her offeree that her offer is irrevocable for three months and one day, or four months, or six months, or one year then, in each such case, it's irrevocable for *three months* and no more.

QUESTION 2. Wallace manufactures light bulbs, and Shep makes electric sockets. They exchange these signed writings:

June 1, Shep: I offer you type 47 electric sockets for $1 each, quantity 20,000, to be shipped by us to your facility at your convenience. The offer is firm, open, and irrevocable until midnight on September 15.

> **September 5, Shep (again):** I have heard nothing from you regarding my June 1 offer. I now withdraw it.
> **September 6, Wallace:** You made your offer firm until September15. By that date we'll let you know if we wish to accept.

On September 15 Wallace decides to accept Shep's offer. Does he have the power to do so?

A. Yes, because he reasonably expects that Shep will honor his written statement
B. Yes, because Shep is a merchant who made his offer by signed writing
C. No, because Shep effectively revoked on September 5
D. No, because when Wallace contacted Shep on September 6, he did not attempt to accept

ANALYSIS.   If the case did not concern goods, the common law would govern and the answer would be clear: Shep's offer would expire by revocation on September 5. Because the problem does concern goods, the common law does not govern; the case turns on UCC §2-205.

Shep made an offer on June 1, proclaiming it irrevocable through September 15. The period June 1 to September 15 exceeds three months. Notwithstanding Shep's promise, he was free to revoke after August 31. On September 5, he did so, and the offer terminated. The answer, therefore, is "no"; on September 15, Wallace had no power to accept.

A and **B** say "yes," so they're wrong. Each also supplies its own erroneous reasoning.[2] According to **A** the offer is extant on September 15 because Shep, a merchant, made it by signed writing. But those facts render the offer irrevocable for no longer than three months. At midnight on August 31, it became revocable and on September 5, Shep revoked. **B** invokes the phrase "reasonable expectation," and too many students believe that all things "reasonable" are happy and right. Realize, please, that a statement might refer to reasonableness and still be wrong. Evidently, Wallace did expect that Shep would hold his offer open until September 15 and, quite arguably, his expectation was reasonable; after all, it's not unreasonable to expect a promisor to keep his promise. Reasonable or not, however, Wallace's expectation conflicted with law. Shep was entitled to revoke his offer on September 1, regardless of Wallace's expectations and regardless of how "reasonable" they might be.

D says "no," but its reasoning is wrong, wrong, wrong. True it is that Wallace did not try to accept the offer on September 6 — but so what? The offer expired on September 5. If, on September 6, Wallace had tried to accept he would have been "too late," just as he is on September 15. The answer would be, still, "no." **D** is wrong.

---

2.   All right answers are alike but every wrong answer is wrong in its own way. See Leo Tolstoy, *Anna Karenina*, Chapter 1, first line.

C correctly says "no," that Wallace has no power on September 15 to accept Shep's offer. The reason? On August 31, the offer turned revocable. On September 5, just as C reports, Shep effectively revoked it. C is right.

3. Don't Misunderstand the Three-Month Provision

Let's think again about Shep and ask: Why did Shep's offer not expire at midnight on September 1, three months from the day on which Shep made it? Let's answer: The passage of three months from June 1 does not by itself *revoke* Shep's offer. Rather, it makes Shep's offer revo*cable*. As of September 1, Shep acquired the *right* to revoke. But if he chose not to exercise that right, his offer, like any offer, would live on until it expired for some other reason such as rejection, passage of time, or death or incapacity of the offeror or offeree.

Imagine, for example, that as September 1 comes and goes Shep does not revoke his June 1 offer. Notwithstanding that three months have passed *since* June 1, the offer continues on; Shep has the *power* to revoke, but he does not do so. For so long as (a) Shep does not revoke, and (b) the offer does not expire for some other reason (Chapter 6), Wallace may, if he wishes, accept it. Imagine, now, that three years pass. Shep has not revoked and Wallace has not attempted to accept. Certainly there has passed a reasonable time since Shep first made his offer; at some time during the three year period, the offer certainly expired — because, as with any offer, it expires, on its own, after there passes a reasonable time from the date on which it is made. (Chapter 6, section D).

Suppose now that on July 15 Wallace tells Shep, "I have thought about your June 1 offer; I'm not going to accept it." That's a rejection; the offer dies. Through August 31 it was *irrevocable*, but that did not render it immune to death by some other cause. On July 15, it died by rejection.

QUESTION 3. Bonnie is a professional dancer, and Sarah sells dancers' garb. On October 1, Sarah sends Bonnie this signed writing: "I'm offering you the Xavier tights model 9 in your size for $350. The offer is guaranteed for two weeks." On October 2, Bonnie calls Sarah and rejects the offer. Three days later, on October 5, Bonnie changes her mind, calls Sarah, and says, "I'd like to have the tights after all." Sarah says that she's no longer willing to sell the tights for $350. Bonnie sues Sarah alleging breach of contract. In defending herself, Sarah should direct the court's attention to

A. the common law mirror-image rule.
B. the three-month limitation embodied in UCC §2-205.
C. Bonnie's communication of October 2.
D. the fact that Bonnie's October 5 statement was not made by signed writing.

ANALYSIS. Think first about the story and then about the question. Regarding the story, consider the legal significance of every fact, communication, and event. On that basis, assess the relevant rights and liabilities.

Sarah deals professionally in dancers' garb. In this transaction, she's a merchant. On October 1, by signed writing, she offers to sell goods, promising not to revoke for two weeks. With that we conclude: Under UCC §2-205, Sarah cannot revoke for two weeks — *period* (even though the common law would allow her to do so). On October 2, Bonnie telephones Sarah and rejects the offer; she "kills" it. Between these ladies there then stands no offer at all. Sarah's two-week guarantee evaporates.

So much for the story. Let's consider the question. Among the answer choices we're to find that fact or precept of law that best helps Sarah establish that she and Bonnie formed no contract.

A refers to the common law mirror-image rule. That rule is vitally important in this case as air conditioning is vitally important in Antarctica. We're *not* dealing with an offeror who proposed one exchange and an offeree who assented to another. The mirror image rule is entirely irrelevant. **A** is wrong. **B** suggests that the UCC §2-205 three-month limitation bears relevance. But it doesn't. Sarah's offer was irrevocable for two weeks; it doesn't "hit" the three-month ceiling.

D joins **A** and **B** in the dumper. It tries to "make hay" from the fact that on October 5 Bonnie attempted to accept not by writing, but by spoken word. UCC §2-205 makes writing relevant in only one respect: If an offeror is to make her offer irrevocable for some period, *she* must do so by signed writing. So long as the offer endures (as we learned in Chapter 9, sections A and B), the offeree may accept in any manner that the offeror prescribes or, if she prescribes none, then in any that is reasonable. True it is that on October 5, Bonnie attempted to accept by spoken word only. But that's irrelevant. If on that date the offer had been extant, Bonnie's spoken words would have accepted it.

Now comes **C**, telling us that Sarah should defend herself by pointing to Bonnie's telephone communication of October 2, in which Bonnie rejected the offer. That's the key to Sarah's defense. By rejection, the offer died on October 2. On October 5, Bonnie's attempt to accept was ineffective. **C** is right.

4. *What If the Merchant Doesn't Prescribe a Time Period for Irrevocability?*

In showing you UCC §2-205, we hid some of its "stuff." Let's reveal it.

> An offer by a merchant to buy or sell goods in a signed writing which by its terms gives assurances that it will be held open is not revocable ... during the time stated *or if no time is stated, [it is irrevocable] for a reasonable time,* but in no event may such period of irrevocability exceed three months[.]

With the italicized words now added, UCC §2-205 comes to mean this:

(1) *If by signed writing a merchant offers to buy or sell goods, declaring the offer irrevocable for a specific period, then it is irrevocable for that period, with a ceiling, however, of three months, and (2) if such a merchant declares his offer irrevocable but specifies no time period for which it will remain so, then, by implication of law, he declares his offer irrevocable for a reasonable time, with that same ceiling, however, of three months.*

Suppose that by signed writing a merchant makes an offer to buy or sell goods, concluding it with this sentence: "By the way, I won't revoke this offer." Because the merchant specified no period of time for which her offer would remain irrevocable, the law reads her last sentence thus: "By the way, *for a reasonable time,* I won't revoke this offer, but in no case is it irrevocable for more than three months."[3]

QUESTION 4. Biff is a professional juggler. Shelley sells carnival equipment. The parties exchange these signed writings:

(1) **April 10, Shelley:** I have twelve surplus juggling pins: height — 9 inches; color — blue/yellow striped; bottom circumference — 3 inches. I'm ready to sell them to you for $3 each. Think it over; take your time. Don't worry; I won't withdraw the offer.

(2) **April 11, Biff:** Yes, I'll think it over.

(3) **May 15, Shelley:** Regarding our communications of April, I no longer have the pins in stock. The offer is withdrawn.

(4) **Biff:** But just before you contacted me — just now — I had decided to accept. I do accept.

(5) **Shelley:** Sorry. We no longer have the pins.

(6) **Biff:** I've just told you that I accept your original offer. You're obliged to perform.

(7) **Shelley:** Forget it. We can't.

Which of the following *additional* facts, if proven, would most strengthen Shelley's position that she is not in breach of contract?

A. Shelley's statement 5 on May 15 set forth these additional words: "but for the same price, we have other juggling pins of the same size, different in color."

B. Biff's first statement of May 15 set forth these additional words: "but only on the condition that you reduce the price to $2 per unit; otherwise, I don't want them."

C. On May 15, Biff was not truthful in stating that he had decided to accept just before Shelley contacted him.

D. On April 12, Shelley, by signed writing, sent Biff this message: "That's fine, but please realize that the offer expires in one week."

---

3. As to what constitutes a "reasonable time," see Chapter 3, section D.

ANALYSIS.   Shelley is a merchant. By signed writing, she makes an offer and declares it irrevocable without naming a length of *time* for which it is irrevocable. She loses the power to revoke for the shorter of (a) a reasonable time (whatever, under the circumstances, that might be), or (b) three months (even if that is less than what would otherwise be a reasonable time). Yet, this merchant's "firm offer" might terminate sooner by rejection. Each answer choice presents a fact and we're to find the one that, if added to the story, best supports Shelley's claim that she did not breach a contract.

By making the statement shown in **A** on May 15, Shelley would make a new offer. But that would not free her of the one she made on April 10. There would be "on the table," two offers from Shelley to Biff: the one of April 10 and the new one of May 15. So **A** is wrong. Assessing **C**, we add to the story this fact: On May 15, Biff was not truthful in stating that he had decided to accept just before Shelley contacted him. That fact would matter not at all. Biff said, "I do accept it." Unless the offer had expired before he said that, he would have accepted the offer and formed a contract.

D is tempting but wrong. Once an offeror sets a time period for which his offer will be irrevocable, he can't later shorten it. If we add to the story that on April 12, Shelly told Biff, "the offer expires in one week," we'll be adding an irrelevancy. Such a statement would be insignificant; Shelley's offer would remain irrevocable for (a) a reasonable time (whatever exactly that is under these circumstances), or (b) three months — whichever is shorter. **B**'s amendment to Biff's statement 4 creates not an acceptance but a counteroffer and rejection. If in statement 4, Biff had said all of *that*, he'd have rejected Shelley's offer and thus put it to an end. Biff's later statement purporting to accept would come too late. Consequently, the added fact described at **B** would support Shelley's contention that she committed no breach of contract. **B** is right.

B.   The Mirror-Image Rule, UCC §2-207(1), and "Battle of the Forms"

In commerce, buyers often make offers on their own preprinted forms entitled something like "purchase order." Sellers often accept (or attempt to accept) on their own preprinted forms entitled something like "sales acknowledgment" or "sales confirmation." Imagine that BuyCo constructs large lawns and buys seed from various suppliers. BuyCo makes offers to buy seed on its own preprinted "purchase order" form. The form's front side recites BuyCo's address and contact information, providing blank spaces on which BuyCo personnel write their orders. The reverse side embodies lots of text in teensy type.

SeedCo sells lawn seed. It generally *accepts* (or attempts to accept) offers to buy on its own preprinted "sales acknowledgment and confirmation" form. The form's front side recites SeedCo's address and contact information. It shows blank spaces on which SeedCo personnel "acknowledge" and "confirm" sales (accept offers) and sign their names. The reverse side, too, embodies lots of text in teensy type.

On one occasion, SeedCo and BuyCo conduct this little interaction:

BuyCo to SeedCo (on the front side of its "Purchase Order" form, signed):

PURCHASE ORDER

Please send to our facility: 18 tons of your grass seed #20. Will pay $200/ton.

NOTICE: THIS PURCHASE ORDER IS SUBJECT TO ALL TERMS ON THE REVERSE SIDE OF THIS FORM.

SeedCo to BuyCo (on the front side of its "Sales Acknowledgment & Confirmation" form, signed):

SALES ACKNOWLEDGMENT and CONFIRMATION

Acknowledged and Confirmed: Will send to BuyCo at its facility 18 tons of our grass seed #20 @ $200/ton.
NOTICE: THIS SALES ACKNOWLEDGMENT IS SUBJECT TO ALL TERMS ON THE REVERSE SIDE OF THIS FORM.

Were it not for the "NOTICE . . . REVERSE SIDE" provisions on each form, BuyCo's form would make an offer and SeedCo's an acceptance. Neatly and nicely, the parties would form a contract for the sale of grass seed. But now, look at the two forms' reverse sides and see how they muck up the works.

BuyCo's Purchase Order, Reverse Side
This Purchase Order is made under these terms: (1) All warranties apply. (2) After BuyCo takes possession of the goods it will have 90 days to pay the agreed price. If BuyCo fails to pay within that period Seller may demand interest at the rate of 4% per annum, but (3) will not be entitled to any interest or recovery beyond that amount, notwithstanding that the law might otherwise entitle Seller to additional damages.

SeedCo's Sales Acknowledgment and Confirmation, Reverse Side
Acknowledgment, Confirmation and acceptance are made under these terms: (1) After Buyer takes possession of the goods, it will have 15 days to pay the agreed purchase price. (2) If Buyer shall fail to pay within that period SeedCo may demand interest at the rate of 12% per annum, and will be entitled, further, to all additional damages for which the law otherwise provides. (3) Further, SeedCo expressly disclaims all warranties that the law might otherwise imply concerning the goods to be sold, including but not

limited to any and all warranties of merchantability, warranties of fitness for a particular purpose, wherefore the goods are sold as is and with all faults.[4]

What Would the *Common Law* Make of BuyCo's "Purchase Order" and SeedCo's "Sales Acknowledgment and Confirmation"?

SeedCo's purported acceptance (the "acknowledgment and confirmation" form) fails to mirror BuyCo's offer (the "purchase order") as to three matters:

1. BuyCo's form gives BuyCo 90 days to pay, but SeedCo's form gives BuyCo 15 days to pay.
2. BuyCo's form provides that in the case of breach BuyCo should pay 4 percent interest and be liable for no additional damages, but SeedCo's form requires that BuyCo pay 12 percent interest in addition to all other damages provided by law.
3. SeedCo's form excludes warranties, BuyCo's form does not.

BuyCo's response does not "mirror" SeedCo's offer. Under the common law mirror-image rule,[5] BuyCo makes an offer and SeedCo responds with a counteroffer that acts, also, as a rejection.[6] The parties fail to form a contract.

Yet, businesses operate this way on a daily basis — attempting to make contracts using preprinted forms whose terms conflict. This shoddy practice creates a problem colloquially called "battle of the forms." By rejecting, in part, the mirror-image rule, UCC §2-207 purports to solve it (and in doing so makes shoddy *law*). UCC §2-207 (comment) states:

> This section is intended to deal with . . . the exchange of printed purchase order and acceptance (sometimes called ["confirmation" or] "acknowledgment") forms. Because the forms are oriented to the thinking of the respective drafting parties, the terms contained in them often do not correspond. Often the seller's form contains terms different from or additional to those set forth in the buyer's form.

1. UCC §2-207(1) as Presently Operative in All States

UCC §2-207, Subsection (1), Lesson 1: The "Expression of Acceptance." UCC §2-207(1) invents a legal communication it calls "expression of acceptance" (to which it gives not a word of definition). That phrase refers to a communication that *on its face* — superficially — "looks like," "sounds like,"

---

4. We teach you about warranties in Chapter 23.
5. Chapter 7, section B.
6. Chapter 7, section A.

or "smells like" assent. SeedCo's response to BuyCo's offer *seems*, on its face, to say, "Yes, we'll send you the seeds you've requested at the price you've named." Because of its reverse side, the form is not a true, common law acceptance. Yet it is, under UCC §2-207 "an *expression* of acceptance."

UCC §2-207, Subsection(1), Lesson 2: An Expression of Acceptance Is an Acceptance Even If It Fails to Mirror the Offer. UCC §2-207(1) provides:

> A[n] expression of acceptance . . . operates as an acceptance even though it states terms additional to or different from those offered. . . .

Those statutory words mean that when Party 1 offers to buy or sell goods and Party 2 responds with a message that, on its face, *seems* to say "yes," Party 2 accepts Party 1's offer, regardless of any different or additional terms that Party 2 might put forth somewhere in the same message.

In the seed case, BuyCo made an offer to buy, and SeedCo — *on the face of things* — seems to express its acceptance; Seedco makes an "expression of acceptance." SeedCo may not know it, but it accepted BuyCo's offer, complete with all terms on the front and back sides of *BuyCo's* form. Hence, under UCC §2-207, BuyCo and SeedCo form a contract on *BuyCo's* terms. The terms that SeedCo wrote on the reverse side of its form are *not* part of the contract. Hence, the contract requires SeedCo to supply BuyCo with 18 tons of grass seed at $200/ton. BuyCo has 90 days in which to pay and late payments will incur interest at 4 percent. All warranties apply; none is excluded.

SeedCo Is Bound by Terms to Which It Never Really Agreed?

By law, SeedCo *did* agree to all of BuyCo's terms. Under UCC §2-207, it issued an "expression of acceptance." By law, it accepted BuyCo's offer — *as BuyCo made it*. With UCC §2-207 in place, all persons who receive offers to buy or sell goods ought to know: If, on the surface of things, they say "yes," then they accept the offer — all of it — including the offeror's "fine print." "Fine print" on the offeree's form doesn't count; it's not part of the contract.

2. *What UCC §2-207(1) Does Not Provide*

See and DO NOT FORGET that UCC §2-207(1) nowhere presents the word "merchant." It operates when both parties are merchants, when neither is a merchant, or when one is a merchant and the other not.[7] Notice, too, that UCC §2-207(1) features no form of the word "write" or "sign." It applies when both offer and acceptance are written and signed, when both are written and unsigned, when neither is written or signed, and when one is written (signed or unsigned) and the other not. Put otherwise, UCC §2-207(1) "doesn't care"

---

7. Section C below discusses an exception in which the parties' status as merchants does bear relevance, as provided in UCC §2-207(2).

whether an offer or an expression of acceptance is unwritten, written, signed, or unsigned.[8]

QUESTION 5. Jared operates a retail hardware store. By telephone, Sarah, a plumber, contacts him:

> **Communication 1 (telephone), Sarah:** Do you have in stock a full set of metric combination wrenches?
>
> **Communication 2 (telephone), Jared:** Yes, we do. Give me your fax number or address, and I'll send you a written description and order form.
>
> **Communication 3 (telephone), Sarah:** Thanks very much. Send it by email, please, to Splum@sp.com.
>
> **Communication 4 (email), Jared:** [description of the wrenches, and then] Full set $450 without ratchet kit. If you want the set, we'll assemble it for you right away. You may pick it up at our store any time tomorrow.
>
> **Communication 5 (email), Sarah:** I'll take it, but please include ratchet kit at your ordinary price.

Jared then assembles the wrenches and readies them for Sarah.

> **Communication 6 (email), Jared:** We have assembled the wrenches for you, but we do not have any ratchet kits. Please come and take the wrenches. For payment we accept cash, credit card, or debit card.
>
> **Communication 7 (email), Sarah:** Without the ratchet kit I have no interest in the wrenches. Thanks very much, but I won't be making the purchase.
>
> **Communication 8 (email), Jared:** You have a contractual obligation to purchase the wrenches, and you have no right to the ratchet kit.

Which of the following facts best supports Jared's position?

A. Sarah initiated the contact with Jared; Jared did not initiate contact with Sarah.
B. In reliance on Sarah's statements, Jared assembled the wrenches.
C. In this circumstance, both Sarah and Jared are merchants.
D. Wrenches are goods.

---

8. Section E below discusses one situation, involving a "confirmatory memorandum," in which the matter of writing *is* significant.

ANALYSIS. Examine the parties' conversation and characterize their statements.

Communication 1 is a "mere" invitation to deal.
Communications 2 and **3** are two more invitations to deal.
Communication 4 is Jared's offer to sell the item.
In **Communication 5**, Sarah writes, first, "I'll take it." With that single sentence, she issues an "expression of acceptance," which means that *she accepts Jared's offer, exactly as Jared made it.* She has formed with Jared a contract for the purchase and sale of a good.

And What About Her Instruction That the Transaction Include Another Item — The Ratchet Kit? Sarah added her request for the ratchet kit *after* she made her "expression of acceptance": "I'll take it." The request, therefore, is akin to the fine print on the back of a purchase or sales forms. It doesn't count. It's not a part of her contract. Again, when Party X offers to buy or sell goods and Party Y responds with what UCC §2-207 calls an "expression of acceptance," Y accepts X's offer *as X makes it.* Whatever else Y might write or say does not become part of the contract. The same, of course, applies if Y offers to buy goods and X responds with an "expression of acceptance." Whatever else X might write or say does not become part of the contract.

Now Maybe You Ask, What About the Mirror-Image Rule Discussed in Chapter 7? And we answer: The mirror-image rule belongs to the common law. Where an offer concerns anything other than the sale of goods, it's alive and well. UCC Article 2 addresses contracts for the purchase and sale of goods. It's a statute. It overrides the common law (Appendix, section A.4, last paragraph). Where an offer concerns the sale of goods, the mirror-image rule has lost its standing. UCC §2-207 supplants it.

Jared is right because (1) the transaction concerns the sale of goods, (2) Jared made an offer, and (3) Sarah issued an "expression of acceptance" as that phrase operates in UCC §2-207. Those three facts support Jared's position; they cause the parties to form a contract. Read the answer choices and determine which reflects one or more of those same three pivotal facts.

A is wrong. Whether two parties form a contract does not depend, ever, on which of them first contacted the other. **B** is just as bad. These parties form a contract with Communication 4, an offer, and Communication 5, an (expression of) acceptance. Nothing that happens afterward alters that reality. After receiving Communication 5, Jared assembled the wrenches. If he had not done so, these two would have a contract just the same.

The statement in **C** is very true and consummately irrelevant. Yes, both these parties are merchants as Article 2 defines that word (section A.1 above and Appendix, section D.4). Sarah is a plumber. Hence, by her occupation she holds herself out as having knowledge or skill peculiar to wrenches. Jared operates a hardware store; in this transaction he too is a merchant. That these two folks are merchants, however, has not a whit to do with the fact that they formed a contract. UCC §2-207(1) applies to any buyer and any seller whether they be merchants or not (Appendix, section D.4).

D correctly reports that wrenches are goods. *That's* why UCC Article 2 applies, and that's why the mirror-image rule does not. *That's* why Sarah's response "operates as an acceptance" even though it states terms "additional to or different from those offered." *That's* why the parties form a contract, and that's why **D** is right.

3. *An Offeree Can Save Herself from UCC §2-207*

UCC §2-207 puts an offeree at risk whether she's a buyer or seller. If she issues an expression of acceptance, she's "stuck" with the offeror's terms. She can avoid that fate if she expressly states that her acceptance is conditional on the offeror's assent to her new and different terms. Look again at UCC §2-207(1), to which we now add and italicize some text earlier concealed:

> A[n] expression of acceptance . . . operates as an acceptance even though it states terms additional to or different from those offered . . . *unless acceptance is expressly made conditional on assent to the additional or different terms.*

"Unless" means "but not if." Let's redraft UCC §2-207(1) so you'll better understand it. The provision really means:

> *(1) When one party offers to buy or sell goods, and the offeree responds with an expression of acceptance, that expression of acceptance operates as an acceptance even though it does not mirror the offer, except that (2) it does not operate as an acceptance if the offeree expressly states that her expression of acceptance is conditional on the offeror's assent to the new or different terms that she, the offeree, in her expression of acceptance, sets forth; in that case the offeree's expression of acceptance is a counter-offer and, ordinarily, a rejection.*

What?

Suppose Simcha makes Bretain this offer: "I offer to sell you 200 widgets for $200, delivered to you next Monday morning." Bretain responds, "I accept, but please deliver on Tuesday, not Monday." He then adds a footnote plainly visible, easy to read: "My acceptance is conditioned on your agreement to all of the terms I have here set forth." On its face, the response reads "yes," meaning that Bretain issued an expression of acceptance. The first clause of UCC §2-207 (1) would make it an acceptance were it not for the *second* — the one that begins with "unless" — the one in our redrafting that begins "except that (2) . . ." Bretain's footnote (plainly visible, easy to read) puts his expression of acceptance within the second clause. Consequently, *this* expression of acceptance does not operate *as* an acceptance.

UCC §2-207(1) tells us that Bretain's response is not an acceptance, but it doesn't tell us what it *is*. That means we must remember: Where statutes are silent, the common law governs. So, in order to characterize Bretain's response, we look to the common law (Appendix, section D.5).[9] The common law generally provides that a non-mirror-image acceptance is a counteroffer and rejection. Bretain's response is just that — a counteroffer and rejection.

QUESTION 6. SellCo installs and repairs computer systems. BellCo creates computer software. On July 18, the parties begin to exchange signed writings:

July 18, BellCo:

PURCHASE ORDER

We understand that you wish to sell an IXM system, with all current software. We wish to purchase it and will pay $40,000, including installation. Our offer stands firm; it will not be withdrawn for 30 days.

July 19, SellCo: Thank you. Please expect our response within three days.
July 20, BellCo: We have decided not to purchase the system.
July 21, SellCo:

SALES CONFIRMATION

Agreed: We will deliver one IXM system to your offices. Installation requires an additional $5,000 charge.

THIS CONFIRMATION IS WHOLLY AND FULLY CONDITIONED ON BUYER'S ASSENT TO EACH AND EVERY ONE OF ITS TERMS.

July 22, BellCo (by telephone): Thank you for your "sales acknowledgment," but as we advised you on July 20, we no longer wish to buy the system.
July 23, SellCo (by signed fax): We accept your original proposal exactly as made.
July 24, BellCo (by signed fax): As we have twice advised you, we no longer wish to purchase the system.

---

9. If you have not yet read that portion of the Appendix, please do so now!

If SellCo brings an action against BellCo for breach of contract, SellCo will

A. prevail, because on July 23, it manifested assent to all of BellCo's proposed terms.
B. prevail, because BellCo's initial offer was irrevocable for 30 days.
C. not prevail, because on July 20, BellCo effectively revoked its offer.
D. not prevail, because on July 21, SellCo rejected BellCo's offer.

ANALYSIS.   UCC §2-207(1) provides that if a merchant, by signed writing, offers to buy or sell goods and declares his offer firm/irrevocable for some particular time period, then the offer is irrevocable for the time stated (but for no longer than three months). Further, if any person (merchant or not) responds to an offer to buy or sell goods with an expression of acceptance, then he accepts the offer as made *unless he expressly provides that his assent is conditional on the offeror's assent to each and every term set forth in the expression of acceptance.* In that case, says §2-207(1), the offeree's expression of acceptance does not operate as an acceptance. Although §2-207(1) tells us what the offeree's response is not, it doesn't tell us what it is. Where the UCC is silent, the common law governs. And the common law, we know, tells us that the response is a counter-offer and, ordinarily, a rejection.

BellCo is a merchant. By signed writing, it offered to buy SellCo's computer system, stating that its offer was firm for 30 days. For that period, therefore, the offer was irrevocable and BellCo had no power to revoke it. Its July 20 attempt to do so was ineffective, and the offer remained open. On July 21, however, SellCo responded with a non-mirror-image expression of acceptance. That response *would* operate as an acceptance of BellCo's offer were it not for the fact that SellCo expressly provided that *its* assent was conditional on *BellCo's* assent to all of its terms. Consequently, SellCo's response did not operate as an acceptance. It was a counteroffer and rejection, meaning that on July 21, SellCo rendered BellCo's offer inoperative and thus terminated its own power to accept. When, on July 23, SellCo attempted to accept the offer unconditionally, it accomplished nothing.

According to **A** and **B**, SellCo prevails. Both are wrong. As for a reason, **A** reports that SellCo assented fully to BellCo's offer on July 23. SellCo did that, but it had rejected the offer two days earlier on July 21. Its mirror-image assent on July 23 came too late. **B** correctly tells us that BellCo's offer was irrevocable for 30 days. Nonetheless, it was susceptible to *rejection*, and on July 21, SellCo did reject it. **C** correctly states that SellCo will not prevail, but its reasoning is wrong. BellCo's offer was irrevocable for 30 days from July 18. On July 20, its attempt to revoke was without effect.

D, alas, speaketh truth. It says that SellCo will not prevail because, on July 21, it rejected BellCo's offer. That's right; it did, and by doing so, it put the offer to death. On July 23, its attempt to accept was ineffective. **D** is right.

QUESTION 7. (This question is similar but not identical to the preceding question.) WellCo raises funds on behalf of charitable organizations. In its offices, it uses computers. It owns an old IXM computer system that it wishes to sell. BestCo, a computer hardware consulting company, wishes to buy it, and the parties communicate:

July 18, BestCo by signed writing:

PURCHASE ORDER

We understand that you wish to sell an IXM system, with all current software. We wish to purchase it and will pay $40,000, including installation. Our offer stands firm; it will not be withdrawn for 30 days.

July 19, WellCo: Thank you. Please expect our response within three days.

July 20, BestCo: We have decided not to purchase the system.

July 21, WellCo:

SALES CONFIRMATION

Agreed: We will deliver one IXM system to your offices. Installation requires an additional $5,000 charge.

July 22, BestCo (by telephone): Thank you for your "sales acknowledgment," but as we advised you on July 20, we no longer wish to buy the system.

July 23, SellCo (by signed fax): We accept your original proposal exactly as made.

July 24, BestCo (by signed fax): As we have twice advised you, we no longer wish to purchase the system.

If WellCo brings an action against BestCo for breach of contract, WellCo will

A. prevail, because it responded to BestCo's offer with an expression of acceptance.

B. prevail, because WellCo assented to BestCo's terms within three days of July 18, as it stated it would.

C. not prevail, because WellCo's July 21 response did not mirror BestCo's offer.

D. not prevail, because on July 20, BestCo caused the offer to terminate.

ANALYSIS.   WellCo is not a merchant, but that's irrelevant. In response to BestCo's offer, it issued an expression of acceptance under UCC §2-207(1) and did not condition it on BestCo's assent to all of its terms. WellCo's expression of acceptance operates *as* an acceptance — of BestCo's offer — all of it, exactly as made by BestCo. The parties formed a contract on BestCo's terms.

C and D are wrong because they state that SellCo will not prevail. As for C, it's true that SellCo's July 21 response did not mirror BestCo's offer, but under UCC §2-207, that's irrelevant. WellCo issued an expression of acceptance, and so accepted BestCo's offer *as BestCo made it.* D is wrong too. BestCo is a merchant; its offer was irrevocable for 30 days from July 18. B correctly states that WellCo will prevail. That it assented within three days of July 18, however, is irrelevant. If WellCo had issued its expression of acceptance on July 19, July 20, or at any time before BestCo's offer expired, the parties would form a contract and WellCo would prevail.

A correctly reports that WellCo will prevail, and its reasoning is right: WellCo responded to the offer with an expression of acceptance. The response operated *as* an acceptance, and the parties formed a contract. That's why A is right.

C.   What the Law Does with the Offeree's New or Different Terms: UCC §2-207(2)

The common law provides, generally, that if two parties form a (bilateral) contract then, by a new offer and acceptance, they may agree to modify it. Suppose, for example, that Gary and Jacqueline form a contract in which Gary promises to pay Jacqueline $30 for proofreading his manuscript by August 1. On July 20, Jacqueline makes an offer to alter their contract: "I'll proofread the text *and* retype it at no charge if you'll extend my deadline to October 1." If Gary accepts, the contract is modified; Jacqueline must proofread *and type.* Her deadline is *October 1.*

There is much more to the matter of modified contracts. As is fully elaborated in Chapter 14, section B, the common law requires that a modification exact consideration from both parties. UCC Article 2, however, does not.

UCC §2-207, Subsection (2), Lesson 1: The Offeree's Additional Terms Are an Offer to Modify the Contract.   Now we know: When, having received an offer for the purchase or sale of goods, an offeree responds with an "expression of acceptance," he accepts the offer, as made. If his response includes terms that don't conform to the offer, they don't belong to the contract. That raises this question: *What is the significance of those terms?* UCC §2-207 subsection 2 (clumsily and ineptly drafted) provides that they are "proposals for addition to the contract." Taken together, subsections 1 and 2 mean this: *If an* *offeree receives an offer for the purchase or sale of goods, and she responds with a non-mirror expression of acceptance, there simultaneously occur these two events: (1) the offeree accepts the offer as made, so that offeror and offeree form a contract on the offeror's terms, and (2) the offeree offers to modify that contract — the one just formed — according to such of her terms as do not mirror the offer.*

Consider these signed writings:

(1) **Ethel:** I am prepared to sell you 20,000 widgets for $20,000, delivered to your warehouse, packed in cardboard boxes, stapled shut. Do you wish to purchase?

(2) **Rohan:** Yes, definitely, and after you apply the staples you will, please, seal the boxes with one-quarter-inch tape.

Ethel makes an offer to sell goods, and Rohan issues a non-mirror-image expression of acceptance. When he does that, there simultaneously occur these two events: (1) Rohan accepts Ethel's offer as made; the parties form a contract on Ethel's terms, and (2) Rohan makes an offer to modify that very same contract — the one just formed. He proposes that Ethel, after stapling the boxes, should seal them with one-quarter-inch tape.

It is for Ethel to accept or not Rohan's offer to modify the contract in that way. If she accepts, then the terms of the contract undergo change: After stapling the boxes, Ethel must seal them with one-quarter-inch tape. If she does not accept, the contract remains as initially formed: Ethel is to shut the boxes with staples; the one-quarter-inch tape has no place in the contract.

Ethel may accept the proposal by announcing her assent to Rohan in any reasonable way (Chapter 9, section B). (Under some circumstances, she accepts by silence, as discussed in section D, below.)

QUESTIONS 8 & 9. On May 1, Powex contacts Genex by signed writing: "After much research, we are prepared to purchase your Genex Model T-12 generator for $2 million. Please deliver all component pieces and parts to our main office. On delivery, we will make payment by certified check." In response, Genex sends Powex a signed Sales Confirmation form: "Sold — Genex Model T-12 generator for $2 million, components to be delivered to buyer's facility. Sale is subject to terms printed on the reverse side."

On the reverse side, in small print, there appears this text: "For all sales of equipment, the parties agree that (1) the buyer will allow only Genex to assemble the equipment and will permit no other party to do so; (2) Genex will assemble the equipment and, for that service, the buyer will pay an additional 10% of the purchase price noted on the front side hereof."

QUESTION 8. If Powex makes no response to Genex's Sales Confirmation, the parties

A. have no contract, because Genex's sales confirmation amounts to a counteroffer and rejection.
B. have no contract, because Powex's offer does not include any term that concerns assembly of the generator.
C. have a contract for purchase of the generator, but no contract for its assembly.
D. have a contract for purchase of the generator and for its assembly.

QUESTION 9. Assume now that Powex responds to Genex's Sales Confirmation with this signed writing: "Very well; we are agreed." The parties

A. have no contract, because Genex's sales confirmation form amounts to a counteroffer and rejection.
B. have no contract, because Powex did not assent to Genex's proposal as to assembly of the generator.
C. have a contract for sale of the generator, but no contract for its assembly.
D. have a contract for sale of the generator and for its assembly.

ANALYSIS. Powex offers to buy a generator in component pieces with no provision as to how or by whom the components will be assembled. Genex issues an "expression of acceptance" that adds a term of its own: Genex is to assemble the components, and in exchange, Powex is to pay an additional $200,000 (10% of the $2 million purchase price). Simultaneously, therefore, Genex (1) accepts Powex's offer as made, thus forming a contract on Powex's terms, and (2) offers to modify that very same contract by adding the assembly term. It is then for Powex to accept or not Genex's offer to modify the contract in that way.

As for Question 8. We are to assume that Powex makes no response to Genex's sales confirmation form. Consequently, the parties form a contract according to Powex's offer, and the assembly term does not become a part of it.

A and B state that the parties formed no contract, which means both choices are wrong. A characterizes Genex's sales confirmation as a counteroffer and rejection. If the common law governed, that would be correct. Under UCC §2-207(1), however, the sales confirmation is an "expression of acceptance." Hence, it acts (a) as an acceptance and, simultaneously, (b) as a proposal to modify the contract thus formed at that same moment. B implies that the parties would form a contract only if Powex were to accept Genex's proposal to modify the contract. That's false. With Genex's "expression of acceptance," the parties form a contract on Powex's terms.

D states that the parties' contract includes Genex's additional term. That's false because Powex did not accept it. **C** correctly reports that the parties formed a contract for the sale of the generator, but not for its assembly. **C** is right.

As for Question 9.   We are to assume that Powex received Genex's sales confirmation and responded, "Very well, we are agreed." With that response, Powex accepted Genex's offer to modify the contract, and the assembly term became part of it. **D** is right.

D.   Offeror's *Silence* as Acceptance of Offeree's Additional Terms

Suppose Offeror and Offeree are in the widget business. Offeror makes Offeree this offer: "Will sell to you 400 widgets for $400, delivered to you on May 1 between noon and 1 P.M." Offeree responds: "Yes, we'll buy. When you deliver the widgets you will also supply an invoice." To that proposal Offeror makes no response.

Let's assess the facts for their legal significance.

Fact: Offeror makes an offer to sell goods. Offeree responds with an expression of acceptance ("Yes, we'll buy"). *Legal consequence*: The parties form a contract on Offeror's terms.

Fact: Offeree's response includes a term not set forth in the offer. *Legal consequences*: (1) Offeree proposes to modify the parties' contract by adding that term to it, and (2) if Offeror accepts Offeree's proposal to modify the contract, then that term becomes part of it.

1.   Sometimes the Offeror Accepts the Offeree's Proposal by Remaining Silent

UCC §2-207(2) provides, in substance: *If an offeree responds to an offer with an expression of acceptance that fails to mirror the offer, meaning that (1) he accepts the offeror's proposal as made, and (2) he proposes to modify the contract thus formed, — then — the offeror's silence constitutes an acceptance of the offeree's proposal to modify the contract if, as rarely is so, the answers are (1) "yes," (2) "no," and (3) "no," to these three questions:*

(1) Are both parties merchants?
(2) In his offer, did Offeror announce that he would reject any additional terms put forth by the Offeree?
(3) Is Offeree's additional term material to the bargain — does it alter, in a significant way, either party's contractual burden or benefit?

Again, if (and only if) the answers are (1) "yes," (2) "no," and (3) "no," the offeror's silence amounts to his acceptance of the offeree's proposal to modify the contract.

In our case, the answers *are* (1) "Yes": Both Offeror and Offeree are merchants, (2) "No": Offeror did not, in his offer, state that he would reject any new terms proposed by the Offeree, and (3) "No": The proposed modification does not significantly alter either party's burden or benefit. By remaining silent, Offeror accepts Offeree's proposal to modify the contract; when he delivers the widgets he must, also, supply an invoice. If Offeror wants not to accept the proposal, he must not remain silent; within a reasonable time he must "speak up" and object to it.

UCC §2-207(2) nowhere invokes the *word* "silence" or the phrase "silence as acceptance." Neither does it, in so many words, refer to the three questions and answers we've described. Rather, it provides:

> The [offeree's] additional terms are to be construed as proposals for addition to the contract. Between merchants such terms become part of the contract unless:[10]
>> (a) the offer expressly limits acceptance to the terms of the offer;
>> (b) they materially alter it; or
>> (c) notification of objection . . . is given within a reasonable time[.]

The words "between merchants" create our question 1: "*Are both parties merchants?*" Provision (a) creates our question 2: "*Did Offeror announce in his offer that he would reject any additional terms put forth by the offeree?*" Provision (b) creates our question 3: "Is Offeree's additional term material to the bargain — does it alter, in a significant way, either party's contractual burden or benefit?" If the answers are (1) "yes," (2) "no," and (3) "no," the words "such terms become part of the contract" together with provision (c) create the result that the offeree's silence constitutes his acceptance.

QUESTIONS 10-13. WaxCo is in the business of selling wax to candle manufacturers. CandleCo manufactures candles. On August 10, with a signed, preprinted "Available for Purchase" form, completing various of its blank spaces in handwriting, WaxCo makes CandleCo this offer: "Will ship to you @$200 per ton, *15* tons of *WaxCo Z-25* Candle Wax, color *White.* Total price: *$3,000.* Delivery within *10* days of your acceptance. Will unload and stack boxes on your receiving platform."

---

10. Because the word "unless" appears just before the colon, the burden of proving that none of the three conditions (a), (b), or (c) applies rests with the party (ordinarily the offeror) who asserts that the offeree's additional terms are not part of the contract. The other party bears the burden of proving that both parties are merchants. As to the relationship between the word "unless" and burden of proof, see Chapter 21, section A.

On August 11, by signed, preprinted "Purchase Order" form, completing various of its blank spaces in handwriting, CandleCo responds by signed writing.

QUESTION 10. For this question, assume that on August 11, CandleCo responds thus: "As per your offer of *August 10*, please ship. Additional Comment(s): *You will stack boxes in piles of three.*" Making no response to CandleCo, WaxCo delivers the wax and stacks the boxes in piles of four (not three). CandleCo sues WaxCo alleging that WaxCo was contractually obliged to stack the boxes in piles of *three*. WaxCo maintains that the parties' contract included no such requirement. Which of the following facts, if proven, best supports WaxCo?

A. In the wax industry, sellers ordinarily deliver boxes and stack them in piles of four.
B. Many times in the past, WaxCo has delivered wax to CandleCo, stacking the boxes in piles of four.
C. The difference between piles of three and piles of four materially alters WaxCo's obligation.
D. WaxCo and CandleCo have never before done business with each other.

ANALYSIS. Under UCC §2-207(1) and (2), CandleCo's expression of acceptance produces, simultaneously, these two legal consequences: (1) the parties form a contract on WaxCo's terms, and (2) CandleCo proposes to modify the contract so that WaxCo will stack the boxes in piles of three. WaxCo's *silence* accepts CandleCo's proposal if (and only if) to the three questions earlier described the answers are, respectively, (1) "yes," (2) "no," and (3) "no." A given fact will support WaxCo if, for any of the three questions, it fails to provide the answer just mentioned.

Choice **A** fails to address any of the three questions. Whether WaxCo's silence amounts to its acceptance is unrelated to the way in which wax sellers customarily stack boxes. **B** and **D** are wrong because they, too, state irrelevancies.

C is correct. If stacking piles of three would materially alter WaxCo's contractual burden, then the answer to question 3 is "yes," meaning that WaxCo's silence does not constitute its acceptance. That's why **C** is right.

QUESTION 11. For this question, assume that on August 11, CandleCo responds thus: "As per your offer of *August 10*, please ship. Additional Comment(s): *Because personnel will not be in vicinity of receiving platform, your delivery personnel will knock* *twice on front office door to notify us that you have delivered the goods."* Making no response, WaxCo delivers the wax and leaves *without* knocking on CandleCo's front door. By failing to do that, does WaxCo breach a contract?

A. Yes, because its silence accepted CandleCo's proposed modification to the contract
B. Yes, because the parties formed their contract with signed writings
C. Yes, because under the relevant circumstances CandleCo's proposed modification was reasonable
D. No, because WaxCo gave no assent to CandleCo's proposal that it should knock on the door

ANALYSIS. When CandleCo issues its "expression of acceptance," it forms a contract with WaxCo on WaxCo's terms. Simultaneously, CandleCo proposes to modify that very same contract so to require that WaxCo, when completing delivery, knock on its front door. To that proposal WaxCo makes no response, meaning that WaxCo accepts only if its silence constitutes acceptance. That in turn requires (1) that both parties be merchants, (2) that the proposed addition not materially alter the contract, and (3) that WaxCo's initial offer not limit acceptance to the terms of the offer.

Both parties are merchants, and CandleCo's proposed modification certainly does not materially alter the contract. Further, WaxCo's offer did not limit CandleCo's acceptance to the terms of the offer. Consequently, WaxCo, by silence, did accept CandleCo's proposal. The contract includes the door-knocking term. WaxCo is in breach.

Choice **D** tells us that WaxCo is not in breach, so it's wrong. **A**, **B**, and **C** all state, correctly, that WaxCo *is* in breach. **B** implies, however, that WaxCo would not be in breach if the parties had communicated without signed writings. That's false. Nothing in UCC §2-207(1) *or* (2) refers to writings, signed or unsigned. With **C**, the question writer hopes you'll grab onto the word "reasonable" because it seems so very right. But nothing in UCC §2-207(2) makes relevant the *reasonableness* of an offeree's proposed modification. **C** is wrong.

A correctly tells us that WaxCo accepted CandleCo's proposed modification, which it did — by silence. In failing to knock on CandleCo's door, WaxCo breached. **A** is right.

QUESTION 12. (Door knocking again.) For this question, assume that WaxCo's "Available for Purchase" form, sent on August 10, includes, on its front side, this language: "SEE ADDITIONAL TERMS ON REVERSE SIDE." The reverse side features this text: "The buyer's acceptance is limited to the terms shown on the front side. WaxCo will not accept any additional terms that the buyer might propose."

On August 11, CandleCo responds thus: "As per your offer of August 10, please ship. Additional Comment(s): Because our personnel will not be in vicinity of receiving platform, your delivery personnel will knock twice on front office door to notify us that you have delivered the goods." Making no response to CandleCo, WaxCo delivers the wax and leaves *without* knocking on the front door. By failing to do that, does WaxCo breach the parties' contract?

A. Yes, because both parties are merchants
B. Yes, because knocking on the door would not materially increase WaxCo's contractual burden
C. Yes, because under the relevant circumstances CandleCo's request was reasonable
D. No, because WaxCo limited CandleCo's acceptance to the terms of its offer

ANALYSIS.   Again, CandleCo accepts WaxCo's offer and simultaneously proposes to modify the contract so to require that WaxCo knock on its front door. This time, however, on the reverse side of its "Available for Purchase" form, WaxCo expressly states that it will not accept any additional terms the buyer might propose. That's part of WaxCo's offer for which, therefore, the answer to our question 3 is "yes"; Offeror announced in his offer that he would reject any additional terms put forth by the offeree. For that reason, WaxCo does not accept CandleCo's proposal. The contract includes no door-knocking term, and WaxCo commits no breach.

According to **A**, **B**, and **C**, WaxCo *is* in breach, and for that reason, they're wrong. As for **A**, it's true that the parties are merchants, but that represents only the first of three necessary conditions ("yes," "no," "no") through which the offeror's silence makes for acceptance of the offeree's new or different terms. **B** correctly states that CandleCo's proposal makes no material alteration to the contract, but that represents only the second of the three necessary conditions. **C**, once again, presents the word "reasonable," to which the question writer hopes you'll mindlessly attach yourself. **C** is wrong. We're left with **D**, which states that WaxCo is *not* in breach because it limited CandleCo's acceptance to the terms of its offer. That's exactly right. On the reverse side of WaxCo's form, we read: "WaxCo will not accept any additional terms that the buyer might propose." That means the answer to question 3 is "yes," and that means WaxCo's silence does not accept CandleCo's proposed door-knocking term. **D** is right.

QUESTION 13. For this question, Waxco's "Available for Purchase" document is as originally described; it presents no text on its reverse side. With that in mind, assume that on August 11, CandleCo, on its own "Purchase Order" form, responds thus: "As per your offer of *August 10*, please ship. Additional

Comment(s): *Please include 15 tons of same product, in color blue @ same price — $200/ton, for total price of 30 ×* $200 = $6,000." On August 12, WaxCo replies, "Sale confirmed as per your August 11 Purchase Order." WaxCo delivers the white wax but not the blue wax. By failing to deliver the blue wax, does WaxCo breach the parties' contract?

A. Yes, because both parties are merchants
B. Yes, because CandleCo proposed an addition to the contract, and WaxCo accepted it
C. No, because CandleCo's proposed addition materially alters the contract
D. No, because CandleCo's request was a proposal to modify the contract, and WaxCo did not accept it

ANALYSIS. The parties first form a contract on WaxCo's terms. Simultaneously, CandleCo proposes to add a term requiring that WaxCo sell CandleCo a substantial amount of additional product. That proposal would make a material alteration to the contract. WaxCo's silence, therefore, would not act as its acceptance.

But WaxCo is *not* silent. After receiving CandleCo's purchase order — its "expression of acceptance" — WaxCo responds: "Sale confirmed as per your August 11 purchase order." With that response, WaxCo expressly accepts CandleCo's proposal. As thus modified, the contract requires that WaxCo deliver both white and blue wax. WaxCo delivered only the white wax. It breached.

C and D state that WaxCo didn't breach, so they're wrong. D incorrectly reports that WaxCo failed to accept CandleCo's proposal. With the August 12 sales confirmation, WaxCo *did* accept it. As for C, it's true that the blue-wax term materially alters the contract, but that's irrelevant because WaxCo expressly accepted it. A correctly tells us that both parties are merchants, but that, too, is irrelevant. If the parties had not been merchants, still, the blue-wax term would belong to the contract because, once again, WaxCo expressly accepted it. B accurately tells us that WaxCo is in breach and correctly states the reason — WaxCo accepted CandleCo's proposal. It did so not with silence, but with its August 12 response. B is right.

E. UCC §2-207 as Wonderful Model of Terrible Draftsmanship: "Different" and "Additional" Terms

Although UCC §2-207(1) tells us that an "expression of acceptance . . . operates as an acceptance even though it states terms additional to or different from those offered," UCC §2-207(2) goes on to describe the fate only of "additional" terms; it says nothing of the "different" ones. That peculiarity raises these questions:

- Did the drafters really mean to distinguish "different" terms from "additional" ones, or did they by sheer (characteristic) carelessness use both words in subsection (1) but only the one word in subsection (2)?
- If the drafters did intend to distinguish "different" terms from "additional" ones, (a) what exactly is the distinction, and (b) what is the fate of the "different" terms?

In answering these questions, the jurisdictions differ and create (roughly) three schools of interpretation, which we'll name School 1, School 2, and School 3.

1. School 1 Jurisdictions

These jurisdictions (very sensibly) assume sloppiness on the drafters' parts and read the word "additional" in subsection (2) to mean "additional or different." Consequently, these jurisdictions make no distinction between "different" and "additional" terms. They apply subsection (2) to any term that the offeree introduces in his expression of acceptance. Such term is a proposal to modify the contract. The original offeror may accept it or not. (And, if the offeror accepts it, the term becomes part of the contract.)

Illustration: White Widgets.   Sandy and Barney are merchants. They conduct this exchange:

Sandy: We will sell you 10 white widgets for $10, delivered on Monday before noon.
Barney: Agreed, but deliver *after* noon, and leave an invoice in our mailbox.

Barney expresses acceptance to Sandy's offer, but introduces two terms of his own: One calls for delivery after noon, whereas Sandy proposes to deliver *before* noon. The other calls for Sandy to leave his invoice in Barney's mailbox. That's a matter that Sandy's offer doesn't address. School 1 courts do not ask to know whether either of these terms "differs" from or "adds" to the offer. Both are newly introduced by the offeree. To a School 1 court, both represent the offeree's proposal to modify the contract. As for the three questions described above, the answers are "yes," "no," and "no." If the offeror responds with silence, both of the offeree's new/different terms join the contract.

2. Schools 2 and 3 Jurisdictions: Generally

These jurisdictions do recognize a difference between "additional" and "different" terms because the code drafters (seem, perhaps, to) create one. In these jurisdictions, if an offeree's term conflicts with any of the offeror's stated terms, then it "differs" from the offer. Otherwise, it "adds" to it.

Illustration: "Different" vs. "Additional."   Reread the exchange between Sandy and Barney. Barney expresses acceptance of the offer, and introduces two terms it does not include. One calls for delivery after noon, and it contradicts the offer, which provided for delivery *before* noon. That term, therefore, "differs" from the offer. The other calls for Sandy to leave an invoice in Barney's mailbox. Sandy's offer states not a thing about the invoice, wherefore the buyer's mailbox term "adds" to it.

3. School 2 Jurisdictions: Discarding the "Different" Terms

These jurisdictions regard the offeree's "additional" terms as proposals for addition to the contract so that UCC §2-207(2) applies to them. If the offeror assents, expressly (or by silence when circumstances satisfy the three relevant conditions), they become part of the contract. If the offeree's terms "differ" from (conflict with) the offeror's terms, they amount to nothing. They are not, even, proposals to modify the contract.

School 2 Illustrated.   Reread the exchange between Sandy and Barney. School 2 courts would wholly discard the buyer's statement as to delivery. They would regard it not even as a proposal to modify the contract. These same courts would treat the invoice term under subsection (2) as a proposal for addition to the contract, which the offeror might accept, expressly (or by silence if circumstances satisfy the three relevant conditions).

4. School 3 Jurisdictions: The "Knockout Rule"

Likely representing a majority, School 3 jurisdictions treat the offeree's "additional" terms under subsection (2) as does School 2; such terms are proposals to modify the contract. As to any of the offeree's terms that "differ" from the offer, School 3 applies a court-made "knockout rule" and discards both the offeror's *and* offeree's term. If the term is somehow essential to the contract, then by "gap filling" they replace it with a "reasonable" one under UCC §2-204(3) (Chapter 4, section C).

School 3 Illustrated.   Reread the exchange between Sandy and Barney. A School 3 court would apply subsection (2) to the offeree's invoice/mailbox term, as would a court of School 2. It would also "knock out" (remove) from the contract both the offeror's and offeree's terms as to delivery and replace them with a "reasonable" delivery term under UCC §2-204(3).

5. Be Forewarned

With the inexplicable chaos it wreaks on this point (and others), UCC §2-207(2) makes a mockery of the drafters' professed wish to clarify the law and render it "uniform" throughout the states. UCC §2-207(2) is a disgrace to legal draftsmanship and to its drafters. Professor Brian Blum calls it "ugly and misshapen."[11] According to Professor Grant Gilmore, it is "the greatest statutory mess of all time."[12] (Both those authorities are too kind.) Take UCC §2-207 with skepticism, disdain and "who knows what, really, it means."[13]

QUESTIONS 14-16. SahlCo manufactures planting pots. BahlCo pots plants for sale to retail customers. On March 1, BahlCo contacts SahlCo by signed writing: "We need 2,000 red clay pots, Model 14-D; priced as per last time — $1/unit = $2,000. Please deliver to our warehouse. Will pay with our business check handed to your driver on delivery." SahlCo responds with a signed sales confirmation form: "Sold to: BahlCo. Red clay pots, Model 14-D; #2,000. Price: $1/unit. Total: $2,000. This Sales Confirmation Includes All Terms Set Forth on Reverse Side."

The reverse side of SahlCo's form includes this text:

(1) Full payment to be made by check sent to SahlCo by U.S. Mail.
(2) For contracts that call for delivery by SahlCo, delivery driver will telephone the buyer within 10 minutes of delivery time, and the buyer will post a receiving agent at its receiving platform/facility.

BahlCo receives the sales confirmation form, but makes no response to it.

QUESTION 14. With respect to the two terms set forth on the reverse side of SahlCo's sales confirmation form, a School 1 jurisdiction would likely hold that

A. both terms become part of the contract.
B. term (1) becomes part of the contract, but term (2) does not.
C. term (2) becomes part of the contract, but term (1) does not.
D. neither term becomes part of the contract.

QUESTION 15. A School 2 jurisdiction would likely hold that

A. both terms become part of the contract.
B. term (1) becomes part of the contract, but term (2) does not.

---

11. Brian Blum, *Contracts: Examples and Explanations* 115 (5th ed. 2010).

12. Mark E. Roszkowski, *Symposium on Revised Article 2 of the Uniform Commercial Code — Section-by-Section Analysis*, 54 SMU L. Rev. 927, 932 (2001) (quoting letter from Professor Grant Gilmore to Professor Robert Summers, Cornell U. School of Law (Sept. 10, 1980), *reprinted in* Richard E. Speidel et al., *Teaching Materials on Commercial and Consumer Law* 54-55 (3d ed. 1981).

13. — together, always, with contempt for the drafters who, in their 2003 proposed amendments, not yet adopted by any state (without apologizing for what was written forty years earlier), eliminate from §2-207 both subsections (1) and (2) and offer, instead, a new and useless provision (born of the original subsection (3), not yet discussed).

C. term (2) becomes part of the contract, but term (1) does not.
D. term (2) becomes part of the contract, but term (1) does not, and is replaced by a "reasonable" term of the court's choosing.

QUESTION 16. A School 3 jurisdiction would likely hold that

A. both terms become part of the contract.
B. term (1) becomes part of the contract, but term (2) does not.
C. term (2) becomes part of the contract, but term (1) does not.
D. term (2) becomes part of the contract, but term (1) does not, and it is replaced by a "reasonable" term of the court's choosing.

ANALYSIS. BahlCo offered to buy goods and SahlCo responded, via sales confirmation, with an expression of acceptance that, on its reverse side, presented two terms not found in BahlCo's offer. Term (1) provides that BahlCo should make payment by mail, and thus contradicts BahlCo's offer, in which BahlCo proposed to pay on delivery. Term (1) "differs" from the offer. Term (2) requires that on receiving a phone call BahlCo must post personnel at its receiving platform to accept delivery. BahlCo's offer did not touch on that topic, so term (2) "adds" to it.

Both of SahlCo's terms alter the contract only in trivial ways; they are not material. Both parties are merchants, and BahlCo, in its offer, did not limit acceptance to the offer's terms. Answers to the three questions are: "yes," "no," "no."

As for Question 14. In applying UCC §2-207(2), a School 1 jurisdiction makes no distinction between "different" and "additional" terms. In view of BahlCo's silence — its failure to object to SahlCo's new terms — both terms likely become part of the contract. **A** is right.

As for Question 15. A School 2 court treats the offeree's "additional" terms under UCC §2-207(2). Consequently, term (2) is SahlCo's proposal to modify the contract. Because BahlCo responds to it with silence (and because circumstances satisfy the three relevant conditions), it becomes a part of the contract. Term (1), however, "differs" from BahlCo's terms. School 2 jurisdictions disregard it entirely. For these reasons, **C** is right.

As for Question 16. A School 3 court applies the "knockout rule." Like the School 2 courts, it treats the offeree's "additional" terms under UCC §2-207(2). Consequently, term (2) is SahlCo's proposal to modify the contract. Because BahlCo responds with silence, it becomes a part of the contract. Term (1), however, "differs" from BahlCo's terms. Under the "knockout rule," both the offeror's and offeree's payment terms drop out. Then, under UCC §2-204(3), the court replaces them with a term it considers reasonable. For these reasons, **D** is right.

F. Back to UCC §2-207(1): The "Written Confirmation"

With regret, we must show you now that UCC §2-207(1) refers not only to an offer and expression of acceptance, but also to something it calls a "written confirmation." In full, UCC §2-207(1) provides:

> A definite and seasonable expression of acceptance or a written confirmation which is sent within a reasonable time operates as an acceptance even though it states terms additional to or different from those offered or agreed upon, unless acceptance is expressly made conditional on assent to the additional or different terms.

With this jumble of words, lacking in proper punctuation, the code drafters disgorge some ill-digested meal of half-cooked thought, leaving for others the task of cleaning up.

Tearing the sentence into what are two separate thoughts, we find (a) a provision concerning offer and acceptance, already studied; and (b) a provision that attempts to deal with two parties who form a contract orally or "informally," whereafter one of them confirms the contract in a writing sent to the other. To understand the meanings of these two separate components, we must further dissect this ill-born sentence (if it be one).

Although the drafters do not define the term "written confirmation," their so-called Official Comment 1 indicates that "written confirmation" means a writing sent by either party to the other, *after* both parties have already formed a contract orally or "informally." The drafters explain that the reference to "written confirmation"

> is intended to deal with [the situation in which] an agreement has been reached either orally or by informal correspondence between the parties and is followed by one or both of the parties sending formal memoranda embodying the terms so far as agreed upon and adding terms not discussed.

The reference to written confirmation would seem, then, to address these parties:

Jack (by spoken word): I'd like to buy from you 200 widgets for $200.
Jill (by spoken word): Sure; I'll send them to your warehouse.
Jill (signed writing): This confirms our agreement under which you will buy and I will sell 200 widgets for $200; delivery to be made by me this Friday, March 10.

The statutory provision then *seems* to tell us that Jill's confirmatory memorandum "operates as an acceptance even though it states terms additional to or different from those . . . agreed upon."

But the memorandum *can't* "operate as an acceptance." The parties have already formed their contract, meaning they have *already achieved offer and acceptance.* If the reference to written confirmation means anything — *anything at all* — it means only that

1. the additional (and different?) terms set forth in the memorandum are proposals for addition to the contract, which the recipient may accept or not; and
2. if the memorandum's recipient responds with silence, then the additional (and different?) terms become part of the contract under the conditions described in UCC §2-207(2).

Beyond that, the reference to "confirmatory memorandum" means nothing, and no learned lawyer can disagree.

Let's Do the Drafters' Job for Them and Render §2-207 Comprehensible

Read UCC §2-207(1) as though it had two separate parts (a) and (b), followed then by UCC §2-207(2):

> *(1)(a) When one party offers to buy or sell goods and the offeree responds with an expression of acceptance, that expression of acceptance operates as an acceptance even though it does not mirror the offer, meaning that the parties form a contract on the offeror's terms. However, if the offeree expressly states that his expression of acceptance is conditional on the offeror's assent to the new or different terms, then the expression of acceptance is not an acceptance but, instead, a counteroffer and rejection;*
>
> *and, separately,*
>
> *(b) If two parties form a contract orally or by an exchange of informal writings, and one (or each party) sends a confirmatory memorandum to the other that includes terms different from or additional to those of the contract,*
>
> *then — in both these cases 1(a) and 1(b) —*
>
> *(2)(a) generally, the additional terms are to be construed as proposals for addition to the contract, and it is for the original offeror or recipient of the memorandum to accept them or not*
>
> *but*
>
> *(b) if in response to the proposal the original offeror or recipient of the memorandum remains silent —does not object to the proposal within a reasonable time — then in that case, the original offeror or recipient of the memorandum is deemed to accept the offeror's or sender's proposed terms if and only if the answers are "yes," "no," and "no" to these three questions:*
>
> *(i) Are both parties merchants?*
>
> *(ii) In her offer, did the original offeror "in advance" reject any new or different terms the offeree might propose?*
>
> *(iii) Do the offeree's or sender's proposed terms materially alter the parties' rights and duties?*

QUESTION 17. BenCo and SenCo deal professionally in pianos and piano parts. On May 10, BenCo telephones SenCo: "Can you ship to us two full sets of plastic piano key tops at your catalog price?" SenCo replies, "Yes, we'll ship them on Tuesday." That same afternoon, by fax, SenCo sends BenCo this writing, signed and dated: "Sold to BenCo. Two full sets of plastic piano key tops at catalog price. Payment to be made by check deposited directly to SkyBank using our direct deposit number: 5090319079." BenCo receives the document but makes no response to it. Seven days later, BenCo receives the key tops with a bill showing the catalog price of $200. Is BenCo contractually obliged to make payment by depositing a check directly into SkyBank?

A. Yes, because the request is reasonable under the circumstances
B. Yes, because it is for a seller to decide how he shall be paid
C. Yes, if that requirement does not materially affect the contract
D. No, because SenCo sent the confirmation after the parties had formed their contract

ANALYSIS. If, for the sale of goods, two parties form a contract orally or by an exchange of informal writings, and one sends a confirmatory memorandum to the other that includes terms different from or additional to those of the contract, then the additional terms represent proposals for addition to the contract (UCC §2-207(1)). If both parties are merchants, and the offeror responds to the proposal with silence, he accepts it if the answers to our three questions are "yes," "no," "no" (UCC §2-207(2)).

Here BenCo and SenCo form an oral contract for the sale of key tops. Thereafter SenCo dispatches a written confirmation in which it sets forth a term not included in the contract, to wit, the payment provision. That term does not *conflict* with the offer, so it's an "additional" one. According to all jurisdictional "schools," when SenCo issues the memorandum the new term proposes to modify the contract. The answers to our first two questions are "yes" and "no." There is, perhaps, some argument as to the third question — whether SenCo's newly proposed terms materially alter the parties' contract. Hence we can conclude that if it does materially alter the contract, it does not become part of it. If the new term does not materially alter the contract, then it does become part of it.

According to **A**, BenCo must make the direct deposit because such represents a reasonable request under the circumstances. Friendly words do not a right answer make. UCC §2-207(2) nowhere makes relevant the reasonableness or unreasonableness of an offeree's additional term. **B** makes a false statement of law. Decisions on payment (or anything else) belong no more to the seller than to the buyer. All contractual terms require *mutual* assent (even if, at times, one manifests his assent by silence). **D** correctly reports that the confirmation came forth after the parties formed their contract. That means, of course, that it can't be an acceptance, as explained above. Nonetheless, an offeree's additional terms set forth in a written confirmation do become part of the contract if the answers to our three questions conform to UCC §2-207(2). **C** correctly reports that the parties adopt the offeree's direct deposit term so long as it does not materially affect their contract. **C** is right.

G.   The Closer

QUESTION 18. While surfing the Internet, Beth sees an advertisement for an electric toothbrush called SensaDent. Among other boasts, the advertisement states that the product is "long-lasting." The advertisement invites readers to click on a link, and Beth does so. Her screen then displays a "SensaDent Purchase Request." She completes its required fields, supplying her name, telephone number, mailing address, email address, credit card number, and card expiration date (together, of course, with the three-digit security code on its reverse side).

The form provides one additional field entitled "Additional Requests or Comments (Optional)." In that field Beth writes:

> I shall have the right to return the item and receive a full refund of the purchase price by certified check (not by credit to my credit card account), within ten years of purchase, if during that period the item should fail to function perfectly.

Having thus completed the purchase request, Beth clicks on the words "I authorize SensaDent to charge $75 to my credit card. SUBMIT." One minute later, Beth receives from SensaDent this email:

> Congratulations! Your Purchase Request is accepted, and the sale is complete. The sum of $75 will be charged to your credit card, and your SensaDent toothbrush will ship within three weeks.
>
> **SensaDent Limited Warranty**
> SensaDent warrants that its product will be free from defects in operation for three years after delivery to the buyer. If the product should fail within that period, then, upon returning the defective product to SensaDent, the buyer will receive a refund of the purchase price IN WHATEVER FORM OF PAYMENT WAS USED TO PURCHASE THE PRODUCT. The product carries no warranties beyond the face of this document.

Five days after Beth receives SensaDent's congratulatory email she hears by telephone from a SensaDent representative.

> **SensaDent:** We have just read the additional comment you submitted with your online purchase request form. We warrant the product for three years, not ten, as you were advised in our congratulatory email. Further, refunds are made through the same form of payment as that used to purchase our product — in your case, by a credit to your credit card account. If those terms are not acceptable to you, we'll cancel your order.
>
> **Beth:** Those terms are not acceptable to me, and neither is it acceptable that you cancel my order. I want the product, and I want it on the terms put forth in what you folks call my "SensaDent Purchase Request."
>
> **SensaDent:** I'm sorry; we can't agree to that.

Making no charge to her credit card, SensaDent, by certified mail, advises Beth that it has cancelled her order, whereupon Beth visits her lawyer to ask whether SensaDent is in breach of contract. The lawyer answers, "No, certainly not, because you and SensaDent never *formed* a contract." Beth's lawyer is most likely

A. right, because SensaDent cannot be bound by terms to which it never knowingly agreed.

B. right, because SensaDent took no payment from Beth and canceled her order.

C. right, because in this transaction SensaDent is a merchant.

D. wrong, because Beth made an offer and SensaDent accepted it.

ANALYSIS.   The saga starts with SensaDent's advertisement. UCC Article 2 is silent on the subject of advertisements, so common law governs. SensaDent's ad was not an offer but a mere invitation to deal. (See Chapter 5, section A.) When Beth completed the purchase request, *she* made an offer whose terms included her demand for a ten-year right to a refund. SensaDent (lacking a good lawyer) responded by advising Beth that it had accepted her "order." It thus issued an expression of acceptance under UCC §2-207(1). Its terms differed from those of Beth's offer, but UCC §2-207(1) makes that irrelevant. Consequently, when SensaDent dispatched its congratulatory email, it accepted Beth's offer, exactly as Beth made it. The parties formed a contract on Beth's terms. Beth's lawyer is wrong.

Telling us that the lawyer is right, **A** and **B** put forth incorrect statements of law. Under UCC §2-207(1), SensaDent *can* be bound by terms to which it never knowingly agreed. Further, if one forms a contract to sell goods (or anything else), he cannot extricate himself by returning the buyer's purchase price. **A** and **B** make excellent compost. **C** states that Beth's lawyer was wrong.

Why? Because SensaDent is a merchant. Yes, SensaDent *is* a merchant, but who cares? It doesn't matter. Nothing in UCC §2-207(*1*) turns on the word "merchant." **C** is wrong.

According to **D**, Beth's lawyer is wrong because Beth made an offer and SensaDent accepted it. That's exactly right. Beth made an offer. SensaDent responded with an expression of acceptance, which operates *as* an acceptance notwithstanding that it carries terms different from those of the offer. **D** is right.

 ## Silver's Picks

1.	A
2.	C
3.	C
4.	B
5.	D
6.	D
7.	A
8.	C
9.	D
10.	C
11.	A
12.	D
13.	B
14.	A
15.	C
16.	D
17.	C
18.	D

12

Consideration, Part I

A.   What's a Contract?

Nonlawyers often think "contract" means a *writing*, formally drafted and ceremoniously signed. They're wrong. Many contracts are embodied in signed writings. We call them "written contracts." Many arise from speech alone. They're "oral contracts." Some arise without words at all. They're born of communicative *behavior*, with nary a word of type or talk. Those are "contracts implied in fact." All such creatures are contracts, and all arise by the same legal mechanism: *Two (or more) parties form a contract when they manifest **mutual assent** to a **bargain** that exacts from each some* **consideration**.

EVERYONE STOP.   If your contracts class begins here, with the topic of consideration, then before proceeding with this chapter and before proceeding with your course, please (for your own good) go to Chapter 2 and read sections A, B, and D. If you like, skip the multiple-choice questions. (When your class covers contract formation, you'll read Chapter 2 in full. That's when you'll address its multiple-choice questions.)

1. How Two Parties Manifest Mutual Assent

Two parties form a contract when the first makes an offer that the second accepts, each providing **consideration to the other.**

We'll understand the meaning of "consideration" only after we know the difference between a "naked promise" and a "contractual promise" (our own term—very useful).

B.   Naked Promise vs. Contractual Promise

You know the meaning of "promise." One makes a promise when she pledges to another that she will or will not do some particular thing. When two parties form a (bilateral)[1] contract, each makes a promise to the other. Consider this offer and acceptance:[2]

Corporation A (offer): If you will service all of our payroll accounts for the coming year we will pay your usual fee of $300 per hour.

Corporation B (acceptance): We accept.

Corporation A proposes an exchange of promises. Specifically, it proposes that (1) B promise to service all of A's payroll accounts in exchange for which (2) A should promise to pay B $300 per hour. Corporation A thereby makes an offer.

When B accepts A's offer, the two proposed promises come to life so that each party *makes* to the other its promise as proposed in A's offer. At the moment B says (or writes) "We accept," (1) A makes a contractual promise to pay B's usual hourly fees and (2) B makes a contractual promise to service A's payroll accounts. Together the two contractual promises make a *contract.*

1. The Law Enforces Contracts

The law enforces the promise that each contracting party makes to the other, meaning it enforces promises embodied *within a contract*. But if one makes a

---

1. "Bilateral contract" refers to the ordinary contract with which you are familiar in ordinary life—the contract in which two parties, A and B, agree that A will do something for B and in exchange that B will do something for A (paying him money, providing him with some service or whatever). The law recognizes, also, what it calls a "unilateral contract," described in footnote 4 and fully discussed in Chapter 9, section C.

2. As we explain in Chapter 1, Party A makes an offer to Party B when she proposes a bargain, a "this" for a "that," a *quid pro quo*: "I will promise to do thing X if you will promise to do thing Y." Party Y accepts her offer if, simply, he assents to it: "Okay," "It's a deal," "I accept," "Great, let's do it." If A makes a promise *without* proposing a bargain—"Here's my offer: I promise to do thing X"—she doesn't *make* an offer. And if she doesn't make an offer, B has nothing *to* accept. Even if B responds with, "I accept your offer," the parties don't form a contract.

Students whose teacher begins here, with the topic of consideration, need to know for now that "offer" and "acceptance" make a contract. Your class will study the ins and outs of that subject later in the course. (See Chapter 1, the section entitled, "Contracts Professors Aren't Cut from a Single Cloth.")

promise *outside* of a contract, the law does not ordinarily enforce it. Suppose Robert Waith creates and signs this writing: "I, ROBERT WAITH, do hereby put forth, to keep and honor, unconditionally and without exception of any kind, this solemn promise: To my nephew, WALLACE WAITH BANNINGTON, on his twenty-first birthday, August 9, 2030 I will give my Symington Swiss gold watch, which watch will then be his wholly, fully, and forever."

Because Robert's promise does not follow from an offer and acceptance by which he and his nephew exchanged promises, it does not belong to a contract. It's not a "contractual promise" (our own term, meaning a promise that belongs to a contract). It's an ordinary everyday promise from one person to another motivated, maybe, by generosity, affection, filial tradition, or who knows what. In the law's words, an ordinary everyday promise that doesn't belong to a contract is a mere "gratuitous promise" or "donative promise" or, most commonly, a "naked promise." When you want to sound lawyerly use the Latin, *nudum pactum*; it means "naked promise"; a promise made in exchange for nothing.

Whether it comes from parent to child, wife to husband, friend to friend, or multinational corporation to the whole of the American public—whether it be made by spoken word or formal writing, signed, witnessed, and notarized, in pencil, pen, or blood—a promise that does not belong to a contract is unenforceable. A gratuitous promise—naked promise—*nudum pactum*—is unenforceable.

2. The Law Doesn't Hold Us to Our Word?

No; generally speaking, it doesn't. It holds us to our *contracts* but not (generally) to the ordinary promises we make to one another day in and day out. Let's write a rule:

(1) When by forming a contract, Party 1 makes a promise to Party 2, the law requires that she keep it. If she breaks it, Party 2 has an action against her for breach, but (2) if Party 1 makes to Party 2 a mere gratuitous promise—a naked promise—nudum pactum, the law does not enforce it. Party 1 may break her promise for any reason or no reason, and Party 2 has no legal remedy.

From Chapter 2, we know that two parties form a contract if and only if one makes an offer that the other accepts.[3] Further, one makes an offer only if he proposes a *bargain*—an arrangement in which two parties make an exchange. "Bargain" refers to a "trade," a "swap," a "this" for a "that," or, in Latin, a *quid pro quo*. A contract always reflects a *bargain*. That's why the Restatement definition of offer centers on that word. Restatement (Second) of Contracts §24 provides:

> [One makes an offer when to another party she proposes] a *BARGAIN* so made as to justify [the other] in understanding that his assent to that *BARGAIN* is invited and will conclude it.

---

3. Chapter 2, sections A, B, and D.

One accepts an offer and thereby forms a contract, if he manifests assent to the bargain it proposes (Restatement (Second) §50(1)).

A contract, therefore, reflects a *bargain* to which two parties commit themselves. Since the law enforces only contractual promises—promises that inhere within a *bargain*—Party Y's promise to Party X is enforceable only if in exchange Party Y gets something back from Party X.

3. *That Brings Us to the Word "Consideration"*

Because two parties form a contract only when they mutually commit to a bargain, simple logic produces this inescapable conclusion: *Two parties form a contract only if they agree to a bargain, meaning that (a) each provides something to the other, and, accordingly, (b) each receives something from the other. The "something" that each party provides to the other is the consideration he gives. The "something" that each party receives from the other is the consideration he gets in exchange for the consideration he gives.* Consequently, the law features statements like these:

- "To form a contract each party must provide consideration to the other."
- "No promise is enforceable unless it is 'supported by' consideration from the promisee" (meaning that no promise is enforceable unless the promisee gives for it ("supports it with") some promise or performance[4] of his own).
- "Any promise not supported by consideration from the promisee is a naked promise, unenforceable."

Look again at the contract between Corporations A and B. It arose when B accepted A's offer. At that moment, each party became bound by its promise to the other.

> **Simple Question:** What consideration does Corporation A receive for its promise to pay $300 per hour?
>
> **Simple Answer:** As consideration for its promise to pay $300 per hour, Corporation A receives Corporation B's promise to service its payroll accounts.
>
> **Simple Question:** What consideration does Corporation B receive for its promise to service Corporation A's payroll accounts?
>
> **Simple Answer:** As consideration for its promise to service Corporation A's payroll accounts, Corporation B receives Corporation A's promise to pay it $300 per hour.

---

4. This chapter concerns only "bilateral" contracts—contracts in which each party makes a promise(s) to the other. Unilateral contracts are those in which A makes a promise to B and in exchange B puts forth not a promise to do what the offeree wants of him, but the very doing of it; A to B: "I *promise* to do thing X if you will *do* thing Y. No promises, please, just do it." In such cases, B accepts A's offer if and only if he *does* thing Y, and the doing of it is the consideration he gives for A's promise. All of this we explain in Chapter 9, section C.

Hence, it's important that you understand this statement 1: "A promise supported by consideration *is* enforceable, and a promise not supported by consideration is *not* enforceable." You must also understand that it's equivalent to this statement 2: "Contracts are enforceable, but gratuitous promises are not."

4. Come Again? How Are These Two Statements Equivalent?

Look at the first clause of each one. Statement 1: "A promise supported by consideration is enforceable." Statement 2: "Contracts are enforceable. . . ." We know that a promise supported by consideration is a promise given by one person in exchange for a promise (or performance)[5] given by another. If two parties exchange promises, then by definition they mutually commit to a bargain, which means they form a contract. Consequently, a promise supported by consideration *means* a promise that belongs to a contract.

Let's now examine the second clause of each statement. Statement 1: "a promise not supported by consideration is not enforceable." Statement 2: "gratuitous promises are not [enforceable]." A promise not supported by consideration is a promise for which nothing is given in exchange; it's a promise that's *not* part of a contract. "Gratuitous promise" carries the same meaning: A gratuitous promise (naked promise, *nudum pactum*, donative promise) is a promise given in exchange for nothing—a promise not tied to a contract. Hence, "a promise not supported by consideration is not enforceable" *means* "gratuitous promises are not enforceable."

QUESTION 1. Hazel works for MedCo, and she happens to be an enthusiastic basketball fan. Nancy is her supervisor. Nancy approaches Hazel: "I have two tickets for this Friday night's game at the Garden. I'm going to give them to you tomorrow as an early birthday present." Hazel replies, "Thank you!" Is Nancy legally obliged to honor her promise?

A. Yes, because she manifested a serious intention to honor it
B. Yes, because she made it in consideration of Hazel's birthday
C. No, because she received no consideration for it
D. No, because she did not make it in writing

ANALYSIS. Neither of these parties proposed a bargain to the other. Asking for nothing in exchange, Nancy promised Hazel a gift, meaning she made a naked promise, unenforceable.

---

5. See *supra* note 4.

A implies that one is bound by her naked promise if she manifests a serious intention to honor it. There's no such rule. One may make a naked promise with the utmost solemnity and still it's unenforceable. **A** is wrong.

B invokes the word "consideration," but does not use it properly. Hazel's birthday represents Nancy's *reason* for giving Hazel the tickets, but Hazel's birthday is not consideration for her promise; it doesn't represent something that Hazel gives to Nancy. **B** is wrong.

D correctly states that Nancy need not keep her promise, but incorrectly implies that one who makes a naked promise in writing must honor it. That, of course, is false, and **D** is wrong.

And so we come to **C**. It tells us that Nancy need not keep her word, and correctly states the reason: "[Nancy] received no consideration for the promise." It would be right also to say, "No, because Nancy made only a naked promise," or "No, because Hazel promised nothing to Nancy in exchange for Nancy's promise," or "No, because Nancy's promise did not belong to a contract," or "No, because the arrangement between Hazel and Nancy did not call for a *quid pro quo*." All such statements mean that Nancy made to Hazel a plain old ordinary everyday promise, and by law one who makes that kind of promise is free to break it.

On the other hand, if (a) Nancy had said, "As an early birthday present I'll give you tickets for Friday night's game at the Garden if you'll stay one hour late at work on Thursday night," and (b) Hazel had responded, "Okay," then Nancy and Hazel would form a contract. Each would be legally obliged to keep her promise.

In any case, **C** is right.

QUESTION 2. LifeTime Inc. publishes a monthly magazine that derives revenues from advertising. As a promotional strategy the company offers various businesses the opportunity to advertise free of charge in three consecutive issues of its magazine. On April 1, a LifeTime representative telephones SportsWear:

LifeTime: We're calling to tell you that free of charge in the next three issues of our magazine, we'll publish your standard full-page advertisement.

SportsWear: We thank you. Please put your promise in a signed writing; we'd like to see it in black and white.

LifeTime sends SportsWear this signed writing:

Confirmation of Binding Contractual Promise
This confirms that LifeTime will publish, free of charge, SportsWear's standard full-page advertisement in three consecutive issues of its monthly magazine.

Thereafter, LifeTime's management decides against its free advertising program. There follows another conversation with SportsWear.

> **LifeTime:** Please know that we have changed our mind about the free advertising. We won't be publishing your ad.
> **SportsWear:** You made a signed written promise and we intend to hold you to it.

Alleging breach of contract SportsWear sues LifeTime. LifeTime contends that it has no obligation to honor its promise. If the court decides against SportsWear, its reason will most likely be that

   I. SportsWear itself did not sign the writing entitled "Confirmation of Binding Contractual Promise."
  II. LifeTime's promise was not embodied within a contract.
 III. LifeTime withdrew its offer before SportsWear accepted it.
 IV. LifeTime's promise was mere *nudum pactum.*
  A. I only
  B. III only
  C. I and II only
  D. II and IV only

ANALYSIS. A contractual promise is enforceable. A naked promise is not. When LifeTime first contacted SportsWear, it proposed no trade, no bargain. Instead, asking nothing in exchange, it promised to publish SportsWear's advertisement free of charge. Consequently, LifeTime proposed no bargain; it made no offer. Neither did SportsWear respond with any offer of its own. Rather, SportsWear requested that LifeTime restate its promise in writing. LifeTime did so. It matters not a whit that LifeTime titled its document with the words "binding" and "contractual." LifeTime proposed no bargain and so made no offer. It made only its own promise in exchange for nothing.

These events lead to a single conclusion that we might state in a variety of ways:

1. Neither of these parties proposed a bargain to the other, meaning neither made an offer to the other, meaning these parties never formed a contract. Consequently, LifeTime's promise is not a contractual promise, and the law will not enforce it.
2. LifeTime's promise does not belong to a contract, meaning it is a mere gratuitous promise, and for that reason it's unenforceable.
3. SportsWear gave no consideration for LifeTime's promise and for that reason the promise is unenforceable.
4. LifeTime's promise was unsupported by consideration from the promisee (SportsWear), wherefore it is unenforceable.

Each of those statements is equivalent to every other. They mean that LifeTime made SportsWear a mere gratuitous promise; the parties formed no contract. Examine options I through IV and determine which is/are equivalent to that same statement.

Option I tells us that SportsWear did not sign LifeTime's writing. So what? If SportsWear *had* signed the writing in ink and in blood, before 1,000 witnesses and 10,000 notaries, then, still, the writing would bespeak only a naked promise. The writing and signature are irrelevant.

According to option III, LifeTime withdrew its "offer" before SportsWear accepted it. That statement is false for the simple reason that LifeTime *made* no offer. It made a promise but proposed no bargain.[6] Option II states that LifeTime's promise did not belong to a contract. That's true and it's the reason LifeTime is free to dishonor its word.

Option IV makes the same statement we see at option II. Because LifeTime's promise does not belong to a contract, it's a mere naked promise or, in Latin, *nudum pactum*. **D** names options II and IV, so **D** is right.

C.   Consideration and Value

For their own peculiar reasons, two parties might agree to a bargain in which they exchange values that are unequal by any normal measure.

1. *Adequacy of Consideration: A Tale of Two Cities*

Party A owns a $100 million building in Manhattan. Party B owns a tiny little spot of waterfront land in Pago Pago. It's worth $10,000. Party A wants the Pago Pago property. Party B is willing to part with it only in exchange for the Manhattan building. The parties form an agreement in which A promises to convey the Manhattan building to B and in return B promises to convey the Pago Pago property to A.

Notwithstanding that the properties differ in market value, each party promises *something* to the other, meaning each gives and receives consideration. The agreement constitutes a contract and both promises are fully enforceable. *So long as two parties reciprocally manifest genuine intention to form a bargain, the law does not inquire into the value that each conveys to the other.* When asking whether Party A gives consideration to support Party B's promise, we don't ask whether the two promises are equal in market value. With respect to consideration, *value is irrelevant.* As Restatement (Second) §79 cmt. c explains:

> Valuation is left to private action in part because the parties are thought to be better able than others to evaluate the circumstances of particular

---

6. See *supra* note 2, and Chapter 2, sections A and B.

transactions. . . . Ordinarily, therefore, courts do not inquire into the adequacy of consideration.[7]

And, as the Indiana Supreme Court ruled in 1861:

> [Contracting parties] have a right to make their own bargains. The owner of a thing has the right to fix the price at which he will part with it, and a buyer's own judgment ought to be his best guide as to what he should give to obtain it. The consideration agreed upon may indefinitely exceed the [market] value of the thing for which it is promised and still the bargain stands. The doing of an act by one at the request of another, which may be a detriment or inconvenience, however slight, to the party doing it, or may be a benefit, however slight, to the party at whose request it is performed, is a legal consideration for a promise by such requesting party.[8]

2. *"Sham Consideration": Ava and Bonnie*

Ava owns a horse named Ever After. She visits her lawyer.

> **Ava:** In seven years my niece Bonnie will turn twenty-one. At that time I want her to have my horse. Can I promise her such a gift and know that it will be legally enforceable?
> **Lawyer:** If, in exchange for your promise, Bonnie pays you $1, the two of you will form a contract and your promise will be enforceable.

Ava's lawyer prepares this document:

> Bonnie Betts ("Bonnie") and Ava Anson ("Ava") hereby agree that: (1) Bonnie will, immediately after executing this agreement, pay to Ava the sum of $1 in exchange for which (2) on Bonnie's twenty-first birthday Ava will convey to Bonnie her horse, Ever After.

Ava signs the document, presents it to Bonnie, and Bonnie signs too. Bonnie then asks, "Do you really want my dollar?" "No," Ava responds, "but you must go through the motions of paying it to me in order that my promise be legally binding. That's what my lawyer told me." Bonnie pays Ava $1. Seven years later, on Bonnie's twenty-first birthday, Ava disavows her promise and refuses to give Bonnie the horse. Let's ask: Does Bonnie have an action against Ava for breach of contract?

When one wishes to render her naked promise enforceable, she and her promisee ordinarily name as "consideration" a petty sum such as $1 or $10 or $25, but no amount of money, however large, constitutes consideration if each party causes the other to understand that its purpose is to create the *false appearance* of consideration when in fact Party A manifests her intent[9] to make

---

7. See Hardesty v. Smith, 3 Ind. 39, 41 (1851).
8. Schnell v. Nell, 17 Ind. 29, 31-32 (1861).
9. With respect to contract law, "intent" does not have its ordinary meaning. Party A's "intent" is not that which is truly in her own head. Rather, it is that which a reasonable person in Party B's position attributes to her on the basis of her words and/or behavior. (See Chapter 2, section B.)

a gift to Party B. Where A and B write or speak of "consideration" from B to A but both understand that B doesn't really want it, the purported "consideration" is not in fact consideration. So it is commonly said that "*sham consideration is no consideration.*"

Restatement (Second) §71 cmt. puts it like this:

> [A] mere pretense of bargain does not [create consideration] as where there is a false recital of consideration or where the purported consideration is merely nominal.

Because Bonnie gave no consideration for Ava's promise, these parties formed no contract. Ava's promise was mere *nudum pactum,* unenforceable.[10]

3. *Hold It. We Just Learned That One's Promise Constitutes Consideration Regardless of Value*

Yes, we did and that's true. If in exchange for some promise, Promisor[11] asks Promisee for $1, the dollar might constitute true consideration or, on the other hand, a sham. If circumstances are such as cause Promisee reasonably to understand that Promisor truly, genuinely, wants the dollar in exchange for her promise, then the dollar constitutes consideration. If, on the other hand, Promisee reasonably understands (or *should* understand) that Promisor intends her promise as a gift, and asks for the dollar only to create the *appearance* of consideration, then the dollar is sham consideration; Promisor's promise is not enforceable.

Illustration: The Garage Sale.   At Franco's garage sale Gary spots a lamp tagged "25¢."

(1) **Gary:** Are you truly selling this lamp for 25¢? I know all about lamps, and this one is worth, maybe, $100.

(2) **Franco:** Well, I appreciate your honesty but we just want to be rid of the thing. We tagged it at 25¢, and that's all we want. Will you pay the quarter?

(3) **Gary:** Yes, I think so. May I come tomorrow to pick up the lamp?

(4) **Franco:** Yes, and you can pay the quarter then too. Deal?

(5) **Gary:** Deal.

At statement 4 Franco puts forth a proposal. In light of the circumstances, including the conversation that preceded it, a reasonable person in Gary's

---

10.   The parol evidence rule, however (Chapter 20), might prevent both parties from offering evidence as to the conversation they held before executing the document, in which case evidence of the sham would not reach the fact finder.

11.   All over the law there are splattered the suffixes "or" and "ee." The "__or" party is the one who does something. The "__ee" party is the one to whom, on whom, or for whom it's done. A landlord is the lessor, and her tenant is the lessee. One who donates to a charity is a donor, and the charity is his donee. One who makes a promise is a promisor. The party to whom she makes it is her promisee.

position would understand that Frank's promise to convey the lamp was truly conditioned on Gary's promise to pay 25¢. A reasonable person in Gary's position would believe that Franco was serious about the 25¢ price, even though he now had reason to believe that its market value was much higher. Consequently, Franco truly proposes a bargain; he tenders his own promise to convey the lamp asking, in exchange, for Gary's promise to pay 25¢. Hence, with statement 4, Franco makes an offer. When, at statement 5, Franco accepts, the parties form a contract.

4. "Liquidated Value": When Disparate Value Does Matter

The word "liquidate" has several meanings. In one sense, it means "transform to monetary value." If we say that a business owner "liquidates her inventory," we mean that she sells it all in exchange for money; she reduces it to its monetary value. If we say that a monetary investment is not "liquid," we mean that it is not subject to easy divestment and conversion back to money. When we say "the value of item X is fully liquidated," we mean that all reasonable persons would agree on its value in monetary terms — that its monetary value is not a matter on which reasonable persons can differ.

The simplest case of an item fully liquidated is ordinary currency itself. An ordinary quarter is worth twenty-five cents, and an ordinary dollar bill is worth a dollar. In the law's estimation, that's indisputable; no sane person can think otherwise. If Party A promises to convey an ordinary dime to Party B and Party B, "in exchange," promises simultaneously to convey one ordinary nickel to Party A, the parties do not form a contract. In net effect, A has promised to give B five cents in exchange for nothing.

Suppose Stock X is listed on the Chicago exchange. Party A owns two shares and Party B owns one. Instant by instant, they cannot know what their shares are worth in monetary terms, but they do know and we all know that each share always has the same value as every other. Imagine (for whatever reason) that A promises to convey his two shares to B who, in exchange, promises simultaneously to convey his single share to A. The law will not enforce their agreement, because it's not a *contract*. In net effect, A promises to give B one share of stock in exchange for nothing, meaning that B gives no consideration for A's promise, meaning that A makes a mere gratuitous (naked) promise, unenforceable. The rule is this: *If two parties purport to contract for an exchange of items that, as a matter of indisputable reality, are of different liquidated values, then one of the parties fails to give consideration and the two fail to form a contract.*

Sometimes a Nickel Is Worth More Than Five Cents

If Party A and Party B agree that (1) Party A will give Party B an ordinary 40¢ postage stamp and in exchange that (2) Party B will give Party A an ordinary $1.00 postage stamp, the two parties don't form a contract. The values of the stamps are fully liquidated. In essence, B has promised A a gift of 60¢ and, as we now know well, one's promise to make a gift is unenforceable because it is not supported by consideration.

On the other hand, some postage stamps are collector's items. Their value is not equal to the monetary amount shown on their face. Suppose the U.S. Postal Service produces a 48¢ stamp that embodies a little mistake: George Washington's picture is upside-down.

That 48¢ postage stamp might be worth thousands of dollars. The nickel in Abraham Lincoln's pocket on the night he died is worth far more than five cents. Its value is not "liquidated." If A agrees to pay B $100,000 for *that* nickel, the parties form a contract.

In 1861, in Indiana (for reasons related to a will contest), D promised to pay P $600 in exchange for P's promise to pay D one cent. The court held D's promise unenforceable:

> It is true, that as a general proposition, [difference in the value of exchanged considerations] will not vitiate an agreement. . . . But this doctrine does not apply to a mere exchange of sums of money, of coin, whose value is exactly fixed, but to the exchange of something of, in itself, indeterminate value, for money, or, perhaps, for some other thing of indeterminate value. In this case, had the one cent mentioned, been some particular one cent, a family piece, or ancient, remarkable coin, possessing an indeterminate value, extrinsic from its simple money value, a different view might be taken. As it is, the mere promise to pay six hundred dollars for one cent . . . was simply [a promise] to make a gift.[12]

QUESTION 3. The law will LEAST likely regard as a contract which of the following exchanges?

A. X will, *today*, convey to Y $100,000; Y will, *today*, convey to X the first U.S. postage stamp, issued in 1847, bearing a stated value of 5¢.

B. X will, *today*, convey to Y 100 ordinary single-dollar bills; Y will, *today*, convey to X four *ordinary* twenty-dollar bills.

C. X will, *today*, convey to Y one eight-ounce bottle of Coca-Cola for which X paid $1; Y will, *today*, convey to X one bottle of Pepsi-Cola for which Y paid 90¢.

D. X will, *today*, lend Y $100,000; Y will, *one year from today*, repay the $100,000 together with an additional $5,000.

ANALYSIS.   If two parties agree to exchange items or services that differ in their fair market values, each nonetheless provides the other with consideration. It's only when the values of the items exchanged are indisputably liquidated and indisputably unequal that one fails to give the other consideration.

---
12.   Schnell v. Nell, 17 Ind. 29, 31-32 (1861).

A refers to the first U.S. postage stamp for which the stated value is 5¢. Such a stamp is no ordinary 5¢ stamp; it's a collector's item. Its value today is unrelated to the words "five cents" printed on its surface. Hence, its value is not liquidated; it's worth any price on which a buyer and seller agree. **A** is wrong. As for **C,** Coca-Cola and Pepsi-Cola are two different things. We cannot say as a matter of absolute undeniable reality that to all persons one is worth more than the other, notwithstanding that their retail prices differ. **C** is wrong. **D** represents an ordinary loan at 5 percent annual interest. It's true that $105,000 indisputably exceeds the value of $100,000. But $105,000 one year hence isn't necessarily more valuable than $100,000 today. (For reasons related to the "time value of money," money "now" is normally worth more than money "later.") **D** is wrong.

As for **B,** 100 ordinary single-dollar bills have a value, indisputably, of $100. Four ordinary twenty-dollar bills have a value, indisputably, of $80. X promises Y $100. In exchange, Y promises at the same time to pay X $80. Under ordinary circumstances, the arrangement reflects not a contract but Y's naked promise to give Y $20. **B** is right.[13]

D.   Make Friends with This Phrase: "Bargained for"

When learning about consideration, be ready for the phrase "bargained for," because you're going to read and see statements like these:

- Consideration must be *bargained for.*
- One's promise (or performance) constitutes consideration only if it is *bargained for.*
- In order that Party B's promise serve as consideration for Party A's promise, Party B's promise must be *bargained for.*[14]

This two-word phrase reflects nothing more than the fundamental rule you already know: A promise is enforceable only if it belongs to a contract.

1. Let's Explain That: Mary and Alice

Mary and Alice are roommates. On Saturday morning they talk:

> **Mary:** I think we've let the yard go for too long. I'll mow the lawn today if you'll trim the shrubs today.
> **Alice:** Okay — agreed.

---

13. *Maybe.* Suppose Party X desperately needs four quarters in "exact" change for use in a washing machine. So desperate is he that he agrees to pay Y $5 for four quarters. In that circumstance, the quarters are not "ordinary" ones.

14. See also Restatement (Second) §71.

In its essence, Mary's offer proposes that each party "sell" her promise to the other and, reciprocally, that each "buy" the other's promise. Mary proposes to sell Alice her lawn mowing promise, charging as a "price" *Alice's* promise to trim the shrubs. Concomitantly, Mary proposes that Alice "sell" Mary her promise to trim the shrubs, with Mary to pay Alice as a "price" *her* promise to mow the lawn. When Mary makes the proposal, she "bargains for" Alice's promise. When Alice assents to it, she "bargains for" Mary's promise. Simultaneously, the parties form a contract. All of that means, really, that: *A promise is "bargained for" if and only if it belongs to a contract—if and only if it belongs to an offer that the offeree accepts.*

Compare Mary and Alice to roommates Marvin and Alex:

> **Marvin:** I think we've let the yard go for too long. I'll mow the lawn today.
> **Alex:** That's great. In exchange, I'll trim the shrubs today.

Alex says he will trim "in exchange" for Marvin's promise to mow. Nonetheless, Alex makes his promise in *appreciation* of Marvin's, but *not in exchange* for it. Neither of these parties ever proposed a *bargain* to the other. Marvin did not say, ever, "I'll mow the lawn if you will trim the trees." Alex did not say, ever, "I'll trim the shrubs if you will mow the lawn." Rather, Marvin promised to mow the lawn asking nothing back from Alex. With Marvin's promise already in place, and in the spirit of cooperative gratitude, Alex promised to trim the shrubs asking nothing back from Alex. Stated otherwise, neither party made an offer to the other, which means that neither accepted an offer *from* the other, which means that the parties did not form a contract, which means neither promise belongs to a contract, which means that neither has been "bargained for." Once again, we reveal this simple truth: *A promise is "bargained for" if and only if it belongs to a contract—if and only if it arises by offer and acceptance.*[15]

QUESTION 4. For the five years 2015-2019, Nancy has lived with and cared for her elderly uncle Moses. At the beginning of year six, Moses's sister takes up the task. Nancy departs to begin the long awaited schooling she has thus far deferred. Grateful for Nancy's services, Moses creates a document entitled "Promissory Writing." He signs it and gives it to Nancy. Nancy reads it:

IN CONSIDERATION OF and IN EXCHANGE FOR THE care, devotion, and affection she has shown and given me during these last five years I, Moses Shev, by this instrument to which

---

15. The Restatement writers put it thus: "(1) To constitute consideration . . . a return promise must be bargained for. (2) A . . . return promise is bargained for if it is sought by the promisor in exchange for the promise and is given by the promisee in exchange for that promise." (Restatement (Second) §71.) These ALI/Restatement folk are a lubberly lot. They seem not to know that by their very own precepts and definitions they have stated only this: A promise is bargained for if it belongs to a contract.

> I have set my hand and signature on this 26th day of February, 2019 do promise that should I live to the age of 90 (ninety) years I will, on my 90th (ninetieth) birthday give to my niece Nancy Shev the exact sum of $1 million.

Two years later, Moses turns 90 but refuses to pay Nancy the $1 million he promised. Nancy brings an action against him for breach. Moses's attorney contends that Nancy gave no consideration for the promise, which fact, he says, renders it unenforceable. Nancy's attorney maintains that the years of service to which Moses expressly referred were Nancy's consideration for the promise. If the court rules for Moses, which of the following might it likely state as its reason?

   I. Nancy cannot demonstrate that her service had a monetary value of $1 million, wherefore Moses received no consideration for his promise.

  II. Nancy did not sign the promissory writing, wherefore Moses's promise does not belong to a contract and is, therefore, unenforceable.

 III. Moses did not bargain for Nancy's service, wherefore he gave his promise without consideration.

 IV. The promissory writing does not represent a bargain, wherefore Moses's promise is unenforceable.

  A. I and II
  B. II and III
  C. III and IV
  D. I, II, III, and IV

ANALYSIS. After Nancy completes her five years of voluntary service, Moses makes his promise in *appreciation* of it, but not in *exchange* for it. Nowhere in these parties' dealings did either propose to the other an "I'll do X if you'll do Y." That means neither made an offer, which means neither made an acceptance, which means the parties formed no contract, which means that Moses made not a contractual promise, but a naked promise, unenforceable. Many will say that Nancy's devoted service fails as consideration because it was not "bargained for"—because Moses did not demand Nancy's service in exchange for his promise. He couldn't do that, of course, because he made his promise when Nancy had already performed her five years of service. And that means no more than this: Moses's promise did not belong to a contract.

Option I implies that Moses's promise is unenforceable because Nancy's service might be worth less than $1 million. We know better. One promise (or performance) may constitute consideration for another regardless of relative values (section C above). Option II reports that Nancy did not sign the promissory writing. That's irrelevant too. Signed or unsigned, by Moses, Nancy,

John Hancock, or Solon the Sage, the document sets forth only a naked promise. If Nancy had signed it, then, still, she would be beneficiary of a $1 million promise — naked and unenforceable.

Having eliminated options I and II, we eliminate also **A**, **B**, and **D**. That leaves us with **C**, which cites only options III and IV.

According to option III, Moses did not "bargain for" Nancy's service. That's true. His promise did not come forth through offer and acceptance; it did not belong to a contract and for that reason was not enforceable. Option IV makes a correct and equivalent statement — that the writing did not amount to a contract. **C** is right.

E.   Past Consideration

1. *"Past Consideration Is No Consideration"*

Loitering about the law is this pest of a "rule": *Past consideration is no consideration*. That "rule" represents yet another form of the one just studied: In order that a promise (or performance) serve as consideration, it must be "bargained for," which means, really, that a promise is enforceable if and only if it belongs to a contract.

We know, now, that if B does some service for A *after which* A purports to make a promise in "consideration" thereof, A's promise is a mere *nudum pactum*, unenforceable. Some courts will write that A did not "bargain for" B's service, wherefore B's service is not consideration. Others, regrettably, write: "Past consideration is no consideration."

Accordingly, some 185 years ago in Vermont, defendant promised to pay money to plaintiff, "in consideration that" plaintiff had in the recent past done some service for defendant. The court ruled defendant's promise unenforceable, explaining that a "promise made on a past consideration is not binding . . . it is nudum pactum."[16] One hundred seventy-six years later, a Montana employer employed defendant. After defendant had worked for four months, the employer presented him with a writing labeled "agreement." It recited defendant-employee's promise not to compete with plaintiff, his employer. According to the writing, defendant made his promise "in consideration" of the salary plaintiff had paid him during the previous four months. The court held defendant's promise unenforceable: "The basic precepts of black-letter contract law teach us that 'past consideration is not sufficient to support a promise.'"[17]

Think again of Moses and Nancy. First, Nancy cared for Moses. Then, in appreciation for what she had already done, Moses promised her $1 million,

---

16.   Barlow v. Smith, 4 Vt. 139, 143 (1832).

17.   Access Organic, Inc. v. Hernandez, 175 P.3d 899, 903 (Mont. 2008).

asking nothing new in exchange. As already noted, some authorities will state that Nancy's services fail as consideration because they were not "bargained for." Others will say, "past consideration is no consideration." And you should now see that the two statements mean one and the same thing: *A promise that does not belong to a contract is mere nudum pactum, unenforceable.*

QUESTION 5. Jill has a large leak in her roof, but lacks the funds necessary to repair it. Her friend Jack voluntarily makes the repair. Three months later Jill learns that Jack is short of funds; he can't pay his rent. She contacts him and says, "I'll pay the $2,000 you owe for rent." When Jack protests that he cannot accept such a large sum, Jill responds, "You repaired my leaking roof when I couldn't afford to pay for it. I now promise you something in exchange. In consideration of the roof repairs you made for me, I will pay your August rent." Does Jack's roof repair serve as consideration for Jill's promise?

   I. Yes, because Jill made her promise expressly citing the roof repair as consideration
  II. Yes, because Jill manifested her serious wish to pay Jack's rent in exchange for the roof repair
 III. No, because the roof repair constitutes only past consideration
  IV. No, because Jill did not bargain for the roof repair
   V. No, because Jill did not record her promise in writing
   A. I and II
   B. I, II, and III
   C. III and IV
   D. IV and V

ANALYSIS. In principle, we've seen this case before. Party X does a favor for Party Y. Gratefully, Party Y promises something to Party X "in consideration" of what Party X has done. By law Party X's service is *not* consideration for Y's promise; Y's promise is *nudum pactum*, unenforceable. In this case, Jack is X and Jill is Y. Jack's prior service is not consideration for Jill's promise, and we may state the reason in multiple ways, including these:

- In making her promise, Jill did not "bargain for" Jack's service; she did not say to Jack, "I'll pay your rent if you will repair my roof." She could not do so because she promised to pay the rent after Jack had already repaired the roof.
- Jack's service was mere "past consideration," which is "no consideration."
- Jill's promise did not belong to a contract.

Options III and IV make two of the statements just mentioned, so they're correct. Options I and II incorrectly state that Jill's promise is enforceable, and each makes (or implies) its own false statement of law. As for option I: A promisor does not receive "consideration" by writing or speaking that *word*. As for option II: One does not create consideration by earnestly thinking her promise to be given "in exchange" for a service previously received. Jill made her promise because she *appreciated* Jack's prior service, but not *in exchange* for it. Option V correctly states that Jill's promise is unenforceable, but its reasoning is wrong. If Jill had put her promise in a signed writing, it would be "bupkis" just the same. C endorses only options III and IV, and so **C** is right.

2. Yet Another Redundant Statement: "Love and Affection Are Not Consideration"

Suppose Daughter cares for Father in his old age. In gratitude Father, by signed writing, makes this promise: "In consideration of the love and affection shown me by my daughter for many years, I hereby promise that one year from today I will give her my farm, to wit, the real estate described in Volume 113 Page 422 of the Ashton County Land Records."

The "love and affection" to which Father refers came to him before he made his promise. Hence, he did not make his promise *in exchange* for his daughter's love. He did not make it as part of any bargain that either party ever proposed to the other. His promise is unenforceable because it doesn't belong to a contract.

Nonetheless, legal history is replete with promisors who cite love and affection as the "consideration" for their promises. For that reason, there arose in the courts the statement that "love and affection are not consideration." The statement means, really, that past consideration is no consideration. *That* statement means really, that consideration must be "bargained for." And *that* statement means no more and no less than this: A promise is enforceable if and only if it belongs to a contract. And, finally, a contract requires, first, that one party make an offer to another. One makes an offer, in turn, only if she proposes a bargain—a "this" for "that"—a *quid pro quo*.

F.   An Exception to the Consideration Doctrine: "Moral Obligation"

Notwithstanding all that we've taught, most jurisdictions do enforce one form of naked promise on a theory some call "moral obligation" or "moral consideration." Suppose that on January 1, Lamar and Damon form a contract under which Lamar lends Damon $1,000, Damon promising to repay it with 5 percent interest on or before December 31 of the same year. Damon's promise is, of course, enforceable. It belongs to a contract. As consideration, Damon receives Lamar's $1,000 loan.

On December 31, Damon fails to repay, but Lamar takes no action against him. Six years then elapse, and still Lamar takes no action. In the relevant jurisdiction, the statute of limitations pertaining to contracts and debts provides: "As to any breach of contract or unpaid debt, a plaintiff who fails to bring his action within six years from the time of default shall have no right of recovery." With six years passed since the time Damon defaulted, Lamar loses his right to sue for the debt. Legally, then, *Damon no longer owes Lamar the money*; his "slate" is "clean."

Imagine that Damon then contacts Lamar and says (or writes), "My debt has been discharged by the statute of limitations, but rest assured that I will pay you the $1,000 anyway—within six months from now." From all that we now know, Damon's new promise ought to be unenforceable. Although Lamar furnished consideration for Damon's *original* promise to repay made six years earlier, Damon gives this subsequent promise in exchange for nothing. The statute of limitations has discharged the original debt wherefore, by law, Damon owes Lamar nothing. Yet for his own reasons Damon promises to pay the $1,000 that he does not (any longer) owe. Damon's newly made promise to pay Lamar $1,000 is *nudum pactum*.

Nonetheless, in most jurisdictions one's promise to pay an old debt, discharged by operation of law, is enforceable because, it is said, the promisor has received "moral consideration," or his consideration inheres in his "moral obligation" to make the payment. With these words, the law means to say that the original loan, although discharged, serves as consideration for the subsequent promise in a way that squares with "good morality" (if not good logic). Hence, one's new promise to pay a debt discharged by operation of law (usually by a statute of limitations) *is* enforceable. The promisee has received no consideration as we otherwise know that word. Nonetheless, for this purpose the law long ago invented the phrase "moral consideration" and with it, in most jurisdictions, renders such promises enforceable as an exception to the general precepts we've studied thus far.

In those jurisdictions, the applicable rule is this: *If, for a contract under which one party owes a debt to the other the relevant statute of limitations expires but the debtor thereafter promises to pay the debt (fully or in part), his promise is enforceable on the theory of "moral obligation" or "moral consideration" notwithstanding the absence of any new consideration from the creditor.*

Restatement (Second) §82(1) takes that view, but (happily) avoids the phrases "moral consideration" and "moral obligation."

> A promise to pay . . . an antecedent . . . indebtedness is binding if the indebtedness . . . would be [enforceable] except for the effect of a statute of limitations.

Among those jurisdictions that recognize "moral consideration", most have modified the common law by statute,[18] providing that any such promise is enforceable only if set forth in a signed writing. In North Dakota, for example,

---

18. See Appendix, section D.4.

one's promise to pay an old ("antecedent") debt discharged by the statute of limitations is enforceable, but "no [such] . . . promise is sufficient . . . unless the same is contained in some writing signed by the party to be charged thereby . . . ." N.D. Cent. Code §28-01-36.

QUESTION 6. In a jurisdiction that recognizes "moral consideration," Solomon's business supplies fabric to wholesalers. Bennett is a fabric wholesaler. By signed writing, on November 1, 2012, the parties form a contract under which Solomon is to sell and deliver to Bennett on December 1 a quantity of cotton cloth for which Bennett will pay Solomon $50,000 on or before December 31. Solomon delivers the cloth on December 1, but by the 31st, Bennett fails to pay. On the next day, January 1, 2013, and on the first day of every month for *six years* through and including December 31, 2018, Solomon's automated office procedures send billing statements to Bennett's office, each one requesting payment of $50,000 "within 30 days."

Meanwhile, for all billing statements it receives, from all vendors, every month, Bennett's automated office procedures print a "Billing Acknowledgment" form that reads: "This office acknowledges a debt in the amount shown on your most recent billing statement and will pay the debt by the last day of the current month." On or about the second day of each month, Bennett's clerical assistant presents all such acknowledgment forms to Bennett, who hurriedly and routinely signs each one, whereafter the assistant mails one to each vendor who has provided Bennett a billing statement that month. Consequently, for each of the seventy-two monthly billing statements Solomon sends Bennett over the six-year period January 1, 2013 through December 31, 2018, Bennett sends Solomon an acknowledgment form. In response to Solomon's December 31, 2018 billing statement, Bennett's office mails its acknowledgment form on January 2, 2019. Solomon's office receives it on January 5.

As to claims for breach of contract and failure to pay debts, the state's period of statutory limitation is six years. Consequently, as to the $50,000 Bennett owes Solomon, the statutory period expires on December 31, 2018, six years after Bennett was first obliged to pay it.

On February 1, 2019, Solomon engages a financial consultant who studies Solomon's business including its accounts receivable (meaning moneys owed to it). On discovering the $50,000 unpaid by Bennett since December 31, 2013, the consultant advises Solomon to bring suit. On March 15, 2019, Solomon does bring suit. Is Solomon entitled to recover the $50,000 from Bennett?

A. Yes, because one's debt to another continues, even after the statutory period of limitation expires
B. Yes, because Bennett sent Solomon an acknowledgment form after the statutory period of limitation expired
C. No, because after the statutory period of limitation expired Bennett made Solomon no express promise to pay the $50,000
D. No, because Bennett ceased to owe Solomon the $50,000 as of December 31, 2018

ANALYSIS.   On December 31, 2018, the six-year period of limitation passed; as of that date, Bennett owed Solomon nothing. Yet two days later, on January 2, 2019 by the acknowledgment form he hurriedly signed, Bennett (unwittingly) promised to pay the debt. Ordinarily, the promise would amount to *nudum pactum. But* in this case, it's a promise to pay a preexisting debt discharged by a statute of limitations. Consequently (in this jurisdiction), it's enforceable on the theory of "moral consideration."

C and D tell us that Bennett's promise is *not* enforceable. Both are wrong. According to C, Bennett made no "express promise" to pay the debt. That's false. Each of Bennett's signed acknowledgment forms referred to Solomon's most recent billing statement and thus constituted an express promise to pay the $50,000 debt. D correctly states that Bennett's debt expired with the passage of six years, but ignores the fact that his new promise, made two days later, revives it. A accurately states that Solomon will recover from Bennett, but its reasoning is flatly contrary to law. When the relevant statutory period of limitation expires, one's debt ceases to exist; he need not pay it — ever.

B tells us that Bennett's promise is enforceable because, with the acknowledgment sent to Solomon on January 2, 2019, Bennett promised to pay a debt that the statute of limitations had discharged. And, although Bennett got nothing back for this new gratuitous promise, the cotton cloth he originally received constitutes "moral consideration." Or, as some would say, the consideration Bennett receives inheres in the discharge of his "moral obligation" to pay (what once was) his debt. B is right.

G.   The Closer

QUESTION 7. Benito is a graduate student. On September 15, 2019, he asks his friend Lannette for a $10,000 loan.

> **Lannette:** Why do you need the loan?
>
> **Benito:** The new semester has begun, and I'm $10,000 short on the tuition I owe. Classes have started and I've been attending them, but the bursar is demanding that I pay.
>
> **Lannette:** That's a lot of money, but I will never forget how you traveled across the country to visit me last year when I needed emotional support. Certainly I'll make the loan; you'll pay it back only if and when you're able. It will take me a week or two to get a hold of the money, but I'll put my commitment in a writing that you can show to the bursar. Maybe she'll leave you alone until the money comes through.

Lannette then creates and signs this writing:

> September 15, 2019
> To Whom It May Concern:

In consideration of (i) my long-standing friendship with Benito Bourne, and (ii) the help he has given me and the sacrifice he has made for me in several specific instances, and (iii) his need to pay school tuition, I, the undersigned Lannette Lindstom as Lender, do hereby promise and commit myself to lend to the said Benito Bourne the sum of $10,000 at 1% annual interest, the loan to be made on or before October 1 of this year, 2019.

> **REPAYMENT TERMS:** The said Benito Bourne is to repay the loan and/or interest when and only when, if and only if, at any time in the future he feels himself ready, willing, and able to do so and otherwise not at all, neither loan principal nor interest.

On October 1, Lannette tells Benito, "I'm sorry, but I've changed my mind about the loan. I don't think I can afford to part with the $10,000." Benito visits his lawyer who correctly advises him that Lannette's promise is unenforceable for lack of consideration from Benito. The lawyer is correct because

I. notwithstanding her signed writing, Lannette made no promise to lend Benito $10,000.
II. Benito promised nothing in return for Lannette's commitment.
III. among the matters that Lannette cites as consideration for her promise, none was bargained for.
IV. within Lannette's signed writing none of the terms provided at items (i), (ii), or (iii) truly describes consideration from Benito to Lannette.
V. Benito did not sign the writing.
A. I
B. II and III
C. I, II, III, and V
D. II, III, and IV

ANALYSIS.   According to option I, Lannette made no promise. That's false. She did make a promise; she promised to lend Benito $10,000. Her promise is not *enforceable*, but she did make it. Since option I is false, **A** and **C** must be wrong. That leaves **B** and **D**, both of which cite options II and III, meaning that II and III must be true. The two choices differ in that **D** cites, also, option IV. If option IV is false, **D** is wrong and **B** is right. If option IV is true, **B** is wrong and **D** is right.

In option IV, clause (i) as consideration for making the loan, Lannette cites her long-standing friendship with Benito. What goes for love and affection goes, too, for long-standing friendships. Lannette makes her promise *because* of friendship, not *in exchange for it.*

Clause (ii) cites help given and sacrifice made — in the past. Some will read it and say "past consideration is no consideration." Better it is to recognize that Lannette makes her promise *because* of Benito's help and sacrifice, not in *exchange* for it. In clause (iii), Lannette states yet another reason for which she promises the loan. But Benito's need for tuition is a fact. Lannette cannot and does not receive it *in exchange* for her promise. And what of the "repayment terms"? Their 48 words come to this: Benito need never repay the loan — ever; the "loan" is, really, a gift.

All references that appear in option IV are bases on which a lawyer should conclude that Lannette has made only a naked promise, unenforceable. Since option IV is true, **D** is right. We know that without examining III or V, but let's look at them anyway.

Option III is true. Among all things that Lannette cites as "consideration" for her promise, none has come to her in exchange for her promise; none was bargained for. As for option V, it's true that Benito did not sign the writing. That, however, is a "so what?" Had Benito signed the writing in ink, holy water, wine, or blood — still he would be giving nothing to Lannette in exchange for her promise. Still, her promise would be mere *nudum pactum*, unenforceable. Options II, III, and IV are true; I and V are false. **D** is right.

 Silver's Picks

1.	C
2.	D
3.	B
4.	C
5.	C
6.	B
7.	D

13

Consideration, Part II

A. "Legal Detriment" and "Legal Benefit"

In section B of this chapter, we'll at long last define "consideration," but first, let's befriend a few more words and phrases. Judicial opinions treat us to proclamations like these: (1) "One gives consideration when she suffers a 'legal detriment,'" (2) "One gives consideration when she suffers a 'loss of legal freedom,'" and (3) "One gives consideration when she confers on another a 'legal benefit.'" KNOW THAT THOSE THREE STATEMENTS HAVE IDENTICAL MEANINGS.

1. "Legal Detriment"

Just below, we depict eight agreements. Understand that "agreement" is different from "contract." An agreement might or not be, also, a contract—its promises might or might not be enforceable. In section B, we'll look again at these eight agreements and determine whether each is or is not a contract. Right now, we'll assess each for the creation of legal detriment.

Al and Bob

> **Al:** I'll drive you to the bank on Monday afternoon if, on Tuesday, you'll wash my car.
> **Bob:** I accept.

Resulting Agreement:

Al will drive Bob to the bank on Monday.
Bob will wash Al's car on Tuesday.

It's obvious, of course, that before the parties form this agreement no law requires that Al drive Bob to the bank or anywhere else. Al promises to do what the law does not otherwise require of him. Conclusion: Al's promise causes him to suffer a legal detriment.

Before the parties form this agreement, no law requires that Bob wash Al's car. With this agreement, he promises to do what the law does not otherwise require of him. Conclusion: Bob's promise causes him to suffer a legal detriment.

BuyCo (Widget User) and SellCo (Widget Seller)

BuyCo: We might need widgets in 2020. Then again we might not. Understand, please, that we won't commit to purchasing even a single widget. But, we propose to promise this: If, in 2020, we do buy widgets, we'll buy them only from you, no one else. We'll pay $1 per widget. In exchange, we want your promise that if we do need widgets, you'll provide them to us in any quantity we order, for $1 each.

SellCo: We accept.

Resulting Agreement:

If BuyCo buys widgets at any time during the year 2020, it will buy them from no one other than SellCo and it will pay $1 per widget.
If BuyCo does order widgets—and maybe it won't—SellCo will provide them for $1 each.

Obviously, once again, before the parties form this arrangement, no law requires that BuyCo buy its widgets from SellCo. BuyCo is free to buy widgets, if at all, from any seller it chooses. It promises not to do—to refrain from doing—what the law otherwise allows. Conclusion: BuyCo suffers a legal detriment.

Before the parties form this agreement, no law requires that SellCo provide any widgets to BuyCo, not at $1 per unit or any other price. With this agreement, SellCo promises to do what the law does not otherwise require of it. Conclusion: SellCo suffers a legal detriment. (In Chapter 14, section A.2, we have more to say about this sort of contract—a "requirements contract.")

Mother and Janelle (age 22)

Mother: If, for these next two coming years, 2019 and 2020, you promise that when driving your car you will always obey the posted speed limit, I will pay you $5,000 today.

Janelle: I accept.

Resulting Agreement:

> Mother will pay Janelle $5,000 today.
> For all of 2019 and 2020, Janelle will obey the posted speed limit.

Before the parties form this agreement, Mother is under no legal obligation to pay Janelle $5,000 or any other amount. With this agreement, she promises to do what the law does not otherwise require of her. Conclusion: Mother suffers a legal detriment.

On the other hand, before the parties form this agreement, the law does require that Janelle obey posted speed limits. With this agreement, she promises to do what the law on its own already requires of her. Conclusion: Janelle does *not* suffer a legal detriment.

Father and Jake (age 22)

> **Father:** If, for these next two coming years, 2019 and 2020, you promise that when driving your car you will not ever exceed the speed of 40 miles per hour regardless of the posted speed limit, I will pay you $5,000 today.
>
> **Jake:** I accept.

Resulting Agreement:

> Father will pay Jake $5,000 today.
> For all of 2019 and 2020, regardless of the posted speed limit, Jake will drive no faster than 40 miles per hour.

Before the parties form this agreement, Father is under no legal obligation to pay Jake $5,000 or any other amount. With this agreement, he promises to do what the law does not otherwise require of him. Conclusion: Father suffers a legal detriment.

Before the parties form this agreement, the law does not on its own require that Jake drive at a speed below the posted limit. He may move at 50, 60, or 70 miles per hour if the posted limit so provides. With this agreement, Jake promises not to do—to refrain from doing—what the law otherwise allows. Conclusion: Jake suffers a legal detriment.

Wesley and Quenton

> **Wesley (by signed writing):** I want to establish a medical laboratory, and your Spring Street building would be perfect for that purpose. In three months, I will buy your building for $10 million if during that period I am able to secure a license to use it as a medical laboratory. If I can't secure the license, then I won't buy it. In exchange, I want your promise that if I do secure the license, you will sell me the building for $10 million.
>
> **Quenton (by signed writing):** Agreed.

Resulting Agreement:

If but *only if* he is able to secure a license to operate it as a medical laboratory—conditional on that—Wesley will purchase the building and pay
Quenton $10 million.

On that same condition, Quenton will sell Wesley the building for
$10 million.

Wesley does not promise to buy the building, but he does make a *conditional* promise to do so. If he succeeds in securing the license, he will buy the
building. Before the parties form this agreement, Wesley is legally free to secure
the license and not buy any building—not Quenton's or any other. With this
agreement, he promises to do what the law does not otherwise require of him.
Conclusion: Wesley suffers a legal detriment. (In Chapter 14, section A, we
provide a more elaborate treatment of conditional promises as consideration.)

Before the parties form this agreement, Quenton is free not to sell his
building to Wesley or anyone else. With this agreement, he promises to do
what the law does not otherwise require of him. Conclusion: Quenton suffers
a legal detriment.

Beth and Hernan, March 1, 10:00 A.M.

Hernan: If you promise to type my 100-page manuscript by March 15,
I will promise to pay you $700 on March 16.
Beth: Okay. It's a deal.

Resulting Agreement:

Beth will type the manuscript and complete the work by March 15.
Hernan will pay Beth $700 on March 16.

Before the parties form this agreement, no law requires that Beth type
Hernan's manuscript, and no law requires that Hernan pay Beth any amount
of money. Each of them promises to do what the law does not otherwise
require. Conclusion: At 10:00 A.M., each suffers a legal detriment.

Beth and Hernan, March 1, 10:30 A.M.

Beth: I have re-thought our agreement of thirty minutes ago. For my
pay, I want more than $700. Here's my proposal: As already agreed, I'll
promise to type the manuscript by March 15. In exchange, you promise
to pay me not $700 but $1,000.
Hernan: I accept.

Resulting Agreement:

Beth will finish the work by March 15.
Hernan will pay Beth $1,000 on March 16.

Before the parties form this 10:30 A.M. agreement, their 10:00 A.M. agreement requires that Hernan pay Beth $700. By law — not statutory law, but the law of contract — Hernan must pay Beth that amount, and no more. With this 10:30 agreement, Hernan promises to pay Beth $300 "extra." He promises to do what the law does not otherwise require of him. Conclusion: At 10:30 A.M., Hernan suffers a legal detriment.

Before the parties form this 10:30 A.M. agreement, their 10:00 A.M. agreement requires that Beth type the manuscript by March 15. With this 10:30 A.M. agreement, she promises only to do that same thing — what the law (the 10:00 A.M. agreement) on its own already requires of her — to type the manuscript by March 15. Conclusion: At 10:30 A.M., Beth suffers no legal detriment.

Ward (Police Officer) and Kathe (Community Resident)

Kathe: Crime in our community seems to be increasing lately. As you patrol the area, please watch for suspicious behavior. If you'll promise to do that for one year, I'll promise to pay you $10,000 today.
Ward: I accept.

Resulting Agreement:

As Ward patrols the area, he will watch for suspicious conduct.
Beth will pay Ward $10,000 today.

Before the parties form this agreement, the law does not require that Kathe pay Ward $10,000 or any other amount, ever. With this agreement, she promises to do what the law does not otherwise require of her. Conclusion: Kathe suffers a legal detriment.

Before the parties form this agreement, Ward, a police officer, by the terms of his employment, is legally obliged to watch for suspicious behavior while on patrol. With this agreement, he promises to do what the law already requires of him. Conclusion: Ward does not suffer a legal detriment.

George and Harriet

George: If you will promise to take me waterskiing on your boat next weekend, I will either (a) drive you to the fair tomorrow or, if I don't, I will (b) pay a cab driver to take you there.
Harriet: I accept.

Resulting Agreement:

Harriet will take George waterskiing next weekend.
George will either (a) drive Harriet to the fair or (b) pay a cab driver to do so.

Before the parties form this agreement, Harriet has no legal obligation to take George waterskiing. With this agreement, she promises to do what the law does not otherwise require of her. Conclusion: Harriet suffers a legal detriment.

Before the parties form this agreement, George has no obligation to drive Harriet to the fair. Neither need he pay anyone else to do so. By promising to do one or the other, George promises to do what the law does not otherwise require of him. Conclusion: George suffers a legal detriment.

Instead of the phrase "legal detriment," some courts invoke the words "loss of (legal) freedom," which means "legal detriment." For every situation above in which we say that one's promise causes him a legal detriment, we might just as well say instead that it causes him a "loss of freedom" or "loss of legal freedom." Hence, one loses legal freedom when he (a) promises to do what the law does not otherwise require of him, or (b) promises not to do—to refrain from doing—what the law otherwise allows him to do. (Knowing that "loss of freedom" is identical in meaning to "legal detriment," in this book, we will stick, usually, with "legal detriment.")

2. The Meaning of "Legal Detriment"

One suffers a legal detriment when she (a) promises to do what the law does not otherwise require of her, or (b) promises not to do what the law otherwise allows her to do. Hence, in 1933, the U.S. Court of Appeals for the Tenth Circuit wrote that legal detriment is one's "giving up . . . of a legal right[;] the refraining from doing what he has the legal right to do, or the doing of what he has the legal right not to do." Petroleum Refractionating Corp. v. Kendrick Oil Co., 65 F.2d 997, 999 (10th Cir. 1933).

For Question 1 below, please keep in mind that it is unlawful for an employer to discharge an employee because of race, religion, sex, unionization, or national origin.

QUESTION 1. Ethel operates a business. To every employee she hires she makes what she calls her "four golden promises," shown in choices A-D below. Which of the golden promises subjects Ethel to a legal detriment?

A. Ethel promises never to discharge an employee because he arrives a few minutes late to work.
B. Ethel promises never to discharge an employee because of his religion.
C. Ethel promises never to discharge an employee because she has joined a union.
D. Ethel promises never to discharge an employee because he was born outside of the United States.

ANALYSIS. The law forbids an employer to discharge an employee because of his religion, because he has joined a union, or because he was born outside of the United States.[1] By law, Ethel may not discharge an employee for any of the reasons mentioned in choices **B-D**. All three of those choices are wrong; none describes for Ethel a legal detriment/loss of freedom. With **A**, Ethel promises to refrain from doing what the law allows her to do. In promising not to discharge an employee for petty lateness, she suffers a legal detriment. It's as simple as that; **A** is right.

3. "Legal Benefit"

"Legal benefit" is the "flip side" of legal detriment. When one party to an agreement suffers a legal detriment, then by definition the other derives a legal benefit. One party to an agreement enjoys a legal benefit if and only if the other suffers a legal detriment. Reciprocally, one party to an agreement enjoys a legal benefit if and only if the other suffers a legal detriment.

In this regard, "benefit" doesn't have its ordinary meaning. Suppose A says to B: I will break your nose if you'll break my toes. B assents. Using the word in its ordinary sense, this arrangement confers no "benefit" on A or B. Each does, however, derive a "legal benefit." No law requires that A break B's nose. Her promise to do so subjects her to a legal detriment and, reciprocally, confers on B a "*legal* benefit." No law requires that B break A's toes. His promise to do so subjects him to a legal detriment and, reciprocally, confers on A a legal benefit.

So It's Simple

If A's promise subjects her to a legal detriment, then it provides B with a legal benefit. If B's promise subjects him to a legal detriment, then it provides A with a legal benefit.

QUESTIONS 2 & 3 Alice and Barry are adults. They agree that for one year, Alice will not smoke and, in exchange, Barry will not drink.

QUESTION 2. Does Barry enjoy a legal benefit?

A. Yes, because abstention from alcohol will benefit his health
B. Yes, because Alice promises to refrain from exercising a legal right
C. No, because apart from this agreement, Alice is free, legally, to smoke
D. No, because Alice's abstention from tobacco will not benefit Barry's health

---

1. If the employee is without legal *permission* to work in the United States, then, of course, the employer may (indeed, must) discharge her. But if she is entitled to work in the United States, the employer may not discharge her simply because she was born elsewhere.

ANALYSIS. Legal benefit and legal detriment are "flip sides" of the same "coin." If two parties form an agreement and one of them suffers a legal detriment, then the other derives a legal benefit — always. In order to determine whether Barry does or does not enjoy a legal benefit, we look at Alice's promise and ask whether it subjects her to a legal detriment. If it does, Barry derives a legal benefit. If it doesn't, he doesn't.

Apart from this agreement, Alice is free to smoke. With this agreement, she promises not to do so — not to do what the law otherwise allows. That means she suffers a legal detriment, and that means Barry derives a legal benefit. The answer, therefore, is "yes." The reason? Alice promises to refrain from doing what the law allows her to do.

C and D say "no," so they're wrong. As a reason, C states that apart from this agreement Alice is free to smoke. That's true, but that's the very fact that makes for an answer of "yes." C is wrong. As for D, legal benefit has not a whit to do with bodily health or any other "benefit" as ordinarily we use that word. D is wrong. A answers "yes," but it too refers to benefit as a matter of bodily health. A is wrong. B tells us that Alice promises not to do what the law otherwise allows. That's why her promise subjects her to legal detriment. And, that's why it confers on Barry a legal benefit. B is right.

QUESTION 3. Does Alice suffer a legal detriment?

A. Yes, because abstention from tobacco will benefit her health
B. Yes, because Alice promises to refrain from exercising a legal right
C. No, because apart from this agreement, Alice is free, legally, to smoke
D. No, because Alice's abstention from tobacco will benefit her health

---

ANALYSIS. With Question 2 we concluded that Barry derived a legal benefit, which means that Alice suffered a legal detriment, which means the answer, here, is "yes." Among choices A-D, we look for a statement that tells us why or how Alice underwent a legal detriment. And it's bingo for B. It tells us that Alice promised not to do what the law otherwise allowed. That fact means she suffers a legal detriment. B is right.

Questions 2 and 3 remind us, once again, that where Party X suffers a legal detriment, Party Y, by definition, derives a legal benefit. Where Party Y suffers a legal detriment, Party X, by definition, derives a legal benefit. It's as simple as that. (And, as earlier noted, remember: To say that one suffers a legal detriment is to say, also, that he "loses legal freedom." Hence if X loses legal freedom, Y enjoys a legal benefit.)

> **QUESTION 4.** Alex invites Joan aboard his sailboat. Joan expresses concern for her safety. Among choices **A-D**, which of Alex's promises would *NOT* confer on Joan a legal benefit?
>
> **A.** Don't worry; I'll have on board all safety equipment required by federal and state regulation.
> **B.** Don't worry; I'll have on board more safety equipment than the law requires.
> **C.** Don't worry; I'll be more careful than any sailor ever has been.
> **D.** Don't worry; I'll see that you're perfectly happy, safe, and comfortable.

ANALYSIS. The rule is simple: With respect to any agreement, one party's legal detriment is the other's legal benefit, and one party's legal benefit is the other's legal detriment. With choices **B-D** Alex promises to do what the law does not require of him. All four promises confer on Joan a legal benefit. With **A**, Alex promises to do what the law on its own does already require of him. That means it subjects him to no legal detriment, and *that* means it confers on Joan no legal benefit. **A** is right.

If we had asked that you identify the promise that did not subject Alex himself to a legal detriment, the answer would be the same: **A**. (And, if we had asked you to identify the statement that does not cause Alex to "lose legal freedom," once again, the answer would be **A**.)

B. Now, at Long Last: What Is "Consideration"?

From Chapter 12, section B.2, we know that (1) two parties form a contract when one makes an offer that the other accepts, and (2) one makes an offer when he proposes to the other a *bargain* — an exchange, a *quid pro quo*, a "this" for a "that" — "I'll do X if you'll do Y."

Defining "consideration" means describing the kind of promise that qualifies as a "quid" or a "quo" — a "this" or a "that."

Very simply, now, here are three forms of the rule that defines consideration, EACH ONE PRECISELY EQUIVALENT TO THE OTHER TWO:

(1) One gives consideration if he himself suffers a legal detriment which means that he confers on another a legal benefit.

(2) One gives consideration only if she promises (a) to do what the law does not otherwise require of her, or (b) not to do — to refrain from doing — what the law otherwise allows.

(3) One receives consideration only if another promises her that he will (a) do what the law does not otherwise require of him, or (b) not do — refrain from doing — what the law otherwise allows.

AGAIN, THOSE THREE STATEMENTS HAVE PRECISELY IDENTICAL MEANINGS; EACH IS THE SAME AS EVERY OTHER.

Most regrettably, many courts mistakenly write that consideration inheres in a benefit to one party "*or*" a detriment to the other, as though one party might suffer a detriment without the other deriving a benefit. They don't really mean (or should not mean) to make that statement. They mean (or should mean) to say that if the agreement at issue (1) shows a legal detriment to A, which means, also, that it confers a legal benefit on B, and (2) shows a legal detriment to B, which means, also, that it confers a legal benefit on A, then each party gives consideration to the other. Bearing in mind the erroneous invocation of the word "or," read what the courts have written for two hundred years and more:

> According to familiar definition, a consideration is a benefit to [one party] or a . . . detriment to the [other.]

Irwin v. Lombard University, 36 L.R.A. 239 (Ohio 1897).

> The consideration of a contract can consist either in a benefit conferred upon [one party] or in a legal detriment to the [other, which means that one party] gives up certain rights . . . which he theretofore possessed or assumes certain duties or liabilities not theretofore imposed upon him.

Lake Land Employment Group of Akron, LLC v. Columber, 804 N.E.2d 27 (Ohio 2003).

> Consideration exists "where there is a detriment to the [one party] or a benefit to the [other]."

In re Cook, 504 B.R. 496, 503 (B.A.P. 8th Cir. 2014).

A "This" and a "That"

In Chapter 2, section B and in the section just above, we say that a bargain is a quid pro quo, an "I'll do this and you'll do that." One's promise qualifies as a "this" or a "that" if and only if, as just stated, it demands that he (a) do what the law does not otherwise require, or (b) not do what the law otherwise allows. In other words, A's promise to B qualifies as a "this" or a "that" if it subjects A to a legal detriment. In still other words, A's promise to B qualifies as a "this" or a "that" if it confers on B a legal benefit.

Now, let's use the eight illustrations from above to identify (a) agreements that do constitute contracts because each party furnishes consideration to the other, and (b) agreements that don't constitute contracts because one of the parties fails to furnish consideration to the other.

Al and Bob

(1) Al proposed that both he and Bob promise what the law did not otherwise require of them, which means he proposed a "this" for a "that," which means he proposed a bargain, which means he made an offer, which means Bob's assent was an acceptance; (2) both parties suffered a legal detriment, which means, reciprocally, that (3) each derived a legal benefit. Those three statements have identical meanings: that each party provided consideration to the other. The parties formed a contract and their promises are enforceable.

BuyCo (Widget User) and SellCo (Widget Seller)

(1) BuyCo proposed (a) its own promise to refrain from doing what the law otherwise allowed and (b) that SellCo promise to do what the law did not otherwise require, which means BuyCo proposed a "this" for a "that," which means it proposed a bargain, which means it made an offer, which means SellCo's assent was an acceptance; (2) both parties suffered a legal detriment, which means, reciprocally, that (3) each derived a legal benefit. Those three statements have identical meanings: that each party provided consideration to the other. The parties formed a contract and their promises are enforceable.

Mother and Janelle (age 22)

(1) Mother proposed (a) her own promise to do what the law did not otherwise require of her but proposed (b) that Janelle should promise what the law, on its own, did already require of her, which means Mother proposed a "this" for herself but no "that" for Janelle—*a "quid" for her but no "quo" for Janelle*—which means she proposed no bargain, which means she made no offer, which means Janelle's assent was not an acceptance; (2) Mother suffered a legal detriment and, reciprocally, Janelle derived a legal benefit; (3) Janelle suffered no legal detriment, meaning that Mother derived no legal benefit. Those three statements have *identical* meanings; Mother's promise qualifies as consideration but Janelle's does not, which means the parties formed no contract, which means Mother made only a naked promise, unenforceable. If Mother decides not to pay Janelle the $5,000, she won't be in breach of contract, because the parties have no contract. Likewise, if Janelle exceeds the speed limit, she will violate traffic law, but she won't be in breach of contract because the parties have no contract.

Father and Jake (age 22)

(1) Father proposed (a) his own promise to do what the law did not otherwise require of him, in exchange for (b) Jake's promise to refrain from doing what

the law otherwise allowed, which means he proposed *a* "this" for a "that," which means he proposed a bargain, which means he made an offer, which means Jake's assent was an acceptance; (2) both parties suffered a legal detriment, which means, reciprocally, that (3) each derived a legal benefit. Those three statements have identical meanings: that each party provided consideration to the other. The parties formed a contract and their promises are enforceable.

Wesley and Quenton

(1) Wesley proposed that both he and Quenton promise what the law did not otherwise require of them, which means he proposed a "this" for a "that," which means he proposed a bargain, which means he made an offer, which means Quenton's assent was an acceptance; (2) both parties suffered legal detriment, which means, reciprocally, that (3) each derived a legal benefit. Those three statements have identical meanings: that each party provided consideration to the other. The parties formed a contract and their promises are enforceable. (Wesley makes a *conditional* promise, a matter that we treat more extensively in Chapter 14, section A.)

Beth and Hernan, 10:00 A.M.

(1) Hernan proposed that both he and Beth promise to do what the law did not otherwise require of them, which means he proposed a "this" for a "that," which means he proposed a bargain, which means he made an offer, which means Beth's assent was an acceptance; (2) both parties suffered legal detriment, which means, reciprocally, that (3) each derived a legal benefit. Those three statements have identical meanings: that each party provided consideration to the other. The parties formed a contract and their promises are enforceable.

Beth and Hernan, 10:30 A.M.

(1) Beth proposed (a) that Hernan promise what the law (the 10:00 A.M. contract) did not otherwise require of him but proposed (b) that she herself would promise what the law (the 10:00 A.M. contract) did already require of her, which means she proposed a "this" for Hernan but no "that" for herself — a "quid" for him but no "quo" for her — which means she made no offer, which means Hernan's assent was not an acceptance; (2) Hernan suffered a legal detriment, which means Beth derived a legal benefit; (3) Beth suffered no legal detriment, which means Hernan derived no legal benefit. Those three statements have identical meanings: Hernan's 10:30 A.M. promise qualified as consideration but Beth's did not; the parties failed to form a new contract that altered their first one, which means that at 10:30 A.M. Hernan made only a naked promise, unenforceable. He and Beth remain bound by the 10:00 A.M. contract; Beth must complete the work by March 15. Hernan need pay her only $700.

Ward (Police Officer) and Kathe (Community Resident)

(1) Kathe proposed (a) her own promise to do what the law did not require of her but proposed (b) that Ward should promise to do what the law did already require of him, meaning she proposed a "this" for herself but no "that" for Ward — a "quid" for her but no "quo" for him — which means she proposed no bargain, which means she made no offer, which means Ward's assent was not an acceptance; (2) Kathe suffered a legal detriment, which means Ward derived a legal benefit; (3) Ward suffered no legal detriment, which means Kathe derived no legal benefit. Those three statements have identical meanings; Kathe's promise qualifies as consideration but Ward's does not, which means the parties formed no contract, which means Kathe made only a naked promise, unenforceable. If Ward fails to watch for wrongful behavior, the police department might discipline him, but he won't be in breach of contract.

George and Harriet

(1) George proposed that both he and Harriet promise to do what the law did not otherwise require of them, which means he proposed a "this" for a "that," which means he proposed a bargain, which means he made an offer, which means Harriet's assent was an acceptance; (2) both parties suffered a legal detriment, which means, reciprocally, that (3) each derived a legal benefit. Those three statements have identical meanings: that each party provided consideration to the other. The parties formed a contract and their promises are enforceable.

QUESTION 5. To say that Party 1 proposes (a) his own promise to do what the law on its own already requires of him, in exchange for (b) Party 2's promise to refrain from doing what the law otherwise allows — and that Party 2 assents to the proposal — is to say that

  I. Party 1 makes an offer but the parties form no contract.
  II. Each party makes a naked promise.
  A. I only
  B. II only
  C. Both I and II
  D. Neither I nor II

ANALYSIS. Party 1 asks that Party 2 promise not to do what the law otherwise allows. She proposes her own promise to do what the law already requires of her. She proposes a "this" for Party 2, but no "that" for herself — a "quid" for him but no "quo" for her. Her proposal is not an offer, which means that Party

2's assent is not an acceptance, which means the parties don't form a contract. In that regard, option I is right. But option I also tells us that Party 1 makes an offer, and that's wrong. Option I is false. That eliminates **A** and **C**.

According to option II, each of these parties makes a naked promise, and that's wrong too. Party 1's "promise" to do what she is already obliged to do means she has promised nothing. That means Party 2 makes a promise in exchange for nothing. Party 2, therefore—*only* Party 2—makes a naked promise. Both options I and II are false. **D** is right.

C.   "Preexisting Legal Duty"

The common law purports to feature this rule: *A party fails to give consideration when he promises only to perform a preexisting legal duty.* That principle presents itself in the Ward and Kathe, Beth and Hernan, and Mother and Janelle cases above.

Before Ward and Kathe made their agreement, the terms of Ward's employment required that he watch for wrongdoing. In promising to do only that very same thing, he promised to perform what was his preexisting legal duty. We can describe his failure to furnish consideration in either of these two ways: (1) he suffered no legal detriment, or (2) he promised only to perform a preexisting legal duty. In his case, they are equivalent statements.

At 10:00 A.M., Beth formed a contract requiring that she type Hernan's manuscript by March 15. As of 10:00 A.M., that was her legal duty. When, at 10:30 A.M., she promised only to do that very same thing, she promised to perform what was her preexisting legal duty. We can describe her failure to furnish consideration in either of these two ways: (1) she suffered no legal detriment, or (2) she promised only to perform a preexisting legal duty. In her case, they are equivalent statements.

Before Mother and Janelle made their agreement, Janelle was bound by law to obey the speed limit. We can describe her failure to furnish consideration in either of these two ways: (1) she suffered no legal detriment, or (2) she promised only to perform a preexisting legal duty. In her case, they are equivalent statements.

Restatement (Second) of Contracts §73 provides: "Performance of a legal duty . . . is not consideration."

QUESTION 6. Lance, a landlord, owns two neighboring residential homes in Roseville. Simeon lives in one and Thad in the other, each as Lance's tenant. By their lease agreements with Lance, both tenants are obliged to "notify the landlord if the premises ever should suffer damage that demands immediate attention."

Every year, Simeon winters in Florida while Thad remains in Roseville. Thad spends every summer in Maine while Simeon remains in Roseville. In the fall of 2018, Thad and Simeon form a contract under which

- Thad will monitor Simeon's home during the winter and contact Lance if it should suffer damage that demands immediate attention;
- Simeon will monitor Thad's home during the summer and contact Lance if it should suffer damage that demands immediate attention.

After the parties form their contract, Lance, knowing nothing of it, approaches Thad.

> **Lance:** Your neighbor Simeon will be away for the winter. I make to you this proposal: You promise to watch his home and to contact me if it suffers any damage that needs immediate attention. In exchange, I'll promise to pay you $500 when Simeon returns home. Are we agreed?
> **Thad:** Yes, it's a deal.

Winter comes and Simeon heads for Florida. All winter long, Thad dutifully monitors Simeon's home. Winter passes, the home is fine, and Simeon returns. Thereafter, Lance learns of the contract between Simeon and Thad. He refuses to pay Thad the $500 he promised. Is Lance in breach of contract?

A. Yes, because in their agreement, both Lance and Thad suffered a legal detriment
B. Yes, because when Thad and Lance reached their agreement, Lance knew nothing of the contract between Thad and Simeon
C. No, because the agreement between Lance and Thad is not a contract
D. No, because Simeon's lease imposed on him a preexisting duty to inform Lance of damage to his own home

---

ANALYSIS.   Think law: If in an agreement between A and B, A promises only to perform a preexisting legal duty, he gives no consideration; he promises to do only what the law already requires of him. As a first event, Thad and Simeon formed a contract requiring that Thad monitor Simeon's home. With that contract in place, Thad then made to Lance that very same promise. He promised to monitor Simeon's home in exchange for Lance's promise of payment. Hence, Thad promised Lance that he would do what he was already obliged to do under his contract with Simeon. He promised to perform a preexisting legal duty. He gave Thad no consideration, which means that he and Lance formed no contract. Although he did not know it, Lance made only a naked promise, unenforceable.

C and D begin with "No," so one of them must be right. Carelessly examined, D looks good. It refers to "preexisting duty" and makes a true statement: It's *true* that before this whole saga unfolded, Simeon, by lease agreement, was obliged to inform Lance of serious damage to his home. But *that* preexisting duty is irrelevant to the question. Thad and Lance failed to form a contract because of *Thad's preexisting (contractual) duty not to Lance, but to Simeon.* D is wrong.

According to C, Lance breaches no contract because he and Thad never formed one. That's true. For want of consideration from Thad, Thad and Lance formed no contract. C is right.

D.   The Closer

QUESTION 7. On May 1, 2019, BuildCo and HotelCo formed a contract by which BuildCo was to build a hotel and complete its work by February 28, 2021. In exchange, HotelCo was to pay BuildCo $30 million. Knowing of HotelCo's plan to open a hotel, GasCo opened a gasoline station near the building site. GasCo speculated that the hotel would bring it business.

In July 2020, GasCo learned that BuildCo was in financial difficulty and might fail to complete the hotel by February 28, 2021. On July 15, GasCo wrote to BuildCo: "We know, of course, that you are building a hotel for HotelCo, and we have heard that financial difficulties might prevent you from doing so. We make this proposal: If you will promise to complete the hotel by February 28, 2021 we will promise to pay you $2 million, beyond the moneys that HotelCo is to pay you." BuildCo wrote back: "Agreed. We will timely complete the hotel." On February 28, 2021, BuildCo completed the hotel. HotelCo has paid BuildCo $30 million, and BuildCo now demands $2 million from GasCo. Is GasCo obliged to pay BuildCo $2 million?

A. Yes, because on July 15 GasCo and BuildCo exchanged signed, written promises
B. Yes, because on July 15 GasCo and BuildCo formed an agreement that called for consideration from each
C. No, because GasCo's promise was *nudum pactum*
D. No, because HotelCo paid BuildCo $30 million

ANALYSIS.   The relevant law is the same as that which governed Question 6 above. On May 1, 2019, HotelCo and BuildCo formed a contract that required BuildCo to build a hotel by February 28, 2021. On July 15, 2020, in exchange for GasCo's promise to pay it $2 million, BuildCo promised GasCo that it would do that very same thing—build the hotel by February 28, 2021. It promised to perform only a preexisting legal duty, meaning that GasCo promised to pay it $2 million in exchange for nothing. GasCo made a naked promise, unenforceable.

The answer is "no," GasCo is not obliged to pay BuildCo the $2 million it promised. So, **C** or **D** must be right. As for a reason, **D** states that HotelCo paid BuildCo $30 million as provided by its contract. That might seem to be relevant, but it isn't. HotelCo owed BuildCo $30 million and whether it had paid it or not, GasCo's promise remains a naked promise, a promise given in exchange for nothing. Just as **C** states, its promise was *nudum pactum*, unenforceable. **C** is right.

 # Silver's Picks

1.	A
2.	B
3.	B
4.	A
5.	D
6.	C
7.	C

14

Consideration, Part III: The Subtleties

A. Conditional Promise as Consideration

Think again of Wesley and Quenton from Chapter 13, section A.

> **Wesley (by signed writing):** I want to establish a medical laboratory, and your Spring Street building would be perfect for that purpose. In three months, I will buy your building for $10 million if during that period I am able to secure a license to use it as a medical laboratory. If I can't secure the license, then I won't buy it. In exchange, I want your promise that if I do secure the license, you will sell me the building for $10 million.
>
> **Quenton (by signed writing):** Agreed.

Wesley made a conditional promise. He promised to buy Quenton's building if — *IF* — he should secure within three months a license to use it as a medical laboratory. Wesley's promise obliged him not, necessarily, to buy the building, but to buy the building — *conditional on* — his success in acquiring the license. Notwithstanding that Wesley might not buy the building, his promise did restrict his legal freedom; it subjected him to a "legal detriment" (and, accordingly, afforded Quenton a "legal benefit"). No longer was Wesley free to secure the license and *not* buy the building. Should he secure the license he'd be required to buy it.

And so it is said that a conditional promise constitutes consideration. For "[i]t is a widely accepted rule of contract law that consideration is not insufficient merely because it is conditional, even though the controlling event may never occur." Charles Hester Enters. v. Ill. Founders Ins. Co., 499 N.E.2d 1319, 1323 (Ill. 1986).

Suppose that just after making his promise, Wesley changes his mind; he doesn't want the building under any circumstance, license or not. For that reason, he "sits on his hands"; he doesn't even apply for the license. He allows three months to pass. Then, having no license to operate the building as a medical laboratory, Wesley tells Quenton, "I did not obtain the license, so I won't be buying your building."

1. *If Wesley Does That, He'll Be in Breach*

In making his offer to Quenton, Wesley expresses his wish to acquire the laboratory license and proposes to buy Quenton's building if he should succeed in doing so. As a reasonable person, Quenton would interpret Wesley's offer to mean, "I will do my honest best to acquire a license to operate a medical laboratory in your building and if I succeed in acquiring it then for $ 10 million I'll buy your Spring Street building, meaning that for that same price you'll sell it to me. Agreed?" Then, when Quenton accepts the offer, the parties form a contract that binds Wesley to two promises (1) to make a serious, diligent attempt to acquire the license and (2) if he succeeds, then to purchase the building. The contract binds Quenton to one promise — that if Wesley succeeds in acquiring the license, he'll sell him the building.

The rule is often stated thus: If in forming a contract, one (a) makes a promise subject to a condition, (b) manifests a wish that that the condition occur, and (c) has its occurrence partially or wholly within his control — then, by law — he promises also that he will make a reasonable, honest, diligent attempt to cause the condition to occur.

Suppose that by signed writing, Buyer and Seller agree on the purchase and sale of realty for $3 million. The contract provides, "Buyer's obligation to buy is conditional on his ability, within sixty days, to obtain a 30-year mortgage loan of $2.5 million, at an interest rate of 6 percent or less." *By law,* Buyer has promised to use honest, reasonable efforts to secure such a loan. He makes an implied promise "to diligently seek to have (the financing) contingency take place." Brack v. Brownlee, 273 S.E.2d 81, 819 (Ga, 1980). If Buyer then "sits on his hands" and makes no quest for the loan, he dishonors that promise, and breaches the contract.

QUESTIONS 1 & 2. Bill Benson wants to buy two adjacent farms, one owned by Sandra Salin, the other by Saul Simmons. But, Benson doesn't want to own either farm unless he owns both. On July 1, by signed writing wholly proper in form and content, Benson makes Sandra this offer:

> OFFER, made today, July 1, 2019: WHEREAS, from SANDRA SALIN ("Salin"), BILL BENSON ("Benson") wishes to acquire certain real property (the "Salin farm") [full legal description of the Salin farm] and wishes also to acquire certain adjacent real property owned by one Saul Simmons (the "Simmons farm") [full legal description of the Simmons farm] NOW, THEREFORE, Benson will, for $1.5 million, purchase the Salin farm only if, however, within 90 days from the date hereof, he succeeds in forming a contract with Saul Simmons, for the purchase of the Simmons farm for a price of $1.5 million or less.

On that same day, July 1, 2019, Sandra reads the document. At its bottom, under Benson's signature, she writes "offer accepted," and signs her name. The parties sign a second copy of the same writing, each keeps one copy, and they separate.

QUESTION 1. For this question, assume that one day later, on July 2, Sandra changes her mind; she doesn't want to sell her farm. She visits her attorney, shows him the signed writing, and asks, "Must I sell my farm to Benson?" With which of the following would the attorney respond *correctly*?

A. "If you revoke your offer before Benson begins to negotiate with Saul, then no, you are not obliged to sell your farm to Benson."

B. "If Benson succeeds in forming a contract for the purchase of Saul's farm, then yes, you will be obliged to sell your farm to Benson."

C. "No; Benson made no promise that he would attempt to purchase Saul's farm, and that renders your promise unenforceable."

D. "No; Benson has given you no consideration, which means your agreement is not a contract."

ANALYSIS. Sandra promises to sell her farm, and Benson promises to buy it if—IF—Benson succeeds, first, in contracting to purchase the adjacent Simmons farm. No law, on its own, requires that Sandra sell her farm to Benson—not under any condition. Hence, Sandra's promise subjects her to a "legal detriment" (and, accordingly treats Benson to a "legal benefit"). Stated otherwise (and more meaningfully) Sandra provides Benson with consideration. It's equally obvious that before making his promise, Benson is free to buy the Simmons farm without then buying the Salin farm too. With his conditional promise, Benson gives consideration to Sandra. These promises belong to a contract; they're enforceable. The answer to Sandra's question is yes — she must sell her farm to Benson *if* Benson succeeds in contracting for the purchase of the Simmons farm.

A says "yes," but it refers to Sandra's "offer." Between these parties there stands, now, not an offer, but — a contract, so **A** is very wrong. **C** is wrong too. By law, whether he knows it or not, Benson does promise that he'll attempt diligently to contract for the purchase of the Simmons farm. **D** reports that Benson has given Sandra no consideration. As just explained, that's false. With his promise — although it be conditional — Benson gave up a legal right and, therefore, suffered a "legal detriment," which means he provided Sandra with a "legal benefit." With **B**, Sandra's lawyer gives good counsel. Sandra must convey her farm to Benson (for $1.5 million), if Benson succeeds in contracting for the purchase of the Simmons farm. **B** is right.

QUESTION 2. For this question, assume that Sandra remains happily committed to her contract. Instead, on July 2, Benson changes *his* mind. He doesn't want to buy either of the two properties, and tries not at all to contract for the purchase of the Simmons farm. Ninety days pass. On October 15, Benson advises Sandra that he has formed no contract to purchase Saul's farm and, therefore, will not purchase her farm either.

Is Benson in breach of contract?

A. Yes, because his offer to Sandra was irrevocable
B. Yes, because he made no proper attempt to bring about the condition tied to his promise
C. No, because his promise was subject to a condition that did not occur
D. No, because the parties' agreement exacted no legal detriment from Sandra

---

ANALYSIS. Benson's offer plainly led Sandra to understand that he sought to buy these two adjacent properties — that he *wanted* to contract for the purchase of Saul's farm. By law, therefore, together with his conditional promise to buy Sandra's farm, Benson promised diligently to pursue the contract with Saul. Having failed to make any effort in that direction, Benson dishonored that promise and breached the contract. The answer, therefore, is "yes."

C and **D** say no, so they're wrong. **D** incorrectly reports that the agreement subjected Sandra to no legal detriment. That's false. **C** correctly reports that as for Benson's promise, the relevant condition failed to occur; Benson did not succeed in contracting to purchase Saul's property. But Benson failed in his duty diligently to *seek out* such a contract meaning that he dishonored his (legally implied) promise, and thus breached his contract. **A** says "yes," but its reasoning is from — nowhere. To begin, between these parties there stands not an offer, but a contract which is enforceable. Second after Benson made his offer, before Sandra accepted it, nothing made it irrevocable. **A**'s references to "offer" and irrevocability are from — the beyond. **B** correctly reports that Benson breached his contract by failing to make a reasonable/diligent attempt to secure a contract for the purchase of the Simmons farm and — **B** is right.

2. *"Requirements" and "Outputs" Contracts*

In Chapter 13, section A.1, you read of an agreement between BuyCo and SellCo. BuyCo promised that if it should need any widgets during the year 2020, it would purchase them from SellCo — and only from SellCo — for $1 each. In exchange, SellCo agreed to sell BuyCo any widgets that it might request. Although it might turn out that BuyCo orders not a single widget during the year, still, BuyCo provided SellCo with consideration. It made the conditional promise that *if*, during 2020 it should purchase widgets, it will purchase them from no one other than SellCo.

This particular form of conditional promise creates what's called a "requirements contract." Contracts teachers like to introduce that phrase and then make a big fuss over it, which they shouldn't. Buyer and Seller form a requirements contract when Buyer agrees that during some Period Y, if Buyer needs ("requires") some quantity of a Commodity X, he'll buy it only from Seller; as for Commodity X, during Period Y, he'll buy from no one else.

Whatever your contracts teacher says about requirements contracts — whatever the fuss and fracas she makes of it — know that the topic comes only to this: When Buyer and Seller form a requirements contract, Buyer does provide Seller with consideration. Even though, for the period at issue, Buyer does not promise to buy even a single unit of the relevant commodity, he does provide Seller with consideration; he loses legal freedom; he suffers a "legal detriment," meaning he treats Seller to a "legal benefit:" he foregoes the right, for Period Y to buy Commodity X from anyone other than Seller. (Minnesota Lumber Co. v. Whitebreast Coal Co., 43 N.E. 774 (1895).)[1]

---

1. When referring to "requirements contracts," the authorities always depict a buyer who, for some stated period, as to some commodity, commits to meeting *100%* of his needs by purchasing from the seller with whom he contracts. Understand that if the buyer should make such a commitment only as to 90%, 80%, 60%, or 20% of his needs, he would form what we might call a quasi-requirements contract which, too, would subject him to a loss of legal freedom, and from him exact consideration.

QUESTION 3. Sealco manufactures seals, gaskets, and flanges. Bonaco manufactures a variety of plumbing products into which it incorporates jetline gaskets. On April 1, by signed writing, Sealco and Bonaco form a contract that includes these three paragraphs, 7, 8, and 9:

> 7. The parties acknowledge that Bonaco has and owns, now, a large supply of the jetline gaskets it uses in manufacturing various of its products, and cannot predict that during the coming period April 1 through March 31, that it will or will not have a need to acquire additional ones. Bonaco promises, covenants, and agrees that *if* it should have need of such additional units and should, therefore, purchase the same during the said period, it will purchase them from Sealco only.

> 8. In exchange for Bonaco's promise, covenant, and agreement as set forth in paragraph 7 immediately above, Sealco agrees to sell to Bonaco all such units, if any, as Bonaco may request, each for a price of $25 (twenty-five dollars) unless through no fault of its own, Sealco is itself unable to secure such units through its ordinary and customary channels and sources. Nothing herein shall prevent Sealco from selling such product during such period to other purchasers.

> 9. To each other, the parties make no promises or commitments beyond those set forth in Paragraphs 7 and 8 above.

In June, from Sealco, Bonaco orders a large number of jetline gaskets, and stands ready to pay $25 per unit. Sealco advises Bonaco that it has decided to raise its price and will sell the units to Bonaco for $29 per unit. Bonaco complains that Sealco is in breach of its contract, to which Sealco responds, "We have no contract, because you have given us nothing, promised us nothing. With the agreement we signed, you promised not even to buy a single gasket. The agreement is unenforceable for lack of consideration on your part."

Is Sealco right?

A. Yes, because Bonaco made only a naked promise
B. Yes, because Sealco made only a naked promise
C. No, because Bonaco made a legitimate conditional promise
D. No, because in June, Bonaco did order a large number of gaskets.

ANALYSIS. As your contracts teacher will want you to know (and she'll make a big deal about it), these parties formed a "requirements contract." And here's what *makes* it a requirements contract: Bonaco, the buyer, promises to fill all of his requirements for jetline gaskets by purchasing them from Sealco and only Sealco. Bonaco doesn't promise to buy even a single gasket, but promises that if—*IF*—it should buy any, it will buy them from Sealco. And the point? Only that Bonaco's promise does qualify as consideration, as does any ordinary conditional promise. Sealco is wrong; Bonaco provided it with consideration, and the agreement constitutes an enforceable contract.

Options **A** and **B** say "yes," so they're wrong. With both **A** and **B**, the writer refers to a "naked promise." One makes a naked promise/gratuitous promise/*nudum pactum*, when, in exchange for his promise—he gets nothing (Chapter 12, section B). To say that one makes a naked promise is to say that the promisee has given him no consideration in exchange for it. Here, as we know, Sealco did not make a naked promise because Bonaco did provide Sealco with consideration; Bonaco promised that if it should buy jetline gaskets during the year at issue, it will buy them only from Sealco. So much for option B.

Sealco promised Bonaco that it would sell Bonaco all jetline gaskets that Bonaco sought to buy (subject to the condition that Sealco itself be able to secure them). Hence, Sealco provided Bonaco with consideration, meaning that Bonaco made not a naked promise but, instead, for its promise took back consideration from Sealco. That takes care of option **A**.

D, too, goes out to the curb. It's true that in June, Bonaco ordered gaskets. (That's how all the trouble began.) But if it hadn't done so, Sealco would still be wrong. Each of these parties gave consideration to the other. And, as for Bonaco, the consideration lay in its conditional promise that should it buy gaskets, it would buy them only from Sealco. And your contracts teacher will swoon when you report to her that *that* fact brands this agreement a "requirements contract." **C** is right.

And Now for the Flip-Side; an "Outputs Contract"

Sarico manufactures a great many products, including—sometimes—PX Tubing. Barico, in its business, uses lots of PX Tubing. By signed writing the parties form an agreement that includes these three paragraphs, 7, 8, and 9:

> 7. The parties acknowledge that, in and for its business, Barico annually purchases large quantities of PX Tubing, and that Sarico at times manufactures or may manufacture that same commodity. For the coming period April 1 through March 31, not knowing that it will or will not manufacture PX Tubing in any quantity at all, Sarico promises, covenants, and agrees that if it should manufacture PX Tubing, it will sell all of it to Barico for $10 per linear foot.

> 8. In exchange for Sarico's promise, covenant, and agreement as set forth in paragraph 7 immediately above, Barico agrees to buy all such PX Tubing, if any, as Sarico manufactures, for the price just specified, but nothing herein shall prevent Barico from purchasing such commodity elsewhere as well.

> 9. To each other, the parties make no promises or commitments beyond those set forth in Paragraphs 7 and 8 above.

And *That's* an Outputs Contract

Buyer and Seller form an outputs contract when, as to some Commodity X, for some Period Y Seller agrees that she will sell Buyer *all* that she produces (or otherwise acquires). As is analogous to its reciprocal—the requirements contract—the outputs contract does not call on Seller to make, acquire, or sell a single unit of Commodity X. It may be that for Period Y, Seller provides Buyer with not a single unit of the stuff. Nonetheless Seller's promise does qualify as consideration; it's a conditional promise; if—IF—Seller does, in fact, manufacture (or otherwise acquire) any quantity of Commodity X, she must sell all of it to Buyer. Hence, Seller suffers a "legal detriment" and, accordingly, affords Buyer a "legal benefit," because she foregoes what would other be her right to manufacture Commodity X and sell it to others or, if she chose, sell it to no one.

3. *Back to Benson and the Two Farms; Conditions Wholly Outside One's Control; Fortuitous Events*

Benson could not, of course, create a contract for the purchase of Saul's farm unless, at least, he attempted to do so. Hence, occurrence of that condition was partly within the control of Benson himself. (And, as we just said, the law imposes on him an obligation to make the attempt.) One's promise might also be conditional on an event not at all within his control—conditional on a "fortuitous event."

Consider a homeowner who, from an insurance company, purchases a hurricane insurance policy.[2] The homeowner's obligation is to pay the insurance premiums (price of the insurance). The insurance company's obligation is to compensate the homeowner if—on the condition that—her home is damaged by a hurricane. The occurrence of the hurricane is not at all within the insurance company's control; it happens or it doesn't. That kind of conditional promise—an obligation to perform subject to a fortuitous event—is called, also, an "aleatory" promise. It subjects the insurance company to a legal detriment. It constitutes consideration and, of course, an insurance contract/policy represents a contract. "In an aleatory contract, one or both parties' performance is conditional on the happening of a fortuitous event." Jackson National Life Insurance Company v. Receconi, 827 P.2d 118, 125 (N.M. 1992).

Restatement (Second) of Contracts §76 cmt. c states:

> A party may make an aleatory promise, under which his duty to perform is conditional on the occurrence of a fortuitous event. Such a promise [is] consideration[.]

---

2. Insurance policies are also called "insurance contracts."

QUESTION 4. Harry owns a racehorse named "Thunder." It's a "mudder," meaning that it runs best on a wet, muddy track. Harry plans to enter Thunder in the upcoming National Horse Race. Jackson is a jockey, famous for his ability to ride mudders and famous, too, for his unwillingness to ride a mudder on a dry track. Harry and Jackson agree that if, on the day of the race, the track is muddy, Harry will ride Thunder. If it's dry, he won't. In exchange, Harry promises to pay Jackson $5,000, unconditionally, when the race is over. That means he promises to pay Jackson even if the track is dry, meaning that Jackson does not ride in the race. He agrees to pay Jackson even if, as things turn out, Jackson does nothing. On the day of the race the track is dry. Another jockey rides Thunder. Jackson does nothing. Because the track is dry, Thunder finishes in last place. When the race is over, Jackson demands that Harry pay him $5,000. Is Harry obliged to pay Jackson the $5,000 he demands?

A. Yes, because Jackson's promise constituted consideration to Harry
B. Yes, because Thunder did run the race
C. No, because Jackson made only an aleatory promise and Harry made an unconditional one
D. No, because as matters turned out, Harry derived no benefit from Jackson's promise.

ANALYSIS.   If a Party A commits himself to a performance conditional on the occurrence of some fortuitous event, he makes an "aleatory" promise, and an aleatory promise constitutes consideration. If, in exchange, Party B makes a promise—conditional or not—A and B form a contract, and both their promises are enforceable. Here, Jackson promises that if the track is muddy, he'll ride. If it's not, he won't. In exchange, Harry promises to pay Jackson $5,000, unconditionally, whether or not the track is wet and whether or not, therefore, Jackson rides. Each of these two provides the other with consideration; Harry and Jackson form a contract, and both their promises are enforceable.

The answer, therefore, is "yes," which eliminates **C** and **D**. According to **C**, Harry's promise is unenforceable because Jackson's promise is conditional/aleatory and Harry's is not. **C** makes a true statement, but a wrong conclusion. An aleatory promise is good consideration for any other promise, conditional or not. **D** incorrectly invokes the word "benefit." Jackson's promise subjects him to a legal *detriment*, meaning that *Harry* enjoys a legal benefit. The race's outcome has not a thing to do with that truth. **D** is wrong. **B** says "yes," but its reasoning is for the junk yard. Whether Thunder had run the race or not, Harry would owe Jackson the $5,000 he promised. **A** tells us that Harry must pay Jackson, and its reasoning is right. Jackson's promise is consideration for Harry's promise. The parties formed a contract, which means Harry's promise is enforceable. **A** is right.

B.   Consideration, Contractual Modifications, and UCC §2-209(1)

In Chapter 13, sections A and B, you read of Hernan and Beth. They formed a contract at 10:00 A.M., and at 10:30 A.M. tried to modify it. At 10:30 A.M., Hernan agreed to pay Beth $400 more than the 10:00 A.M. contract required, but Beth promised to do only what the 10:00 A.M. contract already demanded of her. Hence, at 10:30 A.M. Beth provided no consideration to Hernan and the attempted modification failed. The parties remained bound by their 10:00 A.M. contract.

Modification of an existing contract requires that one party make an offer to modify and the other accept. As is so of any offer, an offer to modify an existing contract must introduce a new *bargain*, meaning it must propose that each party to the original contract suffer some new legal detriment. As is more commonly stated: *Two parties modify an existing contract only if, in that regard, each provides new consideration to the other.*[3]

1.   The UCC Abandons That Rule

UCC §2-209(1) provides: "An agreement modifying a contract within this article needs no consideration to be binding." The Code rule thus departs significantly from the common law.

Consider this. On May 1, by signed writing, Sabrina contracts to sell Brent 10,000 widgets for $10,000. She is to make delivery on July 1. On June 1, Sabrina by signed writing contacts Brent: "I know we agreed on a price of $10,000, but I think it's too low. I'll deliver the widgets on July 1, the purchase price to be $11,000. Agreed?" By signed writing Brent responds: "Yes." Brent now promises to pay $1,000 more than the May 1 contract requires, and Sabrina promises nothing new; she will do only what the original contract already requires. By common law, the modification would be unenforceable; the parties would be bound, still, by the original contract and its $10,000 price. But the contract concerns the sale of goods, and UCC Article 2 governs. Under UCC §2-209(1), the modification is effective. Sabrina is obliged to deliver 10,000 widgets on July 1. Brent must pay $11,000.

QUESTIONS 5-7. On September 1, Roofer and Owner form a contract under which (a) Roofer will repair Owner's roof on or before October 1 and, in exchange, (b) Owner will pay him $1,500.

---

3. The rule (a) that modification of an existing contract requires consideration from both parties is but one application of the broader rule (b) that one gives no consideration when she promises only to perform a preexisting legal duty. When we say that at 10:30 Beth furnished Hernan with no consideration, we might just as well say that she promised only to perform a preexisting legal duty.

QUESTION 5. For this question, assume that on September 12, Owner says to Roofer, "I'd like you also to replace my gutters by, let's say, October 3. Will you do that without any increase in price?" Roofer responds, "Certainly. I'll finish the roof repair by October 1, as agreed, and I'll replace the gutters by October 3." After the parties conduct that September 12 conversation, Roofer is obliged to

A. repair the roof by October 1 and replace the gutters by October 3.
B. repair the roof and replace the gutters, all by October 3.
C. repair the roof by October 1 and nothing more.
D. repair the roof by October 3 and nothing more.

ANALYSIS. On September 1 each of these parties made a contractual promise, fully enforceable. Roofer was to complete a roof repair by October 1, and Owner was obliged to pay $1,500. On September 12, they attempted to modify their contract. In doing so, Roofer promised to replace gutters by October 3, which the original contract did not require. Owner promised *nothing*. He was to pay only $1,500 as already required by the September 1 contract. Under the new agreement, Roofer is allowed until October 3 to replace the gutters, but under the original contract he had no duty to replace the gutters at all. Roofer's promise to replace the gutters belongs to no contract; neither does the date October 3. Both parties are bound by their original contract and nothing more. Owner must pay $1,500, and Roofer must make the roof repair by October 1. **C** is right.

QUESTION 6. For this question, assume that on September 12 Owner speaks to Roofer: "I'd like you also to replace my gutters. If you agree, I'll give you until October 3 to finish the whole job—roof and gutters. Will you do that without any increase in price?" Roofer replies, "Certainly. I'll finish the roof repair and the gutter replacement by October 3." After the September 12 conversation, Roofer is obliged by contract to

A. repair the roof by October 1 and replace the gutters by October 3.
B. repair the roof and replace the gutters, all by October 3.
C. repair the roof by October 1 and nothing more.
D. do nothing.

ANALYSIS. Under the original contract, Owner was entitled to demand that Roofer complete the roof repair by October 1. With this new/modified agreement, he promises not to make that demand. He moves the deadline to October 3. In exchange, Roofer promises to replace the gutters, which the original contract did not require. Both parties suffer legal detriment, meaning each party provides consideration to the other. Roofer gives his promise to replace the gutters and, for the roof repair, he enjoys a two-day extension. Owner gives the two-day extension for the roof repair and receives Roofer's promise to replace the gutters. The parties effectively modify their contract and their promises, as revised, belong *to* their modified contract. All are enforceable. Owner must pay $1,500 and, by October 3, Roofer must repair the roof and replace the gutters. **B** is right.

QUESTION 7. Shane sells books wholesale to retailers. Brenda is a retailer. On February 1, by signed writing, Brenda and Shane form a contract under which Shane will sell Brenda 500 copies of the novel *Snowmaker*, to be delivered on March 1, Brenda to pay a total purchase price of $750. On February 3, Brenda contacts Shane by signed writing: "Our contract calls for you to deliver 500 copies of *Snowmaker* on March 1. We'd like to have an additional twenty-five copies, 525 in all for the same $750 total, all to be delivered by February 15. Agreed?" Shane writes back, "Agreed." As of February 3, Shane's contractual obligation is to deliver

A. 500 copies of the book by March 1.
B. 500 copies of the book by February 15.
C. 525 copies of the book by March 1.
D. 525 copies of the book by February 15.

ANALYSIS. The parties formed a contract for the sale of goods. UCC §2-209(1) permits them to modify it without regard to consideration. On February 3, they attempted a modification under which Shane, in exchange for nothing from Brenda, promised to deliver twenty-five additional books, and all 525 books — fourteen days early.

By common law, the parties would fail to modify their contract. They would be bound by their original contract and nothing more. Shane's promise to deliver the additional twenty-five books would be *nudum pactum*, as would his promise to make delivery fourteen days earlier than first agreed. Under UCC §2-209(1), however, the modification is effective. The parties are bound by their contract *as modified* on February 3. Brenda need pay only $750 and Shane must deliver 525 books on February 15. **D** is right.

C. More on Contractual Modifications: Settlement of Claims, Substituted Contract, Executory Accord, Accord and Satisfaction

1. *The Rule of* Foakes v. Beer

Borrower, a professional roofer, needs a loan. On January 1, Lender lends him $10,000 in exchange for his promise to repay that amount twelve months later, on December 31, together with $500 in interest. On December 1, Borrower contacts Lender.

> **Borrower:** I won't be able to repay all that I owe, and I know that will put me in breach. If you'll forgive the breach, I will pay you $6,000, on the due date, December 31. Is that acceptable?
>
> **Lender:** Yes, it is; I accept.

On December 31, Borrower tenders[4] $6,000 to Lender as agreed. Lender refuses it and demands the full $10,500 originally owed him. Under the common law, Lender is within his rights; he need not honor the "settlement" to which he agreed, because Borrower gave no consideration for Lender's willingness to take less than the amount he was owed. Lender is entitled, still, to collect from Borrower the full $10,500 originally owed him.

This is often called the "rule of *Foakes v. Beer*."[5] *When a creditor, in settlement of a fully liquidated[6] debt, agrees to take less than he is owed, his debtor giving him no new consideration in exchange, he need not abide by his agreement; he is entitled to the full amount of the debt originally owed him.* This "rule of *Foakes v. Beer*" is but a corollary to a more fundamental one: Two parties can effectively modify an existing contract only if each, in that effort, gives consideration to the other.

2. *When a Debt or Other Obligation Is Not Fully Liquidated; Substituted Agreement and Executory Accord*

We have dealt with the case in which two parties form a contract and subsequently alter (or attempt to alter) it. If the common law applies, they may do so only if each provides some (new) consideration to the other. If UCC Article 2 governs, then they may modify their contract even though one party provides no consideration to the other.

Separate from the simple case of a modified contract as just discussed, the law recognizes two other seemingly related terms: (1) "substituted agreement,"

---

4. One "tenders" a payment or performance when he shows that he is ready, willing, and able to deliver it.

5. L.R. 9 A.C. 605 (H.L. 1884).

6. "Liquidated," as used here, means an amount of money that is, under prevailing circumstances, clear, plain, and not plausibly subject to any good faith dispute.

and (2) "executory accord." Just below, we'll tell you what these two phrases mean. Know, however, that they rear their heads *only* in this situation: Two parties form a contract, and later, one of them alleges that the other has breached, which the other might admit or deny.

Lender and Borrower, Episode II

We deal again with the $10,000 loan, payable, with interest, on December 31. This time, the parties have no conversation on December 1. Rather, December 31 comes 'round and payment is due.

> **Borrower:** I can't repay what I owe you.
> **Lender:** Well, then, you're in breach.
> **Borrower:** I know. I'm sorry.

Here, Lender alleges a breach and Borrower acknowledges it. Now, again, suppose Lender agrees to accept $6,000 and, in exchange, Borrower agrees to repair Lender's roof in April. This time, the new agreement requires that each provide consideration to the other. Lender gives consideration by forgoing his right to be paid $10,500. Borrower does so by promising to do something different from what the original agreement required.

Suppose now that April passes, and Borrower does not repair the roof; he breaches the *new* agreement. That raises this question: In view of Borrower's breach of the new agreement, does Lender have an action for the $10,500 originally owed him, or does he have only an action for the damages (if any) that arise from Borrower's failure to repair the roof? Here's the answer: *If the new contract is a substituted agreement, the original contract terminates.* Lender's rights inhere in the new agreement only. He has no action for the $10,500. If, on the other hand, the new contract is an executory accord, then Borrower's failure to honor the new obligation — his failure to "satisfy" it — allows Lender to sue either for (a) $10,500 owed him under the original contract or, if he prefers, (b) damages for Borrower's failure to repair the roof.

Meanings: Substituted Agreement vs. Executory Accord

A "substituted agreement" is, really, a plain old ordinary modification like those discussed in section B above. Yet, for some reason (or no reason), when one party alleges that the other has breached and, in that setting, the parties modify their contract, we don't *say* "modified contract." Instead we say, "substituted agreement." (Don't ask why. Just do it.)

The law finds a substituted agreement only if, in response to the allegation of breach by one against the other, the parties very plainly, clearly, and expressly manifest an intention that their new contract should fully supersede the original one — that they are taking the original contract and "throwing it out." When, on that basis, a court does decide that the new contract is a substituted agreement, the law treats it as it treats any ordinary modified contract as discussed in section B above (meaning, under the common law, that in forming the substituted agreement, each party must provide consideration to the other). Each party's rights and duties belong to the new substituted agreement, and the original agreement is defunct.

However, unless the parties in such a situation do *very* plainly and expressly manifest such an intention, the law identifies their new agreement — their resolution of the alleged or threatened breach — as an executory accord. And where two parties do attempt to settle a dispute by altering the terms of their original agreement, it's relatively rare that a court attributes to them a substituted agreement. Usually, it rules that they have formed an executory accord.

In this case, Borrower and Lender made no plain, clear, and express showing of an intention that their new agreement wholly supersede the original. They formed an executory accord. If Borrower fails to honor ("satisfy") the executory accord, Lender may sustain an action against him for (a) the $10,500 owed under the original agreement or, if he prefers, (b) the damages caused him by Borrower's failure to repair the roof.

3. "Accord and Satisfaction" as a Defense to Breach of Contract

The Executory Accord; Gary and Frances, Episode I

On September 1 Frances and Gary form a contract under which
(1) Frances, on October 1, is to play ten violin pieces at Gary's cocktail party, and
(2) Gary is thereafter, on that same night, to pay Frances $3,000.

On October 1, the party starts. Frances plays the ten pieces, whereafter Gary complains, *sincerely and genuinely*, that as to many notes, Frances had played "out of tune." Frances maintains, sincerely and honestly, that she played every piece in *perfect* tune.

Without knowing whether Frances did or did not play out of tune, we do know that the parties are in *honest, good faith dispute* regarding that question. Gary genuinely believes that Frances played out of tune. Frances genuinely believes she did not. Whatever the truth, each party's position is honestly held. Frances and Gary converse:

Gary: So, we disagree.
Frances: Yes, we do.
Gary: I think you were often out of tune.
Frances: I think not.
Gary: I propose that we settle our dispute on these terms: You play one *more* piece tonight, and, furthermore, I'll reduce your pay; I'll pay you, tonight, $2,500 instead of $3,000.
Frances: OK, it's a deal.

These parties just formed an executory accord. As for consideration, Frances makes two promises (either one of which alone would suffice in that regard). She promises (1) to play an extra piece, not required under the original contract, and (2) to accept a payment of less than the $3,000 to which the original contract entitled her.

Let's ask: What consideration does Gary provide? Let's answer: Gary, we said, alleges in good faith that Frances breached her contract. Consequently, if he so chose, he would be justified in bringing an action against her.[7] He might, of course, fail to prove the breach and, therefore, lose the suit. But, so long as he honestly believes Frances has breached, he is entitled to *bring* the suit. *By forgoing that right he gives consideration.* Hence, these parties form an executory accord in which (1) Frances promises to do what the original contract does not require of her, and (2) Gary promises to forgo his right to bring suit for a breach he honestly alleges.

The Satisfaction

Suppose that after these parties form their executory accord, Frances plays the additional piece. She thus *satisfies* the executory accord — she does what it requires of her. If Gary right away pays the promised $2,500, he too satisfies the executory accord. The parties thus achieve "accord and satisfaction," and each loses her or his rights under the original contract.

But suppose now that after she plays the additional piece and takes Gary's $2,500, Francis regrets having made the settlement. She stands ready to prove, she thinks, that she originally gave a pitch-perfect performance, and she wants the additional $500 that, under the accord, she gave up. She brings an action against Gary under the original contract, seeking a $500 recovery. At trial, as his defense, Gary proves the accord and satisfaction just described. For that reason, Frances recovers nothing. And, once again, that is so even if to the court's satisfaction, she proves that her performance was, in fact, perfectly in tune. The accord and satisfaction terminates her rights under the original contract. (Let's not confuse you. In section C.2 above, we said this: If two parties form an executory accord and one of them fails to honor it, then, in that case, the other, at his option, may sustain a suit under *either* the original contract or the executory accord. But if two parties form an executory accord and both then honor/"satisfy" it, they lose their rights under the original contract.)

Let's state a rule: *If (1) Parties A and B form a contract; (2) Party A in good faith asserts that Party B has breached; (3) as a voluntary resolution, the parties form an executory accord, which means that each must provide consideration to the other; and (4) each party satisfies the executory accord, then neither party may thereafter assert her rights under the original contract. If either one,*

---

7. One has *no* right to bring an action as to any allegation that he, himself, believes to be false. If he does so, he commits the tort of malicious prosecution and/or abuse of process.

as plaintiff, attempts to do so, the other may properly plead the defense of "accord and satisfaction," which, when proven, defeats the plaintiff's claim.

Remember and understand, please, that two parties cannot (under the common law) modify their contract unless each provides consideration to the other. That is so whether they purport to undertake an ordinary, outright modification, a substituted agreement (which is, really, the same thing, except that the term is used only when the modification arises from an allegation by one that the other has breached), or an attempt to settle a dispute by executory accord. Mindful of that, suppose Gary secretly and honestly believes that Frances has played her violin with perfect intonation. Suppose, further, that (a) Gary nonetheless insists, dishonestly, contrary to what he truly believes, that Frances has played out of tune, and (b) Frances, who badly needs money, agrees to Gary's proposed agreement to resolve his claim.

If, later, in court, Frances attempts to enforce the original contract, and proves (somehow) that Gary asserted her breach dishonestly, then the court will (is supposed to) rule that the new agreement does not constitute an executory accord, because the parties are not in *honest* dispute as to the quality of Frances's performance. Rather, the new contract constitutes an attempt to modify a preexisting contract with Gary providing no consideration to Frances. In essence, the arrangement is one in which Party A makes a promise to Party B, "in exchange" only for Party B's promise to perform what the law already requires of him, as discussed in Chapter 12, sections D and E.

Here, then, is the "flip side" of the rule stated just above: *With respect to a contract between two parties, A and B, if Party A, without a good faith belief, asserts that Party B is in breach, the two parties are ineligible to form an executory accord; their attempt to do so is ineffective. Party A retains the right to recover under the original contract, and Party B cannot effectively assert the defense of accord and satisfaction.*

When One of the Parties Fails to Give Satisfaction; Gary and Frances, Episode II

Let's return to the facts of Episode I: Gary asserts a good faith (honest) claim that Frances has played out of tune, and the parties form their executory accord as earlier described. Suppose that Frances plays the additional violin piece pursuant to the accord, but Gary doesn't, on that same night, pay the $2,500 as required. Rather, he decides to "think it over," and ultimately tenders payment on the next day. Frances refuses the money and decides instead to sue for the full $3,000, standing ready to prove she did not play out of tune.

Gary can*not* effectively assert the defense of accord and satisfaction because although the parties reached an executory accord as settlement of their dispute, Gary did not *satisfy* it; he did not timely tender his $2,500 payment. Having failed to satisfy the accord, he leaves Frances free to enforce the original contract. If she proves that she properly performed—that she played every note correctly—she is entitled to the full $3,000 originally promised her.

Let's expand our rule: *If two parties, A and B, form a contract, and Party A later sues B for breach, B may effectively assert the defense of accord and satisfaction if he proves that (a) in an effort to settle a good faith allegation of breach, the parties formed an executory accord, and (b) that he satisfied it. If he proves that the parties formed an executory accord but does not prove that he satisfied it, he has no such defense. In that case, Party A is entitled to pursue her action under the original contract. If she can, after all, prove that she did not breach it, she recovers the damages to which the original contract entitles her.*

QUESTIONS 8 & 9. On May 1, Lender lends Borrower $25,000, to be repaid on April 30 of the next year by ordinary personal check, together with interest of 5 percent, for a total of $26,250. On April 29, Borrower contacts Lender and explains that she cannot pay the full amount.

QUESTION 8. Borrower asks whether Lender will accept $22,000 as a "settlement of the debt." Lender agrees. Borrower sends Lender a check for $22,000, together with a signed note indicating that the check is tendered "in full settlement of what was otherwise my total debt to you of $26,250." Lender deposits the check; three days later, Lender sends Borrower a signed writing: "Your check has cleared; you owe me nothing."

Lender then decides that he wishes to recover the additional $4,250 originally owed him, and he brings an action against Borrower. The court issues judgment for Lender in the amount of $4,250. The court's reason for not enforcing the parties' settlement is most likely that

I.   the parties reached an accord, but the fact that Borrower owed Lender a liquidated debt of more than $22,000 means they failed to achieve satisfaction.
II. in order that two parties effectively modify a contract between them, whether as an executory accord or in any other circumstance, each must provide the other with consideration.
III. by first informing Lender, on April 29, of her inability to pay, Borrower gave Lender no fair and reasonable notice of her wish to settle the debt.
IV. the parties were not eligible to achieve accord and satisfaction.

A.   I and IV
B.   II and IV
C.   III and IV
D.   I, II, II, and IV

ANALYSIS.   Between these parties, there is no dispute as to the amount that Borrower owes. Her debt is fully liquidated. Nonetheless, she asks Lender to accept less than she owes him, and Lender, receiving no consideration, agrees to do so. The absence of a (good faith) dispute as to the amount Borrower owes means the parties cannot effectively form an accord, meaning that they cannot achieve accord and satisfaction. Option IV is true. In order to modify a contract (under the common law), whatever the circumstance, each must provide the other with consideration. Option II is true.

Option I offers a sort of double-talk, presenting, meanwhile, a "friendly face." It correctly states that Borrower's debt is liquidated. Incorrectly, however, it reports that these parties formed an accord, but because of the liquidated debt could not achieve satisfaction. That's wrong. Because Borrower's debt was fully liquidated, meaning they were not and could not be in dispute as to its amount, they could not and did not form an executory accord.

Option III invokes the happy phrase "fair and reasonable," and on all faces, puts a happy smile. It sounds oh so very right, but it's oh so very wrong. Call Borrower's notice monumentally fair, wretchedly unfair, outstandingly reasonable, or abjectly unreasonable; it doesn't matter. In this context, no notice of any kind makes a difference to the legal outcome. Lender is entitled to the additional $4,250 for the reasons cited in options II and IV only (which are, in essence, the same). **B** is right.

QUESTION 9. Assume now that on April 29, after advising Lender that she does not have the funds to pay her full debt of $26,250, Borrower says, "If you will accept $22,000 instead of $26,450, I'll pay you today, two days early. Furthermore, I'll pay you not by ordinary check but by certified check."[8] Lender agrees. On that same day, Borrower engages a courier service that delivers to Lender a certified check in the amount of $22,000. Lender deposits the check, which clears three days later.

A few days later, Lender undergoes a mood change. He sues Borrower for the additional $4,250 originally owed him. The court issues a judgment for Borrower. Its reason for enforcing the parties' settlement is most likely that

I. Borrower paid two days before she was obliged to and did so in a manner that went beyond her contractual obligation.

---

8. As you'll learn in a course called "Negotiable Instruments" or "Payment Systems," Party A issues to Party B a certified check by first writing his own ordinary personal check to B, then taking the check to his own bank and asking the bank to certify it. The bank places various writings on the surface of the check indicating that it is "certified." Once a check is certified, payment is positively guaranteed by the bank; the bank is liable on the check (as otherwise it is not). Before the bank certifies a check, it examines the customer's account, assures itself that the relevant amount is available, and then sets that amount aside, in order to pay on the certified check when Party B presents it for payment. It is sometimes said that "a certified check is like cash." The reason is that the bank must, by law, pay it. The funds are guaranteed to be present and available, and the issuer of the check (Borrower in this case) has no power to "stop" payment on it (as he otherwise would have). Such, among many other matters, is the subject matter of UCC Articles 3 and 4.

II. Lender received consideration in return for his willingness to accept less than the amount originally owed him.

III. in exchange for Lender's willingness to accept less than the amount originally owed him, Borrower conferred on Lender a legal benefit.

IV. in connection with the altered agreement, each party provided the other with consideration.

A. I and IV

B. II and IV

C. III and IV

D. I, II, II, and IV

ANALYSIS.   These parties are not in dispute as to the amount Borrower owes Lender or the date on which payment is due. As in Question 6, they are not eligible to achieve accord and satisfaction. However, as can any two contracting parties, they can modify their contract so long as, in the process, each provides the other with consideration. (Recall from Chapter 12, section C, that the law does not question the relative value of each party's consideration.)

The parties in this case effectively modified their contract. Lender agreed to accept $22,000 in lieu of the full $26,250. Borrower agreed to pay two days early (itself, adequate consideration) and to pay by certified check instead of ordinary check (also adequate consideration in and of itself). Every one of the options, in its own way, states that the parties achieved an effective modification of their contract, because each provided the other with consideration. Hence, **D** is right.

4. Tender of Check as Offer of Accord; Deposit as Acceptance

Suppose Jocelyn and Dante agree that Jocelyn will repair Dante's bicycle, with Dante thereafter to pay her $100. When Jocelyn announces completion, Dante proclaims in good faith that her performance is defective. He declines to pay the $100. Instead, Dante sends Jocelyn a check for $75 together with a letter stating, "because I believe you did not properly repair the bicycle, I offer this check for $75 as full and final payment, with the understanding that each of us is fully discharged of all contractual duties."

The letter is Dante's offer of an executory accord. The check is his simultaneous *tender* of satisfaction. Jocelyn may accept the offer or not. If she returns the check to Dante, she does *not* accept. If she simply deposits the check, she *does* accept, and at that moment the parties form an executory accord. If Dante's bank pays Jocelyn's bank (meaning the check "clears"), Dante satisfies the accord, and Jocelyn loses her right to the $100.

It does not matter that Dante and Jocelyn never communicate with each other about the dispute. It matters only that Dante, in good faith, alleges a breach. If he then tenders his check for $75, he makes an offer of accord. When

Jocelyn deposits it, she accepts the offer and the parties create an executory accord. And in many jurisdictions, that is so even if Jocelyn writes above her endorsement "without waiver of rights," or "under protest." *One who receives a check in an amount less than she thinks she is owed, together with a legitimate offer of accord, must not deposit it, unless she is willing to forgo what she thinks to be her contractual rights.*

Now, let's ask: Who decides that Dante made his allegation in good faith? As always, the ultimate answer comes from *a court or jury*, which makes this decision as it makes all others—upon an evaluation of evidence. Suppose that after Dante's check clears, Jocelyn insists on collecting the additional $25 that he withheld. She sues Dante in small claims court for $25, alleging his contractual obligation to pay her that amount. As a defense, Dante asserts accord and satisfaction. Jocelyn insists that the parties formed no true accord because, she says, Dante did not in good faith believe that her services were deficient.

It falls on Dante to show that he did in good faith believe Jocelyn had failed in her obligations. He tries to do that, perhaps, by (1) testifying himself as to why and on what basis he found the repairs defective; and/or (2) calling in a bicycle repair expert who, after examining the bicycle, offers his opinion on the quality of the repair and whether any person could, in good faith, believe the repair to be defective; and/or (3) presenting the bicycle itself as an exhibit and showing the court on what basis he believed the repair to be improper.

If, ultimately, the court finds that Dante did in good faith believe that Jocelyn's work was defective, then Dante succeeds in his defense of accord and satisfaction. If it finds otherwise, he does not; it will issue judgment for Jocelyn in the amount of $25.

D.   The Illusory Promise and Alternative Promises

1. *The Illusory Promise*

Let's examine four versions of an offer from Alvin, each of which Betty accepts:

> **Alvin (Version 1):** I'd like you to promise to tutor me in calculus for eight hours on Sunday, without charging me.
> **Betty:** I accept.

Alvin purports to make an offer but does not propose that he himself will suffer any legal detriment. Consequently, he proposes no bargain, wherefore he makes no offer, which means that Betty's assent is not an acceptance, which means the parties form no contract. Stated otherwise: The parties' agreement is not a contract because it exacts no consideration from Alvin. Betty's promise belongs to no contract. It's *nudum pactum*, unenforceable. She need not tutor Alvin at all.

> **Alvin (Version 2):** If you'll promise to tutor me in calculus for eight hours on Sunday, I'll do nothing for you in exchange.
> **Betty:** I accept.

This time, Alvin expressly states that he promises nothing. Again, the agreement exacts no consideration from Alvin, and the parties form no contract. Betty's promise is *nudum pactum*, unenforceable.

> **Alvin (Version 3):** If you'll promise to tutor me in calculus for eight hours on Sunday, I'll promise to pay you $400, but I don't promise to *keep* my promise; I might not pay you at all.
> **Betty:** I accept.

Once again, Alvin promises nothing. With one clause he proposes his "promise" to pay and with the next he withdraws it. The parties form no contract.

> **Alvin (Version 4):** If you'll promise to tutor me in calculus for eight hours on Sunday, I'll promise to pay you $400, but please understand that I reserve the right, privilege, entitlement, prerogative, and option unconditionally to dishonor that promise and, therefore, to withhold and refrain from making such payment wholly or in part, permanently or temporarily, with or without notice, if for any reason or no reason, at my own whim and discretion, I should so choose or decide.
> **Betty:** I accept.

This time Alvin promises a great big *mouthful* of nothing. He "promises" to pay $400 but then reserves the right not to pay it for any reason or no reason. Again, Betty promises to tutor Alvin, and Alvin promises *nothing*. With all four of his proposals, Alvin gives no consideration, the parties form no contract, and Betty's promise is unenforceable.

In the fourth version, with all of those fancy words, Alvin creates the superficial appearance — *the illusion* — of a promise but, in fact, makes none. If, as Alvin does in version 4, one purports to make a promise, but then by some attached term reserves the right to dishonor it unconditionally, at his sole whim, for any reason or no reason, then he makes an "illusory promise." An illusory promise is that which, on its surface, might seem to create a commitment but when fully studied comes to nothing because the "promisor" leaves himself wholly free, unconditionally, to honor or dishonor it, as he pleases. An illusory promise is no promise at all. In version 4, Alvin's proposal is exactly the same as proposals 1, 2, and 3. In effect, he says to Betty, "I would like you to tutor me on Sunday for eight hours and in exchange I promise *nothing*."

Here's the relevant rule: *If a party purports to make a promise, but by some attached term or provision provides that he may dishonor the promise, unconditionally, for any reason or no reason, at his sole whim, then he makes not a promise but an illusory promise, which is no promise at all and does not constitute consideration.*

2. Illusory Promise vs. True Conditional Promise

In section A of this chapter, we learned that one's conditional promise constitutes consideration. "If the track is muddy, I will ride your horse in the race." That's a conditional promise, and it constitutes consideration for any promise given in exchange. The promisor obliges himself to perform if there occurs some true condition — a matter not governed by his own arbitrary whim. He promises *something* that the law does not otherwise require of him, and so suffers a legal detriment. Consider this: "If I can obtain a $2 million, 30-year loan at 6 percent interest or less, I promise to buy your real estate." By law, this promisor obliges herself to pursue the loan and, if she obtains it, to purchase the land. She thus promises *something* that the law does not otherwise require of her.

Compare those promises to this one: "If I want to, I will ride your horse in the race." Here the promisor commits to a performance "conditioned" on his own unbridled desire. By law, one's own unbridled desire is not a condition. Rather, it negates the "promise" to which it is tied. This promisor has made an illusory promise. In the law's eyes he has said, "I promise *nothing*."

It's important that we supplement the rule of conditional promises so that it expressly distinguishes between a conditional promise and an illusory one:

> *(1) If in forming a contract, one (a) makes a promise subject to a condition, (b) manifests a wish that that the condition occur, and (c) has its occurrence partially or wholly within his control—then, by law—he promises also that he will make a reasonable, honest, diligent attempt to cause the condition to occur.*

> *(2) If one so describes his promise as to leave himself free to honor or dishonor it at his sole unbridled whim, then he makes not a conditional promise but an illusory promise, which is no promise at all.*

3. Avoid Confusion: Naked Promise vs. Illusory Promise

From Chapter 12, section B, remember that a naked promise is a genuine promise for which the promisee gives no consideration. It's a real promise, but the law won't enforce it because it is unsupported by consideration (meaning it belongs to no contract). An illusory promise is no promise at all. If Party A makes a true promise and Party B, in exchange, makes an illusory one, then (1) B makes no promise at all, and (2) A makes a naked promise — a real promise, but because she receives no consideration, she need not honor it. It's unenforceable.

QUESTION 10. DevCo is a real estate developer and ConCo a builder. By signed writing, DevCo and ConCo form an agreement under which DevCo purports to hire ConCo to construct a housing development.

The writing embodies 50 pages and 550 paragraphs. Paragraphs 1-20 identify the parties and define various terms. Paragraphs 21 and 22 provide:

> 21. ConCo will erect the housing development described herein, according to the timetables, schedules, specifications, and standards also provided herein.
> 22. DevCo will pay ConCo $25 million on each of the four dates herein named.

Paragraphs 23-549 describe the timetables, schedules, specifications, and standards by which ConCo is to perform. They also describe the dates on which DevCo is to make its four $25 million payments. Paragraph 550 provides:

> The parties agree that any promise or commitment made by ConCo hereunder is conditioned on ConCo's determination that it wishes to honor it, which determination ConCo alone shall make if and as it wishes.

In this agreement

   I. ConCo makes no promise.
  II. ConCo makes only an illusory promise.
 III. DevCo makes no promise.
 IV. DevCo makes a naked promise.
  A. I
  B. I and II
  C. I, II, and III
  D. I, II, and IV

ANALYSIS. The parties signed a lengthy document filled primarily with definitions, schedules, timetables, specifications, and standards. At paragraphs 21 and 22, each party purports to make its promise: DevCo is to pay, and ConCo is to build. The last paragraph provides that ConCo need honor its promise only if and as it wishes and thus renders ConCo's promise illusory. An illusory promise is no promise, and in this agreement ConCo promises nothing. DevCo *has* made a promise—a real one. It promises to pay. Because ConCo has provided no consideration in exchange, DevCo's promise is unenforceable; it's a promise given in exchange for nothing—*nudum pactum.*

Options I and II are true; ConCo made an illusory promise and that's no promise at all. Option III is false. DevCo promised to pay. Option IV is true. DevCo made its promise in exchange for nothing, wherefore its promise was *nudum pactum,* unenforceable. **D** is right.

E.   Implied Consideration

In various circumstances, contract law *implies* that a contracting party has agreed to one term or another. Chapter 4, section C, taught of implied "gap fillers." From section A of this chapter, we know that for one who makes a conditional promise the law implies a promise also that she will devote reasonably diligent efforts attempting to bring the condition about. We learn now of another circumstance in which the law implies a promise.

Jake and Enid

Jake manufactures tires, and Enid operates several retail tire stores. On June 1, 2014, Enid and Jake form an agreement in which, for one year, Jake allows Enid the exclusive right to sell his tires. The substantive portion of the agreement provides:

> Jake hereby promises that Enid will, for one year from this date, have the exclusive right to carry, market, and sell tires manufactured by Jake, and that Jake will not, therefore, during that period, allow any other retailer to carry, market, or sell such tires.

Seven months later, on January 1, 2015, Jake wants to dishonor his commitment; he wants other retailers to carry and sell his tires. Jake consults his lawyer, who examines the written agreement and concludes that it does not amount to a contract. "This agreement," the lawyer says, "recites your promise to give Enid an exclusive right to sell your tires, but it exacts no consideration from Enid. Enid promises nothing. You have received no consideration for your promise; it's unenforceable. You may break it."

The lawyer is wrong; because he did not, apparently, read this book, he doesn't know this common law rule: *When Party A conveys to Party B an exclusive right to sell, market, or distribute his goods or service, Party B implicitly promises that she will, through reasonable commercial efforts, attempt to promote and sell the good or service.*

Here, Jake is Party A and Enid Party B. Jake conveys to Enid the exclusive right to carry and sell his tires. *By law*, Enid promises that through reasonable commercial efforts she will attempt to sell the tires. She is obliged, therefore, to sponsor such advertising and marketing as would be usual and customary for a retailer in her circumstance attempting to sell a particular brand of tires. In effect, the law reads the agreement to mean this:

> Jake hereby promises that Enid will, for one year from this date, have the exclusive right to carry, market, and sell tires manufactured by Jake, and Jake will not, therefore, during that period, allow any other retailer to carry, market, or sell such tires. *In exchange, Enid promises that she will resort to such means and measures as are usual in her industry in an effort to market and sell such tires.*

Consequently, even though the writing shows no express promise from Enid, Enid does, by law, make a promise, and that promise provides consideration to Jake. The parties form a contract, and Jake's promise is enforceable. If Jake allows another retailer to sell his tires, he commits a breach. The rule applies not only under the common law, but under UCC Article 2 as well. UCC §2-209(2) provides:

> A lawful agreement by either the seller or the buyer for exclusive dealing in the kind of goods concerned imposes . . . an obligation by the seller to use best efforts to supply the goods and by the buyer to use best efforts to promote their sale.[9]

QUESTION 11. Shirley is a real estate broker. Tamara is a homeowner who wishes to sell her home. Tamara ("Seller") engages Shirley ("Broker") to represent her in the sale. By signed writing, the parties form an agreement with this substantive provision:

> Seller promises and agrees that for six months, Broker will have the exclusive right to list and show the home, and to offer it for sale on Seller's behalf. During that six-month period, therefore, Seller will not herself show the home to any prospective buyer and neither will she allow any other person to do so.

The remainder of the writing carries various incidental terms, but recites no promises or commitments from Shirley. Tamara wishes to break her promise and allow another broker to show her home. Is she free to do so?

A. Yes, because she made only a naked promise
B. Yes, because her agreement with Shirley does not amount to a contract
C. No, because she received consideration from Shirley
D. No, because she made her promise in a signed writing

ANALYSIS.   By agreement, Tamara gave Shirley the exclusive right to show her home and offer it for sale. Although Shirley did not expressly make any promise in exchange, the law attributes to her an implied promise to direct reasonable commercial efforts to show the home and offer it for sale. In effect, the law adds this to the end of the parties' signed agreement: "During that same six-month period, Broker will employ such means and measures as are

---

9. For a celebrated case citing an analogous rule, see Wood v. Lucy Lady Duff-Gordon, 222 N.Y. 88, 90 (1917) (plaintiff did not "promise in so many words [to] use reasonable efforts to . . . market [defendant's] designs," [but] "such a promise is fairly to be implied").

usual, customary, and reasonable in her industry in an effort to show Seller's home and offer it for sale."

With this agreement, therefore, Tamara promised Shirley a six-month period of exclusivity, and Shirley promised Tamara that during those six months she would attempt to sell the home. Each party promised to do what the law, on its own, did not require of her. Each provided the other with consideration. The parties formed a contract, and if either breaks her promise she will be in breach.

According to **A**, Tamara made only a naked promise. If the law did not imply Shirley's reciprocal promise, that would be true. But the law does imply a promise from Shirley, meaning that the parties formed a contract. Tamara's promise belongs to that contract and is not, therefore, a naked promise. **B** states that the parties did not form a contract and, as just explained, that's false. **D** correctly reports that Tamara may not break her promise, but its reasoning is wrong. The rule at issue does not require a writing. If these parties had made their agreement without a writing, then, still, they would form a contract.[10]

C is correct. It accurately states that Tamara may not break her promise and correctly states the reason: She received consideration for it.

F.   Enforcing a Promise to Avoid Injustice

1. Promissory Estoppel

Suppose Olivia's uncle Noah says to her, "As a graduation present, I'll give you a car. Count on it." Delighted with the prospect of owning a car, Olivia plans a weekend car trip. She makes reservations for a two-night stay at a motel, thereby incurring a nonrefundable obligation of $200. Thereafter, Noah tells Olivia that he has changed his mind about the car: "I'm sorry; I won't be getting it for you." Olivia is out $200, and the law of contract affords her no remedy. Uncle Noah has made a naked promise, and the parties have not formed a contract. Stated otherwise, Olivia has given Noah no consideration for his promise, wherefore Noah's promise is *nudum pactum*.

Appended today to the law of contract, however, is the doctrine of "promissory estoppel," rooted not in law but in equity.[11] It renders Noah's promise enforceable — not *fully* enforceable, but enforceable to the extent necessary to make Olivia whole. The rule of "promissory estoppel" provides: *If one makes*

---

10. Unless some statute within the relevant state requires that a real estate brokerage contract be set forth in a signed writing.

11. Appendix, section E. Because the doctrine arises from equity, in some jurisdictions, a plaintiff who brings an action in promissory estoppel is not entitled to a jury trial. C & K Engineering Contractors v. Amber Steel Co., 3 Cal. 3d 1, 5 (1978).

a promise receiving no consideration in exchange, and the promisee reasonably and foreseeably relies on it to her detriment, then the promise is enforceable to the extent necessary to rectify any resulting unfairness. Restatement (Second) §90 states it thus:

> A promise which the promisor should reasonably expect to induce action or forbearance on the part of the promisee or a third person and which does induce such action or forbearance is binding if injustice can be avoided only by enforcement of the promise. The remedy granted for breach may be limited as justice requires.

Noah, receiving no consideration, made Olivia a promise and, indeed, told her to "count on it." As a reasonable person, he should have foreseen that Olivia might do just that and commit herself to some cost, expense, or detriment[12] as a result. Relying on the promise, Olivia did suffer a detriment by committing herself to a $200 expenditure. Very likely, a court will enforce Noah's promise, not in full, but to such degree as is necessary to avoid "the injustice." The car Noah promised has a value, say, of $20,000. If the promise had belonged to a contract, Noah would have to pay that full amount in order to fulfill Olivia's "expectation interest."[13] But the promissory estoppel doctrine won't require that he pay that much. Rather, it will likely require that he pay Olivia $200 — the loss she sustains through her reasonable "detrimental reliance" on the promise. That's ordinarily the amount necessary to avoid "the injustice."

Doesn't This Rule Reverse Everything We've Learned About the Need for Bargain and Consideration?   No, it doesn't. To begin, it operates only if the court finds that the promisee has (1) *relied* on the promise (2) *reasonably*, (3) to her *detriment*, (4) in a way that was *foreseeable* to the promisor, (5) so to cause a resulting *injustice*. Further, when the rule operates, it does not render the naked promise enforceable in full. Rather, it enforces the naked promise only to the extent necessary to correct the resulting "injustice." In the case of Noah and Olivia, that's a difference between $200 and $20,000.

QUESTION 12. Becky, age 92, has only $25,000 to her name and is fearful that she will outlive her financial resources. On August 10, 2015, she describes her concern to her wealthy great-nephew Logan. On that same day, by signed writing, Logan makes her this promise: "When you exhaust the $25,000 that you now have, I will provide you, as a gift, any

---

12. The word "detriment" in this context does not refer to legal detriment as used earlier. It means only some cost or burden.
13. Chapter 25, section D.

amount of money you request, up to a maximum of $50,000 per year, for the remainder of your life."

In September 2015, Becky's grandson Thane asks Becky for $25,000. Unable to resist, and believing that she can turn to Logan for any money she may need, Becky gives Thane the $25,000 in her bank account—all that she has in the world. Becky then contacts Logan. Revealing what she has done, she asks him for $25,000. Logan responds, "I did not make my promise to you so that you could give your money away to Thane. I'm not going to keep the promise." To what extent does the doctrine of promissory estoppel require that Logan keep his promise of August 10, 2015?

A. Not at all, because Becky did not reasonably or foreseeably rely on it
B. To the extent of $25,000, because that is the extent to which Becky relied on it
C. To the extent of $50,000, because that is the amount he promised to pay per year
D. Fully, because Becky was reasonable in believing that Logan would honor his promise

ANALYSIS. Logan can dishonor his promise without committing a breach of *contract*, since these parties formed none. His promise was *nudum pactum*. Under the doctrine of promissory estoppel, the promise *is* enforceable, but only to the extent that Becky relied on it, reasonably, and in a way that was reasonably foreseeable to Logan. Logan made his promise in response to Becky's concern for her financial future. He had no cause to imagine that Becky would rely on it so as to give all of her money to Thane. Becky's reliance was neither reasonable nor foreseeable to Logan. For that reason, Logan need not keep his promise—at all. Consequently, **A** is right. (But, if you think that under the circumstances (a) in giving away her last $35,000 as she did, Becky was reasonable in relying on Logan's promise, and (b) Logan, as a reasonable person, should have foreseen that Becky might do so—then—the right answer would be **B**.)

2. The Offeree Who Relies on an Unaccepted Offer

For an offeree who relies on an offer he has not yet accepted, the law sponsors a doctrine similar to that of promissory estoppel. Restatement (Second) §87(2) provides:

> An offer which the offeror should reasonably expect to induce action or forbearance of a substantial character on the part of the offeree before acceptance and which does induce such action or forbearance is binding as an option contract to the extent necessary to avoid injustice.

Illustration: BigCo and ConCo.   BigCo intends to build a school building and invites contractors to submit bids on the project. ConCo wishes to submit a bid. Before doing so, it needs to know how much it will spend on commissioning an electrical contractor to take charge of the relevant electrical work. ConCo contacts both ElectriCo and LightCo, providing them with specifications pertaining to the school building, asking to know how much each will charge for the relevant electrical work.

ElectriCo advises ConCo: "Regarding the BigCo school building, we are prepared to do the electrical work for $1.5 million, payment to be made in five equal installments, as we complete 20 percent, 40 percent, 60 percent, 80 percent, and 100 percent of the work." LightCo makes an offer on similar payment terms, but the total amount for which it asks is $1.7 million. Relying on ElectriCo's offer, ConCo contacts BigCo and offers to build the building for $30 million. BigCo accepts ConCo's offer, whereupon ConCo decides to accept ElectriCo's $1.5 million offer. Before it does so, however, ElectriCo revokes, whereupon ConCo accepts LightCo's $1.7 million offer.

ConCo brings an action against ElectriCo, seeking to recover $200,000, the difference between the amount it would have had to spend under ElectriCo's offer and the amount it must spend on accepting LightCo's offer. At trial, ConCo proves that (1) in setting its own bid to BigCo at $30 million, it relied on ElectriCo's $1.5 million offer, (2) if it had had only LightCo's bid and not ElectriCo's bid, it would have set its bid to BigCo at $30.2 million, and (3) that BigCo would have accepted that bid, wherefore ConCo lost $200,000 in profit as a result of ElectriCo's revocation.

What does the law say? ConCo and ElectriCo did not form a contract, so ConCo has no cause of action against ElectriCo for breach *of contract*. Nonetheless, ElectriCo made an offer, knowing that ConCo might rely on that offer in making its bid to BigCo. ConCo did just that and offered to build the building for $30 million, instead of the $30.2 million it would have demanded in the absence of ElectriCo's offer. ConCo's offer likely satisfies the conditions attached to Restatement (Second) §87(2). ConCo reasonably relied on ElectriCo's offer in a manner that was foreseeable to ElectriCo. As a result, it suffered a $200,000 detriment. Probably, ElectriCo will be held to pay ConCo $200,000. See Drennan v. Star Paving Co., 333 P.2d 757 (Cal. 1958).

G.   The Closers

QUESTIONS 13 & 14. By signed writing, Nancy and Don contract for the manufacture by Don of three new sails for Nancy's sailboat. The contract price is $12,000, and the contract specifies that the three sails will be suitable to function on Nancy's sailboat, with Nancy to have a reasonable opportunity to test their function before making payment to Don. Pursuant to the contract, Don inspects Nancy's boat and then begins to manufacture the sails: one a mainsail, one a jib sail, and one a mizzen sail. When Don announces completion of his work, he delivers the sails to Nancy. Before paying the agreed contract price, Nancy immediately tests their function on her sailboat.

QUESTION 13. After conducting the test, Nancy concludes that the mizzen sail is, to some noticeable degree, not suitable for use on her vessel. She contacts Don by writing: "The mizzen sail is not quite right. It doesn't hang properly and doesn't trim quite right. I will send a check for $8,000 as payment in full under our contract." Nancy does then send an $8,000 check to Don, together with a letter: "I submit this check in accordance with my last writing, in which I described problems with the mizzen sail."

Don deposits the check, it clears, and the $8,000 moves to Don's bank account.

Thereafter, Don asks Nancy when she intends to pay the remaining $4,000 of the contract price. Nancy responds that she does not intend to pay it. She refers Don to the two writings she sent him after testing the sails, and to the $8,000 check she sent with the second one. Don responds that he never agreed to accept $8,000 as full payment and that he has taken the $8,000 only as a partial payment of the $12,000 owed to him. Nancy refuses to pay any additional amount. If Don brings an action against Nancy for the remaining $4,000 of the contract price, and Nancy proves at trial that she honestly believed the mizzen sail was unsuitable to her vessel, judgment should be for

A. Don, because he received no consideration for the reduction in the contract price from $12,000 to $8,000
B. Don, because he never agreed to accept $8,000 as satisfaction of the $12,000 that Nancy owed under the contract
C. Nancy, because Don's failure to perform one-third of the contract justifies her in withholding one-third of the price
D. Nancy, because under these circumstances, Don's receipt of the $8,000 discharged her duty to pay the full $12,000 contract price

ANALYSIS. In good faith, Nancy believes that Don has breached the contract. She tenders a check that, in light of her earlier message, amounts to her offer of an executory accord. By depositing it, Don accepts her offer and the parties do form an executory accord. When the check clears, Nancy satisfies her obligation under the accord and thus achieves accord and satisfaction. **A** is utterly wrong. By forgoing her right to withhold payment and/or to sue on her good faith belief that Don had breached, Nancy does provide consideration. **B**, too, is for the birds. By depositing Nancy's check, Don accepts her offer of an executory accord. To many, both **C** and **D** might seem right. But we don't know, for a fact, that Don did or did not fully perform his contract. We know only that Nancy, in good faith, *believed* he had not done so. **C** implies, as a fact, that Don breached his contract but, once again, we don't know that he did or did not do so. **D** properly identifies Nancy as the prevailing party and, in its way, correctly states the reason. When Don receives the $8,000, Nancy satisfies the executory accord. Hence Don loses his rights under the original contract. That's why **D** is right.

QUESTION 14. Now assume that when Nancy tests the sails, she finds them satisfactory. She sends Don this signed writing: "All of the sails function well, and I thank you for your work. However, five other sail makers tell me that $12,000 is out of line—that they would have done the same work for $8,000. For that reason, I will send a check for $8,000 as payment in full under our contract." Nancy does send an $8,000 check to Don, together with a letter that states, "I submit this check in accordance with my last writing, in which I noted that your $12,000 price was excessive." All other facts are as set forth in Question 11. Is Don entitled to receive the remaining $4,000 of the $12,000 contract price?

A. Yes, because Nancy's debt to Don was fully liquidated
B. Yes, because Don never expressly agreed to reduce his price by $4,000 after Nancy complained of it
C. Yes, but only if Nancy failed to believe in good faith that $12,000 exceeded the prevailing market price
D. No, because the parties achieved an accord and satisfaction

---

ANALYSIS. Many students choose **D**, but it's wrong. It is not Nancy's right that Don charge her the "going" rate for his service. Don may charge her anything he wishes (so long has he does not, in any way, intentionally deceive her). Even if it's true that Don's price is "out of line," Nancy has no right to sue him. In proposing to pay Don less than the contract requires, therefore, she gives up no right to bring an action against him. In exchange for her proposal that Don accept $8,000 instead of $12,000 she proposes, really, that Don sacrifice a contractual right in exchange for nothing.

B is wrong. Even if Don had expressly agreed to reduce his price when Nancy complained of it then, still, under the "rule of *Foakes v. Beer,*" Don would be entitled to collect the additional $4,000. **C** is just as bad. Even if Nancy honestly (and, indeed, correctly) believes that Don's price is excessive, she has no right to have it reduced. Her proposal to reduce the price provides no consideration to Don.

That leaves **A**, which correctly states that Nancy's debt to Don is liquidated; it is indisputable no matter that Nancy thinks it too high. Because it's indisputable, Nancy is obliged to pay it—absolutely wherefore, once again, her proposal called for no consideration from *her*. When Don deposited the check and received the $8,000, he got $4,000 less than he was owed. For giving up that money, he received nothing back. The parties failed to form an executory accord and so could not achieve accord and satisfaction. **A** is right.

 Silver's Picks

1.	B
2.	B
3.	C
4.	A
5.	C
6.	B
7.	D
8.	B
9.	D
10.	D
11.	C
12.	A
13.	D
14.	A

15

The Statute of Frauds: A "Defense" in a Suit for Breach

A. The Statute of Frauds: What It Is and What It Means

You now know well that two parties may form a contract without a writing. Yet, as explained in Chapter 2, section C, it's one thing to form a contract and another to *prove* you've done so. When we record contracts on paper, we usually do so to create evidence of what we've done, lest there later be a dispute as to whether and on what terms we contracted. In some cases, however, we put our contracts in writing for another reason. For as we've *not* yet learned, some contracts are enforceable *only if* set forth in writing.

In 1677, the British Parliament identified six kinds of contracts that, it believed, created too many plaintiffs bringing too many fraudulent actions—claiming to have formed contracts with their defendants when, in fact, they had not. Fraudulent claims, Parliament believed, frequently arose in connection with

1. contracts for the sale of an interest in land;
2. contracts for which it was impossible for both parties to complete their performances within one year;

3. contracts in which one agreed to be surety/guarantor for another's obligations;
4. contracts for the sale of goods at a price equal to or greater than ten pounds sterling;
5. contracts made in consideration of marriage;
6. contracts in which the executor or administrator of an estate promised to answer for damages out of his own funds.

For that reason, Parliament passed "An Act for the Prevention of Frauds and Perjuries." Regarding those six kinds of contract, the statute provided that no plaintiff could sustain an action for breach unless he could show that the contract had been recorded in a writing that the *defendant had signed*.

In America, all states have enacted statutes derived from the old British "Statute of Frauds" (now repealed in England, as it happens). By custom, lawyers and courts refer to all such statutes collectively as *the* "Statute of Frauds," treating them as a single rule of law that operates throughout the nation. When, without specifying a state, we say "the Statute of Frauds," we do not refer to a single statute. Rather we refer generally, to a rule embodied in fifty separate statutes enacted by fifty separate states, all of them founded originally on the old English law. Now know this: In many if not most states, there appears in the Statute of Frauds the phrase "party to be charged." It means (almost always) "the defendant."[1] With that, let's look at a prototypical Statute of Frauds:

> Unless set forth in a written memorandum, signed by the party to be charged, no action may be sustained for the breach of any contract (1) for the sale of an interest in realty, (2) not to be fully performed within one year of its making, (3) in which one person promises to answer for the debt or default of another, or (4) made in consideration of marriage.

Further, UCC §2-201(1), drawn from the British Statute of Frauds and enacted now in every state, replaces "ten pounds sterling" with "$500." And, instead of "party to be charged," it employs the phrase "party against whom enforcement is sought," meaning, once again, "the defendant":

> [A] contract for the sale of goods for the price of $500 or more is not enforceable . . . unless there is some writing sufficient to indicate that a contract for sale has been made between the parties and signed by the party against whom enforcement is sought[.][2]

---

1. As just noted, the "party to be charged" is, ordinarily, the defendant. That is, when plaintiff sues defendant attempting to enforce a contract, the defendant is the "party to be charged"; she is the party against whom the plaintiff seeks to enforce the contract. It might happen, however, that a plaintiff brings an action against a defendant on some other basis and the defendant in that action asserts a contract as a defense or counterclaim, in which case the plaintiff becomes the party to be charged. The party to be charged is the party in the substantive position of a defendant, whether she is the defendant in fact (as is the usual case) or a plaintiff against whom the defendant asserts a counterclaim.

2. The most recent amendments to the UCC, not yet adopted by any state, raise the relevant amount from $500 to $5,000. UCC §2-201 (as amended, 2005).

In most U.S. states, the Statute of Frauds applies to five kinds of contracts (for which we'll provide illustrations a little further on). They are:

1. *Contracts for the sale of an interest in land.* If two parties form a contract for the purchase and sale *of an interest in land,*[3] neither party as plaintiff may enforce it against the other as defendant unless the contract is set forth in a writing ("memorandum") signed by the defendant.
2. *Contracts for which the parties cannot complete performance within one year.* If two parties form a contract for which they cannot possibly complete performance within one year of the date on which they form it, then neither party as plaintiff may enforce it against the other as defendant unless the contract is set forth in a writing ("memorandum") signed by the defendant.
3. *Suretyship contracts.* If two parties form a contract under which one agrees to be surety or guarantor for the contractual obligation of some third person, neither party as plaintiff may enforce it against the other as defendant unless the contract is set forth in a writing signed by the defendant.
4. UCC §2-201(1) provides that if two parties form a contract for the sale of goods at a price of $500 or more, neither party as plaintiff may enforce it against the other as defendant unless the contract is set forth in a writing signed by the defendant.
5. *Contracts formed in consideration of marriage.* If two parties form a contract in which one party's obligation is to marry some third person, neither party as plaintiff may enforce it against the other as defendant unless the contract is set forth in a writing signed by the defendant.

These five contracts, it is said, "fall within the Statute of Frauds," meaning that the Statute of Frauds applies to them, meaning that they are enforceable only if set forth in a writing signed by the defendant.

1. Illustration: Contracts for the Sale of Interest in Land

Shayna and Belle I.   Shayna owns Blackacre, and Belle wants to buy it. In the presence of ten reliable witnesses, Shayna says to Belle, "I'll sell you Blackacre for $1 million. We'll meet in my lawyer's office one week from this Monday at noon. At that time, you'll hand me a $1 million certified check, and I'll hand you the deed to Blackacre. Agreed?" Belle answers, "Yes, agreed." Shayna subsequently decides not to proceed with the land sale, and Belle brings an action against her.

Shayna and Belle formed a contract that falls within the Statute of Frauds. They created no writing, and for that reason neither can enforce the contract against the other; the contract is unenforceable. Belle stands ready with ten

---

3. As you'll learn when studying real property, "interests in land or realty" include a fee simple, a life estate, a remainder, and many other so-called estates. All illustrations in this text will concern sales of a fee simple, which means a transfer of full and complete ownership. When, in ordinary speech, we speak of buying land or buying a house, we mean buying a fee simple.

witnesses to prove that she and Shayna did, certainly, form a contract. Nonetheless, the Statute of Frauds forbids the court to enforce it, because Belle cannot present a writing signed by Shayna, her defendant — "the party to be charged."

Shayna and Belle, II. Suppose after the parties agree orally on the purchase and sale of Shayna's land, they decide to put their agreement in writing. Seated in Shayna's office, they create two copies of a document that fully describes Blackacre and all other details tied to their agreement. Belle signs both copies, whereupon Shayna says, "We do have a contract, certainly, but I'd like to read the document, carefully, once more before I sign. Leave a copy with me, please. After I sign, I'll send it to you. You can then send me the copy with your signature." Belle leaves the documents with Shayna, and she departs.

Shayna studies the document and decides not to sign it. Furthermore, she decides not to proceed with the sale of her land. Hence, Belle brings an action against her for breach. Again, ten witnesses stand ready to testify to the conversation in which the parties made their agreement. Nonetheless, the Statute of Frauds forbids the court to enforce it against Shayna. Even though Belle presents a writing that *she* has signed, she does not present one *signed by Shayna* — her defendant — "the party to be charged."

Shayna and Belle, III. With respect to story II just above, change one fact: Shayna continues in her wish to sell the land, but Belle decides not to buy it. Let's ask: Can Shayna sustain an action against Belle? Let's answer: Yes, because Shayna will come to court with a writing signed *by Belle* — her defendant — "the party to be charged."

One Party Can Enforce the Contract, but the Other Can't? That's right. Consider two parties, A and B, who form a contract that falls within the Statute of Frauds and then record it in writing. Suppose first that A signs the writing, but B does not. In that case, B can enforce the contract against A, but A can't enforce it against B. Now suppose that B signs the writing, but A does not. In that case, A can enforce the contract against B, but B can't enforce it against A. Suppose, finally, that both A and B sign the writing. In that case, each party can enforce the contract against the other.

2. *Illustration: Contracts for Which the Parties Cannot Complete Performance in One Year*

Laura and Garath. On December 1, 2019, by spoken word, Laura and Garath form a contract under which Garath will serve as Laura's secretary from January 1, 2020 through December 31, 2020 at a weekly salary of $900. Nineteen days later, on December 20, 2019, Laura tells Garath that she won't honor the agreement; she won't employ him.

The parties made their contract on December 1, 2019. It's a logical impossibility that December 31, 2020 should fall within a year of that date.

Consequently, the contract is within the Statute of Frauds. Absent a writing signed by Laura, Garath can't enforce it. As with any contract within the Statute of Frauds, that's so even if Garath can prove unequivocally that he and Laura did, truly, form a contract (orally).

Jason and FinaCo.   Jason is 79 years old, healthy and hearty. FinaCo sells lifetime annuities, and Finn is FinaCo's president. On March 1, 2020, Jason and Finn orally agree that (1) on June 1, Jason will pay FinaCo $500,000, the bulk of his life's savings, and (2) beginning July 1 and on the first day of every month thereafter, for the rest of Jason's life, FinaCo will pay Jason $8,000.

Jason, we said, is in good health. Probably, he will live for more than one year, but it's *possible* that he won't. It's *possible* that FinaCo will make its last $8,000 payment on July 1, August 1, September 1, or at any time within one year of March 1, 2020. That means the parties *might conceivably* complete performance within one year of the date on which they form their contract. Hence, the contract does *not* fall within the Statute of Frauds; it requires no writing or signatures. If either party breaches, the other may enforce it as any two parties may ordinarily enforce any oral contract (provided, of course, that they can prove its existence).[4]

3. Illustration: Contracts in Consideration of Marriage

A "contract in consideration of marriage" means a contract for which one party's consideration is his promise to marry another. It does not include, however, the marriage contract between two persons who commit to marry each other.

Ryan and Frank.   Frank is Abigail's father. He and Ryan form a contract in which Ryan promises to marry Abigail and Frank, in exchange, promises to pay Ryan $100,000 on the wedding day. The parties record their contract in writing. Ryan signs it; Frank doesn't. One week before the wedding, Frank concludes that Ryan is "a bum" (which he is). He (a) tells Ryan that he won't honor the agreement—he won't pay the $100,000, and (b) orders him to "get out of town."

Let's ask: Can Ryan enforce the contract against Frank? Let's answer: No. For his part of the bargain, Ryan promises to marry Abigail. That means the contract is made "in consideration of marriage"; it falls within the Statute of Frauds. The writing is signed by Ryan, but not by Frank—the party whom Ryan wants to sue—"the party to be charged." Ryan can't enforce the contract; he has no action for breach. As with any contract within the Statute of Frauds, that's so even if Ryan can prove, unequivocally, that he and Frank did, truly, form a contract.

---

4. Separate from the Statute of Frauds doctrine, however, every state has imposed a plethora of regulations relating to the sale of life insurance and annuity contracts. The creation of signed writings is among them.

4. Illustration: Suretyship Contracts

One becomes a "surety" when he agrees to guarantee another's contractual performance.

AlCo, BondCo, and Client. Al is a builder and Ben is a bondsman.[5] On March 1, Al forms with Client a contract requiring that Al construct an office building, for which Client is to pay $20 million. Client worries that Al might suffer insolvency ("go broke") and be unable to finish his work. For that reason, on April 1, Client forms a contract with Ben. It provides that (1) Client will pay Ben $50,000 on May 1, and (2) if Al should become insolvent, and fail to complete the building, Ben will pay Client a sum of money sufficient to have some other builder finish the job. Client and Ben record their contract in a writing. Client signs it, but Ben does not.

The contract requires that Ben act as a surety in respect of Al's performance. That means it falls within the Statute of Frauds. Suppose that on May 1, Ben announces his decision not to bond Al's performance and refuses to accept Client's $500,000. Let's ask: Can Client enforce the contract against Ben? Let's answer: No; he can show no writing signed by Ben, his defendant — "the party to be charged." As with any contract within the Statute of Frauds, that's so even if Client can prove, unequivocally, that he and Ben did, truly, form a contract.

5. Illustration: Sale of Goods for $500 or More

TileCo and ClayCo. ClayCo manufactures tiles, and TileCo installs tiled bathrooms. On June 1, ClayCo and TileCo form an oral contract whereunder ClayCo is to supply TileCo with two tons of tile, delivered on July 1. On delivery, TileCo is to pay ClayCo $7,000. The parties do not record their contract in writing. On June 12, TileCo contacts ClayCo and states that it no longer wishes to purchase the tiles, and will not do so.

The contract calls for the sale of goods at a price greater than $500, and so it falls within the Statute of Frauds, meaning, in this case, UCC §2-201(1). ClayCo can show no writing signed by TileCo, its defendant — "the party against whom enforcement is sought." Hence, ClayCo cannot enforce the contract against TileCo; it can't sustain an action for breach. As with any contract within the Statute of Frauds, that's so even if ClayCo can prove, unequivocally, that it did, truly, form a contract with TileCo.

---

5. A bonding company or "bondsman" is roughly analogous to an insurance company in that it sells a guaranty — an assurance — that if some specified risk should arise, it will pay compensation.

QUESTION 1. To say that a contract "falls within the Statute of Frauds" is to say that

A. it is recorded in a writing signed by both its parties.
B. it is not recorded in a writing signed by either party.
C. it is recorded in a writing signed by one of its parties.
D. it is unenforceable unless recorded in a writing signed by the party against whom enforcement is sought.

ANALYSIS. The question tests only your understanding of the phrase "within the Statute of Frauds." That phrase applies to contracts that are enforceable only if set forth in a writing signed by the defendant—"the party to be charged." That a contract is "within the Statute of Frauds" does not tell us that its parties have or have not recorded it in writing, or that either or both have signed one. That a contract is "within the Statute of Frauds" means only this: It's one of the contracts that the Statute of Frauds "talks about"; it's unenforceable unless recorded in a writing, signed by the defendant. **A**, **B**, and **C** are wrong. **D** is right.

QUESTION 2. Which of the following contracts falls within the Statute of Frauds?

I. A contract, written and signed by both parties, under which one party agrees to sell land to another
II. A contract, unwritten, under which one party agrees to sell land to another
III. A contract, written and signed by one party, in which one party agrees to employ another for a period of two years
IV. A contract, unwritten, in which one party agrees to tend to a forty-year-old patient for so long as the patient lives
A. II only
B. IV only
C. I, II, and III
D. I, II, III, and IV

ANALYSIS. Again, the question tests only your understanding of the phrase "within the Statute of Frauds." All of the contracts mentioned at options I, II, and III are unenforceable unless set forth in a writing, signed by the defendant. All of them are "within the Statute of Frauds." (And because they are within the Statute of Frauds, contracts I and II are unenforceable. Contract III is enforceable only by the party who did not sign, against the party who did.) Contract IV does not fall within the Statute of Frauds because the forty-year-old patient might not live for a year. **C is right.**

QUESTION 3. Which of the following contracts, if breached by A, is enforceable by B?

I. An oral contract, whereunder A agrees to sell land to B
II. A written contract, signed only by B, whereunder A agrees to employ B for a period of two years
III. A written contract, signed only by A, whereunder B agrees to employ A for two years
IV. A written contract, signed by both parties, whereunder A guarantees payment of her son's debt to B
V. A written contract, signed only by A, whereunder B agrees to marry A's daughter and A agrees to pay B $500,000

A. I and II
B. III, IV, and V
C. I, II, III, and IV
D. I, II, III, IV, and V

ANALYSIS. All of these contracts are within the Statute of Frauds, meaning that all are of a type to which the Statute of Frauds applies. Some are written and signed by A. Those are the ones B can enforce.

Option I describes a contract for the sale of an interest in land. The contract falls within the Statute of Frauds. B, who wants to sue A for breach, cannot show a writing signed by A. B can't enforce the contract (and neither, for that matter, can A).

Option II tells of a contract that falls within the Statute of Frauds' one-year provision. It is set forth in a writing signed by B but not by A — "the party to be charged." Hence, B can't enforce it against A. (Yet, because B signed, A would be able to enforce it against B.)

Option III describes a contract between A and B that falls, also, within the Statute of Frauds' one-year provision. The contract is recorded in writing and signed by A. B *can* enforce the contract against A (but because B did not sign, A would *not* be able to enforce it against B).

In option IV, we read of a contract that falls within the Statute of Frauds' suretyship provision. It is recorded in a writing, signed by A and B. Consequently, it's enforceable by B against A (and would be enforceable by A against B as well).

Option V describes a contract made in consideration of marriage. It's recorded in a writing signed only by A. The contract is enforceable by B against A (but would not be enforceable by A against B).

Party B can enforce contracts III, IV, and V, but not contracts I or II. **B** is right.

QUESTION 4. On December 1, 2015, Sabrina and Barry form an oral contract under which Barry is to (a) decorate Sabrina's retail store for Christmas Day 2016 and then, *after* Christmas, (b) take the decorations down. Sabrina is to pay Barry $15,000 on or before December 1, 2016. Twelve months later, on December 1, 2016, Sabrina comes to Barry with her $15,000 check. Barry refuses to accept it and tells Sabrina that he will not perform; he won't decorate her store for Christmas. Sabrina sues Barry for breach. Barry moves to dismiss the suit, citing the fact that he signed no contractual writing. Should the court grant his motion?

A. Yes, because the agreement exacts no consideration from Sabrina
B. Yes, because the Statute of Frauds renders the contract unenforceable
C. Yes, because the agreement reflects a bargain in which neither party suffers a legal detriment
D. No, because Sabrina, if she wished, might have paid Barry before December 1, 2016

ANALYSIS. The parties form their contract on December 1, 2015. It's possible, of course, for Barry to decorate Sabrina's store for Christmas of 2016 in late November 2016, which time will fall within one year of December 1, 2015. Yet, Barry is to take down the decorations *after* Christmas. As a matter of logic, it is *not* possible that December 26, 2016, should fall within one year of December 1, 2015.

Sabrina is to pay Barry on or *before* December 1, 2016, meaning she might pay him one hour, one day, one week, or one month after the parties form their contract. *She can* complete her performance within one year of December 1, 2015. Yet, in order that a contract not fall within the Statute of Frauds, it must be possible that *both* parties complete performance within the one-year period. Barry can't do that. Since the contract is within the Statute of Frauds, and the parties have created no writing at all, neither can enforce it against the other.

Choices **A** and **C** refer to lack of consideration, but each party did provide consideration to the other; Sabrina promised to pay, and Barry promised to decorate. **A** and **C** are wrong. **D** is wrong too. Although one contracting party might possibly perform within the one-year period, the contract is, nonetheless, within the Statute of Frauds if the other cannot.

B tells us that Sabrina can't enforce the contract because the Statute of Frauds renders it unenforceable. That's exactly correct. **B** is right.

B.   The Meanings of "Writing" and "Sign"

Ironically, the law disdains its own rule. Surrounding the Statute of Frauds is another judicial doctrine to this effect: *Because the Statute of Frauds may deprive a contracting party of a contract genuinely formed, it is to be very narrowly construed so to allow the parties to enforce contracts they truly have made.* With that premise, the law is stunningly malleable in the meanings it gives to the words "writing" and "sign."

In order that two parties create "a writing," they need not put black ink to business-grade paper stock. They might make marks and scratches on tissues, paper towels, or candy wrappers, and thus create a "writing." If A and B form an oral contract, and A then sends B a signed napkin, on which she describes the contract, A has signed "a writing." B may enforce the contract against her. If B responds, with a signed dust rag, on which she, too, describes the contract, then she, too, has signed "a writing." B can enforce the contract against her. Taken together, the two documents, napkin and rag, make "*a* writing," signed by A and B.

Now we'll address the word "signature." With respect to the Statute of Frauds, a signature is any mark, stamp, or symbol that manifests one's intent to authenticate her identity. One's initials, one's first name only, or last name only set forth in type or in handwriting, cursive, print, or scribble constitutes her "signature," as does one's fingerprint. As characterized by Restatement (Second) of Contracts §134 and cmt. a, a signature

> . . . may be any symbol made or adopted with an intention, actual or apparent, to authenticate the writing as that of the signer.
>
> *a. Types of symbol.* The traditional form of signature is of course the name of the signer, handwritten in ink. But initials, thumbprint or an arbitrary code sign may also be used; and the signature may be written in pencil, typed, printed, made with a rubber stamp, or impressed into the paper. Signed copies may be made with carbon paper or by photographic process.

C.   Part Performance: Removing a Contract from the Statute of Frauds

Without a writing, two parties might form a contract falling within the Statute of Frauds, and then begin to perform. Under some circumstances, their performance or partial performance "removes the contract from the Statute of Frauds," meaning that one party (or both) can enforce it even though it is *not* set forth in a signed writing.

1. Part Performance and the Land Sale Contract

With respect to an unwritten (or unsigned) contract for the sale of land, most courts hold that certain forms of part performance allow the buyer to enforce the contract against the seller (although part performance does not, normally, allow the *seller* to enforce it against the *buyer*). If the buyer has paid the full purchase price, many (but not all) courts allow him to enforce the contract even in the absence of a writing signed by the seller. In such a case, the buyer is not normally entitled to recover monetary damages. Rather, he is entitled to the equitable remedy of specific performance, described in Chapter 30, section B.[6] Similarly, if, with Seller's permission, Buyer occupies the premises and makes improvements,[7] then, too, most courts allow him to enforce the contract without a writing signed by Seller.[8]

Illustration: Benita and Sheldon.   On January 1, without a writing, Benita and Sheldon contract for the sale of Sheldon's vacant land. The contract calls for a closing date of March 1. On February 1, not yet owning the land, Benita asks Sheldon's permission to begin her occupancy. Sheldon is agreeable, whereupon Benita enters the land and begins to build a small home. On February 25, Sheldon tells Benita that he no longer wishes to part with the land and that he will not proceed with the sale.

The February 1 contract falls within the Statute of Frauds. Ordinarily, neither party would have power to enforce it without a writing signed by the other. However, when Benita enters on the premises and begins to make improvements, the contract undergoes such "part performance" as — *maybe, depending on the state and the court* — removes it from the Statute of Frauds. In that case, Benita can enforce the oral contract against Sheldon.

2. Performance and the One-Year Provision

If, without a writing, two parties form a contract that they cannot fulfill within one year, and one of them *fully* performs, then, most courts will declare that both parties may enforce the contract. From Question 4 above, consider Barry and Sabrina. Their Christmas decoration contract falls within the Statute of Frauds. Suppose now that before Barry renounces the agreement, Sabrina

---

6. The emerging view, however, is that payment of the purchase price does not entitle the buyer to specific performance, because he can recover the relevant monies by way of restitution. Restatement (Second) of Contracts §129, and Chapter 28, section B.

7. One makes "improvements" to realty by clearing it, building on it, or otherwise altering it in some way that enhances its utility over the long term. One improves realty when she makes "a permanent addition to or betterment of real property . . . designed to make the property more useful or valuable." Finn v. McNeil, 23 Mass. App. Ct. 367, 502 N.E.2d 557, 562 (App. Ct. 1987) (citations omitted).

8. The conceptual and historical bases of that rule are subject to debate. Some authorities, including the Restatement, assert that such an exception to the Statute of Frauds rule inheres, really, in the fact of the buyer's detrimental reliance, and that the Buyer should be entitled to specific performance only if he has been substantially prejudiced through his occupancy and the making of improvements. Restatement (Second) of Contracts §129.

tenders him the full $15,000 contract price, and Barry takes it. In most states, Sabrina's full performance would render the contract fully enforceable by both its parties. Similarly, if Barry had decorated the store and, after Christmas, disassembled the decorations, his full performance would render the contract enforceable by both its parties; If Sabrina had not yet paid him, she would, now, have to do so.

3. *Part Performance and the Sale of Goods*

Regarding contracts for the sale of goods, the modern-day Statute of Frauds inheres in UCC §2-201(1), adopted in every state. It provides that a contract for the sale of goods at a price of $500 or more requires a writing signed by the party "against whom enforcement is sought." UCC §2-201(3)(a) renders the signed writing *un*necessary if (i) the contract calls for specially manufactured goods that (ii) are not suitable for sale to other of the seller's customers, and (iii) the seller has begun, in some substantial way, to produce or acquire them (or the means necessary to produce them).

Stripped to its essence, UCC §2-201(3)(a) means that the contract is enforceable if the seller has relied on it to his detriment, with (a) "reliance" meaning that she has begun, to a substantial degree, to make or procure the goods, and (b) "detriment" meaning that the goods at issue are not, in ordinary course, salable to others (because they are somehow "unique" or customized for the buyer). Further, UCC §2-201(3)(c) removes a contract from the Statute of Frauds to the extent that (i) the seller has received and accepted the buyer's payment, or (ii) the buyer has received and accepted the goods. In either such case to *that* extent, each party may enforce the contract against the other.

Suppose that on May 1, without a writing, Buyer and Seller agree that for $10,000 Seller will manufacture and sell to Buyer a strange, weird, bizarre-looking, uniquely designed, custom-made bedspring. On May 15, Seller forms a contract with Vendor for the purchase of various parts he needs to create this oddly conceived article. The contract calls for the sale of goods at a price greater than $500. When first formed, therefore, it falls within the Statute of Frauds. The law then "removes it from" the Statute because (1) Seller is to specially manufacture the goods (the goods are to be custom-made), (2) he cannot, in ordinary course, sell them to other customers (because they are of so strange a nature), and (3) he has begun, in a substantial way, to procure necessary parts. The contract is, now, enforceable even though neither party signed any writing.

As to part performance of a suretyship contract or a contract made in consideration of marriage, there is such difference among the states as to prevent us (or anyone else) from stating any general rule.

QUESTION 5. Without a writing, Kevin as seller and Taylor as buyer contract for the purchase and sale of Kevin's farm. Thereafter, Kevin declines to proceed with the sale, and Taylor sues for specific performance. Which of the following additional facts, if proven, would most likely allow Taylor to sustain his action against Kevin?

A. Before Kevin announced his intention not to proceed, Taylor, with Kevin's permission, moved onto the farm and built a new barn.
B. Eight persons saw and heard the parties form their contract, and each is willing to so testify.
C. After the parties formed their contract, Taylor prepared and signed a writing that accurately described the agreement.
D. Before the parties formed their contract, each, by signed writing, declared to the other his tentative interest in concluding an agreement for the sale of the farm.

ANALYSIS. Without a writing, these parties formed a contract for the sale of land. Their contract falls within the Statute of Frauds. Ordinarily, then, neither would be entitled to enforce it against the other. However, where two parties contract for the sale of an interest in land, part performance often "removes" the contract from the Statute, allowing the buyer to enforce it against the seller (but not (usually) the seller to enforce it against the buyer). The two circumstances most likely to remove the contract from the Statute are that (1) the buyer fully pays the purchase price, or (2) with the seller's permission, the buyer occupies the land and makes improvements to it.

B refers to witnesses who saw and heard the parties form their contract. No such circumstance will remove it from the Statute of Frauds. Neither, certainly, would a writing have any such effect if signed only by Taylor, the *plaintiff*. Hence, **B** and **C** are wrong. **D** reports that before forming their contract, the parties wrote, signed, and exchanged invitations to deal. To that we say, "so what?" No such fact removes any contract from the Statute of Frauds.

According to **A**, Taylor, with Kevin's consent, moved onto the premises and made improvements to it. That means he has given such part performance as (in most states) is sufficient to remove the contract from the Statute of Frauds. **A** is right.

D.   The Closer

> **QUESTION 6.** Bernard Bailey and Sahar Scott are long-time friends and business associates. For several months, Bernard has spoken to Sahar about the possibility of purchasing a parcel of Sahar's land. As Bernard and Sahar sit together one evening at a (dull) Chamber of Commerce meeting, Bernard takes hold of a wet cocktail napkin. On it he writes, in crayon, "About your land, 28 Pate Street, Addington, MT 78420 (Volume 909 land books, page 187), I'll buy it for $940,000—let's close by the end of the week. Deal?" Bernard passes the napkin to Sahar. Sahar reads the message and takes from her pocket a piece of crumpled notepaper, personalized with her full name printed at its top. On the paper, with an eyebrow pencil, she circles her name, and writes, "Okay." Sahar passes her message to Bernard. On the following day, Bernard calls Sahar by telephone. "Let's set a date for closing, so I can pay you the $940,000 purchase price and you can hand me a deed to the Pate Street property." Sahar responds that she has changed her mind: "I'm not going to sell." Can Bernard sustain an action against Sahar for breach of a contract to sell the land?
>
> **A.** Probably not, because Bernard did not sign his name on the cocktail napkin
> **B.** Probably not, because the napkin and notepaper constitute two separate writings
> **C.** Probably, because Sahar "signed" her notepaper
> **D.** Probably, because the contract falls outside the Statute of Frauds

ANALYSIS.   Of this, there's no doubt: Bernard offers to buy Sahar's land and Sahar accepts; these two form a contract. The contract provides for the sale of an interest in land, meaning that it's within the Statute of Frauds. Neither party can *enforce* the contract unless it is recorded in a "writing" "signed" by the other (his or her defendant/the party to be charged). In all states, the words "writing" and "signed" are (*very*) liberally construed.

Here, the cocktail napkin and the notepaper together constitute *a* writing. Sahar's name printed at the top of the notepaper qualifies as her "signature." That she drew a circle around it makes that all the more certain. The parties did, therefore, record their contract in a "writing," "signed" by Sahar. That means the answer is "yes." Bernard can enforce the contract against Sahar.

A and B say "no," so they're wrong. As for A, it's true that Bernard has not signed the writing, but it's also irrelevant. When a contract falls within the Statute of Frauds, one party can enforce it against the other whether he himself has or has not signed a writing. It is necessary only that his *defendant* have signed one. As for **B**, two or more separate papers addressing the same subject qualify as "*a* writing." **B** is wrong. **D** correctly answers "yes," but its reasoning is "way" wrong. This contract does fall within the Statute of Frauds. It's enforceable because it conforms to the relevant requirements; it is recorded in a writing (the napkin and notepaper together), signed by the party to be charged (via Sahar's name, printed (and, moreover circled)).

   C tells us that Bernard can enforce this contract because Sahar "signed" the writing, which is true because her name appears on the notepaper. Her name there printed and circled qualifies as her "signature." Without it, Bernard would be unable to enforce the contract, and so **C** is right.

 # Silver's Picks

1.	**D**
2.	**C**
3.	**B**
4.	**B**
5.	**A**
6.	**C**

16

Incapacity to Form
a Contract

A. Rescission, Status Quo Ante, and Unjust Enrichment
B. When Minors Form Contracts
C. When Mentally Impaired Adults Form Contracts
D. When Incompetent Persons Contract for Necessaries
E. The Closers
✦ Silver's Picks

A.   Rescission, Status Quo Ante, and Unjust Enrichment

Under some circumstances, two parties may form a contract that a court or they themselves later "rescind," meaning the contract undergoes "rescission"; it is "undone." Rescission (an enormous topic in itself) is appropriate when a contract is premised on a "mistake" (Chapter 22, section B); "duress" (Chapter 20, section A); "undue influence" (Chapter 20, section B); "illegality" (Chapter 17); or fraud.[1] Further, as this chapter teaches, a contract may undergo rescission when one of its parties lacks "mental capacity."

For right now, let's know this: When a contract undergoes rescission, it "disappears," retroactively, to the time at which it was formed. The law goes back in time and "unforms" it. The contract goes away; it's erased; it vanishes. In the law's eyes, it ceases to exist and *never did exist*.

---

1. One commits fraud, a common law tort, when (1) she knowingly makes a materially false statement to another, (2) intending that the other party believe her, (3) the other party does believe her and, (4) for that reason, suffers harm. Hanson v. Ford Motor Co., 278 F.2d 586, 591 (8th Cir. 1960).

Daphne and Assureco.   Daphne contacts Assureco, an insurance company, and states her wish to buy disability insurance (thereby making an invitation to deal). Assureco sends her its application form and asks that she complete it (thereby *responding* with *its* invitation to deal). The application form describes Assureco's disability insurance policy and the annual premium (price) that Daphne will have to pay for it. It requires that Daphne disclose information concerning her health. Asked whether she has ever been diagnosed with a heart condition, Daphne writes "no," even though she *has* had a heart condition and knows it; Daphne deliberately answers untruthfully.

On October 1, Daphne submits her application, which constitutes her offer to buy the insurance. On October 15, Assureco "approves" it, meaning it accepts the offer. The parties form a contract requiring (1) that Daphne pay an annual premium of $6,000, and (2) that Assureco pay Daphne $50,000 yearly for the remainder of her life *if* she should become disabled. Because Daphne made a materially false statement concerning her health, the contract, unbeknownst to Assureco, is founded on a fraud.

For one year, Daphne pays her annual premium of $6,000. Then, her pre-existing heart condition does, in fact, disable her. She claims her benefit from Assureco. Assureco investigates and learns the truth—that Daphne falsely withheld information about her heart condition. On that basis, it refuses to pay.

Daphne sues Assureco for breach. Citing Daphne's fraud, Assureco counterclaims for *rescission* of the contract. The court orders the contract rescinded and requires, also, that Assureco return to Daphne the $6,000 she paid it.

Why Does the Court Do That?   To say that a contract undergoes rescission is to say that it disappears, retroactively, to the time at which it was formed. By (a fiction of) law, the contract never existed. It is extinguished *nunc pro tunc*.[2] If, under the contract (before it vanishes), either party receives from the other any money, property, or service, the law demands that she return it.[3] That's because one enjoys an "unjust enrichment"[4] if, from another, she takes and retains property or some other benefit pursuant to a contract that, by law, *never existed*. For that reason, rescission of a contract ordinarily requires that each of its parties restore the other to "status quo ante"—to the financial position each occupied before the contract was formed. To sound like lawyers all the more, we invoke the word "restitution"[5] and recite this rule:

> When a contract undergoes rescission, then to avoid unjust enrichment to either of its parties, each must make to the other such restitution as restores

---

2. The Latin phrase *nunc pro tunc* means literally "now for then," or "retroactively."
3. This precept and the notion of rescission generally arose first in *equity* and has since been adopted by the law. See Appendix, section E.
4. "Unjust enrichment" is a great big topic in itself. We address it in Chapter 28.
5. "Restitution" is a great big topic too, intimately tied to "unjust enrichment" and fully addressed in Chapter 28.

her to status quo ante—to the financial position she occupied before the contract was formed.

In *Black on Rescission and Cancellation* §1, we read:

> To rescind a contract is . . . to abrogate and undo it from the beginning; . . . [to] restore the parties to the relative positions which they would have occupied if no such contract had ever been made. Rescission necessarily involves a repudiation of the contract and a refusal of the moving party to be further bound by it. But this by itself would constitute no more than a breach of the contract or a refusal of performance, while the idea of rescission involves the additional and distinguishing element of a restoration of the status quo [ante]. . . .

And Restatement (First) of Restitution §65 provides:

> The right of a person to [rescission] and restitution . . . is dependent upon his return . . . to the other party [of] anything which he received as part of the transaction.

All that we have just discussed explains why Assureco must return to Daphne the $6,000 she paid it. Assureco must restore her to status quo ante—to the financial position she occupied before the parties formed their contract, so to ensure that it enjoys no unjust enrichment.[6]

QUESTION 1. Nanette owns a 90-foot sailing yacht but knows nothing of the sea. She wants a licensed captain to take charge of the vessel, and seeks to hire one. Carp represents himself as a licensed captain with decades of experience on the oceans. On May 1, the parties form a contract under which Nanette is to (a) pay Carp $200,000 per year, and (b) allow him to live aboard the vessel rent free. In exchange, Carp is to pilot the vessel whenever Nanette wants to use it, usually inviting business guests to accompany her.

When the parties form their contract, Nannette pays Carp his first year's salary of $200,000. Carp immediately takes up residence aboard the yacht. Over the course of May, June, and July he pilots it 30 times, for a total of 300 hours, as Nanette treats her business guests to luxurious cruises. Carp performs well; Nanette is pleased with him.

On August 1, however, Nanette learns that Carp has no captain's license and little experience. She petitions the court and moves to rescind

---

6. As explained in the Appendix, section E, there is a difference between "law" and something called "equity." There once were, and to a degree still are—courts of law and courts of equity, each separate from the other. Accordingly, some of our rights and obligations arise from law and others from equity. Appendix, section E, entitled "Law vs. Equity" addresses that subject, and we recommend that you read it *now*. If you do, you'll better understand all that you study in law school, from day 1. If you don't—well, don't blame us for the consequences. In any case, do know that "unjust enrichment" is a doctrine not of law, but of "equity." When one recovers in unjust enrichment, she does not recover under contract *law* or any other body of *law*. She recovers in equity.

the contract. If the court rescinds the contract, it should give such judgment also as will assure that

I. the parties complete their performances for the remainder of the year.
II. Carp returns to Nanette $200,000.
III. Carp pays Nanette for the value he derived by using the vessel as a residence.
IV. Nanette pays Carp for the fair market value that corresponds to 300 hours of his services as captain.

A. I and II
B. I and III
C. II, III, and IV
D. Neither I, II, III, nor IV

ANALYSIS.   When a court rescinds a contract, it renders the contract inoperative from the outset. The contract is "undone." And, to the extent possible, the law requires that each party restore the other to the position he occupied before the contract arose—to status quo ante—so that neither enjoys an unjust enrichment.

In performing under this contract, Nanette (a) paid Carp $200,000, and (b) allowed him to live rent-free aboard her yacht. Carp served competently as a captain for 300 hours. In order that the parties be restored to status quo ante, Carp must (a) return to Nanette the $200,000 she paid him, and (b) pay Nanette the fair market value[7] of his tenancy aboard the yacht. In turn, Nanette must pay Carp a fair market value for 300 hours of his professional service. Hence, **C** is right.

B.   When Minors Form Contracts[8]

In most (if not all) of the fifty states, one reaches adulthood on her eighteenth birthday (although at one time the critical age was twenty-one). Before that she is a "minor," also called an "infant." By common law, a minor/infant lacks the mental *capacity* to form a contract. That is (generally) so whether she be a two-year-old toddler or a seventeen-year-old college freshman studying molecular biophysics (with a minor in Hegelian philosophy).

---

7. Fair market value is a matter of fact. Where, by law, one party owes another the fair market value of some good or service and the parties themselves cannot agree on what *is* the fair market value, then, as with any other contested fact, the answer must come from a court (and in the case of a jury trial—from a jury).

8. Please remember that where UCC Article 2 is silent, the common law governs. On the subject of incapacity, Article 2 *is* silent; it says nothing. In this section B, illustrations might involve goods or services. In either case, the common law governs.

Illustration: Kelly and Marcie I. Kelly, an adult, owns a retail business, "Bicycles Are Best." On September 1, seventeen-year-old Marcie visits the store and declares her wish to buy a bike. Kelly helps her select a bike, tells her that its price is $289, informs her that it will be ready in two days, and takes from her a $50 deposit. Later that day, Marcie regrets what she has done. She doesn't care about the bike and wants back her $50 deposit. She tells the story to her mother, who then telephones Kelly: "My daughter Marcie is a minor. She wants to extricate herself from her contract with you, and demands return of her $50 deposit." With that, the contract dies, and Kelly must return the deposit. That's because *a contract between a minor and an adult is "voidable" at the minor's option,* which means the minor is empowered to rescind it, whereupon she renders it void — dead, erased, *nunc pro tunc.*

In this context, by tradition, most lawyers don't use the word "rescind," although they'd certainly be right to do so. Rather, you'll hear and read that a minor's contract with an adult is voidable and, therefore, that the minor has the power to "void" or "disaffirm" it. But do remember that when a minor is said to "disaffirm" or "void" a contract, she elects, really, to *rescind* it.

As already noted, when a contract undergoes rescission, its parties must, ordinarily, restore each other to status quo ante. In this case, Kelly, an adult, receives money *from* Marcie, an "infant." Consequently, Kelly must return to Marcie the $50 deposit, and we now know this much: A contract formed between a minor and adult is voidable at the minor's option, which means that the minor may, if she chooses, rescind ("disaffirm," "void") it. If she does so, then, by law, (1) the contract is extinguished, *nunc pro tunc,* and (2) the adult must return or make payment for any value the minor conveyed to him.

Illustration: Kelly and Marcie II. Suppose now that Marcie does not rescind the contract. On September 3, she returns to Kelly's store, pays the $239 still due, and takes the bike. Then, after keeping and riding it for one month, she regrets the purchase and wants her money back. Marcie (or an adult on her behalf) tells Kelly that she elects to disaffirm the contract, and to have back the full $289 purchase price.

Even after Marcie pays the purchase price, takes the bicycle, and uses it, she retains the right to rescind (void, disaffirm) the contract. If she elects to do so, the contract vanishes, retroactively, and Kelly must make restitution to Marcie in the amount of $289. Marcie, in turn, must (a) return the bicycle to Kelly, or (b) pay Kelly whatever is its fair market value when she disaffirms the contract.

An Adult Must Return a Minor *Fully* to Status Quo Ante, But a Minor Need Not Do That for an Adult

Now, let's ask: What if, as certainly will be the case, the bike has suffered wear and tear that drops its value below the $289 Marcie paid for it? Let's answer: A minor who disaffirms her contract need not *fully* return the adult to *status quo ante.* She must return any property she has acquired under the contract, or pay whatever is its market value *at the time she disaffirms the contract.* If she returns the property, she need not account for any wear and tear it has suffered while in her hands. If she pays for the property, she need not account for the amount of reduction in its value while it was in her hands.

Marcie, therefore, must return the bicycle to Kelly, whatever its condition, or pay Kelly its value, whatever that is, *at the time she disaffirm/voids the contract.* She need not worry about wear, tear, or depreciation. If Marcie doesn't have the bike because it's been lost or stolen, Kelly must, still, refund the whole purchase price, but Marcie need pay Kelly nothing at all.[9]

Illustration: Kelly and Marcie III.   Let's take one more look at Kelly and Marcie with yet another alteration in the facts: Marcie pays the purchase price and takes the bike. One year later, she turns eighteen, and on the very *next* day, she wants her money back. Kelly must return the money, because:

If a minor forms a contract with an adult, her right to disaffirm it endures until she reaches majority (adulthood), and for a reasonable time thereafter.

In this regard, one day certainly falls within a reasonable time. Kelly must return to Marcie the $289 she paid her, and if Marcie still has the bike, she need only (a) return it to Kelly, whatever its condition, or (b) pay Kelly the amount of its *present* market value, however low that might be. If she no longer has it, she need pay Kelly nothing.

We have just said that a minor retains her right to disaffirm her contract until a reasonable time after she reaches majority. The law features, also, this reciprocal rule:

If, after forming a contract, a minor reaches majority and within a reasonable time thereafter fails to disaffirm it, then, by implication of law, she affirms it and loses her right to disaffirm.

If, during the six months (or so) after she turns eighteen, Marcie makes no attempt to disaffirm her contract, it ceases to be voidable. She is "stuck" with it. If she asks to have her money back, Kelly need not (and certainly *will* not) return it.

Three More Illustrations.
1. Facts: Phillip is twelve years old. Kacy is an adult. By contract, Phillip promises to give Kacy his computer, and Kacy promises to give Phillip her stereo music system. Phillip's computer is worth $200. Kacy's music system is

---

9.   The rule is old: "[I]t is well settled that it is not a condition of the disaffirmation by an infant of a contract made during infancy that he shall return the consideration received by him if, prior to such disaffirmation and during infancy, the specific thing received has been disposed of, wasted, or consumed, and cannot be returned." MacGreal v. Taylor, 167 U.S. 688, 698 (1897). And, as we've just explained, the rule survives, full strength today: "[A minor may] disaffirm all obligations under a contract, *even for services previously rendered,* without restoring consideration or the value of services rendered to the other party." Fife v. Facebook, 905 F. Supp. 2d 997 (N.D. Cal. 2012).

worth \$50.[10] The parties make the trade. Three years later, when he is fifteen, Phillip disaffirms the contract. At that time, the computer in Kacy's possession has a value of \$40. The music system in Phillip's possession is broken, obsolete, and worthless.

The Rule: *When a minor disaffirms his contract, the adult must afford the minor restitution for all value he receives under the contract, but the minor need not make such full restitution to the adult. The minor need only (a) return such property as is actually in his possession, or (b) pay whatever value it has at that time.*

Rule Applied to This Case: Phillip is a minor. He forms a contract with Kacy, an adult, under which the parties trade properties. Phillip then disaffirms the contract, and at that time still has the property he took from Kacy. Whatever its condition or value, he must return it to her but need do nothing more. Kacy, the adult, must restore Phillip to full status quo ante — to the true financial position he occupied before the parties made the trade.

The Result: Kacy must (a) return the computer to Phillip, together with an additional \$160 to account for its loss of value, or (b) keep it, if she likes, and pay Phillip the full \$200 of value it had when the parties made the trade. Phillip need only return to Kacy the worthless music system (if she wants it). He need not pay her a dime.

2. Facts: Pablo is an adult. Patience is a fourteen-year-old girl. The two form a contract under which Patience is to paint two portraits of Pablo, with Pablo to pay her a total of \$200 when she completes them. The actual fair market value of Patience's service is \$1,000 — \$500 per portrait. Patience paints one portrait and then disaffirms the contract.

Rule: *When a minor disaffirms her contract with an adult, the minor need only (a) return such property as is actually in her possession, or (b) pay whatever value it has at that time; she need do nothing more. Yet, the adult must afford the minor full restitution for all value he receives from her. As to property, the adult must restore to the minor the full value with which the minor has parted under the contract. As to services the minor provides him, the adult must pay not the agreed contract price, but the true fair market value of the service[11] whether that's greater than, less than, or equal to the contract price.*

Rule Applied to This Case: Patience is a minor and Pablo an adult. Pursuant to their contract, Patience took no property from Pablo. Rather, she afforded him \$500 in service.

Result: Pablo must pay Patience \$500. Patience need do nothing for Pablo (although Pablo does retain the one portrait she painted).

---

10. As discussed in Chapter 12, section C, the difference in values is irrelevant to the matter of consideration; it does not invalidate the contract.

11. The law does not, in this regard, assume that the fair market value of property is equal to the price that a buyer paid for it or to the value of property that the buyer traded for it. Fair market value creates a question of fact for the court (or, in a jury trial, for the jury).

3. Facts: Lester is an adult and Negev a seventeen-year-old who owns an automobile.[12] The two form a contract under which Lester will repair Negev's vehicle, and Negev will pay him $400 when the work is done. Lester completes the repair, and Negev promptly disaffirms the contract.

Rule: *When a minor disaffirms a contract, he must, to the adult, return to the adult any property (or its value) he retains under the contract, but he need not pay the value of any service with which the adult has provided him.*

Rule Applied to This Case: Negev acquired no property from Lester. He did derive a service, but for that he need not pay.

Result: Negev need pay Lester nothing.

Now, Let's State One Big, Happy Rule

If a minor forms a contract with an adult, then

   (1) (a) the minor may disaffirm (void, rescind) the contract at any time until he reaches adulthood and for a reasonable time thereafter.[13]

   (b) (i) The minor may, if he wishes, affirm the contract when he reaches adulthood, but cannot do so while still a minor, and (ii) once the minor disaffirms the contract he cannot ever affirm it—not as a minor and not as an adult. Disaffirmation is final.

   (c) If the minor reaches adulthood and fails to disaffirm the contract within a reasonable time thereafter, then by law he affirms it.

   (2) If the minor exercises his right to disaffirm the contract while still a minor or (within a reasonable time) as an adult, then

   (a) the adult party to the contract must (i) return (make restitution for) the money and/or the monetary value of any property he received from the minor; and (ii) make payment (restitution) also for the fair market value of any services with which the minor has provided him.

   (b) (i) If from the adult the minor has received and still possesses property, then (1) he must return it, or pay what is then its fair market value, no matter how low that might be, and regardless of its value or condition, and he need do nothing more, but (2) if the minor no longer has the property, he need give or pay the adult nothing; and (ii) for any service the minor has received from the adult, the minor need not make any restitution at all.

---

12.   That one may lack capacity to form a contract does not mean he lacks capacity to own property. All persons, including minors, may own property. If one lacks the capacity to *manage* his property, then a parent or guardian is empowered to do it for him. Even in those cases, however, the minor or other incompetent party continues as owner.

13.   The cases decided on this point seem always to involve a minor who formed a contract shortly before attaining adulthood. To our knowledge, no reported case concerns, for example, a nine-year-old who forms a contract with an adult and wishes to disaffirm it on turning eighteen, nine years later. If you find one, let us know.

QUESTION 2. Peter, age twenty-two, is a skilled auto body worker. Paul, age seventeen, is skilled in piano repair. Peter and Paul agree that Peter will paint Paul's car and Paul will repair Peter's piano. Peter then paints Paul's car, but Paul does not repair Peter's piano. Peter sues Paul for breach, whereupon Paul disaffirms the contract.

The legal result will be that

I. Paul must pay Peter the fair market value of the paint job with which Peter provided him.
II. Peter must pay Paul the fair market value of the piano repair Paul failed to provide him.

A. I only
B. II only
C. I and II
D. Neither I nor II

ANALYSIS. Peter, an adult, forms a contract with Paul, a minor. Peter performs under the contract, but Paul does not. Paul then disaffirms the contract and thus puts it to an end. Because Paul didn't perform, Peter received nothing from him. Consequently, Peter need make no restitution to Paul. Paul retains the value of his painted car, but that represents a *service*. Because Paul is a minor, he need make no restitution for it. Fair or unfair, right or wrong, Paul has a newly painted car, and he need pay nothing for it. **D** is right.

C. When Mentally Impaired Adults Form Contracts

Criminal and common law alike have had difficulty defining such mental incompetence as frees an adult from responsibility for what he says and does. In order truly to understand the law surrounding that question, one must devote considerable study and then, still, he'll finish by throwing up his hands. Nonetheless, with respect to contracts, we'll teach you the standard lyrics to the standard tune, warning you, however, that the rules are far easier to state than apply. The Restatement (Second) of Contracts purports to express modern law on the subject, and for that purpose, it is perhaps as good (and as bad) as any other summary authority.

Restatement (Second) §15(1) divides mentally incapacitated adults into two groups: those who, because of mental illness or defect, (1) do not understand "the nature or consequences" of their agreements, and, on other hand,

(2) do understand their agreements, but as to the relevant subject matter demonstrate an inability to *behave* reasonably:

> A person incurs only voidable contractual duties by entering into a transaction if by reason of mental illness or defect
>
> (a) he is unable to understand in a reasonable manner the nature and consequences of the transaction [and that applies even if the other party has no reason to know of the defect], or
>
> (b) he is unable to act in a reasonable manner in relation to the transaction, and the other party does have reason to know of his condition.

To category 1 belongs the profoundly impaired or intellectually challenged adult who speaks assent to a proposal or signs his name to paper not knowing what it means or what consequences will follow. Category 1 includes, also, those with understanding severely impaired by alcohol, drugs, or the like. To category 2 there belongs, for example, a compulsive buyer or hoarder with an uncontrollable irrational urge to buy, possess, and accumulate things for which she has no earthly use.

When such an incapacitated adult forms a contract, he has the option to rescind (disaffirm, void) it, as does a minor. When before doing so, however, he receives from the competent party any money, property, or service, the Restatement treats him less generously than it does a minor. The incapacitated adult who disaffirms his contract (on his own or through a guardian) must generally make restitution in full for *all* money, property, or service he has received from the competent party. The competent party must, of course, make corresponding restitution for any value *he* has received. Stated otherwise, where a mentally incompetent party of either category 1 or 2 forms a contract, he may rescind/void/disaffirm it, but each contracting party must restore the other to full status quo ante.

Once Again, Let's State One Big Happy Rule

> *(1) (a) When with a competent adult a mentally impaired person forms a contract, he or his legal representative may fully and wholly disaffirm it if at the time he forms the contract his impairment renders him unable to appreciate the nature or consequences of his actions; (b) that is so whether, at that time, the competent adult does or does not have reason to know of the impairment; and (c) when such a person does disaffirm, each contracting party must restore the other to full status quo ante by the return of property, the payment of money, or both.*
>
> *(2) (a) When with a competent adult a mentally impaired person forms a contract, he or his legal representative may disaffirm it if (i) at the time he forms the contract the mentally impaired person does understand the nature and consequences of his actions, but suffers an impairment that renders him unable to behave reasonably as to the subject matter of the contract, and (ii) the competent adult knows or has reason to know of the impairment; (b) if the impaired party effectively disaffirms, each contracting party must restore the other to full status quo ante by the return of property, the payment of money, or both.*

(3) Once either such impaired party effectively disaffirms the contract at issue, he cannot then affirm it, he cannot restore it, and the contract is permanently undone.

Three Illustrations.

Illustration 1. Facts: A is a competent adult who sells clothing retail. Unbeknownst to A, B is so seriously impaired as not to understand the nature or consequences of his actions. A and B form a contract for the sale of a $500 suit of clothes. B pays the $500, and A hands him the suit. For three weeks, B wears the suit, tearing it and staining it to "kingdom come." B's guardian learns of the events. She contacts A and announces B's wish to rescind the contract.

Rule: *If a competent person forms a contract with an adult who does not understand the nature or consequences of his actions, then, whether the competent person does or does not have reason to know of the disability, the incompetent party may, at his option (through a guardian, perhaps), rescind (disaffirm/void) the contract. If he does so, each party must (a) return the other to full status quo ante by payment of money and/or return of property valued as of the time he first acquired it, and (b) pay the other the fair market value of any services the other has performed.*

Rule Applied to This Case: A forms a contract with B, an adult who does not understand the nature or consequences of his actions. B disaffirms the contract. A must return to B all value B conveyed to her, and B must return to A all value A conveyed to him. In both cases, the law assesses "value" as of the time the parties formed their contract.

Result: The contract is rescinded. A must return B's $500. B must pay A such value as the suit had when A parted with it. (Since the law allows that the sale price might be different from the contract price, that amount might or might not be equal to $500. See *supra* note 5.)

Illustration 2. Facts: A is an automobile dealer. B is an adult who understands the nature and consequences of his actions. B is, however, a compulsive purchaser of cars, although A has no reason to know that. Propelled by his compulsion, B contracts with A for the purchase of an automobile, with A charging him a perfectly fair price. B takes the car and drives it for one month. Thereafter, he attempts to disaffirm the contract.

Rule: *If Party A forms a contract with an adult Party B who understands the nature of his actions but who, with respect to the contract, is unable to behave reasonably — A having no reason to know of B's impairment — then Party B has no right to rescind the contract.*

Rule Applied to This Case: A had no reason to know of B's impairment. B has no power to rescind.

Result: The contract is not rescinded. B keeps the car; A keeps his money.

Illustration 3. Facts: A is, again, an automobile dealer. B is an adult who understands the nature and consequences of his actions. However, B is a compulsive, uncontrolled purchaser of cars. B arrives at A's dealership with his brother C. C tells A of B's addiction to car buying. Nonetheless, A contracts with B for the sale of a car at a fair price. B takes the car and drives it for one month. Thereafter, B attempts to disaffirm the contract.

Rule: *If a Party A forms a contract with an adult Party B who understands the nature and consequence of his actions (knows what he is doing) but is unable to behave reasonably in the transaction, and A has reason to know of B's impairment, then Party B may disaffirm the contract. If he does so, each party must compensate the other for all value the other conveyed to him, "value" being assessed as of the time the parties formed their contract.*

Rule Applied to This Case: A knows of (has reason to know of) B's disability, meaning B has power to disaffirm the contract. A must return the money B paid him, B must either (a) return the car together with payment that accounts for its loss of value, or (b) keep the car and pay A the value it had when A parted with it.

Result: The contract is rescinded. A must return B's purchase price, and B must return the car, together with payment for any decrease in its value, or keep the car and pay A its full value at the time the parties formed their contract.

D.   When Incompetent Persons Contract for Necessaries

When an incompetent person, child or adult, (a) forms a contract by which she secures "necessaries"—goods or services reasonably essential to her survival—and (b) then elects to rescind it, she must pay the fair market value (not the contract price) of all goods *and* services provided her. Necessaries include, for example, food, clothing, shelter, and medical care.

Suppose an eight-year-old child, hungry and alone, enters a retail store. He asks for food and clothing, promising to pay at some later time. The retailer obliges him. Thereafter, the child (or someone on his behalf) might pay the agreed price and be done with it. He might, on the other hand, take the goods, consume them, and then elect to rescind the contract. If he does that, he must pay the seller not the contract price to which he agreed (since the contract no longer exists), but whatever the court names as the *fair market value* of the goods given him (which, once again, might or might not differ from the contract price). (See *supra* note 5.) That applies even if the child never does agree to pay for these "necessaries." The law itself imposes on the child an obligation to pay this retailer the fair market value of what the retailer gives him.

The Rule.   *If one supplies a minor with "necessaries," and the minor (a) agrees to pay for them, and does not disaffirm his contract, then he (or someone on his* *behalf) must pay the contract price; but if (b) the minor elects to rescind the contract or never does agree to pay for them in the first place, he (or someone on his behalf) must pay the supplier their fair market value.*

E.   The Closers

QUESTIONS 3-5. State X is selling tickets for a lottery it will conduct on May 2. It announces that on May 1 at 12:00 noon it will cease to sell any tickets. At one minute before noon on that day, May 1, Larry arrives at the ticket sales office and buys two tickets for $50 each. Immediately afterward, the state closes the sales office and ceases to sell tickets. Leaving the office, Larry runs into Lucy, a stranger who has come to the office hoping to buy a lottery ticket. Unbeknownst to Larry, Lucy is a wildly compulsive, uncontrolled gambler. He hears her say, "Oh, no, it's just after noon. I missed my chance to buy a lottery ticket."

For $1,000, Larry offers to sell Lucy one of his tickets. Lucy accepts, and the parties consummate the sale. A few seconds later, Larry meets Victor, also a stranger who has arrived at the sales office hoping to buy a ticket. Victor is a chronic alcoholic, who at this moment is totally "trashed," "plastered," "sloshed," and "stewed," not to mention "wholly wasted," with "three sheets to the wind." Walking in a zig-zag, reaching out to the air for balance, and grossly slurring his speech, Victor shouts, "I don't know where I am, who I am, or what day it is, but it looks like I'm too late to buy a lottery ticket." For $1,000, Larry offers to sell Victor his second ticket. Victor says, "Yeah, okay buddy, here's a thousand bucks in cash." Larry takes the cash and gives Victor the ticket.

Later on that same day, May 1, Lucy contacts Larry: "I paid you $1,000 for a $50 ticket because I am a compulsive, uncontrolled gambler. That was a big mistake. I hereby renounce my contract with you. I'll return the ticket to you, and I want back my $1,000." Larry responds, "No way." Still later that day, Victor sobers up. On his floor, he sees a lottery ticket and a receipt showing that he bought it from Larry for $1,000. From the receipt, he acquires Larry's telephone number and contacts him: "Apparently I bought a $50 lottery ticket from you this morning, for $1,000. I don't remember a thing about it, but I do know I was completely tanked. I didn't know what I was doing. I'll return the ticket to you, and I want back my $1,000." Larry responds, "Forget it."

On the next day, May 2, the state conducts its lottery and announces that ticket number 2321 has won $20 million. That's the ticket in Lucy's possession. Ticket number 2322 has won $10 million. That's the ticket in

Victor's possession. Larry contacts Lucy: "I've changed my mind. Bring me the ticket, and I'll give back your $1,000." Lucy responds, "No way." Larry then contacts Victor: "I've changed my mind. Bring me the ticket, and I'll give back your $1,000." Victor responds, "Get lost." Larry visits a lawyer and tells him the whole story. He then asks, "Am I entitled to have back the two tickets?"

QUESTION 3. As to the ticket in Lucy's possession, the correct answer is

A. yes, because a mental disturbance caused Lucy to purchase the ticket.
B. yes, because once Lucy disaffirmed the contract she could not reinstate it.
C. no, because Lucy could not and did not disaffirm her contract.
D. no, because it is Lucy's option, at her pleasure, to affirm, disaffirm, or reinstate her contract with Larry.

QUESTION 4. As to the ticket in Victor's possession, the correct answer is

A. yes, because Victor successfully disaffirmed the contract after which he could not and did not reinstate it.
B. yes, because Victor's intoxication resulted from his own decision to drink.
C. no, because Victor had no memory of his interaction with Larry.
D. no, because Larry had reason readily to know that Victor had no understanding of the transaction between them.

ANALYSIS.   This story turns things upside-down and inside-out. Each of two mentally impaired buyers wants, at first, to disaffirm the contract formed with a competent person, who does not want to allow either one to do so. Then, for obvious reasons, everyone wants to reverse course. Each of the impaired parties wants to keep the contract alive, so as to retain the winning tickets. The competent party wants the contracts to die, so as to *have back* the winning tickets.

As for Question 3.   Lucy's mental impairment belongs to category 2 (described in section C above). When buying the ticket, she knew what she was doing; she appreciated the nature and consequences of her action. But, as a compulsive gambler faced with an offer of lottery tickets, she was unable to behave reasonably, unable to restrain herself. Lucy's category 2 mental impairment would allow her to disaffirm only if Larry, when forming the contract, had reason to know of it. He didn't. Notwithstanding her proclamation, Lucy did not disaffirm the contract. It remained in force. The answer is "no," Larry is not entitled to have back the lottery ticket he sold to Lucy. **A** and **B** say "yes," so they're wrong.

A implies a false statement of law. There's no general rule that allows one to disaffirm a contract simply because some mental disturbance causes her to form it. A category 1 impairment allows for disaffirmation. A category 2 impairment allows for disaffirmation only if the unimpaired contracting party (Larry) has reason to know of it at the time of contracting. There are a host of other mental disturbances, impairments, and illnesses, none of which warrants disaffirmation. So **A** is wrong. (If when Larry sold Lucy the ticket, he had reason to know of her gambling problem, then Lucy would have the right to disaffirm the contract.) **B** operates on a false premise, to wit, that Lucy successfully disaffirmed the contract. She didn't because she had no right to do so. So **B** is wrong, leaving us with **C** and **D**, one of which (we hope) is right.

D makes a false statement. Larry had no reason to know of Lucy's gambling addiction, meaning Lucy had no right to disaffirm her contract. Further, if one does have a right to disaffirm a contract and does so, she cannot then reinstate it. **D** goes to the dumper. **C** correctly reports that Lucy failed to disaffirm her contract with Larry. Lucy understood the nature and consequences of the contract, but was unable to behave reasonably as to its subject matter. Larry knew nothing of that, so Lucy had no right to disaffirm. Hence, she keeps the ticket for the reason that she did not and could not successfully disaffirm the contract. **C** is right.

As for Question 4.   When Victor bought his ticket, he was so intoxicated as *not* to understand the nature or consequences of what he was doing. As soon as he proclaimed to Larry his wish to "undo" the contract, he—unlike Lucy—successfully disaffirmed it. Having done so, he had no power to reinstate it. Consequently, Victor and Larry must restore each other to status quo ante. Larry gets the ticket and Victor the $1,000.

C and **D** say "no," so they're wrong. Furthermore, **C** implies a false statement of law. A fully competent person might form a contract and then forget he has done so. His poor memory affords him no right to disaffirm it. **D**, too, is legally incorrect. If X, a competent adult, forms a contract with Y, who does not understand the nature or consequences of his actions (category 1), Y is empowered to disaffirm it *regardless* of what X did or did not know about Y's disability. (Y's knowledge that X is mentally impaired would be relevant only if Y's impairment belonged to category 2, as did Lucy's.)

We're left with **A** and **B**. According to **B**, one who causes his own incapacity is not entitled to disaffirm his contract. There's no such law. **B** is wrong. **A** says "yes," and correctly states the reason: Once a mentally impaired party (or an infant) disaffirms a contract, he has no power to reinstate/reaffirm it. The disaffirmation stands. That's the law, and that's why **A** is right.

Should there arise a case with facts as peculiar as these, it would likely produce protracted litigation. A court might play fast and loose with the relevant rules. No good lawyer dealing with this case would rely on standard statements of the so-called rules as predictors of the outcome. The truth is, we have little idea of how a state supreme court would really decide this case. We're willing to say **A** is "right," but that doesn't mean it's *real*.

> **QUESTION 5.** Lucy's demand that Larry refund her $1,000 is best characterized as
>
> I. a successful disaffirmation of her contract with Larry.
> II. an offer to sell her ticket back to Larry, which offer Larry rejected.
> A. I only
> B. II only
> C. Both I and II
> D. Neither I nor II

ANALYSIS. As we know, when Lucy told Larry that she wanted to "renounce" the contract, she did not disaffirm it. Option I is false. Now we're asked, "What *did* she do?" She doesn't know, but we do. She made an offer to sell the lottery ticket back to Larry for $1,000. It was for Larry to accept or reject the offer. Had he accepted it, he would be obliged to return Lucy's money and Lucy would be obliged to return the ticket. Larry, however, responded with "no way," meaning he rejected the offer. Option II is correct and the right answer is **B**.

 # Silver's Picks

1.	C
2.	D
3.	C
4.	A
5.	B

17

Illegal Contracts

A. Illegal Contracts: The Basics

Some agreements create what the law calls "illegal contracts." Classically, it is said that illegal contracts are void—not voidable, but void. Neither party can enforce one against the other. In the law's eyes, the contract does not exist; the parties never formed a contract. English law adopted that precept centuries ago. In 1775 Lord Mansfield wrote, "The principle . . . is this; 'ex dolo malo non oritur actio: No court will lend its aid to a man who founds his cause of action upon an immoral or an illegal act.'" Holman v. Johnson, 1 Crown 341 (K.B. 1775).

And What Makes a Contract "Illegal"?

With respect to illegal contracts, "illegal" does not refer to law as we usually use that word. It doesn't refer, necessarily, to violations of constitution, statute, administrative regulation, ordinance, or court order.[1] Rather, by modern

---

1. When we normal people hear the word "law" we think of legislative enactments: statutes, regulations, ordinances. Many law professors, with their heads in the clouds, think they have (or pretend to have) a philosophic bent. When *they* think of legislative enactments, they invoke the phrase "*positive* law," by which they mean man-made law. They deem that phrase significant because they distinguish it from something they call "natural law." To those who believe in it, natural law refers to rights and duties that derive, somehow, from some higher source, separate from rules that human beings create. President Kennedy (whose head was *not* in the clouds) made *poetic* reference to the idea when he said, "[T]he rights of man come not from the generosity of the state but from the hand of God." (But never again, in public, did he refer to "God.") For more, see Jonathan A. Jacobs, *Reason, Religion and Natural Law* (Oxford University Press 2012).

common law and according, also, to some older judicial authorities, a contract is "illegal" if, in a court's opinion (guided, of course, by judicial precedent), it conflicts with "public policy." In this context, "public policy" refers to human behavior, whether or not prohibited by legislative enactment, that promotes (in the judiciary's mind) morality, public welfare, and values central to a free and ordered society.

Thus characterized, "public policy" remains, still, poorly defined.[2] Nonetheless, we can illustrate its meaning with a few simple stories.

And Here, from Two Hundred Years Ago, Is a Good One

In 1799, plaintiff, owner of a sailing ship, formed a contract with defendant, a sea captain. The contract provided that (1) plaintiff would let his ship out to defendant and (2) defendant would (a) sail it from Boston to the African coast, (b) load it with slaves, (c) sail to the West Indies, (d) sell the slaves and collect the sales monies, (e) sail back to Boston, and (f) pay over to plaintiff two-thirds of the money thus collected. Defendant did all that the contract required, except for item (f); on returning to Boston, he refused to pay any money over to plaintiff. So came the litigation and so came Justice Joseph Story's decision:

> Certainly this action cannot be maintained. The traffic in slaves is a most odious and horrible traffic, contrary to the plainest principles of natural justice and humanity. [I]t cannot have a legal existence. . . . The voyage was, in its very elements, infected with the deepest pollution of illegality; and the present action is brought between the very parties who formed and executed this reprehensible enterprise.

Fales v. Mayberry, 2 Gall. 560 (Cir. Ct. Dist. R.I. 1815).

Two More Illustrations.

Valdez and Ian.   Valdez, married to Wanda, is involved also with a paramour whom he plans to meet on Monday night. Not wanting Wanda to know that, Valdez and his friend Ian agree that (1) Valdez will pay Ian $50, and (2) if Wanda should ask Ian about Valdez's whereabouts on Monday night, Ian will say, "On Monday night Valdez was with me, playing cards."

The agreement calls for Ian to practice deceit on Valdez's wife regarding a concern central to marriage, which, in turn, constitutes a cherished social institution. Further, the agreement helps Valdez pursue marital infidelity, which, too, contravenes "good" morals. Hence, the agreement calls for behavior that violates "public policy." Most judges would brand it an illegal contract (notwithstanding their own frequent participation in similar conduct).

---

2.   See Horner v. Graves, 7 Bing. 735, 743 (1831) ("Whatever is injurious to the interests of the public [violates] . . . public policy."); Richardson v. Mellish, 2 Bing. 229, 252 (1824) (Burroughs, J.) ("Public policy . . . is an unruly horse and . . . you never know where it will carry you."); 3 Samuel Williston, *The Law of Contracts* §1630 (1920) ("[P]ublic policy is a variable thing. It must fluctuate with the circumstances of the time.").

Suppose that on Monday afternoon, Valdez pays Ian the $50 and on Monday night, he visits his paramour. On Tuesday, Valdez's wife asks Ian, "Do you know where Valdez was last night?" Ian decides to tell her the truth. "Not with me," he says, "I think he was with a girlfriend." Ian thus breaches his contract with Valdez. If Valdez brings an action against him for breach, the court will likely award him nothing, because the contract was "illegal," wherefore the law will not enforce it; it's void; legally, it doesn't exist.

Imagine now that the agreement calls for Valdez to make payment not on Monday, but on Tuesday. On Monday night, Valdez visits his paramour. Ian receives no call from Wanda, but on Tuesday he does ask Valdez for the $50. Valdez refuses to pay. If Ian brings an action against Valdez, the court will award him nothing because the contract is illegal, void, nonexistent. It's not enforceable — not for Ian, not for Valdez, "not for nobody."

Bilea and Dale.   On Thursday night, Dale wants to visit his mother. Bilea has a car, on which one tail light is "burned out." Nonetheless, in exchange for $25, Bilea agrees to drive Dale to his mother's home. The contract calls upon Bilea, literally, to violate the law — a traffic regulation — but all courts would agree that it doesn't contravene "good" morality or any value important to a free and ordered society. Hence, it doesn't violate public policy, and no court would call it an illegal contract. If either party breaches, the law will enforce it against the other.

So there you have it. An illegal contract is a contract that contravenes public policy and, as a general rule, it's void, unenforceable, empty of legal existence.

B.   Recovery on Illegal Contracts: Restitution for Unjust Enrichment

We've just learned that an illegal contract is void, meaning that when it's breached, neither of its parties may recover under the law of contract. Nonetheless, under some circumstances, if one party defaults, the other might recover not damages for breach of contract, but monetary compensation for "unjust enrichment."

"Unjust Enrichment"? What's That?

Let's take some time out from illegal contracts for a little chat about "unjust enrichment." It's Sunday, and two strangers A and B sit near each other at the beach, each with blankets, beach bags, sandals, and the usual collection of clutter. From A's beach bag out flies a $10 bill. Aloft in the wind, it reaches B, and B catches it. Let's ask: Does A have an action against B for the recovery of

$10? Plainly, she has no action for breach of contract since these parties never formed one. She has no action in trespass, negligence, assault, battery, defamation, nuisance, or in any of the other "garden variety" actionable wrongs (except, maybe, for "conversion" (Chapter 2 section F, footnote 4)).

Suppose X visits her friend Y at Y's home. While there, X asks Y to change five $20 bills into a single "C note." Y agrees to do so. X hands Y the five $20 bills and Y places for X a single $100 bill on the coffee table at which the parties are sitting. When X departs Y's home, she inadvertently leaves the $100 bill on Y's coffee table. When X asks to have the $100 bill back, Y refuses and insists on keeping it.

Let's ask: What action does X have against Y? Y hasn't stolen the money; she hasn't taken it wrongfully in any way. X, by oversight, left it in Y's home. Again, this aggrieved party, X, has no right of recovery in any garden variety cause of action (except, once again, maybe, for "conversion").

In the cases just described, X and A do have a right to recover through an action called "unjust enrichment." The remedy for unjust enrichment is not called "damages"; it's called "restitution." In short form, the relevant rule is that: If Party B is unjustly enriched at the expense of Party A, then Party A is entitled to such restitution as will correct the injustice. Restatement (First) of Restitution §1 provides:

> A person who has been unjustly enriched at the expense of another is required to make restitution to the other.

The word "unjust," of course, is "soft" and creates the most difficult of the problems tied to unjust enrichment. It should go without saying, therefore, that the Restatement writers, a bootless bunch, offer no definition of that word. So here, from us to you, is the rule of unjust enrichment, in full form complete with the meaning of "unjust."

Unjust Enrichment.
(1) A first party is unjustly enriched when, fortuitously, by chance, by serendipity, by grace of God or good luck, by "windfall" — at the expense of some second party — she enjoys a benefit in money, property, or service, meaning that
(2) the benefit does not come to her
(a) as a gift from another, or
(b) as consideration under an enforceable contract, or
(c) through any other dynamic that renders it earned or deserved, wherefore
(3) by judicial award, the first party must pay to the second such restitution as corrects the injustice.

Unjust Enrichment and Illegal Contracts.   That two parties form an illegal contract means that for at least one or both of them, participation, purpose, or performance violates public policy. The participation, purpose, or performance of the other might or might not violate public policy as well.

Illustration: Both Parties' Participation Offends Public Policy; No Restitution for Either One.   For $50,000 X hires Y to kill Z. In forming their agreement, both parties offend public policy (big time), X by hiring Y to kill Z, and Y by promising to kill him.

Suppose the contract requires that X pay Y in advance, before Y does "the job." X does pay Y $50,000. Y then defaults; he doesn't kill Z. X is "out" $50,000, for which he has received nothing back; Y is "up" by $50,000, for which he has done nothing in exchange. But X can't sustain against Y a suit for breach of contract, because the contract is illegal; it doesn't exist. Instead, X sues Y alleging that Y has been unjustly enriched at his expense. He asks for "restitution" of $50,000, the amount that will correct the injustice. And guess what—he won't get it. As to this illegal contract, X is a "bad guy." He has asked that Y kill X and in doing so he has, of course, violated public policy.

Now suppose the contract calls for X to pay Y after Y does "the job." Y does kill Z, but X refuses to pay him. Again, Y cannot maintain against X a suit for breach of contract, because the contract is illegal. So Y sues X alleging that (1) he performed a service for X, (2) that he did not do so in order to make X a gift, (3) that X has failed to pay him and, therefore, (4) that X has derived an unjust enrichment at his expense. The court will award Y nothing, because as to this illegal contract, Y (like X) is a "bad guy." He promised to commit a killing, and that too violates public policy.

Illustration: Only One Party's Participation Offends Public Policy; Restitution for the Other.   For ten years, Fenn has worked full time for Esta. Needing additional income, he asks Esta for extra work—for "overtime" hours. Esta offers him ten additional hours per week, but says she won't pay the "time and a half" overtime wage required by law. Rather, she'll pay Fenn only his ordinary hourly pay. Fenn accepts the arrangement.

These parties have formed a contract that conflicts with a significant policy of public well-being: A worker should receive a relatively greater rate of compensation for overtime work. The contract is (probably) "illegal." As to this illegal contract, Esta attempts to exploit her employee—to "get away" with receiving overtime service without paying overtime wage. Her participation in the contract offends public policy. Fenn, on the other hand, doesn't want to "get away" with anything. He is, simply, willing to work for a wage lower than the one to which he is lawfully entitled. His participation does not offend public policy. As to this illegal contract, Esta is a "bad guy"; Fenn is not.

Now suppose that (1) the agreement calls for Esta to pay Fenn in advance, (2) Esta does pay Fenn in advance, (3) Fenn fails to perform his extra ten hours of work, and (4) Esta sues asking that Fenn pay her restitution for his unjust enrichment: the payment for which he gave nothing in exchange. A court will likely dismiss her suit. She formed an illegal contract in which her participation offends public policy; she's a "bad guy."

Now suppose that (1) the contract calls for Esta to pay Fenn after he completes the overtime work, (2) Fenn performs the overtime work, (3) Esta (for whatever reason) refuses to pay him anything—not even the ordinary wage, and (4) Fenn sues Esta alleging that he has provided Esta with labor/service, and that Esta, therefore, retains the value of that service at his expense. A court will likely afford Fenn a recovery; restitution for Esta's unjust enrichment. Again, Fenn does not recover for breach of contract, because his contract with Esta is void for illegality. He recovers not damages for breach of contract, but restitution for unjust enrichment.

How Much Does Fenn Recover? Fenn recovers the "fair market value" of the "benefit" he has "conferred" on Esta. As is fully explained in Chapter 28, section B, "benefit conferred," the usual measure of restitution for unjust enrichment, means the fair market value of property or service with which the plaintiff parted. When deciding on Fenn's restitution award, the court will not assess "benefit conferred" by reference to the wage provided in his contract with Esta. As to an award of restitution for unjust enrichment, the law makes its assessment outside of and apart from the contract.

What? Suppose a contract calls for A to provide B with service X, for which B is to pay A $1,000. A performs the service, but B does not pay him. If (for reasons of illegality or other circumstances),[3] the law awards B a recovery not for breach of contract, but in restitution, it will identify the "benefit" that A "conferred" on B without regard to the $1,000 contract price. Rather, it will hear evidence as to the "fair market value" of A's service. It will then decide what is the fair market value of A's service and award that amount to A.

In awarding restitution to Fenn, after hearing evidence, the court might decide that the fair market value of his service happens to correspond to the statutory overtime pay rate. It might, on the other hand, decide that the fair market value is the "going rate" in the community for the work Fenn performed. In any case, the court is to identify fair market value as a matter apart from the contract wage because, once again, the contract between Esta and Fenn is void—nonexistent. One can't recover for breach of contract if he has not formed one.

Illustration: No Unjust Enrichment and No Restitution for Fenn. Let's alter the story of Esta and Fenn. After they form their overtime contract, Esta quickly announces her intention to dishonor it. She instructs Fenn not to work, and actually prevents him from doing so. Fenn sues her. If this contract

---

3. With respect to contracts/agreements, illegality is not the *only* circumstance under which the law awards a recovery in restitution. Other such circumstances are described in Chapters 23 and 28.

were not illegal, contract law would afford Fenn an action for Esta's breach; he'd be able to recover the pay promised him under the contract, regardless of the fact that he performed no work.[4] But the contract is illegal and any recovery to which Fenn might be entitled requires that he confer some benefit on Esta, so as to make for unjust enrichment. However, Esta prevented Fenn from performing. Therefore, Fenn provided Esta with no money, property, or service. He conferred on Esta no benefit; Esta enjoyed no "enrichment" at Fenn's expense. (She enjoyed no enrichment at all.) Fenn recovers zilch.

Brief Summary: The Law of Illegal Contracts.

(1) If and only if two parties form a contract whose terms offend public policy — whether or not they contravene statute, regulation, or common law — their contract is "illegal," wherefore it is void and hence, unenforceable by either party.

(2) If either party performs under the contract, and his participation does not offend public policy, then, to the extent he has parted with his own money, property, labor, or service, he is entitled to restitution for unjust enrichment in an amount equal to whatever the court identifies as the fair market value of that with which he has parted, which amount is called, also, the "benefit" he has "conferred" on the other.

QUESTIONS 1 & 2. Tollins operates a construction business. Santos approaches him and asks for employment. "Can you operate a back hoe?" asks Tollins. Santos says yes, and Tollins continues: "My one remaining back hoe failed the legal safety inspection, but if you're willing to take your chances, you're hired — $30 per hour, 40 hours per week, Monday to Friday, 9:00 A.M. to 5:00 P.M. You'll be paid every two weeks, on Friday at 5:00 P.M.; twenty weeks of work guaranteed if you'll guarantee me that you'll remain for those twenty weeks." Santos agrees: "It's a deal." Let's assume this: Because Tollins authorizes Santos to operate an instrument that is, by law, unsafe, his participation in the agreement violates public policy.

QUESTION 1. Santos performs his work for two weeks, and the back hoe functions well. When he requests his pay of $2,400 ($30/hour × 80 hours), Tollins refuses to pay, asserting that he is short of funds. He further advises Santos that he must "let him go" for that same reason. Alleging Tollins's failure to honor his agreement, Santos sues Tollins. The court should

I. rule that the contract is enforceable against Tollins.

---

4. She would recover damages, however, only to the extent that she exercises a duty to "mitigate." (See Chapter 26, section A.)

II. award Santos $2,400 because that is the amount to which the contract entitles him.
A. I only
B. II only
C. I and II
D. Neither I nor II

ANALYSIS.   Set your brain upon the law. These parties formed a contract under which Santos was to operate heavy machinery that had failed to pass a legally required safety inspection. The contract is illegal—not because it happens to violate a legislative enactment but because, as we said, the operation of such unsafe machinery contravenes public policy. That means the contract is void; it doesn't exist. Hence, neither party can sustain an action or derive recovery for breach of contract. Option I is false.

Tollins is a "bad guy"; Santos is not. Because Tollins dishonored his promise, Santos worked for no pay. Tollins has been enriched at Santos's expense. Santos is entitled to recover not for breach of contract but for unjust enrichment. According to option II, Santos recovers $2,400 because such is the amount to which the contract entitles him. Wrong, wrong, wrong. For unjust enrichment, the court will award Santos restitution in an amount based not on the terms of the illegal contract, but according to the "benefit conferred" on Tollins, which is equal to the fair market value of Santos's services. Yes, Santos will recover the fair market value of his services, but options I and II are false. **D is right.**

QUESTION 2. Assume now that Santos works for ten weeks, and Tollins pays him $2,400 every other Friday, as agreed. On Friday of the twelfth week, Santos asks Tollins, "Can you pay me today for these past two weeks—eleven and twelve, and pay me, also, in advance, for the next two weeks—thirteen and fourteen? I'm very short of cash." Tollins responds, "You've been working for twelve weeks, performing wonderfully and handling that back hoe without difficulty. So my answer is yes." Tollins pays Santos $2,400 for weeks eleven and twelve, and an additional $2,400 for work to be performed during weeks thirteen and fourteen. On that Friday, Santos truly intends to do his work during weeks thirteen and fourteen, but on Monday of week thirteen, he changes his mind. He fails to appear for work. Neither does he appear on Tuesday—nor ever again. Tollins sues Santos for dishonoring his obligations (a) to work for a full twenty weeks, and (b) to earn the $2,400 paid him in advance. In relation to this suit,

I. Tollins will be able to enforce the contract against Santos.

II. Tollins will recover the $2,400 he paid Santos for the two weeks' work Santos did not perform.
A. I only
B. II only
C. I and II
D. Neither I nor II

ANALYSIS.   No one can enforce an illegal contract. Option I is false, so **A** and **C** are wrong. As to this illegal contract, Tollins is a "bad guy"; he attempted to "get away" with the use of a back hoe that, by law, was unsafe. For this illegal contract, Tollins's participation and purpose violated public policy. Santos has, certainly, at Tollins's expense, enjoyed an unjust enrichment of $2,400. Nonetheless, the court will award him zip. Again, **D** is right.

QUESTIONS 3 & 4. Rory owns a suburban home where zoning regulations forbid him to build a yard fence higher than five feet without first obtaining permission (a "variance") from the local zoning board. He wishes to build a yard fence six feet high and offers to pay Ben $1,000 for building it. Ben asks Rory whether he has obtained the necessary zoning variance, and Rory answers, truthfully, "no." Nonetheless, Ben accepts the offer and builds the fence. Thereafter, Rory refuses to pay.

QUESTION 3. Is the contract illegal?

A. Probably, because it conflicts with a lawfully enacted governmental regulation
B. Probably, because it conflicts with traditional notions of sound morals
C. Probably, because both parties knew of the zoning ordinance when they formed their contract
D. Probably not, because it does not conflict with public policy

ANALYSIS.   A contract is not illegal simply because it contravenes some legislative statute or administrative regulation. **A** is wrong. A contract is illegal only if it conflicts significantly with public policy. Public policy, in turn, refers to moral values that are conventionally "good" ones and, in general, values consistent with notions of a stable, free, and ordered society as a court understands them. The zoning ordinance at issue here bespeaks no such concerns. Certainly it does not conflict with traditional notions of good moral values as stated in **B**. Neither is it relevant, as stated in **C**, that the parties knew of the zoning ordinance. **A**, **B**, and **C** are plainly wrong. **D** is right.

QUESTION 4. To what recovery is Ben entitled?

A. None
B. The fair market value of his services
C. The amount promised him under the contract
D. His usual and customary rate for performing substantially similar work

ANALYSIS.   Because the contract does not offend public policy, it's not ille-gal. It's enforceable. Ben has an action for breach of contract. He is entitled to recover the amount promised him under the contract, whether it's more or less than the fair market value of his services or his customary rate of pay. **A**, **B**, and **D** are wrong. **C** is right.

C.   Illegal Contracts: The Latin Vocabulary

We have recited rules that refer to a party whose "participation" in a contract does or does not violate public policy. Although the courts follow them, many don't state them as we do. Rather, the rules as many courts state them are a confused mixture of vestigial remains—fossils buried in the legal turf in which contract law has grown. So remember the rules as we've taught them to you, but know that the courts (and maybe your teachers too) are likely to state them in different terms. Let's explain.

1. Malum in Se *vs.* Malum Prohibitum

You know, of course, that an "illegal" performance refers to behavior that violates public policy (as the court interprets that phrase). The relevant pub-lic policy might or might not be reflected in a legislative enactment. Think of Rory, Ben, and the six-foot fence. Although the contract contravened a zoning ordinance, it was not "illegal" because the erection of such a fence does not violate public policy. When examining a contractual performance that contravenes a statute, regulation, or ordinance, many older decisions and some modern ones invoke the Latin phrases *malum in se* and *malum prohibitum.*

Malum in se* means, literally, "wrong in itself." Murder, rape, arson, and blackmail represent statutory law that, to all legal minds, represent *malum in se. Malum prohibitum* means "wrong only because the law prohibits it." For a court that invokes those terms, "*malum in se*" is by and large equivalent to "violates public policy." "*Malum prohibitum*" is by and large equivalent to "violates a legislative enactment, but not public policy."

With respect to Rory, Ben, and the fence, some courts would rule: "Although the contract violates a zoning ordinance, it does not violate public policy. It is not, therefore, an illegal contract." Other courts might rule: "Although the contract violates a zoning ordinance, the ordinance represents only a *malum prohibitum*. The parties did not, therefore, form an illegal contract." Both courts reach the same result for the same reason. Their meanings are identical. They differ only in the language by which they express it.

2. *Comparative Wrongfulness and "Pari Delicto"*

It once was widely said and still is sometimes said that if (a) two parties X and Y form a contract that assigns to each party an "illegal" performance, but (b) Y's performance constitutes a greater public policy violation than does X's, and (c) X's performance does not violate public policy to such a degree as makes it a "moral turpitude" (meaning X is not to murder, rape, blackmail, bomb a church, or sell "coke" to children), then X will be able to recover restitution for unjust enrichment, but Y will not. On the other hand, if a contract calls for both parties seriously to contravene public policy, they are said to be in *pari delicto*, meaning, literally, that they are equally "bad." In such a case, the court "leaves the parties where it finds them"; it awards neither one a recovery from the other.

Let's Get That Straight

Case 1.   X has "drug connections." X and Y agree that (a) Y will convey to X $200, (b) X will use that money to purchase "coke," (c) X will retain three-quarters of the cocaine and deliver one-quarter to Y, (d) X will sell his cocaine to three children, (e) Y will sell his cocaine to one child, and (f) X and Y will then divide equally the moneys they receive. As to items (a)-(e), both parties perform. X collects $500 from each of three children—$1,500 in all. Y collects $500 from one child. Y then demands that X pay him $500 so that X and Y will retain $1,000 each. X refuses. Y sues X, seeking restitution in the amount of $500 by which, he says, X has been unjustly enriched.

The situation, in the abstract: X and Y formed a contract under which both were to violate public policy. Y, who sold cocaine only to one child (arguably) committed a lesser public policy violation than did X, who sold cocaine to three children. Nonetheless, Y's performance showed "moral turpitude," and the parties are in *pari delicto*.

The result: Y recovers nothing.

Case 2.   In State Z, no person may buy, sell, or possess marijuana. All such acts (we'll assume) constitute violations of public policy, but none constitutes "moral turpitude." From Y, X wishes to obtain a small amount of marijuana for his wife, to alleviate the nausea caused her by cancer chemotherapy. He agrees to pay Y $100. In exchange, Y agrees to procure the marijuana and deliver it to him. X pays Y the $100. Y keeps the money and does not procure the marijuana. X sues Y alleging that in the amount of $100, Y has been unjustly enriched at his expense.

The situation, in the abstract: The parties have formed an illegal contract calling for both to deliver performances that violate public policy. In view of X's purpose (concerning his wife's illness), his participation does not violate public policy to such a degree as does Y's. Neither does X's participation involve "moral turpitude."

The result: X is entitled to restitution for Y's unjust enrichment.

3. *Illustrations Involving the Cases Already Examined*

Think of section A above and the contract between X and Y for the killing of Z. X's participation violates public policy in a "big way," and so does Y's. Suppose X pays Y his $50,000 fee in advance, Y fails to do the job, and X sues demanding restitution for the $50,000. The court, of course, will throw X's case out of court, and throw X out the window. Earlier, we said that such is the result because both parties violated public policy, and that's true. Some courts, however, would note that each party's promised performance does more than violate public policy; each, also, involves moral turpitude.

With that, such a court would express itself thus: "Each party committed himself to a performance that wholly violates public policy. Hence, the contract is illegal. Neither can recover for breach. And, as for restitution and unjust enrichment, I note this: Each party agreed to a performance that did more than violate public policy. Each committed himself to moral turpitude. Therefore, the parties are in *pari delicto*; this court will leave them where it finds them. X recovers no restitution for unjust enrichment."[5] If it just so happens that Y, at X's expense, retains $50,000 for which he did nothing, then so be it.

Suppose, on the other hand, that Y performs first; he commits the killing. If X then refuses to pay and Y sues, the court will throw him and his case out the window for the same reason; the contract called for both parties to violate public policy and, furthermore, their promised performances constituted moral turpitude. Stated otherwise, they formed an illegal contract, and they are in pari delicto; neither recovers anything from the other.

Think again of the slave ship case described in section A above. The court ruled that the contract made for a gross violation of public policy and added, "A party alleging his own [moral] turpitude shall not be heard in a court of justice to sustain an action founded upon it; and, where the parties stand in pari delicto, the law leaves them, as it finds them[.]" Fales v. Mayberry, 2 Gall. 560 (Cir. Ct. Dist. R.I. 1815).

With more refinement, consider again the case of Santos, Tollins, and the back hoe (Questions 1 and 2 above). With his willingness to have Santos

---

5.   The state's attorney, however, will take a different route. She will see that these two miscreants are "tossed" in prison for conspiracy to commit murder for hire.

operate an unsafe machine and put him at risk of injury, Tollins violated public policy. Santos's willingness to operate the machine was, perhaps, a violation of public policy as well. If so, however, it was a lesser violation than the one Tollins committed, and did not, certainly, involve any moral turpitude. If, as in Question 1, Santos sues Tollins for failure to pay, the court will acknowledge the contract's illegality, but nonetheless award Santos restitution for Tollins's unjust enrichment.

Let's Make All of This Easy; Follow This Yellow Brick Road

When you're faced with a problem in which plaintiff sues defendant on a contract that is, perhaps, illegal, follow this "yellow brick road."

(1) <u>Ask yourself</u>: Does either party's promise violate public policy?

(a) <u>Yes</u>: The contract is illegal. Plaintiff cannot recover for breach of contract. Go to question 2.

(b) <u>No</u>: The contract is not illegal. Plaintiff can recover for breach. Go no further.

(2) Does plaintiff's promise violate public policy?

(a) <u>Yes</u>: Go to question 3 (And if, furthermore, it violates a legislative enactment, it represents a *malum in se*.)

(b) <u>No</u>: Plaintiff recovers restitution for unjust enrichment (but only if defendant has in some way been unjustly enriched). Go no further. (But if his promise does, nonetheless, violate some legislative enactment, then it is a mere *malum prohibitum*.)

(3) Does plaintiff's promise call for lesser a violation of public policy than does defendant's?

(a) <u>Yes</u>: Go to question 4

(b) <u>No</u>: The parties are in "*pari delicto*"; plaintiff does not recover restitution for unjust enrichment. He recovers nothing. Go no further.

(4) Does plaintiff's promise bespeak moral turpitude?

(a) <u>Yes</u>: Since plaintiff's promise involves a lesser public policy violation than does plaintiff's, defendant, too, has committed himself to moral turpitude. The parties are in pari delicto. Plaintiff does not recover restitution for unjust enrichment. He recovers nothing. Go no further.

(b) <u>No</u>: Plaintiff recover's restitution for unjust enrichment (but only if defendant has in some way been unjustly enriched). Go no further.

QUESTION 5. One would likely commit a *malum in se* if he violated

I. this ordinance: "Notwithstanding that one may hold a fishing license issued by Town Hall, he may not fish in the Town Pond unless, when doing so, he has the license in a pocket, purse, or otherwise on his person."

II. this statute: "No person may enter a public library carrying an alcoholic beverage anywhere on his person or in his personal effects notwithstanding that the vessel is or is not sealed in a closed container."

A. I only
B. II only
C. I and II
D. Neither I nor II.

ANALYSIS. The question does not concern illegal contracts per se. Rather, it asks that you know the meaning of *malum in se*. *Malum in se* refers to behavior that to any reasonable person is wrong in itself, behavior that would be wrong even if no legislative enactment proscribed it. As earlier stated, murder, arson, burglary, and rape are, certainly, wrongs in and of themselves, and they would be wrong even if no legislative enactment rendered them unlawful. On the other hand, one who fishes and forgets to bring his fishing license with him does not, certainly, commit an act that is wrong in itself. Such behavior is "wrong" only because some legislative enactment renders it unlawful. The same is so of one who, while in a public library, in his pocket, carries a sealed mini-bottle of wine, intending to drink it with dinner, later in the evening. Both options I and II represent conduct that is *malum prohibitum*, not *malum in se*. **D** is right.

QUESTION 6. Gary and Charles agree that (a) Gary will steal two paintings X and Y from Museum, (b) Gary will deliver the paintings to Charles, (c) Charles will sell the paintings to Fence and share equally with Gary the moneys that Fence pays. Gary steals both paintings, but tells Charles that he was able to steal only painting X. He hands painting X to Charles, and Charles sells it to Fence. Charles then learns that Gary had in fact stolen painting Y and was "holding out" on him. Consequently, Charles refuses to share with Gary any of the monies that Fence paid him. Gary sues Charles demanding a judgment in the amount of one-half the monies Fence paid Charles, and Charles counterclaims demanding one half the fair market value of painting Y. If the court concludes that the parties have behaved with equal wrongfulness, it will

A. award Gary the money he requests as damages for Charles's breach of contract.
B. award Charles the amount of money he requests as restitution for Gary's unjust enrichment.
C. award no recovery to either party because they are not in *pari delicto*.
D. deny recovery to both parties because they are in *pari delicto*.

ANALYSIS. Follow the yellow brick road and you'll stop at step 3(b); the parties are in *pari delicto*. Neither can recover from the other. Why not?

These parties formed an illegal contract, and neither, therefore, can recover under the law of contract; neither can recover for breach. Regarding then, the matter of restitution for unjust enrichment, some courts would write, "Pursuant to their contract, both parties were to commit equally poor behavior in serious violation of public policy. Hence, as for unjust enrichment, this court will make no award to either one." Other courts might reach the same result for the same reason, but state it thus: "The parties formed an illegal contract, and they are in *pari delicto*. Hence, as for unjust enrichment, neither is entitled to restitution from the other."

A tells us that the court will make an award to Gary, so it's wrong. Furthermore, even where one party does recover for dishonor of an illegal contract, he does not recover damages for breach. He recovers, if at all, restitution for the opposing party's unjust enrichment. **B** correctly refers to restitution for unjust enrichment, but it reaches the wrong result. Charles gets nothing; **B** is wrong. **C** reaches the right result but misstates the relevant law. These parties are in *pari delicto* and that's why neither recovers anything. **D** reaches the right result for the right reason. These parties are in pari delicto; both have violated public policy to the same degree. That's why neither recovers restitution from the other. **D** is right.

D. The Closers

QUESTIONS 7-9. Lafayette operates a fruit stand, and Habel is his customer. When Habel asks to purchase a peach, Lafayette explains that he has but one peach, ten days old. "It looks all right and it's probably good," Lafayette says, "but the state law against distribution of potentially poisonous foods prevents me from selling you any fruit that is more than three days old, unless it is refrigerated, which this peach is not. And, who knows—maybe it's not safe." Habel responds, "I'll take my chances," and the parties contract for the sale of the peach, at a price of $1.

QUESTION 7. Immediately after forming the contract, before either party has performed, Lafayette decides not to sell Habel the peach and refuses to do so. To what recovery is Habel entitled?

A. None
B. The fair market value of the peach
C. $1
D. The customary charge in the community for a peach

ANALYSIS. Follow the yellow brick road and you'll stop at 4(b), but you'll recognize that Lafayette has not enjoyed any unjust enrichment. So, Habel recovers nothing.

A food safety regulation, certainly, reflects public policy. The contract is illegal, wherefore it is void and unenforceable. Habel has no action for breach of contract. Further, he has not performed under the contract. He has parted with no value in money, property, labor, or service, meaning that Lafayette has enjoyed no unjust enrichment. He is entitled to no recovery at all. He recovers nothing — *nada, rien, nusquam, zilch* — which means **A** is right.

QUESTION 8. Assume that Lafayette hands the peach to Habel and that Habel then refuses to pay for it. To what recovery is Lafayette entitled?

A. None
B. The fair market value of the peach
C. $1
D. The customary charge in the community for a peach

ANALYSIS. Walk the yellow brick road and you'll find yourself at 3(b). The contract is illegal, wherefore it is void and hence unenforceable. Lafayette has no action for breach of contract. Moreover, Lafayette is the seller of the forbidden fruit, wherefore his participation in the contract violates public policy. The law will not aid a willful wrongdoer; *ex dolo malo non oritur actio.* Notwithstanding that he has parted with the peach and that Habel (might) enjoy it, the law will award Lafayette nothing. **A** is right.

QUESTION 9. Assume that Habel pays Lafayette $1. Lafayette then refuses to hand him the peach and refuses, also, to return the dollar. Habel brings an action against Lafayette. If a court allows Habel to recover, it will award him

A. the fair market value of the time devoted to forming the contract with Habel.
B. the fair market value of the peach.
C. $1.
D. the customary charge in the community for a peach.

ANALYSIS. The contract is illegal, wherefore it is void and hence unenforceable. Habel has no action for breach of contract. Arguably, Habel's participation in the contract violates public policy since he has knowingly purchased and intends to ingest food that is, legally, substandard. If the court should so conclude, then Habel will recover nothing. With its first few words, "If a court . . . ," the question hypothesizes that Habel does recover, and you're asked to identify the appropriate form of recovery.

Because the court cannot enforce the contract, it will award restitution for unjust enrichment. Habel will be entitled to have the fair market value of any benefit he has conferred on Lafayette in money, property, labor, or service. In this case, Habel's payment of the $1 purchase price confers on Lafayette a benefit of that same amount (since the fair market value of a dollar is always a dollar). **C** is right.

 # Silver's Picks

1.	**D**
2.	**D**
3.	**D**
4.	**C**
5.	**D**
6.	**D**
7.	**A**
8.	**A**
9.	**C**

18

How We Interpret Contracts

A. You've Already Mastered Most of This Topic

From Chapters 2 and 3 you know that (1) a contract arises by offer and acceptance, (2) the terms of the offer have such meaning as would be given them by a reasonable offeree under all prevailing circumstances, and (3) an offeree accepts only if he assents to all of the offeror's terms without addition or exception.[1] That means (4) the terms of any true acceptance are identical to those of the offer, wherefore (5) the terms of the resulting contract are the same as those of the offer (which are the same as those of the acceptance) — all of which means, finally, that:

A contract's terms have such meaning as a reasonable offeree and offeror would give them under the prevailing circumstances.[2]

---

1. Except that under UCC §2-207, an offeree might accept an offer without a mirror-image assent (Chapter 11, section B).

2. Remember that when two parties form a contract, the offer and the acceptance always have the same meaning. If they do not, then the parties don't form a contract, as happens in a rare case, such as *Peerless*, where each of two parties gives a different meaning to the same word or phrase, both of them reasonable under the prevailing circumstances (see Chapter 3, section C). That is true even in respect of UCC §2-207(1) (see Chapter 11, sections B-E).

We can state the same rule thus:

A contract's terms have such meaning as conforms to the parties' reasonable understandings and expectations.

Darlene is a Canadian citizen visiting Idaho. She wants to buy a car. On an Internet site called "Ibuy," Chester advertises a car for sale, setting forth his address and telephone number in Boise, Idaho. Darlene responds to the advertisement with an email that bears her electronic signature: "I have seen the vehicle you advertised on 'Ibuy.' I'll take it for $7,000. I'll send you a check today. Are we agreed?" With *his* electronic signature, Chester responds, "Yes."

Darlene sends Chester a check drawn on her Canadian bank, for 7,000 *Canadian* dollars. Chester receives it and telephones Darlene: "When we agreed on $7,000, I meant 7,000 *U.S.* dollars, not Canadian dollars. The check you've sent is worth only $6,300 in U.S. dollars." Darlene responds, "I'm from Canada, so I thought in terms of Canadian dollars. I'm only willing to buy for $7,000 *Canadian* dollars — $6,300 U.S. dollars."

These Parties Are in Dispute as to the Meaning of "Dollar."   Within a contract, a word's meaning, we know, is that which reasonable persons would give it under the circumstances that surround them when they form the contract. The advertisement referred to an Idaho address, and Idaho is in the United States. When Darlene offered to buy the car, Chester was justified in believing that she meant to pay 7,000 American dollars. When Chester accepted, Darlene *should* have understood that he assented to a price of 7,000 American dollars. Regardless of what Darlene herself truly thought or intended, these parties contracted for a price of 7,000 dollars, U.S. currency.

We have just interpreted a disputed contractual term. In this contract, "dollar" means "U.S. dollar." We did so according to this rule: Contractual terms have such meaning as reasonable persons would give them under the relevant circumstances.

In its own horribly tortured way, the Restatement (Second) of Contracts §20(2)(b) states the same rule:

> Where the parties have attached different meanings to a promise or agreement or a term thereof, it is interpreted in accordance with the meaning attached by one of them [and not the other] if at the time the agreement was made . . . that party had no reason to know of any different meaning attached by the other, and the other had reason to know the meaning attached by the first party.

Let's take hold of Restatement §20(2) and "plug in" the facts pertaining to Chester and Darlene:

> Where the parties have attached different meanings to a promise or agreement or a term thereof [as happened here with Chester, Darlene, and the word "dollar"], it [the word "dollar"] is interpreted in accordance with the meaning

attached by one of them [Chester, in this case] if [as happened in this case] at the time the agreement was made . . . that party [Chester] had no reason to know of any different meaning attached by the other [Darlene], and the other [Darlene] had reason to know the meaning attached by the first party [Chester].

When Darlene said "dollar," Chester thought she meant "U.S. dollar." In Restatement terms, he had "no reason" to think otherwise (meaning his understanding was reasonable under the circumstances). When Charles accepted the offer, Darlene "had reason to know" that in his mind, "dollar" meant "U.S. dollar" (meaning that she should reasonably have understood him to mean "U.S. dollar"). Hence, the Restatement dictates that in this contract, "dollar" means "U.S. dollar." Its tortuous sentence comes to mean only this: A contract has such meaning as would be given it by reasonable persons under the relevant circumstances.

B.   "Requirements" and "Outputs" Again

In connection with consideration, Chapter 14, section A(2) dealt with requirements and outputs contracts. Here, with respect to interpretation, we deal with the *words* "requirements" and "outputs."

Tileco manufactures tiles. Bathco designs and constructs hotel bathrooms. In each of ten years 1-10, the two companies have formed and performed under contracts related to tiles—Tileco as seller, Bathco as buyer. Each contract, dated January 1, has provided:

> At prices specified elsewhere herein, during the one-year term of this contract, (a) Bathco will meet all of its requirements for tiles by making purchase orders only from Tileco, and (b) Tileco will fill all such orders.

On average, during Years 1-10, Bathco has purchased 500,000 100-packed units ("units") of tile annually. In Year 2, it purchased only 425,000 units, the least it required in any of the ten years. In Year 7, it purchased 565,000 units, the most it required in any of the ten years.

On January 1, Year 11, the parties again from a contract that includes the provision shown above. During the months January through August, Bathco orders a total of 490,00 units, and Tileco fills all of its orders. In September, there comes to Bathco an unexpected opportunity to perform services, in expedited fashion, for a large hotel undergoing renovation. For that reason, on September 1, Bathco orders from Tileco *1.9 million* units of tile—nearly four times more than it has ever previously ordered during an entire year.

> **Tileco to Bathco:** We can't fill your order for 1.9 million units; we don't have that many on hand and can't manufacture them during this month or, even, within the next *twelve* months.
> **Bathco to Tileco:** Well, then, you're in breach of your contract.

Is Tileco in Breach of Contract?

The answer goes to this simple question: As reasonable persons, under the prevailing circumstances, how should Tileco and Bathco understand the word "requirements" as it appears in the contractual provision cited above? More specifically, the question is: With Bathco, in Years 1-10, having purchased between 425,000 and 565,000 units annually, does the word "requirements"—as reasonably construed *this* year—oblige Tileco to furnish a total of *2.39 million* units—490,000 during January through August and 1.9 million more in September?

The answer lies not in any special rule about the word "requirements," but in the fundamental one you already know. Contracts arise from offer and acceptance; an offer has such meaning as is given it by a reasonable offeree under the prevailing circumstances; an offeree's response constitutes an acceptance only if it "mirrors" the offer in every respect.[3] Hence, the terms of a contract are the terms of the offer[4] as the reasonable offeree and offeror should construe them.[5]

Whether as to this Year 11 contract the offeree was Tileco or Bathco, we need only ask:

With Bathco, in Years 1-10 having purchased 425,000 to 565,000 units annually, would Tileco or Bathco, in January, Year 11, reasonably understand "requirements" to include a total annual order of 2.39 million units, 1.9 million of which come forth in September?

Any competent court would answer, "no." Further, UCC §2-306(1) (needlessly) provides:

> A term which measures the quantity by . . . the requirements of the buyer means such actual . . . requirements as may occur in good faith, except that no quantity unreasonably disproportionate to any stated estimate or . . . to any normal or otherwise comparable requirements may be demanded.

The Same Goes For "Output"

Where, as to some Commodity X, during some Period Y, a buyer agrees to purchase all of a seller's "output"—meaning all that she produces or otherwise has available for sale—"output" has such meaning as reasonable persons would give it under the circumstances that surround them when they form their contract.

---

3.   Except, arguably, where UCC §2-207 applies.
4.   —or counteroffer.
5.   But see footnote 2 above.

Chainco and Guardco

Chainco manufactures chain. Guardco designs and constructs security systems for which it uses large quantities of 3/16" stainless steel chain. In each of ten years 1-10, the two companies have formed and performed under contracts, each dated January 1, and providing:

> At prices specified elsewhere herein, during the one-year term of this contract, (a) Guardco will purchase from Chainco all of Chainco's outputs of 3/16" SS Chain, meaning all such chain that, during such year, Chainco produces or otherwise has available for sale and (b) Chainco will sell such chain to no other party or entity but will sell it to Guardco exclusively.

On average, during Years 1-10, Chainco has annually produced 15 million linear feet of 3/16" SS Chain, and Guardco has purchased all of it. In Year 4, Chainco produced 14.1 million linear feet, its lowest output for any of the ten years. In Year 6, it produced 15.4 million linear feet, its greatest output for any of the ten years.

On January 1, Year 11, the parties again form the contract that embodies the provision shown above. During January through August, Chainco produces 14 million linear feet of the chain and Guardco buys all of it. Then, in September, Chainco acquires another chain manufacturing company and with that purchase, acquires 20 million linear feet of 3/16" SS Chain fully manufactured and ready for sale.

> **Chainco to Guardco:** We have available, now, 20 million linear feet of 3/16" SS Chain all of which, of course, you're obliged to purchase. So get ready for delivery and payment.
>
> **Guardco to Chainco:** We can't buy that much chain. We have neither funds sufficient to pay for it nor space sufficient to store it.
>
> **Chainco to Guardco:** Well, then, you're in breach of contract.

Is Guardco in Breach of Contract?

No; contracts arise from offer and acceptance; an offer has such meaning as is given it by a reasonable offeree under the prevailing circumstances; an offeree's response constitutes an acceptance only if it "mirrors" the offer in every respect.[6] Hence, the terms of a contract are the terms of the offer[7] as the reasonable offeree and offeror would construe them.

Whether as to this Year 11 contract (a) Chainco was offeror and Guardco offeree or (b) Guardco was offerror and Chainco offeree, both knew that for ten years Chainco's annual "output" of the relevant commodity fell between 14.1 and 15.4 million linear feet. Now, in Year 11, neither could reasonably have read "output" to mean (14 million + 20 million) = 34 million linear feet.

---

6. Except, arguably, where UCC §2-207 applies.
7. —or counteroffer

UCC §2- 306 (1), *in full*, addresses both words "requirement" and "output":

> A term which measures the quantity by the output of the seller or the requirements of the buyer means such actual output or requirements as may occur in good faith, except that no quantity unreasonably disproportionate to any stated estimate or in the absence of a stated estimate to any normal or otherwise comparable prior output or requirements may be tendered or demanded.

C.   "Usage of Trade," "Course of Dealing," and "Course of Performance"

The law never tires of fashioning words and phrases that add nothing to its good, basic principles. Here, now, we explore three of them.

1. "Usage of Trade"

The phrase "usage of trade" refers to usages and interpretations common among persons belonging to a particular trade, industry, or commercial community. As Restatement (Second) §222(1) provides:

> A usage of trade is a usage having such regularity of observance in a place, vocation, or trade as to justify an expectation that it will be observed with respect to a particular agreement.

Within most industries, for example, "working day" means eight hours. "Full time" means forty hours per week, fifty weeks per year. In the retail sales industry, the phrase "bird dog" means one who sends prospective buyers to some particular seller. In the real estate industry, a "FISBO" is one who attempts to sell his home without an agent's help. Among medical interns and residents, "boxcars" means death. Among gamblers, "house" means casino. Among bartenders and their patrons, "rocks" means ice cubes. All such expressions represent usage of trade.

2. "Course of Dealing"

"Course of dealing" refers to two parties who have, in the past, formed contracts with each other. It represents the meanings and interpretations that *they* explicitly or implicitly adopt for the contracts they form, so much so as to create a private code between themselves, which might differ from the prevailing usage of trade. Restatement (Second) §223(1) provides:

> A course of dealing is a sequence of previous conduct between the parties to an agreement which is fairly to be regarded as establishing a common basis of understanding for interpreting their expressions and other conduct.

Suppose that by usage of trade within the widget industry, "single" means one widget, "double" means two widgets, and "triple" means three widgets. Now suppose that Party B frequently buys widgets from Party S, and suppose that over time these parties have developed a little code of their own, different from the prevailing usage of trade. When B wants 100 widgets, she orders "a single," and S sends her 100 widgets. When B wants 200 widgets, she orders "a double," whereupon S sends her 200 widgets. When she wants 300 widgets, she orders "a triple," whereupon S sends her 300 widgets. This private code, developed between these two parties, represents their "course of dealing," and it happens to differ from the prevailing usage of trade.

3. "Course of Performance"

The phrase "course of performance" applies only to a contract that calls for *multiple occasions of performance.* Suppose B has two warehouses, warehouse 1 and warehouse 2, separated by twenty miles. B and S have a history in which B has repeatedly bought widgets from S under contracts that call for delivery to "B's warehouse." S has always delivered to B's warehouse 2, and B has never objected. According to the parties' course of *dealing*, therefore, delivery to "B's warehouse" means delivery to warehouse 2.

Now suppose B and S form another contract for the sale of widgets. Unlike their previous contracts, this one calls for multiple occasions of performance; it requires that S deliver to "B's warehouse" 450 widgets on January 2, and 450 widgets on the first day of every month from February through December, thus creating twelve occasions for performance. B is to pay $45,000 for each such lot of 450 widgets, three days after S makes delivery.

On January 1, S delivers 450 widgets to warehouse 1, as he had never done in the past. Without objection, B's agent accepts them and, without objection, B pays the $45,000 purchase price on January 5. The same occurs in February, March, April, May, June, and July. On the first day of each such month, S delivers 450 widgets to warehouse 1. Without objection, B's agent accepts them and, without objection, B timely pays the appropriate purchase price. These parties have established a "course of performance," meaning an interpretation developed by their behavior as they perform *this very contract*—whereby "B's warehouse" means warehouse 1. Their course of performance thus differs from their course of dealing, by which "B's warehouse" means warehouse 2.

As Restatement (Second) §202(4) provides:

> Where an agreement involves repeated occasions for performance by either party with knowledge of the nature of the performance and opportunity for objection to it by the other, any course of performance accepted or acquiesced in without objection is given great weight in the interpretation of the agreement.

4. A Hierarchy

In the law's eyes, a reasonable person, in interpreting a contractual term, would or should be keenly aware of any usage of trade, course of dealing, and/or course of performance relevant to the circumstances. Consequently, all such concepts are highly relevant to contractual interpretation. Furthermore, (UCC) §2-208(2) establishes a hierarchy among them. Where course of performance and/or course of dealing and/or usage of trade *conflict*, course of performance ranks first; it trumps course of dealing. Course of dealing ranks second; it trumps usage of trade. Usage of trade ranks third.

QUESTIONS 1 & 2. Within the woodget industry, "two hits" means 2,000 woodgets. Between 1997 and 2018, Bana and Soo have formed many contracts for the purchase and sale of woodgets. With respect to their contracts, they have developed a private language by which "two hits" means only *200* woodgets. On January 2, 2019, Bana and Soo form a contract under which Soo is to deliver to Bana "two hits" of woodgets on the fifth day of every month, January through December. Bana is to pay $10 for each woodget that Soo delivers. For the months January through June, Soo delivers only *20* woodgets and for each such month, Bana accepts and pays for them without objection.

QUESTION 1. With respect to this most recent contract,

 I. by usage of trade, "two hits" means 2,000 woodgets.
 II. by course of dealing, "two hits" means 200 woodgets.
III. by course of performance, "two hits" means 20 woodgets.
 A. I only
 B. I and II only
 C. II and III only
 D. I, II, and III only

ANALYSIS.   You're asked only to know the meaning of three phrases: "usage of trade," "course of dealing," and "course of performance." The parties to this contract are two persons in the business of buying and selling woodgets. In that industry, "two hits" means 2,000 woodgets, and such, therefore, is the usage of trade. Option I is true, so **A** is wrong. We're told also that as to their previous contracts, *these two parties* have established a "code" whereunder "two hits" means only 200 widgets. Hence, option II is true. If option III is true, then **D** is right. If it's false, **B** is right.

It's true. In performing *this very contract*, which calls for multiple deliveries of "two hits," Soo has repeatedly delivered only 20 woodgets, and Bana has repeatedly accepted them without objection. Consequently, for this contract, "two hits" by *course of performance* means 20 woodgets. Option III is true, and **D** is right.

QUESTION 2. July 5 arrives. Soo delivers to Bana 20 woodgets. Bana protests: "You should be providing me with 2,000 units. That's what 'two hits' means in our industry. And certainly you should be providing me with no fewer than 200 units because that's what you've always provided in the past when our contract called for 'two hits.' I won't accept this shipment, you're in breach." Is Bana correct in alleging that Soo has breached with respect to the July 5 delivery?

A. Yes, because the July 5 delivery does not conform to usage of trade
B. Yes, because the July 5 delivery does not conform to the parties' course of dealing
C. No, because the July 5 delivery conformed to the contract, as properly interpreted
D. No, because Soo cannot be charged with knowing a usage of trade once she and Bana have established a course of dealing

---

ANALYSIS. When a conflict arises as to the three phrases we've discussed, the law provides this ranking: course of performance ranks first, course of dealing ranks second, and usage of trade ranks third. In this case, as already noted, the parties established a course of performance (which, once again, is possible only for a contract that calls for multiple occasions *of* performance). According to their course of performance "two hits" means 20 woodgets. That meaning trumps both their course of dealing, in which "two hits" means 200 woodgets, and usage of trade, by which "two hits" means 2,000 woodgets.

Soo delivered 20 units and, pursuant to course of performance for *this* contract, that's what "two hits" means; Bana is wrong. The answer, therefore, is "no," which means that **A** and **B** are wrong. **A** fails to recognize the hierarchy. It's true that the July 5 delivery contravenes usage of trade, but that doesn't matter. Course of performance overrides usage of trade. **B**, too, overlooks the hierarchy. It's true that the July 5 delivery contravenes the parties' course of dealing, but that too is irrelevant. Course of performance trumps usage of trade *and* course of dealing.

We're left with **C** and **D**, both of which correctly answer "no." **D** is double talk at best and, more likely, false. Soo is in the woodget business, and the law *does* charge her with knowledge of the relevant usage of trade. That she does or does not know the usage of trade, however, is irrelevant to this question.

These parties established a course of dealing, and that's the standard by which the law, in this case, construes "two hits." Hence, Soo delivered the appropriate quantity; she performed according to the contract, as properly interpreted. **C** is correct.

But **C** doesn't mention course of performance. Why not? Because the question writer wants to see you choose the right answer without relying on some word or phrase to which you give "magical" meaning. He could have written:

- **C.** No, because pursuant to the course of performance that these parties established, the July 5 delivery conformed to the contract
- **C.** No, because on earlier occasions of delivery, Soo delivered 20 units without objection from Bana, meaning the parties established a course of performance under which "two hits" meant 20 units
- **C.** No, because pursuant to the course of performance, the parties established in performing this very contract, "two hits" means 20 units, and course of performance supersedes both usage of trade and course of dealing

The writer offered no such choices because a multiple-choice question tests your ability to reason and your ability to read for meaning. Your knowledge together with your *reasoning—reasoning—reasoning*—should tell you that for this contract on July 5, "two hits" means 20 units. Hence, Soo performed according to the contract. We need not see the phrase "course of performance" to know that **C** is right.

D. Interpretation of Writings

Recall and/or review the discussion of signed writings in Chapter 2, section C. As explained there, most contracting parties record serious business agreements in writing. That is, they form a written, signed contract. If a dispute later arises, proper interpretation requires that we probe the history of the final written contract.

1. Draft Contracts

Before signing their final writing, contracting parties often exchange unsigned drafts, each draft usually representing an invitation to deal. When one party signs a writing, then generally he is the offeror because his signature manifests his definite willingness to enter the bargain the writing describes. If and when the other signs that same writing she, as offeree, accepts by manifesting her assent to the bargain that the offeror proposes.

Suppose Wendy is a writer and Pablo a publisher. After discussing the possibility of Pablo's serving as publisher for Wendy's latest novel, Pablo sends Wendy an unsigned draft contract, Draft 1. It outlines all details that are customary to a contract between author and publisher — author name, book title, book length, advances, royalties, copyrights, licenses, derivative works, and what not. Draft 1 is Pablo's invitation to deal. (If he had signed it, it would be his offer, but he didn't, so it's a mere invitation to deal.)

Wendy makes changes to the draft, so that it becomes Draft 2. She sends it to Pablo, unsigned. Draft 2 is Wendy's invitation to deal. Pablo makes changes to Draft 2, so to create Draft 3, which he *signs* and sends to Wendy. Because Pablo signed Draft 3, it's his *offer*. If Wendy were now to sign, she'd accept and the parties would form a contract according to the terms of Draft 3. But suppose Wendy doesn't sign. Instead, she makes changes, thus creating Draft 4. She signs *that* and sends it back to Pablo. Draft 4 is Wendy's *counteroffer*. Pablo receives it, reads it, and signs. Now, finally, the parties have a contract whose terms are those of Wendy's counteroffer and Pablo's acceptance (which, of course, "mirrors" the offer/counteroffer (Chapter 7, section B)).

When two parties form a contract through this common process of changing and exchanging drafts, they don't usually retain the unsigned ones. Rather, each keeps a copy of the final, signed document and both forget all about the unsigned drafts. If the signatures are dated, then, ordinarily, the first party to sign is offeror and the second is offeree. If both parties sign on the same date (or leave their signatures undated), the document does not indicate who is offeror and who is offeree. And generally, when two parties form a written contract, lawyers do not think in terms of offeror and offeree. They think in terms of a *contract* by which both parties are bound, the terms of which appear in the writing. If (years later, perhaps) the parties find themselves in dispute as to the meaning of some term, then their lawyers will certainly introduce (conflicting) evidence of what reasonable parties would have understood under the relevant circumstances. They'll adduce evidence concerning usage of trade, course of dealing, and course of performance if any such thing is relevant, but they will not ordinarily trouble to identify the offeror and offeree.

2. Printed and Handwritten Terms

Suppose on February 1, 2019, Buyer and Seller are about to sign a contractual writing, thus evidencing their mutual assent to its terms. The document represents Seller's preprinted form, several pages long. Paragraph 19 appears thus:

> 19. Buyer shall pay Seller the full purchase price named above one year from the date hereof with interest of 7 percent.

At the last minute, before either party signs, Buyer states that he needs only one month — until March 1, 2019 — in which to pay the purchase price, and that he wants to pay no interest. In the margin of the page, Seller handwrites, so that that portion of the document appears thus:

> 19. Buyer shall pay Seller the full purchase price named above one year from the date hereof with interest of 7 percent.

Let's ask: In the event of a conflict, which term governs—the one in print or the one in handwriting? Let's answer: *If in a written contract, a preprinted or typewritten (computer-written) term conflicts with a handwritten term, the handwritten term ordinarily controls.* That's because the handwriting presumably reflects that on which the parties separately and specifically agreed subsequent to the creation of the printed/typed text. Restatement (Second) §202(d) reflects the principle with this:

> [S]eparately negotiated or added terms are given greater weight than standardized terms or other terms not separately negotiated.

3. *Writings Are Construed Against the Drafter*

Often, two parties adopt or sign a contractual writing that one of them has on his own prepared and submitted, wholesale, to another for her signature. That is always the case, for example, when two parties form a written contract pursuant to a preprinted form that one of them supplies. If after forming their contract they should come to dispute the meaning of some term, it is said that "the writing will be construed against the drafter," which means, really, this:

If two parties A and B form a written contract upon a preprinted form or other document wholly prepared by A and a dispute arises as to the meaning of a term, then if (in the court's judgment) the term is ambiguous, it will be given the meaning that favors B, the party who did not prepare the document.

Restatement (Second) §206 provides:

> In choosing among the reasonable meanings of a promise or agreement or a term thereof, that meaning is generally preferred which operates against the party who supplies the words or from whom a writing otherwise proceeds.

Why Do We Resolve the Ambiguity in Favor of the Party Who Did Not Prepare the Document?

The fact that one party prepares a contractual document is itself a *circumstance* under which the parties form their contract. The law's assumption is that the drafter chooses her words carefully and in writing the document resolves every ambiguity in her own favor. Both parties should assume, therefore, that any remaining ambiguity is to be resolved in favor of the *other* party. Some courts view the rule, simply, as one of fundamental fairness: "The rule of resolving ambiguities against the drafter "does not serve as a mere tie breaker; it rests upon fundamental considerations of policy." Goddard v. S. Bay Union High Sch. Dist., 79 Cal. App. 3d 98, 104 (1978).

Full purchase price to be paid on March 1, 2019, no interest.

QUESTION 3. On January 1, 2014, JKLM Radio Inc. and Kelly Kant form a written contract under which Kant, for five years, is to serve JKLM as a radio weather forecaster. The written contract is set forth on a preprinted form provided by JKLM, with some entries made by handwriting. Paragraphs 2 and 29 provide:

> **2. Term of Employment:** The parties agree that Employee will serve for *five* period(s) of *one* year.

Now look at paragraph 29. In its heading, the word "Period" is squished in between "Term" and "of." With that handwritten word sitting there, JKLM would have the right, at its option, to rehire Kant:

> *Period*
> **29. Additional Term ^ of Employment:** Employer will have the option to rehire Employee at the same annual salary and under the same contractual terms as those provided herein.

Following paragraph 29, there appear the parties' signatures and, underneath both, the date of January 1, 2015.

In December 2018, when the five-year contract period has nearly expired, JKLM advises Kant that it wishes to rehire him for an additional five years. Kant refuses, stating that JKLM has the right to rehire him only for one additional year. JKLM sues Kant for breach of contract, citing Kant's unwillingness to be hired for an additional five-year period.

JKLM argues that the word "Term" in the heading for paragraph 2 refers to five years, as provided in the substance of paragraph 2 itself. The heading for paragraph 29, says JKLM, should be read with the printed word "Term" and without the handwritten word "Period." Therefore, paragraph 29, JKLM contends, means that at the end of the first five-year term, it is entitled to rehire Kant for an additional "term"—an additional five years.

Kant agrees that his initial term of employment was five years, but that according to paragraph 2, the five-year term comprised five separate *periods* of one year each. Each employment *period*, he says, was one year. The heading for paragraph 29, he argues, should be read with the word "Period," not the word "Term." Read that way, Kant reasons, it gives JKLM a right to hire him for one additional year only.

In paragraph 29, the fact that "Period" is handwritten whereas "Term" is preprinted argues for

A. JKLM, because a printed term generally carries greater weight than does a handwritten term.
B. JKLM, because the printed term likely represents usage of trade.
C. Kant, because a handwritten term generally carries greater weight than a printed term.
D. Kant, because the addition of the handwritten term shows that the parties had a course of dealing.

ANALYSIS.   It's important to Kant's position that the heading to paragraph 29 be read with the word "Period" and without the word "Term." Important to JKLM's position is that the heading be read the other way 'round. By common law, a handwritten term carries greater weight than does a conflicting printed (or typewritten) term. Consequently, the fact that "Period" is handwritten favors Kant and works against JKLM.

A is opposite to the truth; a handwritten term carries more weight than a printed term. B incorrectly invokes the phrase "usage of trade." Usage of trade refers to the usages, "codes," and private languages that obtain within a given industry. The fact that JKLM, in its form, chose to use a particular word does not render that word a part of its "usage of trade." A and B are wrong.

D improperly cites the phrase "course of dealing," which refers to meanings that two parties implicitly adopt by virtue of their patterns of behavior in performing *their* contracts. The fact that Kant and JKLM agreed, during their negotiations, to handwrite the word "Period" in between the printed word "Term" is wholly irrelevant to the phrase "course of dealing." With A, B, and D so terribly wrong, C had better be right—and it *is*. It tells us, simply, that a handwritten term carries greater weight than does a printed term, for which reason the handwritten word argues for Kant. C is right.

E.   The Closer

QUESTION 4. GlassCo sells window glass to window manufacturers. PaneCo is a window manufacturer. Both parties are located in the city of Alton, where, among buyers and sellers of window glass, the phrase "my place" refers to one's factory headquarters. PaneCo has its factory headquarters on Main Street and its executive offices on High Street.

On October 1, PaneCo contacts GlassCo by signed writing. Stating a price, he orders 100 panes of glass, to be delivered to "my place." GlassCo responds by signed writing with an acceptance. Thereafter, GlassCo's truck driver, Anne, delivers the 100 panes to PaneCo's executive offices on High Street and, for whatever reason, PaneCo makes no objection. It pays the purchase price and with its own trucks moves the panes to its factory on Main Street. On November 1, the parties form another contract for the purchase and sale of glass panes delivered to "my place." Again, Anne delivers to PaneCo's executive offices, and again PaneCo raises no objection.

Six months later, on May 1, GlassCo and PaneCo form a new contract for the purchase and sale of 400 glass panes to be delivered to "my place," in four installments of 100 units each on June 1, July 1, August 1, and September 1. On June 1 and July 1, GlassCo's driver on duty is not Anne, but Derek. In both months, June and July, Derek delivers the window panes to PaneCo's factory headquarters. PaneCo accepts the delivery without objection. On August 1, Anne is once again on duty. As before, she brings the window panes to PaneCo's executive offices, but this time PaneCo refuses the delivery and proclaims that GlassCo is obliged to deliver to the factory headquarters, not to the executive offices.

Citing PaneCo's refusal to accept and pay for the window panes, GlassCo brings an action against PaneCo for breach. The litigation raises only the issue of whether GlassCo tendered the August 1 delivery to the appropriate location. GlassCo asserts that it had tendered delivery to the proper location. PaneCo asserts that it did not.

PaneCo would best support its position by observing that the appropriate place for delivery, in this case, is governed by

A. usage of trade.
B. course of performance.
C. course of dealing.
D. the parties' intentions.

ANALYSIS. These parties formed a contract for the sale of goods, meaning that UCC Article 2 governs. In interpreting a contract, UCC Article 2 provides that course of performance trumps course of dealing, which trumps usage of trade. In this case, usage of trade would require that GlassCo deliver to PaneCo's factory. However, the parties had a prior course of dealing reflected in their contracts of October 1 and November 1. For those contracts, GlassCo delivered to PaneCo's executive offices and PaneCo did not object. As between these two parties, therefore, *usage of trade* calls for delivery to the factory but *course of dealing* calls for delivery to the executive offices.

Then, under the May 1 contract, which called for multiple performances, the parties established a course of *performance*. For the first two installments tied to that contract, GlassCo delivered to PaneCo's factory and PaneCo did not object. Consequently, between these parties, as of July 1, usage of trade dictated delivery to the factory, course of dealing called for delivery to the executive offices, and course of *performance* called for delivery to the factory. Course of performance trumps course of dealing, which trumps usage of trade. PaneCo should cite that law and point out that in this case course of performance requires delivery to the factory, not to the executive offices. Consequently, **B** is right.

Silver's Picks

1.   **D**
2.   **C**
3.   **C**
4.   **B**

19

The Parol Evidence Rule

A. The Parol Evidence Rule: "Few Things Are Darker Than This"[1]

The so-called parol evidence rule is a tangled mass of misunderstanding. Everywhere it rears its misshapen head, it spawns debate, dissent, discord, dysfunction, demoralization, disaffection, depression, dejection, and disgust—not to mention thousands of judicial decisions devoid of sense, coherence, and consistency. No two authorities seem ever to agree on the rule's purpose, meaning, operation, or application. Referring to the parol evidence rule, in 1898 Professor Thayer wrote:

> Few things are darker than this, or fuller of subtle difficulties[.] The chief reason is that most of the questions brought under this head are out of place;

---

1. James B. Thayer, *A Preliminary Treatise on the Law of Evidence* 390 (1898).

331

there is a grouping together of a mass of incongruous matter, and then it is looked at in a wrong focus.

James B. Thayer, *A Preliminary Treatise on the Law of Evidence* 390 (1898). Concerning the puzzlement that surrounds the parol evidence rule, in 1904 Professor John Henry Wigmore wrote:

[T]he so-called parol evidence rule is attended with confusion and an obscurity which make it the most discouraging subject in the whole field of evidence. [T]he present condition of the subject is beyond endurance; unless improved, it threatens . . . irrational and incurable chaos.

4 Wigmore, *A Treatise on the Stem of Evidence in Trials at Common Law* 3368 (1904). In 1952, Professor Arthur Corbin wrote:

The cases that consider and purport to apply the so-called "parol evidence rule" are so variable and inconsistent as to be the despair of the teacher, the lawyer, and the judge.

Corbin on Contracts (one volume edition) 534 (1952). And in 1992, a Missouri court wrote that, with respect to the parol evidence rule,

We, in Missouri, no different [from] the courts in most other jurisdictions, have used a variety of principles, chosen randomly with no consistency . . . . The principles of one source . . . are not necessarily consistent with the principles of another[.] Thus, the random selection of principles from more than one source to resolve parol evidence issues has made the parol evidence rule a deceptive maze rather than a workable rule.

John C. Byers, Inc. v. J.B.C. Investments, 834 S.W.2d 806 (Mo. App. 1992).

All of these authorities are absolutely right. On its surface, the parol evidence rule is a morass of confusion, inconsistency, and misunderstanding. *Beneath* its surface, it is—that same morass of confusion, inconsistency, and misunderstanding. Yet, you must know about the parol evidence rule. You must know, at least, what it's *said* to be, and immerse yourself temporarily in the abject muddle that comprises its core. You must see for yourself what it is, what it is not, and—maybe—that it's nothing at all. Then, too, you must know exactly how to deal with it in your contracts class.

Notwithstanding the diverse misunderstanding that surrounds the parol evidence rule, virtually all modern authorities (and teachers) agree that despite its name, it is a substantive rule of contract law, not a rule of evidence. So when you speak of the parol evidence rule, begin, always, by saying "Despite its name, it's not a rule of evidence, but a substantive rule of contract law." That starts you moving in what all will agree is the right direction. From there, the terrain is replete with pits, potholes, and perils. But heed our teaching, and, to the extent possible, you'll master the parol evidence rule free of the confusion that surrounds it (maybe).

QUESTION 1. The parol evidence rule is

I. a rule of evidence.
II. a substantive rule of contract law.
III. clear and well understood throughout the states and enjoys consistent
and coherent interpretation and understanding.
A. II only
B. I and II only
C. II and III only
D. I, II, and III

ANALYSIS. About the parol evidence rule you know this much:

(1) All authorities agree that it is a mass of confusion and inconsistency.
That eliminates option III, which eliminates choices **C** and **D**. Option II makes
a true statement, meaning that the answer is **A** or **B**, depending on whether
option I is true or false. Despite its name, the parol evidence rule is not a rule
of evidence but a rule of contract law. I and III are false, II is true, so **A** is right.

B.   The Kind of Problem That the Rule Addresses

On October 8, in the presence of ten witnesses, Abe and Betsy reach an oral
agreement:

> **Abe:** I'll pay you $300 to set up my new computer and make it operate
> together with all of its peripherals.
> **Betsy:** I'll do it for $400; I'll finish by Friday, October 11, three days from
> now; and I'll warranty my work for a year.
> **Abe:** It's a deal; let's put it in writing.

Betsy then creates this writing:

> In consideration of $400 to be paid to her by Abe Abrams, Betsy Best will
> set up Abe's newly purchased computer so that it operates properly, together
> with its peripherals, all such work to be completed by October 11 of this year.
>
> *This is our full and final agreement.*

Before signing, with ten witnesses still present and listening, the parties
continue to talk:

> **Betsy:** So, shall we sign?
> **Abe:** The writing doesn't mention your one-year warranty.

Betsy: Don't worry. I'll shout it, now, before all ten of these folks: "I warrant that my work is good for one year."

Abe: Okay — so the warranty is absolutely a part of our agreement, right?

Betsy: Right.

The parties then sign the document. Betsy sets up the computer exactly as promised, and Abe pays her $400. One month later, the system goes down. Abe telephones Betsy asking that she honor her warranty and examine the system. Betsy responds:

Betsy: Our written contract provides for no warranty.

Abe: That's right, but you assured me that your work carried a one-year warranty.

Betsy: I worked hard enough for $400. I won't do any more.

Abe: Ten witnesses heard you make your one-year warranty a part of our agreement.

Betsy: We also have a signed, written contract in which we mention no such warranty, so I say you have no case against me.

Abe brings an action against Betsy alleging that she has failed to honor her warranty. Betsy's lawyer takes this position: "Whether Betsy did or did not orally make the one-year warranty is irrelevant. After forming their oral contract, these parties, with their signatures, adopted a *writing* — and that writing mentions no warranty. By failing to include in the writing the warranty term on which they orally agreed, they failed, legally, to include it in their contract. Even if Betsy did, orally, make the one-year warranty, the writing supersedes it."

Abe's lawyer takes this position: "The parties' contract includes all terms on which they actually agreed. The writing is *evidence* of the terms on which they agreed, but it does not have the final say on that point. The true contract between these parties includes not only the terms of the writing but also another term — the one-year warranty. And if, as we are certain, our evidence is adequate to prove that Betsy made the one-year warranty, then the warranty is part of the contract."

We can't yet tell you who wins. We can only tell you that such is the kind of dispute to which the parol evidence rule is addressed. In more abstract terms, we can say that the parol evidence rule governs this question: *If* (1) as to some subject (such as the installation of a computer system) two parties first form an oral contract[2] and (2) then create a writing that purports to recite the contract's terms, but (3) fail to include in the writing some term(s) on which they did genuinely agree, *then* (a) is the contract, by law, limited to that which is in the writing, or (b) does it include also the terms on which the parties truly, provably agreed but failed to include in their writing?

---

2. To make matters worse, the parol evidence rule as now commonly stated is relevant not only to an oral contract later reduced to writing, but also to a *written* agreement followed by a *later* writing on the same subject matter. See section H below.

Abe and Betsy's oral contract included Betsy's one-year warranty. Their writing failed to mention it. In Abe's and Betsy's case, therefore, the parol evidence rule will decide this question: Are Abe's contractual rights limited to the writing, in which case he has no one-year warranty, or do they include also the warranty on which the parties did truly agree, but failed to record in their writing?

QUESTION 2. The parol evidence rule

  I. concerns the definition of signatures as to those contracts that are unenforceable unless set forth in writing.
 II. concerns the enforceability of terms upon which two parties orally agree but then fail to include in a writing that purports to represent their contract.
III. is a substantive rule of evidence that concerns the relative probative values of signed and unsigned writings.
 A. II only
 B. I and II only
 C. III only
 D. II and III only

ANALYSIS.   About the parol evidence rule you now know *this* much:

(1) All authorities agree that it is a mass of confusion and inconsistency.

(2) Despite its name it is not a rule of evidence, but a substantive rule of contract law. That eliminates option III. Further, the rule is in no way concerned with the difference in probative value between signed and unsigned writings, so option III is false for that reason too.

(3) It concerns, generally, this question: When two parties form an oral contract and then purport to reduce it to writing, is their contract then limited to the terms *of* the writing or does it include, also, terms on which they orally agreed but failed to set forth in writing? That squares very nicely with option II. That means the answer is either **A** or **B**, depending on whether option I is true or false.

And Option I Is — False.   Don't confuse the parol evidence rule with the Statute of Frauds. They're unrelated. The Statute of Frauds (Chapter 15) identifies those contracts that are unenforceable unless recorded in a writing "signed by the party to be charged." Because that doctrine turns, in part, on the word "signed," it concerns also the definition (for its own purposes) of "sign"/ "signature." The parol evidence rule, although it does *relate* to writings, does not provide that any particular kind of contract must be in writing or that, if it is, it must be signed. Options I and III make false statements. Option II makes a true one, so **A** is right.

C.   Before We *State* the Parol Evidence Rule, We Introduce the Word "Integration"

Before *stating* the parol evidence rule we introduce you to the terms "integration," "partial integration," and "total integration." Fundamentally, the verb *integrate* means to take many and join them as one. In the realm of contract law, the word refers to two parties who (1) form a contract orally or, perhaps, by creating several writings, all of which, together, embody their agreement, and (2) then finally settle on *one writing* (as is common) that they "intend" and "adopt"[3] as a *final* expression of their *contract*. An integration brings the parties' prior discussions, drafts, tentative agreements, oral promises, and understandings together in a single final writing that *appears* to recite what the parties finally understand as the terms of their agreement.

Integrations come in two flavors, "partial" and "total." Partial integration means a contractual writing that the parties "intend" as a final expression of their agreement regarding the terms it does recite, but not as a complete expression of *everything* on which they in fact agreed. Total integration means a contractual writing that the parties "intend" to be both (a) *final* as to all of the terms it recites and (b) *complete*, meaning they "intend" the writing to represent a full, final, exhaustive, and exclusive recitation of any and every term on which they agreed, so that nothing, but *nothing* else is a part of their contract. Finally, if the parties create a writing that they "intend" not to be final, even as to those terms stated *in* the writing, then they create no integration at all.

QUESTIONS 3 & 4. Shayna and Chris agree orally that Chris will act as supervisor and manager of Shayna's commercial ice skating rink, Monday through Friday from 9:00 A.M. to 5:00 P.M. Shayna is to pay Chris an annual salary of $150,000, in twelve monthly installments of $12,500 each, on the first day of each month. While negotiating, the parties exchange a number of notes and conduct a number of conversations. Ultimately, they agree, orally and by handshake, to the terms described above, and to an additional fifty terms as well. Thereafter, in cursive, they sign their first names only to this short writing, labeled "Employment Contract":

The undersigned Shayna Signorelli ("Employer") and Chris Matus ("Employee") hereby agree, finally and unconditionally, that

---

3. Although the conventional manner of "adopting" (assenting to) the terms of a writing is by signature, the parol evidence rule does not limit itself, per se, to signed writings. It is possible for two parties to record their contract in writing and then, without signing it, manifest their mutual assent to its terms. In that case, they have adopted the writing.

> Employee will serve as Employer's general manager, on an ordinary full-time basis and that he will be paid for his service an amount satisfactory to him. Employee acknowledges that the skating rink operates from 8:00 A.M. to 10:00 P.M. seven days per week.

QUESTION 3. If a judge concludes that the writing is a partial integration and not a total integration, her reason will most likely be that

A. the writing names itself an "Employment Contract" and therefore must represent, in part, terms on which the parties have finally reached agreement.
B. the writing is dated and signed by both parties, each setting forth his or her cursive signature.
C. the writing specifies the number of days per week and hours during which the skating rink operates.
D. in her opinion, the parties intended the writing as a final statement as to some of what each would do for the other, but they did not intend it fully to state all on which they had agreed.

ANALYSIS. The question tests only the superficial definition of "partial integration" as we describe it above. A partial integration (whatever its significance, to be discussed in section G below) refers to two parties who first form an oral contract and then reduce it to a writing which, in a judge's opinion, they "intended" as a final expression of those terms that do appear in the writing, but not as a complete expression of all terms on which they agreed. **D** very plainly and simply restates that definition, and that's why **D** is right.

QUESTION 4. If the judge were to conclude that the writing constitutes no integration at all, she would most likely do so because

A. in her opinion, it fails to state some of the terms on which the parties actually agreed.
B. in her opinion, the parties did not "intend" the writing to be final even as to the terms it states.
C. each of the parties signed with a first name, but not a last name.
D. it does not refer to itself as an integration of the parties' agreement.

ANALYSIS. This question requires that you know the definition of "integration." An integration is a document that, as to the terms it does set forth, the parties "intend" to be a final expression of their agreement either (a) as for the provisions it embodies (partial integration) or (b) absolutely and completely (total integration). If in a judge's opinion the parties did not intend the writing to be final as to anything, then the writing is no integration at all. **B** restates that simple rule, and that's why **B** is right.

The "guts" of the parol evidence rule, and the confusion that swirls around it, lie in the meaning (or meaninglessness) of "partial" and "total" "integration." We address that subject in sections E and F below. But, now, with what little we've told you about that topic, let's, at least (and at last), *state* the parol evidence rule. Until we get to section H, we're going to omit two of the rule's words, and mark them with two blank lines.

D.   The Parol Evidence Rule *Stated* (with Two Words Omitted for Now)

The parol evidence rule:

> *(1) If contracting parties first form an oral _____ _____ contract and then create a writing that they adopt as a <u>partial</u> integration of their agreement, then*
>
> *(a) no term on which the parties orally agree, prior to or contemporaneous with their adoption of the writing, is enforceable if that term contradicts the writing's terms, but*
>
> *(b) any oral terms that are consistent with the writing and, therefore, do no more than add to it, are enforceable.*
>
> *(2) If contracting parties first form an oral _____ _____ contract and then create a writing that they adopt as a <u>total</u> integration of their agreement, then no term on which the parties agree, prior to or contemporaneous with their adoption of the writing, is enforceable whether it is or is not consistent with the writing; the terms of the writing are the terms of the contract.*

Leaving aside, still, how we determine that a writing is an integration and, if it is, that it is a total or partial integration, let's illustrate the rule's operation when a court has already made that determination (however it does so).

Illustration 1: When the Court Has Determined That a Writing Is a Partial Integration.   Bart owns a white house that needs painting. He plans to be away on vacation for the month of February. On February 1, 2019, in the presence of five witnesses (Al, Bob, Carol, Dave, and Ethel), Bart orally forms a contract with Andy under which (1) Andy, during the month of February, will paint Bart's house; and (2) Bart will pay Andy $2,000 in advance. They agree that Andy will paint the house in the color "robin's egg blue," shown as color #375 in the Bartholomew Mohr paint catalog. The parties then sign this writing:

> The undersigned parties, Andy Anderson ("Andy") and Bart Bennett ("Bart"), agree that Andy will repaint Bart's house at 223 Amiel Avenue, Carson City,

Nevada 89701. Andy will begin work tomorrow, Monday, February 2, 2019 and will finish no later than February 10, 2019. In exchange, Bart will pay Andy $2,000, immediately upon the mutual execution of this writing. The parties acknowledge that Bart will be away from his home during the relevant period.

Just after the parties sign, Bart pays Andy the $2,000. He then departs on vacation. Andy timely paints the house—*white*. On returning home, Bart complains to Andy that he didn't paint the house in robin's egg blue. Andy points out that the signed contract doesn't specify color. Bart counters, "Well, the writing doesn't mention color, but I know and you know that we agreed on the color robin's egg blue. Al, Bob, Carol, Dave, and Ethel know that too." Bart brings an action against Andy for breach of contract. At trial, Bart's lawyer calls Al as his first witness:

> **Bart's lawyer:** Did you hear Plaintiff and Defendant make any kind of agreement on February 1, 2015?
> **Al:** Yes, I did.
> **Bart's lawyer:** On what subject did they agree?
> **Al:** They agreed that while Bart was away, Andy would paint his house.
> **Bart's lawyer:** Did you hear them agree on anything concerning the color of paint to be used?
> **Al:** Ye . . .
> **Andy's lawyer:** Objection, Your Honor.
> **Court (to Al):** Don't answer yet, please.
> **Court (to Andy's lawyer):** What's your objection?
> **Andy's lawyer:** The parol evidence rule forbids Plaintiff to introduce this testimony. The parties executed a writing, a copy of which has been admitted as Defendant's Exhibit 1, which Your Honor has before you. As Your Honor can see, the writing describes the parties' agreement as to the painting of plaintiff's house.
> **Court (interrupting):** Counsel to my chambers.

In chambers:

> **Judge (to Andy's lawyer):** Continue, please, Counselor.
> **Andy's lawyer:** Thank you, Your Honor. As I was saying, and as you can see, these parties reduced their agreement to a writing that makes no mention of color—none. Furthermore, it shows itself to be final and complete. It is a total integration of their agreement. Pursuant to the parol evidence rule, any oral agreement these parties made prior to adopting the writing is ineffective and unenforceable. Consequently, the jury should not hear any of Plaintiff's evidence intended to show that the parties agreed, orally, on any particular color. Hence, the Court should not permit his attorney to ask any witness whether or on what color the parties agreed orally. The terms of the writing are the terms of the contract.

Judge (to Bart's lawyer): What is your response, Counselor?

Bart's lawyer: We expect this witness to explain that the parties agreed before adopting their writing that Defendant should paint Plaintiff's house in a particular color—other than the color in which he actually painted it. And it is our position, Your Honor, that the parties' writing is by no means a total integration of the parties' agreement. It is only a partial integration, which the parties did intend as a final expression of the terms it presents, but not as a *complete* expression of all terms on which they agreed. Because the writing is a partial integration of the parties' agreement, we have the right to prove, if we can, that before adopting the writing the parties agreed, orally, on a term that is consistent *with* the writing. Since the writing says nothing about color, an agreement as to color is consistent with it; such a term would neither contradict nor conflict with any of the writing's terms; it would merely add to them. Consequently, the Court should admit the evidence with which we want to show that the parties did, orally, agree on a color other than the one in which Defendant painted it.

Court: To resolve this dispute, I must apply the parol evidence rule. If the parties intended this writing as a total integration of their agreement, then the terms of the writing are the terms of the contract. In that case, I can admit no evidence as to any terms on which the parties orally agreed before they adopted the writing. On the other hand, if these parties intended the writing as a partial integration of their agreement, then I may admit evidence of terms on which the parties agreed orally before they adopted the writing, so long as those terms have the effect of adding to the writing's terms without contradicting them.

I have examined the writing and I find that the parties intended it to be final as to the terms it states, but that they did not intend it as a complete expression of all terms on which they agreed. I find, therefore, that the writing constitutes only a *partial* integration of their agreement. The writing makes no mention of color. Consequently, if these parties did reach an agreement, orally, as to color, that agreement would not conflict with or contradict the writing's terms. Rather, it would add to them. For that reason, I rule that Plaintiff may present witnesses who will testify that the parties orally agreed as to the color in which Defendant should paint Plaintiff's house. If the jury finds that the parties did indeed make such an oral agreement, then it is part of the parties' contract. Let's return to the courtroom.

In the courtroom:

Court: The court reporter will read back the last question and the witness will answer.

Reporter: Did you hear them agree on anything concerning the color of paint to be used?

Al: Yes, they agreed on the color.

Bart's lawyer: Do you remember on what color they agreed?

Al: Oh, yes, Bart was insistent on it and Andy absolutely agreed—the house was to be painted in a Bartholomew Mohr paint called robin's egg blue. They said that and shook hands. They then signed a piece of paper.

Illustration 2: Partial Integration with a Change in the Story. Suppose now that after reaching their oral agreement, including their understanding as to the color robin's egg blue, Bart and Andy date and sign *this* writing, which, for some reason or other, expressly refers to the color white:

> The undersigned parties, Andy Anderson ("Andy") and Bart Bennett ("Bart"), agree that Andy will repaint Bart's house at 223 Amiel Avenue, Carson City, Nevada 15459. Andy will paint the house white. He will begin work on this next Monday, February 2, 2015, and will finish no later than February 10, 2015. In exchange, Bart will pay Andy $2,000, immediately upon the mutual execution of this writing. The parties acknowledge that for the relevant period, Bart will be away from his home.

Imagine, again, that the parties go to trial and that Bart wants to present his evidence—five witnesses plus his own testimony to prove that notwithstanding the writing, the parties definitely agreed on the color robin's egg blue. And imagine too that the court rules this writing a *partial* integration.

A prior oral agreement that Andy should paint the house blue and not white would certainly contradict the writing. "Blue" is not consistent with "white." Hence, under the parol evidence rule, such a prior agreement—even though the parties really did reach it—is ineffective; it's not a part of their contract. Consequently, the court does not allow Bart even a chance to prove that the parties agreed on robin's egg blue. For even if they did, it's not a part of the contract. The court rules Al's testimony inadmissible; the jury is not to hear of this irrelevancy.

Illustration 3: When the Court Has Determined That the Writing Is a *Total* Integration. Suppose now that in front of five witnesses, Deborah and Elena agree orally that while Deborah is away on vacation, Elena will paint her house Nevada white. The parties agree also that Elena will sand and finish the wood on Deborah's front door. They shake hands, and shortly thereafter Elena presents Deborah with this writing, labeled "Contract":

> **WHEREAS** Elena Pagonis ("Elena") warrants that she has all professional skills, knowledge, and expertise germane and necessary to the performances hereinafter assigned and allocated to her; and
>
> **WHEREAS** Deborah Durbin ("Deborah") wishes, for a price, to avail herself of such skill, knowledge, and expertise,
>
> **NOW, THEN,** the parties do agree that Elena will repaint Deborah's house at 447 Chance Avenue, Reno, Nevada 89501, pursuant to the following terms and conditions:

(1) Elena will paint the house using Bartholomew Mohr paint color #287, "Nevada white."

(2) If Elena is unable, through no fault of her own, to obtain the kind and color of paint hereinbefore described, then she shall, pursuant to professional judgment, use a paint of substantially similar color and quality, such professional judgment to conform to standards of the relevant profession.

(3) Elena will supply her own equipment, including but not limited to ladders, paint brushes, rollers, pans, rags, tapes, covers, and shields.

(4) Elena will purchase the paint as necessary and all other chemical products including, but not limited to, thinners and brush cleaners, and for these expenses Deborah will reimburse her on completion of her performance as hereinbefore and hereinafter described and specified.

(5) As between themselves, Elena is serving not as Deborah's employee, but as an independent contractor, wherefore Deborah's duties and liabilities to Elena or to third persons are governed by that relationship except to the extent that applicable law provides otherwise meaning, *inter alia*, that as to any attempt by any third person or persons to hold Deborah liable for any alleged damage arising as a result of or in direct relation to Elena's acts or omissions as pertinent hereto, Elena will indemnify Deborah and hold her harmless.

(6) Elena will begin work on this next Monday, February 2, 2019, and will finish no later than February 10, 2019.

(7) The parties acknowledge that Deborah will be away from her home during the relevant period.

(8) In exchange for all that Elena does as hereinbefore prescribed and described, Deborah will pay Elena $2,000, immediately upon the mutual execution of this writing.

(9) Should Elena fail to complete the work/performance as hereinbefore agreed, prescribed, and described then, except to the extent that any such failure shall be due to the fault of Deborah, Elena will repay to Deborah $100 for each day of delay.

(10) The contract represented hereby shall, should the occasion arise, be construed and enforced according to the laws of Nevada.

TO THE FOREGOING terms and conditions the parties do commit themselves and, therefore, to this writing they do set their signatures on the date(s) of:

_____   _____
February 1, 2015   February 1, 2015

After Deborah examines the writing, she says to Elena, "The writing doesn't state that you'll sand and finish the wood on the front door." "Oh, I see you're right," replies Elena. "Well, I'm certainly going to do that. We've agreed to it, and of course I'll do it." Deborah is reassured. Without adding to the writing, both parties sign it.

Deborah returns from vacation to find a freshly painted Nevada white house and an untouched front door. Deborah contacts Elena to complain that she did not sand and finish the wood on the front door. Elena denies that she had any obligation to do so because, she says, "the written contract makes no mention of it." A lawsuit follows, and there arises once again the question of whether Deborah's lawyer may attempt to prove, with the testimony of five witnesses and that of Deborah as well, that Elena promised to sand and finish the wood, even though the writing features no term to that effect.

> **Deborah's lawyer:** Your Honor, we seek to prove that these parties orally agreed to a term that is perfectly consistent with the writing, for nothing in the writing contradicts a term by which Defendant is obliged, in addition to painting the house, to sand and finish the wood on its front door.
>
> **Elena's lawyer:** That may be true, Your Honor, but we believe that the writing is a total integration. Consequently, any term to which the parties orally agreed but failed to include in the writing is not a part of their contract, whether it does or does not contradict the terms of the writing. The terms of the writing *are* the terms of the contract.
>
> **Court:** Defendant's lawyer correctly states the parol evidence rule, and Plaintiff's lawyer has no quarrel with him on that point. The rule provides that if two parties first form an oral contract and then reduce it to a writing that they intend to be final as to the terms it states and, furthermore, a complete expression of all terms on which they agreed, then they have created a total integration of their agreement. In that situation, no term to which the parties agreed, orally, before adopting the writing is a part of their contract, unless the parties include it *in* the writing.
>
> Having examined this elaborate writing, replete with terms that address a variety of contingencies and possibilities, I conclude that these parties intended it as a final expression of all terms it states and, furthermore, a complete expression of all terms on which they agreed. They intended that it be a final and complete expression of their agreement. The writing is, therefore, a total integration. Consequently, no term on which these parties agreed belongs to their contract unless it appears in the writing. This writing makes no mention of sanding or refinishing of any wood, wherefore no such term is part of this contract, even if the parties really did agree to it. The jury is to hear no evidence that the parties made any such agreement, meaning that Plaintiff may present no such evidence.

This judge concluded that these parties reduced their oral agreement to a *total* integration. Consequently, the terms of the writing *are* the terms of the contract. Elena's oral promise to sand and finish the wood is unenforceable, no matter how many witnesses stand ready to testify that Elena truly made that promise; no matter that the term is consistent with the writing; no matter that Elena herself might stand ready to acknowledge under oath, on the witness stand, her promise to sand and finish the wood. A total integration "wipes out" any term to which the parties orally agreed and then failed to include in the writing.

E.   The Major Confusion: Deciding That a Writing Is an Integration, Total or Partial

In the first house painting case, the judge ruled Bart and Andy's writing a partial integration. Yet, he did not explain how he reached his ruling, except to say, "I have examined the writing." In the second case, he gave no reason as to why he ruled Deborah and Elena's writing a total integration, except to say, "Having examined this elaborate writing, replete with terms that address a variety of contingencies and possibilities, I conclude that these parties intended it as a final expression of all terms it states and, furthermore, a complete expression of all terms on which they agreed."

Like many others who have applied the parol evidence rule, the judge took his ruling from the "gut"—for the law offers no trace of a settled, workable rule as to how a court should determine that two parties did or did not "intend" their contractual writing as an integration or, if they did, that they intended it as a partial or total one.

What Authorities Say on the Subject.   It's commonly *said* that on this matter the law features two opposing views. Before describing them, we advise you that probably no jurisdiction ever has adopted either one. Rather, the way in which courts make the determinations just described usually falls on a line that extends between the two—or, just as frequently perhaps, on a line that begins and ends nowhere, having nothing to do with either such view. Moreover, the "view" that any court purports to take in explaining a decision on this point usually lacks any logical connection to the ruling it ultimately issues.

1. The "Four Corners" or "Williston" View

Historically, Professor Samuel Williston (1861-1963) is regarded as one of America's two greatest expositors of contract law. With respect to the parol evidence rule, lawyers, judges, and teachers often speak of a "Williston view." According to the so-called Williston view (also called the "four corners" view), a judge determines whether a given writing constitutes (1) no integration or (2) a partial or (3) a total integration—by examining the writing itself and nothing more. That is, a judge confines herself to the "four corners of the document."

She is first to ask herself this question: Does the writing show finality as to any term at all? If her answer is "no," then the writing is not an integration at all. The parol evidence rule does not apply, wherefore the terms of the parties' contract are those to which they manifested their mutual assent, through offer and acceptance, by whatever mode they did so including, of course, spoken word. If her answer is "yes"—the writing does show finality as to at least one of its terms—then it *is* an integration, either partial or total.

In that case, the judge asks herself this second question: Is the writing "complete on its face"? Does it show finality as to all that is necessary to a contract for the kind of performances it describes? If her answer is "no," then the writing is a partial integration. If her answer is "yes," the writing is a total integration.

According to the Williston view, therefore, the whole of the determination is made by examination of the writing itself; the court hears no extrinsic evidence (evidence outside the writing) as to whether and to what extent the parties "intended" the writing as an integration.

Illustrating the Williston View, I.   Think again of Elena, Deborah, the house painting, and the front door. Imagine this time that the parties date and sign this writing:

> The undersigned parties agree that Elena will perform service as to the house, as agreed, Elena to begin and finish as agreed. In exchange, Deborah will give consideration as agreed.

The words of this writing are insufficient to show agreement as to *anything*. In terms of the Williston view, it shows finality as to nothing. Consequently, it is not an integration at all, and the parol evidence rule does not apply. Should these parties fall into dispute and litigation, the Williston view will require that the court permit either one to introduce evidence of any kind to show that the parties did or did not form a contract and what, if any, were its terms.

Illustrating the Williston View, II.   Imagine now that Deborah and Elena, having had their same conversation, date and sign *this* writing:

> The undersigned parties, Elena Pagonis ("Elena") and Deborah Durbin ("Deborah"), agree that Elena will paint Deborah's house at 447 Chance Avenue, Reno, Nevada 89501, color as agreed. Elena will begin work on this next Monday, February 2, 2015, and will finish no later than Monday, February 10, 2015. In exchange, Deborah will pay Elena immediately upon the mutual execution of this writing. The parties acknowledge that Deborah will be away from her home during the relevant period.

This writing shows finality as to some matters, but not as to others. The phrase "color as agreed" makes plain that the writing is not final as to color. The writing's failure to specify Elena's fee means that it's not final as to that matter either. Yet, the writing shows finality as to the fact that Elena *will* paint Deborah's house and the dates on which she will start and finish her work. Hence, it shows some finality and, according to the Williston view, it's a partial integration. Either party may introduce evidence of an oral agreement as to any term, earlier adopted, that does *not contradict* the writing.

Illustrating the Williston View, III.   Let's now look at the long writing Elena and Deborah adopted when first we met them. Before going further, reread their written contract from Illustration 3.

Under the Williston view, this writing is, certainly, "complete on its face," meaning that one who examines it objectively sees in it all terms that a house painting contract ought to have (and more). Reading this writing, two reasonable parties would have no question about what each is to do. Hence, under the Williston view, the writing is a total integration, and its terms *are* the terms of the contract. Neither party may seek to prove that the contract includes anything more or anything different.

Consider, for example, Item 6: "Elena will begin work on this next Monday, February 2, 2015, and will finish no later than February 10, 2015." Suppose Elena truthfully asserts that just prior to signing the writing, before 1,000 witnesses, the parties agreed that she would have until February 15 if the average low temperature for the days February 2 through February 10 fell below 40° F. Suppose further that *Deborah* is prepared to *admit* to that agreement. Nonetheless, that term is not part of the parties' contract. Why not? Because it's not in the writing, and when the writing is a total integration, the writing is the contract, the contract is the writing, and that's that.

2. The "Corbin" View

We said that Williston is regarded as one of America's two greatest expositors of contract law. Professor Arthur Corbin (1874-1967) was the other. According to the so-called Corbin view of the parol evidence rule, a court cannot decide that two parties "intended" a writing as an integration, partial or total, without examining all facts and circumstances in place when they adopted it, including the facts of whether, before adopting it, they had made any other agreements on the same subject. As is so throughout contract law, "intent," according to this view, should refer to what each party led the other reasonably to understand. Stated otherwise, the Corbin view considers that no writing can prove itself to be anything at all but ink on paper. In a disputed case, the writing is one item of admissible evidence as to what the parties, under all circumstances, should have understood to be the terms of their agreement. Admissible also, however, is any and all evidence, including the parties' conversations, statements, and agreements, as to what significance the writing should have.[4] The Corbin view thus *eliminates* the parol evidence rule. Should a court adopt the Corbin view of the parol evidence rule, it would, in fact, abolish the rule, and that is what Professor Corbin truly believed should happen.[5]

Consider the second house painting case in which the parties orally agreed that Andy should paint Bart's house blue, after which the parties signed a writing that specified the color white. In determining that the parties' writing was an integration, partial or total, Professor Corbin would admit evidence of

---

4. We have just purported to summarize, in a few sentences, Professor Corbin's views on the parol evidence rule. Know, please, that he himself wrote hundreds of pages in order to do so. *See generally* 3 *Corbin on Contracts* §§573-596 (2d ed. 1960).

5. As Professor Corbin wrote: "It would be better if no such rule ever had been stated[.]" Arthur L. Corbin, *The Parol Evidence Rule*, 53 Yale L.J. 603, 631-632 (1944).

all circumstances surrounding the parties when they adopted it, *including any statements they made to each other.* For this purpose — the purpose of establishing the parties' "intent" as to the writing — Corbin would have the court admit evidence of Andy's promise to paint the house blue. On that basis, it would decide that the parties did not *intend* the writing even as a partial integration of their agreement, since the writing was at odds with what they had truly agreed.

Consider, now the third house painting case, in which Deborah complains that Elena failed to refinish her front door. If the court had followed the Corbin view, then before finally characterizing the writing, it would have admitted evidence of all circumstances surrounding the parties when they adopted it, *including Elena's promise to sand and refinish the front door.* Since that testimony (if believed) shows that the parties omitted a term on which they had agreed, the court would rule the writing not to be a total integration. The Corbin view thus renders it impossible for any "parol evidence rule" to exclude evidence of agreements that parties make prior to adoption of a writing.

The Corbin View Predominates Today, or So They Say.   It is said that modern law leans toward the Corbin view — toward admitting "extrinsic evidence" (evidence outside the writing) in order to determine that a writing is or is not an integration, partial or total. The Restatement (Second) of Contracts illustrates the point. It devotes ten sections to the parol evidence rule (§§209-218), each accompanied by comments and illustrations. Not one of its illustrations draws a conclusion that a given writing is or is not an integration, partial or complete. And although its writers obviously *purport* to recognize the parol evidence rule, the net effect of their rules, comments, and illustrations, if scrupulously studied, is probably to abolish it (and the writers do not even see that they have done so).

Restatement (Second) §213 first states the parol evidence rule in conventional terms:

> (1) A binding [partially] integrated agreement discharges prior agreements to the extent that it is inconsistent with them.
> (2) A binding completely integrated agreement discharges prior agreements to the extent that they are within its scope[.]

Subsection 2 means, then, that a total integration ("binding completely integrated agreement") supersedes ("discharges"), any prior agreement on the same subject matter ("within its scope").

Comment b then provides:

> To apply this rule, the court must make preliminary determinations that there is an integrated agreement and that it is inconsistent with the term in question. Those determinations are made in accordance with all relevant evidence, and require interpretation both of the integrated agreement and of

the prior agreement. The existence of the prior agreement may be a circumstance that sheds light on the meaning of the integrated agreement[.]

Restatement (Second) Contracts §214 provides:

> Agreements and negotiations prior to or contemporaneous with the adoption of a writing are admissible in evidence to establish
> (a) that the writing is or is not an integrated agreement;
> (b) that the integrated agreement, if any, is completely or partially integrated. . . .

Comment a reads thus:

> *Integrated agreement and completely integrated agreement*: Whether a writing has been adopted as an integrated agreement and, if so, whether the agreement is completely or partially integrated are questions determined by the court preliminary to determination of a question of interpretation or to application of the parol evidence rule[.] Writings do not prove themselves; ordinarily, if there is dispute, there must be testimony that there was a signature or other manifestation of assent. The preliminary determination is made in accordance with all relevant evidence, including the circumstances in which the writing was made or adopted. It may require preliminary interpretation of the writing; the court must then consider the evidence which is relevant to the question of interpretation.

Restatement (Second) §210 provides:

> (1) A completely integrated agreement is an integrated agreement adopted by the parties as a complete and exclusive statement of the terms of the agreement.
> (2) A partially integrated agreement is an integrated agreement other than a completely integrated agreement.

Comment b then reads thus:

> That a writing was or was not adopted as a completely integrated agreement may be proved by any relevant evidence. A document in the form of a written contract, signed by both parties and apparently complete on its face, may be decisive of the issue in the absence of credible contrary evidence. But a writing cannot of itself prove its own completeness, and wide latitude must be allowed for inquiry into circumstances bearing on the intention of the parties.

Taken together, the Restatement's material on the parol evidence rule is shot through with ambiguity, evasion, and inconsistency. The Restatement writers leave the parol evidence rule just as they found it: a morass of circular statements that lead nowhere. And notwithstanding the elaborate pretense to an exacting scholarly analysis, these ten sections of the Restatement — if they do anything at all — abolish the parol evidence rule altogether.

F.   The Merger Clause

Within a contractual writing, a "merger clause" is a provision, whatever its words, that characterizes the writing itself *as* a total integration. Each of the following three provisions constitutes a merger clause (whether or not it is *entitled* "merger clause"):

> **Merger.** This writing represents the entirety of the parties' agreement, and it supersedes any and all prior agreements the parties may have reached on this same subject matter.
>
> **Entire Agreement.** The parties hereby agree that this writing represents a merger of all to which they may have agreed or considered on this subject matter, and that it therefore represents a full and final integration of their agreement.
>
> **Total Integration.** This document fully, finally, and totally integrates the parties' understandings and agreement as to its subject matter, wherefore no prior agreements or understandings on such subject matter is or are operative.

1. The Effect of Merger Clauses According to the Williston View

According to the Williston view, a writing that is not "obviously incomplete" *and* sets forth a merger clause is a total integration. Those who thus describe the "Williston view" give no definition of "obviously incomplete." Let's suppose that the phrase means a writing that "shows finality as to nothing"— the same writing that constitutes no integration at all. We might then come to this conclusion: According to the Williston view, a contractual writing that is otherwise a partial integration becomes a total integration if it features a merger clause. With that in mind, let's add a merger clause to the signed writing we earlier called a partial integration under the Williston view:

> **Agreement:** The undersigned parties, Elena Pagonis ("Elena") and Deborah Durbin ("Deborah"), agree that Elena will paint Deborah's house at 447 Chance Avenue, Reno, Nevada 89501, color as agreed. Elena will begin work on this next Monday, February 2, 2019, and will finish no later than February 10, 2019. In exchange, Deborah will pay Elena, as agreed, immediately upon the mutual execution of this writing. The parties acknowledge that Deborah will be away from her home during the relevant one-month period.
>
> **Merger/Entire Agreement:** The parties agree that this writing represents a full, final, and total integration of their agreement on this subject matter and that no prior terms or agreements bearing on the same are relevant hereto or binding on either of them.

Maybe the Williston view means to say that this writing, otherwise a partial integration, is, *with* its merger clause, a *total* integration. But if it's a total integration, meaning that the writing *is* the contract, it leaves us with these two questions: (1) How shall a court identify the color in which Elena is to paint the house? (2) How shall it determine what fee Deborah is to pay her? The answer to both questions is, plainly: It can't. Hence, with respect to the so-called Williston view (not really Professor Williston's view), the significance of a merger clause remains a mystery.

2. The Effect of Merger Clauses According to the Corbin View and the Restatement

The Corbin view gives merger clauses no significance at all. Under the Corbin view, no writing, however long and elaborate, can, on its own, "decide" that it is a complete expression of the parties' agreement. That view carries a good deal of logical appeal. All will agree that a signed paper, blank in all respects except for a merger clause, cannot constitute a "complete and final expression" of anyone's agreement about anything.

Likewise, the Restatement gives merger clauses no significance at all. We know that because it makes not even a mention of merger clauses.

G. The Parol Evidence Rule in Real Legal Life

In real life, as noted at the beginning of this chapter, there is no agreement on how a court should determine whether a given writing is an integration and, if it is, whether the parties "intended" it as a partial or total integration. Courts write of the Williston and Corbin views, but none adheres to either with any consistency. No *court could* possibly do so. For the Corbin view amounts to a negation of the rule. The so-called Williston view (which was *not* Williston's view) is devoid of logic and wholly unworkable. In parol evidence cases today, some courts, on some days, make their judgments on this critical question by looking exclusively to the writings themselves. Others claim to look only to the writings, but then in fact consider exogenous circumstances as well.

There is, still, no true parol evidence rule on which the jurisdictions agree. As Professor Farnsworth writes, "Surprisingly little light is shed on the problem by the hundreds of decisions resolving the issue of whether an agreement is completely integrated. Opinions often fail to set out the text of the writing in full, and each case turns on its own peculiar facts." E. Allan Farnsworth, *Contracts* 435 (3d ed. 1999). And, as discussed above, the Restatement writers purport to recognize and state the parol evidence rule but, in our opinion, unwittingly abolish it.

As for the merger clause, a court that finds a writing to be a total integration will cite to a merger clause, if there be one, as additional support for its conclusion. But that same court, it appears, would call that same writing a total integration without the merger clause. Substantially every contractual writing formally drafted by an attorney does feature a merger clause. And in practical terms, if a court is faced with two credible arguments as to whether a writing is a partial or total integration, the merger clause will usually cinch the case for the party who argues that it is a total one.

Illustration: Effect of a Merger Clause.   Let's create another dated and signed writing for Elena and Deborah:

> The undersigned parties, Elena Pagonis ("Elena") and Deborah Durbin ("Deborah"), agree that
> (1) Elena will repaint Deborah's house at 447 Chance Avenue, Reno, Nevada 89501. Elena will begin work on this next Monday, February 2, 2019, and will finish no later than February 10, 2019.
> (2) The front door is to be refinished, also as agreed.
> (3) In exchange, Deborah will pay Elena $2,000 immediately upon the mutual execution of this writing. The parties acknowledge that Deborah will be away from her home during the relevant four-week period.
> (4) This writing constitutes the full and final expression of the parties' agreement as to this subject matter.

For a court inclined toward the Williston/four corners rule (as most courts still claim to be), items 1, 2, and 3 leave room for debate as to whether the writing is (a) complete on its face and, therefore, a total integration, or (b) final only as to some matters and, therefore, a partial integration.

Item 1 does not expressly mention color. On that basis, one might argue that it is complete as to the facts that Deborah must paint the house, but incomplete as to color. On the other hand, the writing provides that Deborah will *re*paint the house, which one might take to mean "paint in the same color as now shows itself on the house."

Consider item 2: "The front door is to be refinished, also as agreed." That provision, one might argue, renders the writing incomplete as to what Elena must do with the front door. One might, on the other hand, argue that the provision means only that the front door is to be repainted along with the rest of the house.

Faced with two plausible arguments as to the writing's status—partial or total integration—the judge must, of course, make a decision. To the extent that the judge limits his examination to the "four corners of the document," and where, in the court's mind, the question of total versus partial integration is arguable, the merger clause gives it a reason to decide that it is a total integration.

Before you answer Questions 5 and 6, please go back to section E of this chapter and reread Restatement (Second) §214. Then take on Questions 5 and 6.

QUESTIONS 5 & 6. Aiden planned to produce a film called *The Whole Nine Days*. He wanted Madison to serve as director. The two conducted highly detailed discussions about

- the duties each would perform,
- the way in which each would perform, and
- what would occur in the case of a great many contingencies and conditions.

Among the hundreds of terms on which they orally agreed were these:

(1) Aiden would produce the film and Madison would serve as director.
(2) Madison would take custody of all moneys the film earned each year, and distribute them once on July 31 and again on December 31.
(3) Profits would be divided equally except for the first year, when they would be divided 60 percent to Aiden, 40 percent to Madison.

Finally, after weeks of discussions and after reaching, orally and by handshake, all of the agreements mentioned above, the parties conversed thus:

> **Madison:** We've agreed on hundreds of details. Shall we put the whole thing in writing?
>
> **Aiden:** Yes, eventually we should, but that will require lawyers and lots of time. Why don't we put in writing, for now, a general statement of our agreement and, specifically, our agreement as to division of profits? Once we've done that, we'll get going on the project and, as we do, we'll have our lawyers hammer out a writing in full.
>
> **Madison:** Okay, let's do that.

The parties then created, dated, and signed this writing, entitled "Memorandum of Agreement":

> This writing concerns the creation of a film to be entitled *The Whole Nine Days* for which Aiden Anderson will be producer and Madison Maise director. Anderson will provide such funding as Maise requests up to a maximum amount of $5 million. The parties will generally share any profits that the film earns, with Maise to receive, hold, and take custody of all moneys derived from the film until such time as they are divided. The parties agree that this is the entirety of their agreement.

Notwithstanding their stated plans, the parties never did create another writing. They made the film, and, in 2015, it began to deliver profits. Madison took custody of all moneys and deposited them in a bank account. On December 28, 2015, he advised Aiden that he would, in three days, divide the monies, 50 percent to each of them. Aiden spoke up: "If you'll remember, just prior to signing the writing we agreed that we would divide the first year's profits 60 percent to me and 40 percent to you, because the whole film was my idea." Madison replied, "I remember that, but our writing provides that we will "generally share" the profits. It says nothing about a 60/40 division for the first year." Madison distributed the profits 50/50. Aiden now sues Madison, demanding an additional 10 percent.

At trial, Aiden offers to testify to the conversation that he and Madison had just before signing the agreement. Further, he is prepared to produce three witnesses, all of whom are also prepared to testify that they heard Madison and Aiden agree to the 60/40 first-year division. Madison objects to all such testimony on the basis that the writing called for a general sharing of profits, which, Madison argues, means a 50/50 distribution to each party. The court must then decide whether the writing is a partial or total integration.

QUESTION 5. If the court adopts the Restatement's view of the parol evidence rule, it will most likely

A. exclude the evidence Aiden offers, because the writing features a merger clause.
B. exclude the evidence Aiden offers, because it will restrict itself to the four corners of the document.
C. admit the evidence Aiden offers, because a total integration allows for enforcement of oral agreements made prior to the execution of the writing.
D. admit the evidence Aiden offers to determine the parties' "intentions" as to the significance of the writing.

ANALYSIS. Restatement (Second) §214 provides that "[a]greements and negotiations prior to or contemporaneous with the adoption of a writing are admissible in evidence to establish (a) that the writing is or is not an integrated agreement; (b) that the integrated agreement, if any, is completely or partially integrated." Consequently, for that purpose, this court will admit evidence of the parties' oral agreement. **A** and **B** are wrong.

Further, **A** implicitly mischaracterizes the Restatement view. It's true, as **A** says, that the writing does feature a merger clause; it's in the last sentence. The Restatement, however, gives no significance to a merger clause; it makes no mention of one. **B** sings the "four corners …" song composed by Williston. We are dealing in this case with the *Restatement* view. It implicitly rejects the four corners precept.

C has the law upside-down. Once a court finds a writing to be a total integration, it *won't* entertain evidence of any agreements outside the writing; the writing is the contract and the contract is the writing. Further, C expressly presupposes a decision on the very question the court must answer — whether the writing is a partial or total integration. Finally, it incorrectly states the rule. In the case of a partial integration, a court will not hear evidence of a prior agreement that *contradicts* the writing. C is for the fireplace.

D conforms to the Restatement's provisions on the parol evidence rule. It tells us that the court will admit the evidence of the prior agreement to determine that the writing is a total or partial integration. For that reason, D is right (maybe).

QUESTION 6. If the court adopts the so-called Williston view of the parol evidence rule, it will most likely

A. exclude the evidence Aiden offers, because of the writing's final sentence.

B. exclude the evidence Aiden offers, because in the case of a partial integration, the terms of the writing are the terms of the contract.

C. admit the evidence Aiden offers, because in the case of a total integration, Aiden is allowed to testify to the prior oral agreement.

D. admit the evidence Aiden offers to determine the parties' "intentions" as to the significance of the writing.

ANALYSIS. As to whether a writing is a partial or total integration, or no integration at all, the Williston view provides that a court is to restrict itself to the "four corners of the document." In doing so, a court is first to ask itself whether (in its opinion) the writing is "obviously incomplete." If its answer is yes, then the writing is no integration at all. If it's no, then the writing is an integration, partial or complete. The court is then to ask itself if the writing sets forth a merger clause. If the answer is "no," the writing is a partial integration. If the answer is "yes," it's a total integration; the writing is the contract and the contract is the writing.

This writing is not (we think) "obviously incomplete." It names the parties, it describes what each will do, and it does state that they will "generally share" the profits. A reasonable judge can't look at this writing and call it "obviously incomplete." Further, the writing's last sentence characterizes the writing as the parties' entire agreement on its subject matter. It's a merger clause. Hence, according to the "Williston view," the writing is a total integration. A correctly tells us that the writing's last sentence produces the outcome. That's right. The last sentence is a merger clause. Without that, the writing would be a partial integration. The merger clause renders it a total integration. The writing is the contract and the contract is the writing. A is right.

H. "Confusion Now Hath Made His Masterpiece":[6] The Two Missing Words

Throughout this chapter, we have dealt with the parol evidence rule in terms of two parties who first form an *oral* agreement and then, as to the same subject matter, create and adopt a writing. Cases that call forth the parol evidence rule do usually involve that situation. (The word "parol" means "by the mouth" or "by the spoken word.")

Nonetheless, all modern authorities (purport to) agree that the parol evidence rule applies not only to prior *oral* agreements, but also to prior *written* ones. Hence, for law school purposes, a full statement of the rule requires that we account for that notion:

The Parol Evidence Rule *in Full*

(1) If contracting parties first form a contract and then reduce it to a writing that the parties intend as a partial integration of their agreement, the writing cannot be contradicted by evidence of any prior agreement, written or oral, or any contemporaneous oral agreement, but it may be supplemented by evidence of consistent additional terms on which the parties earlier agreed.

(2) If the parties intend the writing as a total integration/complete and final expression of their agreement, then the writing cannot be varied by evidence of a prior agreement, written or oral, or any contemporaneous oral agreement.

In terms of its application to written agreements, the rule probably means no more than what is otherwise true: A later agreement supersedes an earlier one. Furthermore, despite the rule's broad statement, purportedly excluding evidence of prior written agreements, it cannot be true and *is* not true (except pursuant to UCC §2-209; see Chapter 14, section B) that a later written agreement supersedes an earlier one if the later one fails to exact consideration from both its parties. If,

(1) by writing, A and B agree that A will perform a service for B in exchange for $1,000, and then

(2) by subsequent writing agree that the fee will be $800, the subsequent writing cannot supersede the earlier one, for it represents a modification in which A gives no consideration.

Recognizing those truths, the notion that the parol evidence rule applies not only to prior and contemporaneous oral agreements but also to prior *written* agreements is of very dubious significance. Do know, however, that current statements of the rule do refer, also, to prior written agreements.

---

6. William Shakespeare, *Macbeth*, act 2, sc. 3.

I.   Important Qualifications

1. *Collateral Agreements*

Suppose Buyer and Seller (1) first agree orally on the sale of a violin for $1,500; (2) then, at the same meeting, agree on the sale of a dog located 100 miles away for $200; and (3) then reduce to (signed) writing, finally and completely, their agreement as to the violin but not the one concerning the dog. All authorities agree that even in the face of a total integration, a prior agreement (oral or written) that is truly separate from the one to which the writing applies is enforceable as an oral contract that stands in its own right, apart from the one reduced to writing.

Abstruse and incomprehensible as always, the Restatement writers try to state that same rule. Here for your entertainment is its §212(2):

> A binding completely integrated agreement discharges prior agreements to the extent that they are within its scope.

That sentence means: "A total integration supersedes prior agreements to the extent that they address the same substance and subject matter." Hence, the law recognizes, notwithstanding the parol evidence rule, that two parties might at the same meeting form two separate contracts and then reduce to writing only one of them. The second, it is then said, is "collateral" to—meaning *separate from*—the first. The parol evidence rule does not affect the collateral agreement; that agreement stands independent of the other. That it fails to appear in the writing is insignificant.

In order that an agreement qualify as a collateral one, it must, of course, show a separate consideration and, in the court's opinion, bear on a separate subject matter. Any court would agree that Buyer and Seller above formed two *separate* agreements because the matter of dog and violin are so plainly distinct. The agreement concerning the dog is "collateral" to that which concerns the violin. It stands on its own as an enforceable oral contract.

QUESTION 7. Isaac and Renee agree orally that Isaac will build a garage on Renee's land in exchange for $40,000. Renee then adds, "Would you be willing also to construct a cement walkway leading from my house to the driveway?" Isaac replies, "Yes. That will cost you an additional $5,000." Renee says, "Fine." The parties then create and sign a writing. It's long, elaborate, and exhaustively detailed, complete with a merger clause. It provides that Isaac will build a garage and that Renee will pay him $40,000. It makes no mention of a walkway and no mention of any $5,000 amount.

Isaac builds the garage, whereupon Renee pays him $40,000. She then asks him to begin work on the walkway. He refuses. Renee brings suit, and the court determines that the writing is a total integration. Nonetheless, the court allows Renee's lawyer to prove the agreement concerning the walkway. Ultimately, it is satisfied that the parties did orally agree on the $5,000 walkway construction. It rules the agreement enforceable, notwithstanding that the parties failed to include it in their writing. The court most likely came to the conclusion(s) that

I. construction of the walkway and garage represented different and distinct undertakings.
II. Renee was obliged to pay not $45,000 for garage and walkway, but $40,000 for the garage and $5,000 for the walkway.
A. I only
B. II only
C. Both I and II
D. Neither I nor II

ANALYSIS. With respect to the parol evidence rule, one agreement is collateral to another if, in the court's opinion (a) it pertains to a separate subject matter, and (b) it shows a separate consideration. Unlike the matter of violin and dog, this story creates a close case. When the parties agreed on the building of the walkway, they also agreed that Renee would pay Isaac $5,000 beyond the $40,000 she was to pay for the garage. Certainly some courts would rule that these parties (1) having first agreed on the garage and the $40,000, (2) then *added a provision to their then existing oral contract*, so that they (3) ultimately formed a single contract requiring that Isaac build a garage and walkway for $45,000. Because their writing, a total integration, makes no mention of walkway or $5,000, these courts would rule that the parol evidence rule renders the walkway agreement unenforceable.

This court evidently thought otherwise. Knowing of the "collateral agreement" rule, it thought the parties (1) first formed a $40,000 contract for construction of a garage, (2) then formed a separate $5,000 contract for the construction of a walkway, and then (3) reduced the first one to writing, leaving the second as an oral agreement, fully enforceable in its own right. This court concluded, therefore that the walkway agreement was collateral to the garage contract — that walkway and garage were separate subject matter and that the additional $5,000 was a separate consideration to be paid for the walkway only. Both I and II apply. **C** is right.

Some refer to this collateral agreement doctrine as an "exception" to the parol evidence rule, but that notion is misconceived. The parol evidence rule purports only to affect *a contract* that two parties first form and then reduce to a final written expression. It does not purport to address any *set of contracts* formed by two parties at or near the same time.

2. *Interpretation, Fraud, Duress, Mistake*

Although the parol evidence rule may forbid two contracting parties to enforce agreements and terms omitted from their writing, it does not stop them from introducing evidence of prior discussions to establish the meaning of words and phrases that appear *in* the writing. Hence, if a partial or total integration features the term "blue," or "market price," or "unit," either party may introduce evidence of conversations and negotiations to show that the parties should reasonably have understood "blue" to mean *navy* blue or "market price" to mean opening price on the London market, or "unit" to mean bushel. To those ends, any evidence including usage of trade and course of dealing are admissible. Further, parol evidence is admissible always to show fraud, duress, or mistake (mutual or unilateral). None of these realities constitutes a true exception to the parol evidence rule.

3. *Conditions Precedent*

Suppose Jermaine and Ty, after protracted negotiations, create a ninety-page writing, exhaustively detailed, complete with merger clause, under which Jermaine, as owner of twenty-four patents, is to license all of them to Ty for $40 million. The parties are poised to sign the writing, but before they do, Ty says, "Can we agree that this contract will not be effective unless my lawyer approves it?" Jermaine says, "Yes." The parties do then sign. Notwithstanding the parol evidence rule, *that* oral agreement is effective. Jermaine is obliged to contact his lawyer and seek her approval. And, if the lawyer disapproves of the arrangement, the contract does not operate. This stands as a true exception to the parol evidence rule, for it allows the parties to enforce a term not included in their writing—that each party's duty to perform is subject to the condition precedent that Ty's lawyer should approve their arrangement.

J.   The Most Important Thing of All: How the Courts Will, *Really*, Apply the Parol Evidence Rule

Having said, now, that there's no way to make "heads or tails" of the parol evidence rule, we must nonetheless give you a meaningful way to work with it. So, although no other authority ever has quite stated the rule in this way, we advise you that, whatever courts might say about the rule, they apply it, by and large, <u>in this way</u>:

> *(1) If a contractual writing is complete on its face, meaning that on its own, it appears to provide all terms necessary to a contract dealing with its subject matter, then it is an integration, either partial or total; and*

(a) if such a writing features a merger clause, then it is a total integration, meaning that the writing is the contract, the contract is the writing, and that's that; but

(b) if such a writing does not feature a merger clause, then it is a total integration or partial integration depending on whether or not the court deems important/material/critical the term at issue — the one omitted from the writing that one of the parties seeks to include in the contract.

(2) If a purported contractual writing is not complete on its face, meaning that it fails to provide one or more terms necessary to a contract dealing with its subject matter, then whether or not it features a merger clause (a) it is no integration at all, and (b) the contract at issue includes any and all terms that are proven by any and all evidence including the writing and all else.

That's as close to any true parol evidence rule as we (or anyone) can come.

K.   The Closers

QUESTIONS 8 & 9. Eston is producing a fashion show at a local arts chamber on May 10. He asks Falil to serve as announcer. Falil expresses interest, and before several witnesses, the parties talk and negotiate. Eston begins: "Well, it will require two rehearsals of about four hours each. Then the show itself will last for about two hours. I thought perhaps I'd pay you—for the two rehearsals and the show—$2,000 total." Falil replies, "That's fine; I'll do it. I'd like to be paid $1,000 after the first rehearsal and $1,000 at the completion of the show. Also, if I should put more than twenty hours into all of these efforts, I'd like to be paid an additional $50 for each such hour." Eston says, "It's a deal."

The parties then agree on every other detail they can think of, including rehearsal dates and times, Falil's wardrobe, and music to accompany the show. After the parties agree on all details, Falil asks, "Shall we put all of this in writing?" Eaton answers, "I don't think we need to, do we?" "I guess not," Falil says, "but I would like to put in writing some general statement to the effect that I will serve as announcer and how much I will be paid." On March 12, the parties create and sign this writing, which they label "Contract":

Eston Eaves and Falil Ford acknowledge, between them, an agreement under which (1) Eston Eaves will produce a fashion show at the Hazelton Arts Chamber on May 10 of this year and (2) Falil Ford will serve as announcer for a total compensation of $2,000, no less and no more.

QUESTION 8. On April 9, Eston calls for the first rehearsal and Falil properly performs his part. At the rehearsal's end, Falil asks Eston for his first $1,000 payment. Eston refuses to pay, asserting that "according to our contract of March 12, I need pay you only $2,000, which I will pay after the show itself is complete." Falil counters, "Don't you remember that before signing that short writing we agreed that you would pay me $1,000 after the first rehearsal and $1,000 after completion of the show itself?" "Yes," says Eston, "but we didn't put it in the writing, so as far as I'm concerned I need not do it. But I'll ask my lawyer her opinion." Eston consults with his attorney, who knows how the parol evidence rule is traditionally conceived. She advises him, "You are probably obliged to pay in installments as you agreed, even though the writing recites no such obligation." Apparently, the attorney believes that

I. the March 12 writing was a partial integration.
II. there were several witnesses to the parties' March 12 conversations.
III. payment in two installments would not contradict the March 12 writing.
A. I and II only
B. II and III only
C. I and III only
D. I, II, and III

ANALYSIS. Orally, these parties formed a detailed contract, and then created a writing. In their writing they failed to include Eston's promise to pay Falil in two installments. If that term is a part of the contract, notwithstanding its absence from the writing, then it must be so that (1) the writing is a partial integration, and (2) the term adds to the writing without contradicting it. Consequently, if Eston's lawyer understands the parol evidence rule and concludes that the prior oral agreement is binding — that Eston is obliged to pay in separate installments — she must have reached those two conclusions (however she did so). Options I and III make statements identical to those conclusions, meaning that the answer is **C** or **D**, depending on whether option II is true or false.

Option II makes an irrelevant statement. Again, the parol evidence rule is not a rule of evidence; it is a substantive rule of contract law. When two parties first form an oral (or written) agreement and then reduce it to a writing from which they omit one or more of its terms, the parol evidence rule provides this: Depending on whether the writing is a partial or total integration, the omitted terms are or are not enforceable. As to *how* and by what quantity of evidence the oral agreement, if enforceable, is to be proven, the parol evidence rule has nothing to say. (That, indeed, *is* a question of evidence law.) Options I and III belong to the right answer. Option II does not. **C** is right.

> **QUESTION 9.** The parties conduct the fashion show on May 10 as planned. By the time it's over, Falil has devoted twenty-six hours to the whole effort. He reminds Eston of their oral agreement under which Eston would pay him, in addition to the $2,000, another $50 for each hour he worked beyond twenty hours. Falil claims that he is owed a total of $2,300. Eston acknowledges the oral agreement, but nonetheless refuses to pay the additional $300, noting that "our actual contract provides for total payment of $2,000, no less and no more." If the parties' writing is a *partial* integration of their agreement, is Eston obliged to pay the additional $300 as orally agreed?
>
> **A.** Yes, because the writing is not a total integration
> **B.** Yes, because Eston acknowledges that component of the oral agreement
> **C.** No, because the writing expressly voids all prior oral agreements
> **D.** No, because that component of the oral agreement is inconsistent with the writing

ANALYSIS. Orally, these parties formed a contract providing that Eston should pay Falil $2,000 plus $50 per hour to the extent that he worked beyond twenty hours. They then created a writing that, we are told to assume, was a partial integration of their agreement. Consequently, any term on which the parties orally agreed before adopting the writing (a) *is* admissible if it adds to the writing's terms, without contradicting them, but (b) is inadmissible if it conflicts with the writing's terms.

The writing expressly provides that Falil's "total compensation" will be $2,000, "no less and no more." The prior oral agreement that allows for the possibility of payment greater than $2,000 is *inconsistent* with the writing; the writing refers to $2,000 and "no more," whereas the oral agreement provides for $2,000 plus the possibility of more. The oral agreement thus contradicts the writing and so does not become a part of the contract.

A answers "yes," so it's wrong. That the writing is only a partial integration does not render the oral agreement enforceable. If the prior oral agreement were consistent with the partial integration, then it would belong to the contract. But this oral agreement *contradicts* the writing because of the words "total" and "no more." As for **B**, Eston's acknowledgment of the oral agreement is irrelevant. If the term on which the parties orally agreed contradicts the partial integration, as it does, it is not a part of the contract, acknowledgment or not. **C** correctly answers "no," but it makes a peculiar statement. The writing does *not* provide, in so many words, that "prior oral agreements are void," meaning it does not expressly void the prior agreements. **C** is wrong.

D correctly answers "no" and properly states as its reason that the oral agreement contradicts the writing. That's why **D** is right.

 # Silver's Picks

1.	A
2.	A
3.	D
4.	B
5.	D
6.	A
7.	C
8.	C
9.	D

20

Duress, Undue Influence, and Unconscionability

A. The Doctrine of Duress
B. The Doctrine of Undue Influence
C. The Doctrine of Unconscionability
D. The Closer
✦ Silver's Picks

A. The Doctrine of Duress

Suppose X makes an offer to Y and asks, "Do you accept?" Y responds, "No, definitely not." X then repeats her offer, this time with a knife at Y's throat, saying, "How about now—*now* do you accept?" Rapidly and readily, Y says, "yes."

The doctrine of duress provides: *If parties A and B form a contract and B, by unlawful threat, has coerced A's assent, then at A's option, the contract is voidable.*[1] Restatement (Second) of Contracts §175(1) provides similarly:

> If a party's manifestation of assent is induced by an improper threat by the other party that leaves the victim no reasonable alternative, the contract is voidable by the victim.

In the knife case, therefore, this long-standing rule provides that X and Y form a contract, but the contract is voidable by Y.

---

1. Regarding the meaning of a "voidable" contract, see Chapter 16, section B.

1. So When Is a Threat "Improper"?

A threat is improper when one has no "legal right" to make it. Generally, that means that a party threatens to commit criminal or tortious conduct. Each of the following constitutes an improper threat:

- "Sign this settlement document or I'll sue you, even though I have no good claim against you, and I'll allege the right to garnish your wages even before the trial begins." That constitutes a threat to commit a tort called "vexatious litigation."
- "I offer to buy your car for $100. Accept or I'll destroy it." That constitutes a threat to commit a crime, generically called vandalism, and a tort called trespass to property.

Suppose Buyer and Seller legitimately contract for the purchase and sale of a service and thereafter Seller says:

- "I won't perform the contract unless you agree to pay more than the contract price on which we have already agreed." Seller has threatened the unlawful behavior of contractual breach.[2]

One who threatens to exercise a right or discretion to which he is otherwise entitled, not for its legitimate purpose but for personal gain, also makes an improper threat. In most instances, that too is a crime or tort. Suppose S was once convicted of embezzlement. She has served her sentence and now lives as a good and productive citizen in a community of persons who don't know of her conviction. B proposes to buy S's home for $200,000. S says she is not willing to sell it for that price. Nonetheless, B prepares and signs a writing whose terms require that S sell her home to him for $200,000. He presents the writing to S, saying, "Sign or I'll tell the entire community of your criminal past." He has made an improper threat (and has, in most states, committed the crime generically called blackmail or extortion, depending on the nature of the threat).

QUESTION 1. Thaddeus, Vore's employee, steals $10,000 from Vore's safe. Vore knows nothing of the theft, but unbeknownst to Thaddeus, Banya witnesses it and shortly thereafter creates, dates, and signs this writing titled "Agreement":

Agreement: March 12, 2019; 8:00 a.m.

Banya Banes, "Payee," hereby agrees not to report to Vore Volee or to any other person or authority the activities and conduct she witnessed on the part of Thaddeus Thames on the evening of

---

2. Of course, any resulting "modification" would be unenforceable for lack of consideration, showing that courts invoke the duress doctrine, as they do so many others, when they should rest on other fundamental rules of contract. Modification of a contract, like formation itself, requires consideration from both contracting parties (except as to contracts for the sale of goods; see Chapter 14, section B).

> March 11, 2019 between the hours of 6:00 P.M. and 7:00 P.M., in exchange for which the said Thaddeus Thames agrees to pay her $5,000 within 24 hours.
>
> Banya approaches Thaddeus, presents him with the writing, and says, "Sign or I'll report you to Vore and to the police. You know very well what I'm talking about." Thaddeus reads the writing and signs it. The parties
>
> A. formed no contract, because Banya did not make her offer in good faith.
> B. formed no contract because Thaddeus manifested no assent to Banya's offer.
> C. formed no contract because Banya made only a gratuitous promise.
> D. formed a contract voidable at Thaddeus's option.

ANALYSIS. The doctrine of duress provides that when an offeree accepts an offer in response to an offeror's improper threat, the parties form a contract that is voidable at the offeree's (victim's) option.

One generally has a right to report another's misconduct to whomever she pleases (unless she is bound, for example, by a professional confidence). But one commits a legal wrong (blackmail) when she offers not to exercise that right and to "keep quiet," demanding value in exchange for her silence. The abuse of such a right constitutes an improper threat, which in turn means the resulting agreement between blackmailer and victim is voidable for duress.

Banya has misused her right, precisely as described above (and, therefore, likely committed blackmail). Prevailing legal thought provides that the parties formed a contract voidable by Thaddeus, the victim, for duress. **A** is wrong for stating that the parties did not form a contract. They did. Further, as to the failure of good faith, Banya, in making her offer, likely committed the crime of blackmail, but that does not mean, exactly, that she made her *offer* in bad faith. She made it honestly in the sense that (as far as we know) she intended to keep her promise of silence. Further, one who proposes a bargain in bad faith — intending at the outset not to honor her own part of it — does not fail, for that reason, to make an offer. She likely commits a fraud, but her proposition stands nonetheless as an offer.

Regarding **B,** most authorities, including Restatement (Second) §175, would hold that Thaddeus did manifest assent by signing the paper and that he did thereby form a contract.[3] The contract is voidable at Thaddeus's option,

---

3. Logic (but not "black letter law") dictates that an "assent" elicited by duress is not an acceptance. An offeree accepts, after all, when he says or does that which would lead the offeror reasonably to believe that he assents — truly, by free will — to all terms of the offer (Chapter 2, section D). When, under unlawful threat, an offeree purports to "accept" an offer, an offeror cannot reasonably believe that he has truly assented to the offeror's proposed bargain. Logic dictates that an "assent" produced by duress is no acceptance at all and, in logic, such parties should fail to form a contract. That the law does recognize a contract — a voidable contract — probably reflects its wish to punish the wrongdoer by "sticking" him with the "agreement" he forcibly obtained, should the offeree wish to enforce it.

but it is a contract nonetheless. **C** states, once again, that the parties formed no contract and that's wrong. Further, it's wrong to characterize Banya's commitment as a gratuitous promise. One makes a gratuitous promise when she makes it in exchange for nothing. A gratuitous promise is unenforceable because the promisee gives no consideration, meaning the parties form no contract (Chapter 12). That's not this case. In exchange for her promise, Banya took, in exchange, Thaddeus's promise to pay her $5,000. **A**, **B**, and **C** are wrong, so **D** had better be right. And it is. According to prevailing legal thought, these parties formed a contract, Thaddeus doing so under duress. The contract is therefore voidable at his option. **D** is right.

2. What If the Threat Comes from a Third Person?

Restatement (Second) §175(2) provides:

> If a party's manifestation of assent is induced by one who is not a party to the transaction, the contract is voidable by the victim unless the other party to the transaction in good faith and without reason to know of the duress either gives value or relies materially on the transaction.

Suppose at

> Time 1, with a gun to B's head, A says to B, "If C makes you an offer, you'd better accept it," then
> Time 2, C comes to B with an offer, and B proclaims his assent.

Let's ask: Is the contract between C and B voidable? Let's answer: It depends. If, at time 2, when B proclaimed his acceptance, C knew or had reason to know of A's improper threat, then the contract is voidable at B's option. But if C did *not* know and had no reason to know what A had done and, furthermore, C has relied to his detriment on the contract, then the contract is not voidable. B must honor it. (B's remedies for the wrong are (1) to sue A for her wrongful conduct in making the threat and (2) to report her to police/prosecutorial authorities for criminal prosecution.)

QUESTION 2. Vincent, a married man, owns Blackacre. Fern makes a signed written offer to buy it for $1 million, and Vincent rejects the offer, both parties acting honestly in all respects. Diana is Fern's daughter. She badly wishes that her mother own Blackacre. Without Fern's knowledge, Diana approaches Vincent and says, "If my mother makes another offer for Blackacre, you'll accept it. If you don't, I'll tell your wife about the affair we had." Fern again presents Vincent with her written offer to buy Blackacre for $1 million. Because of Diana's threat, Vincent accepts and signs the writing. Is the resulting contract voidable at Vincent's option?

A. Yes, because Vincent's assent followed from Diana's improper threat

> **B.** Yes, if Fern had a basis on which to know the substance of Diana's conversation with Vincent
> **C.** Yes, if Fern knew of Diana's affair with Vincent
> **D.** No, if after forming the contract Fern acted in reasonable reliance on it, to her detriment

ANALYSIS.   If B and C form a contract, B having assented to its terms because a third party, A, subjected him to an improper threat, then (1) if C knows or has reason to know of A's threat, the contract is voidable at B's option, and (2) if C did not know of A's threat *and* C has relied to his detriment on the contract, then the contract is not voidable; B must honor it. In this case, Fern is Party C (the offeror), Vincent is Party B (the victim), and Diana is Party A (the wrongdoer). In order that the contract be declared voidable, it takes only the single showing (a) that Fern knew or should have known what Diana did to render the contract voidable, or (b) that Fern did not rely on the contract to her detriment. Conversely, it takes *two* showings to render the contract fully enforceable: (1) that Fern did not know or have reason to know what Diana did, and (2) that Fern reasonably relied on the contract to her detriment.

The story tells us nothing as to whether Fern did or did not know of Diana's threat to Vincent. Consequently, a correct answer choice, be it "yes" or "no," must provide us with facts on that subject. **A** fails to do that; reading **A** we still do not know the state of Fern's knowledge regarding Diana's threat to Vincent, and so we cannot say its "yes" answer is correct. **A** is wrong. **C** fails in the same way. It posits that Fern knew of the affair, but says nothing as to what Fern knew of *Diana's threat*. Without that information, we still cannot answer "yes" or "no." That leaves **B** and **D**.

D posits that Fern reasonably relied on the contract. That alone is not sufficient to render the contract enforceable. In order that **D** be correct, it would have to posit also that Fern neither knew nor had reason to know of Diana's threat to Vincent. But **D** is silent on that point, and so we cannot answer the question "yes" or "no." **D** is wrong.

B posits that Fern "had a basis" on which to know "the substance of Diana's conversation with Vincent." Those words mean that Fern had reason to know of Diana's threat. That additional information allows us to conclude that **B** is right.

B.   The Doctrine of Undue Influence

The rule of undue influence arose in equity (see Appendix section E), but the common law has now adopted it. Before reciting it, let's look at a couple of cases.

Case 1:   Yul inherits from his grandfather a 100 percent interest in his grandfather's business. He leaves day-to-day operation of the business to Mary, who has served as the grandfather's business manager for decades. At some point, Mary decides that she wishes to purchase for herself, for her own purposes, certain real property owned by the business, a transaction to which Yul would have to agree. Knowing that the property is worth $50 million and believing that it will soon appreciate dramatically, Mary "advises" Yul to sell her the property for $10 million. Trusting Mary, Yul forms a contract to sell Mary the property.

Here's the rule: *If (1) the relationship between parties A and B (i) affords A a position of "dominance" over B or (ii) justifies B in trusting in A's judgment and (2) A, abusing such dominance or trust, for her own purposes, induces B to form a contract with her, then on the grounds of "undue influence," at B's option, the contract is voidable.*

Most courts would rule that Yul and Mary have such relationship as justifies Yul in trusting Mary's judgment. Most would further rule that Mary induced Yul to enter the contract for her own purposes and thus abused Yul's trust. Consequently, on the ground of undue influence and, more specifically, abuse of trust, it would (should) rule the contract voidable at Yul's option.

Case 2:   Wendy cares for Genna, a sick, weak woman of ninety-eight. Genna depends on Wendy for her care, day to day, hour to hour, minute to minute, microsecond to microsecond. Genna's physician visits her at her home, which she has not left for seven years. Wendy wants to purchase all of Genna's stock in ABC Corporation for $10 per share when, as Wendy knows, each share is indisputably worth $90. Wendy prepares and presents to Genna a writing that calls for Genna to sell her the shares for $10 each. Genna reads it and says, "I don't think I can do this without advice from an attorney or accountant." "Sign now," Wendy says, "or I'll cease to take care of you; I'll resign." Genna signs.

Any sane court will rule that (1) Wendy's position in Genna's life was one of dominance, and that (2) she used her position to induce Genna's acceptance and, therefore, (3) on the ground of undue influence and, more specifically, abuse of dominant position, the contract is voidable at Genna's option.

Let's ask: Why is that not a case of duress? Most authorities would likely answer that Wendy's threat is not an "improper" one, as that term operates in the duress doctrine. By resigning her position, Wendy would not be committing a tort or crime. Neither would she thereby exercise, for an illegitimate purpose, some discretion that is hers (although that's debatable). On the other hand, the existing contract under which Wendy cares for Genna (probably not in writing) likely includes, implicitly, Wendy's promise not to leave her post without such notice as will allow Genna to secure a replacement. Consequently, if Genna reasonably understands Wendy's statements as a threat to leave her side immediately, without giving her opportunity to find a new caregiver, then, probably, Wendy *has* made an improper threat and the contract is voidable on both the grounds of duress (*and* undue influence.[4])

C.   The Doctrine of Unconscionability

Through 1950 or so, contract law did not concern itself with the fairness of contractual terms. The common law nowhere provided that a contract was enforceable only if its terms were fair, or unenforceable if they were not.[5] The common law bound two parties to their agreement whether its terms were consummately fair or so inexpressively and repulsively one-sided as to offend the conscience of right-thinking persons. "A deal was a deal," and "a contract was a contract."

In 1962, the Uniform Law Commission promulgated the Uniform Commercial Code, which all states have now adopted in one version or another. UCC §2-302 invested contract law, for the first time, with a rule that takes account of *fairness*: "If the court . . . finds [a] contract . . . to have been unconscionable at the time it was made the court may refuse to enforce [it]." Section 2-302, of course, is statutory and so does not represent the common law. Further, UCC Article 2 applies only to contracts that concern the sale of goods, and to no others.

But between 1962 and the present, the doctrine of unconscionability as thus created by the UCC wiggled its way into the common law.[6] In all states, it now applies to contracts for the sale of goods, pursuant to UCC §2-302, and to all other contracts as well, by modern common law. Restatement (Second) §208, promulgated in 1972, provides:

> If a contract or term thereof is unconscionable at the time the contract is made, a court may refuse to enforce the contract, or may enforce the remainder of the contract without the unconscionable term, or may so limit the application of any unconscionable term as to avoid any unconscionable result.

Hence, contract law does, today, concern itself with the fairness of contractual terms. For contracts involving the sale of goods, UCC §2-302 provides that a court may refuse to enforce a contract or contractual term if it is

---

4. In view of the deceit that usually accompanies a case of undue influence, it might be that most cases of undue influence are, also, cases of fraud and, where the defendant is a fiduciary, a breach *of* his fiduciary duty.

5. Courts of equity, however, have for centuries taken account of a contract's fairness or unfairness when deciding to enforce it. We discuss that matter later in this chapter and, more elaborately still, in Appendix, section E.

6. For example, in 1965, borrowing from UCC §2-302, the U.S. Court of Appeals for the D.C. Circuit first announced that the D.C. common law would thenceforth render a contract unenforceable where "the element of unconscionability is present at the time a contract is made." Williams v. Walker-Thomas Furniture Co., 350 F.2d 445, 449 (D.C. Cir. 1965).

unconscionable. As for other contracts, the common law now embodies an analogous provision, as reflected today in the Restatement.

1. *How and by Whom Is It Decided That a Contract Is Unconscionable?*

Under UCC Article 2 and by common law, the question of unconscionability is one of law, not fact, which is a fanciful way of stating that even in a jury trial, it belongs to the judge, not the jury. If, as to a suit for breach of contract, one party asserts that the agreement (or one of its terms) is unconscionable, the court holds a hearing, without a jury, to decide whether that's so.

The courts are not unanimous in their conception of an unconscionable contract. Yet, they do reflect some meaningful commonality as to the applicable criteria. The best general statement we (or anyone) can make on the matter is "soft" and a little uncertain of shape. Nonetheless, it's meaningful:

If, in evaluating a contract, a court finds (a) unfairness in the bargaining process ("procedural unconscionability") and, in light of that unfairness, (b) "oppression" of one party ("substantive unconscionability"), then it will find the contract unconscionable.

Let's take those words apart and see what they mean.

Unfairness in the Bargaining Process: "Procedural Unfairness."   Modern decisions indicate that as to two parties A and B, the *bargaining process* (meaning the combined processes of invitation to deal, offer, and acceptance) that ultimately spawns a contract is itself unfair to Party B when the court finds, singly or in combination, to some critical degree, that

1. Party B lacked a meaningful opportunity to understand the contract's terms (leading to "unfair surprise"), and/or
2. Party A subjected B to some form of "pressure," and/or
3. Party A presented the terms to B as a take-it-or-leave-it proposition so that B had no opportunity to negotiate (in which case the contract is termed a "contract of adhesion"), and/or
4. Party A knew that B was subject to some infirmity or weakness.

As to a given bargaining process between two parties, a court "weighs" the total "quantity" of the four factors. If it sees some critical "quantity" of *total* unfairness, whether one or all four factors be present, then it will find the resulting contract infected by an unfair bargaining process.

Let's Explain Further.   Think of the four factors just mentioned. By crude metaphor, imagine that each has "weight"—that each is measurable in pounds. Suppose, further, that a given judge believes that ten pounds of these factors, in any combination, create an unfair bargaining process ("procedural unfairness"). Imagine, now, that, as to a given contract between Parties A and B, the judge finds to the extent of

- two pounds, that A lacked meaningful opportunity to understand the contract's terms;
- five pounds, that B exerted pressure on A;
- three pounds, that B proposed the terms to A as a take-it-or-leave-it proposition;
- one pound, that B knew A was suffering from some degree of dementia.

In sum, the process carries, in this judge's mind, eleven pounds of unfairness, which amount exceeds her ten-pound threshold, wherefore she finds that the parties formed their contract pursuant to an unfair bargaining process.

Oppression: "Substantive Unconscionability/Unfairness."   Generally, the authorities agree on (varied iterations) of this statement: *A contract or its terms are oppressive, meaning "substantively unconscionable/unfair" if the court finds that, under the circumstances that surround formation, the terms are so harsh or one-sided as to shock the conscience of the court.*

"Circumstances that surround formation" means the bargaining process, which we just considered. In other words, procedural unfairness (unfairness in the bargaining process) and substantive unfairness (oppressiveness of terms) do not reflect separate inquiries. Rather, the nation's courts deem a given term substantively fair or unconscionable depending on the nature of the bargaining process, which is, perhaps, the only relevant "circumstance" that surrounds the parties when they form their contract.

If a court deems a bargaining process perfectly fair, then never, it seems, will it find the contract's terms substantively unfair. If the court deems the bargaining process unfair, then the term at issue may be unfair, depending on how the court evaluates it in light *of* the unfairness that infected the bargaining process. As to one bargaining process, a given term might be perfectly fair. As to another, that same term might be *un*fair.

Illustration 1: A Term That in Light of the Bargaining Process Is Fair.   Pam is a savvy, sophisticated lady who operates an investment bank. She contacts ConCorp to secure its consulting services. After brief discussion, ConCorp presents Pam with its standard written form contract prepared by its lawyers, with its blank spaces completed so that they (1) name Pam as the "Client," (2) describe the services ConCorp will deliver, and (3) set forth ConCorp's fee of $500,000.

At ConCorp's offices, holding the writing already signed by ConCorp, Pam says to ConCorp's representative, "Before I read this document, are you negotiable on any of these terms?" "Perhaps," is the answer. "Why don't you and your lawyer read it and get back to us with any changes you propose?" Pam reads the document together with her attorney. The two of them note that the writing sets forth this clause entitled "Arbitration Option"[7]:

---

7. In nearly any legal dispute, two parties may waive their right to litigate in court and instead choose arbitration. In all states, and under federal law where relevant, such parties are bound by the arbitrators' decision. Except in very limited circumstances, arbitration decisions are unappealable.

If either party hereto should assert that the other has breached this contract, then, at ConCorp's option — if and only if ConCorp so decrees — the parties will not, in that regard, resort to judicial litigation, but will instead submit the cause to binding arbitration pursuant to the Commercial rules and regulations of the American Arbitration Association. In this respect, Client shall have no reciprocal option; the decision that any allegation of breach should be resolved by judicial litigation or by arbitration shall rest solely with ConCorp, wherefore Client renounces his/her right to make any choice or decision in that regard and renounces, also, therefore, what would otherwise be his/her/its right to have the relevant dispute adjudicated by a court of competent jurisdiction.

After she and her attorney study the writing in full, Pam tells ConCorp's representative that she wants to eliminate or amend the arbitration clause. In response, ConCorp consults with its attorney, considers Pam's proposal carefully, but ultimately decides that it is not willing to eliminate or modify the arbitration provision. When Pam receives this news, she says, "Well, I've already thought about it and, although I'd prefer to eliminate or modify the arbitration clause, I do need your service and I am, reluctantly, agreeable to signing the document as it is." She then signs on the "dotted line."

After three months, Pam asserts that ConCorp's performance is defective. The parties fail to settle the dispute between themselves, and Pam announces her intention to bring suit for breach of contract. ConCorp informs Pam that the dispute will be resolved by arbitration, and not by a court. Pam protests: "My attorney regards the arbitration clause as unconscionable; it's entirely one-sided. It allows you the option to compel arbitration, but gives me no such right. It requires that I waive my right to sue in court, if you so decree, but it exacts no such waiver from you." The parties then find themselves in court before a judge, who must decide whether the arbitration clause is unconscionable and hence whether it is enforceable.

Without question, any judge would rule this arbitration clause enforceable. She would hold a hearing and hear evidence, first, on the bargaining process, evaluating it according to the four factors previously described. No doubt, she would observe the following:

1. Pam had full opportunity to understand the arbitration provision, she consulted with her own attorney as to its significance, and she did in fact understand it, wherefore it subjected her to no "unfair surprise."
2. ConCorp did not in any way subject Pam to pressure.
3. Although ConCorp was ultimately unwilling to remove or modify the arbitration provision, it did seriously *entertain* Pam's proposal and so did not present its terms to Pam as a take-it-or-leave-it proposition, meaning that ConCorp did not victimize Pam with a "contract of adhesion."
4. ConCorp had no reason to suspect any weakness or infirmity on Pam's part (and, indeed, Pam had none).

Then, having thus evaluated the bargaining process, a judge would examine the arbitration clause and conclude that it is not, under these circumstances (the bargaining process), oppressive. Upon those findings, in turn, the court would certainly decide that the arbitration clause is not unconscionable and that ConCorp has every right to enforce it.

Illustration 2: Under Other Circumstances, the Same Arbitration Clause Is Unfair.   Suppose Jackson visits a hospital emergency room in severe pain, with dizziness, nausea, and partial paralysis of his right arm. Before treating him, hospital personnel present him with a document entitled "Contract for Emergency Room Treatment," demanding that he sign. Frightened and in pain, he does so immediately. Unbeknownst to him, the document includes this provision labeled "Arbitration Option":

> If in connection with or as alleged result of treatment given to Patient, Patient should allege or contend that Hospital or any of its personnel has committed professional negligence or medical malpractice and if the parties are unable, themselves, to resolve the resulting dispute, then, at Hospital's option, and only at Hospital's option, Patient shall submit his cause to binding arbitration pursuant to the rules and regulations of the United States Arbitration Organization, and Patient shall bring his action in court only if Hospital does not decree that he/she shall submit it to arbitration. Patient understands and agrees that he/she has no corresponding right and that should Hospital have cause to bring action against Patient for, without limitation, payment, then it shall, in that case too, have the sole, exclusive option to choose between litigation and arbitration, wherefore, in either such instance, Patient waives what would otherwise be his/her right to pursue judicial litigation.

Emergency room personnel do not treat Jackson for thirty hours, insisting that he has no serious condition and that he "can wait." In fact, Jackson is suffering from a meningeal infection, which is curable with timely diagnosis and treatment. But for lack *of* timely diagnosis and treatment, Jackson is rendered permanently blind and deaf.

Jackson alleges medical malpractice by the hospital and its employees. He wants to sue in court. The hospital insists that the matter be submitted to arbitration. The parties find themselves in court before a judge, who must decide whether the arbitration provision is unconscionable and, therefore, whether it is enforceable.

We borrow the foregoing facts, by and large, from *Weidman v. Tomaselli,*[8] where the court made the following observations as to the four factors relevant to unfair bargaining:

1. The patient had no meaningful opportunity to know of the arbitration provision.
2. The urgency of the patient's situation subjected him to "pressure."

---

8.   365 N.Y.S.2d 681 (City Ct.), *aff'd,* 386 N.Y.S.2d 276 (App. Div. 1975).

3. The hospital had presented the contractual document to the patient as a take-it-or-leave-it proposition, wherefore it gave rise to a "contract of adhesion."
4. The patient's condition itself created a temporary infirmity or a weakness, and the hospital had plain and obvious reason to know that.

Then, evaluating the arbitration provision, the court observed that the purported waiver of the fundamental right to bring a civil action in a court of law is not enforceable under such circumstances; this arbitration clause was unconscionable.

As to what renders a contract or term unconscionable, we now have sufficient basis to articulate something akin to a rule: *As between two parties, A and B, a contract or contractual term is unconscionable as to Party A if, in the court's determination, the relevant bargaining process was, in sum total, unfair because to some critical degree:*

> *(1) (a) Party A lacked a meaningful opportunity to understand the contract (or the relevant term), thus producing "unfair surprise"; and/or*
>
> *(b) Party B subjected A to "pressure"; and/or*
>
> *(c) Party B presented the terms to Party A on a take-it-or-leave-it basis, so that A had no opportunity to negotiate (in which case the contract is termed a contract of "adhesion"); and/or*
>
> *(d) Party B knew that Party A was subject to some infirmity or weakness;*
>
> *and*
>
> *(2) In light of the unfairness in the bargaining process ((1)(a-d)), the contract or terms at issue are harsh, oppressive, or so one-sided as to shock the conscience of the court.*

So let's understand this: In order that a court deem a contract or term substantively unconscionable, it must first ask itself if the contract at issue suffers from procedural unconscionability. If its answer is "yes," then and only then can it ask itself if the contract or term is substantively unconscionable. Consequently, the very same term appearing in two different contracts might be enforceable in one and unconscionable in the other if, in one case, the court deems the bargaining process fair and in the other it does not.

QUESTIONS 3 & 4. Augusta is a wealthy and sophisticated businesswoman. Brigid is a poor widow, unable to read or write. With eight young children in her care, Brigid barely keeps her family fed and clothed by working her very small farm and laboring separately late into every night as a seamstress. Correctly believing that Brigid urgently needs money, Augusta approaches her with what she calls an "offer of kindness": "I am prepared to give you $100 right now, which you need never repay, in exchange only for such consideration as is provided in this document, which I have already signed. If you sign right now, I will immediately pay you the $100."

The document provides that Augusta will pay Brigid $100 on the execution of the writing and, in consideration of that payment, Brigid will, three years later (a) convey to Augusta all of her property, real and personal, regardless of its market value (except for one set of clothes for Brigid and each of her children), and (b) work ten hours per week as Augusta's personal seamstress for five years, without compensation. As consideration for all of that, Augusta promises only $100.

Brigid signs the document, whereupon Augusta immediately pays her $100. Three years later, Augusta demands that Brigid honor the terms of their contract; when Brigid learns what the contract provides, she refuses to honor its terms. Augusta brings suit against Brigid in a court *of law* (as opposed to a court of equity), seeking monetary damage equal to the market value of Brigid's property, real and personal, plus the amount necessary to engage a seamstress ten hours weekly for five years. Brigid secures a lawyer who agrees to represent her pro bono[9] and who asserts that the court should not award damages. Brigid's lawyer offers to present evidence showing that the bargaining process was extremely unfair and the terms shockingly one-sided.

QUESTION 3. Assume all foregoing events occur in 1880. The court rejects the defendant's contentions and ultimately issues a judgment against her for the monetary damages Augusta requests. Its reasons might include these:

I.   Under the common law of 1880, the fairness of a contract's terms was not relevant to their enforceability.
II. A reasonable person would regard the contract as fair to both its parties.
III. One hundred dollars is adequate consideration for all of Brigid's promises.
A. I only
B. I and II
C. I and III
D. I, II, and III

---

9. The Latin phrase "pro bono" means, literally, "for the good" or "for the good of it." When, on occasion, lawyers work without pay, for charitable purposes, they need some fancy Latin phrase to mark the occasion. They don't use the simple phrase "without charge" or "just to be nice." Instead, they say, "I'm doing the work *pro bono*," as though the Latin somehow elevates their undertaking above that of all others who work charitably.

ANALYSIS.   Before 1950 or so, the common law took no account of a contract's fairness. If two parties formed a contract by (what passed for) mutual assent (usually embodied, of course, in offer and acceptance), then they were bound by its terms no matter how unjust anyone might think them to be. If two parties formed a contract and one of them breached it, the common law offered its usual remedy of monetary compensation ("damages")[10] without accounting at all for the contract's fairness.

Option II is false because no reasonable person would deem this contract fair to Brigid and, more to the point, the 1880 common law did not "care" whether contractual terms were fair. As to contract law, the matter of fairness was irrelevant. Because option II is false, **B** and **D** are wrong, leaving us with **A** and **C**. Both **A** and **C** include I, but **C** includes III as well. Option I, therefore, *must* be true, and it is: It's true for the same reason that option II is false. Pursuant to the common law of 1880, fairness was irrelevant to a contract's enforceability. If option III is true, then **C** is right. If option III is false, **A** is right.

Option III is true. As discussed in Chapter 12, section C, courts do not ordinarily inquire into the adequacy of consideration; the common law features no general requirement that consideration by one party be equal, in objective value, to that given by the other. That was true in 1880 as it is now. Option I is true, II is false, and III is true. **C** is right.

QUESTION 4. Now assume all foregoing events occur in 2019. The court accepts the defendant's contentions and dismisses Augusta's suit. Its reasons might include these:

  I. Modern common law allows a court to refuse enforcement of what it deems to be an unconscionable contract.
  II. Brigid had no meaningful way to understand the writing at the time she signed it.
  III. Monetary compensation is a legal remedy.
  A. I only
  B. I and II only
  C. II and III only
  D. I, II, and III

ANALYSIS.   As its principal remedy, the *law* (as opposed to equity) offers monetary compensation ("damages"), and a suit for breach of contract is a suit *in law* (Appendix, section E). Option III is correct. **A** and **B** omit it, so

---

10. See Chapter 25.

they're wrong. That leaves **C** and **D**, which means that option II *must* be correct, and it is; one of the factors that creates an unfair bargaining process is unfair surprise, meaning that one of the parties had no meaningful opportunity to know of the contract's terms (the first factor on our list of four factors). Brigid was unable to read, and Augusta gave her no description of the writing's terms. When Augusta demanded that Brigid convey all of her property to her and serve her as seamstress, Brigid suffered an unfair surprise.

C and **D** differ in that **D** includes option I and **C** does not. If option I is true, **D** is right. If it's false, **C** is right. And — it's true. By modern common law, a court may refuse to enforce — to award damages for — breach of a contract it deems unconscionable (as reflected in Restatement (Second) §208). Options I, II, and III are true. **D** is right.

QUESTIONS 5 & 6. As Bella emerges from TarMart Store, Sidney approaches and offers her a membership in "Consumer's Club." He explains that Consumer's Club members are entitled to enormous discounts on an equally enormous number of goods. Bella, wearing a large hearing aid, responds, "I don't understand." Sidney says, "Take from your bag one item that you just purchased in TarMart." Bella pulls out a package of twelve Snow-White soap bars, marked $10.95. Sidney then opens the Consumer's Club catalog to show the same package of twelve Snow-White soap bars priced at $6.95.

As Sidney reaches into Bella's grocery bag for another item, Bella says, "I don't think I'm interested." Sidney responds, "But you should be — it's good for you and your family. Think of all the money you'll save — money that you can put toward your family's other needs!" Bella asks, "What'd you say? I don't hear so well." Sidney repeats his pitch and again opens his catalog. "I'm not sure I understand how the club works," Bella says, "and I really have to go." "Well, just sign right here at the bottom of this page," answers Sidney, "and you can go with the happy knowledge that you belong to Consumer Club." Bella, worn down and running late, says, "All right, where do I sign?" Sidney points. After glancing at the document's tiny print, Bella signs. Sidney hurriedly gives Bella a copy of the writing, and departs.

Unbeknownst to Bella, the writing's terms provide that

- Consumer Club's catalog prices are subject to change without notice.
- Members must pay a $200 membership fee within thirty days of signing, and suffer a $25 penalty for every month or partial month for which such payment is late.
- Members who order less than $1,000 worth of merchandise from the catalog per year must pay a $300 "failure to purchase" charge.

- Members must pay an annual renewal fee, which is subject to change without notice.
- Members not wishing to renew must contact Consumer's Club by signed writing six months before their memberships end. (The document, however, provides no address or other contact information for Consumer's Club.)
- Consumer's Club does not send bills or requests for fee or penalty payments, but requires members to keep track of all required fees and send them as outlined in the signed writing.

Four years after Bella signs the document, Consumer's Club contacts her and demands payment of $2,000 in membership fees, $1,200 in penalties, and $4,000 in annual "failure to purchase charges," for a total of $7,200. Bella refuses to pay, Consumer's Club brings suit, and Bella's attorney asserts that the contract is unenforceable for the reason that its terms are unconscionable.

QUESTION 5. In deciding the question of unconscionability, the court should consider evidence tending to show that

I. Bella's hearing aid was visible to Sidney.
II. The document's writing was printed in very small type.
III. Sidney had once been convicted of criminal mischief.
IV. The terms gave very little to Bella and took much from her.
A. I only
B. I and III only
C. I, II, and IV only
D. I, II, III, and IV

ANALYSIS. The rule of unconscionability requires first that the court find compelling evidence of an unfair bargaining process. So let's see about that: The writing was set forth in very small type, depriving Bella of a meaningful opportunity to read it, and hence to understand it, thus subjecting her to unfair surprise. Option II, therefore, describes evidence relevant to the matter of unfair bargaining process/procedural unconscionability. The correct answer should include II, meaning that **A** and **B** are wrong.

Sidney subjected Bella to high-pressure sales talk, even after Bella made clear that she was not interested. Bella made plain to Sidney that her hearing was impaired, and her hearing aid was visible to him. That means Sidney had reason to know of her infirmity, wherefore option I makes a true statement. The correct answer must include options I and II, which leaves us, still, with **C** and **D**. As for substantive unconscionability, Consumer Club designed its writing on the philosophy of get-the-most-give-the-least, and surely its terms are so abjectly one-sided as to shock the conscience of any (sane) judge. They are in the nature of what we colloquially call a "scam." Option IV, therefore, describes evidence relevant to substantive unconscionability, and the correct answer must include it. We're left, *still*, with **C** and **D**. They differ in that **D** includes option III and **C** doesn't. If option III is true, the answer is **D**. If option III is false, it's **C**. And—it's false. As to this contract, Sidney's criminal record or other facets of his background are not relevant to unconscionability/ unfairness, procedural or substantive. Options I, II, and IV make true statements; III does not. **C** is right.

QUESTION 6. Beyond the facts already described, Bella's assertion of unconscionability would be most strengthened if she were able to show (1) that she asked Sidney if she could have time to read the document, and (2) that Sidney responded,

A. "No, but if you choose not to sign today we might contact you again if you'll provide me with your contact information."
B. "Certainly you may take home a copy of the writing and read it. But if you wish to join Consumer's Club, we'll require that you sign this document as it is; we won't change it in any way."
C. "Yes, but our offices have not yet approved any proposed changes to this writing."
D. "Yes, but be aware that our fees and charges might increase between now and the time, if ever, that you sign."

ANALYSIS.   None of the four choices concerns the contractual terms themselves. Rather, each adds a fact to the bargaining process, and we should search for that which touches most closely one of the four factors that create unfair bargaining/procedural unconscionability. In **D**, Sidney tells Bella about one of the writing's terms, to wit, that prices, fees, and charges are subject to change. Arguably, Sidney thus exerts pressure by implicitly encouraging Bella to sign then and there. **D** reflects *some* pressure, wherefore **D** *could* be right. But maybe one of the other choices beats it.

In **C**, Sidney warns Bella that his offices have not yet approved changes to the writing. On the one hand, that raises the specter of an adhesion contract (where terms are presented as a take-it-or-leave-it proposition), but on the other, it suggests that the offices might have *considered* proposed changes to the document's terms and would *consider* any that Bella proposes. **C** is not outright wrong; neither is it strikingly correct. In **A,** Sidney does nothing objectionable, but in **B** he expressly informs Bella that the terms are nonnegotiable—that to join the club, she'll have to sign the document as is. With that, certainly, Sidney presents the document as a take-it-or-leave it proposition, meaning that he proposes a "contract of adhesion." Among the choices, there-fore, **B** touches most closely one of the four factors that create unfair bargain-ing and so, **B** is right.

2. Unequal Bargaining Power

Two parties are said to have unequal bargaining power if one of them is somehow "holding all the cards." If, in the desert, A is dying of thirst and B has an abundance of water for sale, A and B have unequal bargaining power. A urgently needs what B has, but from A, B *needs* nothing. Consequently, B might demand from A $1 million for a glass of water.

More realistic situations of unequal bargaining power are those in which many buyers need or wish to secure some very scarce good or service and one or a few sellers have the commodity available. In such situations, the sellers (it is said) have the superior bargaining power. They are in a position to demand a very high price for what they have to sell. Similarly, a buyer might have superior bargaining power. Imagine that a poor but bril-liant chap named Inventor patents a process that will allow BigRichCorp, the world's only widget manufacturer, to create widgets at one-tenth its present costs and thus increase its profits by billions of dollars. Because BigRichCorp has no competitors, Inventor's process would be useful *only* to BigRichCorp. But BigRichCorp can get along without Inventor's pat-ented process, certainly much better than Inventor can get along without some kind of payment from BigRichCorp. These two parties, therefore, have unequal bargaining power. Inventor needs badly what BigRichCorp has to give (money), but BigRichCorp doesn't so badly need (or need at all) Inventor's device.

Does Unequal Bargaining Power Render a Bargaining Process Unfair? Both the Restatement (Second) §208 cmt. b and UCC §2-302 cmt. 1 say "no." The Restatement, however, states that as to any allegation of unconscionabil-ity, the fact of unequal bargaining power should heighten the court's sus-picion that one of the four relevant factors operates. Furthermore, courts frequently do cite unequal bargaining power, without consistency or explana-tion, as a factor that bears on procedural unconscionability. Consequently, we should consider that on some days in some courts for some cases, the factors that tend to create an unfair bargaining process are not four in number, but five — the fifth being "unequal bargaining power."

3. Unconscionability in the Equity Courts

To the law, unconscionability is something relatively new, but in equity courts, it's centuries old. As described in Appendix section E, our Anglo-American legal system once sharply separated courts of law from courts of equity. Today, in America, to a very significant degree, equity and law remain conceptually distinct,[11] but in most (but not all) states, and in the federal system, the same court*houses* serve both the jurisdictions of law and equity. The law court's judges double as the equity court's chancellors when a petitioner invokes the court's equitable jurisdiction.

What Do You Mean, "Invoke the Court's Equitable Jurisdiction"? For a more elaborate answer to that question, see Appendix, section E. (And NOW would be better than later.) Reduced to very simple terms, we may say this: Whether one brings his suit "at law" (in a court of law) or "in equity" (in a court of equity) depends on whether he seeks (1) monetary damages, in which case he brings an action at law, or (2) a court order/injunction, in which case he brings an action at equity.[12] He who brings a suit at equity is termed not a plaintiff but a "petitioner," and his opponent is not a defendant, but a "respondent." The imposing figure seated at the bench, clad in a black robe, removes her hat labeled "judge" (figuratively speaking) and dons the one labeled "chancellor in equity."

When one petitions an equity court, the chancellor first asks herself whether, in her opinion, the petitioner has suffered an "injustice" for which the "law offers no adequate remedy," which means, really, that she asks herself, "Are monetary damages inadequate to compensate this petitioner for the wrong done him, or does the law fail, even, to offer a cause of action that he can pursue?" If she answers "no," meaning that the petitioner does have an adequate remedy at law, then the petitioner is not eligible for equitable relief (an order/injunction), and the chancellor dismisses his case. If the chancellor answers "yes," meaning that the petitioner (in her opinion) has no adequate remedy at law, then, generally, she issues the order the petitioner requests or, in any event, such order/injunction as, in her opinion, is necessary to correct the injustice.

Suppose, for example, by signed writing, Seller contracts to sell Buyer a Rembrandt original for $900,000. Buyer tenders the purchase price but Seller then refuses to convey the painting; he breaches the contract. Buyer wants the painting—*that* painting. Seller owns it and, obviously, Buyer cannot buy it elsewhere. Consequently, Buyer believes that monetary damage will not compensate him for Seller's breach. It is not clear, even, that Buyer has suffered *any* monetary damage; he does not have the painting but he still has his $900,000. He wants that for which he bargained—the painting itself—and he stands ready to pay for it.

---

11. And don't let anyone tell you otherwise. Too many law students, hearing the statement, tried and true, that "law and equity have merged," come to believe that there is no difference between them. No impression could be more misguided. The two are, still, distinct. Be ignorant of that truth, and when you're in practice, some case will show you that you don't know what you're doing. Take a course called "Remedies."

12. When, as is so in the modern era, a *statute* expressly provides for the remedy of court order/injunction, it's kind of "up for grabs" as to whether an action brought under the statute is at law or equity. On the one hand, the remedy is classically equitable. On the other, the right to the remedy arises from a statute, and statutes are creatures of law.

Hence, Buyer brings not an action for breach of contract in a law court but, instead, a petition in equity demanding "specific performance" of the contract, which means a court order requiring that seller convey the painting for the agreed price. Quite likely, the chancellor (that same robed figure who functions as a judge in "cases at law") will issue the order for specific performance; Seller will be required to sell Buyer the painting or face imprisonment for contempt of court.

Equity's "Clean Hands" Rule. As instruments of "justice," the equity courts are to view every contest before them with an eye toward doing "justice" overall. Over the centuries, to serve that objective, they created a variety of defenses that respondents might assert against petitioners. If a petitioner seeks equitable relief but respondent shows that the petitioner himself, in connection with the very matter at issue, has behaved so badly as not to deserve the "justice" he seeks, then the chancellor is to dismiss the petitioner's case upon the ground that he has not come to a court of equity with "clean hands."

Let's add a fact to the Rembrandt case to illustrate the point. Buyer's first name is "Thief." He badly wants the Rembrandt painting and is willing to pay $900,000 to have it. Hoping he might not have to pay at all, he attempts, first, to steal the painting. Seller catches him in the act and demands an explanation. Buyer answers, "Well, uh, I really like the painting; I was just looking at it with the plan of making you an offer to buy it." Seller responds, "Oh, really? Really? Is that so? So what's your offer?" Buyer replies, "$900,000." Seller accepts the offer, and the parties create a perfectly structured writing that calls for Buyer to buy and Seller to sell, for $900,000, the Rembrandt original painting. Both parties sign and thus form a contract.

Buyer then tenders the purchase price and Seller, deciding he does not wish to sell, refuses the money and declines to convey the painting. Buyer brings an action "in equity" (meaning in a court of equity), requesting an order of specific performance—an order to Seller that he accept the purchase price and convey the painting, or face imprisonment for contempt of court.

Hearing Buyer/Petitioner's evidence of the events, the chancellor concludes that he has "suffered an injustice for which the law offers no adequate remedy"—that no amount of monetary damage is assessable and that none will make Buyer whole. On that basis, she is prepared to issue an order of specific performance—to order that Seller accept the purchase price and convey the painting to Buyer. However, Respondent/Seller demonstrates to the chancellor's satisfaction that before contracting to buy the painting, Buyer attempted to steal it. On that basis, the chancellor decrees, "This Petitioner, the buyer, has come to the equity court with unclean hands, and so I will not issue the order of specific performance to which he would otherwise be entitled."

Clean Hands and Unconscionability. We wrote, earlier, that the doctrine of unconscionability is new to the *law* over these last seventy years or so, and that's true. It is not, however, new to courts of *equity*. If as to an alleged contractual breach one seeks a court order of specific performance, then he is seeking an equitable remedy and is, therefore, "in" an equity court, subject to the defenses that equity has devised, including that of "clean hands." We noted above that a Buyer who attempts to steal a good that he later contracts to purchase comes to equity without clean hands. A petitioner's hands are similarly unclean if he seeks specific performance of a contract as to which he himself has subjected the respondent to a grossly unfair bargaining process, together with grossly one-sided terms. That means, really, that in the equity courts, a doctrine equivalent to that of unconscionability has operated for centuries.

In Campbell Soup v. Wentz, 172 F.2d 80 (3d Cir. 1948), Campbell Soup, Inc. had contracted with a grower/seller for the purchase of carrots. The grower/seller refused to honor the contract and Campbell's Soup sought specific performance, meaning it invoked the court's "equitable jurisdiction." Campbell's alleged that the kind of carrot at issue was virtually unobtainable except from this particular grower, and that the law's remedy of monetary damages offered no adequate relief.

The court agreed that monetary damages would not do justice and that specific performance would be an appropriate remedy were it not for the fact that the contract made too hard a bargain and too one-sided an agreement to entitle Campbell's Soup, Inc. to relief in a court of equity, "which is," wrote the court, "a court of conscience."

So, now we know: If, before 1952 (or so) a plaintiff brought an action *at law* for breach of contract, meaning that he sought the law's remedy of monetary damages, he was entitled to recover regardless of the fairness or unfairness of the relevant bargaining process or contractual terms. Today, the law embodies a doctrine of unconscionability; a law court may deny recovery to a plaintiff who sues at law for breach of contract if, in the court's opinion, the bargaining process and terms are so unfair as to render the contract unconscionable.

If, *two hundred years ago*, a petitioner alleged a breach of contract and brought action in an *equity* court for specific performance, unconscionability of the contract (bargaining process and/or terms) would render him ineligible for relief pursuant to the "clean hands" rule, and that continues to be so today. To law, unconscionability is relatively new. To equity, it's centuries old.

D.   The Closer

QUESTION 7. Do yourself a favor, please, and *read Appendix section E*, as you should already have done. (It will serve you well throughout the rest of your law school years and legal career.) Then read this next story. It's similar to that of Augusta and Brigid (Questions 3 and 4 above). This one, however, occurs in Texas in 1880 and involves a court of equity.

Belle is a poor widow, unable to read or write. Caring for nine young children (two of them invalids), she barely keeps her family fed and clothed by working her very small farm and laboring separately late into every night as a seamstress. As a seamstress, Belle is uniquely talented. Cruella is a wealthy and sophisticated businesswoman. An engineer has advised her that oil is likely located beneath Belle's small farm. Correctly believing that Belle urgently needs money (always), Cruella approaches her with an "offer of love."

Cruella: I am prepared to give you $10 that you need never repay. You need only sign this document, which states that I have given you $10. I'm very serious about wanting to help you, dear, so I've already signed. Look, here's a $10 dollar bill. Sign right now and I'll give it to you.

Belle: Well, Miss Cruella, I don't know my letters; I can't read words. Does the paper say anything else? Does it say only that you've given me $10? Is there more?

Cruella: Just a little bit. It states that years from now—years from now, dear, you'll do a few small things for me—some sewing, for example. Really, dear, it's nothing much.

Belle: That's very kind of you. I do know how to write my name, so I'll sign.

The document provides that Cruella will pay Belle $10 on the execution of the writing and, in consideration of that payment, Belle will, three years later, (a) convey to Cruella all of her property, real and personal, regardless of its market value (except for one set of clothing for Belle and each of her children), and (b) work thirty hours per week as Cruella's personal seamstress for five years, without compensation. It expressly provides that the $10 is consideration for all of Belle's property and work as a seamstress, and that Belle is satisfied with such consideration. Belle signs, and Cruella promptly pays her $10.

Three years later, Cruella demands that Belle convey to Cruella all of her property, real and personal, with the exceptions provided in the writing. She further demands that Belle begin working as Cruella's personal seamstress thirty hours per week. By this time, Belle has heard rumors about oil beneath her farmland. Hearing Cruella's demands, she refuses to comply. Cruella engages a lawyer and sues Belle. She asserts that there is uniqueness in Belle's properties and in her skills as a seamstress. Money, she says, can't buy what Belle owes her "under our contract." She wants not a monetary judgment but a court order that Belle do as the contract requires.

On that basis, Cruella goes to an equity court and petitions for a court order directing that Belle convey all of her property to Cruella, and serve Cruella as a seamstress thirty hours weekly for five years. Cruella's lawyer convinces the equity court that Belle's properties and services are unique, so that no monetary recovery at law will do her justice. But the chancellor nonetheless declines to issue the order Cruella seeks. His reasons might include

I. that under the common law of 1880, the fairness of a contract's terms was not relevant to their enforceability.
II. that the agreement between Belle and Cruella was so unfair as to offend the "King's conscience."
III. that equity courts do not aid those who come to it with unclean hands.

A. I
B. II only
C. II and III
D. I, II, and III

ANALYSIS. Equity courts are "courts of justice," with jurisdiction limited to situations in which, as the chancellor sees them, a petitioner has suffered an injustice for which the law (meaning common law or statute) offers no adequate remedy. Consequently where, in the chancellor's opinion, the petitioner has a legitimate grievance (has "suffered an injustice" such as would "offend the King's conscience") that monetary damages cannot correct, the court of equity will ordinarily issue a remedy in the form of an injunction or court order.

Yet, precisely because its mission *is* to "do justice," the equity court won't order specific performance of what it deems to be an unfair contract, for to do so would be to participate in an injustice. Stated in terms of a celebrated equitable maxim, "One who seeks equitable relief must come to court with clean hands,"[13] meaning that if, as to the very matter at issue, a petitioner has himself behaved badly (in the chancellor's opinion), then the equity court will not entertain his complaint of injustice. Consequently, an equity court will not aid a petitioner who first draws another into a wretchedly one-sided contract and then complains that the other has breached.

In this case, Cruella drew Belle into an abusive agreement knowing, moreover, that Belle could not read the contractual document. Further, Cruella told Belle that she would not have to repay the $10. Arguably, such was "technical," "legal" truth, but her statement was grossly misleading, since it implied, perhaps, that the money was Cruella's gift. Hence, with respect to this contract, Cruella behaved badly — very, very badly. Such is a reason that an equity court

---

13. There's another equitable maxim of similar meaning: "One who seeks equity must do equity."

would likely deny her a remedy—even though, by *law* (in 1880), Belle was in breach.

Option I is true but wholly irrelevant. In 1880, the common law took no account of fairness. Yet, this proceeding is not at law but at equity. The chancellor does not look to law for his decisions—he looks to precepts of what he sees as justice. **A** and **D** include option I, so they're wrong. That leaves us with **B** and **C**. Both include option II, which must therefore be correct. And it is; the agreement is so one-sided and oppressive as to "offend the King's conscience." If option III is true, **C** is correct. If option III is false, **B** is correct. And—option III is true. It cites the relevant equitable maxim. Having lured Belle into so heinously abusive an agreement, Cruella comes to court without "clean hands," and that's a reason for which equity denies her relief. Option I is false. Options II and III are true. **C** is right.

 # Silver's Picks

1.	**D**
2.	**B**
3.	**C**
4.	**D**
5.	**C**
6.	**B**
7.	**C**

21

Condition and Contingency

A. Conditional and Unconditional Duties: Conditions Precedent, Conditions Subsequent, and Conditions Concurrent

Nearly every American law student stumbles when she reads the phrases "condition precedent," "condition subsequent," and "condition concurrent." That shan't happen to *you* because we'll make their meaning crystal clear — right here, right now.

1. Let's Understand the Difference Between Conditional and Unconditional Contractual Duties

Contract 1. A and B agree that (1) A will drive B to Boston on March 1 and that (2) B will pay A $100 on his arrival there.

A's duty is to drive B to Boston on March 1, period — no ifs, ands, or buts. A's obligation is *unconditional*.

Contract 2. Now suppose this: Highway 100 leads to Boston. It's been closed for a while but is due to reopen soon. C and D agree that (1) C will drive D to Boston on March 1 *if* Highway 100 reopens by that date, and (2) D will pay C $100 on arrival in Boston. C's duty is to drive D to Boston on March 1 *only if* Highway 100 reopens by that date. C's duty is *conditional*, in this case, on the reopening of Highway 100.

QUESTION 1. By signed writing, Daniel and Melissa reach an agreement with these terms:

The undersigned parties Daniel Thorne ("Daniel") and Melissa Wright ("Melissa") understand and acknowledge:

That Daniel is currently negotiating actively and in good faith toward the formation of a contract with Harmony Hall under which Daniel will, if the negotiations succeed, deliver and be paid for a singing performance at that facility on the evening of August 18, 2019; and

That Melissa is an able and experienced piano accompanist.

Now, therefore, the parties agree:

Item 1: Melissa will and does now commit herself to remain available to provide Daniel with piano accompaniment during and throughout the concert described above.

Item 2: In exchange for the commitment just described, Daniel will pay Melissa the sum of $400 on the execution of this agreement.

Item 3: Should the aforementioned negotiations succeed, Melissa will provide the accompaniment, and Daniel will pay Melissa an additional $600 at the conclusion of the concert.

Item 4: The nature, type, and condition of the piano itself will lie within the discretion of Harmony Hall, and in that regard Melissa will raise no dispute.

Having formed the contract,

A. Melissa has undertaken a duty conditional on Daniel's successful completion of his performance at Harmony Hall.

B. Melissa has undertaken a duty conditional on the formation of a contract between Daniel and Harmony Hall.

C. Daniel has undertaken a duty conditional on the good faith of Harmony Hall's negotiations with him.

D. Daniel has undertaken a duty conditional on Harmony Hall's ability to furnish a piano satisfactory to Melissa.

ANALYSIS.   For her part in this contract, Melissa assumes two duties: (1) Item 1 requires that she be *available* on August 18 to accompany Daniel, with no ifs, ands, or buts. She "will and does now commit herself to remain available." That duty is unconditional. (2) Item 3 requires that she actually provide the accompaniment "should the aforementioned negotiations succeed," meaning the negotiations between Daniel and Harmony Hall, as described in the contract's first sentence. *If* Daniel and Harmony Hall do form a contract, meaning that Daniel will in fact perform, Melissa must provide the accompaniment. Otherwise, she need not do so. So Melissa's duty actually to furnish the accompaniment is conditional.

Daniel, too, assumes two duties: (1) Item 2, with no ifs, ands, or buts, requires that he pay Melissa $400 as soon as the parties execute the writing. (That's Melissa's payment for remaining, so to speak, "on call.") Daniel's duty to pay $400 is unconditional. (2) Item 3 requires that he pay Melissa an additional $600 "should the aforementioned negotiations succeed." That obligation arises only if Daniel and Harmony Hall form a contract (the same condition that applies to Melissa's duty to provide accompaniment). So Daniel's duty to pay $600 is conditional.

A correctly states that Melissa assumes a conditional duty, but it misrepresents the condition; it tells us that Melissa has a duty conditional upon Daniel's successful completion of his performance. With the word "successful," the question writer sets you a trap. Don't fall in. Melissa's duty to provide accompaniment arises "should the *negotiations* succeed," meaning that Daniel and Harmony Hall form a contract. The success or failure of the performance itself is irrelevant to Melissa's obligations. **A** is wrong.

C correctly states that Daniel assumes a conditional duty, but Daniel's duty is not conditional on Harmony Hall's "good faith." The agreement does invoke the *words* "good faith," but they form no part of the condition to which one of Daniel's duties is subject. Daniel's obligation to pay Melissa the additional $600 is conditional on the success of his negotiations with Harmony Hall — on his formation of a contract with Harmony Hall. Hence, **C** is wrong.

D invokes the word "satisfactory" and thus attracts students who, when reading contract item 4, fix on the words "condition" and "satisfaction" without reading the whole of that provision. Item 4 means that Melissa will not assert dissatisfaction with the piano Harmony Hall provides. Nothing in item 4 creates a conditional obligation. **D** is wrong.

That leaves **B**, which correctly tells us that Melissa's duty to accompany Daniel is subject to the condition that Daniel and Harmony Hall succeed in their negotiations — that they form a contract. **B** is right.

See here, as elsewhere, that the three incorrect choices draw on words that appear in the contract, a common trapping technique. The one correct choice does the opposite. It doesn't invoke any words that appear in the contract. Rather, it takes a phrase from the contract ("should the negotiations succeed") and requires that you understand it as a reference to the formation of a contract between Daniel and Harmony Hall.

2. Conditions Precedent and Subsequent

Knowing now the difference between conditional and unconditional duties, we'll distinguish a condition "precedent" from a condition "subsequent." Examine these two promises:

Promise 1: I will go to the fair if tomorrow's weather is good.
Promise 2: I will go to the fair unless tomorrow's weather is bad.

Promises 1 and 2 seem to create the same result. In good weather I go to the fair; in bad weather I don't. Yet, the law sees a subtle difference between them.

Promise 1: The Condition Precedent. Promise 1 is subject to an "if"; I am obliged to go to the fair *if* tomorrow's weather is good. At the time I make the promise, my obligation is not fully mature. Rather, it's a seedling that might or might not take root. If, when tomorrow arrives, the weather is good, my duty blossoms, ripens, and comes to life. If the weather is bad, it doesn't. With that in mind, we say that under promise 1, my duty is subject to a "condition precedent." Something stands "in front" of it. Some event or circumstance must occur before my duty comes fully to life. A condition precedent is marked by the words "if," "only if," "but only if," or some phrase of like meaning.

Think again about my duty to go to the fair under promise 1. We've said that it's subject to a condition precedent. The condition precedent is that tomorrow's weather be good. We might express that same thought thus: "Good weather tomorrow is a condition precedent to my duty to attend the fair."

Promise 2: The Condition Subsequent. Look at promise 2: There's no "if" about it. My duty is *not* subject to a condition precedent. It's full born as soon as I make my promise. Yet, the duty might "die" before I'm ever called on to perform it. I have promised to go to the fair tomorrow without an "if," but I'll be *relieved of that duty* if tomorrow's weather is bad. With bad weather, my duty disappears. Put otherwise, my duty arises as soon as I make the promise, but bad weather will *discharge* it.

When a promise is so worded as to create a current duty that is subject to discharge by some subsequent event or circumstance, we say the duty is subject to a "condition subsequent." Something is standing "in back" of it. The duty exists as soon as the relevant promise is made, but on the occurrence of some condition, it disappears. A condition subsequent is marked by the words "unless," "but not if," or words of similar meaning.

Regarding promise 2, we might say, "My duty to attend the fair is subject to the condition subsequent, that tomorrow's weather be bad," or "Bad weather tomorrow is a condition subsequent to my duty of attendance at the fair."

Here's a rule that might make the whole thing easier: *Whatever a contract's language, (1) if the condition at issue <u>creates</u> one's obligation to perform, then his duty is subject to a condition precedent, and (2) if the condition at issue <u>discharges</u> one's obligation to perform, then his duty is subject to a condition subsequent.*

QUESTION 2. By signed writing, Chantalle and Bob form a contract of purchase and sale:

1. PURCHASE AND SALE
Except in the event that she shall not be able to acquire the product named below, Chantalle will sell, supply, and deliver to Bob thirteen tons of Genetech Solvent, Formula 2, at a price of $20,000 per ton, delivery and payment to be made as described in paragraph 2 below.

2. DELIVERY AND PAYMENT
Delivery is to be made on August 15 of this calendar year by Chantalle to Bob at Bob's warehouse facility, and the purchase price described above is to be paid by Bob, conditional on and subsequent to actual delivery.

3. RIGHT OF FIRST REFUSAL AS TO SUBSEQUENT PURCHASES
If Chantalle does supply and deliver the product as provided in paragraphs 1 and 2 above, then Bob will for all subsequent months in the present calendar year afford Chantalle a right of first refusal to sell to and provide Bob with all Genetech Solvent that Bob may require during that period.

Pursuant to the contract between Chantalle and Bob,

A. Chantalle's acquisition from Bob of a right of first refusal is a condition subsequent to Chantalle's duty to deliver Genetech Solvent to Bob.
B. Payment by Bob to Chantalle of the purchase price is a condition precedent to Chantalle's duty to acquire the Genetech Solvent.
C. Delivery by Chantalle of Genetech Solvent to Bob's warehouse facility is a condition subsequent to Bob's duty to pay.
D. Unavailability of Genetech Solvent is a condition subsequent to Chantalle's duty to supply Bob with that product.

ANALYSIS. Examine the duties each party assumes. Determine which are conditional, on what conditions they depend, and whether each condition *creates* an obligation to perform (condition precedent) or *discharges* an obligation to perform (condition subsequent).

Chantalle's duties arise in paragraphs 1 and 2. Chantalle promises to supply and deliver Genetech Solvent, and there's no "if" about it. Chantalle's obligation, however, is discharged on the occurrence of a condition. It's subject to an "unless," even though that word doesn't appear. Look at paragraph 1's first five words: "except in the event that." They mean "unless." The contract provides that Chantalle must supply Genetech Solvent to Bob, but that her obligation to do so is discharged if she is unable to acquire it. Chantalle's duty is subject to a condition subsequent. The "except" clause makes that so even though, physically, it appears *before* the promise to "sell, supply, and deliver."

Bob's duties flow from paragraphs 2 and 3. At paragraph 2, Bob agrees to pay the purchase price—subject to an "if." Bob is required to pay "conditional on and subsequent to" actual delivery. We may restate Bob's promise thus: "If Chantalle delivers, then, in that case, Bob will pay." Bob's obligation is *created* by the happening of Chantalle's delivery. It's subject to a condition *precedent*, and that's true even though the word "subsequent" appears in the sentence. As used here, that word means only that Bob is to pay Chantalle after she makes delivery.

At paragraph 3, Bob affords Chantalle a right of first refusal as seller of all Genetech Solvent Bob might buy during the year. That duty, too, carries an "if"—Bob will honor the right of first refusal only "if Chantalle does supply and deliver the substance as provided in" paragraphs 1 and 2. The happening that Chantalle make the delivery *creates* Bob's obligation to afford Chantalle the right of first refusal. It's subject to a condition precedent; it matures—ripens—only if Chantalle delivers.

We've identified three conditional duties:

1. Chantalle's inability to acquire the product is a condition *subsequent* to her duty to deliver;
2. Chantalle's actual delivery is a condition *precedent* to Bob's duty of payment; and
3. Chantalle's actual delivery is a condition *precedent* to Bob's duty to afford her a right of first refusal.

A states that Chantalle's acquisition of the right of first refusal is a condition subsequent and, specifically, that it is a condition subsequent to her duty of delivery. That's false. Chantalle's acquisition of a right of first refusal is not, itself, a condition at all. It's a duty that Bob owes her (subject to a condition precedent). **A** is wrong. According to **B**, Bob's payment of the purchase price is a condition precedent to Chantalle's duty to acquire the Genetech Solvent. That, too, is all wet. Payment by Bob to Chantalle is no condition at all. It's a duty that Bob owes Chantalle, and it's *subject* to the condition precedent that Chantalle actually deliver. **B** is wrong.

C tells us that Chantalle's delivery is a condition subsequent to Bob's duty to pay. It's true that in this contract Chantalle's delivery is a condition. But it's a condition *precedent* to (a) Bob's duty to pay, and (b) Bob's duty to afford Chantalle a right of first refusal. **C** is wrong.

D tells us that Chantalle's duty to deliver is subject to a condition subsequent. That's true. Chantalle is obliged to deliver unless she is unable to acquire the product. Her inability to acquire the stuff *discharges* her obligation to sell and deliver it. Consequently, unavailability of product is a condition subsequent to Chantalle's duty to supply Bob with Genetech Solvent. That's what **D** says and that's why **D** is right.

3. *Why We Care About the Difference Between Conditions Precedent and Subsequent: Burden of Proof*

Suppose Arthur and Beth contemplate a written contract for the washing of windows. They consider these two alternative drafts:

> **Draft 1:** Arthur will wash Beth's windows on Monday if the weather is fair, and Beth will pay Arthur $100 for the job.
>
> **Draft 2:** Arthur will wash Beth's windows on Monday unless the weather is foul, and Beth will pay Arthur $100 for the job.

Under draft 1, Arthur's duty to wash is subject to a condition precedent—that Monday's weather be fair. Under draft 2, Arthur's duty to wash is subject to a condition subsequent—that Monday's weather be foul. Draft 1 is better for Arthur; draft 2 is better for Beth, and here's why:

Suppose the parties adopt draft 1, and Arthur fails to wash the windows. If Beth wants to sustain an action against Arthur, she must plead and prove (1) that the parties actually formed the contract, (2) that on Monday, *the weather was fair,* and (3) that Arthur did not wash the windows. Those *three* propositions are essential to Beth's prima facie case.

Now suppose the parties adopt draft 2, and suppose again that Arthur fails to wash the windows. Beth sues. Under draft 2, Arthur's duty to wash arises without any condition precedent. True enough—it will be discharged if the weather is foul, but unless *Arthur* can show that the weather was foul, his failure to wash is a breach. That means, under draft 2, Beth need only plead and prove (1) that the parties formed the contract, and (2) that Arthur did not perform. Those *two* propositions make out Beth's prima facie case. If Arthur wishes to show that the weather was foul, *he'll* have to put on a defense and prove it.

Here's the rule: *In an action for breach of contract, (1) if a defendant's duty is subject to a condition precedent, the burden of proving that the condition occurred is on the plaintiff, and (2) if a defendant's duty is subject to a condition subsequent, the burden of proving that the condition occurred is on the defendant himself.*

Continue to think about draft 1, draft 2, and Beth v. Arthur. Suppose the evidence shows that on Monday the weather was somewhat cloudy, a bit cold (45°), wet, and a little drizzly. Some jurors might think such weather "fair." Others might think it "foul." If Beth sues Arthur under draft 1, the court will instruct the jury that "if, on the evidence, you are in doubt about the status of the weather as fair or foul, then you must find that Beth has failed to meet her burden and return a verdict for Arthur." On the other hand, if Beth sues Arthur under draft 2, the court will instruct the jury that "if, on the evidence, you are in doubt about the status of the weather as fair or foul, then you must find that Arthur has failed to meet his burden of defense and return a verdict for Beth."

Alternatively, imagine this: (1) evidence shows that the contract was formed, (2) evidence shows that Arthur failed to wash the windows, but (3) for some reason, *no* evidence is admitted on the status of the weather. Under draft 1, Beth loses and Arthur wins. That's because Beth failed to show occurrence of the condition that would make Arthur's duty come alive. Having failed to show a duty, Beth cannot show a breach. Under draft 2, Beth wins and Arthur loses. That's because Beth has shown that Arthur had a duty and Arthur has failed to show that his duty was discharged.

QUESTION 3. By signed writing, StarCo and PumpCo form an underwriting contract:

> StarCo Inc., a licensed underwriter, and PumpCo, a corporation engaged in the business of manufacturing peristaltic pumps, mutually wishing to undertake a public offering of PumpCo shares, do agree:
>
> **Item 1:** StarCo will and hereby does firmly commit itself to selling, on PumpCo's behalf, through public offering, two million shares of PumpCo common stock, pursuant to applicable law and regulation, unless PumpCo shall fail diligently, appropriately, and timely to file such registration statements as, for this purpose, are required by applicable state and federal law.
>
> **Item 2:** StarCo warrants[1] and promises that in selling the PumpCo shares as described in paragraph 1, it will receive from buyers thereof a price no lower than $2 per share.
>
> **Item 3:** PumpCo agrees that of the monies StarCo collects from such buyers, PumpCo will allow it to keep, as its commission, 5 percent if, in fact, StarCo does, as described in items 1 and 2, sell the said shares for no less than $2 each.

StarCo fails to sell any of the PumpCo shares, and PumpCo brings an action against StarCo for breach of contract. PumpCo's complaint alleges (1) the formation of the contract described above, and (2) StarCo's failure to sell any of the PumpCo shares. PumpCo's complaint does not, however, allege that PumpCo itself had diligently, appropriately, and timely filed such registration statements as were required by applicable law.

---

1. The meanings of "warrant" and "warranty" are fully discussed in Chapter 23.

> Because PumpCo fails to make that allegation, StarCo moves to dismiss the complaint. Should the court grant StarCo's motion to dismiss?
>
> A. No, because if PumpCo did not file the registration statements, StarCo must plead and prove that fact in its own defense
> B. No, because the contract nowhere includes PumpCo's promise that it will file the registration statements
> C. Yes, because the filing by PumpCo of the registration statements is a condition precedent to StarCo's duty to sell the shares
> D. Yes, because PumpCo's complaint does not specifically allege that StarCo failed to use reasonable commercial efforts in trying to sell the PumpCo shares

ANALYSIS. If StarCo's duty is subject to a condition precedent, then plaintiff PumpCo must plead (and prove) that the condition occurred. If, on the other hand, StarCo's duty is unconditional or subject to some condition subsequent, PumpCo need only plead and prove that the parties formed their contract and that StarCo failed to perform.

StarCo's duty to sell the shares arises from item 1: "StarCo will and hereby does firmly commit itself to selling" the shares. But that duty is subject to an "unless"; "StarCo will and hereby does firmly commit itself to selling the shares *unless* PumpCo shall fail diligently, appropriately, and timely to file" the registration statements. That means StarCo's duty is subject to a condition subsequent. As a plaintiff alleging StarCo's breach, PumpCo need not plead or prove that it *did* file the statements. Rather, StarCo must show, if it can, that PumpCo did *not* do so. For that reason, PumpCo's complaint makes out a prima facie case and is not subject to dismissal. The right answer, then, should state in substance "no," PumpCo's complaint should not be dismissed because it is not PumpCo's burden to plead or show that it filed the registration statements. Rather, it's StarCo's burden to show that PumpCo did not do so.

C and **D** say "yes," the complaint should be dismissed. For that reason, they're wrong. Further, **C** continues in error by reporting that StarCo's duty to sell is subject to a condition precedent; it is in fact subject to a condition subsequent. As for **D**, "reasonable commercial efforts" have nothing—but *nothing*—to do with this contract or controversy. Under the contract, StarCo's duty is to sell the shares. That it does or does not use reasonable commercial efforts in doing so is irrelevant.[2] **B** correctly answers "no," PumpCo's complaint should not be dismissed. Its reasoning, however, is wrong. It's true that

---

2. This case is unlike those discussed in Chapter 14, section E. In those cases, from one of the parties, the contracts do not expressly exact consideration. But, because of the surrounding circumstances, as described in Chapter 14, section E, the law implies a duty on that party's part to devote reasonable commercial efforts to the sale or distribution of the other's commodity.

PumpCo does not promise to file the registration statements, but that is not the reason StarCo's motion should be dismissed. **B** is wrong.

A correctly answers "no," PumpCo's complaint should not be dismissed because StarCo, if it wishes to avoid the contract, must plead and prove that PumpCo failed to file the statements. That's exactly right. StarCo bears the burden of showing, if it can, the occurrence of that condition, in which case its duty is discharged. Hence, **A** is right.

4. *Conditions Concurrent*

Often two parties agree on a transaction but do not specify who will perform first. Suppose it's August 1. Buyer and Seller contract for the purchase and sale of Blackacre. They agree to consummate the transaction (conduct the "closing") on October 1. As is common for real estate sales contracts, this one is silent on the matter of who, at the closing, "goes first." Hence, it leaves open this question: Is Buyer obliged first to pay the selling price after which Seller is to hand Buyer the deed, or is Seller obliged first to hand over the deed after which Buyer is to pay the purchase price?

When a contract fails, expressly or impliedly, to provide that one of the parties will perform before the other, then the law provides that neither need perform until the other first *tenders* his performance.

"Tender" Performance? What's That?

A party tenders his performance when he shows that he's ready, willing, and able to perform. Suppose it's October 1. Buyer and Seller meet for their closing. Buyer says to Seller, "Hand me the deed and then I'll hand you my certified check for the purchase price." Seller says to Buyer, "No, you hand me the check and then I'll hand you the deed." Neither is willing to "go first."[3] As long as these two idiots sit there doing nothing, neither has tendered his performance, and so neither is in breach. Now suppose Seller says, "Here's the deed [he holds it up]. As soon as you hand over the check, I'll hand you this deed." When Seller does that, he *tenders* his performance. As soon as Seller tenders his performance, Buyer must actually *perform*; he must hand over the check. Then, when Buyer does so, Seller must hand him the deed.

The law, at some point, invented the phrase "condition concurrent" and hitched it to the situation just described. When two parties form a contract that does not (expressly or impliedly) provide who should perform first, we say that each performance is a condition concurrent to the other.[4] We mean, simply, that (1) neither Party 1 nor Party 2 need perform until the other first tenders

---

3. See Dr. Seuss, "The Zax" in *The Sneetches and Other Stories* (Random House, 1961, 1998).

4. The phrase "condition concurrent" ought never have been conceived. In truth, when we say that two promises are conditions concurrent to each other, we're really describing a particular form of condition precedent—that the tender of performance by each party is a condition *precedent* to the other's obligation to perform.

performance; and (2) if Party 1 does tender her performance, then — and only then — Party 2 must actually perform. After Party 2 performs, Party 1 must perform. Put otherwise, whichever party first *tenders* her performance creates in the other the duty actually to *perform* — first.

QUESTION 4. On May 1, Desi and Yan form a signed written contract requiring that Desi conduct a marketing study and prepare a report on the product that Yan manufactures and distributes. In exchange, Yan will pay Desi $25,000. The contract provides: "The parties will meet at Yan's offices on November 1, at which time they will make the exchange of payment for marketing report — marketing report for payment." On November 1, Desi arrives at Yan's office with the complete marketing report in his briefcase. In his desk drawer, Yan has a cashier's check for $25,000, made payable to Desi. Yan asks for the marketing report. Desi says that he won't remove the report from his briefcase until Yan pays him. Yan says that he won't pay until Desi gives him the report. Is Desi in breach for failing to hand Yan the marketing report?

A. Yes; by refusing to deliver the report, Desi fails to honor his contractual promise
B. Yes; Yan has no duty to make payment until Desi first tenders the marketing report
C. No; Desi has no assurance that Yan genuinely intends to pay him
D. No; absent Yan's tender of payment, Desi is under no duty to perform

---

ANALYSIS. Desi and Yan formed a contract that did not provide for the order in which they'd perform, meaning that each performance was a condition concurrent to the other. Neither party here was willing to tender performance, and since neither party tendered performance, neither was in breach.

A says "yes," Desi was in breach, so it's wrong. As for the reasoning, it's true that Desi has made a contractual promise to deliver the report, but he need not honor it unless and until Yan tenders payment. As for **B**, it's true that Yan had no duty to pay until Desi tendered the report, but that means only that Yan is *not* in breach. It doesn't mean that Desi *is* in breach. **C** is tempting because one might think of Yan's tender as an assurance that Yan does in fact have the check and intends to pay. If none of the choices was better than this, **C** would be correct.

But **D** is better than **C**. It states the relevant rule of law: Neither party is obliged to perform until the other first tenders performance. As for whether Desi breached the contract, the answer is "no" — precisely because, absent Yan's tender, Desi need not perform. So **D** is right.

B. Waiver of a Condition by the Party It Is "Intended to Benefit"

1. Which Party Is a Condition "Intended to Benefit"?

It is said that most conditions precedent or subsequent are "intended to benefit" one of the contracting parties. A court determines that a condition is or is not intended to benefit a particular party by interpreting the contract according to the ordinary rules of interpretation (Chapter 18). Suppose X and Y form a contract that subjects one of their performances to a condition—precedent or subsequent. If the condition is tied to X's performance, then it is "intended" to benefit X. If it's tied to Y's performance, then it's "intended" to benefit Y. It's as simple as that.

To illustrate, let's return to C, D, and the trip to Boston. C and D agree that (1) C will drive D to Boston on March 1 if Highway 100 reopens by that date, and (2) D will pay C $100 for C's service. C promises to transport D, subject to a condition *precedent*—that Highway 100 reopen by March 1. The condition affords C a (legal) protection. If it fails to occur, C is "off the hook," and D doesn't get his ride. The condition is "intended" to benefit C, not D.

The same would apply if the highway's reopening were a condition *subsequent* to C's duty: "C will drive D to Boston on March 1 unless Highway 100 fails to reopen by that date." With *that* formulation, C is, *ab initio*, under a duty to furnish the transportation on March 1, but the law releases him if Highway 100 does not reopen (for which the burden of proof rests on him). Again, the condition is intended to benefit C, not D.

2. If a Condition Is Intended to Benefit Party 1, Then Party 1 May "Waive" It, But Party 2 May Not

Suppose D decides he doesn't want to go to Boston. He wants a "way out" of his contract with C. Imagine, then, that Highway 100 doesn't reopen by March 1. D is delighted. He contacts C: "Well, the highway hasn't reopened, so it's all off. I'm not going to Boston. You don't drive and I don't pay. Thanks anyway." D can't do that, and here's why: The condition regarding the highway is intended to benefit C, not D. D has no right to assert the condition's nonoccurrence as a basis on which to dishonor *his* obligation. If C wants to proceed even though the condition has not occurred, then the contract goes forward; C drives and D pays.

On the other hand, suppose again that on March 1, the highway has not reopened. C contacts D: "Highway 100 has not reopened, so I'm not going to drive you to Boston." That's C's right. Again, the condition is intended to benefit C, and C—but not D—is entitled to assert the condition's nonoccurrence as a basis for withholding performance.

Suppose again that on March 1, the highway isn't open. C contacts D, but this time he says, "The highway isn't open, but I've decided that I will, anyway, drive you to Boston." D has nothing to say about that; *he* can't escape his obligation. C is entitled to waive the condition, meaning that he can, if he wants, insist on proceeding with performance even though there did not occur the condition subsequent that would discharge him.

Here's the rule: *(1) If two parties, 1 and 2, form a contract in which Party 1's obligation to perform is subject to a condition precedent or subsequent, then (a) Party 1 may, as he wishes, assert the condition as a reason for withholding his performance, or waive the condition and insist that both parties perform even though the condition does not occur, but (b) Party 2 has no such right; if Party 1 insists on performance, Party 2 must perform.*

In short form, the rule is stated thus: *With respect to a contract where a performance is conditional, the party whom the condition is intended to benefit may waive it, but the other may not.*

QUESTIONS 5 & 6. On June 1, 2015, by signed writing, JelCorp and NetCorp form a contract that bears these terms:

Item 1: JelCorp hereby promises to buy from NetCorp, for the price of $450,000, NetCorp's Hubdie machine, delivery to be made by NetCorp to JelCorp at JelCorp's main processing center on September 9, 2015, except that JelCorp need not make the purchase if, before August 1, 2019, the U.S Congress repeals the presently effective accelerated depreciation statute applicable to the purchase of a Hubdie machine.

Item 2: NetCorp promises, in accordance with item 1 above, to deliver the Hubdie machine to JelCorp.

On July 1, 2019, the U.S. Congress repeals the accelerated depreciation statute applicable to the purchase of a Hubdie machine.

QUESTION 5. JelCorp contacts NetCorp: "As you may know, Congress has repealed the accelerated depreciation statute. Nonetheless, we wish to proceed under our contract and purchase the machine." NetCorp responds, "We no longer wish to sell it to you at the $450,000 price. And since Congress has repealed the law to which our contract refers, we need not proceed." If NetCorp refuses to deliver the Hubdie machine, will it breach its contract with JelCorp?

A. Yes, because the condition has no intended beneficiary

B. Yes, because JelCorp did not insist on the condition

> **C.** No, because the contract is subject to a condition precedent that Congress not repeal the accelerated depreciation statute
> **D.** No, because repeal of the accelerated depreciation statute is a condition subsequent to JelCorp's promise

ANALYSIS. The contract subjects JelCorp's promise to a condition subsequent. JelCorp promises to purchase and pay for the Hubdie machine (whatever *that* is), but then by using the words "except that" gives itself an "out." It need not purchase if Congress repeals the accelerated depreciation statute pertaining to a Hubdie purchase.

Remember (or reread) section A.2 above: If a condition *creates* one's obligation to perform, it's a condition precedent. If a condition *discharges* one's obligation to perform, it's a condition subsequent. JelCorp makes a promise to purchase and pay for the Hubdie machine and then invokes the words "except that . . . ." Those two words are like "unless," or "but not if." They indicate that some condition will discharge JelCorp's obligation to buy. They make for a condition subsequent. And, since the condition applies not to NetCorp's obligation, but to JelCorp's, it's intended to benefit JelCorp.

The answer to Question 5 is, first of all, "yes," NetCorp will be in breach. The reason is that NetCorp is not the condition's intended beneficiary; it has no power to insist on the condition. In the face of JelCorp's willingness to purchase, NetCorp's failure to deliver the machine is a breach. **A** correctly answers "yes," but thereafter makes no sense. All conditions are intended to benefit one (or occasionally both) parties. This one is intended to benefit JelCorp. **C** incorrectly answers "no"; it's wrong for that reason alone. Furthermore, it mischaracterizes the condition with the word "precedent"; the relevant provision is a condition subsequent. **D** correctly characterizes the condition with the word "subsequent," but it incorrectly answers "no."

B doesn't jump out as the right answer, but it *is* the right answer. It does not mention the critical point, to wit, that this condition benefits JelCorp and only the condition's beneficiary has the power to insist on it. Yet, **B** makes a statement that's wholly relevant and correct. It answers "yes," and then words the reason in a way that's exactly right (even though the question writer has not used the wording we'd *like* to see). It's true that because JelCorp did not insist on the condition, NetCorp must deliver the machine or find itself in breach. If JelCorp *had* insisted on the condition, NetCorp would not be in breach for failing to deliver the machine. Implicit (and sort of hidden) in **B** is the reality that only JelCorp has the power to insist on the condition and, therefore, the power to waive it. **B** is right.

QUESTION 6. JelCorp contacts NetCorp: "As you may know, Congress has repealed the accelerated depreciation statute. We are not willing to purchase. Please do not deliver." NetCorp responds, "We don't insist on the condition that concerns the depreciation statute. We're ready to proceed and expect you to purchase." If JelCorp refuses to pay for the machine, does it breach its contract with NetCorp?

A. Yes, because the provision concerning the depreciation statute is a condition precedent to NetCorp's promise
B. Yes, because the provision concerning the depreciation statute is a condition precedent to JelCorp's promise
C. No, because the contract is subject to the condition that Congress not repeal the accelerated depreciation statute
D. No, because repeal of the accelerated depreciation statute is a condition subsequent to JelCorp's promise

ANALYSIS. JelCorp's promise to purchase is subject to a condition subsequent; its duty to purchase is discharged if and when Congress repeals the statute. Congress did repeal the statute and thus released JelCorp from what was otherwise its obligation to purchase. The answer, therefore, is "no," JelCorp is not in breach. The reason is that its obligation to purchase was subject to a condition subsequent, and the condition occurred.

A incorrectly answers "yes." It mischaracterizes the condition with the word "precedent" and ties the condition to NetCorp's promise, whereas it belongs to JelCorp's promise. **A** couldn't be more wrong. **B** incorrectly answers "yes," and it too mischaracterizes the condition with the word "precedent." **C** correctly answers "no" but ties the condition to "the contract," and that's not quite right. Properly characterized, a condition attaches to one or the other of the parties' promise(s). It's poor form to characterize a condition as a provision attached to the whole of a *contract*. Even if the terms expressly provide that "this contract is subject to the condition that . . . ," still the condition belongs, truly, to a promise(s), not to "the contract." In this case, the condition is tied to JelCorp's promise, so that a lawyer should (but certainly might not) know better than to state, in this case, that the condition applies to "the contract." **C** is bad; let's not talk any more about it.

D correctly answers "no," JelCorp will not be in breach, and it correctly states the reason, to wit, that its promise is subject to a condition subsequent. The condition has occurred, and thus relieved JelCorp of its obligation to purchase. **D** is right.

3. Sometimes a Condition Seems to Benefit Both Parties When, Really, as Usual, It Benefits Only One

Some conditions precedent or subsequent are intended to benefit both parties. But beware. Even when a condition *applies* to both parties' promises, it may be intended to benefit only one of them. Or then again, it may be just as it seems: intended to benefit both.

Let's use the Boston trip to illustrate. Let's recast the initial conversation:

D: Do you think you might be able to drive me to Boston on March 1?
C: Yes, for $100 or so, but Highway 100 is closed.
D: So what? There are other routes to Boston.
C: Well, I won't do it unless I can travel Highway 100.
D: Well, all right, I suppose I'll agree to that.

C and D then create this writing: C and D agree that (1) if Highway 100 reopens by March 1, then, for a fee of $100, to be paid on arrival in Boston, C will drive D to Boston; and (2) D will pay C $100 for C's service.

The writing begins by stating a condition — that Highway 100 reopen by March 1. It then recites the two parties' promises, so that superficially the condition appears to attach itself to both sides of the contract. Read literally (and hence, superficially), the terms provide that if the highway does not reopen by March 1, neither party need perform. Yet, the parties' antecedent conversation makes plain that D is indifferent to the travel route. It is C to whom Highway 100 is important. Mindful of "intention" under contract law — reading the words to mean as, under all prevailing circumstances, reasonable persons would understand them — the condition is intended to benefit C.

Consider these contractual terms:

If, by May 1, the zoning board approves Buyer's plan to build a hotel on Blackacre, now owned by Seller, then on June 1, for a purchase price of $12 million, Seller and Buyer will undertake and proceed with the purchase and sale of Blackacre.

The writing first states a condition — that the zoning board should approve Buyer's plan to build a hotel on Blackacre. It then recites the two parties' promises, so that on its face the condition appears to attach itself to both parties' promises. Read literally (and hence superficially), the terms provide that if the zoning board does not issue its approval, then neither party need perform.

Read with a mind toward "intention" — the intentions that two reasonable persons would attribute to each other — we can conclude that Seller cares only to sell the property and receive her money; she doesn't care about the zoning board or the hotel. Buyer wants the Board's approval; he doesn't want Blackacre unless he can build the hotel on it. Hence, on the basis of the contractual words alone, without evidence of any surrounding circumstances, a court will likely conclude that the condition is intended to benefit Buyer.

Here's a Condition Intended, Truly, to Benefit Both Parties

Consider these contractual terms:

> Subject to the condition that there should occur a snowstorm tomorrow as the weather forecast currently predicts, A will arrive at B's business premises no later than 4:30 A.M. and plow all snow from the parking lot by 9:00 A.M. For that service, B will pay A $500.

The occurrence of the snowstorm is a condition precedent tied to both A and B. Plainly, neither party need perform if the snowstorm, as predicted, does not occur. The condition benefits A in that it relieves him of the obligation to plow the snow (beginning at 4:30 A.M.). It benefits B in that it relieves him of the obligation to pay. (The fact that A probably wants it to snow so that he'll make $500 does not alter this truth: If it does not snow as the weather forecast predicts, he won't have to do a thing; he'll be unburdened of his obligation. Suppose, for instance, that the prediction is for eight inches of snow. A wakes up in the morning and sees that it has snowed not at all. He can, at least, say to himself, "Good, I can stay in bed.")

4. If One Promises to Waive a Condition, Is He Bound by His Promise?

Suppose again that on February 1, C and D form a contract under which C agrees that if Highway 100 reopens by March 1, he'll drive D to Boston. D will pay C $100 on arrival there. C's promise, of course, is subject to the condition precedent that the highway reopen by March 1. Now, on February 15, C contacts D:

> **C:** I don't think Highway 100 will reopen by March 1. I've decided, however, that I'm willing to take old Route 4. So I'll drive you to Boston on March 1. Count on it.
>
> **D:** That's great.
>
> **C:** I'll see you on March 1.

On February 18, C contacts D again:

> **C:** I've changed my mind again. I don't want to travel on any route other than Highway 100. So we're back to our original agreement. If Highway 100 opens by March 1, we go. If not, we don't.
>
> **D:** No, no, no. You promised just three days ago that you would perform regardless of whether Highway 100 reopens. You waived the Highway 100 condition.
>
> **C:** Well, now, I'm "unwaiving" it.
>
> **D:** You can't do that; you'll be in breach.

Let's ask: Is D right? Must C keep his promise of waiver? In Chapter 14, section B, you learned that to modify an existing contract, each party must provide the other with consideration—just as each must do in forming the contract to begin with. By waiving—promising not to insist on—the Highway 100 condition, C gives up a contractual right and receives nothing back for it. If the law requires that he keep the promise—if it holds him to the waiver—then, in effect, it binds him to a contractual modification for which he receives no consideration.

Yet, the law might hold him to the waiver anyway, and the relevant rule draws on the notion of "detrimental reliance" (as does the doctrine of promissory estoppel addressed in Chapter 14, section F). The rule provides (in part, for now): *If a contracting party waives a condition intended for her benefit, then (1) she may effectively retract the waiver before the other party has reasonably, foreseeably, and detrimentally relied on it, but (2) she is bound by the waiver once the other party has reasonably, foreseeably, and detrimentally relied on it.*

Let's apply the rule to the Boston travel case in its most recent incarnation: (1) C waived the condition on February 15, and (2) he attempted to retract his waiver on the 18th, three days later. Suppose, first, that on February 16, D, in reliance on C's waiver (a) confirmed his business appointment for that day; (b) purchased nonrefundable airline tickets for $600, with which his wife and children could fly to Boston on March 3 when his business would conclude; and (c) for that same purpose, made nonrefundable hotel reservations for the week of March 3 to March 10. C's attempt to retract his waiver would be ineffective; the law would bind him to it. If, on the other hand, D had not altered his position at all in reliance on the waiver, then C would be free to retract it.

But One Can Always Retract His Waiver If the Relevant Condition Goes to His Principal Contractual Purpose

Please reread the hotel/zoning board contract in section B.3 above. Now suppose this: On April 29, Seller contacts Buyer: "I have some information indicating that the zoning board is not going to approve your proposal by May 1. So that I may make plans, tell me, please: Are you willing to buy the property even if the board does not give its approval by May 1?" The Buyer replies, "Yes, I'll buy it anyway." Buyer has purported to waive the condition precedent tied to his performance. A court would likely rule, however, that this particular condition goes to the essence of Buyer's purpose in forming the contract. Both parties understood (or should have understood)—*when they formed the contract*—that Buyer wished to own Blackacre to build a hotel on it. With the condition thus touching on Buyer's principal contractual purpose, the waiver is retractable, and that is so even if Seller relies on it to his detriment, reasonably and foreseeably.

If the zoning board fails to approve Buyer's proposal by May 1 and then on June 1, Seller wishes to proceed with the purchase and sale, Buyer may still, if he wishes, insist on the condition and refuse to buy the property. And that's so even if to his detriment, Seller has relied on Buyer's waiver.

Let's add to the rule of waiver retractability and nonretractability (leaving for now, space for a few more words at the end):

(1) If two parties 1 and 2 form a contract in which Party 1's obligation to perform is subject to a condition precedent or subsequent, then (a) Party 1 may, as he wishes, assert the condition as a reason for withholding his performance, or waive the condition and insist that both parties perform even though the condition does not occur, but (b) Party 2 has no such right; if Party 1 insists on performance, Party 2 must perform.

(2) When Party 1 waives a condition, then (a) if the condition is material to her principal contractual purpose she may, always, retract the waiver, regardless of whether, how, or to what degree Party 2 relies on it, but (b) if (i) the condition is not material to Party 1's principal contracting purpose and (ii) Party 2 reasonably and foreseeably relies on the waiver to his detriment, then the waiver is nonretractable; _____ .

Restatement (Second) of Contracts §84 provides:

[A contractual] promise to perform all or part of a conditional duty . . . in spite of the non-occurrence of the condition [meaning the promisor waives the condition tied to his promise] is binding . . . unless . . . occurrence of the condition was a material part of the agreed exchange [or, more precisely, it pertains to the promisor's principal purpose in forming the contract]. [When that is not so], the promisor can make his duty again subject to the condition [meaning he can retract his waiver] by notifying the promisee . . . of his intention to do so if . . . [retraction of the waiver] is not unjust because of a material change of position by the promisee . . . [meaning the promisee has not relied on the waiver reasonably, foreseeably, and to his detriment].

QUESTIONS 7 & 8. FanCo and FireCo form a contract that includes these terms:

Paragraph 12: FanCo hereby promises and agrees that it will monitor the activities of FireCo's 400 franchisees throughout the United States, Europe, and Asia, and report its findings to FireCo once every three months in writing, according to details and specifications described in paragraphs 3 to 11 above, but FanCo will have no such obligation as to any nation if there should come to exist a state of war between it and any other nation anywhere.

Paragraph 13: Every three months, FireCo will pay FanCo $4 million, representing $100,000 per franchise, except that it will make no payment as to any franchise for which during any three-month period FanCo fails to issue a report for any reason, including the reason referenced in paragraph 12 above.

> **QUESTION 7.** If FireCo announces a waiver of the condition set forth in paragraph 13, beginning with the words "except that," and FanCo reasonably and foreseeably relies on the waiver to its detriment, will FireCo be empowered, thereafter, to retract its waiver?
>
> A. Yes, because as to this contract FireCo's principal purpose is to receive FanCo's reports
> B. Yes, because FanCo has the power to insist or not insist on a condition intended for its benefit
> C. No, because reasonable, foreseeable reliance always renders a waiver nonretractable
> D. No, because such retraction would subject FanCo to an unfair surprise

ANALYSIS. Regardless of the promisee's reliance, a promisor cannot — even if she wants to — make a nonretractable waiver as to a condition that goes to the essence of her contractual purpose. As for this contract, FanCo's principal purpose is to receive payment. FireCo's principal purpose is to receive *reports*. Paragraph 13 subjects FireCo's promise to pay $100,000 for each report to the condition that it *actually receive the report*. That condition goes to the heart of FireCo's purpose in forming this contract. If FireCo announces its waiver of that condition, it *can*, thereafter, retract the waiver and reinstate the condition no matter how or to what degree FanCo has relied on it. The answer, therefore, is "yes" — FireCo is empowered to retract its waiver. The reason is that the condition goes to the essence of FireCo's contractual purpose.

D incorrectly answers "no," so it's wrong. As a reason, it offers up some happy-sounding "fluff" concerning "an unfair surprise." C, too, incorrectly answers "no," so it's wrong. Then it makes the false statement that detrimental reliance always renders a waiver nonretractable; wrong again. Detrimental reliance is necessary to but not sufficient for nonretractability. Stated otherwise, nonretractability requires, always, detrimental reliance. But a waiver does not, in every case, become nonretractable simply because the promisee has detrimentally relied on it. Nonretractability requires, also, that the condition at issue be immaterial to the promisor's principal contractual purpose.

B correctly answers "yes," but it reports an irrelevancy. It's true that FanCo (and any contracting party) has the power to insist or not on a condition intended for its benefit. But this condition is intended to benefit *FireCo*, not FanCo. B's observation is wholly irrelevant to the question. A correctly answers "yes" and correctly states the applicable reason: FireCo's principal contractual purpose is to receive FanCo's reports. Consequently, it can waive the condition that it receive the reports, but may always retract the waiver. Hence, A is right.

QUESTION 8. If FanCo announces a waiver of the condition set forth in paragraph 12, beginning with the words "but FanCo will have no such obligation," and FireCo reasonably and foreseeably relies on the waiver to its detriment, will FanCo be empowered, thereafter, to retract its waiver?

A. Yes, because as to this contract FireCo's principal purpose is to receive FanCo's reports
B. No, because FireCo has the power to insist or not on a condition intended for its benefit
C. No, because reasonable, foreseeable reliance renders this waiver nonretractable
D. No, because such retraction would subject FireCo to an unfair surprise

ANALYSIS. This condition (subsequent) relieves FanCo of its duty to monitor any franchisee if the nation in which it sits goes to war. Quite obviously (as any court would likely rule), FanCo wants freedom from the obligation to travel to or enter into nations at war. The condition expressly attaches itself to FanCo's promise and plainly is intended for FanCo's benefit. Yet, it does not pertain to FanCo's principal contractual purpose. Surely, any court would rule that, although FanCo might well regard the condition as terribly important, FanCo did not form this contract to distance itself from war among nations. It did so to sell its service—to receive payment. Hence, this condition, unlike the one that appears in paragraph 13, is ancillary to its beneficiary's principal contracting purpose.

According to the rule written above, if (1) FireCo (somehow) relies on FanCo's waiver reasonably, foreseeably, and to its detriment, and (2) the relevant condition is not material to FanCo's principal contractual purpose, then once FanCo waives the condition, it cannot then "unwaive" it; it cannot then retract its waiver. Here, (1) the condition is ancillary to FanCo's principal contracting purpose, and (2) FireCo (we said) has relied on the waiver. Hence, the answer to this question is "no."

A says "yes," so it's wrong. As for a reason, it states an irrelevant truth—that FireCo's principal purpose is to receive FanCo's reports. For this question it matters not where lies FireCo's principal purpose. The relevance of principal purpose relates to FanCo. **B** is just as bad. It offers another "yes," wrong in itself, and another irrelevant truth—that FireCo has the power to insist or not on a condition intended for its benefit. FireCo does have such power (within limits), but this condition is not intended for *its* benefit; it benefits FanCo. As it did in Question 8, **D** refers us to the "fluffy" concept of unfairness; it's junk.

C is right all the way 'round, and it differs by one word from choice **C** of Question 7. The difference lies in "this waiver" versus "a waiver." *This* waiver is ancillary to FanCo's primary contractual purpose. And so it is that FireCo's reliance on *this* waiver renders it nonretractable. **C** is right.

The Doctrine of "Estoppel" Touches on the Nonretractable Waiver

When stating in fuller form the rule of waiver, retractability and nonretractability, we reserved a blank space. Let's complete it:

> *(1) If two parties, 1 and 2, form a contract in which Party 1's obligation to perform is subject to a condition precedent or subsequent, then (a) Party 1 may, as he wishes, assert the condition as a reason for withholding his performance, or waive the condition and insist that both parties perform even though the condition does not occur, but (b) Party 2 has no such right; if Party 1 insists on performance, Party 2 must perform.*
>
> *(2) When Party 1 waives a condition, then (a) if the condition is material to her principal contractual purpose she may, always, retract the waiver, regardless of whether, how, or to what degree Party 2 relies on it, but (b) if (i) the condition is not material to Party 1's principal contracting purpose and (ii) Party 2 reasonably and foreseeably relies on the waiver to his detriment, then the waiver is nonretractable; Party 1 is estopped to retract it.*

"Estopped" is a form of the word "estoppel," so let's learn about "estoppel." Suppose (1) Shayna has a baby. By judicial proceeding, she alleges that Marvin is the biological father and asks that the court issue a support award against him; (2) Marvin responds by admitting his fatherhood and by demanding shared custody of the child; (3) Shayna, wanting to keep sole custody, responds by alleging now that Marvin is *not* the father.

The court rules:

> This mother, Shayna, first took the position that Marvin was the baby's father and on that basis sought a support award. Faced now with a custody claim, she reverses course, contending that Marvin is *not* the father and has no custodial rights. We hold that she cannot want it one way and then another. That is, we invoke the doctrine of estoppel and rule that Shayna, having first claimed that Marvin was the child's father, will not now be heard to say the opposite. She is *estopped* now to assert that Marvin is not the father, and so whether he is or is not, we shan't entertain her claim that he is not.

Now imagine that, each driving her own car, Ethel and Fran collide. A few days later, Fran receives a letter from Ethel's lawyer:

> We represent Ethel Elanda, with whom you were recently involved in an automobile accident. Having thoroughly investigated the matter, we conclude that you were at fault. We have also thoroughly investigated all aspects and details of the damage to our client's vehicle and we have determined that

it amounts, monetarily, to $2,700. Please write a check to our offices in the amount of $2,700 in order that our client may be properly reimbursed.

Fran refuses, and the attorneys send another letter asserting, again, that they have thoroughly investigated the accident and the damage in all aspects and details. Again, they demand payment in the amount of $2,700, which, they assert, represents the damage done to their client's automobile. Again, Fran refuses to pay. Ethel's attorney brings suit in the amount, not of $2,700, but $11,100, asserting now his readiness to prove in court that the collision damaged Ethel's vehicle to that degree.

Citing the doctrine of estoppel, Fran's lawyer contends that whatever the true damages to Ethel's vehicle, Fran (by her lawyers) may not now claim or be allowed to prove, even if she can, that they exceed $2,700. Even if the vehicle really is damaged to the extent of $11,100, she argues, Ethel and her attorneys are estopped to ask for any more than $2,700. Fran's attorney addresses the court:

Your Honor, Plaintiff's attorneys, having repeatedly demanded that Defendant pay $2,700 upon their claim that they had "*thoroughly investigated* all aspects and details" of the accident and damages, cannot now be heard to say that the damage is three times what their "thorough investigation of all aspects and details" first revealed, upon which they demanded that Defendant pay $2,700. Even if the vehicle truly was damaged to the extent of $11,100, as Plaintiff and her attorneys *now* claim, they should be estopped now to make that claim and estopped, likewise, to present any evidence that would support it. They demanded that Defendant pay $2,700 in accordance with their "thorough investigation." Under the doctrine of estoppel, they should not and cannot now be heard to say that the damages were greater than that.

The court might well agree and rule that Ethel (and her attorneys) are estopped to claim $11,100 after first purporting to have conducted a thorough investigation as to every aspect and detail of the damage and, on that basis, making a demand for $2,700.

The Doctrine of Estoppel Stated. The doctrine of estoppel provides generally:

A first party will not be heard to assert against a second what would otherwise be a proper position if, as to the matter at issue,
    (a) the first has induced the second to believe she would not take such a position, wherefore the other, on that belief, has reasonably, foreseeably, and detrimentally relied; or
    (b) the position she first asserts so contravenes some statement or stance she has earlier taken as to create incongruity that amounts to injustice.

Part (a) of the foregoing definition applies to the Boston travel case in which D relied on C's waiver by committing to the purchase of airline tickets and hotel accommodations. C is estopped to retract his waiver; that's clear. Part (b) applies to Shayna, who first demands a support award, claiming that Marvin fathered her child and then, faced with a custody dispute, flip-flops and claims he did not. A fair-minded person wants to say to Shayna: "Having claimed that Marvin was the father to obtain a support award, you're in no position now to claim—and you will not be heard to say—that he's *not* the father." And when fair-mindedness invites a statement such as that, the doctrine of estoppel comes 'round.

Part (b) above applies, likewise, to Fran, Ethel, and the attorneys who first demand $2,700 upon their purported "thorough investigation" but then, when Fran refuses to pay, bring an action for $11,100. The fair-minded person wants to say: "You claimed to have made a 'thorough investigation of all aspects and details' relating to the damage and on that basis you demanded $2,700 from Defendant without her having a day in court. You're in no position now to claim, in court, that the damages are higher—you won't be heard to say so."

There's Much More to Estoppel Than We've Described.   In all (conceptual) directions, estoppel reaches far beyond what we've discussed, and it embodies a variety of types and categories including "estoppel in pais," "estoppel by deed," "collateral estoppel," "estoppel by acquiescence," and "promissory estoppel" (discussed in Chapter 14, section F). Estoppel is not—not at all—limited in application to the law of contracts. All that we've said about estoppel is *correct*, but it's not *complete*. We have only touched on the subject in order to explain why, when a waiver of condition is nonretractable, the words "estoppel" and "estopped" rear their heads. Now you know why they do.

C.   Excuse of a Condition for "Obstruction"

If a condition that benefits Party A will occur or not occur depending on some conduct *of* Party A herself, and B prevents A from fulfilling the condition, then it's excused. Suppose A and B agree that (1) A will mow the lawn using B's lawnmower, and (2) B will pay A $50, on the condition that A refill the lawnmower's gas tank after using it to mow the lawn. A mows the lawn, travels to a gas station, fills a gas can with gasoline, and returns to B's home in order to pour it into the lawnmower's fuel tank. When A arrives at B's home, B refuses to give him access to the lawnmower. B's "obstruction" excuses the condition precedent to his own performance. B must pay A, notwithstanding that the condition is unfulfilled—that A did not refill the gas tank.

D. An Implied Condition Precedent: Substantial Performance, Total Breach, and Partial Breach

The common law provides that an "express" condition—one that the parties explicitly state or write—calls for *full and literal fulfillment*. When C promises to drive D to Boston *if Highway 100 reopens*, his duty arises only if Highway 100 does fully reopen (whatever the court decides "reopen" means). If it's a five-lane highway and only two lanes open, then it has not fully reopened; the condition does not occur, and C has no duty to transport D to Boston (unless the court decides, as is unlikely, that "reopen" includes the opening of only two lanes).

Now Suppose Corp X and Corp Y agree that: (1) Corp X will ship 36 tons of the chemical substance known as Trentoran to Corp Y, if Corp X can secure, for a total of $10,000 or less, a 24-hour rental of 18 trucks, each with a payload capacity of no less than 2 tons; and (2) Corp Y promises to pay $20 million for the Trentoran.

Corp X's promise to deliver the Trentoran is subject to the express condition precedent that it be able to secure for a total of $10,000 or less a 24-hour rental of 18 trucks, each with a payload capacity of no less than 2 tons. If Corp X can secure only 12 trucks, each with a payload capacity of 3 tons, its obligation to fulfill the duty does not arise. We might think that in essence the condition is fulfilled, since 12 trucks with a payload capacity of 3 tons will facilitate the transport of $(12 \times 3) = (18 \times 2) = 36$ tons of Trentoran. Nonetheless, this express condition has not enjoyed complete, absolute, literal fulfillment. Consequently, Corp X is not obliged to deliver the Trentoran.

1. Conditions Implied by Law Call Only for "Substantial" Fulfillment

The law will, at times, impose its own condition upon a party's contractual obligation in order, 'tis said, to "do justice." An implied condition calls not for complete and literal fulfillment, but only for "substantial" fulfillment. The only implied condition of general consequence is described below. It spawns the doctrine of "substantial performance."

Suppose Jack and Jill agree that (1) on Monday Jack will paint the kitchen, and (2) on Tuesday Jill will pay Jack $500. The terms don't seem on their face to provide for any conditions—precedent *or* subsequent.

But, with its doctrine of "substantial performance, the law implies one. The law subjects Jill's duty to this condition *precedent*: that Jack will *substantially perform* the painting of the kitchen. The *law* reads the contract thus:

(1) on Monday Jack must paint the kitchen, and (2) *if Jack substantially performs on Monday*, then on Tuesday Jill must pay Jack $500. The law adds the italicized text as a condition precedent to Jill's duty, pursuant to the doctrine of substantial performance.

Hence, the doctrine of substantial performance creates this rule: *Where a contract provides that Party 1 is to perform first in time and Party 2 is to perform second in time, the law implies as a condition precedent to Party 2's obligation that Party 1 shall timely deliver a substantial performance.*

Think about the kitchen painting contract and imagine that on Tuesday Jill refuses to pay. If Jack sues for breach, he'll have to plead and prove that (1) the parties formed the contract, (2) on Monday he *substantially* performed the painting service, and (3) on Tuesday Jill failed to pay. Stated otherwise, if on Monday Jack fails to give substantial performance, then Jane's obligation to pay does not arise — at all.

And What's "Substantial Performance"?   One furnishes substantial performance when he — pretty much, by and large — performs his obligations, even if he doesn't *fully* and *completely* perform them to perfection in every detail. One substantially performs if, as to his obligations, he leaves undone only a portion that is slight, small, relatively unimportant, or immaterial. It helps, perhaps, to think numerically:

- Performance to the extent of 50 percent, 60 percent, 70 percent, 80 percent, or 85 percent certainly is *not* substantial performance.
- Performance of 99 percent *is* substantial performance.
- Performance to the extent of 90 percent, 92 percent, or 95 percent creates a "gray area"; it might or might not be substantial performance.

Understand, however, that not every performance or breach is readily quantifiable in true numeric terms. Suppose Party A is to deliver a music lesson and Party B alleges that A failed substantially to perform because the lesson was, to a substantial degree, unprofessional. One cannot measure "professionalism" in numbers. Hence, in many (maybe most) cases, the numerical guide set forth above is valuable only in figurative terms.

Suppose Xavier and Thalia form a contract by which they agree that

> **Item 1:** Xavier will clean Thalia's fireplace on Wednesday and then clean any areas of the nearby floor that become unclean as a result, so as to restore the surrounding area to its original condition, completing all work by 5:00 P.M. sharp — no delays or extensions.
>
> **Item 2:** Thalia is to pay Xavier $100 on Wednesday at 5:00 P.M.

Xavier works on the fireplace all day Wednesday. At 5:00 P.M., he finishes cleaning the fireplace, but he has created an ugly mess on the floor that will take, say, another thirty minutes to clean. He says to Thalia, "Well, I have left only to clean the floor. I'll stay and do that now, or I'll come back tomorrow and do it then — whatever you prefer." She replies, "I don't want either. You had until 5:00 P.M. and you haven't finished. I don't want you to stay on now and I don't want you back. I'm not going to pay you — not anything."

Thalia is within her rights. The contract calls for Xavier to perform first in time. Thalia is to perform second. By implication of law, therefore, contract item 2 reads thus: "*If Xavier substantially completes the cleaning of the fireplace (and the surrounding floor) by Wednesday at 5:00 P.M., then* Thalia is to pay Xavier $100 on Wednesday at 5:00 P.M." The italicized words represent the condition precedent imposed by the law. With the fireplace clean and surrounding floor markedly unclean, Xavier has not given a substantial performance. It's hard to assess the breach numerically, of course, but the percentage numbers presented above are useful as figurative guides. Left with a soot-covered floor, no reasonable person can conclude that Xavier's work is done to near perfection. Xavier's failure to clean the floor by 5:00 P.M. is a failure to furnish substantial performance, meaning Thalia's obligation is subject to an unfulfilled condition precedent, wherefore she need not pay.

If Xavier does, by 5:00 P.M., clean the floor, leaving, however, one small speck of soot, then he does, certainly, furnish substantial performance — a performance that is almost entirely complete even though not complete "to the letter" in every single detail. In that case, (1) Xavier *is* in breach (ever so slightly), but (2) Thalia is nonetheless obliged to pay Xavier *in full*. Thalia has an action against Xavier for this teensy breach (if she cares to pursue it), but she must pay *in full* or she herself will be in breach.

QUESTIONS 9 & 10. TCorp binds books, booklets, and magazines. UCorp publishes a magazine called *RoofTop*. In May 2015, UCorp has one million copies of its August issue printed. The copies, however, are not bound. UCorp contracts with TCorp to take possession of the one million copies, bind them, and return them to UCorp by July 25. Relevant portions of the parties' written contract appear below.

The undersigned parties TCorp and UCorp do agree on May 6, 2015, that: [Paragraphs 1-120 not shown]

> **Paragraph 121:** TCorp will bind one million copies of UCorp's magazine *RoofTop* according to the specifications set forth in paragraphs 1-120 hereof, and deliver the said one million bound copies to UCorp in 10,000 bound packages of 100 copies each, all to be delivered on or before July 25, 2015.
> **Paragraph 122:** On or before July 27, 2015, UCorp will pay TCorp a $300,000 fee.

> **QUESTION 9.** On July 25, TCorp tenders delivery to UCorp of 800,000 copies of the bound magazine in 8,000 packages of 100 copies each. TCorp apologizes for not having finished the job and promises to deliver the remaining 200,000 magazines within ten days, on or before August 4. UCorp refuses to accept the 800,000 magazines because they are deficient in quantity. On July 27, TCorp demands payment from UCorp of $240,000, or 80 percent of the total fee. Again, UCorp refuses to accept the magazines and refuses to pay. Is UCorp in breach of contract?
>
> A. Yes, because TCorp promised to complete its work within a reasonable time after the initial due date
> B. Yes, because TCorp furnished 80 percent of its performance and is entitled to 80 percent of the payment provided in the contract
> C. No, because TCorp gave UCorp no reliable basis on which to believe it would complete the work on or before August 4
> D. No, because there has failed to occur a condition precedent to UCorp's obligation to pay

ANALYSIS. If two parties form a contract under which Party 1 is to perform first in time and Party 2 second in time, substantial performance by Party 1 is a condition precedent to Party 2's obligation to perform. Consequently, if Party 1 fails to give substantial performance, Party 2 need not perform — at all.

TCorp and UCorp formed a contract under which TCorp was to perform first in time (on or before July 25) and UCorp was to perform second in time (on or before July 27). By implication of law, UCorp's duty to pay on or before July 27 was subject to the condition precedent that TCorp should, on or before July 25, furnish substantial performance. By law, paragraph 122 of their contract means that *if TCorp furnishes substantial performance on or before July 25, then* on or before July 27, UCorp will pay TCorp a $300,000 fee. The italicized words represent the condition precedent implied by law. On July 25, TCorp furnished performance of only 80 percent, which does not amount to substantial performance. The relevant condition precedent, therefore, did not occur, and UCorp need not pay. For that reason, the answer is "no" — UCorp is not in breach of contract.

A answers "yes," so it's wrong. Further, it misstates the law, implying that Party 1, who fails timely to furnish substantial performance, is entitled to Party 2's performance if he promises to furnish substantial performance within a reasonable time after it is due. There is no such rule. **B** also answers "yes," and it too misstates the law. It's wrong. If Party 1 performs to the extent of 80 percent, she is not entitled to 80 percent of Party 2's performance; she is entitled to nothing.

C correctly answers "no," but its reasoning is wrong. It implies that Party 2 is obliged to perform even if Party 1 fails to furnish substantial performance so long as (a) Party 1 promises to complete performance within a reasonable time and (b) gives Party 2 a reliable basis on which to believe him. Again, there is no such rule.

D correctly answers "no." UCorp is not in breach of contract because there failed to occur a condition precedent to its obligation. That's correct. UCorp's duty to pay is subject to the condition precedent that TCorp substantially perform. TCorp failed to do that, meaning that UCorp need not pay, meaning in turn that by refusing to pay it commits no breach. **D** is right.

QUESTION 10. Assume for this question that on July 25 TCorp tenders delivery to UCorp of 10,000 packages of magazines and advises UCorp: "The total number of magazines in the packages is one million, as agreed, and all but two packages contain exactly 100 magazines, as agreed. One package contains only 99 magazines and another contains 101." UCorp refuses to accept the magazines and, on July 27, refuses to pay. Is UCorp in breach of contract?

A. Yes, because the condition precedent to UCorp's duty was satisfied
B. Yes, because TCorp honestly disclosed its breach
C. No, because TCorp failed to furnish substantial performance
D. No, because TCorp did not deliver a perfect service, as required by the contract

---

ANALYSIS.   If two parties form a contract under which Party 1 is to perform first in time and Party 2 is to perform second, then the law implies, as a condition precedent to Party 2's obligation, that Party 1 will *substantially* perform, not that Party 1 will perfectly perform "to the letter." If Party 1 provides a nearly perfect performance, incomplete or flawed only in some immaterial way, then he is in breach, but has nonetheless given substantial performance, and Party 2 must perform.

These parties formed a contract requiring that TCorp perform first and UCorp second. TCorp timely delivered 1 million bound magazines as required, but deviated ever so slightly from its promise as to packaging. Its failure constitutes a breach, but a breach so small as to mean that it did still furnish substantial performance. Consequently, TCorp satisfied the condition precedent provided by law, and UCorp is obliged to pay (and is entitled, of course, to the magazines that it refused to accept). The answer then is "yes"—UCorp is in breach, and the reason is that TCorp furnished substantial performance, thus fulfilling the condition precedent to UCorp's duty to pay.

C and **D** say "no," so they're wrong. **D** implies that UCorp would be obliged to pay only if TCorp delivered a perfect service. That's not the rule.

TCorp's failure to deliver a perfect service does constitute a (a teeny-tiny) breach. UCorp is entitled to recover any damages it sustains as a result (none in this case), but it may not, for that reason, withhold its own performance. It must pay in full. **C** incorrectly concludes that TCorp failed to furnish substantial performance. Certainly TCorp did furnish substantial performance. **B** correctly answers "yes," but its reasoning is wrong. It implies that one who honestly discloses his breach is entitled to a return performance for that reason. There is no such rule. **B** is wrong.

A is correct. It says "yes," UCorp is in breach, and correctly states the reason. By furnishing substantial performance, TCorp fully satisfies the condition precedent to UCorp's duty to pay. That's why **A** is right.

2. *Some Annoying Vocabulary: Material (Total) Breach and Immaterial (Partial) Breach*

If a contracting party furnishes substantial performance but does not give "letter perfect" performance in every detail, then she has committed an "immaterial" breach, also called a "partial" breach. An immaterial breach is one so slight as not to negate a substantial performance. If as to a contract between Parties X and Y, we say, "X committed an immaterial breach" or "partial breach," we're saying that Party X (1) did furnish substantial performance, and (2) did also commit a (very small) breach entitling Party Y to damages (whatever they are, if any).

If a party commits a breach so large that it negates substantial performance, then he commits a "material" breach, also called a "total" breach. One who performs to the extent of 10 percent, 30 percent, 50 percent, 70 percent, 80 percent, or 85 percent commits a material breach/total breach and, concomitantly, fails to furnish substantial performance.

DON'T THINK THIS: Total breach means failure to perform at all. That's wrong. Again, "total breach" means a breach sufficiently large to negate substantial performance. One who performs his obligation, say, to the extent of 80 percent has committed a "total breach," which has the same meaning as "material breach." AND DON'T THINK THIS: One who partially performs has committed a "partial breach." Again, that's wrong. If one commits a "partial breach"—also called an "immaterial breach"—he has performed almost but not quite—perfectly. Hence, again, to say that one commits only a partial/immaterial/teensy-weensy breach is to say that he does give substantial performance.

In Question 9 above, TCorp delivered only 80 percent of the bound magazines it had promised. Consequently, it committed a material breach/total breach and failed to give substantial performance. That means UCorp had no obligation to pay TCorp anything and had an action against TCorp for damages sustained by its breach. In Question 10 above, TCorp delivered an incomplete, but very *nearly* complete performance and so, TCorp committed only an immaterial/partial breach, meaning that it did furnish substantial performance. Consequently, UCorp was obliged to make full payment but nonetheless had an action against TCorp for the damages (if any) it suffered because of the partial breach.

So understand, please, that (1) the term "total breach" is synonymous with failure to give substantial performance, and (2) the term "partial breach" is synonymous with "a breach so small as does not negate substantial performance." It's simple (but lots of students don't realize that).

3. When It Comes to Goods, Seller's Substantial Performance Is Not Enough to Trigger Buyer's Duty

Under UCC §2-206 (and older law on which it draws), the seller of goods must make a "perfect tender" to trigger the buyer's duty to accept the goods and pay the price. Suppose Buyer and Seller form a contract that calls for Seller to deliver 100 widgets, each wrapped in light blue paper, Seller to deliver the goods to Buyer's facility on July 11, Buyer to pay the purchase price on July 12. On July 11, Seller delivers 100 widgets, all of them in perfect condition, wrapped in *dark* blue paper. Even if all concede that the color of the wrapping paper is a trivial matter, still (with qualifications), Buyer may reject the goods, refuse to pay the price, and sue for Seller's breach. (If a buyer first pays all or part of the purchase price, she is entitled to have it back and can sue for her damages. See Chapter 26, section C.)

E. The Contractual Term That Is Both a Condition and a Promise: A Paradox of Breach

Consider two contractual terms, 1 and 2: By term 1, A promises to do thing X on Monday, in exchange for term 2, by which B promises to do thing Y on Tuesday. Term 1 embodies the promise given by a party who is to perform first in time. As we've just learned, it has significance in two separate respects: (1) It represents A's promise; if she dishonors it, she commits a breach. Separately, (2) its substantial performance represents a condition precedent to B's promise; if A fails substantially to perform (commits a material breach), then B need not perform at all.

Now consider these contractual terms: "1. Buyer, on Wednesday, August 19, will pay Seller $4 million by certified check. 2. In consideration of such promise, Seller will, on Thursday, August 20, convey Blackacre to Buyer."

Term 1 sets forth (a) Buyer's promise to pay by certified check, and (b) two conditions precedent (or one condition in two parts) to Seller's obligation to convey Blackacre. They are (i) the implied condition precedent that Buyer substantially pay the $4 million, and (ii) that he do so by certified check. Suppose that on August 18, Buyer asks Seller whether she will accept a cashier's check rather than a certified check. Seller replies, "Yes, I will," and thereby waives the condition that Buyer pay by certified check.

In reliance on the waiver, Buyer buys a cashier's check, but on the morning of August 19, Seller contacts Buyer to say that she's changed her mind; she wants a certified check after all. Buyer explains, "But it's too late for me to get one today." Seller's attempt to retract her waiver is ineffective because the matter of a certified check versus a cashier's check is not material to Seller's principal contractual purpose, and Buyer has relied on the waiver to his detriment, reasonably and foreseeably. Seller can no longer demand a certified check as a condition of conveying Blackacre. When Buyer arrives at Seller's office and tenders the cashier's check, Seller must deliver the deed to Blackacre.

But, odd though it seems, Buyer is in breach. One can waive a condition precedent (or subsequent) to his promise, but he cannot, without consideration, waive *a promise*; to do that would be to forgo a contractual right without consideration. Where a particular contractual term creates both a promise and an implied condition precedent (as does Buyer's promise to pay by certified check), the promisee (Seller) may effectively waive the component of condition, but not the component of promise.

Most paradoxically, therefore, the condition that Buyer pay by certified check is waived, but his promise to do so (all embodied in the same term) is not. Although Seller cannot refuse the cashier's check, she can, most paradoxically, sustain an action against Buyer for breach — for the dishonor of his promise to pay by certified check. It's a fine point, peculiar, a little crazy — but it's law and (maybe) belongs to the basic contracts course.

F.   The Closers

QUESTION 11. PayCo, a payroll accounting firm, forms a contract with SoluCo, a computer programmer:

(1) SoluCo will create for PayCo, and PayCo will purchase from SoluCo, together with all applicable rights of ownership and copyright, four computer programs to be designed and to function according to the specifications set forth in Appendix A attached to this writing.

(2) The price to be paid by PayCo will be $360,000 in total, on final completion and delivery of all of the four programs to be produced by SoluCo. The first program, as described in Appendix A, shall be due and delivered on January 15, 2019, the second on

February 15, 2019, the third on March 15, 2019, and the fourth on April 15, 2019.

SoluCo timely delivers the first three programs, properly designed and properly functioning. On April 15, 2019, SoluCo notifies PayCo that the fourth program will be delivered one month late, on or about May 15. SoluCo demands that in the interim, PayCo pay it the amount of $270,000 for the three programs already delivered, noting that $270,000 represents three-quarters of $360,000. PayCo refuses to make any payment. All of that means that

I. by failing to deliver the fourth program on time, SoluCo committed only a partial breach.
II. by delivering three of the four programs, SoluCo provided PayCo with substantial performance.
III. by refusing to pay SoluCo any money at all, PayCo committed a total breach.

A. I only
B. II and III only
C. I, II, and III
D. Neither I nor II nor III

ANALYSIS. By failing timely to deliver a full 25 percent of the programs for which the contract called, SoluCo committed not an immaterial/partial breach, but a serious, material/total breach. Consequently, option I is false. To say that a contracting party commits only a partial breach is to say that he commits only a very, very small breach and does, therefore, give substantial performance. That means option II is false as well. SoluCo, who was to perform first in time, did not provide PayCo with substantial performance, meaning it did not fulfill a condition precedent to PayCo's duty to pay. Hence, PayCo had no obligation to pay SoluCo *anything*, and by refusing to do so it committed no breach. Option III, therefore, is false. And so, **D** is right.

QUESTION 12. On March 1, by signed writing, MetalCorp and GreenCorp agree on these contractual terms:

Paragraph 1: GreenCorp will overhaul the landscaping on the 100 acres surrounding MetalCorp's corporate offices according to the specifications set forth in paragraphs 3-20 of this written agreement, GreenCorp to begin work on or about March 1 and to complete its work on or before March 22.

Paragraph 2: MetalCorp will pay GreenCorp (a) $100,000 when GreenCorp begins work; (b) an additional $100,000 when GreenCorp completes such portion of the work as is specified in paragraph 12 of this agreement, the parties agreeing that such work constitutes approximately one-half the total work GreenCorp is to perform; and (c) $100,000 when GreenCorp completes the work—for total payment from MetalCorp to GreenCorp of $300,000.

[Paragraphs 3-11 concern other matters.]

Paragraph 12: On the 50-acre portion of MetalCorp's property called Colleague Quadrangle, rectangular in shape, GreenCorp will plant, along each of the four sides, so many trees as fully cover each such side with no spaces visible between trees.

[Paragraphs 13-20 concern other matters.]

On March 1, GreenCorp begins work and MetalCorp pays it $100,000. On March 12, GreenCorp completes the tasks (approximately one-half the total work) described in paragraph 12, and MetalCorp pays it an additional $100,000. On March 22, GreenCorp announces that it has completed the work, and on March 23 requests that MetalCorp pay the final $100,000 installment.

MetalCorp truthfully informs GreenCorp that "on the Colleague Quadrangle, which represents only 50 acres of our 100 acres, you planted 300 trees. Having done that, you left one of the Quadrangle's four sides with a two-foot space between two of the trees. To conform your performance to paragraph 12 of our contract, you should have planted one additional tree." For that reason, MetalCorp refuses to pay GreenCorp any portion of the final $100,000 installment and, further, refuses to allow GreenCorp to plant the one additional tree. MetalCorp brings an action against GreenCorp for breach. Which of the following facts, if found, is most favorable to MetalCorp?

A. With respect to landscaping and plantings, MetalCorp has always paid serious attention to its Colleague Quadrangle.

B. The Colleague Quadrangle is the only portion of MetalCorp's property used by employees and visitors, and the space between the two trees is sorely noticeable.

C. GreenCorp failed to plant the 300th tree in the Quadrangle because it had run short of trees.

D. Each tree carries a cost of about $40.

ANALYSIS.   To be innocent of breach, MetalCorp must show it had no duty to make the final $100,000 payment. If, by March 22, GreenCorp failed to furnish substantial performance, meaning it committed a material breach, then MetalCorp would have no such duty because, once again, GreenCorp's substantial performance is a condition precedent to MetalCorp's obligation to pay. The correct answer is that which reflects a finding that GreenCorp, by failing to plant the one missing tree, committed a material breach and, therefore, failed to give substantial performance.

D reports that the cost of a single tree is about $40. If that fact is relevant at all, it works not in MetalCorp's interest, but against it; $40 is a minuscule portion of $100,000. **D** therefore is wrong. **C** too is wrong; it states an irrelevancy. GreenCorp's reasons for failing to plant the missing tree are unrelated to the question at issue: Does the missing tree represent a material breach? **A** has some vague overtone of relevance. It suggests that the quadrangle is important to MetalCorp, but that does not allow us to call GreenCorp's omission a material breach (unless B is worse).

B is better, and best among the four. It reports two facts: (1) that the quadrangle is the only portion of MetalCorp's property occupied by employees and visitors, and (2) the absence of the missing tree is significant to its appearance. Those two facts together would make for an argument that GreenCorp's failure to plant this single tree represents a material breach. Hence, **B** is right.

 # Silver's Picks

1.	B
2.	D
3.	A
4.	D
5.	B
6.	D
7.	A
8.	C
9.	D
10.	A
11.	D
12.	B

22

Interpretation as to Allocation of Risk: Mistake, Frustration, and Impracticability

A. Interpretation as to Allocation of Risk

Life is full of risk, and contracts are a part of life. Suppose XYZ stock is traded publicly on the New York Stock Exchange. Divestor owns 10,000 shares of XYZ stock and believes its value will soon decline — he thinks the stock will "go down." Meanwhile, Investor has a tip that XYZ stock's value soon will rise — she thinks the stock will "go up."

Investor pays $1 million for 100 of Divestor's shares of XYZ stock, the transaction mediated by a stockbroker in the ordinary way so that neither party knows the other's identity. Each party knowingly assumes a risk. If the stock goes down, Investor loses and Divestor wins (because he did not suffer a loss; he got out in time to avoid it). Investor wishes she could go back in time, undo the purchase, and have her money back. If the stock goes up, Investor wins and Divestor loses (because he did not enjoy the gain; he got out too soon to reap it). Divestor wishes he could go back in time and have the stock back.

In either case, we know and they know that they can't do that. By law, the gains and losses lie where they fall; the law saddles each party with the outcome of the risk he assumed.

The law that does that is the law by which we interpret contracts. In Chapter 18, section A, we learned that the terms of any contract have such meaning as would be given the offer, as accepted, by a reasonable offeree and offeror under all prevailing circumstances. When two parties contract for the purchase and sale of publicly traded stock, each, as a reasonable person, should know (and usually does know) that her contract implicitly includes this term:

> To the buyer there is allocated the risk that the stock's value will decrease, and to the seller there is allocated the risk that the stock's value will increase. Consequently, neither party on the ground of disappointment as to any such outcome shall have the right to rescind (undo) the agreement hereby recorded or the purchase and sale that follow herefrom.

As to the unknown matter of future increase or decrease of the stock's value, the contract *allocates risk* to each party, and that is so because this contract, like all contracts, carries such terms as reasonable persons under the circumstances would so understand.

Illustration: Blueacre Might Be Hiding Oil.   Suppose Seller owns Blueacre, which is unsuitable for farming, building, or anything else, except that many think oil might lie beneath it. Seller announces that the land is for sale for $20 million. Buyer contacts Seller and the two converse.

Buyer: So, many people think that oil lies beneath your land. What do *you* think?

Seller: I don't know any more than anyone else knows. If I *knew* that oil lay beneath the land, I would keep it, drill, and make billions. But I *don't* know and I don't want to invest any money trying to find out. If oil lies beneath Blueacre, someone else will make the billions. If it does not, someone will lose $20 million, my selling price, plus whatever he invests in finding nothing.

Buyer: Yes, yes, of course. That's right.

Buyer decides to buy. The parties form a signed, written contract and proceed to closing. Buyer pays the purchase price, Seller conveys the land, and Buyer becomes owner. Buyer spends $1 million exploring the land for oil and finds none — not a drop.

Buyer wants his money back. But plainly, the contract does not entitle him to that. As to what should transpire if Blueacre does or does not yield oil, this contract resembles a contract for the sale of publicly held stock. Again, from Chapter 18, section A, the terms of any contract have such meaning as would be given the offer and acceptance by a reasonable offeree and offeror under all prevailing circumstances. The circumstances under which Buyer and Seller formed this contract included, notably, their conversation in which each led the other reasonably to understand that each was taking his chances as to the matter of oil. Seller assumed the risk that he would receive a mere $20 million for property that might harbor billions in oil. Buyer assumed the risk that he would pay $20 million for useless land. Properly interpreted, the contract allocated risks to each of its parties, as just described. The contract does not entitle Buyer to a return of his money should the land prove useless. Neither would it entitle Seller to reverse the transaction if the property produced oil.

Furthermore, if the parties had not expressly conversed about the oil prospects, still, as reasonable persons, they would or should know that their agreement implicitly and unquestionably provided that (1) if the land held oil, Seller would not be entitled to take it back; and (2) if the land held none, Buyer would not be entitled to the return of his money. Say, if you wish, that such is simple common sense. In so saying, you mean that reasonable persons would so understand such an agreement.

Illustration: This Contract for the Sale of Woodacre Is Different.   Now suppose Seller owns Woodacre, which when she purchased it was rich with timber, holding a stand of 140,000 trees. Buyer wants the land for its timber. On May 18, the parties converse.

> **Buyer:** Am I right to understand that Woodacre has a stand of approximately 140,000 trees?
> **Seller:** Yes, that's right.
> **Buyer:** Well, I don't care about the land itself, but I want the timber, which I think to be worth about $12 million. I'll purchase the property for that amount.
> **Seller:** I'll sell for $14 million.
> **Buyer:** It's a deal.

On May 20, the parties create and sign the appropriate writing, and Buyer pays Seller a $2 million deposit. The contract provides that the closing should occur on July 1. Unbeknownst to the parties, all of Woodacre's trees had been destroyed by fire on May 1, nineteen days before they formed their contract. Buyer discovers that fact on June 1 and informs Seller that she will not honor the contract.

> **Buyer:** I've just learned that at the time we formed our contract, the trees were no longer standing on Woodacre; they had burned on May 1.
> **Seller:** Well, *I* didn't know that.
> **Buyer:** I realize that you didn't know that, and I'm not accusing you of any deceit. Still, we both honestly understood that I was to buy and you were to sell property on which there stood some 140,000 trees. In fact, even as we formed our contract, there were no trees on the property.
> **Seller:** Well, what do you want *me* to do about it?

> **Buyer:** I want out. I want back my $2 million deposit and, of course, I don't want to buy the land.
>
> **Seller:** Well, we have a contract for the sale of Woodacre, and I expect you to buy it.

Buyer refuses to buy the property, and Seller sues. Buyer counterclaims for the return of her $2 million deposit. In the conversation Buyer and Seller conducted just before forming their contract, they spoke of the trees as though their presence on Woodacre was a fact, not a possibility. Further, Buyer's statements should have led Seller to understand that Buyer wanted the land only for its trees and that, absent the trees, she would not want to buy it. Thus interpreted, the contract does not allocate to either party any risk as to the presence or absence of the trees. Rather, its terms assume that the trees do sit on Woodacre. The parties have manifested no recognition of a risk that things are otherwise, and hence, no intention to allocate it to either of them.

When that is so—when, as to some fact(s) relevant to their contract, the contracting parties manifest an *assumption of* its truth, meaning they do not allocate to either of them the possibility of its falsehood—the law invokes its so-called doctrines of mutual mistake, frustration of purpose, or impracticability—all similar in concept, but different as to details that, in the law's eyes, make a difference as to which doctrine applies. Let's discuss each such doctrine, one at a time.

B.   Mutual Mistake

The doctrine of mutual mistake provides: *A contract between two parties A and B is voidable by A if (1) when forming their contract, the parties manifest their mutual belief, to the point of absolute fact, that some set of circumstances is in place; and (2) when forming the contract B should, under the circumstances, understand that but for that belief A would be unwilling to enter the contract (except, perhaps, on materially different terms); and (3) that belief is mistaken, then the contract is voidable at A's option.*[1]

Let's apply that rule to the Woodacre case. Before forming their contract, the parties conversed, each manifesting to the other her understanding—not as a chance or possibility, but as an absolute *fact*—that Woodacre held a large stand of trees. Each manifested her absolute unequivocal belief in that fact and, further, Seller should have understood that Buyer would not have agreed to the purchase had she known Woodacre held no trees. They then learned that

---

1.   Most regrettably, many (many) courts invoke the phrase "mutual mistake" in conjunction with the unfortunate phrase "meeting of the minds" (discussed in Chapter 3, section C). Stated otherwise, they write of mutual mistake when faced with two parties, each of whom reasonably attributes to the other a meaning different from the one that the other attributes to him, as occurs in the *Peerless* case (Chapter 3, section C).

at the time they formed their contract, Woodacre had no trees. Consequently, Buyer may void the contract. And if she does, the court will afford her the remedy of rescission, meaning it will "undo" the contract and, for Seller's $2 million unjust enrichment, afford Buyer, also, the remedy of restitution, meaning it will require Seller to refund Buyer's $2 million deposit.[2]

The Restatement (Second) of Contracts §§152 and 153 (which we have here combined into one sentence) states the rule of mutual mistake:

> A mistake is a belief that is not in accord with the facts [and] [w]here a mistake of both parties at the time a contract was made as to a basic assumption on which the contract was made has a material effect on the agreed exchange of performances, the contract is voidable by the adversely affected party. . . .

The phrase "basic assumption on which the contract was made" refers to what we describe in element 1 of the rule, to wit, that each party manifests to the other — to the degree of absolute fact — a belief that some circumstance is in place. The phrase "has a material effect on the agreed exchange of performances" means that one of the parties should know that the other, if he knew the truth, would not form the contract (except, perhaps, on significantly different terms).

QUESTION 1. Walker owns a cow that she cannot breed. A veterinarian thoroughly examines the animal and advises Walker that the cow is infertile. Walker then offers the cow for sale at a price of $1,000, whereas a fertile cow of the same type, variety, and age would command a price of $15,000. On April 1, Sharewood expresses interest in purchasing the cow and asks Walker why her asking price is so low. Walker explains that the cow is infertile. Manifesting his understanding that the cow is indeed infertile and that such is the reason for the low price, Sharewood accepts the offer and thus agrees to purchase the cow. The parties create and sign a writing by which they agree to the purchase and sale of the cow for $1,000. The contract provides that Sharewood will pay the purchase price and that Walker will deliver the cow on May 1.

On April 15, Walker, still possessing the cow, thinks it might be pregnant. Surprised at what she thinks to be so, she calls her veterinarian again. The veterinarian examines the cow and advises Walker that his earlier diagnosis of infertility had been wrong, that the cow is pregnant, and that it had been pregnant for some two months. On May 1, Sharewood tenders the $1,000 purchase price. Walker explains that the cow is fertile and, indeed, pregnant. She refuses the payment, and declines to convey the cow.

---

2. Regarding the law of restitution, see Chapter 29, sections A and B.

> Sharewood sues Walker for breach. Referring to the cow's fertility and citing mutual mistake, Walker attempts to void the contract. Which of the following facts is legally relevant to Walker's claim of mutual mistake?
>
> A. Walker had a reasonable basis on which to believe the cow was infertile.
> B. The parties formed their contract before they were to complete the sale itself.
> C. Each party led the other to understand that he or she took the cow's infertility for a fact.
> D. Sharewood believed the cow was infertile only because Walker had so represented it.

ANALYSIS.   Apply the rule to the facts. Walker can avoid this contract on the ground of mutual mistake if she proves that (1) when the parties formed the contract, each manifested a belief *to the point of fact* that the cow was infertile; and (2) under the circumstances, each should have understood that Walker, had she known the cow to be fertile, would not have agreed to sell it for so little as $1,000; and (3) that the cow was in fact fertile at the time the parties formed the contract.

Referring to the Restatement's formulation, Walker can void the contract if she shows that (1) both parties believed the cow to be infertile, which belief was not in accord with the facts (meaning it was false); (2) their mistaken belief in the cow's infertility was a "basic assumption" on which they formed their contract, meaning each manifested such a belief to the point of fact; and (3) the mistake had a material effect on the agreed exchange of performance (meaning that Sharewood should have known that Walker, if she knew the truth, would not have formed the contract).

All such elements apply to this case, but among the four answer choices, only one is mentioned. The veterinarian advised Sharewood that the cow was infertile, and **A** correctly reports, therefore, that Walker had good reason to adopt that belief. That fact, however, is irrelevant to mutual mistake. The doctrine requires that each party manifest to the other his belief in some fact, which belief they later learn to be false, but it matters not how or why either party comes to manifest that belief or whether he or she does so for good or bad reason. **A** is wrong. **D** is wrong for the same reason; *how or why* Sharewood came to manifest his mistaken belief is irrelevant. **B**, too, cites an irrelevancy. That time does or does not intervene between the dates on which two parties form a contract and on which they actually perform plays no role in the doctrine of mutual mistake.

That leaves **C**, which is correct. **C** recites an element critical to the mutual mistake doctrine, to wit, that each of these parties manifested his or her belief to the point of absolute *fact* that the cow was infertile. Referring to the

Restatement's formulation, these parties manifested a belief that was not in accord with the facts, and that belief served as a basic assumption on which they formed their contract. Hence, **C** is right.

QUESTION 2. Nancy's great uncle dies, leaving his home and its contents to Nancy. Nancy decides to sell the home, and commissions Oliver to empty it for that purpose.

> **Nancy:** I'll pay you $20 per hour if you'll empty the house.
> **Oliver:** I normally charge $35 per hour.
> **Nancy:** What if we agree that you can keep anything you find in the house?
> **Oliver:** Well, what's *in* the house?
> **Nancy:** As far as I know—junk. But who knows? Sometimes old junk is valuable.
> **Oliver:** You're right. Who knows?
> **Nancy:** Do we have a deal—$20 per hour and you keep the junk?
> **Oliver:** Yes.

Oliver empties the house. Buried among items in its attic he seizes on a cluster of 1910 stock certificates, which upon his research reveal a value of $20 million. Nancy learns of the find and insists on having the certificates herself. She engages a lawyer who, on the ground of mutual mistake, brings an action seeking rescission and a return to Nancy of the stock certificates. Oliver contends that mutual mistake does not apply. Which of the following most *weakens* Nancy's position?

A. Nancy deliberately persuaded Oliver to accept less than $35 per hour for his work.

B. In making her offer, Nancy believed the house contained nothing of value.

C. In using the word "junk," the parties manifested their assumption that the home contained nothing of great value.

D. In using the phrase "who knows?," the parties mutually manifested their uncertainty as to the value of the home's contents.

ANALYSIS.   In order that the mutual mistake doctrine apply to this case, Nancy would have to show (1) that before forming their contract, the parties led each other to understand that each believed—not as speculation, but to the point of fact—that the home contained nothing of significant value; (2) that she led Oliver to understand that she would not have entered the contract absent that belief; and (3) that the mutual belief was mistaken—that the home did, in fact, contain one or more items of significant value.

A is a big "so what?" Nancy offered $20 per hour, and Oliver accepted it. **B** is irrelevant and implies a false statement. An offer's terms mean what a reasonable person in the offeree's position would think them to mean. **C** argues *for Nancy's* position. If the parties mutually manifested an assumption that the home contained only "junk," then the stock certificates shows they *were* mistaken, just as Nancy contends.

We're left with **D**, and it's correct. It posits that the parties mutually manifested their understanding that the presence or absence of valuable articles within the home amounted to a risk, each side of it resting on one of the parties. To finish the argument that **D** starts, we would say that the contract, properly interpreted, allocated (a) to Nancy the risk that the home harbored items of significant value and (b) to Oliver the risk that it did not. If as to some circumstance in place at the time they form their contract, two parties manifest their uncertainty, then they allocate the relevant risk between them. They make no "mistake," and the mutual mistake doctrine does not apply. **D** is right.

QUESTIONS 3 & 4. AuctionCorp conducts an auction in which it attempts to sell memorabilia. The auction is "with reserve," meaning that AuctionCorp is not obliged to sell any item unless the highest bid is, in its judgment, *sufficiently* high, in which case it will sell to the highest bidder. At the auction site, AuctionCorp posts a sign that reads: "All sales are final."

Auctioneer: We have here lot 15, a scarf that belonged to Vice President Spiro Agnew, and lot 16, a scarf that belonged to President Abraham Lincoln. I put up first lot 15—the Spiro Agnew scarf. Do I hear $5,000? . . . $500? . . . $50? . . . $5? . . . $1? . . . 50 cents? . . . 1 cent?

Bidder 1: Yes, 1 cent; I'll use it for wrapping fish.

Auctioneer: Sold for 1 cent.

Auctioneer: I show you now lot 16—a scarf that belonged to President Abraham Lincoln. Do I hear . . .

Bidder 1: $50,000

Bidder 2: $500,000

Bidder 1: $5 million

Bidder 2: $50 million

Auctioneer: Do I hear $55 million? Going once, twice—sold for $50 million.

Bidder 1 paid 1 cent and took the scarf labeled lot 15. Bidder 2 paid $50 million and took the scarf labeled lot 16. Three days later, all discover that the auctioneer had accidentally mislabeled the scarves. The lot 15 scarf had belonged to Lincoln and the lot 16 scarf to Agnew.

QUESTION 3. On the ground of mutual mistake, AuctionCorp brings an action against Bidder 1 seeking rescission of the contract and return of the Lincoln scarf. Which of the following facts should AuctionCorp prove and cite as a basis for its claim?

A. That as for this contract Bidder 1 bore the risk that the scarf might have belonged to Abraham Lincoln

B. That AuctionCorp and Bidder 1 manifested their certain belief that the lot 15 scarf had belonged to Vice President Agnew

C. That the auctioneer put up first the scarf he thought had belonged to Vice President Agnew and second the one he thought had belonged to President Lincoln

D. That between the two scarves, the difference in value pertains not to any inherent quality of each, but to their divergent histories

QUESTION 4. On the ground of mutual mistake, Bidder 2 brings an action seeking rescission of his contract with AuctionCorp and a return of his $50 million. He should

A. win, pursuant to mutual mistake.

B. win, because the Agnew scarf has a fair market value substantially less than the $50 million Bidder 2 paid for it.

C. lose, because AuctionCorp posted the sign reading "All sales are final."

D. lose, because AuctionCorp acted in good faith throughout.

ANALYSIS. The situation bears all elements tied to the mutual mistake doctrine, which therefore renders voidable both of AuctionCorp's contracts — that with Bidder 1 and that with Bidder 2. In both cases, Auctioneer and the bidder should reasonably have understood each other to take not as a chance but as a fact that the scarf was what Auctioneer said it was. In Restatement terms, both parties, contrary to the truth, believed lot 15 to be the Agnew scarf, with that mistaken belief constituting a "basic assumption" on which they formed their contract. Bidder 1, as a reasonable person, should have known (and certainly did know) that Auctioneer would not have let the scarf go for 1 cent if he'd known it belonged to Lincoln and not Agnew. In Restatement terms, the mistaken belief had a "material effect on the agreed exchange of performances."

As for the second contract, Auctioneer should have known (and certainly did know) that Bidder 2 would not have paid $50 million for Spiro Agnew's scarf (or for anything that ever pertained to Spiro Agnew except, maybe, his death certificate). Hence, both contracts answer to the doctrine of mutual mistake. Each is voidable by the injured party, the first by Auctioneer and the second by Bidder 2.

The right answer to Question 3 is the one that reflects at least one of the doctrine's elements: (1) that each party manifested to the other his understanding—to the point of absolute fact—that the lot 15 scarf had belonged to Agnew and not Lincoln; (2) that the lot 16 scarf had, in fact, belonged to Lincoln, not Agnew; (3) that Bidder 1 should have understood that Auctioneer would not have accepted 1 cent for Lincoln's scarf.

A does the opposite. It states that the contract did allocate risk. **C** refers to an utter irrelevancy. It is insignificant to the doctrine of mutual mistake of which order the auctioneer put up the two scarves. **D** correctly states that the two scarves carry different values because they have different histories. But the mistake doctrine takes no account of why two items might have different values. **B** states, in substance, that each party manifested his belief to the point of fact that the lot 16 scarf had belonged to Lincoln. That reflects the first criterion tied to the mutual mistake rule, and so **B** is right.

In Question 4, **B**, **C**, and **D** make correct factual statements—all of them irrelevant. No doubt the fair market value of the Agnew scarf is far less than $50 million. Indeed, the auction is potent evidence that the scarf is worth exactly 1 cent. But that does not go to the elements of mutual mistake. Further, it's true that AuctionCorp posted an "All sales are final" sign. Nothing in the law allows any such sign to supersede the doctrine of mutual mistake or to supersede any other law pertaining to contracts. Finally, that AuctionCorp acted honestly is, similarly, irrelevant. The mutual mistake doctrine does not concern the matter of honesty or dishonesty.

A correctly states that Bidder 2 should win because all elements of the mutual mistake doctrine apply to his contract. Hence, **A** is right.

C.   Frustration of Purpose

Suppose it's July 3 and Party A wants to see tomorrow's July 4th parade from a tall building that overlooks Main Street. Party B owns such a building. A explains to B that he wants to see the July 4th parade from a spot high in B's building, and the two agree that B will allow A to occupy a room on the 25th floor of her Main Street building "in order that A be able to view tomorrow's July 4th parade, in exchange for $500 to be paid by A to B at the conclusion of the parade."

Early on the morning of July 4th, a terrorist incident causes the city to cancel the parade. With no parade to see, A has no use for the room. He wants "out" of his contract with B. The mutual mistake doctrine affords A no relief; the parties did not manifest belief in some fact or circumstance *in place at the time they formed their contract*. The situation thus differs from the timber and pregnant cow cases. In the timber case, the parties manifested their belief—to the point of absolute fact—that there stood on Seller's realty, *at the time they formed the contract,* 140,000 trees, when in fact the trees were, at that time, no longer there. In the cow case, the parties manifested their belief—to the point of absolute fact—that the cow, *when they formed their contract,* was infertile, when in fact it was at that time "with calf."

Here, the surprise relates not to a circumstance relevant to the time at which the parties contract, *but to a future event,* the July 4th parade that, contrary to their certain belief—contrary to their basic assumption—did not occur. Upon that (conceptually unimportant) distinction, the law distinguishes between mutual mistake and "frustration of purpose." It provides: *With respect to a contract between Parties A and B, A is discharged from any performance not yet given if (1) when forming their contract, the parties manifest their mutual belief, to the point of absolute fact, that some event will (or will not) occur, (2) when forming the contract B should, under the circumstances, understand that absent the expected occurrence (or nonoccurrence) of that event, A will fail to fulfill his principal purpose in forming the contract, and (3) (through no fault of A), contrary to the parties' mutually manifested belief, the event does not (or does) occur.*

The canceled parade case answers to the rule. A and B mutually manifested a belief—to the point of absolute fact—that the July 4th parade would occur—not that it *might* occur—not that it *probably* would occur, but that it *would* occur. On the basis of A's statements, B should have understood that A would not have rented the room absent his expectation that the parade would occur. Finally, contrary to the parties' belief, the parade did not occur.

Where frustration of purpose applies, it does not render a contract voidable, but rather creates the equivalent of a condition subsequent (Chapter 21, section A) and so discharges the aggrieved party from any remaining obligation to perform. In our July 4th case, A has not yet paid B, and the frustration of his purpose discharges his duty to do so. (If in whole, or in part, A had paid B, A might be entitled to recover his payment as restitution for unjust enrichment.)

D. Impracticability

Think again of the July 4th case. Parties A and B form a contract under which B will allow A to occupy a room in her building on Main Street. Imagine now that the terrorist incident occurs. This time it destroys B's building. But the city doesn't cancel the parade; the festivity goes forward. With the building destroyed, B can't possibly perform her part of the bargain; she can't allow A to occupy the room because room and building are reduced to rubble.

The case differs from the canceled parade case in this way: In that case the unexpected supervening (future occurring) event rendered valueless to A what B was to provide him; cancellation of the parade "frustrated" A's "purpose" in wanting a room high up in B's building. In the blown-up building case, neither party's purpose is frustrated. Rather, the supervening event—destruction of the building—renders it impractical (in this case, impossible) for B to perform. B's duty is discharged upon the doctrine of "impracticability."[3]

The doctrine of impracticability provides: *As to a contract between Parties A and B, not yet fully performed, B is discharged from the duty of further performance if*

(1) when forming their contract, the parties manifest their mutual belief, to the point of absolute fact, that some event will (or will not) occur,

(2) when forming the contract, A should, under the circumstances, understand that the occurrence or nonoccurrence of the event will render it unreasonably difficult or impossible for B to perform, and

(3) contrary to their belief, and through no fault of B, the event does not or (does) occur.

Frustration and Impracticability: The Commonality and the Difference

The Commonality. Both the frustration and impracticability defenses require that a supervening (future occurring) event contravene a mutually manifested assumption as to what the future does or does not hold.

The Difference. They differ as to the *effect* of that unexpected supervening event: (1) if for one of the parties the supervening event strips the other party's performance of the value he justifiably anticipates, we say "frustration of purpose" (that's the canceled-parade case); and (2) if for one of the parties the supervening event makes performance impossible or far more costly, burdensome, or difficult than he justifiably anticipates, we say "impracticability" (that's the blown-up building case).

Where we write of a mutually manifested belief to the point of certainty that some event will or will not occur, the Restatement writers, again, say "basic assumption," and here's how they state the two rules:

Restatement (Second) of Contracts §265 [Frustration of Purpose]

> Where, after a contract is made, a party's principal purpose is substantially frustrated without his fault by the occurrence of an event the non-occurrence of which was a basic assumption on which the contract was made, his remaining duties to render performance are discharged[.]

---

3. The doctrine once was called not "impracticability," but "impossibility." It was said that on such basis one was discharged from her contractual obligation only when she could not *possibly* perform. Taylor v. Caldwell, 122 Eng. Rep. 309 (K.B. 1863).

Restatement (Second) of Contracts §261 [Impracticability]

Where, after a contract is made, a party's performance is made impracticable without his fault by the occurrence of an event the non-occurrence of which was a basic assumption on which the contract was made, his duty to render that performance is discharged, unless the language or the circumstances indicate the contrary.[4]

Finally, remember the difference between these two doctrines and the doctrine of mutual mistake. Mutual mistake operates when the parties adopt their contract upon a manifest (mistaken) basic certainty/assumption, express or implied, that some fact or circumstance is *in place at the time they form their contract*. As for its effect, the mistake might *either* frustrate one party's purpose or render one party's performance impractical/impossible.

QUESTIONS 5-7. ShowCo, located in Pottsfield, produces shows for theater owners. StageCo, located in Cincotti, owns and operates a theater. On July 1, 2019, ShowCo and StageCo form a contract including these terms:

> Whereas StageCo plans to sell seats in its theater for $100 each on such dates and for such performances as are described below, and whereas Morton Green is a world-renowned baritone revered, moreover, for his portrayal of the part of Ko-Ko in the opera hereinafter mentioned, the parties do agree that:
>
> 1. ShowCo will produce, at StageCo's facility, on the dates October 1 to October 15, 2019, inclusive, the comic opera *Mikado*, for which ShowCo will hire, furnish, and pay the entire cast and orchestra, the leading baritone role of Ko-Ko to be played by the celebrity Morton Green; and
> 2. StageCo will, on November 1, pay ShowCo $500,000 for such service.

QUESTION 5. Which of the following facts, if proven, would most likely render the contract voidable by ShowCo on the theory of mutual mistake?

A. On July 1, unbeknownst to either party, Morton Green was dead.
B. On August 1, Morton Green died.

---

4. We are at a loss to explain (1) why when referring to frustration the Restatement speaks only to the expected occurrence of an event that fails to occur, and (2) why when referring to impracticability it speaks only to the *non*occurrence of an event that does occur. Either doctrine might apply in either such situation—where an expected event does not occur or an unexpected event does occur.

C. On July 1, just before forming their contract, the parties mutually acknowledged their understanding that *Mikado* might not be appealing to a Cincotti audience.

D. On August 1, through no fault of StageCo, the Daily-Carta opera company obtained a court order against StageCo forbidding it to present *Mikado* to a paying audience.

ANALYSIS. Mutual mistake operates only if, *at the time they form their contract,* the parties mutually manifest, to the point of certainty/fact/basic assumption, a mistaken belief as to a circumstance *already existing at that time.* The doctrine, of course, requires more than that, but that, first, it demands. **B** and **D** describe supervening events — events that arise in August — *after* the parties form their contract, so both are wrong. **C** also refers to the future — whether an audience will or will not wish to see the opera. Furthermore, **C** describes as an allocated risk the possibility that Cincotti audiences will or will not wish to see *Mikado*. If expressly or implicitly contracting parties do allocate a given risk, then there cannot apply any of the three doctrines of mistake, frustration, or impracticability. **A** reports that Morton Green is dead *on July 1,* and thus hypothesizes a fact in existence *at the time the parties form their contract.* Among these choices, therefore, only **A** cites a fact essential to ShowCo's claim of mutual mistake. **A** is right.

QUESTION 6. Which of the following facts, if proven, would most likely discharge ShowCo's duty to perform on the theory of impracticability?

A. On July 1, unbeknownst to either party, Morton Green was dead.
B. On August 1, Morton Green died.
C. On July 1, just before forming their contract, the parties mutually acknowledge their understanding that *Mikado* might not be appealing to a Cincotti audience.
D. On August 1, through no fault of StageCo, the Daily-Carta opera company obtains a court order against StageCo forbidding it to present *Mikado* to any audience, whether or not the audience pays for the presentation.

ANALYSIS. Like frustration of purpose, impracticability requires a supervening event — an event that occurs *after* the parties form their contract, which event, of course, they manifestly assumed would not occur. (As noted at footnote 5 above, both doctrines apply also when the parties assume that some event will *not* occur and, contrary to their assumption, it does.) Impracticability applies when the supervening event renders it far more difficult, costly, burdensome — or indeed, impossible — for one of the parties to perform. The right answer is that which refers to an event that (a) according to their manifestations at the time they formed their contract, the parties believed certainly would (or would not occur), and (b) whose nonoccurrence (or occurrence) makes it unreasonably difficult or impossible for one of them to perform.

A hypothesizes a fact *in place at the time the parties contract*. For that reason, it's wrong. C, once again, describes not a "basic assumption," but uncertainty — an allocated risk, which is the very circumstance that renders inapplicable all of the three doctrines, mistake, frustration, and impracticability. D does hypothesize an event that occurs after the parties form their contract, but its effect is to render *StageCo's performance* impractical/impossible. We're looking for a fact that renders *ShowCo's* performance impractical/impossible.

B describes an event that occurs after the parties form their contract whose effect is to render it impossible for ShowCo to perform. With Morton Green dead, ShowCo can't secure him for its cast. Hence, B is right.

QUESTION 7. Which of the following facts, if proven, would most likely discharge StageCo's duty to perform on the theory of frustration of purpose?

A. On July 1, unbeknownst to either party, Morton Green was dead.

B. On August 1, Morton Green died.

C. On July 1, just before forming their contract, the parties mutually acknowledge their understanding that *Mikado* might not be appealing to a Cincotti audience.

D. On August 1, through no fault of StageCo, the Daily-Carta opera company obtains a court order against StageCo forbidding it to present *Mikado* to any *paying* audience, but allows StageCo, still, to present it to a non-paying audience.

ANALYSIS. Like impracticability, frustration of purpose applies when there occurs some supervening event that the parties manifestly believed, to the point of certainty/basic assumption/absolute fact, would not occur. (And, as earlier noted, it applies, too, when as a basic assumption, the parties believe an event *will* occur, but it does *not*.) Its effect must be to frustrate for Party 1 that which Party 2 knows or should know to be Party 1's essential purpose in forming the contract.

Here, StageCo formed the contract in order to derive revenue. The right answer, therefore, must describe an event that occurs after the parties form their contract, whose effect is to prevent StageCo from *selling tickets*. **A** describes a preexisting fact or circumstance that renders it impossible for ShowCo to perform. (That's why it's the right answer to Question 5 above.) **B** describes a supervening event that renders *ShowCo's* performance impossible (and so it's the correct answer to Question 6 above). **C**, once again, describes a circumstance as to which the parties manifest uncertainty, which, therefore, cannot answer the criterion of "basic assumption." **D** describes an event that occurs after the parties form their contract, whose effect is to prevent StageCo from charging a price to its audience, thus frustrating StageCo's essential contractual purpose. Hence, **D** is right.

E.   Unilateral Mistake

The courts have little common understanding of what they mean by the phrase "unilateral mistake." They use it in three wholly different contexts, the first of which is absolutely unjustifiable.

Situation 1.   Courts most often invoke the phrase when two parties purport to form a contract but give materially different meanings to some critical word or phrase, both of them reasonable. Such are the cases we described in Chapter 3, section C, to which some courts also apply the phrase "meeting of the minds."[5] The courts shouldn't do that, but they do. (If the *Peerless* situation (Chapter 3, section C) were not so famously tagged with the phrases "meeting of the minds" and "latent ambiguity," many courts would, today, call it a case of unilateral mistake. And, as described in footnote 1 above, courts also invoke "mutual mistake" under those same circumstances. That too is unjustifiable.

There Remain Two Situations in Which Courts Invoke the Words "Unilateral Mistake"; Here They Come

Situation 2.   On May 25, 2019, DemCo, a political organization, asks BusCo, a busing company, if it can transport 200 DemCo members round-trip from Los Angeles to Washington, D.C., some ten months later, with departure from Los Angeles on March 1, 2020, arrival back in Los Angeles on March 15. In response, BusCo contacts LeaseCo to discuss leasing eight buses for the first two weeks of March, and LeaseCo assures BusCo that the buses will be

5.   See, e.g., Beatty v. Depue, 103 N.W.2d 187 (S.D. 1960); *cf.* Fleischer v. McGehee, 163 S.W. 169 (Ark. 1914); Goodrich v. Lathrop, 29 P. 329 (Cal. 1892); Perlmutter v. Bacas, 149 A.2d 23 (Md. 1959); Winkelman v. Erwin, 165 N.E. 205 (Ill. 1929); Stong v. Lane, 68 N.W. 765 (Minn. 1896).

available. BusCo then contacts DemCo offering to transport the 200 DemCo members to Washington, D.C., on the dates specified by DemCo, for a total fee of $40,000. DemCo accepts the offer. On June 1, 2019, the parties reduce their contract to a signed writing providing that DemCo will pay BusCo $40,000 with BusCo, on the specified dates, to furnish the round-trip transportation from Los Angeles to Washington.

In February 2020, BusCo attempts to contact LeaseCo to secure the necessary buses and discovers that on May 31, 2019, just a few months after it had interacted with LeaseCo, LeaseCo had ceased to do business. BusCo wants "out" of its contract with DemCo, stating that its belief in LeaseCo's existence was its own "unilateral mistake." Now, before we probe the relevant law, let's read about situation 3.

Situation 3.   Contractor and Developer form a contract under which Contractor is to construct a building on Developer's land. To fulfill her obligations, Contractor must secure the services of subcontractors — electricians, masons, heating specialists, ventilation specialists, and many others — with whom she plans to form contracts for the purchase of their services.

Contractor asks five electricians to bid on the electrical components of the project. (When one asks for bids, be he a contractor or an auctioneer, he makes an invitation to deal (Chapter 4, section A). A bid, itself, is an offer.) From four of the electricians, Contractor receives these bids: (1) $920,000, (2) $890,000, (3) $1,110,000, and (4) $990,000. The fifth bidder, ElCo, intends to bid $975,000, but in writing the bid, one of its clerks mistakenly writes "$97,500." On receiving ElCo's bid, Contractor immediately writes to ElCo, "We accept your offer." When ElCo discovers its error, it wishes not to perform the work for so little. The $97,500 figure, it says, was its own "unilateral mistake."

These Two Cases Represent Two Very Different Forms of Mistake.   In situation 1, BusCo formed its June 1 contract upon *its own* belief, to the point of basic assumption, that LeaseCo was in business and ready to supply buses. In fact, LeaseCo, like the Woodacre trees, had "burned"; it no longer existed. BusCo made the kind of mistake that underlies the rule of *mutual* mistake, but BusCo *alone* made the mistake. DemCo did not. Hence, the law applies to BusCo the phrase "unilateral mistake."

In situation 2, ElCo did not form its contract with Contractor upon any basic assumption or belief as to a nonexistent fact. Rather, it made a clerical error in transcribing the bid it meant to make. This sort of error, too, the law treats as a unilateral mistake, although in its nature it differs entirely from the mistake at issue in the BusCo case.

The Law Affords Situations 1 and 2 Two Different Treatments.   As to situation 1 — the contracting party who commits the first form of error — the law seldom, if ever, allows him to void the contract. That's because a reasonable contracting party normally understands (even if subconsciously) that his contract allocates to him the risk that he enters it due to some misinformation or misapprehension. One's own misinformation is one's own problem. If BusCo promises to transport passengers falsely (though faultlessly), believing that LeaseCo will make buses available to BusCo, then BusCo's personnel, as reasonable persons, should understand that LeaseCo's disappearance is their problem — that the contract allocates that risk to *them*. (Likewise, as reasonable persons, the DemCo folks should understand that if they fail to secure a sufficient number of passengers to pay BusCo's $40,000 fee, that such is their problem; the contract allocates that risk to DemCo.[6])

As to the contracting party who commits the second form of unilateral mistake — a simple careless error — the law works a discharge if the other party should, as a reasonable person, perceive the error.[7] In the ElCo case above, Contractor received four bids all falling within the "ballpark" of $1 million. She should have known that ElCo did not really mean to offer its service for $97,500 but rather that it had misplaced a comma and then omitted a zero. Certainly a court would rule that the contract is voidable by ElCo. Stated otherwise, ElCo made a careless clerical error, and Contractor should have known that.

So What Do We Know About Unilateral Mistake? We know that when courts write "unilateral mistake," they refer to one of these three very different kinds of mishap:

1. That in which two parties give materially different interpretations to the words on which they purport to agree, both of them reasonable. In those cases, "unilateral mistake" is improperly used. The parties fail to form a contract because they have not achieved offer and acceptance or an *objective* "meeting of the minds." They are addressing, really, a "Peerless" kind of case, incorrectly invoking the phrase "unilateral mistake" (Chapter 3, section C).

---

6. Yet, the Restatement writers, recklessly and without cited authority, describe the law otherwise. According to Restatement (Second) §152, one who makes the sort of unilateral mistake just described may void the contract if (a) the contract does not allocate the risk of the mistake to him, and (b) by enforcing the contract (awarding damages for breach), the court would subject him to "unconscionability." The Restatement writers offer not a whit of authority to support their thinking. Not one of the judicial opinions cited together with §152 invokes any words similar to "allocation of risk" or "unconscionability." And although the cited cases do refer to "unilateral mistake," all inexcusably describe, as discussed above, offerors and offerees who give two different interpretations to the terms of their agreement, *both of them reasonable*. Those cases do not properly belong, even, to the subject of unilateral mistake.

7. Yet again, in this context the Restatement, recklessly and without cited authority, invokes the word "unconscionable." Restatement (Second) §152 provides in full: "Where a mistake of one party at the time a contract was made as to a basic assumption on which he made the contract has a material effect on the agreed exchange of performances that is adverse to him, the contract is voidable by him if he does not bear the risk of the mistake . . . and (a) the effect of the mistake is such that enforcement of the contract would be unconscionable, or (b) the other party had reason to know of the mistake or his fault caused the mistake."

2. That in which two parties form a contract with one of them (but not the other) believing to the point of certainty or "basic assumption" that some fact or circumstance is then in place when in fact it is not. Probably, that sort of mistake never renders a contract voidable.[8]

3. That in which one contracting party commits an ordinary careless error in expression — a "slip" of the pen or tongue. That sort of unilateral mistake renders a contract voidable if the other party knows or should know of the error (which certainly includes any situation in which he himself has *caused* the error).

QUESTION 8. C-Corp, a construction company building a high-rise office building, invites bids from eight plumbing companies in relation to the plumbing for which the project calls. Seven plumbing companies respond with bids that range from $15 million to $16 million. The eighth company, PlumbCo, bids $15.6 million. But in calculating that bid it omits, by simple oversight, to account for a $150,000 expense it would have to bear in completing the project. If it had not made the error, therefore, its bid would have been $15,600,000 + $150,000 = $15,750,000 = $15.75 million, instead of $15.6 million.

C-Corp receives Plumbco's $15.6 million bid and immediately accepts it. It does so even though other of the bids it receives are lower, because C-Corp's president has faith in PlumbCo. After C-Corp issues its acceptance, PlumbCo discover its $150,000 error and seeks to void the contract. In all likelihood, PlumbCo

A. can void the contract because C-Corp received seven additional bids, any one of which it can accept or could have accepted.

B. can void the contract because C-Corp had good reason to believe that PlumbCo had made a simple error in addition.

C. cannot void the contract because such would subject C-Corp to a possible loss of profit.

D. cannot void the contract because, under the circumstances, C-Corp had no reason to believe that PlumbCo had made the error in addition.

ANALYSIS. All authorities agree that if one enters a contract whose terms reflect a clerical error, he may void the contract if the other party, as a reasonable person, *should have known of the error*. In this situation, C-Corp received seven bids, all of them within the range of $15 million to $16 million. PlumbCo's bid fell squarely within that range, notwithstanding its error.

---

8. Yet, the Restatement, without authority or relevant illustration, states that it does so where enforcement would be "unconscionable."

Consequently, C-Corp had no reason to believe that PlumbCo, due to its own error, submitted a bid of $15.6 million instead of $15.75 million. For *that* reason, PlumbCo's mistake does not afford it the right to void the contract.

A and **B** report that PlumbCo can void the contract, so they're wrong. In addition, **A** makes a statement of abject irrelevancy; that C-Corp had other offers available to it plays no role in the doctrine of unilateral mistake. **B** makes the false statement that C-Corp had reason to know of PlumbCo's error. **C** correctly states that PlumbCo cannot void the contract, but its reason is no reason at all: The phrase "loss of profit" has no place in the realm of unilateral mistake. **D** is right in all respects. It tells us that PlumbCo must abide by its contract notwithstanding the error because C-Corp had no reason to think it was "snapping up" an offer that arose through error. Hence, **D** is right.

QUESTION 9. On September 20, EmCo, owner of a property known as the Wrightworth Estate, by signed writing, offers to sell it to ZeCo for $50 million. The Wrightworth Estate has no house on it, but in the same vicinity is a property also owned by EmCo known as the Wentworth Estate, which includes an enormous mansion. Misreading EmCo's offer, ZeCo thinks that it pertains to the Wentworth Estate. Wanting property only with a mansion, ZeCo accepts EmCo's offer, also by signed writing. When ZeCo learns that it has confused "Wentworth" with "Wrightworth," it seeks to void the contract. If the court does not permit ZeCo to void the contract, it might state among its reasons that

I.   the contract implicitly allocated to ZeCo the risk that it had misunderstood EmCo's offer.
II. the contract falls within the Statute of Frauds.
A. I
B. II
C. Both I and II
D. Neither I nor II

ANALYSIS.   The law seldom, if ever, allows a contracting party to void a contract because she (and not the other) enters it through some mistaken belief or assumption. That's because a reasonable person normally understands (even if she does not think in these words) that her agreement allocates to her the risk that she, alone, through no fault of the other party, is misinformed or otherwise acting under a misapprehension. EmCo's error is its own. The contract implicitly allocates to EmCo the risk that it is misinformed or otherwise operating under a misapprehension.

Option II states an irrelevancy. The contract does fall within the Statute of Frauds because it provides for the sale of realty (Chapter 15, section A). That, however, has no bearing on *mistake*. Option I states the relevant truth, and so **A** is right.

F.   The Closers

QUESTIONS 10 & 11. ArmCo is in the business of selling weapons to national governments. On September 1, 2019, the nation of Qarat is at war with Bohrein and, as is widely publicized, the nations are conducting peace negotiations even as they fight. Also on September 1, by signed writing, ArmCo as buyer contracts with WeapCo as seller for the purchase of 100 tanks at $200 million, delivery to be made eleven months later on August 1, 2020. ArmCo forms the contract in order that it be able to supply Qarat and Bohrein with additional tanks if and as the two nations seek to purchase them. ArmCo pays WeapCo $20 million on September 1 and promises to pay the remaining balance on August 15, 2020.

On July 1, 2020, the warring nations reach a peace accord. The war ends. Consequently, ArmCo is unable to sell the tanks. It wants not to pay WeapCo any remaining purchase price.

QUESTION 10. ArmCo's attorney recognizes that ArmCo might not be entitled to a discharge of its obligations. Nevertheless, she decides to argue on ArmCo's behalf. In seeking to obtain a discharge for ArmCo, the attorney would be best advised to cite the doctrine of

A. frustration of purpose, because at the time the parties formed their contract, the peace accord represented a future event.
B. frustration of purpose, because at the time the parties formed their contract, each party understood that it was in no position to know for how long the war would continue.
C. mutual mistake, because when they formed their contract, the parties were mistaken about the likely duration of the war.
D. mutual mistake, because when they formed their contract, the peace negotiations were in progress.

ANALYSIS.   Mutual mistake and frustration of purpose differ most significantly in that (1) mutual mistake requires that the contracting parties be manifestly, mutually mistaken as to a fact or circumstance *in existence at the time they form their contract*, whereas (2) frustration of purpose requires that they be manifestly, mutually mistaken as to the occurrence or nonoccurrence of some *future* event that one party should know will frustrate the other's essential purpose. Both, of course, require that both parties hold their manifest mistaken belief to the point of certainty—that it be a "basic assumption" on which they form the contract.

In this case, ArmCo cannot conceivably establish a mutual mistake as to a fact or circumstance in existence at the time the parties formed their contract. The peace talks were widely publicized and both knew (or certainly should have known) that. If ArmCo is entitled to withhold payment, it would have to resort to frustration of purpose and show that both parties manifested their belief, to the degree of fact—as a basic assumption—that the war would continue for at least eleven months—that the warring parties would reach no peace accord during that period.

C and **D** state that ArmCo should look to the doctrine of mutual mistake, so both are wrong for that reason. Further, **C**, while referring to mutual mistake, cites also a future circumstance, to wit, the likely duration of war. Again, mutual mistake requires that the parties be mistaken as to a fact or circumstance existing at the time they form their contract. **D** refers to a fact in place at the time the parties formed their contract, but that fact is one that each party had reason to know.

B reports that neither party could predict the prospects for war or peace. That suggests that they could not as reasonable persons assume that war would continue. **B** is wrong. **A** correctly refers to frustration of purpose and properly cites to the peace accord as a future event. That's why **A** is right.

QUESTION 11. If ArmCo claims discharge by frustration of purpose, which of the following facts, if proven by WeapCo, would weaken ArmCo's claim?

A. *As* they formed their contract, the parties manifested their mutual belief that the war was certain to endure for more than eleven months.

B. *As* they formed their contract, the parties mutually acknowledged that the war might not endure for eleven months.

C. *After* forming their contract, the parties manifested their mutual belief that the war was certain to endure for more than eleven months.

D. *After* forming their contract, the parties mutually acknowledged that the war might not endure for eleven months.

ANALYSIS. WeapCo will weaken ArmCo's claim of frustrated purpose if its proof negates one or more elements of the relevant rule. **A** affirmatively states one of the doctrine's elements, to wit, that the parties took as a fact — assumed — that war would not end within the period September 1 to August 1. If WeapCo were to prove *that*, it would *strengthen* ArmCo's claim, so **A** is wrong. **C** and **D** refer to the parties' state of mind *after* forming their contract, and that certainly is irrelevant. Both the mutual mistake and frustration doctrines (as well as the impracticability doctrine) require that the contracting parties manifest erroneous beliefs at the time they form their contract. With mutual mistake, the erroneous belief must relate to a fact in existence at that very time. With frustration, it must pertain to the future. Hence, **C** and **D** are wrong.

Now consider **B**. It hypothesizes that WeapCo proves this fact: As these parties formed their contract, they manifested their mutual belief that by August 1 the war might or might not end. If that was their manifest belief, then certainly the war's continuation was not a basic assumption on which they contracted. Rather, it was a matter of uncertainty, with ArmCo, as buyer, assuming the risk that the war might end by the date. Hence, the frustration doctrine would offer no relief to Buyer, and for that reason **B** is right.

 # Silver's Picks

1.	C
2.	D
3.	B
4.	A
5.	A
6.	B
7.	D
8.	D
9.	A
10.	A
11.	B

23

Warranty

A. What's a Warranty?

A warranty is one's contractual promise — his absolute guaranty — that some particular facts or circumstances are or will be in place. A piano tuner makes a warranty if to her customer she says, "I am well qualified to tune pianos." A bicycle seller makes a warranty if to his buyer he says, "this bicycle is perfectly suited for mountain climbing." All authorities divide warranties into two categories: "express" and "implied." An express warranty is one that a seller creates by his own words or behavior. An implied warranty is one that the law creates on its own.

Sometimes expressly and sometimes by implication of law, the purveyor of a good or service warrants that what he sells will be of some specific quality concerning its function, utility, or durability (among other matters). For example, the bicycle seller warranted that "this bicycle" was suited to mountain climbing. Those are the warranties that most often create legal disputes — warranties concerning the quality of a good or service that one party sells to another.

B. Warranties as to Service

1. Nonprofessional Sellers of Service: Express Warranties

When a nonprofessional sells a service, the law implies no warranties. If, however, such a seller makes an express warranty, she is bound by it as she is by any term of her contract. Suppose that on his car's fender, Bard sees a scratch, which he mentions to his next-door neighbor, Lola. Lola says, "I'd be happy to remove the scratch and refinish the affected area." Bard queries, "Do you know how to do that work?" She replies, "Yes. I warrant that after I complete my work, you will be unable to identify the affected area of the car." Bard asks to know "how much," and Lola says "$200." He replies, "It's a deal." The parties thus form a contract under which Lola, for $200, will remove the scratch and refinish the affected area. Further, the contract includes Lola's express warranty that after she completes her work, Bard will be unable to identify the scratched area.

In order to communicate her express warranty, Lola need not use the words "I warrant." She could simply say, "After I complete my work, you will be unable to identify the affected area of the car." Or, when Bard asks, "Do you know how to do that work," Lola might show him photographs of other scratched fenders she has repaired. Bard, as a reasonable person, will justifiably conclude that in promising to repair his fender, Lola promises also that her work will conform to the quality of the photographs she shows him. In that case, too, she makes an express warranty. Lola might (1) use the words "I warrant," or (2) expressly describe the quality of the work she will do, or (3) show Bard a sample of her work as a means of telling him how her work will appear. In every such case, she makes an express warranty.

Express Warranty: A Rule.   *One expressly warrants the service she sells if in forming her contract with her buyer by written or spoken word, description, display, depiction, sample, or simulation—she leads the buyer reasonably to believe in some fact pertaining to its nature, quality, or durability.*[1]

2. *Professional Sellers of Service: Implied Warranties*

Depending on the jurisdiction and the industry, a seller who holds himself out as a professional provider of a service warrants that he will perform in a "good and workmanlike" manner. That phrase, in turn, refers to a performance that would ordinarily be given by one who has the knowledge, training, and/or experience necessary for the successful practice of the seller's same trade or occupation. Where such an implied warranty applies, it means the service provider must perform his work at least as well as would the ordinary reasonable person *in his same profession.*

That warranty does not pertain directly to outcome. The fact that a mechanic agrees to "repair the leaking gas tank" does not imply a warranty that when he completes the job, the tank will not leak. Rather, by law, it implies a warranty that he will think, judge, decide, and perform at least as well as would a mechanic of fair and average ability. If, in doing so, he fails to stop

---

1.   That rule, of course, is but a corollary to a set of more basic ones that we presented at the very beginning of Chapter 18, section A.

the leak, he does not breach any implied warranty. If, on the other hand, he exercises lesser judgment and skill than would the ordinary, average mechanic confronted with the same work, and for *that* reason fails to fix the tank, then, in that case, he breaches a warranty. Such a warranty applies by common law to construction workers, and by statute, in some states, to other providers as well.

QUESTION 1. VentCo installs and repairs heating, air conditioning, and ventilation equipment. BuildCo is a builder. Both are located in a jurisdiction that imposes an implied warranty on all providers of building construction services. In connection with its construction of a residential apartment building, BuildCo, by signed writing, forms a contract with VentCo under which VentCo, for $700,000, is to "perform all services relating to the installation, placement, connection, and adjustment of all vents and related conductors appurtenant to the heating, air conditioning, and ventilation systems in the said building." Although the written agreement comprises thirty-five pages, it nowhere expressly describes the quality of VentCo's work or service. When VentCo announces completion of its work, BuildCo inspects it and finds it unsatisfactory. BuildCo brings an action alleging that VentCo is in breach of warranty.

At trial, BuildCo calls as witnesses various VentCo personnel, who describe in detail the way in which they think about their work, make their judgments, and perform their installations. Separately, BuildCo introduces evidence of the way in which the heating, ventilation, and air conditioning systems, as installed, do and do not function. Thereafter, BuildCo calls as a witness a professional expert in the field of heating, ventilation, and air conditioning systems. That witness will most directly support BuildCo's claim if he testifies that

A. in his opinion, VentCo's work product would not suit the ordinary and reasonable needs of the residents who occupy BuildCo's building.

B. he himself would have performed the work differently from the way in which VentCo performed it.

C. in his opinion, VentCo did not reach its professional decisions with the same care as would a professional in the same field with the ordinary degree of skill.

D. having examined the building's heating, air conditioning, and ventilation systems after VentCo installed them, he would not hire VentCo to do the sort of work for which BuildCo hired it.

ANALYSIS. Under the contract, VentCo made no express warranty as to the quality of its work. Consequently, any breach by VentCo of a warranty must relate to an implied warranty—a warranty that the law imposes on it.

The only warranty that the law imposes on providers of a service (and it does not impose one on all of them; some states impose it only as to construction work) is that of "good and workmanlike" performance, which relates not to the outcome of one's work but to the way in which one performs it (which, of course, does *affect* the outcome). Most relevant to BuildCo's claim in breach of warranty is evidence not as to how the various systems function, but as to how VentCo actually performed its work.

A relates not to how VentCo performed its work but to how the systems will or will not meet the needs of reasonable persons. It's wrong, and the friendly phrase "reasonable persons" can't make it right. **B** relates not to whether VentCo performed as would an average professional in its field, but to how the expert witness himself would have chosen to do the work. It too is wrong. **D** is also off the mark. It tells us only that the expert witness thinks VentCo's work product inadequate to the standards by which *he* would hire a professional in the same field.

C is best; it affords the fact finder a basis on which to conclude that VentCo performed its work in a manner not equal to the standard that prevails among average professionals in its field. That denotes a breach of VentCo's warranty to perform its service in a "good and workmanlike manner," and that's why **C** is right.

C.   Express Warranties Relating to Goods

UCC Article 2 governs warranties related to goods. UCC §2-313 provides:

(1) Express warranties by the seller are created as follows:

(a) Any affirmation of fact or promise made by the seller to the buyer which relates to the goods and becomes part of the basis of the bargain creates an express warranty that the goods shall conform to the affirmation or promise.

(b) Any description of the goods which is made as part of the basis of the bargain creates an express warranty that the goods shall conform to the description.

(c) Any sample or model which is made part of the basis of the bargain creates an express warranty that the whole of the goods shall conform to the sample or model.

(2) It is not necessary to the creation of an express warranty that the seller use formal words such as "warrant" or "guarantee" or that he have a specific intention to make a warranty, but an affirmation merely of the value of the goods or a statement purporting to be merely the seller's opinion or commendation of the goods does not create a warranty.

The definition is much like the common law definition we present in section B above, relating to service, and it carries the same meaning.

QUESTION 2. Channah visits TronCo to purchase a set of wall-mountable shelves on which to place her stereo equipment. The salesperson shows her a set of shelves mounted in its showroom and says, "How about this?" In color, the shelves happened to be black. Channah asks about the price, receives an answer of "$195," and then says, "I'll take it." The salesperson retrieves a large box from the back room. Channah pays $195 and receives a receipt that reads "$195 received for X23 Wall Unit." At home, Channah opens the box and finds shelves that resemble the ones shown to her at TronCo, except that they are white instead of black. Is TronCo in breach of an express warranty?

A. Yes, because the receipt expressly identifies the product for which Channah paid

B. Yes, because of the color difference between the product TronCo supplied to Channah and the one it showed her

C. No, because TronCo made no expression or communication as to the color of the shelves it supplied Channah

D. No, because Channah asked no questions and made no statements about color or preference as to color

---

ANALYSIS. Reread UCC §2-313(1)(c) above. The TronCo salesperson showed Channah the model attached to the walls of the showroom. By doing so, TronCo made an express warranty that the shelves supplied to Channah would conform to the model, which, because of their color, it did not do. The answer therefore, is "yes," and the reason is that the contract included TronCo's *express* warranty that the shelves sold to Channah would be the same color as those she was shown.

C and D answer "no," so they're wrong for that reason alone. Further, C makes a (legally) false statement. By showing Channah its model, TronCo did make an expression as to the color of the shelves it would provide her. D implies that Channah's failure to mention color denies her an express warranty, and that's false. That TronCo showed her the model, making it a "basis of their bargain," creates the express warranty. A correctly reports that the receipt (in some way) identifies the product sold, but that creates no warranty.

B correctly answers "yes" and correctly states the reason: The color of the shelves Channah took home was different from those shown to her. The shelves did not conform to the sample or model presented to her. Hence, B is right.

D. Implied Warranties Relating to Goods

For the sale of goods, UCC Article 2 creates two *implied* warranties: (1) the warranty of "merchantability," which applies to virtually all contracts in which a merchant sells goods; and (2) the warranty of "fitness for a particular purpose," which applies to *some* contracts in which a merchant sells goods.

1. Merchantability

UCC §2-314 provides generally that a merchant who sells a good (to a merchant or non-merchant) implicitly warrants that it is "merchantable," which means it must be of such quality (a) as ordinarily characterizes that same product when sold, generally, throughout the relevant industry, and (b) as renders it suitable to the purpose for which reasonable persons use it. In stating that principle, the Code writers describe merchantable goods as those that are of such quality as "pass without objection in the trade," are of "fair and average quality," and are "fit for the ordinary purposes for which they are used."

2. "Fitness for Particular Purpose"

With the Code's implied warranty of merchantability, a seller promises that his goods are fit for their *ordinary* purpose—that a sponge will absorb water, a grass seed will grow grass, and a paper cutter will cut paper. Labeled by the Code as an implied warranty, it reflects, really, the broader rule that a contract includes such terms and has such meaning as will afford its parties their reasonable expectations. Now you'll see that "the implied warranty of fitness for a *particular* purpose" represents, really, that same rule.

Suppose Buyer contacts Seller, a professional dealer in widgets and widget covers: "I need a 2011 widget cover that will fit over a 1911 widget. Do you have any such thing?" Seller shows Buyer a widget cover and says, "Certainly we do. Here it is. It's $9.99." Buyer buys it. A reasonable person in Buyer's position would take Seller's statement to mean, "For $9.99, I will sell you this widget cover, and I promise it will fit over a 1911 widget."

Contemplating that kind of situation, the Code creates the implied warranty of fitness for a particular purpose, for which the relevant rule is this: *If a commercial seller of any good knows (or should know) (1) of some specific purpose for which the buyer wishes to secure the goods, and (2) that the buyer is looking to the seller's expertise in order that the good should serve that purpose, then, when he contracts to sell his good, he warrants that it will serve that very pupose. If he wishes not to make the warranty, then he must refrain from selling the good.* Here, in its very own words, is UCC §2-315:

> Where the seller at the time of contracting has reason to know any particular purpose for which the goods are required and that the buyer is relying on the seller's skill or judgment to select or furnish suitable goods, there is . . . an implied warranty that the goods shall be fit for such purpose.

Can a Seller Somehow Disclaim the Implied Warranties?   Yes, the Code allows a seller to "exclude" both the implied warranties of merchantability and fitness for particular purpose, but only if she does so according to the dictates of UCC §2-316. That section provides that the seller may exclude the warranty of merchantability (a) orally or (b) by conspicuous writing and that, in either case, she must use the word "merchantability" or words that in "common understanding" indicate the absence of implied warranties. By way of example, the Code cites to the phrases "as is" and "with all faults." A long string of big arcane words supplied by a lawyer will not disclaim the warranty. (And do remember that the seller who relies on an oral statement sets herself up for a potentially difficult task as to proof.)

A seller may exclude the warranty of fitness for a particular purpose *only by* "conspicuous" writing. In the writing, the phrases "as is," "with all faults," and "no implied warranties" are sufficient to work the exclusion. An attempt to exclude the fitness warranty by spoken word is ineffective, as are any words that a reasonable person of ordinary ability cannot understand.

E. The Closer

> **QUESTION 3.** On November 1, 2019, SurfCo contacts PlexCo.
>
> **SurfCo:** We plan to manufacture a new line of vacuum-formed sandwich-riding surfboards and so wish to purchase polyurethane foam.
> **PlexCo:** We have 120 different polyurethane foam preparations. Can you be more specific about the sort you'd like to have?
> **SurfCo:** No, we can't. We know only what we wish to do with it.
> **PlexCo:** Well, we can offer you our #99 polyurethane foam at $100 per commercial unit, delivered to your facility on November 20.
> **SurfCo:** We'll take 100 units.
>
> The parties then create a signed writing identifying SurfCo and PlexCo by name and address. It otherwise provides only this: "PlexCo will, on November 20, 2019, deliver 100 commercial units of its #99 polyurethane foam to SurfCo's facility, with SurfCo to pay $100 per unit for a total price of $10,000." If the #99 polyurethane foam is not suitable for the manufacture of vacuum-formed sandwich-riding surfboards, then, under UCC Article 2, PlexCo is in breach of
>
> A. an express warranty of merchantability.
> B. an express warranty of fitness for particular purpose.
> C. an implied warranty of merchantability.
> D. an implied warranty of fitness for particular purpose.

ANALYSIS.   PlexCo made no express warranty, but under UCC §2-314, it warrants its product to be "merchantable"—that it will serve its ordinary purpose and be of such fair and average quality as is ordinarily provided by sellers who deal in the same or analogous product. The case presents no evidence that PlexCo's product fails in those respects.

But SurfCo informed PlexCo that it needed the polyurethane foam for construction of a vacuum-formed sandwich-riding surfboard, and that it did not know what sort of foam would serve that purpose. PlexCo therefore knew (or should have known) "the particular purpose for which the goods [were] required and that the buyer [was] relying on [its] skill or judgment to select or furnish suitable goods." Consequently, PlexCo made a warranty of fitness for a particular purpose. By law, it promised that the polyurethane preparation #99 would be suitable for the manufacture of vacuum-formed sandwich-riding surfboards. If the product is not fit for that purpose, PlexCo is in breach of that warranty. Hence, **D** is right.

 ## Silver's Picks

1.	**C**
2.	**B**
3.	**D**

24

Third-Party Beneficiaries, Assignment, and Delegation

A. Third-Party Beneficiaries

1. Intended and Incidental Beneficiaries

B is a pianist and C is her next-door neighbor. C frequently hears B play and enjoys her music, until one day he begins to notice that B's piano is falling out of tune. B too knows that her piano is losing tune and forms a contract with A, a piano tuner, under which A will tune B's piano and B will pay him $150. C is not a party to the contract. A breaches; he fails properly to tune B's piano. Consequently, when B plays, C continues to hear piano music that offends his ear. For that reason, C (not B, but C, the neighbor) sues A for breach. Guess what? The court dismisses his suit.

Now suppose F owns a piano and E is her friend. As a gift to her friend, E wishes to have F's piano tuned. E forms a contract with D under which D will tune F's piano and E will pay D $150 for that service. E tells F about the contract she has made with D and F is delighted; as a gift to her, her piano will be tuned. F is not party to the contract. D breaches; he fails properly to tune F's piano. F sues D. The court *sustains* her suit.

Why Dismissal for C but Not F?

In both cases, two persons form a contract, and a third person, not party to the contract, stands, somehow, to benefit from one of the contracting parties' performances. In the first case, C stands to benefit from A's performance; if A properly tunes the piano, C will enjoy music, in tune, floating into his home. In the second case, if D properly performs, F will enjoy a properly tuned piano. We call each of these parties a "third-party beneficiary" of a contract between two other parties. C is a third-party beneficiary of the contract between A and B, and F is a third-party beneficiary of the contract between D and E.

But the law distinguishes between (a) a mere "*incidental* third-party beneficiary" and (b) an "*intended* third-party beneficiary." In the first case, when A and B form their contract, neither has reason to believe that the other intends C to benefit from it (and indeed, neither party did intend that C should benefit from it). And so we say that as to the A and B contract, C is an incidental third-party beneficiary (or, more commonly, "incidental beneficiary"). For that reason — because C is a mere incidental beneficiary — when A breaches, C has no right to sustain an action against him.

In the second case, when D and E form their contract, D, as a reasonable person, should understand (and probably does understand) that E wants F to benefit from it. After all, E agrees to pay D to tune F's piano. E wants F — the piano owner and piano player — to benefit from the tuning. For that reason — because as to the D and E contract, F is an intended beneficiary — when D breaches, F can sustain an action against him.

So, here's the rule:

(1) When (a) two parties X and Y form a contract, and (b) some third person, Z, stands to benefit from X's or Y's performance, then, with reference to that contract, Z is a "third-party beneficiary," either "incidental" or "intended."

(2) If, in forming their contract (a) either of the parties X or Y has reason to understand that the other intends Z to derive that benefit, then Z is an "intended beneficiary," but (b) if neither such party has reason to know that the other intends Z to derive the benefit, then Z is a (mere) "incidental beneficiary."

(3) (a) If Z is an intended beneficiary of the contract between X and Y and either such contracting party commits a breach that deprives Z of his benefit, then even though he is not party to the contract, Z has an action against the breaching party, but (b) if Z is an incidental beneficiary, he has no such action.

Restatement (Second) of Contracts §§302, 304, and 315 provide:

> **§302.** The beneficiary of a promise is an intended beneficiary if recognition of a right to performance in the beneficiary is appropriate to effectuate the intention of the parties and . . . the circumstances indicate that the promisee

intends to give the beneficiary the benefit of the promised performance[.] . . . An incidental beneficiary is a beneficiary who is not an intended beneficiary.

§304. A promise in a contract creates a duty in the promisor to any intended beneficiary to perform the promise, and the intended beneficiary may enforce the duty.

§315. An incidental beneficiary acquires by virtue of the promise no right against the promisor or the promisee.

Again, let's note that behind the veil of doctrines and definitions tied to the status of third-party beneficiaries, the rule truly at work is this one: A contract includes such terms and has such meaning as conform to the parties' reasonable understandings at the time they form the contract. When E offers to pay D $150 to tune F's piano, D should understand the offer thus: "I will pay you $150 to tune F's piano and, of course, I am doing this for F's benefit." When D says, "I accept," he accepts those terms and manifests his understanding that he is tuning the piano for F's benefit.

QUESTION 1. Jeffrey's employer is sending him on a six-month overseas business trip. Not wanting to disrupt his twelve-year-old son Kyle's school year, Jeffrey forms a contract with Kandy under which Kandy promises to live in Jeffrey's house as a full-time caregiver to Kyle, in exchange for which Jeffrey promises to pay Kandy $35,000 for the full six-month period. If Kandy fails properly to care for Kyle, can Kyle himself (through his guardian *ad litem*) sustain an action against her?

A. Yes, because Jeffrey and Kyle have a direct familial relationship
B. Yes, because contract law affords Kyle that right
C. No, because Kyle is not a party to the contract between Jeffrey and Kandy
D. No, because Jeffrey was not within the jurisdiction at the time of the breach

---

ANALYSIS. In relation to a contract between Parties X and Y of which Z is not a part, Z is an intended third-party beneficiary if the contracting parties, as reasonable persons, at the time they form their contract should understand that one (or both) of the promised performances is meant for the benefit of Z. Here, Kyle is Z. The parties should understand that Jeffrey intends Kandy's performance to benefit Kyle. Consequently, the answer is "yes," for the reason that Kyle is an intended third-party beneficiary.

C and **D** answer "no," and they're wrong for that reason. **C** offers a blatantly false statement, implying that no third party ever acquires a right to bring an action for breach. **D** raises a matter of irrelevancy. Whether a party to the contract is or is not within the relevant jurisdiction at the time of breach has no effect whatsoever on the beneficiary's rights (nor on his own, for that matter; when he returns to the jurisdiction, Jeffrey, too, may sustain an action against Kandy).

A accurately reports that Jeffrey and Kyle are family, but that has no bearing on Kyle's status as an intended beneficiary. **A** too is wrong. **B** correctly answers "yes" and correctly states its reason: Because Kyle is an intended beneficiary, contract law does afford him the right to sustain this action. Hence, **B** is right.

2. Creditor Beneficiaries and Donee Beneficiaries

When first the law described its rules of third-party beneficiaries, it distinguished beneficiaries not with the words "intended" and "incidental" but with the designations "creditor" and "donee." It was said that a third-party *creditor* beneficiary could sustain an action for breach but that a third-party *donee* beneficiary could not.

Suppose A borrows $10,000 from C and so owes C that amount. C is A's creditor. Separately, thereafter, A and B agree that A will perform some service for B, in exchange for which B will pay A's $10,000 debt to C. In that circumstance, the law recognized (and in most quarters still does recognize) C as a "creditor beneficiary" of the contract between A and B, meaning that the third-party benefit C stands to derive arises because A actually owed C a debt and formed a contract in which B was obliged to pay it.

Now, suppose G and H form a contract under which G will rebuild H's transmission and H will re-landscape G's yard. Party I is G's next-door neighbor and stands to benefit from the beauty added to G's yard. Neither G nor H owes I any obligation; the benefit of beauty that I stands to derive through the contract between G and H amounts, in older legal terms, to a mere "donation." Consequently, it used to be said that as to the contract between G and H, I was a mere "donee" beneficiary.

And what relevance do these older terms have today? As already noted, modern common law distinguishes between an *intended* and an *incidental* beneficiary. Any creditor beneficiary is also an intended beneficiary; "creditor beneficiary" represents a subset of "intended beneficiary." Hence, it remains so today that the law allows every creditor beneficiary to sustain an action for breach against a contracting party who, by breaching her contract, deprives the creditor beneficiary of his benefit. And although the significance of "creditor beneficiary" is eclipsed now by that of "intended beneficiary," modern courts still invoke the phrase; it's not yet dead.

A donee beneficiary might be an intended beneficiary and might be an incidental beneficiary. In the first piano case above, C was a donee beneficiary and also an incidental beneficiary. In the second piano case, F was a donee beneficiary but also an intended beneficiary. The phrase "donee beneficiary," therefore, is no longer significant to the law of contracts except for historical purposes.

QUESTION 2. StopCo owns a restaurant at the corner of Highways 21 and 22. FuelCo, a gasoline dealer, and BuildCo, a builder, form a contract under which FuelCo is to pay BuildCo $300,000 and BuildCo is to build a gasoline station near the corner of Highways 21 and 22. BuildCo fails to build the gas station and thus breaches its contract with FuelCo. StopCo is disappointed because it expected that the new gasoline station would bring additional clientele to its restaurant. Does the law afford StopCo the right to sustain an action against BuildCo for its breach?

A. Yes, because StopCo reasonably expected and understood that it would benefit from the presence of the new gasoline station

B. Yes, because FuelCo might reasonably expect to benefit from the location of StopCo's restaurant

C. No, because StopCo's expectation was insignificant to BuildCo's and FuelCo's contractual purpose

D. No, because StopCo had chosen its location before BuildCo and FuelCo formed their contract

---

ANALYSIS. StopCo is analogous to the pianist's next-door neighbor. Two parties, FuelCo and BuildCo, contracted manifesting no intention to benefit StopCo; neither had reason to understand that the other was concerned with any gain StopCo might reap from the contract. (And that is true even though FuelCo might have selected the site because of StopCo's presence there. That FuelCo might have sought a benefit from StopCo's presence is not to say that FuelCo formed its contract to benefit StopCo.) As to the FuelCo and BuildCo contract, StopCo is a mere incidental beneficiary. For that reason, the answer is "no."

A and B answer "yes," and they're wrong for that reason alone. A is tempting to some because it correctly states that StopCo's expectation was a reasonable one. Reasonable understandings and expectations are significant insofar as they apply to the *contracting parties*. If either FuelCo or BuildCo had reason to believe that the other wished to benefit StopCo, StopCo would be an intended beneficiary. But neither party had any reason to hold such belief. As for B, FuelCo's expectation that *it* might benefit from *StopCo's* presence does not make StopCo an intended beneficiary.

D correctly answers "no," but its reasoning is all wrong. Let's ask: If StopCo had selected its own site after BuildCo and FuelCo formed their contract, would it then become an intended beneficiary? Let's answer: No, it would not. D is wrong. C correctly answers "no," but some students fail to see its correctness because it does not feature the phrase "incidental beneficiary." Nonetheless, it accurately reports the *reason* that StopCo is an incidental beneficiary; StopCo's well-being played no role in FuelCo's and BuildCo's contractual purpose. C is right.

B.   Assignment

Recall again the broad precept that arises from all we discussed in Chapter 2 (see also Chapter 18, section A): *An offer means whatever, under the relevant circumstances, a reasonable offeree thinks it to mean. The acceptance must mirror the offer, and it means whatever, under the relevant circumstances, the reasonable offeror thinks it to mean. Hence, in all cases except the very rare one typified by Peerless (Chapter 3, section C), the terms of a contract are the terms of the offer from which it arises. That means a contractual term has such meaning as, under all surrounding circumstances, conforms to the reasonable expectations of its parties.* Keep that in mind while reading about X and Y, below.

On Monday Z lends Y $100 and Y must repay him on Friday. Separately, on Tuesday, Y forms a contract with *X*, under which Y will weed X's garden on Wednesday and, in exchange, X will pay Y $100 on Friday. Thinking in terms of contract *rights*/reasonable expectations, we see, of course, that the contract affords X the right to a weeded garden on Wednesday, and Y the right to $100 on Friday. On Wednesday, Y does weed the garden, meaning that on Friday X must pay him $100. On Thursday, Y approaches Z, to whom, as we said, he owes $100 to be paid, also, on Friday.

> **Y speaks to Z:** Yesterday, I weeded X's garden, and for that she owes me $100 to be paid me tomorrow, Friday, the same day on which *I* am to repay *you* the $100 you loaned me. I am going to be away on Friday, so here's what I'm going to do: As for the $100 that X owes me, I'll tell her to pay not me, but you. That way all will be right.
>
> **Then and there, in Z's presence, Y sends X this mobile "text" message:** As you know, on Friday (tomorrow) you must pay me $100 for the work I did in your garden yesterday (Wednesday). Please pay that sum not to me, but to Z. His address is 12 Nora Way, Manton, RA 54098; email: ZZ@Zmail.com.
>
> **Y then turns back to Z:** There you are. Now X owes $100 not to me but to you.

Y Had a Contractual Right to Receive $100 from X, and He Assigned that Right to Z.

When a first party (Y) is owed a contractual right (to be paid $100 by X) and manifests his intention presently to transfer that right to some third party (Z), he is said to "assign" it. In this case, Y assigns to Z his right to collect $100 from X. Y, the party who assigns his contractual right, is the "assignor." Z, the party *to whom* Y assigns his right, is the "assignee." X has a place in all of this, so she too acquires a title. It's her obligation to pay the $100, so the law names her the "obligor."

One Who Assigns a Contract Right Is, By and Large, Like Anyone Who Conveys His Property to Another

Suppose A owns land. She sells it to B. Hence, she conveys her property to B. When she does that, she parts with all of the rights and privileges that accompany ownership and, naturally, loses the right to enforce them. A no longer has the right to occupy the land and she loses the right to sue another for trespass. B, naturally, acquires A's rights. B has the right to occupy the land and the right to sue another for trespass.

A contract right *is property*. (More specifically, it is intangible personal property.[1]) By assigning a contract right, one conveys his property. All that was his belongs to his assignee. He loses his right to have the obligor perform in his favor and loses the right to recover from her if she fails to perform. What the assignor loses, the assignee acquires. The obligor must give her performance to the assignee. If she fails to do that, the *assignee* has an action against her for breach.

So — when Y assigns (conveys) to Z his $100 contract right (his property), the law creates these three consequences: (1) Y loses his rights against X; X owes him nothing; (2) Whatever X does or does not do—whomever she does or does not pay — Z has no right to sue her; (3) Z *acquires* Y's rights, meaning X owes $100 directly to Z; (4) Z is entitled to sustain a suit against X if she fails to pay him.

But Z (the Assignee) Wasn't Party to the Contract

That's true, but Assignor (Y) *was* party to the contract, and had against Obligor (X) a contract right — property. Y took hold of *his* property — the right to have X pay him $100 — and he conveyed it to Assignee (Z). And for that reason, once again, the results are that (1) Y loses his rights against X — X owes him nothing; (2) Whatever X does or does not do—whomever she does or does not pay—Y has no right to sue her because he's "out of it"; (3) Z *acquires* Y's rights, meaning X owes $100 directly to Z; (4) Z is entitled to sustain a suit against X if she fails to pay him.

What If, Whatever Her Reason, X (the Obligor) Wants Only to Pay Y, the Person With Whom She Contracted? Why Should She Be Obliged to Pay Someone (Z, the Assignee) With Whom She Never Did Form a Contract?

Well, let's ask: Why not? If X must pay Z instead of Y, does she fail to fulfill her contractual rights—her reasonable expectations? Let's answer: As the law sees the original contract between X and Y, a reasonable person in X's position should expect to have her garden stripped of weeds and to pay $100 for the service. That she should be asked to pay the $100 to Z instead of Y does not compromise her reasonable expectations. Where the contract provides that Y will weed X's garden, and "X will pay Y $100," the law reads it to *mean that* in

---

1. And, more specifically still, it is a "chose in action."

exchange for a weeded garden, "X will pay $100 to Y *or to any other person as Y directs.*"

Now Know This

In order that an assignee (Z) be empowered to enforce an assignment against an obligor (X), the assignor (Y) must notify the obligor (X) of the assignment. In this case, Y, the assignor, with her "text" message, did notify X, the obligor, that she should pay the $100 to Z, the assignee. Having done that, Y empowered Z to enforce the assignment against X. If Y had not notified X of the assignment, Z would have no right directly against X. X would be free, still, to pay the $100 directly to Y. (*Y* would then, still, owe 100 to Z.) So, know this: When one party, as assignor, assigns his contractual right to a second party, the assignee, the assignee acquires no legal right against the obligor unless and until the assignor notifies the obligor of the assignment. (Some teachers make a big deal about that. Don't ask us why.)

And so, finally, the rule is this: *Ordinarily, a contracting party may assign his contractual rights and if he does so, with notice to the obligor, then (1) the assignor loses his rights against the obligor, (2) the obligor must perform for the assignee; and (3) if the obligor fails to perform, the assignee has an action against her for breach.*

Likewise, Restatement (Second) §317 provides:

> An assignment of a right is a manifestation of the assignor's intention to transfer it, by virtue of which the assignor's right to performance by the obligor is extinguished . . . and the assignee acquires a right to such performance.

QUESTION 3. At noon on Saturday, Alan and Betty form a contract under which (1) on Monday Betty is to perform service S for Alan, and (2) on Wednesday Alan is to pay Betty $10,000. At noon on Sunday, Betty assigns to Charles her rights under the contract with Alan and notifies Alan that she has done so. As a result of the assignment,

I. Betty need never perform service S on Monday.
II. Alan need not pay Betty anything, ever.
III. if Betty substantially performs service S on Monday, Alan must pay Charles $10,000 on Wednesday.
IV. even if Betty does not substantially perform service S on Monday, Alan must pay Charles $10,000 on Wednesday.

A. I and II only
B. II and III only
C. III and IV only
D. I, II, and IV only

ANALYSIS. Here's how things stand at 12:01 p.m. Saturday:

On Monday, Betty must perform service S for Alan. If she does (substantially) perform, then on Wednesday Alan must pay Betty $10,000.[2] Betty's right to be paid on Wednesday is her property. As is land, a boat, a computer, or a sofa, it's *property*. And as we all know, if one conveys her property to another, she loses it and he "gets" it.

At noon on Sunday, Betty assigns (conveys) her contractual right to Charles. She loses it. Charles owns it. He stands, now, in Betty's shoe — in only *one* of her shoes — because when Betty assigns her *right* to Charles, the law doesn't free her of her contractual *duty*. She still wears the shoe that requires her to perform for Alan on Monday. If she doesn't do that, then (a) she breaches her contract with Alan, and (b) the law releases Alan from his contractual duty to pay. If Betty does not (substantially) perform on Monday, therefore, Alan need not pay Charles anything, not on Wednesday, not ever.

If Betty Fails to Perform, Why Should Charles Suffer? When Betty assigns her right to Charles, Charles gets exactly what Betty had — no more, no less. He acquires a right to be paid on Wednesday, subject to the condition precedent that Betty substantially perform on Monday.[3] That's what Betty had and that's what Charles acquires. (Suppose that in 2018, L owns a building in which there lives T, a tenant whose lease entitles him to stay until December 31, 2021. On January 1, 2019, L conveys the building to B. B takes the building *subject to that tenant's right to stay* for three more years, 2019, 2020, and 2021. The building comes to B with that encumbrance. B can't oust the tenant. L owned a building subject to a tenant's right to stay in it. That's what she had and that's what B gets.)

So, on Sunday at 12:01 p.m., things stand thus: (1) On Monday Betty must perform service S for Alan. Otherwise she breaches her contract *with* Alan. Option I is false; **A** and **D** are wrong. If and *only if* Betty does (substantially) perform on Monday, then on Wednesday Alan must pay *Charles* $10,000; III is true, IV is false, and **C** is wrong. That leaves **B**, which reports that options II and III are true. We already know that III is true, so let's examine II. It tells us that Alan need never pay Betty. That's right. Once Betty assigns her contractual right, Charles owns it. Betty doesn't. Options I and IV are false, II and III are true, and **B** is right.

Why Would Charles Accept Property That Gives Him Nothing If *Betty* Fails to Perform? It all depends on the transaction in which he took the assignment. Maybe Charles paid Betty for the assignment and formed a contract with her requiring that she perform on Monday. Betty's failure to perform

---

2. From Chapter 21, section D, recall (or re-learn, please), that if a Party 1 is to perform at time 1, and Party 2 at time 2, then by law Party 2's obligation to perform at time 2 is subject to the implied condition precedent that Party 1 *substantially* perform at time 1.

3. *Id.* (which means please see the footnote just above).

would give Charles an action against her for breach. Or, maybe Charles bought the assignment and formed a contract with Betty under which Charles would pay the price only after she performed on Monday.

C. Delegation

Think again, please, of the original contract between X and Y under which Y will weed X's garden on Wednesday and X will pay him $100 on Friday. This time, let's say Y doesn't assign his rights. Instead, he decides he doesn't want to weed the garden. He forms a separate contract with Z under which Y will pay Z $75 and Z will weed X's garden; Z will do Y's job for him, Y will pay him money for doing it (and Y will make a "profit" of $25 ($100 – $75)). With that arrangement, Y "delegates" his contractual duty to Z. Y is the "delegor" (also called the "delegator" or the "delegating obligor"). Z is the "delegee" (also called the "delegatee"). Because X is the party to whom performance is owed, we name her, in this situation, the "obligee."

Y Can Do That Without X's Permission? Even Though X Contracted for Y's Service, She Has to Accept Performance from Z?

Generally, yes. Where a contract provides that "Y must weed X's garden," the law reads it to *mean*, "Y must see to it that *someone* weeds X's garden." By law, when Z, not Y, arrives at X's garden on Monday ready to remove weeds, X has no good reason to object. So long as Z does eliminate the weeds, he fulfills X's reasonable expectations. That Y himself doesn't do the work gives her no cause to complain.

What if the delegee (Z) does not properly perform for the obligee (X)? What if he does not properly weed X's garden? Who's in breach then? Under the original contract as the law reads it, Y promises to see that X's garden is stripped of weeds. He may have Z do the weeding, but if Z fails to perform, then Y has broken his promise and he — *Y*—is in breach. Restatement (Second) §318 provides: "[D]elegation of performance [does not discharge] any duty or liability of the [delegator]."

So, when it comes to delegation, here's the rule: *(1) Each party to a contract is entitled to receive the performance promised by the other, but neither has, generally, a right to have that other party himself provide it, wherefore (2) if one contracting party delegates his duty and the delegee does in fact perform, the delegator is not in breach, but (3) if the delegee fails to perform, the delegor is in breach and the obligee has an action against him.*

We have just described the common law rule regarding delegation of a contractual duty. Know, please, that UCC §2-210(1) and (2) provide, in substance, for the same thing, so that the rule applies to contracts for the sale of goods (UCC Article 2) and, generally, to all others (common law).

Maybe we've thus far caused you to think that all contract law lives in either the common law or UCC Article 2. It's not true, and that's why, in the last sentence we write the word "generally." And for that reason, we say PLEASE STOP, and read Appendix, section D.4. Then, come back here.

D.   Assignment and Delegation Together

Weeds Again

Let's go back to X, Y, and the weeds. On the morning of Tuesday, April 7, 2019, X and Y form a contract under which Y will weed X's garden on Wednesday, April 8 and X will pay Y $100 on Friday, April 10. On the *afternoon* of Tuesday April 7, Y and Z sign this writing: "With reference to the contract between X and Y, formed this morning April 7, 2019, a copy of which is attached hereto, Y assigns to Z all of his rights and delegates to Z all of his duties, which delegation Z accepts." As a result, there stands:

(1) a contract, still, between X and Y under which (a) Y must see to it that someone weeds X's garden, and (b) X must pay $100 to Y or to anyone else as Y directs.

(2) a contract between Y and Z under which (a) Z must weed X's garden, and (b) Z is entitled to have payment from X.

Finally, there's this: Regarding contract (2), X is an intended third-party beneficiary of Z's promise to weed the garden. Why? When Y and Z form their contract, Z *has* to know that her duty to weed X's garden was intended (by Y) to benefit X.

If Z fails to weed the garden, then (1) he breaches his contract with Y, and Y has an action against him; (2) he deprives X of his third-party benefit, and X has an action against him; and (3) Y breaches his contract with X so that X has an action not only against Z but also against Y.

If Z does weed the garden and X fails to pay him, X breaches his obligation to pay Y's assignee and Z (but not Y) has an action against X.

Assignment & Delegation Together

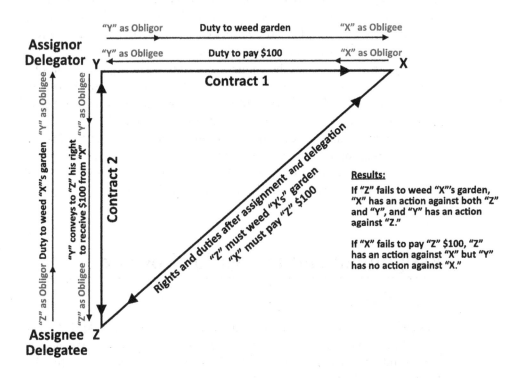

Results:

If "Z" fails to weed "X"'s garden, "X" has an action against both "Z" and "Y", and "Y" has an action against "Z."

If "X" fails to pay "Z" $100, "Z" has an action against "X" but "Y" has no action against "X."

Meet This Phrase: "Assignment of a Contract"

The best way to achieve a joint assignment of rights and delegation of duties is the way in which Y and Z did so. In words, they expressly made plain that Y had, to Z, assigned his rights and delegated his duties.

But read this story: Once upon a time, two parties Q and R formed a contract. Q and S wanted then to form a contract under which Q would assign his rights and delegate his duties to S. For this purpose, some ill-advised lawyer wrote for two parties a document reciting that "Q assigns to S, his contract with R." The lawyer did not write that Q "assigns his rights." He did not write that "Q delegates his duties." He did not write that "Q assigns his rights and delegates his duties." He wrote "Q assigns . . . *his contract.*"

Naturally, that phrase "assigns the contract" later created a dispute as to whether it meant "assign rights," "delegate duties," or both. On hearing of the circumstances and conversations surrounding the agreement in which the phrase appeared, a court ruled, in *that* case that "assignment of the contract" meant "assign the rights and delegate the duties." Then, a few more lawyers and a few more courts, carelessly reading the decision, thought that in all cases "assign the contract" should mean "assign the rights and delegate the duties." For *some* courts, in some jurisdictions, it seems to have become a rule that:

If at time 1, two parties X and Y form a contract and at time 2 Y forms a separate arrangement with a third party, Z, in which Y "assigns the contract," then, because of that particular phrase, there moves from Y to Z an assignment of Y's rights and a delegation of Y's duties. Hence, under the contract between Y and Z, formed at time 2, Z's obligation to Y is that he will perform for X, and Z is entitled to have from X whatever X owed Y under the original contract between X and Y, formed at time 1.

We can't say that today's common law really embraces a rule like that. Many jurisdictions don't "buy" it; according to their judicial decisions, a reasonable person would not take that phrase, in itself, to mean "assignment of rights and delegation of duties." Such jurisdictions think the phrase is ambiguous. In order to interpret it in any given case, they look to the circumstances surrounding the parties at the time they form their contract.

If, on the evidence, the court (or jury on the court's instructions) concludes that before they signed their writing Y and Z lead each other reasonably to believe that there was to be from Y to Z an assignment and a delegation, then that's what the phrase means. If they lead each other to believe that there will be only an assignment or a delegation, then the phrase has the corresponding meaning.

Yet, as to contracts for the sale of goods, we look to UCC Article 2. Section 2-210(5) does actually provide that "assignment of a contract" means assignment of rights and delegation of duties:

> An assignment of "the contract" or of "all my rights under the contract" or an assignment in similar terms is an assignment of rights and unless the language or the circumstances . . . indicate the contrary, it is a delegation of performance of the duties of the assignor and its acceptance by the assignee constitutes a promise by him to perform those duties.

QUESTIONS 4 & 5. On Monday, by signed writing, Sahlia and Bahlia form a contract under which Sahlia will perform on Wednesday morning, and Bahlia immediately thereafter on that same day. On Tuesday, also by signed writing, with a copy of Monday's writing attached, Bahlia and Chalia form a contract under which Bahlia "assigns Monday's contract" to Chalia. Bahlia then sends a copy of the Bahlia/Chalia writing to Sahlia.

QUESTION 4. Is Chalia obliged, on Monday, to give the performance owed to Sahlia under Monday's contract?

I. Yes, almost certainly, if Sahlia and Bahlia are, respectively, the seller and buyer of goods
II. Yes, almost certainly, if Sahlia and Bahlia are, respectively, the seller and buyer of a service
A. I only
B. II only
C. I and II
D. Neither I nor II

ANALYSIS. UCC Article 2 governs contracts for the sale of goods. It provides that "assign the contract" ordinarily means assign contractual rights *and* delegate contractual duties. If Sahlia and Bahlia formed a contract for the sale of goods, then Bahlia's assignment to Chalia of "the contract" means Sahlia must deliver the goods to Chalia and Chalia must, immediately, pay Sahlia the purchase price. Option I is true, which eliminates **D**.

The common law doesn't "buy into" that rule in any comprehensive way. Maybe some jurisdictions adopt it on some days. Others, for sure, do not. They regard the phrase as ambiguous and interpret it in terms of what reasonable parties would expect it to mean under the operative circumstances. Option II is false. I is true, II is false, and **A** is right.

QUESTION 5. For this question, assume that the Sahlia-Bahlia contract calls for the purchase and sale of goods and, again, that Bahlia "assigns Monday's contract" to Chalia. According to the applicable law,

I.   if Chalia fails to take and pay for the goods, Sahlia has an action against Chalia.
II. if Chalia fails to take and pay for the goods, Sahlia has an action against Bahlia.
III. if Sahlia fails to deliver the goods to Chalia, Chalia has an action against Sahlia.
IV. if Sahlia fails to deliver the goods to Chalia, Bahlia has an action against Sahlia.

A. I and II only
B. II and III only
C. I, II, and III only
D. I, II, III, and IV

ANALYSIS. We deal here with a contract for the sale of goods. UCC Article 2 governs, and "assign a contract" means assign rights and delegate duties. Please look at the two diagrams above in sections C and D, respectively. With respect to the S-B contract, B has assigned his rights and delegated his duties to C. As for the assignment of rights, B is the assignor, C the assignee, and S the obligor. As for the delegation of duties, B is the obligor (the one who owes the duty) and, also, the delegor (the one who delegates his duty). Finally, A is, also, an intended third-party beneficiary of the contract between B and C.

If C fails to take and pay for the goods A has an action against B for breach of contract and against C for deprivation of an intended third-party benefit. Options I and II are true. If S fails to deliver the goods to C, then (1) C, as assignee of B's rights, has an action against S. Option III is true, but (2) B, who has fully parted with his rights by assigning them to C, has no action against S. Option IV is false, I, II, and II are true, and **C** is right.

Can B, Somehow, Assign His Rights to C, Delegate His Duties to C, and Get Out of the Whole Thing So He Owes Nothing to A? B can free himself of his obligation to A only if all three parties agree to a "novation," which means that A and B mutually release each other from their original contract and, simultaneously, C and A form a contract in which C promises to take and pay for the goods, and A promises to deliver the goods to C. Again, the law calls that new arrangement a "novation."

One More Thing. The law, it is said, favors the free transferability ("alienability") of property. If two parties form a contract whose terms are silent on the subject of assignment, then each is ordinarily free to assign her rights. A party is forbidden to assign her rights only if the contract so provides, explicitly. If two parties form a contract whose terms are silent on the subject of delegation, then each is ordinarily free to delegate her duties.

BUT even in the absence of an express contractual provision that prohibits delegation, there remains one circumstance under which an obligor is, nonetheless, forbidden to delegate her duties: that in which the would-be delegator owes the obligee a so-called "personal service," as discussed below.

E.   Delegation and the (Silly Phrase) "Personal Service Contract"

Reasonable persons (as the law sees them) do not ordinarily fuss over who it is that weeds their gardens, sweeps their floors, washes their cars, sharpens their pencils, or shovels their snow. They do care, of course, that the work be done, but when properly performed, the quality of those services do not differ with the person who performs them. To the reasonable person, a shoveled driveway is a shoveled driveway regardless of who wields the shovel.

Yet, reasonable persons consider that the work products of a graphic artist, musician, poet, cook, or hair stylist do differ depending on the person doing the work. If X contracts with William Shakespeare to write a sonnet, and Shakespeare delegates the duty to his neighbor's eight-year-old son who has lately said, "I want to try writing poems," X has reason to be dissatisfied.

So, sometimes when Party 1 contracts to buy Party 2's service, both parties should reasonably understand that he wants the service performed by Party 2 *himself*, and no other. In such cases, by implication of law, the contract prohibits delegation by Party 2.

Fay's Portrait

Elan is a renowned painter of portraits. He forms a contract with Fay under which he is to paint Fay's portrait and Fay is to pay him $100,000. Jetta, Elan's daughter, timely arrives at the appointed location, with paints, paintbrushes, and canvas in hand. She truthfully advises Fay that Elan has delegated to her his duty to paint the portrait, wherefore she stands ready, willing, and able to do so.

Of that situation the courts used to say this: "Although a contracting party may generally delegate his duties to another, in the case of a 'personal service contract,' that rule does not apply. One who contracts to deliver a personal service must deliver it himself."[4] The phrase "personal service contract" was mischosen since, by ordinary usage, one who collects the garbage, cleans the furnace, or repairs the roof does personally deliver a service. The decisions make plain that when haplessly writing of "personal service contracts" courts meant and mean to designate those contracts for which the services of a particular person on one side of a contract are critical to the reasonable expectations of the party on the other. More fundamentally, the courts mean to recognize (although they may not know it) that when one party says "I promise to paint your portrait," the other reasonably understands him to *mean*

---

4. "The general rule regarding obligations under a personal service contract is that they are not delegable." Loftus v. American Realty Co., 334 N.W.2d 366 (Iowa 1983). "[A] right to performance of personal service contract requiring special skills based upon the personal relationship between the parties cannot be [delegated]." Munchak Corp. v. Cunningham, 457 F.2d 721 (4th Cir. 1972).

"I—*myself*—promise to paint your portrait," wherefore by law that *is* what he means; that is what he "intends" to promise, and that is the promise he makes. The law does not allow him to delegate.

Let's State the Law of Delegation More Fully

Except as to a contractual duty for which reasonable parties should understand that the obligee contracts for performance given personally by the obligor and not by his delegee — that situation often calling forth the mischosen phrase "personal service contract" — a contracting party may effectively delegate his duty to another and when he does so (1) the obligee has no cause to complain, so long as the delegee does in fact perform; but (2) if the delegee fails to perform, then the obligee/buyer of the service has an action (a) against the original obligor for breach of contract and (b) the delegee for denial of an intended third-party benefit.

It's no surprise, of course, that Restatement (Second) §318 states the matter as badly as this:

> An obligor can properly delegate the performance of his duty to another . . . [but] a promise requires performance by a particular person . . . [if] the obligee has a substantial interest in having that person perform . . . the acts promised.

That section's comment c then runs 'round in circles as well, citing to the old phrase "personal service," meanwhile offering no attempt to define the Restatement's own words, "substantial interest," and failing to relate the relevant principle to that of reasonable expectations, from which, certainly, it arises. Comment c provides:

> Delegation of performance is a normal and permissible incident of many types of contract. . . . The principal exceptions relate to contracts for personal services and to contracts for the exercise of personal skill or discretion.

With its illustrations 1 and 5, §318 does properly report that when A owes money to B, he may effectively delegate to C his duty to pay, but that when A contracts with B to sing, he may not effectively delegate that duty to C, another singer.

QUESTIONS 6 & 7. TeleCo provides television conferencing services, and StockCo is a nationwide stockbroker. By signed writing, TeleCo and StockCo form a contract under which TeleCo, for three years, will service all of StockCo's needs for teleconferencing among its various offices, with StockCo to pay for that service in installments every three months, beginning three months after the parties create their contract. The contract features no provision that concerns assignment or delegation.

QUESTION 6. Before the first three-month period expires and hence before StockCo makes its first payment, TeleCo assigns to ElectriCo its right to receive the first payment from StockCo. TeleCo notifies StockCo of the assignment, and StockCo acknowledges the notice. When its first payment is due, StockCo contacts TeleCo and asks for permission to pay one month late. TeleCo gives permission and so notifies ElectriCo, but ElectriCo objects to the one-month extension. It contacts StockCo and demands immediate payment. In light of the extension that TeleCo has given StockCo, is ElectriCo entitled to immediate payment?

A. Yes, because as to that payment TeleCo and StockCo have no contractual relationship
B. Yes, because StockCo sent no notice to ElectriCo of the extension given it by TeleCo
C. No, because as assignor of a contract right, TeleCo maintains its power under the original contract to modify StockCo's duties
D. No, because ElectriCo's position is subordinate to TeleCo's and ElectriCo is bound by any waiver TeleCo might make in respect of StockCo's obligations

ANALYSIS. When one assigns a contract right, he conveys property to his assignee and so relinquishes all rights and privileges tied to ownership. Had TeleCo not assigned its right to ElectriCo, it would be entitled to payment according to a specified schedule. Upon StockCo's failure to make it, TeleCo would have an action for the breach or, alternatively, the power to allow StockCo an extension. Once TeleCo did make the assignment, it lost all such privileges and passed them to ElectriCo. Consequently, TeleCo had no power to extend StockCo's payment deadline by one month or one moment. That right belonged to ElectriCo, and ElectriCo wants immediate payment. For *that* reason, the answer is "yes."

C and **D** say "no"; they're wrong. Both make statements contrary to the law. As to the right it assigned, TeleCo maintains no power to modify StockCo's duty; neither is ElectriCo's position "subordinate" to StockCo's. **B** correctly answers "yes," but then cites an irrelevancy. An assignor has no power to alter a contractual right it has assigned to another. That is so whether the obligor (StockCo) does or does not notify the assignee that the assignor has attempted to do what he cannot do. **B** is wrong.

A answers "yes" and correctly states the reason. TeleCo assigned to ElectriCo its right to receive from StockCo, StockCo's first payment. As to that payment, TeleCo gave up its contractual relationship with StockCo and so lost its power to deal with StockCo as to StockCo's obligation to make that payment. **A** is right.

QUESTION 7. MeetCo too provides teleconferencing services and is known to have a status, capacity, and reputation equal to TeleCo's. For this question, assume that TeleCo does not assign any right to ElectriCo. Instead, before beginning its performance, TeleCo signs a writing on which it writes "Contract with StockCo is hereby assigned to MeetCo, rights and duties." TeleCo staples to that writing a copy of its written contract with StockCo and delivers the two stapled writings to MeetCo. MeetCo takes the papers and gives back to TeleCo a signed writing on which it writes "Assignment of StockCo's contract with TeleCo is accepted." TeleCo and MeetCo then notify StockCo of these events.

Thereafter, MeetCo visits StockCo's facility and announces its readiness to provide teleconferencing service. StockCo refuses to accept the service on the ground that its contract is with TeleCo, not MeetCo. It then contacts TeleCo, insisting that TeleCo is in breach of contract. Which of the following facts most strongly suggests that StockCo is wrong?

A. TeleCo and MeetCo made their arrangement in writing.
B. The contract provides for the sale of a service, not for the sale of goods.
C. MeetCo is capable of offering service equivalent to TeleCo's.
D. TeleCo not only delegated its duties but also assigned its rights.

ANALYSIS. TeleCo has "assigned its contract" to MeetCo, expressly mentioning "rights" and "duties." It has, in reality, assigned its *rights* and *delegated* its duties. Critical to this question is the delegation. When one party to a contract delegates her duty to some third party, the original obligee (StockCo in this case) has no cause to complain unless the original contract, as fairly interpreted, provides that the obligee is entitled to service from the party with whom she actually contracted. And that is so only if the contract expressly forbids one or both parties to delegate performance or if the service at issue, in the mind of a reasonable person, will differ depending on the party who actually furnishes it (in which case there arises the unhappy phrase "personal service contract").

We are told that this contract featured no provision relating to assignment or delegation. Hence, TeleCo is permitted to delegate (and assign). We're told, too, that MeetCo's abilities are equal to TeleCo's. For both reasons, TeleCo's assignment and delegation are effective. So long as MeetCo performs (or tenders performance in the face of StockCo's refusal to accept it) neither TeleCo nor MeetCo commits a breach.

A, B, and **D** cite factual truths—all of them wholly irrelevant. StockCo would be obliged to accept performance from MeetCo if TeleCo and MeetCo had made their arrangement without a writing. It would be so obliged, too, if the contract were for the sale of goods and if the delegation had not been accompanied by TeleCo's assignment of rights.

C is correct because it cites a matter of significance. If MeetCo were not capable of offering service equivalent to TeleCo's, StockCo would not be obliged to accept MeetCo as provider of the service, and TeleCo would be in breach. **C** is right.

F.   The Closer

> **QUESTION 8.** FlyCo, an airline, forms a contract with ServeCo, a packaged food sales company, under which ServeCo will supply FlyCo with packaged meals suitable for delivery to passengers during flight. The contract is specific as to quantities, time periods, and the nature of the packaged meals. FlyCo pays ServeCo its full fee under the contract and awaits ServeCo's performance. ServeCo then meets with MealCo, which is in the business of preparing packaged meals. ServeCo explains to MealCo its contractual obligations to FlyCo and that FlyCo has fully paid for the services it was to perform. Thereupon, ServeCo and MealCo form a contract under which ServeCo will pay MealCo and MealCo will actually prepare and package the meals to be delivered to FlyCo. MealCo fails properly to perform and, as a result, ServeCo is unable to deliver meals to FlyCo as required by its contract. FlyCo brings an action naming both ServeCo and MealCo as defendants. MealCo moves to dismiss the action as to itself. In reaching its decision, a court might logically observe that FlyCo's status is that of
>
> I.   creditor beneficiary.
> II. donee beneficiary.
> III. intended beneficiary.
> IV. incidental beneficiary.
> A. I
> B. I and II
> C. I and III
> D. I, III, and IV

ANALYSIS. When ServeCo approached MealCo, it owed FlyCo a contractual duty, and ServeCo fully described it to MealCo. Hence, MealCo had reason to know that ServeCo wished to secure MealCo's services to fulfill that same duty. In older legal parlance, FlyCo might well be called a "creditor" beneficiary, and courts do still invoke that phrase. In more modern terms, FlyCo is an intended beneficiary (as is every creditor beneficiary), and for that reason the law affords it the right to sustain an action against MealCo for its breach. A creditor beneficiary cannot be a donee beneficiary, and an intended beneficiary cannot be an incidental beneficiary (although a donee beneficiary might well be an intended beneficiary).

A court might today invoke both the phrases "creditor" and "intended" beneficiary (even though the latter alone is sufficient for this purpose). Consequently, options I and III make true statements. II and IV do not. **C** is right.

 # Silver's Picks

1.	**B**
2.	**C**
3.	**B**
4.	**A**
5.	**C**
6.	**A**
7.	**C**
8.	**C**

25

Breach, Remedies, and Damages, Part I

A. What's a Contract?

Many define "contract" thus: A contract is a promise or set of promises that, when breached, entitles the aggrieved party, by law, *to a remedy*.[1] So crucial is the concept of remedy to the law of contracts that many teachers (and some casebooks) begin the course with that subject. If your teacher is in that group, then begin *this* book right here. Most likely, your teacher's unit on remedies will take you through our Chapter 30. He or she will likely turn then to either offer and acceptance (Chapters 1-11) or consideration (Chapters 12-14).

If your teacher begins with remedies, he or she may well begin with the material set forth in section D, "Calculating the Damages: Expectation Interest and Benefit of the Bargain." Even so, we urge you first to read section B (it's short). Okay? Let's get started.

---

1. That's a better-crafted version of the Restatement's definition.

According to Restatement (Second) of Contracts §1: "A contract is a promise or a set of promises for the breach of which the law gives a remedy. . . ."

If you are beginning this book with Chapter 25, you will not yet know what is meant by the "Restatement." In that case, see Appendix, section C.

B.   Three Little Words: "Breach," "Remedies," and "Damages"

If a contracting party fails to honor one or more of her contractual promises, she commits a breach of contract (unless she has some viable defense[2]). Breach of contract constitutes a *cause of action*, meaning that if a plaintiff alleges facts that describe a defendant's contractual breach (see Appendix section A), the law entitles him to sustain an *action* (lawsuit) through which to prove his allegations and, if he succeeds in doing so, a *remedy*.

"Remedy" refers to some process or device by which the law attempts to right a legal wrong. The law's customary remedy for breach of contract is an award of "monetary damages" (sometimes called, simply, "damages"), meaning a monetary recovery that, in the law's eyes, corresponds to the harm or loss caused the plaintiff by the defendant's breach. So we say that for breach of contract, the usual remedy is damages.

PLEASE STOP! Before going further in this chapter, read (or reread) Chapter 21, section D, which thoroughly discusses material (total) breach and immaterial (partial) breach. It's essential that you do that! Then, come back here. (We'll wait for you.)

Welcome back. Now, please answer Questions 1 and 2.

QUESTIONS 1 & 2. On January 1, Jack and Jill form a contract under which Jack is to build a house on Jill's land, the work to be completed by July 31. When the house is built, Jill is to pay Jack $400,000. On July 31, Jack announces his completion, but unknowingly fails properly to bang one last nail into one last shingle on one corner of the newly built roof. Believing he has done his job, Jack gathers his equipment and leaves. On the morning of August 1, Jill inspects the house and sees a loose shingle. She so advises Jack, who responds, "Well, I've taken all my equipment away, and I have other commitments to fulfill. I can't come back right away to secure one nail in one shingle. I'm sorry. I will be able to return, however, in about ten weeks."

QUESTION 1. Is Jill obliged to pay Jack the $400,000, as provided by their contract?

A. Yes, because if two parties A and B form a contract and A breaches, B has an action against A, but B must nonetheless perform *her* contractual duties

---

2. Defenses include the Statute of Frauds (Chapter 15); incapacity (Chapter 16); illegality (Chapter 17); duress, undue influence, and unconscionability (Chapter 20); mistake, frustration of purpose, and impracticability (Chapter 22). You have studied or will study all such topics earlier or later in your course.

B. Yes, because Jack committed only a partial breach, which means he provided Jill with substantial performance

C. No, because as to two contracting parties A and B, if A is to perform first and B second, any breach by A allows B to withhold her performance

D. No, because Jill gave Jack notice as to his breach and Jack declined to make prompt correction and cure

ANALYSIS. This question tests the law described in Chapter 21, section D: *If Parties 1 and 2 form a contract under which Party 1 is to perform first in time, and Party 1 commits only a partial breach, then Party 2 must nonetheless continue in her performance. If she doesn't do so, then she too is in breach*—total breach.

Jack gave substantial performance; he *almost* fully completed his work. Failure to bang in the last nail *is* a breach, but it's an immaterial breach called, also, a partial breach. Hence, Jill may not withhold her performance. By law, she must pay Jack the full $400,000. She can then sustain an action against him for the damages, if any, caused her by the missing nail, but she can't withhold her own performance—not even a little bit.[3] So the answer to this question is "yes," which shoves C and D out the window. Let's look at them as we say goodbye. **D** implies a false statement of law, to wit, this one: Where Party B notifies Party A that he has committed a breach—even a "teensy" one—then if Party A fails promptly to correct ("cure") it, Party B may withhold her performance. There is no such rule. And that illustrates an important test-taking strategy: As always, read a multiple-choice option *for its meaning* and not for the appearance of familiar words. If the question then confronts you with a rule of which you never have heard, assume that it doesn't exist. (That applies, of course, only if you have studied.)

By omitting the word "material" or "total" before "breach," **C** states that *any* breach by Party A allows Party B to withhold performance. That's false, so **C** is wrong. **A** is wrong for the same reason. Omitting the words "partial" or "immaterial" before "breach," **A** says that Jill would have to perform even if Jack had left the building without any roof at all. **A** and **C** fail to distinguish between partial (immaterial) and total (material) breach.

And what of **B**? It says, "yes," Jill must pay Jack the full $400,000. Why? Because Jack committed only a partial breach. That alone would be enough to make a correct answer. Yet, **B** goes on. To commit only a partial breach, it explains, is to give substantial performance. And we know that if Party A gives

3. In reality, Jill, if honest, would pay Jack all but the amount necessary to place the last shingle. Imagine that she pays Jack $399,900, reserving $100 to hire someone to place the last shingle. She would then be in breach. In theory, Jack would have an action against Jill for the $100, but Jill would have a counterclaim against him for the $100 damage occasioned by his breach. Jack (unless crazy) would accept the $399,900 and the parties would not—*certainly not*—find themselves in court.

substantial performance, then Party B must perform fully. There's no doubt about it: **B** is right.

QUESTION 2. Now assume that on July 31, the house is complete, except that it does not yet have a roof; it has no roof at all. Is Jill obliged to pay Jack the $400,000, as provided by their contract?

A. Yes, because if two parties A and B form a contract and A commits a significant breach, B has an action against A, but B must nonetheless perform her contractual duties
B. Yes, because Jack completed most of his work, and in the case of this partial breach the law does not excuse Jill from honoring her contractual obligations
C. No, because as to two contracting parties A and B, if A is to perform first and B second, a total breach by A deprives B of substantial performance
D. No, because Jill gave Jack notice as to a material breach, and he declined to make prompt correction

---

ANALYSIS. This time Jack committed a total breach. A house without a roof certainly bespeaks a material breach, which entitles Jill to withhold her performance entirely, cancel the contract, and sue Jack for monetary damages. Plainly, then, the answer to this question is "no," Jill is not obliged to pay Jack anything at all. That means we show **A** and **B** to the door. **A** refers to a "significant breach" and thus refers to a material breach — a failure of substantial performance. Where a first party commits a material breach, the second is *not* obliged to perform, because the first party's substantial performance is a condition precedent to the second party's duty to perform. **A** answers "yes," whereas the right answer is "no." **A** is wrong.

B too is a loser. The "yes" makes it wrong, of course, as does the double-talk that follows. We're told that Jack completed most of his work. That's true; he did. Then we're told that he has committed only a partial breach, and that's false. The absence of a roof denotes, certainly, a material breach, even though it represents less than one-half the task of building a house. Jack committed not a partial breach, but a total breach. **B** is wrong.

D properly answers "no" but then implies a false statement of law, invoking the word "material" to trap the unwary. There is no such rule as is given in **D**. If Party A commits a material breach, then B need not perform. Party A can't revive B's duty to perform by curing the material breach. (If she wishes, however, Jill certainly can *allow* Jack to cure the breach and then pay him. Sensible people in Jack and Jill's position behave that way when they can. Lawsuits aren't fun, except for lawyers.)

C, alas, is correct. It correctly says "no," Jill is not obliged to pay Jack any money at all, and it correctly states the relevant law: When a first party commits a material breach, the second need not perform. C is right.

C. Anticipatory Repudiation as Total Breach

Suppose that on February 1, Cook and Darworth form a contract under which Cook is to perform on March 1 and Darworth on March 2. On February 15, Cook tells Darworth: "I regret forming this contract and I won't perform." Cook thus commits an "anticipatory repudiation" (or "anticipatory breach"). Darworth may treat the anticipatory repudiation, immediately, as a total breach. Without waiting until March 1 when Cook's performance is actually due, Darworth may inform Cook that the contract is terminated, and/or contract with some other party to furnish Cook's performance, and/or bring an action for breach. (But as discussed in Chapter 26, Darworth must mitigate his damage or risk losing some of his recovery.)

Restatement (Second) of Contracts §253 provides:

> Where an obligor repudiates a duty before [his performance is due,] his repudiation alone gives rise to a claim for damages for total breach, [and the repudiation] discharges the other party's remaining duties to render performance.

On the other hand, Darworth may sit still and wait until March 1, hoping perhaps that Cook will have a change of heart, retract his repudiation, and perform. For so long as Darworth sits still, Cook is entitled to make such a retraction. If, however, before Cook retracts his repudiation, Darworth advises Cook that he is terminating the contract, and/or contracts with some other party to substitute for Cook, and/or brings suit against Cook, and/or otherwise alters his position in response to or reliance on Cook's repudiation, then Cook loses his power to retract his repudiation. He remains in breach, and Darworth may recover damages.

As Restatement (Second) §253 provides:

> [A] repudiation . . . is nullified by a retraction of the [repudiation] if notification of the retraction comes to the attention of the injured party before he materially changes his position in reliance on the repudiation or indicates to the other party that he considers the repudiation to be final.

So let's write a rule:

> *If with respect to a contract one party manifests her intention not to furnish substantial performance when it comes due, she commits an anticipatory repudiation, whereupon*
>
> *(1)(a) the aggrieved party may consider that the repudiating party has committed a total breach and, in response, without waiting until performance*

is due, advise the repudiating party that the contract is at an end, and take any and all other actions that she would be entitled to take had that party failed to furnish substantial performance on the very day it was due, including the initiation of a lawsuit for total breach, and (b) if the aggrieved party does initiate suit or take any other action in reliance on the repudiation, the contract is at an end and the repudiating party loses his right to reaffirm it; or

(2) the aggrieved party, if she chooses, may do nothing in response, in which case, if the repudiating party retracts her repudiation before the day on which her performance is due, she thereby reaffirms the contract, the aggrieved party loses her right to respond to the breach, and both parties are once again obliged to perform as agreed.

D. Calculating the Damages: Expectation Interest and Benefit of the Bargain

Fairfax is an orchestra leader and Gaelle a planner of corporate events. On April 1, the two form a contract under which Fairfax, before June 6 and (a) at his own expense, will engage twenty-five musicians, thereby assembling an orchestra, and then (b) on June 6, conduct the orchestra at a corporate event to be arranged by Gaelle. In exchange, Gaelle will pay Fairfax, on April 5, a total, final fee of $40,000.

On April 2, Fairfax spends $25 for a list of orchestral musicians available for performance on June 6. Then, on April 6, Fairfax contacts Gaelle: "Your $40,000 payment was due yesterday, April 5, but I haven't received it." Gaelle responds, "I won't be paying because I have decided that I don't want to proceed with our contract. I'm out." Gaelle thus commits an anticipatory repudiation. Fairfax proclaims that he'll take Gaelle to court for breach. Gaelle asks, "Have you made any commitments or payments to anyone because of our contract?" Fairfax replies that he has spent $25 for the musician's list. Gaelle then says that she'll reimburse Fairfax the $25. Not satisfied, Fairfax promises to sue, but Gaelle counters, "Go ahead, but you'll only recover $25."

Gaelle Is Wrong: Fairfax Is Entitled to Much More Than the $25 He Spent "Out of Pocket." Long-standing common law provides that recovery for a plaintiff who suffers breach of contract is not measured by the amount he loses out of pocket. Rather, *for breach of contract, the plaintiff is normally entitled to recover such amount as will move him from the financial position he occupies at the time of breach to the financial position he would have enjoyed had the contract been fully performed by both its parties.* Restatement (Second) §347 cmt. a tells us:

> Contract damages are . . . intended to give [plaintiff] . . . a sum of money that will, to the extent possible, put him in as good a position as he would have been in had the contract been performed.

Suppose Fairfax does sue Gaelle. At trial, evidence makes plain that if both parties had fully performed under the contract, Fairfax would have paid

- $25 for the available musicians list (which he has in fact paid),
- $1,000 for a rehearsal hall, and
- $20,000 in fees to the musicians.

To calculate the appropriate recovery—Fairfax's "damages," we first identify the financial position plaintiff (Fairfax) *would have* occupied if defendant (Gaelle) hadn't breached. We do so by describing the events that *would have* occurred if both parties had fully and properly performed their contract—all on a monetary timeline on which "$00.00" marks the plaintiff's position just before the parties form their contract.

$00.00→	-$25.00→	-$1,000→	-$20,000→	+$40,000→
Fairfax's position just before the parties form their contract	Fairfax buys the available musicians list	Fairfax rents rehearsal hall	Fairfax pays musicians' fees	Gaelle pays Fairfax

= $18,975

Fairfax's expected gain
if both parties had fully
performed their contract

Had both parties fully performed, Fairfax would have enjoyed a net gain of $18,795.

Next, we identify the position that plaintiff *actually* does occupy in the face of Gaelle's breach. Fairfax has received nothing from Gaelle and has spent $25 on the available musicians list.

$00.00→	- $25.00 =	-$25.00
Fairfax's position just before the parties form their contract	Fairfax buys the available musicians list	Fairfax's position in face of Gaelle's breach

When Gaelle breaches, Fairfax is "down" by $25 relative to the time the parties formed their contract. If both parties had fully performed, he'd have been "up" by $18,975. The law awards Fairfax such amount of money as will "move" him from the financial position he occupies in the face of Gaelle's breach—to—the position he would have occupied/*should have* occupied—the position he justifiably "expected" to occupy—in light of full, proper performance by both parties. In this case that amount is

$$[(\$18,975) - (-\$25.00)] = [(\$18,975) + (\$25.00)] = \mathbf{\$19,000}$$

That amount—the amount necessary to "move" plaintiff Fairfax from the financial position he occupies to the one he should occupy—fulfills his "expectation interest"; it affords him the "benefit of his bargain" and, again, by doing so it fulfills/represents his *expectation interest*.

-$25.00→	+ $19,000 =	$18,975
Fairfax's position in face of Gaelle's breach	RECOVERY (Fairfax's expectation interest)	Fairfax's expected gain if both parties had fully performed their contract (benefit of his bargain)

We state the general rule like this: *For breach of contract the plaintiff is normally entitled to recover such monetary damages as will move him from the financial position he occupies in the face of defendant's breach to the financial position he would have occupied had the contract been fully performed by both its parties, thus fulfilling his "expectation interest" and affording him the benefit of his bargain.*

QUESTIONS 3 & 4. On July 1, Sintara and Tanya form a contract under which Sintara is to cut 12 trees on Tanya's property, Sintara to begin her work on August 1 and complete it by August 15. Tanya is to pay Sintara a total of $6,000 in three installments: $2,000 immediately upon formation of the contract, an additional $2,000 on August 1 when Sintara arrives to begin work, and $2,000 when Sintara completes her work.

On July 1, Tanya pays Sintara $2,000 as agreed. On August 1, Sintara arrives, demonstrating that she is ready, willing, and able to begin work. Tanya announces that she will not pay the second or third installments of $2,000 because she is "bowing out" of the contract; she anticipatorily repudiates, thus committing a total breach.

QUESTION 3. Sintara brings an action against Tanya. At trial it is proven that in order to perform, Sintara would have spent $500 in equipment rental, which in light of the breach, she will not in fact have to pay. Sintara is entitled to a total recovery of

A. $6,500 − $2,000 = $4,500
B. $6,000 − $ 500 = $5,500
C. $5,500 − $1,500 = $4,000
D. $5,500 − $2,000 = $3,500

ANALYSIS. For breach of contract, a plaintiff ordinarily recovers such amount as will fulfill her expectation interest or, stated otherwise, as will afford her the economic position she would have enjoyed if both parties had properly performed. If both these parties had fully performed under their contract, Tanya would have received $6,000 and paid $500, for a net expectation interest of $5,500. That amount represents the benefit of Sintara's bargain — Sintara's expectation interest. Tanya did pay Sintara $2,000, so that at the time of the breach, Sintara is "up" by $2,000. To move her from the position of $2,000 to $5,500, the law must award her (from Tanya's pocket) $3,500. **D** is right.

QUESTION 4. Assume now that when Tanya breached, Sintara had already paid the $500 for equipment rental. In that case, the law should afford Sintara recovery of

A. $6,500 − $2,000 = $4,500
B. $6,000 − $ 500 = $5,500
C. $5,500 − $1,500 = $4,000
D. $5,500 − $2,000 = $3,500

ANALYSIS. The change to the story does not affect Sintara's expectation interest; it does not alter the gain she would have derived if both parties had fully performed. That remains at $5,500. The fact that Sintara paid the $500 for equipment rental alters the position she in fact occupies in light of Tanya's breach. It is not + $2,000 but rather + $1,500 ($2,000 − $500). Consequently, the recovery necessary to fulfill her expectation interest is $5,500 − $1,500 = $4,000. **C** is right.

E.   The Closers

QUESTIONS 5-7. On September 1, Team and Legs form a contract under which Legs will play basketball for Team during the months January through April of the following year, and Team will pay Legs a salary of $1 million monthly, on the 30th day of each such month. On September 15, Legs announces to Team that he will not, under any condition, play for Team, and that he will not report to work in January.

QUESTION 5. *Team takes no action in response.* On January 1, Legs does report for play as required by his contract, announcing that he has changed his mind and that he will honor it after all. Team Owner advises Legs that he is not welcome to play, that he will not be paid a salary—that he is "fired." Which party has an action against which party?

A. Team has an action against Legs for total breach, arising from the anticipatory repudiation Legs made on September 15.
B. Legs has an action against Team arising from Team Owner's declaration, on January 1, that Legs was "fired."
C. Each party has an action against the other because each has manifested an intention not to honor the relevant contractual obligations.
D. Neither party has an action against the other because each has behaved improperly as to the other.

ANALYSIS. If Party 1 commits an anticipatory repudiation, Party 2 may consider that he has committed a total breach. Without waiting for the day on which performance is due, Party 2 may announce that the contract is terminated, engage a substitute if he wishes and, in any case, initiate suit against Party 1 for total breach. If, however, Party 2 does nothing at all in reliance on the breach, then at any time up to the moment performance is due, Party 1 may retract his repudiation and reaffirm the contract. Party 2 is obliged, then, to honor it.

Legs commits an anticipatory repudiation on September 15, but Team takes no action in reliance on it. It does not hire another player to take Legs's place. Neither does it initiate suit or advise Legs that it is terminating the contract. When Legs reports for duty on January 1, he reaffirms his contract. When Team Owner then "fires" him, *Team* commits an anticipatory breach by announcing (implicitly) that it will not pay his salary when due. Because Legs reaffirms the contract, Team has no action against him. Because Team then commits its own anticipatory breach, Legs has an action against Team. For those reasons, surprisingly, **B** is right.

QUESTION 6. Assume that in response to Legs's September 15 announcement, Team, on December 31, hires another player to replace Legs. On the next day, January 1, Legs reports for play as required by his contract. Team Owner advises Legs that he is not welcome to play, that he will not be paid a salary—that he is "fired." Which party has an action against which party?

A. Team has an action against Legs for total breach.
B. Legs has an action against Team for total breach.
C. Each party has an action against the other for total breach.
D. Neither party has an action against the other for breach.

ANALYSIS. In this case, Team took action in reliance on the repudiation before Legs attempted to retract it. Team, therefore, has an action against Legs for total breach. **A** is right.

QUESTION 7. Assume now that in response to Legs's September 15 announcement, Team brings an action against Legs for breach. On receiving notice of that action, Legs attempts to retract his repudiation. He promises that he will indeed perform under the contract. May Team proceed with its action?

I. Yes, because the initiation of suit constitutes reliance on Legs's repudiation

II. Yes, because one who commits an anticipatory repudiation loses his right to reaffirm the contract if the aggrieved party brings suit against him
A. I only
B. II only
C. Both I and II
D. Neither I nor II

ANALYSIS. When one contracting party commits an anticipatory breach, the other's initiation of a lawsuit is, by law, a reliance on the breach. If and when the other party begins his suit, the repudiating party can no longer retract the repudiation. The situation is thus akin to that of Question 6 above, in which Team hired a replacement for Legs. In that case and this one, it acted on/relied on the repudiation. Options I and II make true statements, and **C** is right.

 # Silver's Picks

1.	**B**
2.	**C**
3.	**D**
4.	**C**
5.	**B**
6.	**A**
7.	**C**

26

Breach, Remedies, and Damages, Part II

A. Plaintiff Does Not Recover for Damage She Could Reasonably Have Avoided: Mitigation of Damages

1. Mitigation of Damages: The Rule

Several years ago, Marnoff bought a home for $350,000. Now, several years later, its value has increased, so that on May 1 of this year, Marnoff and Namly form a contract for the sale of Marnoff's home to Namly for $550,000, meaning that the sale will afford Marnoff a gain of:

$$\$550,000 - \$350,000 = \$200,000.$$

The contract provides for an August 1 closing.[1] On May 15, real estate values fall. Namly believes he'll save money if he waits a few months before buying a home. On May 20, he tells Marnoff, "I no longer wish to buy your home. I'm not going forward with our contract." Two days later, Orshan offers to buy Marnoff's home for $490,000, but Marnoff rejects the offer. By August 1, the home's value has fallen to $350,000, the amount for which Marnoff himself had purchased it.

Marnoff sues Namly for breach of contract. His lawyer argues, "Had both parties fully performed this contract my client, Mr. Marnoff, would have received $550,000 for his property. The real estate now, however, is worth only $350,000, meaning that my client is entitled to recover damages of ($550,000 − $350,000) = $200,000. That amount will move him from the financial position he now occupies to the financial position he would have occupied had both parties fully and properly performed."

Namly's lawyer responds, "Two days after my client withdrew from the contract, Orshan stood ready to buy the property for $490,000. Had Marnoff sold to Orshan for that amount, he would have had $490,000 in his pocket. The monetary 'distance' between that amount and his expected receipt of $550,000 is:

$$(\$550,000 - \$490,000) = \$60,000.$$

From my client, that's all he should recover. For the remaining $140,000 of his 'damage,' Marnoff has himself to blame—he should have sold to Orshan for $490,000 and thus spared himself $140,000 of his $200,000 loss."

Namly's lawyer is right. The common law has long provided that a party who suffers a breach of contract has an obligation to "mitigate"—lessen—his damages. One who suffers a breach cannot sit idly by and let his damages run upward if there is available to him some reasonable means of mitigating them. The consequence of one's failure to mitigate damages is the reduction of his monetary award by the amount which he himself could have lessened his loss. Marnoff is entitled only to $60,000 in damages; of his $200,000 loss, $140,000 arose because he failed to accept Orshan's $490,000 offer.

What would have occurred if Namly had not breached:

($00.00)→ Marnoff's position before the parties form their contract	+ $550,000→ Namly pays purchase price	− $350,000 = Marnoff parts with home for which he paid $350,000	**$200,000** Marnoff's gain if both parties had fully performed

---

1. The contract for sale of the realty and the sale itself are not the same. The contract obliges each party to appear at a "closing" and perform his part of the sale. At the closing, the seller transfers title and the buyer pays the purchase price.

What would have occurred *if*, in the face of Namly's breach, Marnoff had mitigated his damage by selling to Orshan:

($00.00) → Marnoff's position before the parties form their contract	[+ $490,000] Marnoff receives purchase price from Orshan (as did not happen)	[- $350,000] = Marnoff parts with home for which he paid $350,000 (as did not happen)	[$140,000]→
+ $60,000→ RECOVERY	[= $200,000] Marnoff's position *if in the face of Namly's breach, he had mitigated by selling to Orshan* (as he did not do)		

Recovering only that same $60,000 he would have recovered had he properly mitigated his damage, Marnoff's true financial position is:

($00.00) → Marnoff's position before the parties form their contract	+ $60,000 = RECOVERY	$60,000 Marnoff's true position *in face of Namly's* breach, *and his own failure to mitigate*

By failing to sell his home to Orshan and thereby failing to mitigate his damage, Marnoff costs himself ($200,000 - $60,000) = $140,000.

Knowing, now, of the plaintiff's obligation to mitigate her damages, we must amend the rule stated in Chapter 25, section D — the rule by which we ordinarily calculate a plaintiff's damages for breach of contract: *For breach of contract, the plaintiff is normally entitled to recover (a) a monetary award that will move her from the financial position she occupies in the face of the breach to the financial position she would have occupied if both parties had fully performed, except that (b) the award is reduced by the amount of damage, if any, she caused herself by failing to make a reasonable effort to mitigate.*

2. *What Constitutes a "Reasonable" Effort to Mitigate?*

One who suffers a breach of contract must make such efforts to mitigate her damage as do not expose her to unreasonable risk, cost, burden, or humiliation. Restatement (Second) of Contracts §350 provides that "damages are not recoverable for loss that the injured party could have avoided without undue risk, burden or humiliation."

Investor and Broker are in a contractual relationship requiring that Broker execute Investor's orders to buy and sell stock. For each purchase and sale that Broker executes, Investor is to pay her 1% of the purchase or sale price. On March 1, Investor directs Broker to buy 100 shares of XYZ Stock, the price of which on that day is $1,000 per share, $100,000 in total. In the early morning of the next day, March 2, when the stock price is $1,100 per share, Broker advises Investor that she did not and will not be able to make the purchase for reasons relating to the validity of her brokerage license. She refers Investor to Finn, who is in fact able immediately to make the purchase. "Call Finn immediately" Broker says, "He too will charge you 1 percent for each trade."

But Investor does not call Finn. At 4:00 P.M. on March 2, the price of XYZ stock is $1,200 per share. Then, for each of the days March 3 through March 31, Investor takes no action as the price of XYZ stock increases daily. On March 31, the price of each share, whether for sale or for purchase, is $3,000. One hundred shares are worth $(100 \times \$3,000) = \$300,000$, and Investor, of course, owns none. Thereafter, the stock's price does not increase. It remains $3,000 per share. On April 1, Investor brings suit against Broker, seeking to recover his expectation interest. He asks for $199,000, which he says is equal to $300,000, the value of the stock he would own if Broker had properly performed, *minus* the $100,000 he would have paid for the stock if Broker had properly performed, *minus* the $1,000 commission (1% of $100,000) he would have had to pay Broker:

$$(\$300,000 - \$100,000 - \$1,000 = \$199,000).$$

And That's What He Gets, Right?   Wrong. Investor had the chance easily to mitigate (lessen) his damage. If on March 2 he had contacted Finn and bought the stock for $1,200 per share, he would have enjoyed a gain, still, of:

$$\$300,000 - \$120,000 - \$1,200 \ [1\% \ of \ \$120,000] = \$178,800.$$

Of the $199,000 in damage to which Investor thinks he's entitled, he himself caused $178,800. Hence, he recovers only:

$$\$199,000 - \$178,800 = \$20,200:$$

| $00.00→ Investor's position before contract formation | - [$121,200]→ stock price plus broker's fee Investor *would have paid* had he bought stock on March 2 | + [$300,000] = value Investor's stock *would have had* on April 1, if Investor had bought stock on March 2. |

$178,800→
Investor's position
before recovery,
if he had properly
stock on March 2.

+ **$20,200** =
RECOVERY

$199,000
Investor's position if
both parties had fully
performed

Hence, after recovering $20,200, Investor's *true* position will be:

$00.00→
Investor's position
before contract
formation

+ **$20,200** =
RECOVERY

$20,200
Investor's true position
after recovery

Investor would have enjoyed his expected position of [+$199,000] had he properly mitigated by purchasing the stock through Finn on March 2; the $20,200 recovery would have seen to that. But, because Investor failed to mitigate, the $20,200 recovery affords him a position of only [+$20,200] meaning, once again, that the failure to mitigate has cost Investor $199,000 – $20,200 = $178,800.

$199,000→
Investor's final position
if he had bought the
stock through Finn on
March 2.

- **$20,200** =
Investor's final position
having failed to buy the
stock through Finn on
March 2.

$178,800
What Investor costs
himself by failing to
buy the stock through
Finn on March 2.

3. *Mitigation When an Employer Breaches an Employment Contract*

For an employee who suffers breach of contract by her employer, the rule on mitigation is fundamentally the same. But the law offers more refined a statement of what, in that circumstance, constitutes a reasonable effort to mitigate. *When, by breach of contract an employer terminates an employee, the employee must use reasonable efforts to mitigate her damages by seeking alternative employment of a similar nature, in a similar location, of similar status. If she finds (or could find) such alternative employment but fails to accept it, her recovery is limited to the difference between the financial position she would have occupied had she accepted it and the position she would have occupied had both parties fulfilled their contract.* The phrase "similar status" reflects Restatement §350's word "humiliation."

Let's Illustrate.   Multinational Corporation X hires Raelle as its new president under a ten-year contract at a salary of $10 million per year. For one year, the corporation honors its contract, but then fires Raelle and thus breaches. On those facts alone, Raelle's expectation interest would be:

$00.00→	+ $10 million→	+ $90 million =	$100 million
Raelle's position before forming the contract	Raelle's position in face of breach	**RECOVERY** (Raelle's expectation interest)	Raelle's position if contract were fully performed

Now add these facts: Upon firing Raelle from the presidency, the corporation offers her a full-time job making photocopies at $15/hour, forty hours per week, fifty weeks per year, so that she will earn $30,000 per year for the nine additional years during which she was to have been president. By accepting this alternative employment, Raelle would reduce her damages by:

$$(9 \text{ years}) \times (\$30,000 \text{ per year}) = \$270,000.$$

In that case, her recovery would be

$$\$90,000,000 - \$270,000 = \$89,730,000.$$

But Raelle refuses the copy job, announcing that it would be "humiliating to move from corporate president to corporate photocopier."

Maybe Raelle is a snob, but so is the law. Recall our rule's requirement that any alternative employment be similar in location, nature, and status. Because, relative to a corporate presidency, the photocopying position is not similar in nature or "status," Raelle may refuse the job without reducing her damage award. The law entitles her to the full $90 million difference between the $100 million Corporation X should have paid her and the $10 million it did pay her.[2]

---

2. In 1965, Shirley MacLaine contracted to play the leading role in a movie to be entitled *Bloomer Girl*, for which she was to be paid $53,000 per week of filming. Before production began, the corporate producer abandoned the project, but simultaneously offered the actress the same pay if she would play the leading role in a picture to be entitled *Big Country, Big Man*. Ms. MacLaine refused the offer and sued the producer for breach. Insisting that she had no obligation to accept the *Big Country* role, in mitigation of her damages, she sought to recover all moneys she would have earned from *Bloomer Girl*. Insisting that with respect to the *Bloomer Girl* role, *Big Country* represented work of a different and inferior nature requiring, too, that she work in a dissimilar location, Ms. MacLaine cited these facts: (1) that *Bloomer Girl* was to have been a musical, and *Big Country* a Western, (2) that *Bloomer Girl* was to have been filmed in California, and *Big Country* in Australia, and (3) that the *Bloomer Girl* contract afforded her "directorial approval" whereas the *Big Country* offer did not. The court accepted Ms. MacLaine's position. By affirming summary judgment, it ruled, in substance, that by rejecting the *Big Country* role she would suffer no reduction in her recovery for the producer's breach of the *Bloomer Girl* contract. Shirley MacLaine Parker v. Twentieth Century-Fox, 3 Cal. 4d 175 (1970).

Let's alter the story like this: For the remaining nine years of her original contract, Corporation *Y* offers Raelle the position of executive vice president at an annual salary of $7 million. She refuses the job, thereby refusing alternative employment whose nature and status *are* similar — not identical, but similar — to her job with Corporation X. From Corporation X she'll recover the amount that moves her from the position *she would have occupied had she accepted* the *alternative employment* to the position she would have occupied had Corporation X honored its contract. Of the $90 million Raelle truly lost *she* costs *herself* $63 million by failing to mitigate.

$00.00→ Raelle's position before forming the contract	+ $10 million→ Raelle's position in face of breach	+ $63 million pay Raelle *would have received* if she had accepted employment with Corporation Y (as she did not do)
=$73 million→ position Raelle would have occupied if she had accepted employment with Corporation Y (as she did not do)	+ $27 million= RECOVERY	$100 million Raelle's position if contract were fully performed

Again, by failing to mitigate, Raelle costs herself

($100 million- $37 million) = $63 million.

QUESTION 1. On September 1, Bowman and Chance form a contract under which Bowman is to serve as Chance's public relations consultant for one year at an office five miles from Bowman's home. Chance is to pay Bowman $45,000 in each of the twelve months September through August, so that for the year Bowman will earn $540,000.

All's well for September, October, and November. Bowman does his job, and Chance pays him. On December 1, Chance announces that he no longer needs a consultant, fires Bowman, and refuses to pay him any more. With nine months remaining under the contract, Bowman searches diligently for alternative work. He finds one and only one job, as a parking lot attendant fifty miles from his home at $8 per hour, forty hours per week, for all nine months. From that job, over nine months, he would earn $12,000. If Bowman rejects the parking lot job and sues Chance for damages, he is likely to collect

A. nothing, because he failed to mitigate his damages.
B. the amount he would collect from the parking lot employer over nine months.
C. his regular salary from Chance, for so much time as a reasonable person in his position would need to find alternative employment.
D. an amount sufficient to achieve his full expectation interest without reduction for a failure to mitigate.

ANALYSIS. An employee discharged in breach of contract must make reasonable efforts to seek and accept alternative employment of a similar nature, in a similar location, and of a similar status (meaning without humiliation, as states the Restatement). Bowman's diligent search for alternative employment resulted in only one job offering—as a parking lot attendant, which differed radically in nature from his job with Chance. Further, it was located forty-five miles farther from his home than was his job with Chance, and it offended the law's snobbery because it was not of similar status. This alternative employment fails all three of the pertinent tests: similar location, nature, and status. The law will not reduce Bowman's recovery for failing to accept it. Bowman is entitled to recover the difference between the financial position he would have occupied had both parties fulfilled their contract minus the financial position he occupies in view of the breach.

A gives Bowman nothing "because he failed to mitigate." Failure to mitigate does not reduce one's damages to zero unless mitigation would have done the same. Suppose, for example, a new employer offered Bowman nine months' work as an executive consultant for $45,000 monthly, five miles from his home. By accepting that job, he'd reduce his damages to zero. The law would award him zero, whether he had accepted it or not. The parking lot job, however, offers him only about $1,300 per month. Arithmetically, it would not reduce his damages to zero, even if it did pass all three tests named above.

According to **B**, Bowman is entitled to the amount he would have earned in nine months at the parking lot—about $12,000. That's not the recovery Bowman would derive even if the parking job passed the three tests. Rather, it's the amount the law would *subtract* from his expectation interest in assessing his recovery.

C tells us of law that does not exist: that an employee discharged in breach of contract is entitled to receive his regular salary for so much time as a reasonable person would need to find alternative employment. To one who does not know the law, that's an appealing statement. It features the word "reasonable," and (in a way) it *seems* reasonable. But there's no such law; **C** is wrong. Remember, if you have studied appropriately, and a multiple-choice option states or implies a rule you've never heard of, then it is almost certainly wrong. **C** is a sirens' song; don't let it wreck your ship.[3]

---

3. See Homer, *The Odyssey*, Book XII, lines 36-49 (Circe to Odysseus).

D states that Bowman had no reasonable opportunity to mitigate, and that's true. He diligently searched for alternative employment but could find none that passed the three pertinent tests of nature, location, and status. He is entitled to $405,000 (9 × $45,000), so that he'll achieve his full expectation interest.

$00.00→	- $135,000→	+ **$405,000** =	$540,000
Bowman's position before the parties form their contract	Bowman's position in light of the breach (3 x $45,000)	RECOVERY (Bowman's expectation interest)	Bowman's expected gain

D is right.

B.   The *Common Law* on Expectation and Mitigation for a Buyer of Goods When a Seller Breaches

In Chapter 25 and in section A of this chapter, we've talked about common law rules regarding expectation interest and mitigation. Before there was a UCC Article 2 (or its predecessor the Uniform Sales Act),[4] these common law rules applied to all contracts, including contracts for the sale of goods.[5] Article 2 deals with these matters with its usual asininity. Read it "cold" and your head will spin. But you'll easily understand it if, first, you think about the common law mitigation rule regarding a breach by the seller of goods, and realize that UCC Article 2, in its own ridiculous way, embraces the very same rules.

Wholesaler (Buyer) vs. Distributor (Seller): Four Episodes as the Common Law Dealt with Them

1. *Wholesaler vs. Distributor, Episode I*

It's January 1. Wholesaler and Distributor form a signed, written contract under which Distributor, at a price of $1 per widget, will deliver 100,000 widgets to Wholesaler on February 1, for a total purchase price of $100,000. Wholesaler is to pay Distributor $20,000 immediately as a down payment, $80,000 on delivery, plus a $2,000 delivery charge. Wholesaler has many customers. They're retailers, who will buy the widgets from *her* for $1.50 per

---

4. See Appendix section D.1.

5. Except where a state had enacted some miscellaneous statute of its own. See Appendix section D.4.

widget, so that, if necessary, she stands to resell all 100,000 units for a total of $150,000 ($1.50 × 100,000).

As soon as Wholesaler and Distributor sign their contract, Wholesaler, as agreed, pays Distributor $20,000 as a down payment.

Then, on January 3, Distributor contacts Wholesaler and announces that he will not deliver the widgets; he commits an anticipatory repudiation (Chapter 25, section C). By that time, as between distributors and wholesalers, the market price of widgets has increased. Wholesaler searches for the 100,000 widgets elsewhere and spends $500 conducting the search. On January 3, she finds another distributor willing, without delivery charge, to sell her 100,000 widgets for $120,000 — $20,000 more than she was to pay Distributor. Wholesaler buys the widgets, pays the $120,000 and, as planned, sells them to her customers for a total of $150,000.

So, When Distributor Breached, Wholesaler Responsibly Mitigated by Seeking and Securing Widgets Elsewhere

From Distributor, for his breach, Wholesaler is entitled to recover an amount equal to:

[the financial position she would have occupied absent the breach]
minus
[the financial position she occupies in light of the breach *and her mitigation*].

Had all gone properly, Wholesaler would have

(a) paid Distributor $20,000 (down payment, as she did in fact pay) + $80,000 (remainder of purchase price) + $2,000 (delivery charge), and
(b) resold the goods for $150,000.

$00.00→	- $20,000→	- $80,000→	- $2,000	+ $150,000 =	**$48,000**
Wholesaler's position before contract formation	down payment	remainder of purchase price	delivery charge	resale to wholesaler's customers	whole-saler's expected gain

But, as things truly stand in light of the breach and mitigation, Wholesaler paid $20,000 (down payment) + $500 (searching for substitute goods) + $120,000 (price of the substitute goods) + $00.00 for delivery. She resold the goods for $150,000. She's "up" by only $9,500 and is entitled to the difference:

$$\$48,000 - \$9,500 = \$38,500.$$

($00.00)→	- $20,000→	- $500→	- $120,000→
Wholesaler's position before contract formation	down payment	search for substitute goods	purchase of substitute goods

+ $150,000→
resale to Wholesaler's customers

= $9,500→	+ **$38,500** =	**$48,000**
Wholesaler's actual position in light of breach and mitigation	RECOVERY (Wholesaler's expectation interest)	Wholesaler's expected gain

2. *Wholesaler vs. Distributor, Episode II*

All things are the same as in Episode I, except this: When Wholesaler finds the substitute goods, she does not buy them. In that case, the law would cognize the figures that would have applied if Wholesaler *had* mitigated as she should have. Consequently, her recovery will be, once again, $38,500.

= $9,500→	+ $38,500 =	**$48,000**
Wholesaler's position *if she had properly mitigated*	RECOVERY	Wholesaler's expected gain

By failing to mitigate, and recovering only that same $38,500 she recovered when she did mitigate (Episode I), Wholesaler will occupy a final position of only

= $00.00→	- $20,000→	- $500→
Wholesaler's position before contract formation	down payment	search for substitute goods
= - $20,500	+ **$38,500** =	**$18,000**
Wholesaler's position before recovery, in light of breach and failure properly to mitigate	RECOVERY	Wholesaler's actual position after recovery

By failing to mitigate, Wholesaler will cost herself ($48,000 − $18,000) = $30,000.

3. *Wholesaler vs. Distributor, Episode III*

Let's change the story. On learning of Distributor's breach, without spending any money on a search, Wholesaler immediately finds another distributor willing, without delivery charge, to sell her 100,000 widgets for $100,000, the same as she was to pay Distributor. She buys the goods and sells them to her customers for $150,000 as planned. In that case, an $18,000 recovery makes her whole. It represents the down payment less $2,000 she saves in delivery charge.

$00.00→
Wholesaler's posi-
tion before con-
tract formation

- $20,000→
down payment

- $100,000→
purchase of
substitute goods
($20,000 less than
Distributor's price)

+ $150,000→
resale to
Wholesaler's
customers

= $30,000→
Wholesaler's actual
position
in light of breach

+ $18,000 =
RECOVERY
(Wholesaler's expectation interest)

$48,000
Wholesaler's
expected gain

4. *Wholesaler vs. Distributor, Episode IV*

On learning of Distributor's breach, Wholesaler diligently searches for substitute goods but cannot find any. As a result, she loses her $150,000 sale. Under these circumstances, she recovers a full $68,500, representing $20,000 (the down payment) + $50,000 (the lost profit). That amount, once again, would afford her the full benefit of her bargain, her expectation interest.

= $00.00→
Wholesaler's position
before contract
formation

- $20,000→
down payment

- $500 →
search for substitute
goods

= - $20,500
Wholesaler's position
before recovery, in light of
breach

+ $68,500 =
RECOVERY
(expectation interest)

$48,000
Wholesaler's actual posi-
tion after recovery

C. The *Common Law* on Expectation and Mitigation for a Seller of Goods When a Buyer Breaches

Supplier (Seller) vs. Retailer (Buyer): Three Episodes as the Common Law Dealt with Them

1. *Supplier vs. Retailer, Episode I*

Supplier deals in widgets and has in her warehouse ten million Type A widgets for which she paid 50¢ each, each identical to every other. She also has in her warehouse one million Type B widgets, which are out of production. The one million Type B units were made in 1956, for which, *in* 1956 Supplier also paid 50¢ each. Today, few if any businesses have any use for the Type B product.

Nonetheless, on March 1, Retailer contacts Supplier and wants to know if, by chance, Supplier has in stock any of the "old Type B widgets from the 1950s." Supplier tells Retailer that she has one million units purchased decades earlier. Later that same day, March 1, by signed writing Supplier and Retailer form a contract under which Supplier will deliver to Retailer the one million old Type B widgets on March 10. Retailer will pay, on delivery, $1.00 per unit, for a total purchase price of $1 million.

Since Supplier has paid 50¢ per widget, she properly anticipates a profit of $500,000 [($1.00 − 50¢) × ($1 million)]; that's her expectation interest. On March 8, Supplier packs the widgets and prepares them for delivery to Retailer. On March 9, Retailer contacts Supplier and repudiates: "I've changed my mind. I don't want the widgets. Don't send them." Hence, Retailer breaches; he commits an anticipatory repudiation (Chapter 25, section C).

Coincidentally, on that same day, March 9, a party named LastUser contacts Supplier. He asks, "Do you happen to have any of the old Type B widgets from the 1950s? I need about one million of them." Supplier responds, "Yes, I do. I was just about to sell them to a customer who backed out of his contract with me. So they're available to you at the same price I quoted him; $1.00 per widget, delivered to you, $1 million total, payable on delivery." LastUser accepts, and the parties reduce their agreement to a signed writing.

Supplier takes the one million Type B widgets she had planned to send Retailer and sends them to LastUser, whereupon LastUser pays the $1 million purchase price. Having resold to LastUser for $1 million the one million Type B widgets that Retailer should have purchased, Supplier achieves the monetary position in which she would have stood had Retailer honored his contract. Supplier has the same $500,000 profit she would have derived from the sale to Retailer. If she wishes, now, to sue Retailer for breach, she will recover nothing (except perhaps "nominal damages" of $1 or so).[6] The breach caused her no harm; she's whole.

2. Supplier vs. Retailer, Episode II

Remembering that Supplier has *ten* million Type A widgets, having paid 50¢ for each one, let's change the story. Retailer and EndUser, complete strangers, happen to contact Supplier at the same time. Each contracts to purchase one million Type A widgets for $1 million, so that on each sale, Supplier stands to earn a $500,000 profit. EndUser honors his contract; he buys the widgets and pays the $500,000 price. Retailer repudiates; he breaches, and refuses to purchase the widgets. The one million widgets that Retailer should have purchased remain in Supplier's warehouse.

It is absolutely plain (we hope) that the sale to EndUser does not compensate Supplier for Retailer's breach. Supplier had formed two contracts, each

---

6. Breach of contract is, theoretically, actionable without a showing of damages. If a plaintiff who suffers no harm from defendant's breach of contract wishes nonetheless to bring suit, she is entitled to "nominal damages," usually in the amount of $1 or $10.

unrelated to the other and, since Retailer dishonored his contract, Supplier lost one of her expected $500,000 profits. In order to fulfill her expectation interest, therefore, the law affords her a recovery from Retailer of $500,000. And that simple little story prepares us for . . .

3. Supplier vs. Retailer, Episode III

Remembering, still, that Supplier has ten million Type A widgets, let's alter the story yet again. On March 1, Supplier and Retailer form a signed written contract under which Supplier will deliver to Retailer one million Type A widgets on March 10. Retailer will pay Supplier, on delivery, $1 per unit, for a total of $1 million. As before, Supplier has paid 50¢ per unit and anticipates a profit of $500,000. On March 9, Retailer repudiates; he tells Supplier that he will not purchase the widgets.

On that same day, it just so happens that FinalUser contacts Supplier: "I need one million Type A widgets. Have you got them?" Supplier replies, "Yes, I have ten million of them; nine million in my warehouse and, on my truck, one million units that I was preparing for delivery to another buyer who breached his agreement to buy them. I was about to return them to my warehouse, but I'll deliver them to you tomorrow, March 10, for $1.00 per unit, $1 million total, on delivery." FinalUser agrees, the parties record their agreement in a signed writing, and both parties fully perform.

Retailer has delivered to FinalUser the very same one million widgets she had prepared for Retailer, and she has collected from FinalUser the same $1 million price that Retailer was to have paid. Let's ask: Does Supplier occupy the same position she would have occupied if Retailer had honored his agreement? Let's answer: No, she doesn't, and she has an action against Retailer for $500,000.

That's Because This Episode III Is Really the Same as Episode II.   In episode II, Supplier had ten million Type A widgets. She formed two separate contracts with two separate buyers, each for the sale of one million units, each contract wholly unrelated to the other. EndUser fulfilled his contract, wherefore Supplier, of course, had no action against him. Retailer breached his contract. Supplier was left with a single profit of $500,000, and nine million unsold units in her warehouse. But if Retailer had honored his contract, she would have had two $500,000 profits, and eight million units remaining in her warehouse. Hence, Supplier was entitled to recover from Retailer the full $500,000 profit she lost because of his breach. That we saw quite clearly.

In all meaningful respects, this episode III is the same. Supplier has ten million Type A widgets. She forms two separate contracts with two separate buyers, Retailer and FinalUser, each for the sale of one million units, each contract wholly unrelated to the other. FinalUser performs properly, and Supplier has no action against him. Retailer breaches his contract. Supplier is left with a single profit of $500,000, and nine million unsold units in her warehouse. Just as was so in episode II, if Retailer had honored his contract, Supplier would have had two $500,000 profits and eight million units remaining in her warehouse. Supplier is entitled to recover from Retailer the full $500,000 profit she lost because of the breach.

Between episodes II and III, there *are* two differences, but both are legally meaningless: (1) In episode II, EndUser and Retailer happen to approach Supplier simultaneously, and form their separate contracts at the same time. In episode III, FinalUser approaches Supplier and forms his contract with her after Retailer has already breached; (2) When Supplier hears from FinalUser she is about to take from her truck and return to her warehouse the one million units she had prepared for Retailer.

If Retailer had not committed his March 9 anticipatory repudiation then when, on March 9, FinalUser contracted to buy one million units, Supplier would have gone to her warehouse, removed *another* one million units, and tossed them on the truck. On March 10, she would have made two separate deliveries—one to Retailer and one to FinalUser. From each she would have collected two separate, unrelated amounts of $1 million and, thus derived two $500,000 profits, each unrelated to the other. By selling to FinalUser the same one million units that just happen to be, still, on her truck, Supplier in no way reimburses or compensates herself for the $500,000 profit lost through Retailer's breach. Rather, she saves herself a trip from her truck to her warehouse; that's all.

The Common Law Phrase "Lost Volume Seller."   Here, in episode III, we say that Supplier is a "lost volume seller," meaning that by selling to FinalUser the goods she intended to sell Retailer, Supplier does not make herself whole. She derives one profit whereas she ought to have had two; the volume of her sales on March 10 was one million instead of two million. She lost a sale; she "lost volume."

Let's state a rule: *If as to a contract for the sale of goods, a buyer breaches and the seller sells the relevant goods to some other party, then (1) if, absent the buyer's breach, the seller would nonetheless have made the second sale, she is a "lost volume seller," entitled to recover the profit lost through the buyer's breach, but (2) if, absent the buyer's breach, the seller would not have made the second sale, then the buyer's breach has caused the seller no loss of profit and she is not entitled to recover from buyer the profit she anticipated via the breached contract.*

QUESTION 2. Saul operates an automobile dealership that sells the popular Jip Mangler-X. Whenever Saul's inventory on that vehicle runs low, he buys more from the manufacturer, paying $18,000 for each. On August 1, by signed writing, Saul contracts to sell one Jip Mangler-X to Berringer for $25,000. Berringer agrees to take delivery and pay the purchase price on August 15. When August 15 arrives, Berringer tells Saul that he won't purchase the vehicle; he commits an anticipatory repudiation—a total breach.[7] One hour later, Bennington walks into Saul's showroom wanting to purchase a Jip Mangler-X. For $25,000, Saul sells Bennington the vehicle he had planned to sell Berringer. Saul then brings an action against Berringer seeking damages for $7,000, his lost profit. Should Saul recover that amount?

I. Yes, because he is a lost volume seller

II. Yes, because he would have sold a Jip Mangler-X to Bennington even if Berringer had honored his contract

III. Yes, because the sale to Bennington does not compensate Saul for the profit he would have earned on the sale to Berringer

IV. No, because the resale to Bennington affords Saul the economic position he would have occupied had Berringer honored his contract

A. I only

B. I and II only

C. I, II, and III only

D. IV only

ANALYSIS. Ask yourself: Would seller have made the sale to Bennington if Berringer hadn't breached? The answer is "yes." Bennington's wish to purchase the Jip Mangler-X had nothing to do with Berringer's ultimate refusal to buy one. If Berringer had honored his contract, Saul would have sold Bennington not the very same vehicle he had prepared for Berringer, but an identical vehicle at the same price, deriving the same $7,000 profit. The two contracts are unrelated. Berringer's breach cost Saul $7,000, and from Berringer, he is entitled to recover that amount.

Option IV, therefore is false, so **D** is wrong. Options I, II, and III are different formulations of the same thought, and they all speak truth. Berringer is a lost volume seller; he had sufficient inventory to supply both Berringer and Bennington with vehicles. Option II correctly makes the simple, critical statement that Saul would have sold a vehicle to Bennington even if Berringer hadn't breached. Option III properly states that the sale to Bennington did not compensate Saul for the profit he lost through Berringer's breach. Had Berringer bought the vehicle, Saul would have had not one $7,000 profit, but two. **C** is right.

---

7. See Chapter 21, section D.

D. Uniform Commercial Code Article 2 on Expectation and Mitigation (Including the Lost Volume Seller)

Before we look at the inanity with which Article 2 assesses damages for breaching buyers and sellers of goods, know this: The UCC embodies nine "articles," the first of which is Article 1, entitled "General Provisions." It supplies definitions and rules intended to apply to all the other Code articles if and as the context requires.

UCC §1-305 provides:

> [All] remedies provided by the Uniform Commercial Code must be liberally administered to the end that the aggrieved party may be put in as good a position as if the other party had fully performed.

Article *1*, therefore, tells us this: When a buyer or seller breaches a contract for the sale of goods, the other should recover his expectation interest. It tells us, in essence, to apply the common law.

Yet, in addressing the matter of damages, Article *2*'s writers neither state nor cite that simple provision. They make not a single reference to it. Instead, they treat the subject of damages by dressing it in wigs, robes, jewelry, gloves, and tattoos. They garb it in a real "get-up," replete with a whole big batch of definitions, sections, subsections, parts, and subparts (and, of course, the usual "comments"). But, when stripped of its costumes, Article 2's provisions on damages and mitigation come to *nothing more than* the common law.

Really? Show Me.

1. Buyer's Damages for Seller's Breach as Described in UCC Article 2

When the seller repudiates or otherwise fails timely to deliver conforming goods, then, as the UCC puts it, the buyer may "cover." That word means "buy the goods elsewhere." If she does so, UCC §2-713 entitles her to recover, generally,

- any contract price already paid the seller, *plus*
- the quantity [(cover price) *minus* (contract price)],[8] *plus*
- "incidental damages," *plus*

---

8. Here, we interpret and *paraphrase* Article 2. Article 2 does not, in fact, identify the quantity [(cover price) *minus* (contract price)]. Rather, it entitles the covering buyer to "the difference between the cost of cover and the contract price" (§2-712(2)). With those words, the writers fail to account for a cover price that falls *below* the contract price. Consider a contract price of $100 and a cover price of $60. The "difference" between them is $40. If the law awards plaintiff $40 for that "difference," it overcompensates him.

- "consequential damages," *minus*
- expenses saved as a result of the breach.

"Incidental damage" means ancillary expenses the buyer incurs because of the breach. If, for example, he spends $500 searching for cover, he has "incidental damage" of $500. If seller delivers defective goods and buyer spends $1,000 storing them for seller or returning them to seller, buyer has $1,000 in "incidental damage."

"Consequential damages" refers to damages that are indirectly or remotely caused by the breach.[9] With respect to a seller's breach, a classic example is the middleman buyer who contracts to buy goods, with another contract already in place, by which he plans to resell them to his own customer for a profit. If the seller fails to deliver the goods and, as a result, the buyer cannot resell to his own customer, the buyer's lost profit constitutes "consequential damage."[10] Lost profit is the most common form of consequential damage.

All of This Amounts to a Badly Structured Form of the Simple Common Law Rules Wearing an Article 2 Disguise

Let's revisit Wholesaler vs. Distributor, Episode I: It's January 1. Wholesaler and Distributor form a signed, written contract under which, for $100,000, Distributor will deliver 100,000 widgets to Wholesaler on February 1. Wholesaler is to pay Distributor $20,000 immediately as a down payment, $80,000 on delivery, plus a $2,000 delivery charge. Furthermore, Wholesaler has customers who will buy the widgets from *her* for $150,000 in total. Wholesaler makes the $20,000 down payment.

Then, on February 3, Distributor contacts Wholesaler and repudiates the contract. Wholesaler searches for the 100,000 widgets elsewhere, and spends $500 conducting the search. She finds another seller willing to sell her 100,000 widgets for $120,000, $20,000 more than she was to pay Distributor. That seller does not impose a charge for delivery. Wholesaler buys the widgets, pays the $120,000, and, as planned, sells them to her customers for $150,000.

Applying the common law, we calculated Wholesaler's recovery with this simple monetary timeline:

($00.00) →	- $20,000→	- $500→	- $120,000→
Wholesaler's position before contract formation	down payment	search for substitute goods	purchase of substitute goods

---

9. "Consequential damage" has meaning in many fields outside of contracts and sales. It means, generally, "such damage, loss, or injury as does not flow directly and immediately from [a defendant's wrongful act."] Black's Law Dictionary 467 (rev. 4th ed.).

10. UCC §2-715 cmt. 6; Kunstsoffwerk Alfred Huber v. R.J. Dick Inc., 621 F.2d 563 (3d Cir. 1980).

+ $150,000
resale to Wholesaler's to customers

= $9,500→	+ $38,500 =	$48,000
Wholesaler's actual position in light of breach and mitigation	RECOVERY (Wholesaler's expectation interest)	Wholesaler's expected gain

Now, Let's Calculate Wholesaler's Damages Under Article 2

Under Article 2, Wholesaler is entitled to:
1. contract price (down payment) already paid the seller = $20,000
2. the quantity [(cover price) *minus* (contract price)] + $20,000
3. "incidental damages" (search for cover) + $ 500
4. "consequential damages," *minus* + $ 0
5. expenses saved as a result of the breach
   (delivery charge) – $ 2,000
   $38,500

Now, as we did above, in Wholesaler v. Distributor, Episode II, let's suppose Wholesaler finds the substitute goods but doesn't buy them. From the common law, Wholesaler recovered only that same $38,500 she recovered when she did mitigate, as in Episode I. Our common law monetary timeline told us this:

$9,500→	+ $38,500 =	**$48,000**
Wholesaler's position *if she had properly mitigated*	RECOVERY	Wholesaler's expected gain

Article 2 calculates her damage according to the five items shown above, including consequential damages—BUT—(a) in *defining* consequential damage UCC §2-715(a)(2) provides that the phrase does not include damage that "could reasonably be prevented by cover or otherwise," and (b) for a buyer who does not cover, item 2 does not refer to cover price, but to "market price" at the time the buyer learns of the breach.

1. + contract price (down payment) already paid the seller = $20,000
2. + the quantity [(market price) *minus* (contract price)][11] $20,000
3. + "incidental damages" (search for cover) $ 500
4. + "consequential damages" $ 0
5. expenses saved as a result of the breach (delivery charge) – $ 2,000
   $38,500

---

11. See note *supra*. Here, again, we paraphrase. The writers do not name the quantity [(market price) *minus* (contract price)]. Rather, they provide that the buyer who does not cover is entitled to "the difference between the market price . . . and the contract price" (§2-713(1)). With the words "difference between," they fail to account for a market price that *exceeds* the contract price.

If from $38,500 we subtract $20,500, the amount Wholesaler had spent at the time of the breach, we find, as before, that her true position after recovery is $18,000; she forgoes the $30,000 in damage that she caused herself.

2. Article 2's Treatment of the Lost Volume Seller

As to the lost volume seller, Article 2's writers present so pitiful a poverty of comprehension, so meager a mastery of the matter as, once again, to make a mockery of legal reasoning.

To begin, as for a buyer who breaches by refusing *to* buy, UCC §2-706(1) provides:

> [T]he seller may resell the goods concerned . . . [and] the seller may recover the difference between the contract price and the resale price together with any incidental or consequential damages[.][12]

That rule is worthless. For as we know, a seller may resell the goods intended for the breaching buyer at the same price the breaching party was to pay, in which case [(resale price) − (contract price)] = 0. Yet, if the seller would have made the second sale regardless of the buyer's breach, he is a lost volume seller, entitled to the profit lost through the buyer's breach.

Don't the Article 2 Writers Account for That?

They make the most pathetic of attempts. UCC §2-208(2) provides:

> If the measure of damages provided . . . in Section 2-706 is inadequate to put the seller in as good a position as performance would have done, the measure of damages is the profit . . . that the seller would have made from full performance by the buyer, together with any incidental or consequential damages. . . .

Official Comment 4 then explains:

> Subsection 2 is used in the cases of . . . lost-volume sellers. This remedy is an alternative to the remedy under . . . §2-706, and it is available when the damages based upon resale of the goods . . . do not achieve the goal of full compensation for harm caused by the buyer's breach.

In order to "get it straight," the writers need only have written §2-706(1) **this way:**

> *(1) The seller may resell the goods concerned to another buyer and recover the difference between the contract price and the resale price together with any incidental or consequential damages, but (2) if, regardless of the breach, the seller would have sold identical goods to that same buyer, then the seller is a lost volume seller and the sale to the second buyer is irrelevant to calculation of the seller's recovery.*

---

12. Here, again, note the words "difference between." With respect to a plaintiff seller's damages, Article 2 fails, yet again, to account for a resale price that exceeds the contract price.

3. *What Can We Conclude About Article 2?*

About Article 2's rules regarding expectation interest, mitigation, and lost volume sellers, we can conclude that:

- Article *1*'s writers intended that a breaching buyer or seller should pay damages according to the common law's rule, and UCC §1-305 proves that point.
- Article *2*'s writers were not equal to that task; their provisions on these points offer a morass of misconception and mistake.
- When calculating damages under Article 2, one should first calculate them under the common law and then make the result "fit" Article 2 (which in some cases the Code drafters make impossible through their pervasive inability to address legal concepts of any complexity).

E.   The Closers

> **QUESTION 3.** On June 1, Attly and Bartley form a contract under which (1) Attly is to design a dam on or before August 1, and (2) Bartley is to pay her $250,000 when she completes the design.
>
> Attly begins work and during the month of June spends $10,000 in work-related expenses. On July 1, Bartley advises Attly that he no longer needs the dam design and will not pay her, thereby committing an anticipatory repudiation (Chapter 25, section C). Nonetheless, Attly completes the design, spending an additional $20,000. Attly then sues Bartley for breach, claiming damages of $250,000. She asserts that
>
> **(a)** if Bartley had not breached, she would have received $250,000 and paid $30,000 for a net gain of $220,000;
>
> **(b)** in light of Bartley's breach, she has spent $30,000 and received nothing; and
>
> **(c)** to fulfill her expectation interest, she is entitled to [($220,000 − (−$30,000)] = [($220,000 + ($30,000)] = $250,000.
>
> Attly should recover:
>
> **A.** $250,000
> **B.** $230,000
> **C.** $220,000
> **D.** $210,000

ANALYSIS.   When Attly learned of Bartley's breach, she had spent $10,000. Because she knew that Bartley intended not to pay, mitigation required that she not spend additional sums. By spending yet another $20,000, she "ran up" her damages. Had Attly properly mitigated, her ultimate position would have been negative $10,000 instead of negative $30,000. She herself caused $20,000 of her loss. Hence, she is entitled to [($250,000) − ($20,000)] = $230,000. **B** is right.

QUESTION 4. Brothers Martin and Nate decide to purchase a photocopier—one photocopier for their home. Phil operates a retail electronics store that carries photocopiers. Martin visits Phil's store and contracts for the purchase of a Repro Model 13 photocopier for $1,200. Phil has in stock fifty of these same machines, having paid $700 for each. Further, for that same price, he is free to order from the manufacturer as many additional units as he wants.

Martin and Phil agree that Martin will return on the following day to make payment and take delivery of the machine. Phil immediately sets aside a machine for Martin. One hour later, however, Martin returns to say that he will not purchase the machine. Phil moves the photocopier back to his storage room. Nate then learns what Martin has done, but he still wants the photocopier. He goes to Phil's store, and tells Phil that he wants to buy a Repro Model 13. Phil tells him that the price is $1,200, and Nate agrees to buy. Phil brings out a second machine from his storage room, whereupon Nate pays him $1,200 and takes the machine.

Is Phil entitled to recover from Martin a $500 profit ($1,200 − $700) lost to him because of Martin's breach?

A. Yes, because he is a lost volume seller
B. Yes, because he had sufficient inventory to supply *both* Martin and Nate
C. No, because he did not sell Nate the very same unit he had planned to sell Martin
D. No, because if Martin had purchased a machine, Nate would not have done so

---

ANALYSIS.   Ask the key question: Would Phil have made the sale to Nate if Martin hadn't breached? The answer is "no." Between the two brothers, there never were to have been two sales. Nate bought the photocopier only because Martin did not. Had Martin bought it, Nate would not have done so. Consequently, by selling the photocopier to Nate, Phil recouped the profit he lost through Martin's breach.

As for **A**, Martin's breach didn't cause Phil to lose a sale; Phil is not a lost volume seller. **A** is wrong. **B** correctly states that Phil had sufficient inventory to supply both Martin and Nate, but that's irrelevant to this circumstance. The facts are such that he did not stand to make two sales. The answer "yes" makes **B** wrong. **C** cites a fact that's true but irrelevant. The whole question of whether a seller resells to some other customer, physically, the very same goods that a breaching buyer failed to buy is irrelevant to the lost volume issue. The question is only whether the second sale of an identical good is separate from, independent of, and unrelated to the first. In this case, it's not. **D** correctly says "no" and offers the right reasoning. Between the brothers, there was never to have been more than *one* sale. Hence, **D** is right.

QUESTION 5. Quenn owns a yacht (which is a good; see Appendix, section D). She engages Broker 1 to sell it. Under her contract with Broker 1, Broker 1 is entitled to receive 6 percent of the sale price if he finds a party who contracts with Quenn to buy the yacht at any price above $700,000. Broker 1 is entitled to his commission as soon as such a contract arises. The fact that Quenn or his buyer might then breach does not affect his entitlement to the 6 percent fee.

On March 1, Broker 1 finds a buyer, Remsen, willing to pay $1 million for Quenn's yacht. On March 5, by signed writing, Quenn and Remsen contract for the sale of the yacht at a price of $1 million, the actual payment and transfer of title to occur on April 1. Also on March 5, Quenn pays Broker 1 his $60,000 fee.

On March 10, Remsen contacts Quenn and commits an anticipatory repudiation (Chapter 25, section C). On March 15, Quenn engages Broker 2, with whom she contracts to pay the same 6 percent commission should he find a buyer who contracts to purchase the yacht at a price above $700,000. Quenn also advertises the yacht on her own and spends $1,000 doing so. On April 1, Broker 2 introduces Quenn to Leonards, who stands ready to buy the yacht for $750,000. On April 5, Quenn and Leonards form a contract calling for the purchase and sale of the yacht at that price. Also on April 5, Quenn pays Broker 2 his $45,000 fee. Leonards does purchase the yacht for $750,000 as agreed.

Quenn brings an action against Remsen. Itemized according to the UCC, to what recovery, if any, is Quenn entitled?

A. $45,000
B. $250,000
C. $296,000
D. $300,000

ANALYSIS. Forget about Article 2, and solve the problem, first, by common law, which means, also, that you abide by UCC §1-305. Quenn is entitled to occupy the financial position she would have occupied had both parties fully performed *minus* the financial position she occupies (or would have occupied) having made a reasonable attempt to mitigate. If both parties had fully performed, the result would be:

$00.00→	+ $1 million→	- $60,000 =	$940,000
Quenn's position before the parties form their contract	Remsen pays purchase price	Quenn pays Broker 1	Quenn's expected gain

By engaging Broker 2, and selling the yacht to Leonards, Quenn did make a reasonable attempt to mitigate and succeeded. She is entitled to damages of:

$00.00→	- $60,000→	- $1,000→	- $45,000→	+ $750,000
Quenn's position before the parties form their contract	Quenn pays Broker 1	Quenn pays for advertising	Quenn pays Broker 2	Leonards pays purchase price

= $644,000→	+ $296,000 =	$940,000
Quenn's position after sale to Leonards	RECOVERY (expectation interest)	Quenn's expected gain

Now, force UCC Article 2 to yield that same result:

(1) purchase price paid:	$
(2) [(contract price) − (resale price)]	$250,000
(3) incidental damages	$
(a) advertising:	$ 1,000
(b) commission, Broker 2:	$ 45,000
	$296,000

C is right.

 Silver's Picks

1.	D
2.	C
3.	B
4.	D
5.	C

27

Breach, Remedies, and Damages, Part III

A. Expectation Interest and Foreseeability of Damage: *Hadley v. Baxendale*
B. Expectation Interest When Cost of Performance Exceeds Value of Performance
C. Expectation Damages Require "Reasonable Certainty"
D. The Closer
✧ Silver's Picks

A. Expectation Interest and Foreseeability of Damage: *Hadley v. Baxendale*

It's 1854. Hadley operates a mill. Its shaft breaks, leaving the mill inoperable. By custom, the owner of a mill such as his would ordinarily have a spare shaft so that if one should break, the mill would still operate. Hadley, however, has no such spare. And, for every day the mill is idle, he loses large sums of money. Hurriedly, Hadley contacts Manufacturer, who instructs Hadley to send him the broken shaft itself as a model from which he'll construct a new one.

Baxendale is a courier. Hadley and Baxendale form a contract under which Baxendale will deliver the broken shaft to Manufacturer, Baxendale promising that he'll do so in one day's time. Baxendale has no reason to know that Hadley's mill will remain inoperative until fitted with a new shaft. Alas, Baxendale delivers the broken shaft to the manufacturer not in one day but in one week. Consequently, the mill is idle for that additional week and causes Hadley to lose £200 in revenue. Hadley sues Baxendale, claiming damage of £200.

Faced with (something like) this story, an English court ruled that because Baxendale had no reason to know that plaintiff's mill would remain inoperative without the new shaft, plaintiff's damages did not include the revenue lost through Baxendale's lateness:

> Now we think the proper rule . . . is this: Where two parties have made a contract which one of them has broken, the damages which the other party ought to receive . . . should be such as may fairly and reasonably be considered either arising naturally, i.e., according to the usual course of things . . . or such as may reasonably be supposed to have been in the contemplation of both parties at the time they made the contract, as the probable result of the breach of it[.] . . . Now, in the present case . . . we find that the only circumstances here communicated by the plaintiffs to the defendants at the time the contract was made, were, that the article to be carried was the broken shaft of a mill, and that the plaintiffs were the millers of that mill[.] . . . [And] in the great multitude of cases of millers sending off broken shafts to third persons by a carrier under ordinary circumstances . . . [the miller has a spare shaft and the mill continues to operate].

Hadley v. Baxendale, 156 Eng. Rep. 145, 151 (1854). The rule that denies a plaintiff recovery of damage that is not, under the circumstances, reasonably foreseeable to the defendant is often called, "the rule of *Hadley v. Baxendale.*"

With that, we amend the rule stated in earlier chapters:

For breach of contract, the plaintiff is ordinarily to recover the amount of money that will transform his financial position from

(a) the lesser of that which (i) he occupies in light of the breach, or (ii) should occupy in light of any reasonable opportunity to mitigate, whether he does or does not avail himself of it to

(b)(i) that which he would have occupied if he and the defendant had fully and properly performed, which position constitutes his "expectation interest," known also as the "benefit of his bargain," but (ii) such expectation and benefit do not include the damage that arises because of any fact, circumstance, or event that the defendant had no reason to foresee at the time he and plaintiff formed their contract.

In this regard, Restatement (Second) of Contracts §351(1) provides: "Damages are not recoverable for loss that the party in breach did not have reason to foresee as a probable result of the breach when the contract was made."

QUESTION 1. Harriet plans to attend a business meeting 2,000 miles from her home. She purchases a refundable airline ticket for $1,000 and makes a cancelable hotel reservation for $1,000. Harriet then forms a contract with Indo, a cab driver, under which Harriet will pay Indo $55. Indo will pick up Harriet on Wednesday at 6:00 A.M. and transport her to the airport. Indo neither knows nor has reason to know why or to where Harriet is traveling.

On Wednesday morning, Indo, running twenty minutes late, reaches Harriet's home at 6:20 A.M. As a result, Harriet reaches the airport at 7:20 A.M. She pays Indo $55 and dashes from cab to her boarding gate. Nonetheless she misses her plane by two minutes and, for that reason, misses her business meeting, thus losing a business opportunity that would have paid her, provably, $5 million. After canceling her lodging reservation without penalty, Harriet decides to sue Indo.

Harriet calculates her expectation interest as she sees it. If the driver had properly performed, she would have spent $1,000 for airline tickets, $1,000 for lodging, and $55 for Indo's cab ride, for a total of $2,055. She would have received $5 million. Her position would have been positive $4,997,945. In fact, Harriet spent $1,000 on airfare, but because she did not travel, the airfare was refunded. She paid Indo $55, she canceled the hotel reservation, and she did not, of course, enjoy the $5 million. Her position, therefore, is *negative* $-55. On this basis, Harriet sues Indo, alleging damages of $4,997,945 (the position she would have occupied if both parties had fulfilled their contract—*minus*—the position she in fact occupies in light of Indo's breach:

$00.00→	- $55→	- $1,000→	+ $1,000 =	- $55→
Harriet's position before forming contract	cab fare	airfare	airfare refund	Harriet's position in face of breach

Consequently, Harriet contends that she is entitled to recover:

= - $55→	+ $4,998,000 =	$4,997,945
Harriet's position in face of breach	**RECOVERY HARRIET DEMANDS** (expectation interest as she sees it)	Harriet's position if Indo had honoroed the contract

As *the law* regards her expectation interest, Harriet is most likely entitled to recover

A. $4,998,000, the amount necessary to afford her the benefit of her bargain
B. $55, the amount she paid to Indo
C. $1,000, the amount she spent on the airline ticket
D. $0 because under the rule of *Hadley v. Baxendale*, none of the damage she alleges is recoverable

ANALYSIS.   For breach of contract, a plaintiff cannot recover for any loss not reasonably foreseeable to defendant at the time the parties form their contract. That's the "rule of *Hadley v. Baxendale*." Indo had no reason to foresee that a twenty-minute lateness on his part would occasion damage of so staggering an amount as $4,997,945. Consequently, in calculating Harriet's recovery, the law does not include the $5 million lost business opportunity.

A awards Harriet her full expectation interest and thus includes the damages that Indo could not reasonably have foreseen. It's wrong. **B** reimburses her the cab fare, an expense she would have to have made even if Indo had not breached. It's wrong. **C** gives Harriet reimbursement for her airfare, but she did not, in fact, pay the airfare, since it was refunded to her. **C** goes to the curb. **D** eliminates the $5 million loss not foreseeable to Indo, accounts for the refunded airfare and for the $1,000 she did not spend on lodging. It recognizes that absent Indo's breach she would, still, have had to pay his fare. Apart from the $5 million that Indo could not foresee, Harriet suffered no damage. She recovers nothing. **D** is right.

B.   Expectation Interest When Cost of Performance Exceeds Value of Performance

Suppose Olan and Portia form a contract under which Portia is to build a house for Olan and Olan is to pay her $400,000 when she completes the work. The contract provides that for all internal plumbing, Portia is to use Rodding copper piping. Portia completes the house with perfect conformity to the contract except that she uses Conan copper piping, whose quality is the same as the Rodding product.

Olan obtains three good faith estimates for the cost of replacing the Conan piping with the Rodding product; all three estimates report a cost of $50,000, primarily because the placement would require opening walls, tearing out the Conan piping, replacing it with the Rodding product, and resealing the walls. Olan sues Portia claiming damages of $50,000, which amount, he asserts, he will need to replace the piping and thus afford himself the position he would have enjoyed had Portia properly performed.

Portia admits the accuracy of Olan's estimates, but her own evidence demonstrates that (a) with the Conan piping in place the home's value is $500,000 and (b) with the piping replaced by the Rodding product its value would like-wise be $500,000. Hence, the cost of correcting Portia's performance would be $50,000 whereas the corrected performance would add to the home a value of $0. Olan does not dispute those financial realities.

Nonetheless, Olan insists that his expectation interest — the benefit of his bargain — entitles him to a home with Rodding pipes, and he demands $50,000 in damages. Portia contends that she has, in fact, afforded Olan his expectation interest, since with either form of piping the home is worth $500,000.

That Leaves Us with This Critical Question

When the *cost* of correcting or completing a defendant's faulty performance exceeds the market *value* of the corrected performance, does fulfillment of the plaintiff's expectation interest require recovery of the cost ($50,000 in this case) or only the difference in value ($0 in this case)?

The pat answer to that question turns on the phrase "economic waste," and many law students learn to recite, "When, as to a building or construction contract, the cost of performance exceeds the value of corrected performance and correcting performance would wreak economic waste, then the plaintiff recovers not the cost but the value of correction." The phrase "economic waste" derives from the *first* Restatement of Contracts §348:

> (a) For defective or unfinished construction [plaintiff] can get judgment for either
>
>   (i) the reasonable cost of construction and completion in accordance with the contract, if this is possible and does not involve unreasonable economic waste; or
>
>   (ii) the difference between the value that the product contracted for would have had and the value of the performance that has been received by the plaintiff, if construction and completion in accordance with the contract would involve unreasonable economic waste.

Comment b then provides:

> The purpose of money damages is to put the injured party in as good a position as that in which full performance would have put him; but this does not mean that he is to be put in the same specific physical position[.] There are numerous cases . . . in which the value of [a] finished product is much less than the cost of producing it after the breach has occurred[.] The law does not require damages to be measured by a method requiring such economic waste. If no such waste is involved, the cost of remedying the defect

is the amount awarded as compensation for failure to render the promised performance.

The Restatement nowhere defines its own phrase "economic waste." Neither is that phrase useful in explaining what judges really find themselves doing. A number of courts have purported to state that a plaintiff should recover the cost of a corrected performance, even where it exceeds its value, if the defendant's breach is willful — if he breaches "on purpose" (meaning that the defendant did not in good faith attempt to honor his contract). Yet if defendant's breach is not deliberate/willful then, say some courts, recovery is limited to the monetary value of correcting performance where the cost of performance would be greater.

> Where the contractor's performance has been incomplete or defective, the usual measure of damages is the reasonable cost of replacement or completion[.] That rule does not apply if the contractor performs in good faith but defects nevertheless exist and remedying them could entail economic waste. Then, diminution in value becomes the proper measure of damages.

City Sch. Dist. of the City of Elmira v. McLane Constr. Co., 85 A.D.2d 749, 750 (N.Y. App. Div. 1981).

But the distinction between willfulness and good faith doesn't "hold water." The decisions don't support it. In one celebrated case, plaintiff and defendant formed a contract under which defendant paid plaintiff for the right to remove valuable sand and gravel from his land. Defendant was obliged not only to pay money to plaintiff, but also to restore the land to a certain condition after it completed the removal. Defendant paid plaintiff as required, removed the sand and gravel, but then failed to restore the land. The cost of the restoration would have exceeded $60,000. Yet, *if* restored, the land would have a market value only $12,000 higher than it had when loaded with defendant's mess. Noting that the breach was willful, the court ruled that plaintiff was entitled to have the *cost* of performance.[1]

In an equally renowned decision, the result was opposite. Defendant strip miner formed a contract with plaintiff landowner under which defendant would pay plaintiff for a lease of plaintiff's land and have the right to mine it. The contract further required that when defendant concluded its activity, it was to restore the land. Defendant paid plaintiff as required and mined the land. When finished, however, defendant made no restoration. The court found that restoration would cost $29,000 but would increase the land's value by only $300. On that basis, citing the Restatement's phrase

---

1. Groves v. John Wunder Co., 286 N.W. 235 (Minn. 1939).

"economic waste," the court limited damages to $300.[2] In that case, too, the breach was willful.

The two cases are not reconcilable (as certainly can happen, especially between two separate jurisdictions). Simply and plainly, *there is no reliable rule* whereunder willfulness or innocence of the breach dictates the recovery when cost of correction exceeds its monetary value.

Restatement (First) §346, illustration 2 tells us this:

> A contracts to erect a dwelling for B for $70,000, according to plans and specifications, one of which is the use of "Alpha" pipe for all plumbing. After completion, B learns that A has used "Beta" pipe, an equally good brand. To replace the "Beta" pipe with the "Alpha" would now require tearing down the walls and would cost almost as much as a new house. The value of the house as built is not less than the value of the house as promised. B can get judgment for only nominal damages.

Illustration 4 then tells us *this*:

> A contracts to construct a monumental fountain in B's yard for $5,000, but abandons the work after the foundation has been laid and $2,800 has been paid by B. The contemplated fountain is so ugly that it would decrease the number of possible buyers of the place. The cost of completing the fountain would be $4,000. [B's contract required that he pay $5,000 for the fountain and he has thus far paid only $2,800. He is entitled to $4,000, the cost of completing performance, less the additional $1,200 he would have had to pay ($5,000 − $2,800) as the remainder of the $5,000 contract price.] He can get judgment for $1,800, the cost of completion . . . less the part of price unpaid.

The Restatement writers don't explain — not anywhere, not anyhow — why in illustration 2, plaintiff recovers only the value of performance whereas in illustration 4 he recovers the cost.[3]

So, let's take the Restatement rule and set it aside. Let's state a better rule — the *real* rule — the rule that explains the decisions.

All We Need Do Is Return to the Basic Simple Doctrine of Contractual Interpretation

As we now know well, as recovery for breach of contract, the plaintiff is entitled to so much as will afford him "the position he would have occupied if both parties had fully, properly performed." That's his "expectation interest," the "benefit of his bargain."

---

2. Peevyhouse v. Garland Coal & Mining, 382 P.2d 109 (Okla. 1962).

3. If they meant to imply that a lesser number of potential buyers is equivalent to lower market value, they should have so stated.

All reported cases in which the *cost* of a corrected performance differs substantially from the market *value* of a corrected performance bear on contracts for building, construction, or other activities that touch on realty. Where correcting the flawed performance would occasion the physical destruction or substantial disassembly of a physical structure, then, citing the phrase "economic waste," courts are quite likely to limit recovery to the value of performance.

PLEASE STOP. For those of you whose courses have not yet dealt with contract formation, offer and acceptance, and mutual assent, stop here and read Chapter 2, sections A, B, and D; Chapter 3, section A; Chapter 7, section A; and Chapter 18, section A. Skip the multiple-choice questions for now; just read the text. It will go very quickly (we promise) and give you a leg up in understanding the material in the next part of this chapter. Then, meet us back here.

In earlier chapters, you learned that

- a contract arises by offer and acceptance (with each party providing consideration to the other);
- the terms of the offer have such meaning as would be given them by a reasonable offeree under all prevailing circumstances;
- an offeree accepts only if he assents to all of the offeror's terms without addition or exception; *wherefore*
- the terms of any true acceptance are identical to those of the offer; *wherefore*
- the terms of the resulting contract are the same as those of the offer which are the same as those of the acceptance; *wherefore*
- a contract includes such terms and has such meaning as conform to the parties' reasonable understandings and reasonable expectations.

Consider the Difference Between These Two Contracts.   Here's the first:

> **Party A:** I'd like you to rip up all of the grass and flowers on my residential property. I'll pay you $3,000 for the service.
> **Party B:** Why do you want me to do that?
> **Party A:** Well, I'm somewhat eccentric. I prefer my yard to be absolutely devoid of greenery.
> **Party B:** But that will diminish the market value of your property.
> **Party A:** I know it will, but I don't care. That's the way I want it.
> **Party B:** Okay, if that's what you want — it's a deal.

Here's the second:

> **Party C:** I'd like you to build a house on my land according to the specifications shown in these architectural diagrams. I'll pay $350,000.
> **Party D:** What are your plans for the house after it's built?
> **Party C:** I think it will be worth about $550,000, and I'm going to sell it.
> **Party D:** I agree that it will be worth about that amount. You should make a handsome profit. In any case, I accept. I'll build the house for $350,000.

Now let's compare the two contracts. Any reasonable person in B's position should understand that A's purpose is not to raise his property's value but to strip it of greenery even if that reduces its worth. B, as a reasonable person, should understand that the "position" in which A seeks to be placed is that of a person who owns residential realty devoid of greenery. Both A and B should understand that when these parties make their contract, B makes this promise: "I will strip your property of all grass, plants, and flowers, and if I fail to do that I will owe you the cost of completing that job, regardless of what happens to the value of your property." If B breaches, A's expectation interest should be measured not according to the monetary value of his property, but according to the cost of correcting B's performance.[4]

With regard to contract 2, a reasonable person in D's position should understand that C seeks no particular outcome touching on his own taste, but a structure that he anticipates will be worth more than it costs him to build it. As a reasonable person, D should understand that the position C seeks is to own a house with a value greater than the cost of erecting it. That doesn't mean D guarantees any such result. It means only that if D fails properly to build, C's expectation interest should be measured as the difference between the value the house would have had if properly constructed and the value it has as D improperly built it.

No real case in a real court has ever involved conversations that so explicitly define a contractual purpose as do the two depicted above. Nonetheless, in all real cases in which cost of correcting performance exceeds the value of correction, it is the court's job to determine what, under the circumstances, the parties should reasonably have understood as their objectives in forming a contract. On *that* basis and no other, the court should identify plaintiff's expectation interest according to either monetary value or cost of completing/correcting performance. And whether consciously they know it or not, that *is* what the courts generally do.

So What Rule Can We Write About Cost of Performance versus Value of Performance?

This one:

If (1) two parties P and D form a contract under which D is to perform a service for P, and (2) D breaches, and (3) the cost of completing or correcting D's performance exceeds the market value to be obtained by doing so, then the measure of recovery depends on what D should have understood regarding P's objective in light of all circumstances surrounding the parties — including their own communications — when they formed their contract; and

> *(a) Where such circumstances led or should have led D to understand that P's purpose was to derive increased monetary value, then P's recovery is the value of corrected performance; but*

---

4. See Chamberlain v. Parker, 45 N.Y. 569, 572 (1871) (an owner is "entitled to recover the value of the work and labor that the defendant was to perform, although the thing to be produced had no marketable value").

(b) Where such circumstances should have led D reasonably to understand that P's purpose was not pecuniary, but something else — related, perhaps, to sentiment, emotion, or personal taste — then P's recovery is the actual cost of corrected performance, even though that exceeds its monetary value.

Accordingly, in 1871, the New York Court of Appeals wrote:

[One] may do what he will with his own, . . . and if he chooses to erect a monument to his caprice or folly on his premises, and employs and pays another to do it, it does not lie with a defendant who has been so employed and paid for building it, to say that his own performance would not be beneficial to the plaintiff. Chamberlain v. Parker, 45 N.Y. 569, 572 (1871).

We add to the court's words this clarification:

If the party hired to erect the monument fails to do what *he knows or should know is wanted*, it is not for him to say that correcting his flawed performance would render the monument less valuable than it is with flawed performance in place. It is for him to do as he promised or to pay the cost of having it done.

QUESTION 2. Kinelman is an auto body servicer. Leder owns an old car that once belonged to her grandmother. Leder approaches Kinelman and, as she displays her car, the parties speak:

Leder: How much will you charge to restore this car's body to showroom condition, repainting it in its original color, mint green?

Kinelman: Far more than the car would be worth after I complete the work. I don't recommend that you have me do it.

Leder: Well, it was my grandmother's car, and I love it. So, what would you charge?

Kinelman: $18,000, in advance.

Leder: Yes, let's do it.

Kinelman: Okay.

Leder pays Kinelman $18,000, and Kinelman begins work. In three weeks, he notifies Leder that the vehicle is ready. When Leder arrives at Kinelman's shop, she sees that the Kinelman has painted the car not mint green, but sky blue.

Leder: It's beautiful, but it's the wrong color. I'd like you to repaint it in mint green, the color on which we agreed.

Kinelman: [Kinelman checks his notes.] You're right. I'm sorry, I painted it the wrong color. But, as you say, it's beautiful, isn't it?

Leder: Yes, but I want it to be mint green, the color it was when my grandmother first bought it.

> **Kinelman:** I can't do that. I would have to remove this brand new paint, re-sand, prepare the whole surface of the car, and then apply four coats of mint green. That would take several days of my time — what a waste.
>
> **Leder:** I insist.
>
> **Kinelman:** I'm sorry. I won't do it. The car's value is no different now from what it would be if I were to repaint it in mint green. I won't do it.
>
> Leder sues Kinelman. At trial, undisputed evidence shows that the cost of having a well-qualified auto body expert repaint the vehicle mint green would be $5,000, and the change in color would make no difference to the car's market value. Is it likely that the court will award Leder a judgment of $5,000?
>
> A. Yes, because in order that Leder achieve his proper expectation interest, he needs such recovery as will provide him with a car that is painted mint green
>
> B. Yes, because a judgment of a lesser amount would reward Kinelman for his breach and unjustly enrich him at Leder's expense
>
> C. No, because changing the vehicle's color from sky blue to mint green would cause economic waste
>
> D. No, because when Party A contracts with Party B for the purchase of a service and Party B fails properly to perform it, Party A is entitled to receive only the monetary value of which the breach deprives her

ANALYSIS. Whether cost or value of performance measures the plaintiff's expectation interest depends on the expectations that reasonable parties would have had when they formed the contract. In this case, Leder made plain that her wishes arose from sentiment, not from a quest for monetary gain. Consequently, Leder's expectation interest is to be measured not according to the car's market value, but according to its physical appearance. In this case, then, plaintiff is entitled not to the difference in market value tied to the two different colors, but to the cost of correcting performance.

C and D say "no," so they're wrong. D makes the incorrect statement that a plaintiff is never entitled to receive the cost of completing performance. C invokes the tired phrase "economic waste" (as likely will your contracts teacher) and so misses the point. Some will say that one commits economic waste when she buys a thing or service whose monetary value is less than its price. More sophisticated economics, however, recognizes that value is an individual matter. The mint green is worth more to Leder than to the ordinary person. The restoration of the vehicle, obviously, is worth $18,000 *to Leder*, even though it has no such value to others. Although commonly used in this context, "economic waste" is an unavailing phrase; it gets us nowhere.

B correctly says "yes," but its reasoning is wrong. To award Leder less than $5,000 would not "reward" Kinelman for his breach. Kinelman worked diligently on the vehicle. He took no shortcuts and cut no corners. He simply made an honest mistake as to color. **A** reports the $5,000 figure and reasons correctly. Under the circumstances, Kinelman should have known that Leder was unconcerned with market value — that she expected the car to be mint green. Hence, **A** is right.

C. Expectation Damages Require "Reasonable Certainty"

Starr is a theatrical celebrity. After discussions, Starr and *Watch* magazine form a contract under which Starr will pose for a photograph that *Watch* will print on its January cover. The contract calls for neither party to pay any money to the other.

As the contract requires, Starr poses and *Watch* snaps the photo. *Watch* then decides to publish the picture of some other celebrity on its January cover, thus committing total breach of its contract with Starr. Starr brings an action alleging that the published photo would have benefited her career and enhanced her earnings. At trial, she calls two witnesses, both experts in theatrical publicity. Asked what financial benefit Starr would have derived from the published picture, Witness 1 testifies: "Who knows? It might have brought her millions. It might have brought her nothing. That kind of thing is impossible to predict." Answering the same question, Starr's Witness 2 says, "There's no way to tell — maybe a lot, maybe a little, maybe nothing."

When Starr rests her case, *Watch* moves to dismiss on the ground that Starr has shown no damage. The court rules:

> Whether the action be breach of contract or any other, a plaintiff cannot recover damages that would require a jury to guess or speculate as to their amount. Rather, a plaintiff must present such evidence as, in the court's opinion, will allow the jury to quantify her damages with *reasonable certainty*. This plaintiff has failed to satisfy that requirement. She has presented two witnesses, neither of whom offers any meaningful answer as to whether this bargain would have afforded the plaintiff any benefit at all. Consequently, this Court lacks an evidentiary basis on which to submit this case to the jury on the question of Plaintiff's expectation interest. Plaintiff is entitled only to nominal recovery. Judgment is for the plaintiff in the amount of $1.

The Relevant Rule. *With respect to breach of contract, a plaintiff cannot recover for expectation interest unless she shows with reasonable certainty the* *benefit she stood to enjoy absent the breach.*[5] *If she can make no such showing, then she has, by law, no expectation interest.*

And that raises this question: If plaintiff has no expectation interest, does she recover anything? The answer is "yes," as described in Chapter 28. So, answer the closer and move to the next chapter.

D. The Closer

QUESTION 3. Perry and Della form a contract. Della performs improperly, thereby committing a total breach. The nature of the breach and surrounding circumstances are such that the cost of actually correcting Della's performance will exceed the monetary value Perry will derive from correction. In which of the following cases is a court most likely to award Perry the cost of correcting performance, notwithstanding that it exceeds the monetary value of the correction?

A. Where, at the time Della made the error in her performance, there was no difference between the cost of performing correctly and the cost of performing incorrectly

B. Where no reasonable person would consider significant the difference between the way in which Della did perform and the way in which she should have performed

C. Where the circumstances surrounding the parties at the time they formed their contract should have caused Della to understand that Perry's objective pertained not to monetary gain, but to sentiment

D. Where at the time the parties formed their contract, it should have been plain to Della that Perry hoped to derive a monetary gain

---

ANALYSIS. On the question of recovery when cost of correcting improper performance exceeds its monetary value, neither the courts nor the Restatement offers a meaningful rule. (But for the rules they do state, see section B above.) Among the decisions, in result more than reasoning, a common thread strongly suggests that the rule truly, silently at work is this: When two parties contract for the purchase and sale of a service, and the seller should, as

---

5. The doctrine as to reasonable certainty and proof of the plaintiff's anticipated gain is another redundancy of law. It is but an application of a general (and obvious) rule: The jury will not be allowed to make a finding of fact on any matter unless, in the court's opinion, the trial has produced evidence sufficient for a reasonable person to do so.

a reasonable person, realize that the buyer's purpose is not to enjoy a monetary gain but a fulfillment of sentiment or taste, then, for a seller's breach, the law awards the buyer not the value of corrected performance, but its cost.

A has a nice ring so long as you don't read it for its true meaning. It fabricates a rule, to wit: If, at the time of breach, the cost to the defendant of doing things properly equals the cost of doing them improperly, then the law is more likely to award plaintiff the cost of correcting performance, even though it exceeds the value of correction. What can we say? It's double-talk; nonsense; there's no such rule. So, A is wrong ("*way*" wrong). B is seductive, but only if you don't comprehend the difference between one's *reasonable expectations* and the usual expectations of a *reasonable person*. They're different. The ordinary reasonable person does not want his front and back yards stripped of greenery. Yet, if he contracts for such a thing, then *he* is reasonable in expecting *that result*. Got it? B is wrong because it refers, generally, (a) to what reasonable persons would think significant instead of (b) to *Perry's* reasonable expectations under the circumstances in which he and Della form their contract.

D is opposite to the law. If at the time X and Y perform a contract they should mutually understand that X is hoping to achieve or preserve market value, then if Y breaches, X is entitled only to recover only the monetary cost of correcting performance so that he achieves his expectation interest as both parties understood or should have understood it. Certainly, in that case he does *not* recover cost of performance. D joins A and B in the trash truck.

As for C, think again of Grandma's car, mint green and sky blue. Surrounding circumstances (including conversations) should have caused (and probably did cause) defendant to understand that plaintiff's contractual purpose pertained not to value but to color. Perry's expectation interest, therefore, required that he recover not the value of performance, but its cost. C knows just what it's talking about. C is right.

 ## Silver's Picks

1.	D
2.	A
3.	C

28

Breach, Remedies, and Damages, Part IV

A. Reliance Interest
B. Restitution Interest: Unjust Enrichment, Restitution, and "Benefit Conferred"
C. "Benefit Conferred" in Dollars and Cents: *Quantum Meruit* and *Quantum Valebant*
D. Reliance, Restitution, and the Losing Contract
E. The Closers
⟡ Silver's Picks

A. Reliance Interest

Please reread the *Starr v. Watch* magazine story in Chapter 27, section C. Then add a few facts. Assume that after Watch contacts Starr but before the parties form their contract, Starr spends $2,000 in consulting fees attempting to determine that the photograph will or will not promote her celebrity. She then decides that it will in fact do so, and she accepts *Watch*'s offer; the parties form their contract. Starr then spends $3,000 on clothing and grooming to style her appearance for the photograph. Take special note of this: Starr spends the $2,000 on consulting fees *before* forming the contract. She spends the $3,000 fussing with her appearance *after* forming the contract. That's important.

Here's Why

Starr spends the $2,000 not so that she can perform or prepare to perform under the contract. Rather, she spends that money before she has any contract at all. She spends it in order to determine that she will or will not form one. On the other hand, Starr spends the $3,000 after she forms her contract. She spends that money in order to give or prepare for her performance. When one spends in order to perform or prepare to perform, she spends *in reliance* on her contract. That means Starr spends the $3,000 *in reliance* on the contract. The law accounts for that expenditure by calling it Starr's "reliance interest," and, as discussed more fully below, it's recoverable in the case of breach.

But, an expenditure one makes in order to decide, in the first place, that she will or will not form a contract belongs to no legally compensable "interest." If she does form a contract with another, as Starr formed one with Watch, the other's breach does not entitle her to recover it. Hence, for Watch's breach, Starr can't recover her $2,000 expenditure. It's money she would have spent "anyway"—even if she and Watch had never formed their contract.

In our revised story, as in the original one, *Watch* breaches and Starr sues. And, as before, she can't, with any certainty, establish an expectation interest. But, as we've now altered the facts, she can show that she spent money *in reliance* on the contract. *Because* of the contract—in preparation for her performance *under* the contract—she spent $3,000. Compared to her $00.00 position before she contracted with Watch, Watch's breach puts Starr $3,000 "in the red." Again, the $2,000 expenditure is legally irrelevant; Starr spent that money before the parties formed their contract. The $3,000 belongs to Starr's reliance interest.

	Reliance on contract	
$00.00→	- $3,000 =	- $3,000
Starr's position before the parties form their contract	fussing with appearance	Starr's position in face of breach

When, as in Starr's case, a plaintiff cannot show an expectation interest, the law (usually) awards her an amount equal to her reliance interest. Doing so affords the plaintiff not her expectation interest (since she cannot prove what that might be) but, instead, at least, restores her to *the position she occupied just before the parties formed their contract*. In order to do that—in order to make her "whole," the law must award her $3,000—her reliance interest.

- $3,000→	+ $3,000 =	- $00.00
Starr's position in face of breach	RECOVERY (Starr's reliance interest)	Starr is restored to the position she occupied before forming the contract; she has recovered her reliance interest

Again, Why Do We Assign $00.00 to the Moment Before the Parties Form Their Contract? What About the $2,000 Consulting Fee?

Starr secured consulting services *before* forming the contract. She did so to determine whether she wished to form it or not. She paid $2,000 not in reliance on the contract, which she had not yet decided to form, but in *contemplation* of it. To the moment before the parties form their contract, we always assign the value $00.00. As to an aggrieved plaintiff's recovery, nothing that happens before then "counts." Consequently, amounts that one spends investigating and studying a prospective contract before forming it don't belong to her reliance interest; she has not spent the money in reliance *on the contract*.

With that, let's amend our rule regarding recovery for breach of contract: *For breach of contract, the law's ordinary remedy is monetary damages in an amount that allows plaintiff to enjoy "the benefit of her bargain," meaning the amount necessary to fulfill her expectation interest. BUT, if (in the judge's opinion) evidence is insufficient for a jury to quantify that amount with reasonable certainty, then the law awards the plaintiff such amount as corresponds to her reliance interest, meaning the value of money or property (but not of time, effort, or labor) with which she parted in reliance on the contract.*

QUESTION 1. Orson secures a patent on her new invention. Penn knows of the invention and believes he can, over ten years, earn $500 million manufacturing and marketing it. Consequently, Penn wishes to buy Orson's patent. Orson becomes serious about selling the patent to Penn and Penn becomes serious about buying it from Orson. Each engages an attorney and Penn pays $10,000 for his attorney's services. He also spends $12,000 consulting with technical experts as to what would be involved in manufacturing and marketing the device.

On January 2, 2017, the parties form a contract under which Penn is to pay Orson $1 million immediately; Orson is to convey the patent to Penn one year hence; and Penn, as he sells the device to buyers, is to pay Orson a royalty of 5 percent on each sale.

Penn makes the $1 million payment as required and, over the next year, begins to prepare for manufacture. Spending 100 hours of his time, he secures a factory and equipment, all at a cost of $3 million. On January 2, 2019, Orson refuses to convey the patent, and Penn sues him for breach.

At trial, Penn produces two expert witnesses who testify about the profit Penn would have earned manufacturing and marketing Orson's invention. One witness testifies, "It's very hard to know—maybe a billion dollars, maybe nothing." The other testifies, "These things are highly speculative. It's impossible to say." Both witnesses testify that 100 hours of Penn's labor has a fair market value of $25,000. After Penn presents all of his evidence, the court rules, (a) as a matter of law, that Penn has not shown with reasonable certainty how much money he stood truly to derive if Orson had honored the contract, and (b) that Penn is entitled to recover his reliance interest. Therefore, the court will award him

A. nothing.
B. $22,000, the combined amount he paid a lawyer and consultants.
C. $4 million, the amount he spent after forming the contract.
D. $4 million plus $25,000, the fair market value of his time and effort.

ANALYSIS.   Start with the rule. Then recognize that just before forming this contract, Penn *had already spent* the $22,000 on a lawyer and consultants. That's "on him." He doesn't recover it. **B** is wrong. *After* forming the contract, Penn spends $4 million and invests 100 hours of his time and effort, relying on the contract. Reliance interest does not include the value of time, effort, or labor that plaintiff puts forth in reliance on the contract, so **D** is wrong. Penn does recover the $4 million in *money* he spends in reliance on the contract. Hence, **A** is wrong and **C** is right.

1. Reliance Is a Subset of Expectation

Look again, here, at more elaborate monetary timelines tied to *Fairfax v. Gaelle* from Chapter 25, section D:

What Should Have Occurred

$00.00→	- $25→	- $1,000→	[- $20,000]	+ $40,000 =	$18,975
Fairfax's position before forming contract	spent securing musicians	spent on rehearsal hall	spent on musicians' pay	received from Gaelle	Fairfax's position if contract had been fully performed

What Actually Occurred

$00.00→	- $25→	[- $1,000→]	[- $20,000→]	[+ $40,000→]	- $25
Fairfax's position before forming contract	spent securing musicians	NOT SPENT	NOT SPENT	NOT RECEIVED	Fairfax's actual position in face of breach

- $25	+ $19,000=	$18,975
Fairfax's actual position in face of breach →	**RECOVERY** (Fairfax's expectation interest)	Fairfax's expected gain

The (–$25) represents the amount Fairfax spent on the available musicians list, in reliance on the contract. The $18,975 represents the overall *net gain* he would have enjoyed had both parties fulfilled their obligations [$40,000 (Gaelle's payment)] *minus* [$21,025 (Fairfax's expenses if all had gone properly)]. Fairfax's total recovery, therefore, is equal to the $25 he actually paid in reliance on the contract plus the $18,795 gain he would have derived absent Gaelle's breach. Hence, *expectation interest = reliance interest + expected net gain* (accounting always for one's obligation to mitigate). Further, one (who keeps good records) can usually show the degree to which she made expenditures in reliance on a contract.

The reasonable certainty rule usually raises its head when the plaintiff can't show that *second* portion of her expectation interest: expected net gain. Hence, when writers (and teachers) say that "one recovers his expectation interest only if he can prove it with reasonable certainty," they mean (without knowing it) that one recovers his *full* expectation interest only if he can prove, with reasonable certainty *all* of it: (1) his reliance interest *and* (2) his expected net gain. If he can prove only the first part of it—his reliance interest—then he does recover that portion of his expectation interest. That was so in the *Starr v. Watch* magazine illustration and also of *Penn v. Orson* in Question 1 above. The principle, of course, shows up in the *true* case law.[1]

QUESTION 2. On November 1, Beller and Gall form a contract under which (a) Beller, by February 1, is to design audio speakers for Gall's audio speaker business, and (b) Gall is to pay Beller $400,000 when she completes the work. Relying on Beller timely to complete the design, Gall launches an advertising campaign relating to the new, forthcoming speaker and, in so doing, spends $1 million. Beller, however, never even begins her work and thus breaches the contract. Consequently, Gall withholds payment of the $400,000 and brings suit, alleging that sales of the new speaker, over the next many decades, would have afforded him approximately $100 million in profit. He demands damages of $99,600,000 ($100 million less the $400,000 he would have paid Beller on full performance).

At trial Gall calls witnesses who, to his disappointment, testify that the profit one might derive from a new audio speaker is wholly unpredictable. Several add that a newly designed speaker might yield enormous profits but might just as easily fail to capture any market share at all, causing enormous losses for manufacturers such as Gall. When Gall finishes with his prima facie case, the court rules that he has failed to present any meaningful evidence as to the gain he would have derived through sales of the new speakers. The court also rules that Gall has presented indisputable evidence that he spent $1 million on his advertising campaign. It issues a judgment against Beller for that amount. In doing so, the court has fulfilled

I.   that portion of Gall's expectation interest as to which Gall presented adequate evidence.
II. Gall's reliance interest.

---

1. See, e.g., Sperry & Hutchinson Co. v. O'Neill-Adams Co., 185 F. 231, 239 (2d Cir. 1911) ("In this case, [a]ny attempt to reach a precise sum [as to expected gain] would be mere blind guesswork. Nevertheless, [in reliance on] this contract, the plaintiff made expenditures which otherwise it would not have made.... [P]laintiff was entitled at least to recover these expenses to which it had been put in order to secure the benefits of a contract of which defendant's conduct deprived it.").

> **A.** I only
> **B.** II only
> **C.** I and II
> **D.** Neither I nor II

ANALYSIS. A plaintiff's expectation interest represents the sum of two parts: (1) amounts she expends in reliance on the contract (reliance interest) and (2) (provable) net gain she would have derived absent defendant's breach.

In this case, Gall could not prove the second component of his expectation interest; he could not show what net gain he would have derived from Beller's performance. In awarding Gall $1 million, the court fulfilled his reliance interest or, stated otherwise, fulfilled that portion of his expectation interest that he proved. Both I and II are accurate, so **C** is right.

B. Restitution Interest: Unjust Enrichment, Restitution, and "Benefit Conferred"

1. Restitution and Unjust Enrichment

Aunt, age ninety, decides to give one thousand dollars to Niece in honor of her college graduation. Aunt attends the graduation ceremony. When it's over, she approaches a young woman whom she thinks is Niece. In fact the woman strongly resembles Niece, but she is another graduate named Stranger.

Believing that she is speaking with Niece, Aunt congratulates Stranger: "It's wonderful, Niece to see you graduate." She then hands Stranger $1,000 in cash, and Stranger takes it. Thereafter Aunt discovers her mistake and asks Stranger to return the $1,000. Stranger refuses.

Aunt and Stranger never formed a contract, so Aunt has no action for breach. Stranger did not find the money, so she is not a bailee (Chapter 2, section E, footnote 3). Stranger did not steal the money, so Aunt has no action in conversion (Chapter 2, section E, footnote 4). Mistakenly but willingly, Aunt gave Stranger one thousand dollars. There is no "garden variety" of common law action through which she can recover it.

Is There *Something* That Allows Aunt to Recover?

Yes. Aunt has a right to recover through an action called "unjust enrichment." Unjust enrichment arose not in law, but in equity. (Appendix, section E) Today, the law has adopted it, and unjust enrichment is, now, a *legal* cause of action. The remedy for unjust enrichment is *not* called "damages" but, instead, "restitution." In short form, the relevant rule is: *If Party B is unjustly enriched at the expense of Party A, then Party A may bring an action in unjust enrichment and, as a remedy, recover from B such restitution as will correct the injustice.*

Restatement (First) of Restitution §1 provides:

> A person who has been unjustly enriched at the expense of another is required to make restitution to her.

The word "unjust," of course is "soft," and there abounds a legal literature that debates its meaning. It ought go without saying that the Restatement writers, a bootless bunch, offer no definition of that pivotal word. So here, from us to you, addressing the meaning of "unjust," is the rule of unjust enrichment — in full form:

(1) A first party derives an unjust enrichment when, fortuitously, by chance, by serendipity, by error, by grace of God, good luck, or "windfall"—at the expense of some second party—without wrongfulness on her own part—she enjoys a benefit in money, property, or service, meaning that

(2) the benefit does not come to her

(a) as an intended gift from another, or

(b) as consideration under an enforceable contract, or

(c) through any other dynamic that renders it earned or deserved, wherefore

(3) by judicial award, the first party must pay to the second such restitution as corrects the injustice.

Let's ask: *How much money does Aunt recover?* The rule is this: *For breach of contract, a recovery in restitution is measured by the amount of benefit the plaintiff has conferred on the defendant.* And for short, we say, that the measure of restitution for unjust enrichment is "benefit conferred." As for Aunt and Sandra, it's clear that Aunt's error conferred on Sandra a benefit of $1,000.

Let's Shore Up Our Vocabulary on This Stuff

Unjust enrichment is a *cause of action* in which plaintiff alleges that defendant has been unjustly enriched at her expense.

Restitution is the *remedy* and the *only* remedy by which the court rectifies the unjust enrichment. Where the suit is for breach of contract, restitution takes the form of a money judgment. (In other legal settings it might result in a court order.)

Benefit Conferred are the words that quantify the money a plaintiff receives as his award in restitution.

Please do master the simple relationships among those three terms. Otherwise, as they come up in your contracts class, they'll confuse you.

The doctrines of unjust enrichment and restitution do not, per se, belong to *contract* law. They arise in hosts of cases having naught to do with a contract. And, even with respect to contracts, they arise in several settings

We have touched on unjust enrichment before. In Chapter 16, section A, we did so as to contracts between minors and adults. (If your class has not yet covered this topic, please read, now, Chapter 16, section A, but skip over the multiple-choice questions.) All that we learned about voidability and status quo ante as related to contracts between minors and adults has its historical roots in unjust enrichment.

Similarly, in cases where a defendant successfully asserts the defense of mutual mistake, unilateral mistake, impracticability, or frustration of purpose (Chapter 22), either party might be left with some degree of unjust enrichment, and the law requires that each make appropriate restitution so that all comes out right (kind of). The same applies to discharge for duress and undue influence (Chapter 20).[2] So, restitution for unjust enrichment is a remedy for breach of contract, but it also rears its head (a) in contract law where breach of contract is not at issue, and (b) outside of contract law in a host of settings. But the phrase "benefit conferred" as the monetary measure of restitution belongs only to the law of contracts as discussed here in section C, and in Chapter 29 sections A and B.

QUESTION 3. Among the three terms I - III below, which is/are limited, primarily, to contract law?

I. unjust enrichment
II. restitution
III. benefit conferred

A. I only
B. II only
C. III only
D. I, II, III, and IV

ANALYSIS. The cause of action called "unjust enrichment" arises in a host of contexts within and without contract law. The same is so for restitution which is, in *all* cases, the remedy for unjust enrichment. Hence options I and II are false, meaning we eliminate **A**, **B**, and **D**. That leaves us with **C**. As a measure of restitution for unjust enrichment, "benefit conferred" belongs only to contract law. So, we say: (a) unjust enrichment is a cause of action, for which (b) the remedy is restitution, which, in certain cases related to contracts, entitles the plaintiff to (c) a money judgment equal to the amount of benefit she has conferred on the defendant. Option III is true, and **C** is right.

---

2. See Restatement (Second) of Contracts §376.

2. *Recovery for Breach of Contract vs. Restitution for Unjust Enrichment: Recovery "On" and "Off" of the Contract*

As we know, by issuing to plaintiff a recovery for expectation damages, the law attempts to afford her the position she would have occupied absent defendant's breach. It tries to create a *substitute* for the defendant's performance. Consequently, in awarding *full* expectation damages (which include reliance damages), the law recognizes the contract and, by considering available admissible evidence, takes account of (1) what each party did and did not expend in money; (2) what each party did and did not expend in time, effort, and labor; (3) the consequences that followed from what they truly did and did not do; (4) the consequences that would have followed had they done all they *ought* to have done. When the law awards a recovery for full expectation damages, it thus *enforces the contract*.

The same is so when a court makes an award for reliance only. A plaintiff's reliance interest, we know, represents the position she occupied *before forming her contract* with defendant. It's also a component of her expectation interest; expectation interest = reliance interest + expected net gain. When the plaintiff cannot establish (with such reasonable certainty as a given court demands) the amount of that second component—her expected net gain—she recovers only her reliance interest in order, at least, that she be restored to the position she held before forming the contract, meaning that she is, at least, "made whole."

Hence, in making an award in reliance the law, once again, addresses itself to the contract. By considering available evidence, it takes account of (1) what each party reasonably spent in reliance on—the contract. In issuing plaintiff an award that affords her that position the law, as far as the evidence will allow, once again *enforces the contract*.

Recognize then, that recovery for (1) full expectation or (2) reliance alone represents the law's *enforcement* of the breached contract. And, for short, it is often said that awards for full expectation or reliance alone represent recoveries "on" the contract. Recovery "on" the contract means a recovery that *enforces* the contract, providing the plaintiff with money designed to substitute for defendant's failed performance, whether the recover be for reliance only or for both reliance and expected net gain, which is equal to full expectation interest.

And So What?

Here's the "so what": As already noted, recovery in restitution is not a remedy for breach of contract only. Rather, it reflects the long-standing doctrine of unjust enrichment that applies, also, to many situations not related to contracts. Where, as to a contract, a court awards restitution (the remedy) for unjust enrichment (the cause of action) it does *not enforce* the contract. Rather, it cancels (or some say "rescinds") the contract—makes it go away—so that according to the law, it never existed. Having done that, the court then seeks to take from defendant and return to plaintiff any benefit defendant derived through plaintiff's performance under the contract *less* any benefit that plaintiff might retain from defendant's performance under the contract.

According to this traditional thought, restitution does not constitute recovery "on" the contract. It's a recovery "off" of the contract. When, in response to a breach, a plaintiff seeks restitution, she elects, in theory, to cancel the contract and have back from the defendant anything of value that she conferred on him in attempting to perform. Because restitution carries with it an implicit cancellation of the contract, some speak of the remedy as "rescission with restitution for benefit conferred,"[3] which has the same meaning as does the informal phrase "recovery off of the contract."

QUESTION 4. When defendant commits a breach and plaintiff recovers "off" of the contract,

I. the contract terminates retroactively to the time at which it was formed.
II. defendant must compensate plaintiff for such advantage as he has derived from plaintiff's performance.
III. plaintiff is entitled to fulfillment of her expectation interest.
A. I only
B. II only
C. I and II only
D. II and III only

ANALYSIS. Recovery "off" of the contract refers to (a) an action for unjust enrichment, (b) for which, always, the remedy is restitution, meaning that (c) the monetary award is equal to the amount by which the defendant was unjustly enriched at the plaintiff's expense, which amount is also called, for short, "benefit conferred." As goes the traditional thinking, when a court awards restitution, it rescinds (undoes) the contract. Hence, option I is true. That means the answer is **A** or **C**, depending on whether option II is true, too, and it is. The measure of restitution is the "benefit" plaintiff has "conferred" on defendant. Option III, as expected, makes a false statement. Plaintiff's full expectation interest is relevant to recovery *on* the contract — to monetary damages designed not to rescind it, but to *enforce* it (and the same is so of

---

3. A relatively few modern authorities lately reject the historical distinction between recovery "on" and "off of" the contract. They regard a restitution award as one form of recovery for breach. But we'll stick with the traditional thinking because (a) it still prevails, all over the place, and (b) it makes more sense.

recovery in reliance only, which is one "piece" of expectation interest). Hence, **C** is right.

Let's Summarize What We Know So Far

When two parties form a contract, and one of them breaches the other, as plaintiff, is entitled either to:

(1) monetary damages in such amount as fulfills
    (a) her "expectation interest," which represents the benefit of her bargain — the financial position she would have occupied had the contract been fully performed (subject to her obligation to mitigate damages); or if she cannot show her *full* expectation interest with reasonable certainty,
    (b) her reliance interest alone, which represents the position she occupied just before forming her contract with defendant (and is, also, a *component* of her expectation interest),

OR

(2) an award of such money as fulfills her restitution interest, meaning the amount by which, through her performance, she has afforded the defendant an unjust enrichment, also called the "benefit" her performance has "conferred" on the defendant.[4]

Once again, according to traditional thought, still prevalent in most quarters, (a) expectation/reliance damages represent recovery "on" the contract, and (b) restitution recovery represents recovery "off" of the contract.

3. *Who Decides That Plaintiff Recovers for Expectation, Reliance, or Restitution?*

From the mouths of judges, authors, and teachers, three statements frequently emerge:

1. In a breach of contract action, Plaintiff may "elect his remedy"; he may seek to recover for his expectation, reliance, or restitution interests as he chooses, but he can recover *for only one* such interest — whichever he selects.
2. Ordinarily, the plaintiff will choose to recover for his full expectation interest as that will usually (it is said) yield him the largest recovery.
3. If, however, he cannot show his full expectation interest with reasonable certainty, then he will choose between the greater of his reliance interest (if he has one) and his restitution interest (if he has one).

These three statements embody some truth, but they're tied to a bunch of "ifs," "ands," and "buts." Here, now, is one of the "ifs," "ands," and "buts."

---

4. Regarding this summary, see Restatement (Second) Contracts §344.

4. Restitution Is Available Only When Defendant Commits Total Breach

Because a suit in restitution involves a rescission (the undoing) of the contract, it's available only when defendant commits a *total breach* (covered in Chapter 21, section D and Chapter 25, section C). As Restatement (Second) of Contracts §373 cmt. a tells us: "[Restitution] . . . is available only if the breach gives rise to a claim . . . for total breach and not merely to a claim for . . . partial breach."

When two parties form a contract and one then commits a partial breach, the law will not rescind it. Plaintiff must continue to perform. He may sue for the monetary amount that corresponds to the partial breach, but he can't recover restitution. If, on the other hand, defendant commits a total breach, then the plaintiff may (a) terminate the contract and sue for his expectation or reliance interests or (b) have the court rescind the contract and recover restitution for unjust enrichment.

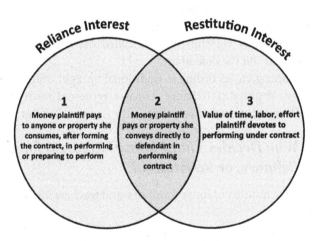

Figure 28-1.   Reliance vs. Restitution Interests

C.   "Benefit Conferred" in Dollars and Cents: *Quantum Meruit* and *Quantum Valebant*

1. Reliance and Restitution Compared

Look just above, please, at Figure 28-1, areas 1 and 2 together, ignoring area 3. When a plaintiff recovers her reliance interest, she is entitled to monetary compensation for all elements in those two areas—everything in the whole of that circle. Hence, reliance damages include any expenditure that the plaintiff makes in (reasonable) reliance on the contract,

- whether or not she confers any benefit on defendant,
- whether she pays it to defendant or to any other person, and
- whether she spends it in preparing to perform under the contract or in actually performing her contractual obligations (but not for any expenditure she makes *before forming* the contract; that's never recoverable, not under any theory).

As Restatement (Second) §349 provides: "As an alternative to [damages for full expectation interest], . . . the injured party has a right to damages based on his reliance interest, including expenditures made in preparation for performance or in performance." Reliance interest is limited to expenditures of money (or property). It does not include the value of any time, effort, or labor, that plaintiff expends or delivers in performing or preparing to perform.

Now, look please at Figure 28-1, areas 2 and 3 together, ignoring area 1. Plaintiff's restitution interest—her right to be paid for "benefit conferred," includes any money paid *to* defendant (area 2) and includes, by curious fiction of law, the value of any time, labor, or effort the plaintiff devotes actually to performing his contractual obligations (area 3), whether or not defendant truly receives or retains any of its value. Suppose B is an architect. A hires him to design a building. B makes it halfway through the work and A then anticipatorily repudiates/breaches the contract (Chapter 25, section C). *Even though A has not taken or retained any portion of the design*, the law supposes that he received a "benefit" equal to the "value" of B's time, labor, and effort.[5]

Restitution interest does not, however, include any time, effort, or labor that plaintiff devotes to *preparing* for performance. In that regard, think again of B, the architect. Imagine that after he forms his contract with A, he spends time and effort cleaning and organizing his office in order to perform his obligations. Because that represents *preparation* for performance, it does not belong to P's restitution interest. Stated otherwise, in the law's eyes, time and effort that plaintiff devotes to *preparing* for performance does not confer a benefit on defendant.[6]

Hence, as Figure 28-1, area 2, demonstrates, reliance and restitution have in common this single element: money (or property) that plaintiff conveys *to* defendant in performing his obligations under the contract.

---

5. We think, that "[because] the law supposes that, the law is a ass." Charles Dickens, *Oliver Twist*, Chapter 51.
6. See Restatement (Second) of Contracts §371 & cmt. a.

2. Now Learn About These Latin Phrases: "Quantum Meruit" and "Quantum Valebant"

The Latin phrase "*quantum meruit*" means, literally, "amount deserved." In contract law, it refers to that component of a plaintiff's restitution interest inherent in the value of time, labor, or effort he actually devotes to performance. On the other hand, "*quantum valebant*" means, literally, "amount of worth" or "amount of value." In contract law, it refers to that component of a plaintiff's restitution interest inherent in the money or property that, in performing her contractual obligations, she pays *to* defendant—only to defendant—not to anyone else. Hence, if we want to "talk the talk," we say that as to breach of contract, plaintiff's restitution interest is the sum of *quantum meruit* and *quantum valebant*.

Look now, please, at Illustration 28-2, in which we've left area 1 blank.

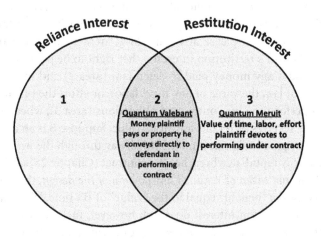

Figure 28-2.   *Quantum Meruit* vs. *Quantum Valebant*

Hence, the figure shows only areas 2 and 3 which, together, make up restitution interest. Let's focus on area 2: money or property that, in performing her contractual obligations, plaintiff pays *to* defendant and not to anyone else. All together, area 2 carries the Latin designation "*quantum valebant*" which means, literally, "amount of worth" or "amount of value." As for breach of contract it really means amount of value or worth conveyed by plaintiff directly to defendant. Now, we can sound like legal hotshots and say, "one component of the restitution interest is *quantum valebant*."

Let's look at Figure 28-2, area 3. There we see the value of time, labor, or effort that plaintiff devotes to performing his contractual obligations. Those items of recovery belong also to a plaintiff's restitution interest and, in Latin, we call them "*quantum meruit*," which means "amount deserved." Now, we can be hotter hotshots and say "restitution interest includes both *quantum valebant* and *quantum meruit*. Reliance interest includes *quantum valebant*, but not *quantum meruit."* We know, too, that *reliance* interest includes more than *quantum valebant.* As shown in Figure 28-1, area 1, it also includes expenditures in money or property that plaintiff spends/consumes in performing or preparing to perform no matter to whom or for whom she spends or conveys it.

QUESTIONS 5 & 6. Hardy is a musical CD distributor. In his possession is a "master recording" made by some celebrated musician (whose name doesn't matter). By signed writing, Hardy forms a contract under which Dollins is to "mix" the recording and, having done so, create one million copies of it. When Dollins has completed the work, Hardy is to distribute the recording worldwide and divide the net earnings equally with Dollins.

Dollins prepares to do his job. For $12,000, he rents equipment; for $8,000, he rents a studio. He then begins to "mix" the recording. After he has spent 5 hours on the work which, according to the evidence, has a fair market value of $2,500, Hardy contacts him and says, "I am not going to distribute the recording. Don't make the mix. It's all off."

Dollins sues Hardy for breach. At trial, he attempts to show how much money he would have derived if (a) he had finished the work, and (b) Hardy had then distributed the recording, with net earnings divided equally between the parties. After Dollins rests his case, the court rules that his evidence is insufficient for a jury to identify the amount of net earnings the recording might have produced.

QUESTION 5. If Dollins then elects to recover his reliance interest, the court should award him

I.   money for *quantum valebant.*
II. money for *quantum meruit.*
III. some money, but no money for *quantum valebant* or *quantum meruit.*
A. I only
B. II only
C. III only
D. I and II

ANALYSIS. Reliance interest embodies (1) *quantum valebant,* which means money or property that plaintiff conveys directly to defendant, and (2) any money that (a) plaintiff spends or (b) property he consumes—in performing or preparing to perform. (That component of reliance recovery is not tied to any special Latin phrase.) Because Dollins elects to recover his reliance interest he is, theoretically, entitled to an award for *quantum valebant.* Since Dollins conveyed no money or property *to* Hardy, *quantum valebant* is zero; he recovers no money for *quantum valebant.*

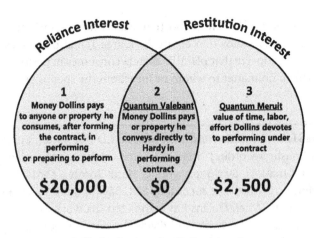

Dollins's reliance and restitution interests

Option I is "out," which means **A** and **D** are wrong. Option II refers to *quantum meruit*, which belongs not to reliance interest but to restitution interest. Since Dollins elects to recover in reliance, he does not recover, as *quantum meruit*, the $2,500 in time/effort/labor he devoted to performance, because *quantum meruit* belongs not to reliance but to restitution. Option II follows option I out the door, and we eliminate **B**. We're left with **C**. Dollins did spend ($12,000 + $8,000) = $20,000 performing, and that money belongs to reliance interest as shown in area 1. Dollins recovers $20,000, meaning Option III is true, so that **C** is right.

QUESTION 6. If, instead, Dollins elects to recover his restitution interest, the court should award him

I. money for *quantum valebant*.
II. money for *quantum meruit*.
III. money, but no money for either *quantum valebant* or *quantum meruit*.

A. I only
B. II only
C. III only
D. I and II

ANALYSIS. Dollins's restitution interest embodies all of the right-hand circle, meaning areas 2 and 3, but not area 1. In theory, Dollins is entitled to *quantum valebant* (area 2), but again, he conveyed no money or property to defendant. His recovery in *quantum valebant* is zero. Farewell to **A** and **D**. Dollins does recover in area 3 — *quantum meruit* — for the time and effort he devotes to performing. Within the designation *quantum meruit*, that stuff represents, fictitiously, a "benefit conferred" by Dollins on Hardy even though, truly, Hardy gets nothing from it. Option II is true. Option III states, among other things, that Dollins recovers nothing for *quantum meruit*, and that's false. Options I and III are false. Option II is true. **B** is right.

3. *Quantum Meruit in Dollars and Cents; Valuing Plaintiff's Time, Effort, and Labor*

When, in performing a contract, plaintiff pays money to the defendant, it's easy to assess its monetary value: $1 is worth $1 and $1,000 is worth $1,000. But if instead or in addition plaintiff devotes time, effort, labor in performing the contract, there arise two measures by which, logically, we might quantify the monetary "benefit" (*quantum meruit*) his efforts (fictitiously or not) "confer" on the defendant.

Scape and Ohn form a contract under which (a) Scape is to cut down all of the trees on Ohn's land, and (b) Ohn is to pay Scape $25,000 when Scape completes the job. Scape completes half of the job, whereupon Ohn advises Scape that he has changed his mind, that he does not want any more trees cut, that he will not pay Scape anything, and that Scape is to leave the land immediately. Scape leaves and Ohn, of course, is in material breach of his contract.

Whatever his reason, Scape elects to recover his restitution interest. He has paid no money and conveyed no property to Ohn. Hence, his restitution interest has no component of *quantum valebant*. But Scape has spent time and effort cutting down trees, and that invests his restitution interest with *quantum meruit*. At trial, Scape proves these two additional facts: (1) to hire a person with Scape's credentials to cut down half the trees on Ohn's land, Ohn would have to pay $18,000; and (2) the value of Ohn's land with half its trees removed has been increased by $90,000.

Let's ask: Do we identify the benefit conferred by Scape's labor (*quantum meruit*) (a) as $18,000, (b) as the $90,000 enhanced value of Ohn's land, or (c) as $12,500, which is equal to [(½ of all work Scape agreed to perform) × (the $25,000 contract fee)]. Stated more abstractly: Does *quantum meruit* equal (a) the fair market value of plaintiff's services, (b) the net increase in financial value that defendant derives, or (c) such portion of the contract price as corresponds to the portion of contractual service plaintiff performs?

Remember and never forget: Item (c) is totally and absolutely out of the question. Any award based in any way on the contract price/fee amounts to enforcement of the contract, and restitution doesn't do that — not ever. Again, restitution, the remedy for unjust enrichment, "throws" the contract "away"; it's a recovery "off" of the contract. So, as for the measure of restitution, the theoretical "candidates" are either (a) the fair market value of plaintiff's services, or (b) the net increase in financial value defendant derives. Now know this: the "usual" measure of benefit conferred is not item (b) but item (a): "the fair market value" of the plaintiff's services. Scape recovers $18,000.

Again: The law measures restitution for services rendered—for *quantum meruit*—according to their "fair market value." Furthermore (and interestingly), the law does not recognize any situation in which the fair market value of plaintiff's services is indeterminable. If plaintiff can show no evidence of what others would charge for the service he performed, then, still, he recovers whatever the jury thinks to be the "fair market value" of his services.

But Sometimes, Some Jurisdictions Measure *Quantum Meruit* According to Item (b)

In some jurisdictions, if a court thinks defendant has breached willfully or, somehow, maliciously, it might award plaintiff the *larger* of fair market value or defendant's financial gain. If the larger recovery happens to be defendant's financial gain, that's what plaintiff recovers. But, again, that's only a "sometimes maybe." Generally, the law measures quantum meruit according to the "fair market value" of plaintiff's services even where the defendant has acted willfully or in bad faith.

So Here's the Rule: The Measure of *Quantum Meruit*. *When defendant breaches and plaintiff seeks recovery in restitution for services she has delivered under the contract, she usually will recover not what evidence shows to be the amount of financial gain that defendant derived from the plaintiff's service, but what evidence shows to be the fair market value of her services.*

But, be ready for this. The Restatement (Second) §371 states it thus:

> If a sum of money is awarded to protect a party's restitution interest, it may *as justice requires* be measured by either
> (a) the reasonable value to the other party of what he received in terms of what it would have cost him to obtain it from a person in the claimant's position, or
> (b) the extent to which the other party's property has been increased in value or his other interests advanced.

The Restatement cites item (b) as one way a court might measure the benefit conferred by defendant's time, effort, and labor. But the common law is otherwise. Only a very few courts in very few situations have awarded restitution according to item (b). Furthermore, we *italicize* the Restatement's phrase "as justice requires" to demonstrate that its writers offer no principle or precept more specific than that. And although the writers gabber on as usual, commenting on their own writing, their comments, also as usual, offer no clarification or sophistication of thought. The comments come to this: It's up to each court to decide on its own what is meant by "justice," and then to choose whether fair market value or actual financial gain better serves that end.

To Scape in his restitution suit against Ohn, the court would certainly refuse to award $90,000. Under the operative circumstances, almost any (sane) judge would consider $90,000 excessive and unjust. It would award Scape $18,000, the fair market value of his service, according to what is, truly, the general rule.

QUESTIONS 7 & 8. Harris and Danforth form a contract under which (1) Danforth is to make a market study for Harris, (2) Harris is to pay Danforth $50,000 immediately on formation of the contract, and another $250,000 when Danforth completes the study and delivers his report. Harris pays Danforth the $50,000 on formation of the contract, but Danforth never begins the study and thus breaches the contract. Harris sues Danforth for breach but cannot show what profit or benefit, if any, he would have enjoyed had Danforth completed the study and delivered his report.

QUESTION 7. If Harris elects to recover for his *reliance* interest, and not his restitution interest, the court should award him

A. $50,000, because that is the amount of benefit he conferred on Danforth.
B. $50,000, because he spent that amount in reliance on the contract.
C. nothing, because he cannot show that he would have enjoyed any benefit if Danforth had fully performed.
D. nominal damages, because he can show no damage, but Danforth is nonetheless in breach.

ANALYSIS. Go back, please and look at Figure 28–1, areas 1 and 2. As for some given contract, they show us that any money (or property) with which the plaintiff parts in reliance on the contract belongs to his reliance interest, whether or not he pays it to defendant or someone else. To the extent a plaintiff makes a payment (or conveys property) *directly to* defendant, in performing, the corresponding monetary amount belongs to both his reliance and restitution interests. Figure 28–1, area 2 illustrates that point, and the figure below illustrates it specifically for Harris and Danforth.

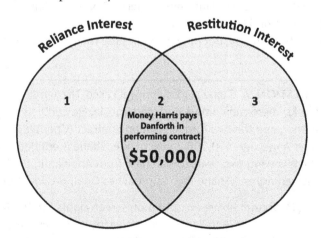

Harris's reliance and restitution interests

Harris paid $50,000 *to* Danforth as part of his contractual performance. That $50,000 belongs to both his reliance and restitution interests. Harris elects to recover not his restitution interest, but his reliance interest. So, the right answer is $50,000, characterized not as a benefit conferred on Danforth (because we say "benefit conferred" only in connection with restitution interest), but as money spent in reliance on the contract.

C and **D** are wrong because they fail to recognize that Harris is entitled to any recovery at all. **A** correctly states that Harris will recover $50,000, but its rationale misses the target. It recites reasons that pertain not to reliance but to restitution. It's wrong. **B**, on the other hand, correctly cites a $50,000 recovery and properly ties it to reliance. **B** is right.

QUESTION 8. If Harris elects to recover his *restitution* interest, the court should award him

A. $50,000, because that is the amount of benefit he conferred on Danforth.
B. $50,000, because he spent that amount in reliance on the contract.
C. nothing, because he cannot show that he would have enjoyed any benefit if Danforth had fully performed.
D. nominal damages, because he can show no damage, but Danforth nonetheless is in breach.

ANALYSIS.   Harris's restitution interest happens to be the same as his reliance interest because he spent exactly $50,000 in reliance on the contract, paying all of it *to* defendant, thus conferring on defendant a $50,000 benefit. For this question Harris elects to recover restitution. Both **A** and **B** correctly recite the $50,000 figure, but only **A** reports the right reasoning. **A** is right.

QUESTION 9. Shane studies a novel called *The Terrible Truth*. From it, he thinks, there can come a profitable movie. He contacts Angelante, the author, and the two form an option contract (Chapter 6, section B). Shane pays Angelante $10,000. In exchange, Shane is entitled at any time during the following two years to purchase from Angelante, for $1 million, all "screen rights." Shane then approaches Gold, president of Gold Studios:

(1) **Shane:** I have an option on screen rights for *The Terrible Truth*, by Anne Angelante. For two years, it entitles me to buy all screen rights for $1 million. It will make a great movie. I want to call it *All News Is Bad News*.
(2) **Gold:** What else?

(3) **Shane:** I have here an elaborate proposal, complete with thirty pages of dialogue. I want you to read it. If after you do so you want the screenplay, I'll write it. And if, then, the screenplay is as good as the proposal, it's a "go"; you produce the film and arrange for a distributor.

(4) **Gold:** And you'll want what in exchange?

(5) **Shane:** If you like the proposal I'm about to hand you, and if the full screenplay is as good as the proposal, then you will (a) pay Angelante the $1 million, (b) produce the film, (c) arrange for a distributor, and (d) pay me 20 percent of net earnings.

Gold reads the proposal and tells Shane, "I like it. Let's take it the next step." Each party engages a lawyer. Together, the lawyers create a lengthy contractual writing that provides for a great many details the parties did not discuss. Among its terms are those that Shane proposed to Gold at (5) above. Both parties sign.

Shane works diligently on the screenplay and timely completes it. He submits it to Gold who, *without* reading it, tells Shane, "It's no good." In fact, Gold has not read the screenplay because, for his own reasons, he no longer wishes to produce the film, even if he should find the screenplay to be excellent. From a source close to Gold, Shane later learns that Gold did not read the screenplay. Shane sues Gold for breach of contract. At trial, Gold, under oath, reluctantly admits that he did not read the screenplay. Witnesses for both parties testify that:

(1) the quality of Shane's screenplay is superb and at least as good as that embodied in the proposal he gave to Gold at their first meeting;

(2) the amount of net earnings that the motion picture might have produced is wholly speculative, not subject, even, to a rough estimate; and

(3) the cost of hiring a writer to produce a screenplay as good as this one would be $250,000.

The court decides that Gold's failure to read the screenplay was a material breach and that no reasonable juror could possibly disagree. Without jury participation, the court issues a judgment in Shane's favor. It should award him

A. nominal damages, because the evidence shows no right of recovery "on" or "off" of the contract.

B. $10,000, the amount he paid Angelante, which constitutes his reliance interest.

C. $250,000, which constitutes *quantum meruit.*

D. $1 million, which represents Shane's expectation interest.

ANALYSIS.   Shane fulfilled his contractual obligations. Had Gold done the same, Shane would have received 20 percent of net profit that the film produced. The court found "as a matter of law" that such amount was purely speculative and could not be quantified. Consequently, Shane's full expectation interest is not assessable. He paid $10,000 to Angelante *before* contracting with Gold, which means he did not pay it in reliance on the contract. Having neither a net expectation nor reliance interest, let's ask if Shane has a restitution interest. The answer is "yes," he does. He devoted time and effort to writing the screenplay. By law, *that* (fictitiously) qualifies as a "benefit conferred" on Gold and, more specifically, *quantum meruit.* Shane is entitled to recover the fair market value of his services, which according to undisputed evidence is $250,000.

A, B, and D name the wrong numbers, so all are wrong. Further, A makes a false statement. The evidence shows that Shane is entitled to no award "on" the contract (meaning he can show no expectation or reliance interest). He is entitled to recover "off" of the contract so to fulfill his restitution interest. B incorrectly identifies $10,000 as Shane's "reliance interest," which it is not. Again, Shane spent that money *before* forming his contract with Gold and so did not spend it in reliance on the contract. D falsely characterizes $1 million as Shane's full expectation interest. If Gold had honored the contract, he would have paid $1 million not to Shane, but to Angelante.

That leaves us with C. It tells us, correctly, that Shane is entitled to $250,000 because that amount is equal to *quantum meruit*—the value of the time, labor, and effort he devoted to performing his contractual duties. C is right.

4. Depending on the Case, Reliance and Restitution Interests Might Be Equal, or One Might Exceed the Other

In *Harris v. Danforth* above, Harris paid Danforth $50,000, and made no other expenditures of property or money. The $50,000 belonged to Harris's reliance and restitution interests; reliance and restitution were equal. In Question 1 above, when Penn and Orson first formed their contract, Penn paid Orson $1 million. That amount belonged to Penn's reliance *and* restitution interests. Further, in preparing to perform, Penn spent $3 million and put forth $25,000 worth of time and effort. The $3 million belonged to Penn's reliance interest, but not to his restitution interest. The $25,000 belonged to his restitution interest, but not to his reliance interest. Hence,

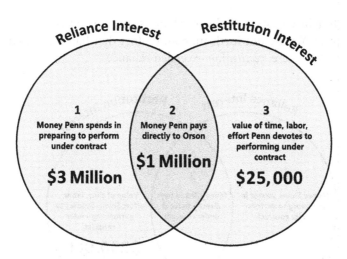

Penn v. Orson (from Question 1 above); Penn's reliance and restitution interests

Penn's reliance interest was:

$3 million + $1 million = $4 million.

His restitution interest was:

$1 million + $25,000 = $1,025,000

Penn's reliance interest exceeds his restitution interest.

In *Dollins v. Hardy* above, Dollins's restitution interest was zero. His reliance interest was $20,000. Again, reliance exceeded restitution. In our revised Starr and *Watch* Magazine case above, Starr conveyed no value *to* Watch, and devoted no time or effort to performing under the contract. Her restitution interest was zero. Yet, after contracting with Watch, she paid $3,000 in preparing to perform, which means she paid $3,000 in reliance on the contract. Again, reliance exceeded restitution.

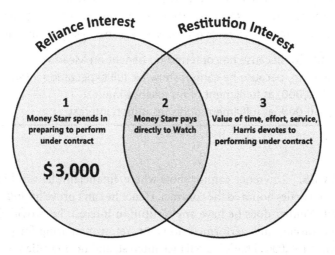

Starr v. Watch (Chapter 27, section C, as modified in this chapter, section A); Starr's reliance and restitution interests

But in Question 9 above, Shane spent no money in reliance on the contract. Yet, he put forth time and effort that had a fair market value of $250,000. There, *restitution* exceeded reliance.

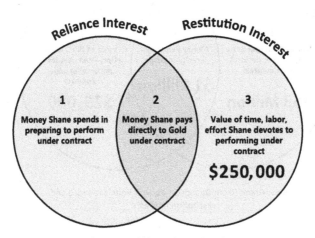

Shane v. Gold (Question 9 above);
Shane's reliance and restitution interest

QUESTION 10. Lawrence and Meadows form a contract under which Lawrence is to market Meadows's patented device for five years, and Meadows is to pay Lawrence a royalty of 8 percent on each unit of product sold. After the parties form their contract, Lawrence begins to prepare for performance. He hires marketing consultants, contracting to pay them nonrefundable fees of $100,000 in total, and he commits to advertisements for a nonrefundable cost of $50,000. After Lawrence makes those $150,000 in expenditures, Meadows commits a total breach. Lawrence cannot show, with any reasonable certainty, how many units he would have sold over the five-year period, and so cannot show what his royalties might have been. By way of remedy and recovery, Lawrence is most likely entitled to

A. nothing, because he conferred no benefit on Meadows.
B. nothing, because he cannot show his full expectation interest.
C. $150,000, as fulfillment of his reliance interest.
D. $150,000, as fulfillment of his restitution interest.

ANALYSIS.   Lawrence cannot show where, financially, he would have stood had both parties honored the contract. Hence he can't prove his *full* expectation interest. Neither does he have any restitution interest; he provided Meadows with no money and performed no labor. Yet, in preparing for performance, he spent $150,000. That's his reliance interest, and he is entitled to recover it.

A and **B** correctly tell us that Lawrence has neither a full expectation nor restitution interest. Yet, by ignoring his reliance interest, they incorrectly report that he recovers nothing; **A** and **B** are wrong. **D** names the right number, but incorrectly attributes it to restitution interest, which is zero. **C** correctly identifies Lawrence's $150,000 reliance interest and awards him that amount. **C** is right.

QUESTIONS 11 & 12. On March 1, 2014, Landers and Cleft form a contract under which Cleft is to study Landers's missiles and devise for them a satellite-directed guidance system, his work to be completed in one year, by February 28, 2015. In exchange, Landers is to pay Cleft a royalty on missile sales, equal to 2 percent of net receipts. For that purpose, Cleft situates himself at Landers's office facilities and for six months studies the missiles, spending no money in that effort. At the end of that period, Landers advises Cleft that he has decided not to develop guidance systems for his missiles, that Cleft should leave Landers's premises, and that "the deal is off." Landers thus commits a total breach of his contract. Cleft sues Landers. At trial, he produces no meaningful evidence as to the receipts that might have been generated through the selling of missiles equipped with the satellite-directed guidance system.

QUESTION 11. By way of recovery and remedy, Cleft is most likely entitled to

A. nothing, because he can show neither a full expectation nor reliance interest.
B. nominal damages, because he can show no actual damage.
C. restitution equal to the fair market value of the time and effort he devoted to the project during the six-month period.
D. recovery in reliance equal to the fair market value of the time and effort he devoted to the project during the six-month period.

ANALYSIS. Cleft offers no evidence that meaningfully quantifies the royalties he stood to earn. Hence, he cannot show his full expectation interest. He spent no money in performing or preparing to perform, so he has no reliance interest. He did devote time and effort to performance. And, although his efforts leave Landers with no financial gain, Cleft did, by (fiction of) law, confer a benefit on Landers equal to the fair market value of Cleft's services.

A correctly states that Cleft has neither full expectation nor reliance interest, but incorrectly awards him nothing. **B** is wrong because it, too, denies Cleft a (meaningful) recovery. **D** correctly states that Cleft should recover the fair market value of his services, but incorrectly refers to his reliance interest. That leaves **C**, which correctly tells us that Cleft should recover the fair market value of his services, properly attributing the award to his restitution interest. **C** is right.

QUESTION 12. By way of recovery and remedy, Cleft is most likely entitled to recover

A. money for *quantum meruit*.
B. money for *quantum valebant*.
C. money for both *quantum meruit* and *quantum valebant*.
D. money for neither *quantum meruit* nor *quantum valebant*.

ANALYSIS. From Question 11, we know that Cleft has neither an expected net gain or reliance interest, which means he has no expectation interest. Neither did he convey money or property directly to Landers, meaning he recovers no *quantum valebant*. Cleft did devote time and effort to his performance and hence has a restitution interest arising from *quantum meruit*. **A** is right.

D. Reliance, Restitution, and the Losing Contract

On April 1, Tripp and Unis form a contract under which Tripp will rewire Unis's house by May 1. Unis will pay him $50,000 when the work is complete. Before forming the contract, Tripp calculates that in doing the work, he will incur $40,000 in expenses, meaning he'll derive a gain of $50,000 minus $40,000 = $10,000. As he does his work, to his surprise, he realizes that his expenses will come to $60,000. Nonetheless, Tripp honors his contract, pays out $60,000 in expenses, and finishes the work on May 1. When he receives $50,000 from Unis, Tripp sustains a loss of $10,000. Hence, he has formed and performed a "losing contract," a contract in which he suffers a loss.

1. The Losing Contract and Reliance Damages

When a plaintiff sues "on" the contract, the law does not require, ever, that the defendant pay more than was his obligation *under* the contract. Let's alter the *Tripp v. Unis* case this way: When Tripp has spent $53,000 in performing, Unis repudiates the contract. By this time, Tripp knows that he has made a losing contract. If both parties were fully to perform, his position would be *negative* $10,000. Therefore, Tripp asks for reliance damages of $53,000. The court will award him only $50,000, because that's the amount Defendant was obliged to pay him. If the law were to award Tripp the full $53,000 he spent in reliance, while the total amount Unis owed him was only $50,000, it would not, in doing so, enforce the contract. Rather, it would punish Unis for her breach—demanding that she do more than the contract required of her.

With That, Let's Write a Rule.   *With respect to breach of contract, a plaintiff who elects to recover his reliance damages cannot recover more than the amount of money (or other value) the defendant was obliged to pay him or, otherwise stated, a defendant will not be held to pay more than she would have had to pay under the contract itself.*

2. For Restitution, the Rule Is Different

Remember that restitution makes a recovery "off" of the contract. Its purpose is not to enforce the contract, but to correct an "injustice." Retroactively, it cancels/rescinds the contract and restores to the plaintiff the benefit conferred on defendant by conveyance *to* defendant of money/property or by devotion of time and effort.

For that theoretical reason, a recovery in restitution isn't limited to the amount of money (or other value) that the contract requires defendant to pay plaintiff. When the court issues a restitution award, it might require that the defendant pay *more* (*much* more) than the contract requires of her. Reciprocally, the plaintiff might recover more than her entitlement under the contract.

Suppose Muir and Boomer form a contract under which Boomer is to build a dam during the ten-month period April through February. During that period, as Boomer needs and requests, Muir is to furnish him with necessary supplies and equipment. Further, Muir is to pay Boomer $2,000 on the first of every month May through February, for a total of $20,000.

Boomer begins performance on April 1. For April, May, and June he works diligently. During that period, Muir properly provides Boomer with supplies and equipment, but fails to make a single $2,000 payment. But Boomer keeps working. Then, in August, September, and October, Muir fails to make a single $2,000 payment and fails repeatedly to provide Boomer with the supplies and equipment he needs. For that reason, on November 1, Boomer stops working. Citing Muir's material/total breach, he declares the contract terminated (Chapter 21, section D). He then brings an action for unjust enrichment and hence, as remedy, seeks restitution.

To the jury's satisfaction, Boomer proves that the fair market value of the services he delivered over seven months was $258,000, even though total payment due him under the contract was only $20,000. Accordingly, Boomer's action in unjust enrichment is a suit "off" of the contract. The court awards him $258,000 because (a) in an action for restitution, the contract, by law, disappears; it plays no role in measuring or limiting the recovery, so that plaintiff's recovery is equal to the fair market value of his performance (plus any money he actually paid defendant)—*minus*—any amount defendant did actually pay plaintiff.

So, even though the *contract* entitled Boomer to only $20,000, Boomer's suit in unjust enrichment affords him judgment of restitution equal to the $258,000 "benefit" he "conferred" on Muir.

That Can Really Happen?   It *did* happen in 1933, with the case of *Boomer v. Muir*.

> To hold that . . . [the contract price] may limit recovery where the contract is afterwards rescinded through the defendant's fault seems to us to involve a confusion of thought. A rescinded contract ceases to exist for all purposes. How then can it be looked to for one purpose, the purpose of fixing the amount of recovery? . . . Generally speaking, the effect of rescission is to extinguish the contract. The contract is annihilated so effectually that in contemplation of law it has never had any existence[.] When the [plaintiffs] rescinded the contract, they put it out of [defendant's] power to enforce it, . . . but [plaintiff] may . . . claim pay [for the fair market value of his services] just as though [the contract] had never existed.[7]

This court writes "rescind" where it should write "repudiate." Muir (the defendant) did not rescind the contract. He *repudiated* it. When Boomer (the plaintiff) sued in unjust enrichment, the *law* rescinded the contract.

In any case, the amount Muir owes to Boomer under a contract does not limit a Boomer's recovery if he sues "off" of the contract in unjust enrichment, and hence for the remedy of restitution, measured by benefit conferred. The law lets the fact finder (ordinarily a jury) award the plaintiff so much as (on the admissible evidence) it (reasonably) finds to be the value of plaintiff's time, effort, and labor, ignoring the payment to which the contract entitled him since, in the case of rescission and suit for unjust enrichment, the contract is erased.

Hence, Plaintiff Might Recover Large Amounts Even When He Gets Himself into a Losing Contract.   Let's revisit Tripp's losing contract with Unis, and change the facts a little. This time, Tripp unhappily discovers that he has *already* spent $60,000 on April 15, halfway through his work. Nonetheless, as an honorable chap, he continues in his obligation, continues spending, and continues rewiring. On April 20, by which time Tripp has spent $63,000 performing his work, Unis advises him that she does not want the work done and that he should leave her house.

Tripp engages a lawyer who, after investigating for several days, tells Tripp of her opinion (a) that Unis has committed a total breach and (b) that Tripp has badly undersold his own service. The lawyer tells Tripp that the value of the labor and service he had provided before Unis breached is approximately $225,000.

On Tripp's behalf, the lawyer brings suit against Unis, electing the remedy of restitution for benefit conferred. At trial, the lawyer presents evidence tending to show that the market value of Tripp's performance falls somewhere

7.   24 P.2d 570, 577 (Cal. Dist. Ct. App. 1933) (citations and appurtenant quotation marks omitted).

between $200,000 and $300,000. The jury returns a verdict for $210,000, and the court enters judgment on the verdict. Hence, depending on the market value of the service he gives (or money he pays) *to* the defendant in performing the contract before defendant breaches, a plaintiff who makes a losing contract and then sues to recover restitution for unjust enrichment might fare better than the contract itself allowed.

E.   Closers

QUESTIONS 13 & 14. TCorp binds books, booklets, and magazines. UCorp publishes a magazine called *RoofTop*. In May 2015, UCorp has one million copies of *RoofTop*, the August issue—printed but not bound. On June 1, TCorp contracts to take possession of the one million copies, so it can bind them, and return them to UCorp. UCorp is to pay TCorp $30,000 on June 15, an additional $10,000 on June 30, and another $10,000 on July 15, for total payment of $50,000. TCorp is to deliver the bound magazines to UCorp on July 30.

QUESTION 13. TCorp begins work on the project, pays $12,000 in various expenses, and binds 500,000 *RoofTop* magazines. On June 15, UCorp fails to pay any part of the $30,000 it owes and announces, further, that it will not proceed with the contract. TCorp is able to prove that if it had finished the project, it would have spent $16,000 more in expenses and, on receiving $50,000 from UCorp, would have derived a gain of $22,000 [$50,000 − ($12,000 + $16,000)]. With respect to UCorp's breach, TCorp may bring an action

  I. "on" the contract.
  II. "off" of the contract.
  A. I only
  B. II only
  C. At its option, either I or II, but not both
  D. Neither I nor II

ANALYSIS.   When a defendant commits a total breach, the plaintiff may choose to sue (a) "on" the contract, meaning she recovers for her full expectation interest or, if she cannot show her expected gain, then her reliance interest, or (b) "off" of the contract, meaning she may rescind the contract and recover for any benefit she has conferred on defendant. Benefit conferred means money (or property) conveyed *to* the defendant, and the market value of time, effort, and labor that plaintiff devotes to performance. By fiction of law, such time, effort, and labor "confer" a "benefit" on defendant whether or not defendant actually takes, retains, or derives value from any of plaintiff's work product.

In this case, UCorp fails to pay any part of the $30,000 it owes on June 15, which $30,000 amounts to 60 percent of all moneys it is to pay under the contract. On April 15, UCorp announces that it will not proceed with the contract and so commits an anticipatory repudiation and material breach. TCorp's reliance interest is $12,000, the amount of money it spent performing the contract when UCorp breached. An award "on" the contract for TCorp's full expectation interest would be

$00.00→	- $12,000→	+ $34,000 =	$22,000
TCorp's position before contract formation	TCorp's position in face of UCorp's breach	RECOVERY (TCorp's expectation interest)	TCorp's expected gain

If TCorp elects to recover "on" the contract it will naturally choose its full $22,000 expectation interest over its $12,000 reliance.

TCorp's restitution interest is equal to the fair market value of the services it delivered in binding 500,000 of the magazines. What that amount might be, we don't know; it remains to be proven in court. It might be more than or less than $34,000. We do know, however, that among recoveries "on" or "off" of the contract, the choice belongs to plaintiff. Hence, **C** is right.

QUESTION 14. Now assume that on June 15 UCorp pays only $29,000 of the $30,000 it owes, promising to make up the $1,000 difference by paying $11,000 instead of $10,000 on July 15. With respect to that breach, TCorp may bring an action

I. "on" the contract.
II. "off" of the contract.
A. I only
B. II only
C. Either I or II, but not both, at plaintiff's option
D. Neither I nor II

ANALYSIS. By paying 29/30 (96.67 percent) of the amount it owes on June 15, UCorp furnishes, by that date, not a complete performance, but a substantial performance. It commits only a partial breach, meaning the law will not rescind the contract. Without rescission, TCorp can't sue "off" of the contract, so it can't sue for the remedy of restitution. Neither can TCorp cancel/terminate the contract. It must continue to perform. As it does so it may sue for the partial breach, but, because recovery will be "on" the contract, the law will limit it to the monetary amount that corresponds *to* the breach which, in this case, is $1,000. Since the partial breach entitles TCorp only to a suit "on" the contract, **A** is right.

 # Silver's Picks

1.	C
2.	C
3.	C
4.	C
5.	C
6.	B
7.	B
8.	A
9.	C
10.	C
11.	C
12.	A
13.	C
14.	A

29

Breach, Remedies, and Damages, Part V

A. Restitution Interest for the Plaintiff in Breach
B. More "Benefit Conferred": Restitution for the Non-Officious Volunteer; Contract Implied in Law and Quasi-Contract
C. The Closer
✦ Silver's Picks

A. Restitution Interest for the Plaintiff in Breach

Party A contracts with Party B. Party A partly performs, then ceases to perform, thus committing a material breach. On some occasions, Party A — the *breaching* party — secures a recovery not for breach of contract, of course, because B hasn't breached. Rather, A sues in unjust enrichment for value with which A's partial performance has provided B — even though it is A himself who has breached.

The rule is that *if Parties P and D form a contract and Party P breaches but has partially performed in a way that left D with a genuine benefit, then Party P — the breaching party — is entitled, from Party D, to recover restitution for unjust enrichment.*

Let's Illustrate: Panwith and Randolph. Panwith and Randolph form a contract under which Panwith will build three cottages on Randolph's land. Randolph will pay him $165,000 upon completion. Panwith begins his work and finishes two of the cottages, paying $20,000 in expenses. He never begins work on the third and thus commits a material breach.

Randolph, certainly, has an action against Panwith for breach of contract, but to what recovery is he entitled? If possessed of his full expectation interest, he would be "out" $165,000 and "up" by three cottages. At the time of the breach, Randolph has paid Panwith nothing and, still, he is "up" by two cottages. He is, in fact, "ahead" of his expectation interest (unless it will cost him more than $165,000 to have another person build the third cottage). Again, because Randolph has spent nothing in performing or preparing to perform, he has no reliance interest. Further, because, again, he has paid Panwith nothing, he has no restitution interest. Notwithstanding Panwith's breach, Randolph is entitled only to nominal damages.

Panwith, of course, has no action for breach of contract because Randolph committed none; he himself is the breaching party. The contract required that Randolph pay Panwith $165,000 after all three cottages were completed, but Panwith never built the third. Nonetheless, Panwith, the breaching party, has provided Randolph with a benefit — not a fictitious one, but a genuine one. He has built two cottages on Randolph's land, and Randolph has acquired them "for free." In this situation, the law finds that Randolph has been "unjustly enriched"; he has enjoyed an unearned benefit at Panwith's expense. (See Chapter 28, section B.) For that reason, the law affords Panwith a cause of action and recovery—not in breach of contract, but in unjust enrichment affording him remedy of restitution (which is, always, the remedy for unjust enrichment (Chapter 28, section B)).

How much restitution does Panwith recover? Here's the rule: *When one party breaches a contract and she herself sues, seeking restitution for unjust enrichment, she is entitled to receive the lesser of (a) the value she has given up in performing the contract or (b) the degree by which the non-breaching party's position exceeds the one he would have held had both parties fulfilled their obligations.*

See How Simply That Works: Panwith and Randolph Continued.   Suppose that when Panwith breaches, Randolph hires Substitute to build the third cottage. Substitute charges $40,000 for the work. Panwith then sues Randolph seeking restitution for unjust enrichment. At trial, evidence shows that:

- Just before Panwith and Randolph formed their contract, Randolph's land was worth $300,000.
- When Panwith breached, the two cottages he had built increased the value of Randolph's land by $140,000 so that its value was $440,000.
- For building the third cottage, Randolph paid Substitute $40,000.
- With the third cottage completed, Randolph's realty increased its value by another $70,000, for a total increase of $210,000, and final value of $510,000.
- Panwith spent $20,000 of his own money in expenses related to his work and *would have* had to spend an additional $10,000 in building the third cottage.

If both parties had fully performed, Randolph would have spent $165,000 and held land worth $510,000. His monetary position would have been/

should have been ($510,000 - $165,000) = $345,000. What actually has happened? Randolph holds a position ($510,000 - $40,000) = $470,000. He is $125,000 "ahead" of the position he would have held if both parties had fully performed. Meanwhile, in partially performing, Panwith spent $20,000. As a breaching party seeking restitution for unjust enrichment, he recovers the *lesser* of $125,000 and $20,000 = $20,000.

Doesn't That Leave Randolph with $105,000 in Unjust Enrichment?   No, it doesn't. It's true that after paying Panwith $20,000 in restitution, Randolph's position exceeds his expectation by ($125,000 − $20,000) = $105,000. That, let's say, is enrichment by good luck. But in the law's eyes, it's not unjust enrichment, because it does not come to Randolph at Panwith's expense. Let's prove that by understanding from just where the $105,000 originates.

Panwith was to build each cottage for ($165,000 ÷ 3) = $55,000. In building each one, he would have spent $10,000 so that his profit per cottage, would have been ($55,000 − $10,000) = $45,000. Had he not breached, his profit for the two cottages he built would have been ($45,000 x 2) = $90,000. Panwith failed to build the third cottage and Randolph found Substitute whose fee was $40,000 instead of $55,000, meaning that because of Panwith's breach, Randolph saved $15,000 on the third cottage. Randolph's $105,000 gain by good luck is the sum of the $90,000 in profit that Panwith would have earned on the first two cottages had he honored the contract, and the $15,000 that Randolph saved on the third cottage. By law, Randolph keeps all of that.

In the law's eyes, there's no injustice in leaving that money with Randolph, the non-breaching party, and denying them to Panwith the party who breached. Yes, Randolph enjoys an unearned gain, but it doesn't come to him *at Panwith's expense.* Having received from Randolph $20,000 in restitution Panwith enjoys the position he occupied before forming the contract. The restitution makes him "whole." He loses nothing. Again, Randolph is undeservedly enriched, but he is not enriched *at Panwith's expense.* He enjoys no *unjust* enrichment.

QUESTIONS 1 & 2. On October 1, Sanford Seretan contracts to sell a parcel of commercially zoned real estate to Barbara Boshen for $2 million. At the time the parties form their contract, Boshen makes to Seretan a $400,000 down payment. The contract provides for a closing to occur on December 1, at which time Seretan will transfer title and Boshen will pay $1.6 million in remaining purchase price. On November 15, Boshen advises Seretan that she will not purchase the property. Seretan immediately advertises the land for sale.

QUESTION 1. After one month, the land's value has increased. Nancy offers to buy it for $3 million, and Seretan sells it to her for that amount.

Thereafter, Boshen notes that Seretan has parted with his land and holds not $2 million, as she was obliged to pay, but (a) the $3 million paid by the new buyer, plus (b) her own $400,000 down payment. Concluding that Seretan has lost nothing from her breach, she asks that he return the down payment. Seretan refuses, and Boshen sues him, seeking restitution for unjust enrichment. The court is most likely to award Boshen

A. nothing, because Seretan is not in breach of contract.
B. $1 million, because that is the amount of Seretan's windfall.
C. $400,000, because that is the amount by which Seretan has been unjustly enriched at Boshen's expense.
D. $1.4 million, because that is the sum of Seretan's unearned down payment and his $1 million windfall.

ANALYSIS. Start with the rule (a good place, always, for lawyers to begin). *When one party (Boshen) breaches a contract and she herself (Boshen) sues, seeking restitution for unjust enrichment, she (Boshen) is entitled to receive the lesser of (a) the value she (Boshen) has given up in performing the contract ($400,000) or (b) the degree by which the non-breaching party's (Seretan's) position exceeds the one he would have held had both parties fulfilled their obligations.*

If both these parties had fulfilled their obligations, Boshen would have paid $2 million and acquired the realty. Seretan would have received $2 million and parted with the realty. What actually has happened? Seretan has parted with the realty and received ($3 million from Nancy) plus (Boshen's $400,000 down payment) = $3.4 million. Relative to where he would have stood under the contract as fully performed, Seretan is "ahead" by ($3.4 million − $2 million) = $1.4 million. Boshen has paid Seretan $400,000. The lesser of $400,000 and $1.4 million is $400,000. That's the amount by which Seretan is enriched at Boshen's expense, and that's what Boshen recovers.

The $400,000 restitution that Seretan pays Boshen leaves him a $1 million gain by good luck. Meanwhile, it restores to Boshen what would otherwise be, for Seretan, an unjust enrichment—an undeserved $400,000 gain at her expense. **C is right.**[1]

QUESTION 2. Assume now that one month after Boshen repudiates, Nancy offers to buy Seretan's land not for $3 million, but for only $1.85 million. Seretan sells for that amount. Thereafter, Boshen asks Seretan to return her $400,000 down payment. Seretan refuses, and Boshen sues seeking restitution for unjust enrichment. The court is most likely to award Boshen

---

1. As discussed in Chapter 30, section A, a contract for the sale of real estate often provides explicitly that if the buyer breaches, the seller may keep her down payment. In this case, of course, the contract featured no such provision.

A. $400,000, because that is the amount Boshen paid Seretan.
B. $250,000, because that is the amount by which Seretan is unjustly enriched.
C. $250,000, because that is the amount by which Seretan has damaged Boshen.
D. nothing, because Seretan is not unjustly enriched.

ANALYSIS.   Once again, think "rule": *When one party (Boshen) breaches a contract and she herself (Boshen) sues, seeking restitution for unjust enrichment, she (Boshen) is entitled to receive the lesser of (a) what she (Boshen) has given up in performing the contract ($400,000) or (b) the degree by which defendant's (Seretan's) position exceeds the position he would have enjoyed had both parties fulfilled their obligations.*

Had both parties fully performed the contract, Seretan would have parted with his realty and received $2 million. What actually has happened? Seretan has parted with his realty and received $2.25 million ($1.85 million + $400,000). His actual monetary position exceeds his expectation position by ($2.25 million − $2 million) = $250,000

Boshen has paid Seretan $400,000, and $250,000 is less than $400,000, That's the amount by which Seretan is unjustly enriched, and that's what Boshen recovers. That leaves Seretan with no particular good fortune, but it does leave him as well off as he would have been if Boshen had fully performed. Meanwhile, it restores to Boshen what would otherwise be for Seretan a $250,000 unearned gain at her expense — $250,000 in unjust enrichment.

D correctly states that Seretan is not in breach, but it ignores all that we've just discussed, to wit, that a breaching party is sometimes entitled to recover restitution for unjust enrichment. **A**, too, is wrong. As explained above, Seretan has been unjustly enriched at Boshen's expense by $250,000, not by $400,000. If we were to award Boshen $400,000, we would leave Seretan with a $150,000 loss; he'd have $1.85 million instead of the $2 million to which he was entitled under the contract. We'd be giving Boshen *more* than Seretan's unjust enrichment. **B** and **C** both report the correct award of $250,000. **C**, however, describes it as damage done by Seretan to Boshen, and that's inaccurate. Seretan has done nothing wrong. Rather, Seretan unjustly retains money at Boshen's expense; he retains what the law calls unjust enrichment, precisely as **B** describes it. **B** is right.

Does There Apply to All of This the Phrase "Benefit Conferred"?
In Chapter 28, section C, with Figures 28-1 and 28-2 we dealt with unjust enrichment and restitution as a remedy for *breach of contract*. There we said that restitution was equal to "benefit conferred" which, in that context, means (1) any amount that plaintiff pays directly to defendant in performing or preparing to perform, plus (2) the fair market value of time and effort/labor

plaintiff expends in performing, whether or not defendant thereby derives any *true* benefit.

Here, we have dealt with something quite different: unjust enrichment and restitution not as a plaintiff's remedy for a defendant's breach of contract, but as a remedy afforded a *plaintiff who herself breaches* a contract, who happens to provide some benefit to the innocent party—the one who has not breached. As we've just taught, *that* plaintiff recovers only to the extent that she parts with value in a way that *truly* benefits the innocent party at her expense (meaning, more specifically that she recovers (a) the lesser of the money with which she parts or (b) the degree by which defendant's financial position exceeds the one he would have held if both parties had fully performed). Fair market value of time and effort play no role in the recovery.

In describing that latter form of recovery in restitution—the one awarded to a breaching plaintiff against an innocent party, some lawyers and judges do, incorrectly, use the phrase "benefit conferred." But recognize and remember that "benefit conferred" for a breaching plaintiff, as described in this chapter, carries a measure quite different from "benefit conferred" as discussed in Chapter 28.

B.   More "Benefit Conferred": Restitution for the Non-Officious Volunteer; Contract Implied in Law and Quasi-Contract

For two separate scenarios, we have identified two separate measures of "benefit conferred." Where a plaintiff seeks restitution as a remedy for breach of contract we assess "benefit conferred" as described in Chapter 28, section C, Figures 28-1 and 28-2. Where from an innocent non-breaching party, a *breaching* party seeks restitution for unjust enrichment, we assess "benefit conferred" (incorrectly used) as described in section A above. We assess "benefit conferred" in yet another way where as here in section B, we address unjust enrichment and restitution for the "non-officious volunteer," beginning with a woman named Olson and a man named Neff.

Nathan Neff and Orella Olson are next-door neighbors. Neff owns a dog. Having intended, first, to board his dog in a kennel, Neff leaves his home to travel on business. In his hurry, he forgets about the dog and unwittingly leaves it in his backyard, tied to a tree. Olson sees the dog there and believes that Neff, if he knew of the situation, would (a) want her to rescue the dog and (b) be willing to pay her for doing so. Consequently, Neff takes the dog into her own home, feeding and caring for it during the four weeks in which Neff is away. Further, during that period the dog becomes sick and needs veterinary attention. Olson sees to that as well, paying the veterinarian her fee. All in all, over four weeks of caring for the dog, Olson spends $500.

When Neff returns, Olson tells him what happened. Neff thanks her. Olson then hands Neff a $700 "invoice," demanding payment of $100 for food, $400 for veterinary bills, and $200 for her time, effort, and attention. Neff refuses to pay.

These parties had no contract. In caring for Neff's dog, Olson did not act pursuant to a contract. By refusing to pay, Neff breached none. But in the law's eyes Neff enjoys an unjust enrichment—an unearned, undeserved gain at Olson's expense. The law entitles Olson to restitution in the amount of "benefit conferred," which in this case is equal to (a) money she spent and (b) the fair market value of time and effort she dedicated.

Restitution for the Non-Officious Volunteer: The Rule (with a Blank Space for Now). *If (1) Party A reasonably concludes (a) that Party B is in serious need of service, money, or property, and (b) that Party B himself is unable or unavailable to meet his own need, and (2) Party A volunteers to meet Party B's need, reasonably, non-officiously, with the reasonable expectation that B would want her to act and would be willing to compensate her for doing so, then by action in unjust enrichment—A is entitled to restitution (a) for money she spends and (b) for the fair market value of time and effort she devotes to that purpose.*

Hold on tight, please, to the word "non-officiously." *In order that a plaintiff recover under the rule, the court or jury must find that she did not "butt in" where she is not wanted. With that in mind, consider this:*

Jake and Janet are next-door neighbors. Jake knows that his house needs painting but has decided, for now, to leave it alone. Jake travels away for several weeks and during that period, Janet hires and pays painters to paint the house. When Jake returns, Janet hands him a bill for the cost of the painting. Jake responds, "Get lost."

The law, too, tells Janet to get lost. She has acted *officiously*, meaning her behavior has been meddlesome. She has interfered and intruded where she did not belong. She could not reasonably have believed that Jake would have wanted her to do as she did and, certainly, she could not have believed that he would be willing to pay her for it. For those reasons, Olson is entitled to nothing.

More Terms: "Contract Implied in Law" and "Quasi Contract."   Olson's recovery represents restitution for unjust enrichment in the amount of benefit conferred which, in this context, is assessed as described above. But in this, the case of the non-officious volunteer, we add to the mix, another term: "contract implied in law," and the closely related phrase "quasi-contract." As already noted, Olson and Neff had no contract, so Olson's recovery is not for breach of any true contract. Yet, in this context, the law, it is said, "implies" a contract; of thin air, it creates one. By refusing to pay Olson for saving the dog, Neff breaches a "contract implied in law." These parties, of course, formed no true contract, but according to law, whether they know it or not they have something "kind of like" a contract. They should be treated *as though* they have a contract. They have "sort of" a contract.

The prefix "quasi" means "very much like, but not really." For that reason the law describes Olson's action against Neff as an action "in quasi-contract," meaning an action for breach of a contract implied in law which, in turn, *really* means: an action in unjust enrichment for restitution in the amount of benefit conferred by a non-officious volunteer upon some person to whom he has reasonably given assistance at his own expense of money and/or time/effort.

With that, let's restate the rule, this time filling the blank: *If (1) Party A reasonably concludes (a) that Party B is in serious need of service, money, or property, and (b) that Party B himself is unable or unavailable to meet his need, and (2) Party A voluntarily meets Party B's need, non-officiously, with the reasonable expectation that A would want her to act and would be willing to compensate her for doing so, then by action in unjust enrichment—in this setting, called, more specifically, an action for "breach of contract implied in law" or an action in "quasi-contract"—A is entitled to restitution (a) for money she spends and (b) for the fair market value of time and effort she devotes to that purpose.*

> **QUESTION 3.** Johnson is away on business. Kohr, his neighbor, inspects Johnson's yard. He thinks it needs more in the way of perennial plants. On his own initiative, making necessary expenses, Kohr plants a large number of perennials in Johnson's garden. When Johnson returns, Kohr presents him with a bill for his monetary disbursements and for his labor, at $20 per hour. In response, Johnson says, "Get lost." Kohr is not entitled to recovery in quasi-contract because
>
> **A.** Johnson was enriched in no way by Kohr's activities.
> **B.** Kohr's behavior was meddlesome.
> **C.** Flowers are not a life-or-death necessity.
> **D.** the rate of $20 per hour is excessive for the kind of work that Kohr performed.

ANALYSIS. The non-officious volunteer recovers in "quasi-contract"—for breach of a "contract implied in law,"—only if he behaves *non-officiously*. No one asked Kohr to take charge of Johnson's garden. Kohr had no reason to think that Johnson, if present, would want him to do so, and no reason, certainly, to expect compensation for what he did.

A makes a false statement (in the law's eyes anyway). Johnson did benefit from Kohr's activities; Kohr spent money and put forth effort enhancing

Johnson's garden. **A** is wrong. **C** is true but irrelevant. One might act non-officiously to save another's property where no life-or-death consequence presents itself. If for that purpose he spends money and/or effort, non-officiously, reasonably believing that the other party would want him to do so, he'll recover restitution for money and effort spent. **C** is wrong. **D** makes a statement that may or may not be true; it's a matter for the jury to decide. But we cannot say, on our own, that the rate of $20 an hour for landscaping work is, per se, unreasonable. Hence, **D** too is wrong. **B** correctly observes that Kohr acted where he had no business doing so; he was meddlesome, meaning he acted officiously. **B** is right.

C.   The Closer

QUESTION 4. Harrison falls out of a train. He's unconscious and badly injured. Bystanders bring him to a hospital where Surgeon operates on him for several hours. Harrison survives for a time, but dies many weeks later, never regaining consciousness. Thereafter, Surgeon demands that Harrison's estate pay for her services. The estate refuses, stating that Harrison formed no contract with her.

Surgeon brings an action against Harrison's estate. As a matter of law, the court rules that, notwithstanding the ultimate death, Harrison's temporary survival represented a benefit conferred on him. On that basis, it issues Surgeon a judgment in an amount equal to (what the jury names as) the fair market value of her services. The state's appellate court affirms the decision. In writing its opinion, is the appellate court likely to invoke the phrases "contract implied in law" or "quasi-contract"?

A. Yes, because the plaintiffs were volunteers, acting non-officiously
B. Yes, because those phrases belong to all suits in unjust enrichment
C. No, because those phrases do not apply to the case of a non-officious volunteer
D. No, because those phrases have no relationship to unjust enrichment, restitution, or benefit conferred

---

ANALYSIS.   For every action in unjust enrichment (no matter what the scenario), the remedy is—restitution, always, always—restitution. And, where a non-officious volunteer sues in unjust enrichment for restitution in the amount of benefit conferred we say, more specifically, that she sues in "quasi-contract," or that she sues for breach of a "contract implied in law."

That's this case. Harrison was unconscious, unable to act for himself. As a volunteer, acting non-officiously, Surgeon attempted to save his life and by prolonging it afforded him a benefit. Should Harrison be allowed to retain the benefit without paying for it, he'll enjoy (in the hereafter) an *unjust* enrichment—an unearned benefit acquired through Surgeon's time and effort. In this, the case of a non-officious volunteer who, for unjust enrichment seeks restitution in an amount equal to benefit conferred, we say, for specificity, that Surgeon recovers in "quasi-contract," or that she recovers for breach of a "contract implied in law." **A** is right.[2]

 # Silver's Picks

1.	C
2.	B
3.	B
4.	A

---

2. This closer is inspired by Cotnam v. Wisdom, 104 S.W. 164 (Ark. 1907). There, even though medical personnel did not, even, prolong the patient's life, still, they were deemed to "benefit" him.

30

Breach, Remedies, and Damages, Part VI

A. Liquidated Damages
B. Specific Performance
C. The Closer
✦ Silver's Picks

A. Liquidated Damages

1. What Are Liquidated Damages?

"Liquidate" has several meanings, one of which is "to reduce or transform to money or cash." One who owns corporate stock might decide to liquidate her investment by selling it, thus converting its value to money. Where one party owes another 5 percent of the value of copyright X, the parties might decide to "liquidate" the amount of the debt by subjecting the copyright to appraisal, taking 5 percent of the result and thus assigning to the debt a cash figure. When two parties form a contract, the law sometimes allows them to create and enforce a "liquidated damage provision."

Meere is a renowned expert in investment, finance, and insurance, so much so that she is thought to have no equal in all of the United States. Greeney contacts Meere, and the parties discuss forming a contract under which Meere will (a) review all of Greeney's investments and insurance policies, and then (b) in writing, report her opinion as to any changes she recommends. Meere will submit to Greeney an itemization of time spent on the project, whereupon within ten days of receiving it, Greeney will pay Meere for her work at the rate of $800 per hour.

Before forming the contract, it occurs to Greeney (or his lawyer) that if Meere fails substantially to perform he'll withhold her payment. But beyond that, he thinks he will sustain a loss — a loss of the uniquely expert services for which he has contracted. Not knowing how he might demonstrate the monetary amount of that loss, he suggests that the parties add to their contract this provision:

> **Liquidated Damages.** If Meere should fail substantially to fulfill her obligations under this contract, then (a) Greeney may withhold all payment that he would otherwise owe her, and (b) Meere will pay Greeney damages of $100,000.

That's a liquidated damage provision, meaning a contractual term by which the parties agree on the monetary amount that, in the case of breach, one (or each) shall pay the other. Meere agrees to it, and by signed writing, the parties form their contract.

Let's ask: If Meere commits a material breach, will a court award Greeney $100,000?

Let's answer: Maybe. Here's the liquidated damage rule:

As to a contract between parties A and B, the law will enforce a liquidated damage provision against A if and only if (1) at the time the parties form their contract, reasonable persons in their positions would think themselves unable to foresee the actual damage to be caused B by A's breach, and (2) also from the perspective of reasonable persons at the time they form their contract, the liquidated amount on which they agree represents a legitimate foresighted attempt to compensate B for A's breach, not so high as to be punitive.

If, for example, Meere and Greeney had agreed to a figure of $10 million, their liquidated damage provision would violate criterion 2. Ten million dollars would not, to persons in their positions, represent a reasonable attempt to compensate Greeney in the event of Meere's breach. An award of that amount would do no more than punish Meere for her breach; it would be punitive.

Suppose Meere agrees to a liquidated damage provision against her, but demands that there be one against Greeney too. As finally formed, the contract includes this:

> **Liquidated Damages.** (a) If Meere should fail substantially to fulfill her obligations under this contract, then (i) Greeney may withhold all payment that he would otherwise owe her, and, further (ii) Meere will pay Greeney damages of $100,000; (b) if Greeney should fail timely to pay Meere the $800 hourly fee, Greeney will pay Meere the sum of $2,500 per hour of service Meere has performed.

Meere submits her report to Greeney, on time, in perfect form. She also provides a document showing that she spent 100 hours producing it, meaning that Greeney owes her ($100 \times \$800) = \$80,000$. Greeney tells Meere that he'll need three weeks to raise that amount. In three weeks he does raise the money, but Meere refuses to accept it. Rather, citing his lateness and the liquidated damage clause part (b) just above, she demands ($\$2,500 \times 100) = \$250,000$.

Meere won't get $250,000 because no court will enforce the liquidated damage provision's part (b). It contravenes the rule's first criterion — that actual damages be difficult to predict in monetary terms. At the time they form their contract Meere and Greeney should conclude quite the opposite — that they can readily foresee the damages to Meere for Greeney's failure timely to pay the hourly fee; $800 per hour is — after all — $800 per hour. Greeney's failure to pay that amount when due would cause Meere damages of exactly $800 for each hour she works. She'll recover $80,000 (plus interest in some amount, depending on the degree of the lateness).

QUESTION 1. On April 1, by signed written contract, Shuva and Bimra agree that Shuva (Seller) will convey his real property to Bimra (Buyer), Bimra to pay a purchase price of $800,000. As a down payment, Bimra is to pay 10 percent of that amount ($80,000) immediately on April 1, and the remaining, $720,000, at a closing to occur on June 1. The contract includes this provision:

> **Down Payment as Liquidated Damage.** The parties agree that if Buyer should fail at closing to purchase the property, then Seller may keep, as liquidated damage, the 10 percent ($80,000) down payment Buyer is to make on the formation of this contract, in which case Seller will be entitled to nothing more.

On May 20, Bimra advises Shuva that she will not purchase the realty, thus committing an anticipatory repudiation and material breach.[1] She has found another property offered by a seller named Shane, and she intends to buy it. Bimra asks Shuva to return her $80,000 deposit. Shuva refuses, claiming that under their contract he is entitled to keep it as liquidated damages. Bimra sues Shuva for unjust enrichment, claiming restitution in the amount of $80,000. The court should rule for *Shuva* only if it finds that

I.   under these circumstances, an $80,000 award is not punitive.
II. on forming this contract, under these circumstances, reasonable persons would find themselves unable to foresee the actual damage to be sustained by Shuva on Bimra's breach.
III. Bimra did not truly intend to purchase Shane's property.
IV. Shane's property is substantially similar to Shuva's.
A. I only
B. I and II only
C. I, II, and III only
D. I, II, III, and IV

ANALYSIS.   Ruling for Shuva means enforcing the liquidated damage clause, which we do only if it answers the applicable rule's two criteria: (1) that as reasonable people *at the time they formed their contract*, these parties believed themselves unable to foresee the actual monetary damage Shuva would suffer from Bimra's breach, and that (2) as reasonable people *at the time they formed their contract*, $80,000 is not so high as merely to subject Bimra to punishment.

Options I and II reflect those two criteria. Hence, they belong to the right answer; we eliminate **A**. Option III refers to a lie told by Bimra to Shuva, and option IV refers to substantial similarity between Shane's property and Shuva's property. Neither of those references is relevant to the problem. The court should enforce the liquidated damage clause (a) whatever is the cause of Bimra's breach and (b) whether Bimra does or does not lie to Shuva about her plan to buy other property. Only options I and II reflect the two criteria that render a liquidated damage clause enforceable. **B** is right.[2]

2. *More About Criterion 1: Actual Damages Difficult to Foresee*

Focus above, please, on the liquidated damage rule, criterion 1. In reverse, it means this:

If (i) two parties A and B form a contract, and (ii) reasonable persons in their positions would think themselves able, meaningfully to foresee the damages B will likely suffer from A's breach, then (iii) the law does not enforce a liquidated damage clause against A. If A breaches, B is entitled to the actual damage he proves, whether it be less or more than the liquidated damage clause prescribes. The liquidated damage clause becomes irrelevant; the court "throws it out."

QUESTION 2. On May 1, Xanzi and Yorta form a contract. On that same day, May 1, surrounding circumstances should cause them to foresee (a) that Xanzi's material breach will cause Yorta damage in the amount of $100,000 to $150,000, and (b) that Yorta's material breach will damage Xanzi in the amount of $400,000 to $500,000. Nonetheless, the contract carries this clause:

Liquidated Damage. If either party should commit a material breach, then she shall pay the other liquidated damages of $5 million.

---

2. Some jurisdictions hold that as to a contract for the sale of realty, a seller's prospective damages for buyer's breach are, as a matter of law, "difficult to foresee." In those states, a 10 percent, 15 percent, or perhaps 20 percent down payment is, by law, reasonable; it's neither excessive nor punitive. Even where the parties' contract does not provide that the down payment will serve as liquidated damage, these states hold that *unless the parties contract otherwise*, a 10 to 20 percent down payment implicitly represents a liquidated damage provision, with the down payment representing the liquidated damage.

Xanzi commits a material breach. Yorta can prove true damages of $6 million, very different from what reasonable parties would have predicted but, as it happens, not so different from the $5 million on which the parties agree. The court should award Yorta

A. $5 million, because on a standard of reasonableness, between the damage named in a liquidated damage clause and that which a plaintiff actually sustains, plaintiff recovers the smaller amount.

B. $5 million, because the contract tied Yorta's agreement to accept that amount to Xanzi's mirror-image agreement also to accept that amount as compensation for Yorta's breach.

C. $6 million, because it is reasonably close to the $5 million figure to which the parties manifested their mutual asset via their liquidated damage clause.

D. $6 million, because when the parties formed their contract, they should have believed that Xanzi's breach would cause Yorta a foreseeable degree of damage.

ANALYSIS. Before assessing the choices, think of the law — the law — *the law*! As to any defendant sued for breach of contract, a liquidated damage clause is unenforceable *if, at the time plaintiff and defendant form their contract,* the damage to be suffered by plaintiff on defendant's breach would be meaningfully foreseeable to reasonable persons in their positions.

As reasonable persons *when forming this contract,* these parties should foresee (i) $100,000 to $150,000 of damage to Yorta should Xanzi breach, and (ii) $400,000 to $500,000 of damage to Xanzi should Yorta breach. Hence, *at the time Yorta and Xanzi form their contract* — whether they be right or wrong— they should believe themselves able to foresee the damage to be done to either of them by the other's breach. So, regardless of what might later turn out to be true, we take the liquidated damage clause and trash it. Legally, it doesn't exist. For that reason, as for any breach of contract, Yorta recovers his true provable damages — $6 million.

A awards plaintiff $5 million, so it's wrong for that reason alone. It then states a rule that's from Mars. It implies that when a liquidated damage clause names one figure and evidence identifies another, the court awards the smaller of the two figures. There's no such rule. The test writer invented it to knock you off balance. Once again, *when a multiple-choice option states or implies a rule of which you've never heard, you must indulge a very strong presumption that it's wrong.* So A is wrong, and the word "reasonableness" doesn't make it right.

B, too, gives plaintiff $5 million, so it's wrong. It too implies a nonexistent rule: The law enforces a liquidated damage clause if it awards the parties equal amounts. That's nonsense; there's no such law. And don't let the words "mirror-image" seduce you, just because you've seen them before (which you have if you've already read Chapter 7). B is wrong.

C correctly awards plaintiff $6 million, but its reasoning is wrong. It too implies a nonsensical, nonexistent rule: when faced with a liquidated damage clause, the court is to award actual damages only if they are reasonably close to the amount named *in* the liquidated damage clause. According to **C**, then, if Yorta's actual damages had been $15 million, the court would award him $5 million. The law provides for no such thing. Alas, **C** is wrong.

That leaves **D**. It awards plaintiff $6 million — his actual damage — and its reasoning hits the bull's eye. When these parties formed their contract, **D** tells us, reasonable persons — whether they be right or wrong — would believe they could, by foresight, approximate the actual damages to be suffered by each party should the other commit a material breach. That fact renders the liquidated damage clause unenforceable. Plaintiff is entitled to recover his true provable damages, whether they be near to or far from those named in the liquidated damage clause. **D** is right.

QUESTION 3. Winston is a screenwriter and Antwon a screenplay agent. On February 1, they form a contract requiring that Winston, by or before December 31, write a screenplay for the largely forgotten novel *Alone But Yet Alive*. Antwon then, for three years, must make diligent commercial efforts to market the screenplay to motion picture producers. If Antwon should be successful in that effort, which he cannot and does not guarantee, Winston will pay Antwon 15 percent of whatever moneys a motion picture production company pays Winston for the screenplay.

The parties and their lawyers justifiably conclude that it is nearly impossible by foresight to quantify the damages Antwon might suffer if Winston should fail to write the manuscript. Similarly, they conclude that as for Antwon's marketing efforts, they cannot know, now, what company, if any, will purchase the screenplay, what price, if any, it might pay, and how much money, if any, Antwon then might owe Winston. Consequently, the parties reasonably believe that they cannot foresee the damages Winston might suffer if Antwon should fail to make diligent marketing efforts. The parties mutually agree simply to assume that if both honor their obligations, the screenplay will be sold for about $20 million. In their contract, they include this:

> **Liquidated Damages.** (a) If Winston should fail substantially in his obligation timely to create the aforementioned screenplay, he will pay Antwon (15% of $20 million) = $3 million and (b) if, after Winston does timely create the manuscript, Antwon fails substantially to exert diligent efforts attempting to market it, then Antwon will pay Winston (85% of $20) = $17 million.

Winston timely completes the screenplay, but Antwon lifts nary a finger attempting to market it. During the next year, another screenwriter named Sarahn writes a screenplay for *Alone But Yet Alive*, hoping to market it to production companies. Shortly after he finishes it, the original author of the novel *Alone But Yet Alive* is involved in a widely publicized scandal whose facts resemble those of her novel. She and her novel gain enormous notoriety, and Sarahn, through a good and diligent agent, sells his manuscript to a production company for $25 million — twice the highest price ever paid for a screenplay.

Thereafter, Winston seeks to recover from Antwon the liquidated damages to which, he says, the contract entitles him. He sues Antwon demanding $17 million, and moves for summary judgment. On evaluating Winston's motion, the court finds as facts that:

(1) at the time the parties formed their contract, no screenwriter had been paid more than $8 million for a screenplay; wherefore

(2) the amount of $20 million as provided in the parties' contract, viewed from their perspective when they formed it, was positively unreasonable, producing recoveries that would be punitive;

(3) as matters evolved, *Sarahn* did sell his screenplay for $25 million, so that a $20 million sales price, examined *today*, turns out not to be unreasonably high.

The court then rules:

This liquidated damage clause is unenforceable. If plaintiff Winston wishes to recover from defendant Antwon, he must prove his damages. He must prove that Antwon, if properly discharging his contractual duties, would have sold Winston's manuscript, and for how much he would have sold it. Let us remember that Mr. Sarahn's manuscript was not the same as plaintiff Winston's and, moreover that he sold it under circumstances no person could have foreseen when Messrs. Winston and Antwon formed their contract.

The court's reason for ruling the liquidated damage clause unenforceable is most likely that

A. at the time they formed their contract, the parties had no reason to believe that either of them would breach.

B. the parties' liquidated damage provision did not treat equally a breach by Winston on the one hand and a breach by Antwon on the other.

C. as to the amount of damage on which two parties agree, the law evaluates a liquidated damage clause in light of all circumstances that surround the breach.

D. as to the amount of damage on which two parties agree, the law evaluates a liquidated damage clause in light of the circumstances surrounding the parties when they form their contract.

ANALYSIS. The enforceability of a liquidated damage clause rides on two criteria, each to be applied from the perspective of reasonable persons under the circumstances that surround them *at the time they form their contract*. If as reasonable persons acting under those circumstances, the parties choose a figure that they should believe so high as to serve the purpose not of compensation but of punishment — then — (a) the clause is unenforceable, meaning that (b) as in any other suit for breach, plaintiff is entitled to such actual damages as he can prove, whether they be more or less than the amount named in their liquidated damage clause. That's true even if, as no one would reasonably have predicted, it turns out that the figure is *not* too high.

In this case, the parties agreed to assume that if both honored the contract, Antwon would sell the manuscript for $20 million, even though no movie manuscript had ever brought a price higher than $8 million. Because of the scandal, wholly unforeseeable, Sarahn did later sell his manuscript for an amount even higher than that. But that fact does not affect the reasonableness of the $20 million figure *at the time the parties formed their contract*. That's why this court ruled their liquidated damage clause unenforceable.

As for **A**: The validity of a liquidated damage agreement does not require that the parties anticipate a breach. That thought has nothing to do with anything. **A** is wrong. **B** too is wrong; the viability of a liquidated damage clause does not depend on mutuality or equality. As we already know, a contract might provide for liquidated damages respecting one party's breach, but not the other's. **C** is nonsense. The reasonableness of a liquidated damage figure depends not on what a court thinks in light of all circumstances surrounding a breach. It depends on what a court, on evidence, thinks reasonable parties should have thought *at the time they formed their contract*. **D** says exactly that, and that's why **D** is right.

3. There Is, Lately, a Different Trend (Maybe)

According, maybe, to a more modern and emerging view, a court may assess the reasonableness of a liquidated damage figure by looking not only backward in time to what the parties should have thought when they formed their contract, but also to the present for reasonableness of amount *in light of what truly has occurred*.

Although very few courts have taken that view, Restatement (Second) of Contracts §356 appears to do so:

> Damages for breach by either party may be liquidated in the agreement but only at an amount that is reasonable in the light of the anticipated or actual loss caused by the breach and the difficulties of proof of loss. A term fixing unreasonably large liquidated damages is unenforceable on grounds of public policy as a penalty.

The three words "or actual loss" seem to mean that a liquidated damage clause is enforceable if it approximates the actual damage a plaintiff suffers from defendant's breach even if the named amount was not foreseeable at the time the parties formed their contract. UCC §2-718(1) provides similarly:

> Damages for breach by either party may be liquidated in the agreement but only at an amount that is reasonable in the light of the anticipated or actual harm caused by the breach[.]

The words "or actual harm" mean the same as the Restatement's words "or actual damage."

Please know this: Even if adopted, that innovation in the law is of dubious significance. It would seem to be relevant only when the plaintiff is, in fact, able to show his actual damage and the liquidated damage clause provides for damages slightly higher or lower than the actual ones. And maybe—*maybe*—the view is endorsed by Equitable Lumber Corp. v. IPA Land Dev. Corp., 381 N.Y.S.2d 459 (N.Y. 1976).

PLEASE STOP and read Appendix, section E. Then, meet us back here.

B.   Specific Performance

1. *What Is Specific Performance?*

A long-standing precept adopted by the equity courts provides that when the law's remedy of money damages is insufficient to rectify the injustice wrought by breach of contract, the injured party may petition the equity court for an order of "specific performance," meaning a court order to the breaching party that he *actually perform his contractual obligation* or, if he refuses, face incarceration for contempt of court.

Suppose Bertha conducts a garage sale where Hattie finds an old 78 RPM recording of her own great aunt Lottie playing the violin. Lottie, in her day (the 1910s), had been a well-known concert violinist. Hattie wants badly to buy the record. Bertha offers it for $5, and Hattie accepts. The parties thus form a contract for the sale of the record by Bertha to Hattie. Hattie roams among the other merchandise for a while and then approaches Bertha to pay for and take the recording. Bertha says she has changed her mind and wants $100 for the record. Bertha, therefore, is in material breach of contract.

Hattie's lawyer tells her that in an ordinary suit for breach of contract, she'll be entitled to recover only the fair market value of the record, whatever that is — $5 or $100. Hattie tells him that no such amount of money will give her what she bargained for. The record she contracted to buy has a special meaning to her. Tearful, she tells her lawyer, that "nothing will do but to have the record itself."

On Hattie's behalf, the lawyer brings an action against Bertha (1) citing Bertha's breach of contract; (2) citing the particular significance of the very recording Hattie contracted to buy from her; and (3) asserting therefore that a monetary award equal to the value of the record will not put Hattie in the same position she would have occupied had the contract been performed. The lawyer then advises the court of his position: (4) that the case is one in which Bertha's breach subjects Hattie to an "injustice for which the law (through a judgment for monetary damages) offers no adequate remedy," and (5) that the court therefore should invoke its jurisdiction as a court of equity and order "specific performance" of the contract, meaning it should issue not a judgment, but rather an *order* to Bertha that she convey the record itself when Hattie tenders her $5.

With that argument on these facts, Hattie's lawyer might well succeed. If she does, the court will likely issue an order of specific performance, meaning an order that Bertha do as she contracted to do or find herself in contempt of court, which in turn subjects her to incarceration (for ten days, perhaps, and then for as long as she refuses still to comply). If, when Hattie tenders $5, Bertha refuses to turn over the record, Hattie's lawyer will return to court asking that it find Hattie in contempt, and send her to jail until she is willing to comply. In theory, the court should do just that (but, in the case of this record and so small an amount of money, it probably won't).

QUESTION 4. With respect to breach of contract, the remedy of specific performance

I.   inheres in a court order, which if disobeyed puts its recipient in contempt of court, for which she is subject to incarceration.

II. is intended to afford the aggrieved party the financial position she would have occupied absent the breach.

III. is no longer available in the United States because the American courts of law and equity are merged.

IV. is available only where the court concludes that a monetary award will not meaningfully afford plaintiff the position she would have occupied absent the breach.

A. I only
B. III only
C. I, II, and III
D. I and IV only

ANALYSIS.   Specific performance is an *equity* court's remedy for breach of contract. It's a court order compelling the breaching party actually to perform. Option I is true. The remedy is intended to afford the aggrieved party the actual position she would have occupied absent the breach — the *actual* position, not the *financial* position. Option II is false. A court is to issue such an order when, in its opinion, monetary recovery (the *legal* remedy) will fail to achieve that end; when *law* offers no remedy that will correct the "injustice." Hence, option IV is true.

Option III reports that specific performance is not available in the United States. That's false. It's available in every American jurisdiction. It's an "equitable remedy," meaning it arose in the English equity courts. When issuing an order of specific performance today, an American court invokes its jurisdiction *as* an equity court. "Merger" does not alter that fact, wherefore option III is false. Only I and IV are true. **D** is right.

2. *Specific Performance as the Remedy in Real Estate Sales Contracts*

Equity considers that all real estate is unique (just as Great Aunt Lottie's record was unique to Hattie).[3] If Seller and Buyer agree on the sale of Blackacre for $500,000, and Seller wrongfully refuses to sell, then (1) equity acknowledges (a) that the return of any purchase price Buyer paid in advance plus (b) any difference between current market value and the contract price will afford Buyer the *financial* position he would have occupied absent the breach, but (2) equity believes that such will not truly afford Buyer *the* position he would have occupied absent the breach.

The monetary award, equity believes, will not allow Buyer to buy equivalent realty because no two parcels of realty are the same. In such a case, if Buyer so chooses, the judge changes "hats" and becomes a chancellor. The court converts itself briefly from a law court to an equity court, whereupon the chancellor issues an order of specific performance. It *orders* Seller to convey the property to Buyer (subject, of course, to Buyer's tender of the purchase price). Should Seller disobey, he'll be in contempt of court, for which the court (once again, acting as an equity court) might incarcerate him until he avows his willingness to obey the order.

QUESTION 5. On May 1, Sasha, owner of Redacre, forms a contract with Basha under which (a) Basha is to make a $75,000 down payment on May 1, and (b) at a closing to occur on July 1, Sasha is to convey Redacre to Basha, with Basha then to pay Sasha an additional $425,000 for a total purchase price of $500,000.

On May 31, Sasha correctly determines that during the previous two months Redacre has increased in value. She contacts Basha and advises

---

3. Realty earned its special place in equity's heart because, in centuries past, English and American economies were largely agricultural. Land, more than any other asset, was the greatest show of wealth. Only one hundred fifty years ago, after all, to his daughter Scarlett, Gerald O'Hara imparted this wisdom: "Why land is the only thing worth working for, worth fighting for, worth dying for, for it's the only thing that lasts."

her that she will return the $75,000 down payment but will not convey the property. Basha receives from Sasha a $75,000 check, and Basha promptly returns it to Sasha. Basha then brings an action against Sasha. Basha is probably entitled, as she chooses, to either

I.   a remedy at law in the form of a judgment in an amount equal to $75,000 plus the difference between Redacre's present value and the $500,000 contract price.
II. a remedy at law in the form of specific performance.
III. an equitable remedy in the form of specific performance.
IV. an equitable remedy in the form of a court order requiring that Sasha convey Redacre to Basha.

A. I only
B. III only
C. I, III, and IV only
D. II, III, and IV only

ANALYSIS.   Orders of specific performance are creatures of equity, not law. Option II characterizes specific performance as a legal remedy, so it's wrong. For a seller's breach of a contract to sell realty, equity is generally willing to grant the remedy of specific performance, since it believes that no parcel of realty is equivalent to any other. Consequently, option III is true. Because specific performance is, in fact, a court order that a breaching party honor his contract by actually performing under its terms, option IV is true too. A buyer of realty may, if he prefers, choose an ordinary legal remedy — a monetary judgment. Hence, I is true as well. Basha may have, if and as she wishes, option I, III, or IV. (III and IV are identical.) **C** is right.

C.   The Closer

QUESTION 6. Adams is a theatrical celebrity. *Showstopper* magazine wants to publish her photo on the cover of this year's January issue. Adams and *Showstopper* contemplate a contract under which Adams will pose for a photograph and permit *Showstopper* to publish it on its January cover; *Showstopper* promises that it will in fact print the photograph on its January cover. Before making any agreement, the parties' lawyers speak:

Adams's Lawyer: There's something I don't love about this arrangement. If you folks breach, my client will be unable to show what damage she suffers beyond any money she spends in

> preparing for the photograph. We will never be able to show what
> gain, if any, she might have derived from the published picture.
>
> **Showstopper's Lawyer:** I agree, that will be hard to show. And now
> that you mention it, if Adams should breach, it will be hard for
> *Showstopper* to show what, if anything, it has lost.
>
> **Adams's Lawyer:** True. I suggest that we include in the contract a
> liquidated damage provision for each of our clients.
>
> **Showstopper's Lawyer:** Yes, I suppose we can do that. You know
> the drill, I'm sure: By law, we must choose an amount that is
> reasonable, not so high as to be punitive.
>
> **Adams's Lawyer:** Yes, I know. I too have read the Glannon Guide to
> Contracts.
>
> **Showstopper's Lawyer:** Exactly. So we're talking about a big
> celebrity and a big magazine. I say that a $100,000 liquidated
> damage provision for each of us will be enforceable.
>
> **Adams's Lawyer:** Agreed.

The lawyers prepare and the parties sign a document that includes these
provisions:

1. Adams ("Celebrity") will pose for a photograph and permit
   Showstopper magazine to publish it on the cover of its forthcoming
   January New Year issue.
2. *Showstopper* magazine ("*Showstopper*") will in fact take the
   photograph and print it on the cover of its forthcoming January New
   Year issue.
3. **Liquidated Damages:**

   WHEREAS the parties hereto do agree that if either should commit
   a material breach, the damages to be suffered by the other, in
   the nature of this contract, will be difficult to quantify and prove,
   and do further agree that in light of that fact, a non-punitive,
   non-excessive amount of damage, reasonably calculated to
   compensate each party for a potential breach by the other, would
   be $100,000, wherefore the parties agree that (a) if Adams should
   materially dishonor its obligations hereunder by refusing to pose
   for the aforementioned photograph or by any other failure, then
   she will pay *Showstopper* damages in the amount of $100,000,
   and (b) if *Showstopper* should materially dishonor its obligations
   hereunder by failing to produce and publish the aforementioned
   photograph, or by any other failure, then *Showstopper* will pay
   Adams damages in the amount of $100,000.

As the contract requires, Adams poses and *Showstopper* snaps the photo.
Showstopper then decides to publish the picture of some other celebrity
on its January New Year cover, and thus commits total breach of its

contract with Adams. Pursuant to their contract, Adams seeks to recover from *Showstopper* $100,000 in liquidated damages.

At trial, Adams introduces the contract and its liquidated damage clause. Adams also introduces expert witnesses who testify that at the time the parties formed the contract there was no plausible basis on which to predict what damages, if any, *Showstopper*'s breach would cause Adams. *Showstopper* does not dispute that evidence but seeks to introduce evidence showing that when *Showstopper* itself breached the contract, another magazine offered to publish Adams's photo on its cover, and that Adams did not avail herself of that opportunity. Adams (through her lawyer) objects to the introduction of that evidence.

> **Adams's Lawyer:** Defendant *Showstopper* does not dispute that at the time these parties formed their contract, it was virtually impossible for reasonable people in their positions to predict what economic damage, if any, either would suffer from the other's breach. Consequently, they settled on a liquidated damage provision not for $100 million, or $10 million, or $1 million, but $100,000. Even if defendant can show now that plaintiff might have turned down an opportunity to have her photograph published in another magazine, such a showing is irrelevant. We object to the introduction of the evidence and, if defendant has no other evidence to present, we move for a directed verdict in our favor.
>
> **The Court:** I sustain the objection. Whatever the situation might truly be now, the validity of the liquidated damage clause depends on whether reasonable parties *at the time they formed their contract* would have believed that damages upon breach would be difficult to show, and that they agreed on liquidated damages that represented a reasonable attempt not to punish, but to compensate. Now, have you anything more to introduce?
>
> **Showstopper's Lawyer:** No, Your Honor, the defense rests.
>
> **The Court:** There is, then, nothing for a jury to consider. Plaintiff's motion for directed verdict is granted. Judgment for plaintiff in the amount of $100,000.

Which of the following changes to the foregoing story would most likely cause the court to *deny* Plaintiff's motion for a directed verdict?

A. The amount of liquidated damage on which the parties agreed was $1 billion.

B. The amount of liquidated damage on which the parties agreed was $25,000.

> **C.** The liquidated damage provision provided for damage of $100,000 in the case of *Showstopper*'s breach, but set no amount of damage for Adams's breach.
>
> **D.** The liquidated damage provision did not include the text in item 3 beginning with "whereas."

ANALYSIS. Think of the law: In deciding to enforce a liquidated damage clause, a court wears the lens of reasonable persons at the time they form their contract. It enforces the provision only if, thus taken back in time, it sees that reasonable parties, when forming the contract, would have thought: (a) "If this breach occurs, it will cause damages difficult to quantify and prove," and (b) "the amount of money chosen as liquidated damage is neither excessive nor punitive, but rather shows a reasonable attempt to compensate the party who suffers the breach."

The law does not require that a liquidated damage provision address a breach by both parties. It may address a breach by only one of them. For that reason, **C** is wrong. The law requires that the applicable criteria apply, but it certainly does not require that the parties, in their contract, *state* their belief that they apply. Hence, **D** is wrong as well. A liquidated damage provision cannot provide for excessive or punitive damages, but (as far as the common law now stands) the parties do not invalidate their liquidated damage provision by choosing a figure that is *lower* than what they might justifiably have chosen. So **B** is wrong, too. **A** refers to liquidated damages in the amount of $1 billion. Faced with that, a judge would laugh the plaintiff out of court. **A** is right.

With the court's refusal to enforce the liquidated damage provision, Adams would have to prove her actual damages, if any.

 # Silver's Picks

1.	B
2.	D
3.	D
4.	D
5.	C
6.	A

31

Closing Closers

Here are some final questions that will test your comprehension of the material covered in Chapters 1-30. Answers and explanations appear at the end, along with references to the chapter and section in which the tested material was taught.

Good luck!

QUESTION 1. Alicia says to Frank, "If you will offer me $100 to shovel the snow out of your driveway this morning, I promise that I will definitely accept. So, you need only make the offer and that will seal the deal." Frank replies, "I hereby offer you $100 to shovel the snow out of my driveway this morning." To his surprise, Alicia counters, "Well, I've changed my mind; I do not accept." If Frank insists that the parties have formed a contract, then his best argument is that

A. if at a first party's request a second party makes an offer, the first has no right then to reject it.
B. notwithstanding that Alicia purported to request an offer from Frank, Alicia herself made an offer that Frank accepted.
C. with their first two communications, Alicia and Frank formed an option contract.
D. one's promise to accept an offer needs no consideration to be binding.

QUESTION 2. George and Jacqueline are friends. On Monday, they meet by chance at a shopping mall. Jacqueline is accompanied by another of her friends whom George has never met; he has never heard of her and she has never heard of him. The friend's name happens also to be Jacqueline. When George encounters the two friends, he says, "Jacqueline, I've been meaning to call you, so I'm glad I've bumped into you. I need twelve illustrations for my next book and, of course, would like you to produce them. I'll need them by December 1, and I'll pay you $1,200. Will you do it?" George's friend Jacqueline does not immediately respond. Rather, the other Jacqueline immediately responds, "Yes, I'll do it." A few seconds later, George's friend Jacqueline says, "No, he means me, and yes, I'll do it." Has George formed a contract with the other Jacqueline?

A. Yes, because when one makes an offer in the presence of two persons, only one has power to accept it

B. Yes, because, by law, the offer went to both women, and the other Jacqueline was first to manifest assent

C. No, because the other Jacqueline knew or should have known that George did not know her *name*

D. No, because the other Jacqueline knew or should have known that George did not know *her*

QUESTION 3. In each of the following cases, Party B proposes a modification to her preexisting contract with Party A. In which case does Party A's silence most likely amount to an acceptance of Party B's proposal?

A. On February 1, Parties A and B form a contract under which B is to empty A's basement on March 1, and A is to pay B $200 when the job is done. On February 15, B sends A an email that reads, "As to our agreement that I empty your basement, I'd like to be paid $250 instead of the $200 on which we first agreed. I assume that you are agreeable." As of February 28, A makes no response.

B. On February 1, Parties A and B form a contract under which B is to empty A's basement on March 1, and A is to pay B $200 when the job is done. On February 15, B sends A an email that reads, "As to our agreement that I empty your basement, I'd like to do the work on March 10 instead of March 1." As of February 28, A makes no response.

C. Party A is a professional seller of used carpenter's tools. Party B is a carpenter. On February 1, A makes to B this offer: "I will sell you the used lathe that you saw in my garage for $300, delivered on March 1 to your home, 46 Shepherd Drive." B promptly responds, "Yes, I accept, but I will not be home on March 1. Please deliver to my next-door neighbor, 48 Shepherd Drive, instead. I will alert her and she'll be there to accept delivery." As of February 28, A makes no response.

D. On February 1, A makes to B this offer: "I will sell you the used lathe that you saw in my garage, delivered to your home, 46 Shepherd Drive, on March 1, for $300." B promptly responds, "Yes, I accept, but I will pay only $200." As of February 28, A makes no response.

QUESTION 4. By signed writing Randolph, an attorney, offers to sell his automobile to Endicott for $400. The writing is complete in all material respects and correctly recites the vehicle's identification number. By signed writing, Endicott responds immediately, "I'd like to think it over for four or five days." Randolph responds with another signed writing: "That's fine." Two days later, Endicott observes someone other than Randolph driving and parking what appears to be Randolph's automobile. After the driver parks the car and emerges, Endicott asks her, "Is this your car?" She responds, "Yes, I bought it yesterday." With the driver's permission, Endicott examines the vehicle's identification number and correctly concludes that the automobile is the same one Randolph has offered to sell him. Later that same day, Endicott reaches Randolph by telephone and says, "I accept your offer to sell me your car." Randolph responds, "I'm sorry, it's sold." Which of the following facts most clearly indicates that Randolph is not in breach of contract?

A. When Endicott attempted to accept Randolph's offer, Randolph no longer owned the vehicle he had offered to sell Endicott.
B. Before attempting to accept Randolph's offer, Endicott learned that Randolph had sold the vehicle to another party.
C. By the time Endicott attempted to accept Randolph's offer, it had expired by passage of time.
D. Randolph, in making his offer, did not expressly provide that it would be irrevocable.

QUESTION 5. Sandoff and Barlow reach an agreement, recorded in a signed writing that embodies twenty-five paragraphs. Paragraphs 1 to 19 describe the parties' promises and set forth a variety of additional terms and conditions. Paragraph 20 provides:

> The parties agree and understand that notwithstanding any other agreements, commitments, or terms hereinbefore set forth, Barlow is free at any time, for good cause, before or after either party begins performance to cancel, renounce, dishonor, and withdraw from all promises, agreements, terms, and commitments by which he is, herein, otherwise bound.

After the parties form their agreement, but before either begins to perform, Sandoff announces to Barlow that he will not honor it. Sandoff claims the right to dishonor the agreement on the ground that Barlow made only an illusory promise, wherefore he and Barlow formed no contract. Which of the following phrases from paragraph 20 most weakens Sandoff's position?

A. "for good cause"
B. "before or after"
C. "purportedly bound"
D. "notwithstanding any other"

QUESTION 6. Chadwick walks through the center of Tarleton City and, for three hours, shouts repeatedly, on and on: "To any person who gives me an Indian head nickel, I will pay $500 right now." After three hours, Sheila and Charise emerge from their two homes, each holding an Indian head nickel. Sheila reaches Chadwick first. She tenders to him her nickel. Chadwick takes it and pays Sheila $500. Charise then reaches Chadwick. She tenders her nickel, but Chadwick rejects it and refuses to pay her.

The matter goes to court, Charise claiming that Chadwick made an offer, that she accepted, wherefore Chadwick owed her $500. Which of the following changes to the facts would most strengthen Charise's claim?

A. Instead of proposing to pay $500 for the nickel, Chadwick had proposed to pay only $200.
B. Instead of shouting "To *any* person . . . ," Chadwick had shouted, "To *every* person . . . ."
C. Instead of dispatching his message by voice on the streets, Chadwick had dispatched it using written flyers left at all homes he passed.
D. Instead of shouting "anyone who *gives* me . . . ," Chadwick had shouted, "anyone who *in exchange gives* me."

QUESTION 7. Jones sends to Kirkwood an unsigned writing in which she states, "I am prepared to refurbish and rebuild your computer—the one we discussed—for $250, payable when I finish the work. Sign below on the line above your printed name, and we'll have a deal (unless I am unable to secure the parts I need for the job)." At the bottom of the writing are two blank lines above which is printed "Signatures." Below one of the blank lines Jones's name is printed and below the other, Kirkwood's name is printed. Kirkwood receives and reads the writing. On the space above his printed name, he signs. He then sends the writing back to Jones. Two days later, Jones receives it. She telephones Kirkwood and says, "I've received back my writing, signed by you, but I have decided not to sign it. We don't have a deal." Has Jones committed an anticipatory repudiation?

A. Yes, because Jones's unsigned writing constituted his offer, which Kirkwood accepted by signing his name and returning the writing to Jones

B. Yes, because Jones made an offer for a unilateral contract and Kirkwood, by signing the writing, began his performance, thus forming with Jones an option contract

C. No, because Jones's unsigned writing constituted only an invitation to deal, meaning that Kirkwood, by signing and returning the document, made not an acceptance but an offer

D. No, because the parenthetical clause in Jones's letter meant that her proposal failed to exact consideration from her

QUESTIONS 8 & 9. Lampert, a professional musician, says to Norberg, a manufacturer of computer motherboards, "I'm interested in buying your land, Blueacre." Norberg responds, "Well, you can have it for $3 million. That's my offer." "I'd like you to promise that you'll hold that offer open for four months so that I may consider it," replies Lampert.

QUESTION 8. The conversation continues: "Absolutely," says Norberg. "The offer is good for four months. I won't take it back." Lampert answers, "Great. Let's put it in writing." The parties then sign a writing that fully sets forth their names and addresses. It describes Blueacre in full legal detail, and provides that

> Norberg hereby offers to convey Blueacre to Lampert for $3 million, this offer not to be revoked or withdrawn for four months.

Is Norberg free, immediately, to advise Lampert that he will not sell him Blueacre and then sell it to some other buyer?

A. Yes, because the prescribed period of irrevocability exceeds three months

B. Yes, because the subject matter of the sale is not a computer motherboard

C. No, because the parties have effectively formed an option contract

D. No, because equity considers that all realty is unique and its owner cannot be compelled to part with it, even if he has contracted to do so

QUESTION 9. Now assume that the parties continue their conversation thus: "Okay," replies Norberg, "but you'll have to pay me $25,000 now for that privilege. Agree to that, and I won't take the offer back for four months." Lampert agrees, again saying, "Great. Let's put it in writing." The parties then sign a writing that fully sets forth their names and addresses. It describes Blueacre in full legal detail, and provides that

> In exchange for $25,000 to be paid by Lampert one month from the date hereof, Norberg hereby offers to convey Blueacre to Lampert for $3 million, this offer not to be revoked or withdrawn for four months.

Is Norberg free, immediately, to advise Lampert that he will not sell him Blueacre and then sell it to some other buyer?

A. Yes, because the prescribed period of irrevocability exceeds three months
B. Yes, because the subject matter of the sale is not a computer motherboard
C. No, because the parties have effectively formed an option contract
D. No, because equity considers that all realty is unique and its owner cannot be compelled to part with it, even if he has contracted to do so

QUESTIONS 10 & 11. On March 1, Janus and Kellman agree, orally, that Janus will replace all windows in Kellman's office building. Kellman is to buy and pay for the windows and all other necessary supplies. Janus is then to install the windows. He is to begin work on April 15 and finish by June 30. Kellman is to pay Janus $1.5 million for the entire job, in three installments: $500,000 on April 15, $500,000 on April 30, and $500,000 when the work is complete on June 30.

QUESTION 10. The parties also agree, as part of that same oral contract, that Janus will repaint all of the building's window sills. Having formed their contract orally, the parties create a writing that fully, exhaustively, and completely describes every detail concerning the way in which Janus is to replace the windows, the kind of windows and sealants he is to use, and the timing by which Kellman will pay him. The writing is silent as to the painting of any window sills, and its last paragraph provides:

> This writing represents the whole of the parties' agreement on this subject matter, wherefore in this regard, no other term on which they might have agreed, by whatever mode, means, or medium, is binding on them.

On April 1, each party has his own copy of the writing, but neither has signed it. By telephone, they speak:

> **Janus:** Well, I have my copy of the writing, and it's fine. Are we agreed—definitely—that this writing is our contract?
> **Kellman:** Yes, we're agreed—definitely—that this writing is our contract.
> **Janus:** Okay, then. Next time we meet we'll sign it. Right?
> **Kellman:** Right.
> **Janus:** So I'll begin work on April 15, and on April 15 you'll pay me $500,000.
> **Kellman:** Yes, that's what our contract requires.
> **Janus:** Very good.

Is Janus obliged to paint the window sills?

A. Probably, because the window sills are separate from the windows
B. Probably not, because the contract would otherwise be unconscionable
C. Probably not, because the writing is most likely a total integration of their agreement
D. Probably not, because neither party signed the writing

QUESTION 11. Now assume that with the oral contract Janus warrants that the windows, as installed by him, will remain free of leaks for ten years. That provision the parties do include in their writing, although as noted in Question 10, they do not include in the writing any term as to the repainting of the window sills. The parties then conduct the same conversation described in Question 10. As of April 15, after the parties have their conversation, have they formed an enforceable contract?

A. Yes, because the parties adopted the writing as a total integration
B. Yes, because the writing specifically includes the warranty term
C. No, because neither party signed the writing
D. No, because the writing is probably a total integration of their agreement

QUESTION 12. On July 1, Buyer calls Seller to say, "I may need some widgets on September 1—3,000 of them. If I decide that I do need them, will you be able specially to manufacture them for me?" Seller replies, "I'm not sure. Let me find out and get back to you." The next day, Seller sends Buyer this signed writing labeled "sales confirmation":

> Regarding our conversation of yesterday: Yes, I'll be able to specially manufacture the widgets—3,000 of them for delivery to you on September 1.

Seller then begins work and tenders 3,000 widgets to Buyer on September 1. Buyer refuses to accept or pay for them. Is Buyer in breach of contract?

A. Yes, because Seller's July 2 writing removed the contract from the Statute of Frauds
B. Yes, because Seller's special manufacture of the goods removed the contract from the Statute of Frauds
C. No, because the parties did not agree on price
D. No, because the parties did not form a contract

QUESTION 13. After attending his cousin's wedding reception, Andrews, fifty years old, with $2,000 to his name—all of it sitting in his pocket as cash—is so wholly inebriated as not to understand his own actions or the results they might produce. Notwithstanding his state of intoxication, he appears to ordinary persons to be sober. In that condition, he enters the Black Bear Smoke Shoppe and there sees for sale a box of ten cigars with a $2,000 price tag, "all taxes included." Black Bear Smoke Shoppe had bought the box of cigars for $1,000. Andrews takes the box to the cashier, who is a stranger, and states that he wishes to purchase it. He then puts on the cashier's counter $2,000 pulled from his pocket. The cashier processes the purchase and hands Andrews the box of cigars. Andrews leaves the store and promptly chain-smokes all ten cigars. On the following day, Andrews returns to the store. He tenders back the cigar box empty of cigars and asks to have back his $2,000. He is entitled to have back

A. nothing, because he smoked all of the cigars.
B. nothing, because his inebriation was not obvious to a reasonable person in the cashier's position.
C. $1,000, the difference between $2,000 paid by Andrews and $1,000 paid by Black Bear Smoke Shoppe to its supplier.
D. $2,000, all of the money he paid for the cigars.

QUESTION 14. Bruce, fourteen years old, enters ElectroniMart, a retail electronics store, and for $300 purchases a device called HiPod. Before the day is out, Bruce decides to sell the HiPod for $250, which he does, then spending the $250 on spray paint, all of which he uses to write graffiti on his high school's exterior walls. Bruce then demands from ElectroniMart a return of his $300, offering the store nothing back in exchange. Is ElectroniMart obliged to return the $300?

A. Yes, because it is in the business of selling electronic equipment at retail
B. Yes, because Bruce is empowered to disaffirm the contract and retains no value related to the HiPod
C. No, because Bruce's use of the spray paint probably violates public policy
D. No, because Bruce voluntarily disposed of the HiPod for money, and knowingly spent the proceeds on another commodity

---

QUESTION 15. Marjorie and Dahlia are nineteen-year-old girls, both of them competent (but stupid). They decide to play their own version of the game called chicken, using trains instead of automobiles. Each girl is to take a turn standing on the local railroad tracks as a train approaches her. She who allows the moving train to come closest to her before jumping off the tracks wins the game. The loser (if she does not lie flattened on the tracks) is to pay the winner $1,000.

After agreeing by offer and acceptance to play the game according to those rules, Marjorie takes the first turn on the tracks. She allows the train to come within thirty feet of her body and jumps from the tracks. Dahlia takes her turn and allows a train to come within twenty-five feet of her body. As winner, Dahlia demands that Marjorie pay her $1,000. Is Marjorie obliged to pay?

A. Yes, because the parties are competent adults, generally free to form their contracts as they wish
B. Yes, because each party's conditional promise to pay $1,000 to the other makes for mutuality of consideration
C. Yes, because neither Dahlia nor Marjorie suffered any harm or injury
D. No, because Dahlia's participation in the contract violates public policy

---

QUESTION 16. By signed written contract, Sanford employs Bella to serve as a pharmacist for one year in Sanford's pharmacy. The agreed compensation is $9,400 per month, payable monthly with ordinary income and payroll taxes to be deducted, thus leaving a monthly take-home amount of about $6,100. Bella begins work, and at the end of the first month, Sanford pays Bella $6,100 (properly withholding and crediting the unpaid amounts). He says, however, that he is dissatisfied with her work. He offers to pay her an additional $9,400 in full if she gives up her employment with him. Bella refuses. Nonetheless, Sanford sends Bella a $9,400 check with a signed note that reads: "I tender this check as per our earlier conversation regarding your employment with me." Bella deposits the check.

On the following day, Bella reports for work at the pharmacy and says to Sanford, "I thank you for the additional check. I will consider it an advance on the salary due me at the end of this month." Sanford responds, "You no longer work here; by agreement, you have given up your employment." Bella brings suit against Sanford for breach of an employment contract. As a defense, Sanford asserts accord and satisfaction. Bella moves to dismiss the defense. Which of the following additional facts, if proven, would most strengthen Bella's position?

A. Sanford's check "bounced"; it did not clear his bank.
B. By depositing Sanford's check, Bella did not genuinely intend to accept Sanford's proposal that she give up her employment.
C. Bella's job performance, although not satisfactory to Sanford, was adequate under ordinary standards prevailing among pharmacists.
D. Bella was reasonably relying on the $9,400 monthly salary to meet commitments she had made before accepting employment with Sanford.

QUESTION 17. At the trial of a suit by Seller against Buyer for alleged breach of a contract for the purchase and sale of Torto Lift Springs, undisputed evidence tended to show:

1. On many occasions during each of the years 2008 through 2013, Buyer ordered Torto Lift Springs from Seller, whereupon Seller, on each such occasion, delivered the goods together with a billing statement showing a "catalog list price" and "billing price" of $1,500 per unit. On each such occasion, Buyer paid the $1,500 per unit, and Seller accepted that amount as full payment.
2. During the years 2014 to 2018, Buyer made no purchases from Seller.
3. On January 1, 2019, Buyer issued to Seller a signed, written purchase order requesting "prompt shipment of 200 Torto Lift Springs; appropriately priced." On January 2, Seller confirmed the order in a signed writing that did not mention price, and then immediately shipped and delivered 200 such units together with a billing statement showing a "catalog list price" and "billing price" of $2,500 per unit. The total bill was $500,000 ($2,500 × 200).
4. On January 2, 2019, Seller's catalog list price for the Torto Lift Springs was, in fact, $2,500 per unit.
5. The average price actually billed for Torto Lift Springs by suppliers other than Seller within 100 miles of Buyer's facility during the

preceding twelve months was $1,900 per unit, although the average *catalog* price for such other suppliers was $2,550.

6. When the goods arrived at Buyer's premises, Buyer examined the billing statement, whereupon she rejected the goods and refused to pay for them, advising Seller that the price was "too high."

In Seller's suit against Buyer, which of the following phrases would least likely appear in the court's charge to the jury?

A. "course of dealing"
B. "prevailing market price"
C. "course of performance"
D. "reasonable price"

QUESTIONS 18-20. On June 1, Georgia Morales receives by mail from Universal Insurance Co. a document entitled "Offer of Life Insurance." Although Georgia has had no previous contact with the company, the "offer" correctly states her name and age. Under its title, the document reads:

> We are pleased to offer you a $2 million life insurance policy. Should you die within the next 20 years, Universal Insurance will pay $2 million to the beneficiary you name. If you wish to accept, complete the health questionnaire that appears on the next page and, in the indicated space, provide the name, address, and social security number of the person whom you wish to receive the benefit under your policy. Send the completed form back to us at the address shown above. Our approval and premium/cost will depend on our evaluation of your responses.

Georgia completes the health questionnaire, reporting the truth as she knows it. Asked if she has ever had any disease of the brain or blood vessels, she answers "no." As beneficiary, she names her daughter Angela Morales, providing Angela's name, address, and social security number. On June 2, Georgia mails the completed form back to Universal Insurance. On June 15, she receives from Universal a second mailing entitled "Insurance Approval." It states:

> Based on your responses to our health questionnaire, we are pleased to advise you that a $2 million insurance policy is available to you, for 20 years, at a cost of $300 per month. The initial beneficiary will be Angela Morales subject to change at any time, if and as you wish. You need only sign and send back

to us the enclosed purchase form in the enclosed envelope, together with a check or money order in the amount of $300.00 for your first month's premium, payable to Universal Life Insurance Co.

The "purchase form" states only this: "I wish to purchase Universal life insurance, as described to me." Georgia signs the form and, together with her $300 check payable to Universal, puts it in the designated envelope. She deposits the envelope in the U.S. mail on June 16.

Although Georgia does not know it, and has no reason to know it, she has been born with a cerebral aneurysm. On June 17, the aneurysm ruptures and she instantly dies. On June 18, Universal receives the mailing she had dispatched on June 16. On that same day, Universal learns of Georgia's death and refrains from depositing her check. It writes to her daughter Angela:

Your mother, Georgia Morales, applied with this office for a life insurance policy naming you as beneficiary. We learned today of her death, and we express our sympathies. We presently hold, undeposited, the check that she tendered to us as her first premium payment. Please provide us with the name and address of the party handling her estate, and we will return the check to him or her.

Angela visits an attorney who, on her behalf, brings an action against Universal, demanding judgment in the amount of $2 million. At trial, undisputed evidence establishes all of the facts described above. Universal argues that it owes nothing to Angela because it never formed a contract with Georgia and, even if it had, (a) it never formed a contract with Angela, and (b) it was freed from its obligations under any such contract on the ground of mutual mistake. As to mutual mistake, Universal observes that when it interacted with Georgia, (1) the cerebral aneurysm was in place, (2) neither Georgia nor Universal knew of it, (3) neither party was at fault for failing to know of it, and (4) Georgia's responses on the health questionnaire were basic assumptions on which the parties had dealt.

QUESTION 18. Did Georgia and Universal form a contract?

A. Yes, when Georgia dispatched her mailing of June 2
B. Yes, when Georgia dispatched her mailing of June 16
C. No, because Universal did not deposit Georgia's check
D. No, because $300 is inadequate to constitute consideration for a promise to pay $2 million

---

QUESTION 19. If Universal and Georgia did form a contract, is Universal entitled to avoid it on the basis of mutual mistake?

A. Yes, because from June 1 to June 16, both parties were justifiably ignorant of the cerebral aneurysm
B. Yes, because as between the two parties, Georgia was in the better position to discover that she had a cerebral aneurysm
C. No, because each party to the transaction deliberately undertook risk
D. No, because Universal did not insist that Georgia undergo a medical examination

---

QUESTION 20. If Universal did form a contract with Georgia and is unable successfully to assert mutual mistake as a defense, does it owe $2 million to Angela?

A. Yes, because both parties should have understood that Georgia wished Angela to benefit from the contract
B. Yes, because Georgia, in effect, assigned her contractual rights to Angela
C. No, because Angela is an incidental third-party beneficiary
D. No, because Angela fails to constitute a creditor beneficiary

---

 Silver's Picks

Question 1.   From Chapter 2, section B, you know that one makes an offer when, to some other person, she proposes an arrangement in such a way as would lead the other reasonably to believe that a definite bargain is proposed to him, that he is invited to assent to it, and that if he does, he will finalize the bargain. You know also that one may make an offer without using the *word* "offer" (Chapter 2, section B). Here, Alicia purported to *solicit* an "offer" of specified terms and promised absolutely that she would accept it; she promised that Frank's "offer" would "seal the deal." Alicia thus *made* an offer (even though she purportedly invited Frank to make one). She invited Frank to assent by *purporting* to make an offer. When, in response, Frank purported to make the offer, he assented to the bargain that Alicia had proposed, and therefore issued an acceptance (even though he termed it an "offer"). That these parties turned upside down the *words* "offer" and "acceptance" matters not. Alicia made an offer and Frank accepted it. **B** is right.

Question 2.   In Chapter 2, section D, you learned that we identify an offeree according to reasonable beliefs: With respect to any offer, an offeree is any person who, under the circumstances, reasonably believes that the offeror has made his proposal to *her* and that *she* is invited to assent to it.

Under these circumstances, the other Jacqueline could not reasonably believe that George intended to make his proposal to her. She knew (or certainly should have known) that George did not know her and would not say, to her, "I've been meaning to call you, so I'm glad I've bumped into you." Hence, she should have known that George was not addressing her. **D** reflects that reasoning, and it's the right answer.

What's wrong with **C**? It tells us that the other Jacqueline was not the offeree because she should have known that George was unfamiliar with her *name*. That's not quite right, and here's how we prove it: Suppose that when the three parties met, George's friend Jacqueline had said, "George, I want you to meet my friend, whose name happens also to be Jacqueline." At that point, the other Jacqueline would have reason to think that George now knew her name. Yet, that would not change our answer from "no" to "yes." When George said, "I've been meaning to call you, so I'm glad I've bumped into you," this lady should know, still, that George was not addressing her, because even having learned her name, he did not know *her*. In concluding that this lady was not an offeree, our critical observation is not George's unfamiliarity with her *name*, but his unfamiliarity with *her*. Hence, **D** is right.

Question 3.   In Chapter 14, section B (and elsewhere), you learned that by common law if two parties first form a contract, they may effectively modify it only if, in doing so, each provides consideration to the other. But you also learned that UCC §2-209(1) departs significantly from that rule when the contract involves the sale of goods, by stating: "An agreement modifying a contract within this article needs no consideration to be binding." Further, UCC §2-207(1) and (2) govern "expressions of acceptance," contract modifications, and a merchant party's silence as assent (Chapter 11, sections B, C, and D).

In **A**, Party B proposes to modify an existing contract without providing that he will give consideration to A. Even if A had overtly purported to accept, the attempted modification would be ineffective. That alone means **A** is wrong. **B** and **D** are wrong for the same reason. In **C**, Party A makes an offer and Party B responds with an "expression of acceptance," thus (1) forming a contract on A's terms and, at the same time, (2) proposing to modify that very contract as to the place of delivery. Note now that (a) both parties are merchants, (b) the proposed change is immaterial, (c) Party A, in his offer, did not object to any change in terms, and (d) after receiving B's response, Party A remained silent for a full four weeks. Hence, Party B's proposed change as to place of delivery likely becomes part of the contract; A's silence acts as his acceptance. (And although the UCC allows two parties to modify an existing contract irrespective of consideration, this particular modification did exact consideration from both parties. B released A from the obligation to deliver to B's home, and A, in exchange, took on a new obligation: to deliver at the next-door neighbor's home.) **C is right.**

Question 4. In Chapter 6, section C, you learned that an offeror may dictate the time at which his offer expires. If he doesn't do that, it expires at such time as is reasonable under the circumstances. On learning that Endicott wished to ponder the offer for several days, Randolph responded, "That's fine." Randolph thus restated his offer (implicitly) and provided that, for at least five days, it would not expire. Two days later, therefore, it had not expired by passage of time. **C is wrong.**

It's true that Randolph offered to sell a good, and that UCC Article 2 applies generally to the transaction. But Randolph is an attorney; for this transaction, he's not a merchant. Consequently, the Article 2 "firm offer" provision (Chapter 11, section A) does not apply to him as to this offer. Even if Randolph's signed, written offer had proclaimed itself irrevocable (with or without stating an associated time period), it *would* be revocable. Hence, **D** is wrong. **A** too is wrong, and here's why: Revocation is effective only when communicated to the offeree (Chapter 8, section A). If one offers to sell a good to one party and then sells it to another (or otherwise loses ownership), he does not, with that alone, communicate revocation to his original offeree. Yet, as you learned in Chapter 8, section C, effective revocation requires no *direct* communication from offeror to offeree. If an offeree learns not from the offeror but from some other source that the offeror cannot or will not stand by her offer, then the offer is effectively revoked. That's what happened here, and **B** properly attributes revocation to that fact. **B is right.**

Question 5. In Chapter 14, section D, you learned that if one purports to make a promise but then by some attached term reserves the right to dishonor it unconditionally, for any reason or no reason, then he makes an "illusory promise," meaning no promise at all. One party who, with respect to a purported contract, makes to the other only an illusory promise gives no consideration, and the two parties fail to form a contract.

Here, however, Barlow does not quite reserve for himself the right to dishonor his promise at his own unbridled whim. Rather, he reserves the right to do so for "good cause." Although the agreement may nowhere define that phrase, those two words do refer to some objective standard that sits apart from Barlow's own unfettered fancy. Hence, a court will take it on itself to decide how two reasonable parties should understand the phrase "good cause" — that it means, perhaps, grave illness, unforeseen weather conditions, family emergency, or the like. Of all phrases listed in answer choices **A** through **D**, only "good cause" arguably means that Barlow's promises (whatever they be) are genuine and not illusory ones. That's why **A is right.**

Question 6.   In Chapter 5, section A, you learned that an ordinary advertisement is a mere invitation to deal, but an advertisement that is extraordinarily specific as to available quantity and/or the person(s) addressed is an offer.

The fact that Chadwick shouts his message personally on the streets tends to make the message more personal than would be a printed advertisement. Hence, **C** is wrong. Chadwick's message clearly contemplates an exchange and adding the *word* "exchange" would make no significant difference. Hence, **D** is wrong. The price that Chadwick proposed to pay is wholly irrelevant to the question of whether he made an offer and, if so, how many persons became offerees. Hence, **A** is wrong.

If Chadwick's message is an offer, then the words "every person" make relatively plain that he directs it at all persons who hear him. The words "any person" arguably mean that he contemplates paying for only one nickel. Pursuant to that argument (a decent one), all who heard Chadwick shouting his message should have understood him to mean that he would pay $500 only to the *first person* who tendered an Indian head nickel. Hence, **B** is right.

Question 7.   In Chapter 5, section C, you learned that *ordinarily* a proposal or "draft contract" that bears a marked space for the proposor's signature is (a) an offer if the proposor has signed, and (b) a "mere" invitation to deal if she has not. But "ordinarily" doesn't mean "always." If she who sends the unsigned proposal makes abundantly clear that she intends it to constitute a definite proposal for a bargain that awaits only the recipient's assent, then the unsigned proposal *is* an offer. The recipient has power to accept it.

B and **D** are wrong. Jones did not demand that Kirkwood manifest his assent by actually making the $250 payment. Hence, she did not make an offer for a unilateral contract (Chapter 9, sections C and D). Jones's parenthetical remark did not create an illusory promise (Chapter 14, section D). Rather, it subjected her commitment to a condition subsequent (Chapter 21, section A).

If Jones had sent this same unsigned writing without its last sentence, then certainly the writing would have constituted only an invitation to deal. By signing the document and returning it to Jones, Kirkwood would make an offer that Jones might accept or not. And in that case, **C** would be right. By including in her message that last sentence, however, Jones made abundantly clear that she intended it to constitute a definite proposal for a bargain. For that reason, **A** is right.

Question 8.   Generally, the common law provides that one who makes an offer may revoke at any time before the offeree accepts. That's so even when he promises not to do so (Chapter 6, section A). Yet, two parties may form an "option contract," which is a contract in and of itself, requiring offer, acceptance, and consideration from both its parties. More specifically, an option contract is a contract in which one party, *for consideration*, agrees to hold an offer open and irrevocable for some stated period (Chapter 6, section C).

These parties have formed no such thing because Lampert gave no consideration for Norberg's promise to hold his offer open. **C** is wrong. As for **D**, it's true that equity regards all realty as unique (Appendix, section E and Chapter 30, section B). That means, only, that when one breaches his contract to sell realty, the buyer might obtain the remedy of specific performance, compelling the seller to convey the realty. Hence, **D** is wrong.

UCC Article 2 provides that if a merchant who by signed writing makes an offer to buy or sell goods and proclaims it irrevocable, the offer *is* irrevocable for any time stated or, if none is stated, for a reasonable time, but in no case for more than three months. This transaction involves the sale not of goods but of realty. Hence, that rule does not apply in any respect. Whether Norberg had specified a time period of three seconds or three hundred years, he would be entitled, immediately, to revoke his offer. (Furthermore, where the Code's "firm offer" rule does apply, an offeror who proclaims his offer irrevocable for four months creates an offer that's irrevocable for *three* months (Chapter 11, section A).) **A** is wrong.

As to motherboards, Norberg is a merchant (Chapter 11, section A). If this signed written offer had pertained to a motherboard, then the Code's "firm offer" rule would apply, and the offer would be irrevocable for three months, not four. Reciprocally, we may say that because the transaction does *not* involve motherboards, Lampert is free immediately to revoke his offer. So, **B** is right.

Question 9.   Question 9 differs from Question 8 in that Norberg promised to *pay* Lampert for the option to accept his offer at any time during a four-month period. These parties thus formed an option contract, and for four months Norberg (the optionor) must remain ready, willing, and able to sell Blueacre to Lampert (the optionee). That's why he is not "free, immediately, to advise Lampert that he will not sell him Blueacre and then sell it to some other buyer." **A**, **B**, and **D** are wrong; **C** is right.

Question 10.   In order that a contractual writing should constitute an integration, the two contracting parties must "adopt" it as an expression of their agreement. Ordinarily, they manifest the adoption by signing, but they need not do it that way. These two parties formed an agreement orally and then reduced it to a writing, which via their conversation, they plainly adopted as a final expression of their contract—even though they did not sign it (Chapter 19, section C, footnote 3). This writing is probably a total integration since it shows finality as to all matters ordinarily necessary to a contract for replacement of windows and, furthermore, features a merger clause (Chapter 19, sections F and G). Consequently, the parol evidence rule renders unenforceable the prior oral agreement as to the window sills. The exception concerning a "collateral agreement" (Chapter 19, section I) is inapplicable here because the oral agreement as to the window sills, we are told, was part of the same oral contract. Hence, **C** is right.

Question 11. In Chapter 15, section A, you learned that the Statute of Frauds applies to all contracts that, in their nature, cannot be fully performed within one year. A contract wherein one warranties his work for ten years cannot complete his performance in one. Until the ten years pass, his performance is not complete. Hence, this contract falls within the Statute of Frauds, which requires that the contract be set forth in a writing, *signed* by any party against whom it is to be enforced. Neither party signed the writing, wherefore, after these parties form their contract and adopt the writing, it is unenforceable under the Statute of Frauds, precisely because they did not *sign* it. **C** is right.

Question 12. The rule given in Chapter 11, section F, concerning UCC §2-207 and the written confirmation, has no bearing on this case. The parties' conversation reveals that they never formed a contract. Seller's "sales confirmation" was in fact an offer, nothing more, and Buyer never accepted it. Seller moved ahead as though he and Buyer had created a contract, but that was his mistake, and the result his problem. Furthermore, because the parties never formed a contract, any matter bearing on the Statute of Frauds or on "gap filling" are similarly irrelevant to the problem. Hence, **A**, **B**, and **C** are wrong. **D** is right.

Question 13. Chapter 16, section C, teaches that when a competent adult forms a contract with an adult who is so mentally impaired as not to appreciate the nature or consequences of his actions, the contract is voidable at the option of the incompetent adult, *whether or not the impairment was objectively apparent*. If the impaired adult elects to rescind the contract, he must, generally, make restitution in full for *all* money or property he has received from the competent party. As is not so for a minor,[1] the amount to be repaid includes the value of any service he received and the value that any property given him has lost by damage, deterioration, consumption, ordinary use, wear, or tear. The competent party must, of course, make corresponding restitution for any value he received from the incompetent one.

Black Bear Smoke Shoppe must return $2,000 to Andrews. Andrews must return to Black Bear Smoke Shoppe (a) the empty cigar box, and (b) the $1,000 in value he turned to smoke. In net terms, therefore, Black Bear Smoke Shoppe must pay Andrews $1,000. With the remaining $1,000 that Andrews paid it, the smoke shop can buy a box of cigars to replace the ones Andrews smoked. Andrews has back $1,000 of the $2,000 he paid the smoke shop and has reimbursed the shop for the value he consumed. **C** is right.

Question 14. By contract Bruce, a minor, bought a good from ElectroniMart. According to the rule given in Chapter 16, section B, Bruce may disaffirm the contract, whereby he rescinds it. That leaves ElectroniMart with unjust enrichment in the amount of $300. It must return that amount to Bruce. Having

---

1. Chapter 16, section B.

sold the HiPod, thereafter spending the proceeds of that sale, Bruce no longer retained any value that came to him via the contract, and a minor (unlike the competent adult of Question 13) need not restore to a competent adult any value except that which he retains at the time he rescinds. Hence, he need return nothing to ElectroniMart. Like it or not, **B** is right.

Question 15.   In Chapter 17, section A, you learned that an "illegal contract" is one that violates public policy, which almost certainly includes a monetary bet in which each party seriously risks her life. And when a party alleges breach of an illegal contract, she does not recover if public policy is offended by her own performance under the contract or by her wish to induce the other to give a performance that violates public policy (Chapter 17, section B).

Here, each party's participation violates public policy: Each risks her life to win a $1,000 bet, and induces the other to do the same. To the left of the word "because," A and B say "yes," so **A** and **B** are wrong. To the right of the word "because," they make irrelevant statements that happen to be true. (As to choice **B**, see Chapter 14, section A.) **C** is ridiculous; a violation of public policy does not require injury of any kind, to anyone, so **C** is wrong. Dahlia wants to enforce a contract as to which her own performance contravened public policy. That's why **D** is right. (Also right would be this: "No, because Dahlia induced Marjorie to risk her life for no good purpose.")

Question 16.   In Chapter 14, section C, you read about "accord and satisfaction" as a defense to an action for breach of contract. It often happens that (1) two parties form a contract, (2) one of them plausibly alleges that the other breached, (3) the other acknowledges (or, more often, denies) that she has breached, and (4) the parties agree to settle their dispute by revising their contract in some way that provides consideration to both. In that situation, the revised agreement is an "executory accord."

Very often, a first party proposes an accord to a second by tendering a check for some amount below an agreed contract price, offering it in final settlement of a dispute as to the second party's alleged breach. By sending such a check, with notice or prior notice that it is offered in settlement as to a *good faith* allegation of breach, the sender offers to make an executory accord. If the recipient deposits the check, she accepts that offer and the parties form the accord. If, however, the sender's check then "bounces," the sender fails to satisfy the accord. In that case, the defense of accord and satisfaction is unavailable to him.

Here, Sanford said he was dissatisfied with Bella's work. If his dissatisfaction arose through some *good faith* belief that Bella was in breach of her contract, then his statements to her, together with his check and accompanying message, made an offer of accord. By depositing the check, Bella accepted the offer (of an accord), thus forming an executory accord. But if Sanford's check were then to bounce, Sanford would fail to give satisfaction (fail to honor his obligations under the accord). Bella would then be free to sue Sanford for breach of the accord or the original contract. In either case, Sanford would lose any possible defense of accord and satisfaction. That's why **A** is right.

Question 17. Since this case concerns the sale of goods, the relevant provisions are those of UCC Article 2 (which on this point are substantially identical to those of the common law). As explained in Chapter 18, section C, according to UCC §2-208(1), "course of dealing" refers to the meanings and interpretations that evolve between two particular parties over the contracts they form with one another over time. "Course of performance" applies only to one contract that calls for *multiple occasions of performance*. It refers to the meanings and interpretation on which the parties, by behavior and silence, appear to agree as they give performance of that one particular contract.

This contract does not call for multiple occasions of performance and so the phrase "course of performance" has no relevance. For that reason, **C** is right.

Question 18. Look for an offer and acceptance. Universal named its first communication "offer" but proposed no bargain; it did not describe what Georgia was to pay in exchange for the $2 million insurance coverage. Rather, it indicated that cost/premium were not yet identified, and further stated that Universal had not yet "approved" the arrangement. As a reasonable person, Georgia could not believe that a definite bargain had been proposed to her. Universal's first communication was a mere invitation to deal, meaning that Georgia's June 2 response was not an acceptance. **A** is wrong.

Universal's June 15 communication proposed that Georgia pay $300 per month for twenty years, in exchange for Universal's promise to pay, if Georgia should die during that period, $2 million to Angela or any other beneficiary whom Georgia might someday name in her stead. Universal thus made an offer. Universal specified the manner by which Georgia might accept (although it did not use the *word* "accept"). She was to sign a paper and send a $300 check. Georgia manifested her assent exactly as Universal requested, and her acceptance was effective on June 16 when she dispatched it (Chapter 8, section A).

That Universal did not deposit her check is irrelevant (in *this* case). **C** is wrong. As for **D**: If Georgia truly agreed to pay $300 per month in exchange for an absolute promise of $2 million, the arrangement might fail to exact consideration from Georgia (Chapter 12, section C). But that didn't happen. Universal promised to pay $2 million subject to the condition precedent that Georgia die (Chapter 21, section A). **D** is wrong, and **B** is right.

Question 19. We interpret contracts according to each party's manifestation of intent—according to the understandings that each party should reasonably attribute to the other (Chapter 18, section A). In Chapter 22, sections A and B, you learned that mutual mistake applies only if two parties form a contract, each manifesting to the other a belief—to the point of fact or basic assumption — that some fact is or is not so. If, on the other hand, two parties form a contract that, properly interpreted, allocates to one or both the risk that some fact is or is not so, then as to that fact, each party takes his chances.

Insurance of any kind is, perhaps, the quintessential contract in which each party leads the other to understand that she knowingly, deliberately, takes on a risk. Any insurer that sells a homeowner's fire insurance policy should understand that the purchaser/insured intends to take the risk that her home will *not* burn and that, in the end, she will have paid insurance premiums without recovering a monetary benefit. The purchaser should reasonably understand that the insurance company takes on the risk that the future is unpredictable and that the home *will* burn. The same applies, of course, to life insurance. Georgia and Universal formed a contract in which each deliberately took a risk as to unknown circumstances, present and future. Georgia took the risk that she might live beyond twenty years and have nothing to show for the $72,000 she will have paid Universal. Universal took the risk that Georgia might die in ten years, one year, one week, or one minute after making her first premium payment. Universal has no defense in mutual mistake. **C** is right.

Question 20.   One assigns her contractual right by manifesting her intention presently to transfer her own existing right to another (Chapter 24, section B). As Universal's offer and hence the resulting contract provide: "The initial beneficiary will be Angela Morales subject to change at any time, if and as you wish." It is Georgia's right, if she should die within the twenty-year period, to have Universal pay $2 million to Angela or to any other person she might later select. Georgia did not transfer *that* right to Angela. **B** is wrong.

One who stands as a third-party beneficiary to a contract formed between two others may sustain an action for breach as to a benefit of which she is deprived (a) if she is an *intended* beneficiary, but (b) *not* if she is a mere *incidental* beneficiary (Chapter 24, section A). Universal knew or should have known that Georgia intended her named beneficiary (Angela, at present) to benefit from this insurance contract. Accordingly, Georgia was reasonable in believing that Universal did know that. Consequently, as to this contract, Angela is an intended third-party beneficiary. **C** is wrong. It's true that Angela is not a creditor beneficiary (Chapter 24, section A), but that doesn't negate her status as *intended* beneficiary. **D** is wrong, and **A** is right.

Appendix: All About Law

A. What *Is* Law, and Who Makes It?

Law is our government's decree as to how we should behave. To the extent that our government is of, by, and for the people, law is our own collective code of right and wrong. For "unlawful" (wrongful) behavior, the government holds us "liable" (responsible). Depending on whether one's unlawful behavior constitutes a civil or criminal wrong, it imposes (a) civil liability or (b) criminal liability.

1. Civil Liability: "Actionable Conduct," "Cause of Action"

Suppose Party P complains to her lawyer, "Party D's cat scratched me." Then she asks, "Can I sue?" In legal terms she means, really: *Has D committed the sort of unlawful behavior that makes him civilly liable for the harm he has caused me?* Stated in more lawyerly form, she means: *Does D's behavior afford me a civil cause of action against him?* Stated in shorter lawyerly form, she means: *Has D committed against me an actionable wrong?*

"Civil cause of action" and "actionable wrong" refer to behavior by one party for which the law affords another the right to sustain a civil action — a lawsuit — and, on proving both the truth of her allegations and the harm caused her — to recover compensation, usually in the form of money (as fully discussed in Chapters 25 through 30).

Most actionable wrongs are called "torts" (from the French noun of the same spelling, which means "wrong").[1] Your first-year law school curriculum will likely include a course called torts, in which you'll study a variety of actionable wrongs ("torts"), including assault, battery, conversion, trespass, defamation, nuisance, negligence, and professional malpractice.

---

1. That, in turn, derives from the Latin word "tortus" which means "twisted."

QUESTION 1. Danielle allows her dog to run free around her community. The dog makes its way into Peter's yard and scratches him. In letting her dog run free so that it scratches Peter, Danielle commits a tort against Peter. That means that

I. Peter has a cause of action against Danielle.
II. Peter has a basis on which to sustain a lawsuit against Danielle.
III. if Peter proves his allegations and his damage, Danielle must compensate him.
IV. Danielle has committed against Peter an actionable wrong.
A. I
B. II
C. I, II, and III
D. I, II, III, and IV

ANALYSIS. To say that Danielle commits a tort against Peter is to make all four of these statements, each roughly equivalent to every other. Hence, I, II, III, and IV make true statements. **D** is right.

2. *Criminal Liability*

One is *criminally liable* when she commits conduct that the government identifies as a crime. Generally, then, the phrase "criminal liability" means "subject to governmental punishment for the commission of a crime."[2]

For most crimes, the law recognizes corresponding torts (although the inverse is not true; most torts do not carry corresponding crimes). One who commits the crime of robbery or larceny also commits the tort of "conversion." For the robbery or larceny, the government prosecutes. For the conversion, the victim may sustain an action in conversion, demanding judgment in the amount of the stolen property's value. One who commits the crime of murder also commits the tort called "wrongful death." For the murder, the government prosecutes. For the wrongful death, the decedent's estate and survivors have an actionable wrong for which they may recover monies. In every state, a driver who operates a motor vehicle while intoxicated commits a crime. For that the government may prosecute and, if it prevails at trial, punish him. If by driving while intoxicated the driver injures someone, then that injured party has a civil cause of action against the driver for the tort of negligence. If by driving while intoxicated the driver *kills* another, he commits homicide for which the state

---

2. To their most serious crimes, most jurisdictions give the name "felony," and to the (relatively) less serious ones the name "misdemeanor." "Felony" usually means a crime that is punishable by one year or more in prison, and "misdemeanor" a crime punishable by less than one year in prison (or by no imprisonment at all). Lesser offenses called "infractions" or "violations" are punishable by fine or community service, but strictly speaking, they do not qualify as "crimes."

may prosecute and, if it prevails, punish him. The deceased's survivors have against him the civil action of wrongful death.

QUESTION 2. Victoria's bicycle is worth $200. Daryl steals it, and for that behavior the state charges him with the crime of larceny. After trial, Daryl is convicted and sentenced to pay a fine of $3,000. Does Victoria receive that $3,000?

A. Yes, because she is the victim of Daryl's crime
B. Yes, because the purpose of the criminal law is to compensate victims of tortious conduct
C. No, because the bicycle's value was less than $3,000
D. No, but Victoria may sustain against Daryl a civil action to recover $200

ANALYSIS.   Criminal law does not compensate victims of wrongful behavior. Rather, it visits punishment on those who commit crimes. Daryl pays his $3,000 fine to the state, and the state keeps it. Hence, **A** and **B** are wrong. **C** correctly says "no," but its reasoning is wrong. If the bicycle were worth 2 cents or $2 million, then, still, Daryl would pay his $3,000 fine to the state, and the state would keep it. **D** correctly states that separate from the criminal charge and conviction, Victoria has a civil cause of action against Daryl. As noted above, it's an action in conversion. Via that action, she will recover from Daryl the $200 value of the bicycle. **D** is right.

3. *All Law, Civil and Criminal, State or Federal, Comes from Government — from One of Its Three Branches — Legislative, Executive, or Judicial*

Every person (other than a foreign diplomat) who is physically present within the United States is subject to the laws of the United States government ("federal law"), and, separately, to those of the state in which he is physically present at any given moment.[3] The civil and criminal law of the United States government, "federal law," generally arises from the U.S. Congress through its enactment of "statutes" (which nonlawyers usually call "laws"). Congress derives its existence and its authority to make law from the U.S. Constitution's Article I.[4] In addition to the statutes through which it creates substantive provisions of law, Congress

---

3.   One might be present in the United States, but not within one of the fifty states. The United States includes fourteen "territories," including, for example, American Samoa, Guam, Howard Island, Midway Islands, Northern Mariana Islands, Puerto Rico, the U.S. Virgin Islands, and Wake Island. One who is located in a U.S. territory is subject to the laws of the United States and to the relevant territorial law.

4.   The Constitution establishes the whole of the federal government, describing and conscribing its powers. It creates and defines the authority of a Congress, a president, and the federal courts.

has created fourteen executive "departments," from which there arise hundreds of administrative agencies (generally called "bureaus" or "offices"). Congress empowers the agencies to promulgate "regulations," and those too, constitute federal law. The agencies exist at Congress's pleasure, and Congress is empowered to abolish any or all of them at its will.

In any given state, law arises from both (1) statutes enacted by the *state* legislature, and (2) *common law* (described and discussed at section A.4 below).[5] And every state legislature, like the federal government, has by statute created administrative agencies, empowering them to promulgate regulations. Those regulations constitute state law, just as federal regulations constitute federal law.

Ultimately, all statutes and common law are subject to "judicial interpretation," also called "judicial construction." When two parties dispute the meaning or applicability of a statute, courts step in to interpret it, and thus to resolve the dispute. Some disputes work their way up to the "court of last resort," meaning the highest court in the relevant jurisdiction, which most (but not all) jurisdictions call their "supreme court." Hence, each of the states California, Colorado, and North Carolina has its own supreme court. The federal government's highest court is, of course, the Supreme Court of the United States.

4. Common Law: Courts Not Only Construe It, They Create It

As to any question for which a state has enacted no constitutional provision, no statute and no administrative regulation, the relevant law comes from precepts, principles, and doctrines that the courts themselves have created over the last 1,000 years, beginning about 150 years after the Norman Conquest of 1066. Under King Henry II of England and his successors, there came to be a system under which judges (1) rode (by horse) about the land hearing and deciding disputes, (2) returned to the King's Court, (3) discussed their judicial experiences, and (4) described in writing the controversies they'd heard and decisions they'd made.

Among the King's judges, there arose an understanding that each should make his decisions consistent with those made by every other. Stated otherwise, the common law came to be a bundle of rules created by judicial decisions, with every judge (supposedly) attempting to make "today's" decision consistent with "yesterday's" decision that some other judge had reached as to a conceptually analogous controversy.

Suppose, for Example, That It's 1381

Judge A faces a controversy in which Parties X and Y have exchanged covenants (signed, written promises): Y covenanted to pay Party X £5 (five Pounds

---

5. Cities, towns, counties, villages, and other municipalities are created by the states in which they sit. Hence, municipal law (enacted by town councils or similar bodies) is, really, state law that is applicable only in some portion of the state.

Sterling), and Party X covenanted to convey a mule to Party Y. Party Y has paid X the £5, but X has decided that he doesn't wish to part with the mule. X stands ready to return Y's £5, but refuses to deliver the animal. Y doesn't want his money back; he wants the mule. Hence, it's for Judge A to decide whether on the one hand (a) Y has a right to *the mule* or, on the other, (b) X has the right to keep the mule as long as he returns to Y the £5 Y has paid him.

Judge A knows that before reaching a decision, he is to learn of any other judge who might have decided an analogous controversy. He discovers that in 1309, Judge Z decided a case in which Party F had covenanted to clean Party G's stables every day for one year, and Party G had covenanted to pay Party F, for the year, £1 at the end of each month — 12£ in all. For two months, Party F cleaned the stables; at the end of each such month, Party G paid him £1. Party F then announced his refusal any longer to clean the stables. He stood ready to return to G the £2 already paid him and, of course, to forego any additional pay. Party G did not want his money back; he wanted Party F to continue cleaning the stables, and stood ready to continue paying him £1 monthly.

And What Does Judge A Learn of Judge Z's 1309 Decision?

Judge A reads Judge Z's decision: "Each of these covenants is independent of the other; each has a life of its own and must be honored as made. That Party F is willing to release Party G from his covenant to pay does not entitle Party F to dishonor the covenant he made to Party G." Having read Judge Z's decision, Judge A feels obliged in *his* case to rule for Party Y, and so he decides, "One party might stand ready to release another from a covenant the other has made him. That, however, does not entitle him to dishonor a covenant he has made to the other. For it appears to be the common law that each of two reciprocal covenants is independent of the other; each must be honored as made, regardless of the other. Whether, in this case, Party Y does or does not return Party X's money, he must come forth with a mule and deliver it to Party Y."

The very phrase "common law" refers to what is *common* to all persons and places — the same everywhere within the nation. Commonality, in turn, demands consistency. That judicial decisions should show consistency gave rise to the notion of "precedent" and the doctrine that courts were bound *by* precedent (which doctrine goes, also, by the Latin phrase *stare decisis*, meaning "to stand by the [earlier] decision").[6] In 1381, Judge A felt obliged to reach a decision consistent with *precedent*—Judge Z's decision of 1309. And, in England it became a common law principle that every judge, deciding every controversy, should look to precedent and issue a decision consistent with it.

---

6. Expect your law school orientation program to steep, shower, and bathe you in that Latin phrase, and to invest it with some sort of silly mystique. Whatever the orientation folk tell you, remember that "*stare decisis*" refers only to the notion that law should, generally, remain constant and consistent; a court's decision made "today" should be consistent with the one it made "yesterday."

Within the thirteen North American British colonies, courts bound themselves by the English common law, reaching their decisions by looking to English decisions as precedent. And when the thirteen colonies became the United States of America, each state by its own constitution or by proclamation of its highest court "accepted" the existing common law of England as it then stood. Each state thus adopted, by and large, the rules and doctrines embodied within the English common law. In reaching their decisions, early American courts searched for precedent in decisions that emanated from both the colonial courts and the courts of England.

Then, as the American courts themselves decided ever more controversies, and as the United States took on ever more states, the state courts came ever more to cite back to their *own* precedents, seldom needing to cite to an English or colonial case. Read a Massachusetts appellate opinion from 1790 and you'll find citations to English precedent. Read a Massachusetts appellate opinion from 1990 and you won't. You'll find citations to Massachusetts precedent (which, of course, has its *origins* in the English common law).

Common Law Is *State* Law, Meaning There Are Fifty Sets of Common Law.   Although we refer to "*the* common law" as though it were a single discrete set of rules, there are really fifty sets of common law — one for each state. Because each state's judiciary *tends* to keep its common law consistent with that of every other, the common law of any one state does not differ *much* from that of any other.[7] Kentucky's common law of contracts might differ a tad from Missouri's on one matter or another; New York's might differ from California's. On some questions, it is often said that there are two views: a minority view and a majority view, meaning that as to some particular matter, in one whole group of states the common law provides one rule and in another group it provides a different one.

In every state, for example, the common law provides that contracts ordinarily arise upon offer and acceptance. Further, in every state, the common law provides that two parties form a contract only if each furnishes consideration to the other (as taught in Chapters 12 to 14). In all states, the common law provides that two parties may not modify an existing contract unless the modification exacts consideration from both. To that last rule, however, the common law in some states recognizes an exception: If D owes money to C, and D agrees to settle the debt by taking less money than he is owed, the common law in a minority of states provides that the agreement is enforceable, notwithstanding the absence of consideration from D to C. The common law of others (a majority) provides that it is not enforceable because D provides no consideration to C. (This whole topic is addressed at Chapter 14, section B.)

So here's the point: When, generally, a lawyer, judge, or teacher refers to "*the* common law" as though it's one uniform set of rules throughout the

---

7. The one exception is Louisiana, which, because of its French colonial history, does not even recognize anything called the common law. Like all other states, Louisiana is bound by federal law including, of course, the U.S. Constitution. Yet, in some significant respects its legal system differs from those of the other forty-nine states.

nation, she takes liberty with legal language. She refers, en masse, to that large body of common law rules as to which each state is by and large the same as every other. But the truth is that here in the United States, there are fifty bodies of common law, one for each state, each, as it happens, similar — but not identical — to every other.

And Is There *Federal* Common Law?   No — not since 1938 when the U.S. Supreme Court decided the case of Erie Railroad v. Tompkins, 304 U.S. 64 (1938). (Certainly, you'll study that case in your first-year civil procedure class.[8])

The U.S. empowers federal courts to decide (a) disputes that arise under federal law itself and, separately, (b) "controversies between . . . citizens of different States" even where no federal law is at issue. In 1798, pursuant to that Constitutional provision, Congress enacted a statute providing that if (1) two citizens of different states should be plaintiff and defendant in a lawsuit brought in federal court as the Constitution allows and (2) the law at issue is common law—then—the federal court should base its decision on the common law "of the several states":

> The laws of the several States . . . shall be regarded as rules of decision in trials at common law, in the courts of the United States, in [controversies between citizens of different states].

28 U.S.C. §1652.

Until 1938, the federal courts read the phrase "laws of the several states" to mean some blend of rules taken piecemeal from the common law of all states, whereby the federal courts assembled and created a general federal common law drawing "this" rule from the common law of State A, "that" one from State B, and "the others" from States C, D, E, or F. And so there came to be by 1938, a general federal common law, created by the federal courts in just that way.

In *Erie Railroad v. Tompkins*, the Supreme Court addressed the phrase "laws of the several States," and ruled that it did not refer to any notion of "general federal common law" assembled by the federal courts as an amalgam of common law provisions of the various states. Rather, the Supreme Court ruled, the Constitution did not allow for any such creature as "federal common law." For a suit between citizens of different states brought in federal court, where no state or federal statute governed, the Supreme Court ruled that the governing common law would be such *state* common law as would apply if the plaintiff had brought the suit in a *state* court. Justice Brandeis wrote:

> [T]he law to be applied in any [such] case is the [common] law of the state. There is no federal general common law . . . [and] no clause in the Constitution purports to confer . . . power upon the federal courts [to create one].

304 U.S. 64, 75 (1938). So — there is no such creature as federal common law.

---

8.   Which, in some law schools, lately goes by other names—because each new generation of law teachers thinks itself innovative when it gives new names to old things.

What Law *Does* Govern When Citizens from Different States Sue in Federal Court?   In a suit between citizens of two different states, X and Y, a federal court must apply either the law of State X or the law of State Y[9] because there is no such thing as federal common law.

QUESTION 3. In State X, by common law decision of the state's highest appellate court, "an advertisement to the general public, however or wherever posted, if otherwise sufficiently definite to constitute an offer, does in fact amount to an offer and, if any person should attempt properly to accept it, a contract arises between that person and the person who issued the advertisement." However, in State Y, by common law decision of the state's highest appellate court, "an advertisement made by newspaper, radio, television, Internet, or other means does not constitute an offer unless it specifically names the party to whom the offer is made." (In a great majority of states, an advertisement made to the general public does not ordinarily constitute an offer (Chapter 5, section A)).

Esther is a State X citizen in the business of manufacturing paper products. On the Internet site u-buy, she sees this advertisement: "Offered for sale 1 Orson Paper Cup Manufacturing Machine Model #4587-A, 2008, used 10,000 hours, $50,000, pay by cashier's, teller's, or certified check. Any person who wishes to buy or to ask a question about this item should contact seller at Goods@ubuy.com." To that e-mail address, Esther writes, "I wish to buy the Orson Paper Cup Manufacturing Machine Model #4587-A, and I accept your offer. Please send instructions as to how I should make payment. I will retrieve the machine at my own expense wherever it is now located or at such other place as you may direct." Esther receives a response, signed by Frances, to this effect: "I posted the u-buy advertisement for the Orson machine. Thank you for your interest, but I have decided not to sell it."

Esther locates Frances and finds that she is a citizen of State Y. Esther brings suit against Frances for breach of contract, exercising her right to bring the suit in federal court. At trial, Esther cites the State X statute and her own State X citizenship. On those bases, she contends that the u-buy posting was an offer. Frances cites the State Y statute and her citizenship in State Y. On those bases, she contends that the u-buy posting was not an offer.

Which of the following, if put forth by the federal court, plausibly represents an appropriate decision?

---

9. Which, according to the state's choice of law rules might refer the court, finally, to the law of a State Z, all such complexities covered, generally, in a law school course called "Conflicts of Law."

> I. The law of State X governs this controversy, wherefore the u-buy posting was an offer, meaning that these parties did not form a contract.
> II. The law of State Y governs this controversy, wherefore the u-buy posting was not an offer, meaning that these parties did not form a contract.
> III. Federal common law governs this controversy, wherefore the u-buy posting was not an offer, meaning that these parties did not form a contract.
> A. I
> B. II
> C. I and II
> D. I, II, and III

ANALYSIS.   The U.S. Constitution affords the federal courts jurisdiction to hear suits between citizens of different states. In 1798, by statute, Congress provided that in such suits the federal court should apply the "laws of the several States." For 150 years, the federal courts took that phrase to signify some mélange of state common law doctrine, which, as assembled by the federal courts, over time, came to be called federal common law or "general common law." But in 1938, the U.S. Supreme Court put an end to that. There was, it said, no such thing as federal common law. The phrase "laws of the several States" as used by Congress meant the common law (or statutory law) of the state whose law would govern a given controversy if it were, in fact, brought in state court.

In this case, the federal court will have to apply the common law of State X or State Y (making that decision according to another complicated body of doctrine called conflict of laws). Options I and II make plausible statements. But this much is sure: The federal court cannot apply to this controversy anything called federal common law because there is no such thing. Option III is clearly unacceptable. **C** is right.

Even Though There Is No Federal Common Law Federal Courts Do, with Their Decisions, "Make Law"; They *Have* To.   The federal courts (by and large) decide cases involving federal law that *others* enact. U.S. Const. art. III. For example, the Constitution's first amendment provides that "Congress shall make no law . . . abridging the freedom of speech[.]" No court had any part in creating that rule. Congress wrote it (in 1798) and the states ratified it.

Now suppose, a century later, Congress enacts a statute forbidding any person to wear on his clothing a button with a message that criticizes the president, or to place on her carriage, in time of war, a sign that reads "Bring Our Troops Home." Suppose now that Citizen X does wear a button that reads "Impeach the President." The FBI arrests him for violating the statute just described. He contends that his button is a form of speech under the first amendment. The U.S. Justice Department contends that it's not.

As to what the first amendment does or does not mean by "speech," the federal courts *must* decide. That's their job. Many in our nation like to say, "It's a court's job to interpret law, not to create it." The statement is meaningless. Such persons don't know that to do its job, a court must, in the very sense to which they object, "make law."

Thousands of times daily, two parties A and B (one of whom might be the federal or a state government) come to court disputing the meaning of some words within a federal statute, regulation, or the Constitution. A insists that the words in a given provision mean "this," and B insists they mean "that." The court's job is to *make a decision as to what the words do mean*. In doing so, it *must* pronounce that the *behavior* at issue is or is not lawful.

Love it or hate it, call it (through ignorance) "legislation from the bench," "judicial activism," or anything else. The federal courts must, when faced with a controversy, take hold of the statutes, regulations, or constitution that others have written, *interpret* them, and so decide that the behavior at issue is or is not lawful.

Consider the Controversial Topic of Abortion.   In 1972, the Supreme Court of the United States decided (with some qualifications) that no state could prevent a pregnant woman from securing an abortion within the first two trimesters of pregnancy. Any state that did so, it ruled, behaved unlawfully. Plainly, the Constitution makes no such statement in "black and white." Rather, the Supreme Court so construed/interpreted various of its provisions as to reach that decision. *Roe v. Wade*, 400 U.S. 113 (1973). (And there is scarcely a Supreme Court decision more controversial than that one.) In 1992, by *reinterpreta*-tion, the Court modified that ruling, holding that a state may, to some degree, restrict a woman's right to procure an abortion during pregnancy's first two trimesters. In that case, it faced a Pennsylvania statute requiring that a pregnant woman (1) if married, notify her husband of her plan to secure an abortion and, (2) married or not, after advising her physician that she wished to abort her pregnancy, wait twenty-four hours before actually undergoing the procedure.

The Court ruled that requirement (1) was unconstitutional; Pennsylvania could not impose that restriction on a pregnant woman; its attempt to do so was unlawful under the U.S. Constitution. It ruled that requirement (2) *was* constitutional; the state's imposition of *that* requirement was lawful. *Planned Parenthood of Southeastern Pennsylvania v. Casey*, 505 U.S. 833 (1992).

But Here's the Point: That Decision Did Not Reflect Federal *Common Law*.   When a federal court decides on the meaning of some word(s) within a federal statute, it announces *statutory law*; it tells the public what the statute *means*. When it decides on the meaning of some word(s) within the U.S. Constitution, it announces constitutional law by advising the public on the meaning tied to some portion of the Constitution. In that way, we might say, casually, that federal judges do "make law," but only by doing their job — by interpreting some statute, regulation, or the Constitution — for which the court did not ask and that it did not write. There is (since the *Erie* decision cited above), no federal *common law*.

What If a State Legislature Enacts a Statute That Conflicts with Its Own Common Law Rule?   Statutes supersede the common law. That's a principle of the common law itself. In Chapter 2, we teach that two parties may generally form a contract without a writing. If, however, some state should enact a statute that no agreement constitutes a contract unless set forth in writing, then such would be the law in that state. For once again, it's a principle of the common law itself that *statutory law supersedes common law*. Stated otherwise, common law governs in any given jurisdiction for only so long as its legislature fails to enact a statute that conflicts with it. Once it does so, the common law on that point ceases to operate.

B. What Is Contract Law, and Who Makes It?

When we use the word "contract," we usually mean a "bilateral contract."[10] A bilateral contract is *an exchange of promises each of which the law enforces by providing, in the case of breach, a cause of action and compensatory remedy.* (Compare "unilateral contracts," discussed in Chapter 9, sections C and D.) Restatement (Second) of Contracts §1 defines "contract" as "a set of promises for the breach of which the law gives a remedy, or the performance of which the law in some way recognizes as a duty."

Throughout the fifty states, contract law is largely common law (see section A.4 above). You won't likely find, in any state, a statute defining "offer," "acceptance," "rejection," or "revocation." Rather, the use, meaning, and significance of all such terms arose, grew, and evolved, slowly, by judicial decision; they belong to the common law.

So Where, in One Place, Is the Common Law of Contracts Written?   It isn't. The common law lies in judicial decisions. In order truly to read the common law of contracts for any given state, one must read, for that state, every judicial

---

10. Historically, the word "contract" referred to three kinds of binding obligation: (1) The "formal contract" which, in turn, referred to (a) the "covenant under seal" (section E below), (b) the "recognizance" (not discussed in this book or in any ordinary law school Contracts course), (c) the negotiable instrument (the topic of a separate course usually called "negotiable instruments" or "payment systems"), and (2) the "simple bilateral contract," which is what we all mean, today, when we say "contract." If ever you cross paths with the phrase "simple bilateral contract," know that it means "contract" as we all, today, use that word and that the word "simple" distinguishes it from what once were called "formal contracts," as described above.

opinion put forth by every judge or, at the very least, every decision put forth by the state's highest court. All together those decisions, for any given state, are that state's common law of contracts.

In the 1800s and early 1900s, some scholars did very nearly that. They include Oliver Wendell Holmes, Samuel Williston, Arthur Corbin, and others. Their scholarly works have gone far to "pull together" the common law so that one may read (their interpretations and understandings of) the common law in organized fashion. Their multivolume treatises (now updated and revised by others) constitute revered authority on the common law of contracts. Judges frequently cite to them as they do, also, to the works of Professors Farnsworth, Calamari, and Perillo, and to various articles written (usually) by law professors who, too, have achieved expertise in the common law of contracts (maybe).

C. Restatement of the Law of Contracts

1. What Are Restatements of the Law?

In Philadelphia, Pennsylvania, there sits an entity called the American Law Institute (ALI), founded in 1923. Among its self-assigned missions is to gather groups of (supposed) authorities on various subjects, and through their conjoined efforts, to "restate" the common law. Each of the ALI's Restatements appears as a set of "rules" partitioned into "sections" that (a) in their form resemble statutes and that, (b) *according to the ALI*, accurately reflect the common law. (In some cases, clearly they do not, and in some others, the rules reflect the common law as the ALI would *like* it to be.)

With the word "*restatement*," the ALI acknowledges that the common law on any subject is *stated* in the thousands of judicial decisions, each made (supposedly) with an attempt at ongoing consistency. The ALI's work-product characterizes itself as a *re*statement of such common law; it represents the ALI's effort to take hold of the judicial decisions and to "restate" their common law principles in a cohesive, accessible form.

The ALI has now put forth a large number of restatements on a variety of common law subjects, including agency, property, torts, trusts and — contracts. The first Restatement of the Law of Contracts, published in 1932, represents the ALI's purported exposition of the common law of contracts as of 1932. The Restatement (Second) of the Law of Contracts, published in 1979, we are to believe, accounts for changes in the common law between 1932 and 1979, and so represents the ALI's purported exposition of the common law of contracts as of 1979 (and just as much, perhaps, its opinion as to what the common law *should* be). Someday, no doubt, will follow Restatements (Third), (Fourth), and so on.

2. So, at Any Given Time, the Most Current Restatement Is the Common Law of Contracts?

No, no, no — don't ever say that. Whatever the Restatement of Contracts might be, it's *not* law. It represents, at best, a private committee's joint opinion as to what is the common law of contracts, based on *its* reading of the cases, and *its* reading of the various scholars who have written on the subject (some of whom themselves participated in writing the first and second Restatements). Nonetheless, rightly or wrongly, state courts around the country regard the Restatement of Contracts with reverence. They refer to it, they *defer* to it, and they cite to it almost as though it *were* law, which it is not.

Whether, on the one hand, the Restatement is a well-conceived work of useful scholarship or, on the other, a recitation of obvious unavailing generalities, empty of intelligent analysis, that avoids always the difficult issues and resolves in trite terms the easy ones — lawyers, judges, and teachers regrettably regard it as an important authority. Some teachers base the whole of their Contracts course upon it. Nearly all refer to it regularly and require that their students (*you*) read many of its provisions. Hence, we cite to it very frequently in this book, for as to some matters you must know its contents.

QUESTION 4. The Restatement (Second) of the Law of Contracts is best described as

A. statutory law.
B. common law.
C. an opinion.
D. a precedent.

ANALYSIS. Restatements of the Law come forth from the American Law Institute, an arm of the American Bar Association. They are not statutes because the American Law Institute is not, certainly, a legislature. They are not common law because the common law inheres only in judicial decisions. They are not precedent because precedents, too, arise from judicial decisions. They represent the opinion of the American Law Institute as to what is or should be the common law of contracts. **C** is right.

3. What We Mean When We Refer to the "Common Law of Contracts"

When we say "common law of contracts," we mean that large body of contract law created over a millennium by the courts of England and the United States, each judge, theoretically, reaching her decisions with an effort to be consistent with her predecessors — an effort to abide by precedent and also, at times, to "break new ground," so that the common law of contracts is said, always, to "grow" (as is so of the common law on any subject).

D.   Statutory Contract Law: Uniform Commercial Code Article 2 and Miscellaneous State Statutes

In 1892, there occurred a first meeting of what is now called the National Conference of Commissioners on Uniform State Laws, headquartered today in Chicago, Illinois. Commonly called the "Uniform Law Commission" (ULC), this entity is not a government agency, but a private not-for-profit association. Nonetheless, by ULC invitation, each of the fifty states (plus a few U.S. territories) names several "commissioners" to participate, on the state's behalf, in the ULC's self-appointed task.

1.   What Is *the ULC's Self-Appointed Task?*

Because we are a nation of fifty states, each with its own power to make common law (via the judiciary) and statutory law (via the legislature), one state's laws sometimes conflict with another's. Where persons partake of interstate transactions, those conflicts raise questions as to the rights and duties of the participating parties. Suppose, for example, that by statute in State B, a check is valid only if dated at its top. Suppose that by statute in State A, a check is valid whether or not dated at its top. If a State A buyer sends to a State B seller a check that is undated at the top, there might well arise the question of whether the buyer has or has not sent a check that's valid. Under statutory law in the state from which the buyer sent it, the check is valid. In the state where the seller received it, it's not — and that's a problem.

Suppose a State A statute provides: "The retail seller of any electronic consumer product automatically, as a matter of law, warranties that the product will function properly for two years after the date of purchase." Suppose a State B statute provides: "The retail seller of any electronic consumer product automatically, as a matter of law, warranties that the product will function properly for three years after the date of purchase." If, by on-line, mail-order purchase, a State B buyer purchases a consumer electronic product from a State A retail seller, there arises the question of whether Seller warrants the product for two years or three years — and that's a problem, too.

In order to transcend such conflicts, the ULC assigned itself the mission of drafting and proposing to each state legislature for enactment various "uniform statutes" addressing areas of commercial law in which interstate conflicts often arise. The thinking ran thus: If every state were to adopt as statutes the laws that the ULC proposed, then as to the subject at issue, the law would be uniform throughout the states and thus unburden interstate transactions from potential conflicts among differing state laws.

Among the several uniform acts that the ULC put forth in its earlier years was one called the Uniform Sales Act of 1906. It concerned those transactions in which two parties formed or negotiated toward a contract for the sale of *goods*. The Uniform Sales Act addressed no other sort of contract; it addressed only contracts *for the sale of goods* (presumably because the purchase and sale of goods often involved interstate transaction, particularly with the advent of railroads). The purchase and sale of service (at that time) was usually a local matter undertaken between persons closely located. (In 1906, American businesses did not engage employees in India to answer customer service telephone lines and instruct us on how to operate our computer equipment.)

About thirty states adopted the Uniform Sales Act, and in those states, therefore, the Act governed contracts for the sale of goods. All other contracts were governed still by the common law, and even contracts for the sale of goods were governed by the common law as to matters on which the Uniform Sales Act was silent. For example, the Act at various points invoked the terms "offer" and "acceptance," but nowhere defined them. Even in those states that adopted the Act, therefore, the definitions of those terms continued to be creatures of the common law (as did all other matters that the Act did not address).

In 1952, the ULC sent a call to all forty-eight states: "Repeal the Uniform Sales Act and certain other of our previously drafted uniform acts related to commercial transactions. Adopt in its place our new Uniform Commercial Code (UCC)." The UCC was (and is) a long statute (hundreds of pages long) partitioned into several "articles," each such article revising and replacing a pre-existing single uniform statute that the ULC had earlier put forth, each of which some (but not all) states had enacted. In 1952, UCC Article 2 dealt (and still deals today) with contracts for the sale of goods, the ULC intending that it replace the Uniform Sales Act. The states were slow to adopt the UCC, and so the ULC revised it in 1955. Even then many states declined to enact it, and so the ULC revised it again in 1962, hoping all states would find it acceptable. And, during the 1960s, all states did adopt the UCC, including its Article 2 (some with minor alterations in language, and Louisiana with very significant alterations).

2. *What's a "Good," Exactly?*

All property is divisible, first, into "real property" and "personal property." Real property means land and all things firmly affixed to it such as a house, driveway, or flagpole. Personal property is all property other than real property. We may then divide personal property into two categories: "tangible" and "intangible." Tangible personal property means (by and large) any personal property that has a physical existence, such as a paper clip or the Hubble telescope; both are tangible personal property. Intangible personal property means personal property that has no physical existence. One's right to enforce a contract is intangible personal property. If one is injured by another's negligence, then his right to recover under negligence law is intangible personal property. A copyright, a trademark, and one's right to receive his income tax refund are all intangible personal property.

Article 2 (UCC §2-205) defines "good" generally as a "movable thing." With certain additions and exceptions set forth in that same section, "movable thing" means, really, tangible personal property. A wristwatch is a good. So is a jet, a nuclear bomb, a safety pin, a contact lens, a ball bearing, a marble, a loaf of bread, and an ocean liner. A patent, contract right, or right to take a gift left by a decedent through a will all qualify as personal property, but they have no physical existence. They constitute *in*tangible personal property; they're not "goods," and UCC Article 2 does not govern contracts regarding their sale. Contracts for the sale of real property or intangible personal property fall within the common law (or within some statute outside the UCC if the relevant jurisdiction has enacted one).

Since first putting forth the Uniform Commercial Code, the ULC has several times revised it, thus, over time, issuing Article 2 in various versions: a 1952 version, a 1955 version, a 1962 version (the one first adopted by substantially all states), and a 2003 version (which the ULC has withdrawn because no state is willing to adopt it; it was junk).

Hence, UCC Article 2 as now enacted in all states (with some variation in text here and there) is, by and large, the 1962 version. For that reason, when we, in this book, refer to UCC Article 2, we refer to the 1962 version, for that's the only version that constitutes law. Further, when we refer generally to "the Code" or to the "UCC," we mean Article 2 of the UCC, 1962 version, for that's the article that specifically addresses contracts — *again, not all contracts, but only contracts for the sale of goods.*

QUESTION 5. When the Uniform Law Commission first completes the writing of any one of its uniform laws, its written work product at that moment constitutes

A. state common law.
B. state statutory law.
C. administrative regulatory law.
D. no law at all.

ANALYSIS. The Uniform Laws Commission is not a governmental entity, and it has no power to enact law. Pursuant to the mission it has declared for itself, it writes what, in its opinion, *would make* good uniform law throughout the states and then submits its work product to the state legislatures, suggesting that all enact it as statutory law. In some cases, the states do adopt the recommended law, and in some cases they don't. If one state adopts the law, then its provisions become law in that state. If another state adopts it, its provisions become law in that state too. If ultimately all states adopt it (as has happened with Article 2), then it becomes statutory law in all states. But — when the ULC first completes writing one of its "uniform laws" and before a first state adopts it, it is no law it all; it represents no more than ULC's *suggestion* to all states that they *enact* it as law. **D** is right.

3. The Code Comes with "Official Comments"

For all of the UCC's provisions, the writers have supplied their own "official comments." These purport to explain the origin, meaning, and application of the Code provisions themselves. When the ULC encouraged all state legislatures to adopt the UCC, it did not proclaim that its official comments should be part of the law per se, and it is said in all states that the official comments do not enjoy the status of law. Indeed, where a state's statute books show the UCC as statutory law, they do not show the official comments; the comments are not a part of the law. The comments are, however, readily accessible, and courts do frequently read and refer to them when interpreting and applying the Code's provisions. In that way, the official comments heavily influence the judiciary's understanding of the Code and therefore certainly do *inform* the law. Without doubt, when asking that you read provisions of the Code, your contracts teacher will ask that you read, too, the relevant official comments.

4. Other State Statutes Related to Contract Law

Beyond UCC Article 2, the various states have enacted, to greater or lesser degrees, miscellaneous statutes that bear on contract law. In those states, *those* statutes form a part of the state's law of contracts; if they conflict with the common law, they supersede it. In Chapter 2, sections E and F, for example, we discuss the common law rules of acceptance by silence and dominion. There we teach this common law rule: if (1) a Party S (Detergent Inc, for example) delivers to Party B's home, an unsolicited, unwanted, unknown product (its new detergent) offering to sell it for a named price, and (2) Party B takes hold of the product using it, consuming it, or otherwise treating it as his own — he then forms a contract requiring that he purchase the product, and he must pay the stated price. That's the common law. But in New York, a statute supersedes the common law by providing that:

> No person, firm, partnership, association or corporation . . . shall . . . offer for sale . . . merchandise, where the offer includes the voluntary and unsolicited sending of such . . . merchandise not actually ordered[.] The receipt of any such . . . merchandise shall for all purposes be deemed an unconditional gift

to the recipient, who may use or dispose of such ... merchandise in any manner he sees fit without obligation on his part to the sender.

N.Y. General Obligations Law §5-332.

So — as to any topic or subtopic you study in your contracts course, there may well be, beyond the common law and beyond UCC Article 2, "this" or "that" miscellaneous statute in "this" or "that" state. In each state, all such statutes represent a part of *that* state's contract law.

5. *So Is the Common Law of Contracts Obsolete?*

No, certainly not. UCC Article 2 governs only *contracts for the sale of goods.* A contract for the sale of any service (including, notably, a contract for construction) is governed still by the common law (except where some miscellaneous state statute supersedes it). And even as to contracts for the sale of goods, where the Code is silent, the common law governs.

QUESTION 6. In any given state, statutes that address contract law include

   I. UCC Article 2, as enacted by the state's legislature.
   II. the Restatement of the Law of Contracts, as enacted by the state's legislature.
   III. miscellaneous statutes, as enacted by the state's legislature.
   A. I
   B. I and II
   C. II and III
   D. I and III

ANALYSIS.   In any given state, the law of contracts is largely a matter of common law. Statutes supersede the common law, and every state has enacted UCC Article 2, a statute that governs contracts for the sale of goods. In every state, therefore, the Code forms a part of statutory contract law. Option I is true. If the UCC and the common law conflict, the Code governs. If as to some matter bearing on contract law, Article 2 is silent, the common law governs. In addition, every state has enacted, to greater or lesser degrees, its own statutes pertaining to contract law. Those form the remaining portion of state statutory law on the subject of contracts. Option III is true. As to any matter on which any such statute conflicts with the common law, the statute governs. The Restatement is *not* a statute. Neither is it common law. It is no law at all. It is, rather, the ALI's opinion as to the state of the common law (and in some cases, as to what the common law should be). When courts must decide contractual controversies governed by the common law, they do frequently look to the Restatement for guidance, but the Restatement isn't law. Options I and III are true, and II is false. **D** is right.

QUESTION 7. If two parties wish to form a contract under which one will build a home for the other, the law governing the formation, interpretation, enforceability, breach, and remedies pertaining to their contract inheres in

A. UCC Article 2 only.
B. UCC Article 2 and any other pertinent state statute.
C. the common law only.
D. the common law and any other pertinent state statute.

ANALYSIS. The question describes a contract that does not concern the sale of goods, and for that reason UCC Article 2 is irrelevant. *Article 2 of the Code applies only to contracts for the sale of goods, and no others.* Let's say it again: *Article 2 of the Code applies only to contracts for the sale of goods, and no others.* **A** and **B** are wrong. If the state has enacted any statute that applies to the contract or controversy at issue, then that statute does certainly apply. As to matters for which there is no statute, the common law applies. **D** is right.

E.   Law vs. Equity

Throughout law school, a student reads and hears of "equity" contrasted with "law." She hears also that equity has "merged" with law, and she is led *wrongly* to conclude that the difference between them is today largely insignificant. Unless she takes a (good — *good*) course called Remedies, Equity, Equitable Remedies (or something like that), she will all too likely graduate law school with a wholly inadequate understanding of what is meant by "equity courts," "equitable jurisdiction," the "merger" of law and equity, and "equity vs. law." When, in her practice, the significance of equity vs. law jumps up to jolt her with reality, she'll have to learn about it *then*, which is why, once again, every law student should take a (*good*) course that teaches equitable remedies.[11]

We can't, in this book, teach you fully (or anywhere *near* fully) about the meaning of equity courts, equitable jurisdiction, or equity vs. law. A full apprehension of equity you shan't achieve by reading this chapter, nor as a first-year

---

11. Alternatively, you might read all six volumes (with footnotes) of John Norton Pomeroy, *Equity Jurisprudence* (1881-1883) (originally three volumes, later expanded to six).

law student, nor in all your years at law school, nor perhaps in your lifetime on this planet. *But, as President Kennedy urged, let us make a beginning.*

Seat thyself in medieval England where the courts of law were, *conceptually*, like our courts of law today. The English law courts developed and applied the common law and in so doing created forms of action, those giving rise today to what we call causes of action. If, however, some party felt he had suffered an injustice for which the law offered no cause of action and hence no adequate remedy, he had the right, under some circumstances (depending on who he was and what year it was) to petition the King for some form of relief — *outside* the law. He thus became not a "plaintiff" in a lawsuit but a "petitioner" who sought the King's own justice. His adversary was not a "defendant" but a "respondent" who, the petitioner asserted, had caused him an *injustice for which the law offered no adequate remedy.*

The King, 'twas said, would hear the matter and test it against "the King's conscience." If by such test he concluded that the petitioner had indeed suffered an injustice for which the law offered no action and hence no remedy, the King (or Chancellor on the King's behalf) *ordered* the respondent to do "this, that, or the other" to give the petitioner his justice.

For example, in medieval England the law had not yet come to the point where it enforced contracts as we know that word. What we today call a contract (more properly, a "simple contract") was then a mere "private agreement," unenforceable at law. Hence, if two parties made an agreement, orally or by signed writing, the law wanted nothing to do with it. One party's breach gave the other no grounds on which to sue. Agreements, per se, were not enforceable; they had no status under the law; the law did not recognize them.

Let's Make That Very Clear.   *Ask yourself:* If on Monday, A and B agree that lavender is the prettiest of all colors, but on Tuesday B changes her mind and decides that wine-red is the prettiest of all colors, does A have a cause of action against B?

Answer yourself: No, of course not. As between two persons, sameness, difference, or change of opinion has no legal status. The law cares naught about it. No person can sustain a suit against the other because the other holds an opinion different from his own, and that's obviously true even if at one time the two of them held the same opinion.

Similarly, in medieval England if Parties A and B formed an agreement by handshake, or by signed writing, the law took no account of it. There was no name for what they had formed except a mere "private agreement." If Party A breached, Party B had no cause of action against him. Party B might learn not to make private agreements with A ever again, but the law offered him no cause of action and, therefore, no remedy or relief.

But the Law Did Furnish a Means to Enforce a Promise: Covenant Under Seal.   If, in 1660, (1) X made a promise to Y, setting it forth in writing; and

(2) X applied to the writing his *seal* ("seal" meaning one's own special stamp-like raised imprint, in those days made of wax); and (3) X delivered the sealed instrument to the promisee, then his promise became a "covenant under seal," and the law enforced it.[12]

Hence, it became the common wisdom that a promise was enforceable when it was set forth in a writing that was "signed, sealed, and delivered" (which in today's parlance means "all done — complete").

An Illustration: Bullworth and Sterling.   Suppose it's November 1, 1621. Bullworth wants to buy Sterling's horse for £5. He wants to make the exchange of money for horse four months hence, on March 1, 1622. Sterling wants to sell the horse to Bullworth for that same price on that same day. The parties want to achieve what we, today, would call a contract for the sale of the horse. They can't do *that*, but here's what they *can* do. Bullworth writes his promise to pay Sterling, on March 1, 1662, the sum of £5. He supplies the document with his seal and his signature. Sterling creates his own writing, promising delivery of the horse, on March 1, 1622, to Bullworth, investing the writing with *his* signature and seal. The parties then meet. Each delivers his writing to the other, so that each has, from the other, a written promise, signed, sealed, and delivered and, therefore, a covenant under seal. Each thus has from the other an enforceable promise. Should either of the parties breach his covenant, then, in order to enforce the promise in court, the other must present the document to the judge.

And on that point, the law took itself quite seriously. Suppose Bullworth and Sterling prepare their signed, sealed, written promises as just described, Sterling covenanting to deliver a horse on March 1, 1662, and Bullworth covenanting to pay Sterling £5 on March 1, 1662. On November 3, 1661, they exchange writings so that each has from the other an enforceable promise, each promise to be performed on March 1, 1662. On December 15, Bullworth accidentally drops Sterling's covenant in the hearth. It burns to ash. No longer possessing the covenant, Bullworth cannot enforce Sterling's promise to deliver the horse. Yet Sterling still has Bullworth's covenant and Sterling must honor it; he must pay Sterling the £5.

You Mean Bullworth Had to Pay the Money but Had No Right to Receive the Horse?   Yes, that was so. But the law didn't then see the situation as we do; it did not consider that £5 was the price of a horse. Bullworth had to pay £5, not for a horse, but rather because (for whatever reason, about which the court did not care) he promised to pay Sterling £5, in a writing signed, sealed, and delivered, wherefore the writing became a covenant under seal — enforceable — period. The *law enforced the covenant*, and cared not a whit about the

---

12. Although the promisor need not have *signed* the instrument to render his promise enforceable, he customarily did so.

reasons for which Bullworth created it. Bullworth had to pay not for a horse but to make good on his covenant.

Bullworth, of course, knows that he made the covenant to Sterling in exchange for Sterling's covenant to deliver the horse, but the *law* took no account of "exchanges" or "bargains." Such things had no legal status. Their status at law was *nada, nilch, zilch* — just as today, for example, a difference of opinion between two persons has no legal status. Quite simply, if one was in possession of another's covenant, signed, sealed, and delivered to him, then he had a right to enforce it regardless of the "whys" and "wherefores" surrounding its creation.

Suppose Bullworth refused to pay the £5 unless Sterling should deliver the horse. Sterling would sue Bullworth for breach of covenant, and the court would award Sterling a judgment for £5.

That Takes Us on a Little Detour: "Judgment" vs. "Order."   When a court issues a *judgment* against some defendant, it does not *order* the defendant to pay the plaintiff. It is up to defendant to pay the judgment. If she doesn't, she is not in "contempt of court"; she suffers no punishment; the court isn't "mad at" her. Rather, the plaintiff must undertake a whole, new separate procedure to collect on his judgment. That procedure involves discovering and locating the defendant's assets and acquiring from the court something called (in many jurisdictions) a "writ of execution," which directs some judicial officer (a sheriff, constable, or someone else, depending on the jurisdiction) to seize the defendant's property, sell it at auction, deliver to plaintiff so much as the judgment requires, and return the excess, if any, to defendant. Or, if the defendant has money in the bank, the writ will direct the judicial officer to seize from the bank the amount of the judgment and pay it to plaintiff. Or, in an amount limited by statute in most jurisdictions, the writ will permit the judicial officer to garnish the defendant's wages, so that her employer withholds, say, 10 percent of her wages every pay period and pays them over to the court, which in turn pays the plaintiff.[13]

So Understand This.   The enforceability of one's promise or covenant, signed, sealed, and delivered, did not arise because the parties had formed an agreement or exchange; the law knew and cared nothing for *agreements*. It looked at each covenant individually. If the instrument was signed, sealed, and delivered, the law enforced it, and *that was that*.

---

13. The matter becomes more complicated when a state legislature (or the U.S. Congress) enacts a statute creating some cause of action specifically authorizing the court to issue, against a defendant, a court *order*. Since the relevant authority arises from the legislature and not from either the common law or equity per se, it is difficult to state confidently that such a court order is an equitable remedy. We are safer saying that such a court order is "in the nature of an equitable remedy." Hence, while all equitable remedies come in the form of court orders, we cannot say that all court orders constitute equitable remedies.

So One *Could*, in Those Days, Make an Enforceable Naked Promise?
Exactly right. There was, at that time, no such concept as "consideration." If, for whatever reason, Party 1 promised by covenant under seal to pay Party 2 on her eighteenth birthday £500, then he was bound to do so — as long as Party 2 could produce the instrument when she reached her eighteenth birthday. Without the paper, she had a right to nothing.

QUESTION 8. The common law developed the legal creature called covenant under seal

A. after it had already invented the enforceable contract in which two parties exchanged promises.
B. because the doctrine of consideration was excessively complex and the law wished to create a device by which one could make an enforceable promise without receiving consideration in exchange.
C. in order that one promise could serve as consideration for another.
D. before it recognized any such creature as an enforceable agreement.

ANALYSIS.   Long before the law recognized that which we now call "contract," one could make an enforceable promise via the covenant under seal. At that time, the law knew nothing of and cared nothing for what it regarded as private agreements between private persons. It did not enforce agreements; it enforced *promises* that were written, signed, sealed, and delivered. In later centuries, the law came to recognize consideration as the substitute for a seal, although the history of that particular development is long and complex. This much, however, is simple and sure: The law recognized and enforced the covenant under seal long before it knew of what we today call a contract — an exchange of promises, each serving as consideration for the other.

A, B, and C all state or imply that the doctrine of consideration predated the covenant under seal. That makes all of them wrong. D makes the simple and correct statement that the law honored, recognized, and enforced the covenant under seal before it developed what we, today, call a contract. Hence, D is right.

End of Detour: Back to Bullworth, Sterling, and the Horse.   Because Sterling holds Bullworth's covenant under seal, the court issues against Bullworth a judgment for £5 in favor of Sterling. Having lost the covenant that Sterling gave him, Bullworth, in 1622, has no *legal* right to the horse for which (in *his* mind) he has paid.

So Bullworth Appeals to the "King's Conscience."   Bullworth petitions the King, asserting that he has suffered an injustice for which the law affords no action and hence no remedy. The King hears Bullworth's plea and hears too from Sterling, the respondent. The King decides that Bullworth is right — that he has suffered an injustice for which the law offers no action and hence no remedy. The King *orders* Sterling to convey the horse to Bullworth. His Highness does not issue a *judgment* at law, for he has no power to do so. He issues an order, and *that*, in 1622, he has power to do. A King's order is a thing quite different from a court's judgment. Should one disobey it, the King will order him imprisoned.

The King Sent His Conscience Around His Realm: "Courts of Equity." To oversimplify a little (or a lot), the King ultimately established what we might call "satellites" of his conscience by setting up equity courts around the realm and appointing "chancellors" to hear "petitions in equity." Hence, one who claimed to have suffered an injustice for which the law would give no remedy needed no longer to take himself to the King's Court and wait in line to see him. Rather, the petitioner might go to an equity court closer to his own location and present his grievance to the chancellor who sat there. Each chancellor, as "keeper of the King's conscience," was to ask himself, in each such case, whether the petitioner had indeed suffered an injustice for which the law offered no remedy. If he answered "yes," then he fashioned an order as, in his judgment, would correct the injustice by requiring the respondent to do or to refrain from doing some certain thing. One who disobeyed the order was incarcerated for "contempt of His Majesty's Court," which phrase was later shortened to "contempt of court."

When the United States first established itself, the federal government and all thirteen states, modeling themselves on the English system, had separate courts of law and equity (courts of equity being sometimes called courts of chancery). In 1938, the federal government "merged" its law and equity courts. The effect was not to abolish the separate *jurisdictions* of law and equity, but rather to house both jurisdictions in the same court buildings. A federal judge, figuratively speaking, had in his closet two hats, one labeled "judge at law" and the other "chancellor at equity." Depending on the nature of the matter before him, he put one or the other atop his head. When there came before the federal court the construction and application of either a federal statute, the U.S. Constitution, or the common law, the judge wore his "law hat"; the interpretation and application of common law and statutes are matters of *law*. When the federal court faced a petitioner who sought a court order to rectify an injustice for which the law offered no remedy, the federal judge donned his "equity hat."

It is said that in most states law and equity are similarly merged. Unfortunately, too many equate the "merger" with the abolition of equity as a separate jurisdiction, and for doing so they're much mistaken. Some states still do retain separate law and equity courts, and in virtually all states some courts of special purpose (the probate court, for instance) remains, still, a court of equity. In any event, you'll hear and read in your first year of law school (probably in civil procedure class) that law and equity are largely merged. Your teacher might (or might not) skate so quickly over the subject as to make you think there is no longer any distinction between equity and law. That (if it happens) does you a terrible disservice. Hence we say again: Take a course called remedies, equity, or equitable remedies. (And if you can't, then read *Examples & Explanations: Remedies*, by Richard L. Hasen (Aspen, 2d ed. 2010). It's a great (*great*) teach-yourself book on the subject.)

For Our Purposes, the Two Most Important Truths About Equity vs. Law Are These.   (1) When a court sits "at law" (as a court of law), an award of monetary damage is (just about) the only remedy it can offer. The law's principal remedy is monetary damages; (2)(a) When a court issues an *order* as opposed to a monetary judgment, it ordinarily invokes its jurisdiction as a court of equity, and (b) it does so only if, in its opinion, the petitioner before it has suffered an injustice for which a legal remedy (monetary award) is either unavailable or unavailing.

QUESTION 9. In general (with exceptions created by statute), when one seeks a court order as opposed to an award of monetary damages, she invokes a court's jurisdiction

A. at law and not at equity.
B. at equity and not at law.
C. both equity and law.
D. neither equity nor law.

ANALYSIS.   Generally speaking, when a plaintiff wins an action at law, she receives the remedy of monetary damages, an award of money calculated (theoretically) to compensate her for the harm done her by the defendant (as elaborately discussed in Chapters 25 to 30). If she seeks a court order, then, generally, she must invoke the court's equitable jurisdiction — ask it to don its "equity hat." She must convince the judge that she has suffered an injustice for which the law affords no adequate remedy.

If she succeeds in that effort, the judge will issue an *order* that the defendant do (or refrain from doing) some particular thing which order will, in the judge's mind, correct the injustice. As a general rule, monetary damages represents the remedy available "at law." A court order represents the remedy available "at equity." Hence, **B** is right.

QUESTION 10. Historically, equity courts and the equitable jurisdiction of today's courts have their roots in

A. common law court orders.
B. court orders authorized by statute.
C. an appeal to the "King's conscience."
D. an appeal to "natural law."

ANALYSIS.   Equity is distinct from law (although the distinction is less visible today than it was 100 years ago). In theory (and in fact, still), the courts of equity are distinct from the courts of law, although the difference today represents not two different court houses or two different judges, but, usually, two different "hats" worn by the same judge sitting in one court house. Hence, equitable jurisdiction, yesteryear and now, is separate from legal jurisdiction and separate, therefore, from the common law. Consequently, **A** and **D**, which refer to "law," are wrong. The tasks of construing and applying statutes belong, also, to the law courts. **B** is wrong. The first equity court was the King's own court, where he entertained petitions from those who alleged that they had suffered an injustice for which the law offered no remedy. The King (or his delegate) then resolved the matter, according to His "conscience." **C** is right.

 Silver's Picks

1.	D
2.	D
3.	C
4.	C
5.	D
6.	D
7.	D
8.	D
9.	B
10.	C

Index